The Philippine Economy

The Philippine Economy

DEVELOPMENT, POLICIES, AND CHALLENGES

EDITED BY
Arsenio M. Balisacan
Hal Hill

OXFORD
UNIVERSITY PRESS
2003

OXFORD

UNIVERSITY PRESS

Oxford   New York
Auckland   Bangkok   Buenos Aires   Cape Town   Chennai
Dar es Salaam   Delhi   Hong Kong   Istanbul   Karachi   Kolkata
Kuala Lumpur   Madrid   Melbourne   Mexico City   Mumbai   Nairobi
São Paulo   Shanghai   Taipei   Tokyo   Toronto

Published by Oxford University Press, Inc.
198 Madison Avenue, New York, New York 10016

www.oup.com

Oxford is a registered trademark of Oxford University Press

Library of Congress Cataloging-in-Publication Data
The Philippine economy : development, policies, and challenges /
edited by Arsenio M. Balisacan and Hal Hill.
   p. cm.
Includes bibliographical references and index.
ISBN 0-19-515897-0; ISBN 0-19-515898-9 (pbk.)
1. Philippines—Economic conditions—1986– 2. Philippines—Economic policy.
3. Philippines—Social conditions. I. Balisacan, A. M. II. Hill, Hal, 1948–
HC455 .P455 2002
330.9599—dc21   2002031180

9 8 7 6 5 4 3 2 1

Printed in the United States of America
on acid-free paper

In memory of José Encarnación, Jr. and H.W. Arndt

Preface and Acknowledgments

The writing of this book has incurred numerous debts, and it is a pleasure to acknowledge the support of the colleagues and institutions that assisted us.

Its origins were laid during Arsenio Balisacan's visiting fellowship at the Australian National University in late 1995. At that time, and in discussion with several colleagues in Canberra, it was decided as a medium-term objective to explore the possibility of setting up a Philippine Economy Research Program involving academics from the Philippines, Australia, and elsewhere.

The editors then began to formulate plans for a book on the Philippine economy, motivated by the consideration that it had been many years since the last broad academic analysis of Philippine economic development. These plans were given a significant boost in 1998 when Felipe Medalla was appointed Socioeconomic Secretary and Director-General of the National Economic and Development Authority (NEDA). His interest in seeing a study of the Philippine economy, looking both backward and forward, coincided very closely with our proposal. We do want to place on record our thanks to Philip for his enthusiasm and support for our work.

With the backing of the Philippine and Australian governments, through NEDA and the Australian Agency for International Development (AusAID) respectively, this project was thus formally conceived in 1999.

We are grateful first and foremost to our authors for their interest and participation in the project and for writing the kind of papers we wanted: analytically informed and with a policy edge.

Both governments have supported this project throughout. We particularly want to thank David Swan, Director of AusAID's Philippines Section, Ruperto Alonzo and Gilberto Llanto, successive Deputy Directors-General at NEDA, and their staff. We are likewise grateful to Professor Dante Canlas, one of our authors and now

Socioeconomic Secretary and Director-General of NEDA under the Macapagal-Arroyo administration, for his interest in seeing the project through to its present form.

Discussants and other speakers at the November 2000 conference in Canberra played an important role in lifting the quality of the papers and proceedings. We wish to thank the following individuals for their contribution in this respect: Ruperto Alonzo, the late Heinz Arndt, Prema-Chandra Athukorala, Romeo Bautista, Jeff Bennett, Kit Collier, Ian Coxhead, Chris Findlay, Ross Garnaut, Barry Hooker, Terry Hull, Gavin Jones, Mario Lamberte, Warwick McKibbin, Ross McLeod, Chris Manning, James Roumasset, and Richard Woolcott.

The Philippine and Australian ambassadors during this period, Delia Domingo Albert and John Buckley, took an active and supportive interest in our work. We wish to acknowledge their important contribution.

We could not have run this project without the able and efficient assistance of Sharon Faye Piza. Melody Garcia and Rashiel Velarde helped greatly during several stages of the project, and Gemma Estrada provided valuable research assistance during the revision stage. Collectively they kept the show on the road.

At the Australian National University, logistics and administration were expertly handled by Julie Zhu and Dzung Phan, assisted at the conference by Lorraine Salazar.

Professor Raul Fabella, dean of the School of Economics, University of the Philippines, kindly facilitated our work and played an active role in the Canberra conference, which we gratefully acknowledge.

Beth Thomson transformed the manuscript from a collection of papers in need of an editor to this final polished version. We are indebted to her for her excellent work under a tight deadline. We also wish to thank Jeff Ducanes for preparing the subject index with care and finesse.

We thank our publishers, Oxford University Press and Ateneo de Manila University Press, for their interest and enthusiasm. In particular we would like to thank Paul Donnelly, Stephen McGroarty, Nancy Hoagland, Ma. Corazon Baytion, and Esther Pacheco.

A word on the history and evolution of the project is warranted. We started off in a moderately hopeful vein. After a shaky beginning, the 1990s turned out to be a pretty good decade for the Philippines. The reform process, which got under way seriously in the very difficult later years of the Aquino administration and accelerated during the Ramos administration, produced a dividend. Growth was quite strong until the onset of the Asian economic crisis, and then at least the country weathered this event quite successfully.

However, as has so often happened in the Philippines, just when the prospects were again looking encouraging for the country, events took a turn for the worse. The early hopes for the Estrada administration—based on an assessment that the president would in effect delegate to his largely able cabinet members—were dashed by a series of scandals, rising nepotism, and corruption. A renewal of the very serious insurgency problems in the south of the country during 2000 and 2001 badly tarnished the Philippines' international reputation. The political impasse was resolved, temporarily at least, in early 2001 with the accession to power of President Macapagal-Arroyo, but domestic political uncertainties lingered. Meanwhile the international outlook also began to sour, initially as the world economy headed for recession, and dramatically following the terrorist attacks on New York and Washington, D.C. of 11 September.

Since the research and writing on which this book draws were essentially completed before September 11, it is pertinent to ask whether these events and their aftermath have implications for the story presented here. Do our arguments and conclusions require a fundamental rethink, and if so, how and why?

The Philippines has become a "frontline state" in the U.S.-driven war against international terrorism. The controversial and long-established American bases in the country were closed over a decade ago, but, in the wake of September 11, Philippine–U.S. military and strategic cooperation quickly intensified. Southeast Asian governments immediately condemned the terrorist attacks, but none has aligned itself more closely with the United States than the Philippines. President Macapagal-Arroyo signaled her intention to cooperate very closely with American anti-terrorist initiatives, in particular the assault on the global network of Al Qaeda cells and sympathizers.

The Philippines has had a long-running Muslim insurgency in the south of the country. In recent years the insurgents have splintered into several groups, ranging from moderates whose agenda calls for greater regional autonomy within the Philippine state to opportunistic and ruthless gangs who practice banditry and kidnapping. With its history of sporadic Middle Eastern interference, Mindanao proved to be fertile ground for Al Qaeda penetration. It is not known with any precision how active this Al Qaeda presence is, but links have been established between it and the Abu Sayyaf rebels. Sections of the more mainstream Moro Islamic National Front are also thought to have some Al Qaeda connections.

The American and Philippine administrations thus had a powerful common interest in waging a war against terrorism and insurrection in the south of the country. The United States believed that the Al Qaeda presence in the Philippines was probably the most established in East Asia. The new Macapagal-Arroyo administration was anxious both to solve the Mindanao problem and to develop closer political and commercial ties with the United States.

The Philippine president met with President Bush and Prime Minister Blair in late 2001 and, notwithstanding nationalist reservations at home, aligned herself closely with the United States. In consequence some 660 American military personnel were dispatched to the Philippines, with their mandate restricted to advisory work rather than combat duty. In return for this cooperation, the United States doubled its development assistance in Mindanao to $55 million and offered a significant increase in military assistance.

It is too early to judge what effect these events will have on Philippine economic development. Ideally one needs to separate out the immediate effects of the terrorist attacks and the medium-term impact of closer engagement with the United States and its allies. These events also occurred against a backdrop of global economic recession in 2001, further complicating the challenges of economic management and recovery.

With regard to the immediate effects, regrettably the Philippines tends to attract international publicity for all the wrong reasons: foreign tourists and business people being kidnapped; prolonged insurrections in the south of the country; and all manner of personal and national tragedies, including earthquakes, typhoons, and interisland ferry accidents. The country's political and commercial terrain is perceived, rightly or wrongly, to be unpredictable and sometimes difficult. In times of international crisis and uncertainty, therefore, the "safe haven" effect works against it. Investors, particularly from distant OECD countries, are inclined to avoid it.

In principle, closer relations with the United States should prove beneficial to the Philippines. But there are no guarantees. The country enjoyed very close commercial and strategic relations with the United States during its first four decades of independence, but that relationship was not able to guarantee rapid economic growth and immunity to crisis. Indeed, one of the clear lessons of international experience is that foreign aid can foster development, but only in the context of a supportive domestic policy environment. Thus, the increased aid flows to the Philippines offer the possibility, but not the certainty, of accelerated economic growth. Whether the foreign largesse translates into improved performance will depend on the ability of the nation's leadership to capitalize on these opportunities. In this respect, September 11 has not altered the fundamental analysis and message of this volume. To the extent that this is a policy-oriented tract, our themes of sustainable growth with equity remain the same.

Where circumstances have altered since September 11 is in the prosecution of the war on rebellion and insurrection in the south. President Macapagal-Arroyo has committed her administration to a full-scale assault, with the aid of American troops. Obviously, a military operation of this nature can only be a part of the solution and, if mismanaged, could aggravate the situation. Former President Ramos demonstrated that it is possible to secure peace—albeit fragile—in Mindanao, when his administration negotiated a settlement. (It is often forgotten, incidentally, that then President Soeharto played a constructive role in this peace settlement. Indonesian politics is now so unpredictable, and the nation so absorbed in its domestic problems, that concerted assistance from this source is not in prospect.) The key to success, now as then, is a deft combination of military force to root out banditry, a recognition of the genuine grievances lying behind the unrest, a willingness to address these economic, social, and religious grievances at their source, and an administrative and financial capacity to implement reform.

On the third element of this equation, the state of the economy, the Philippines displayed surprising resilience in 2001. The economy grew by a quite respectable 3.4%, slightly over 1% in per capita terms. This is about the post-crisis growth rate, that is, for the years 1999–2001. Although far too slow to make a dint on the serious socioeconomic challenges facing the country, this has at least enabled the Philippines to avoid the deeper recessions of several Southeast Asian nations. The economy continued to grow in 2001 because of the return of some semblance of political stability, and the expectation in the business sector that the Macapagal-Arroyo administration would evolve into a pragmatic regime emphasizing sound economic management. The country also managed to avoid the worst of the global recession because, although heavily reliant on the electronics sector, it is still not as internationally oriented as some of its neighbors.

It is therefore unclear what effect the events of September 11 and their aftermath will have on the country's development. There are clear potential negatives. As a frontline state in the U.S.-led war on terrorism, tourists and investors will tend to avoid the country. The deployment of American troops in the war against alleged Al Qaeda influences could backfire if the military operation is poorly executed, or if nationalist sentiment is inflamed to the point where the government's shaky political mandate is weakened further.

But there are potential positives, too. The Macapagal-Arroyo administration is seen as staunchly pro-West, and is likely to benefit from increased aid and improved market access for its exports. If the campaign against the insurrections in the south is managed adroitly, peace could be restored. This would have tremendous potential benefits for both Mindanao and the nation as a whole. Moreover, in times of national crisis there are typically benefits of incumbency (provided of course that the regime did not itself cause the crisis). It is therefore conceivable that the president may have an opportunity to rule the country for almost a decade and to oversee a period of sustained reform and policy continuity. We will have to wait and see whether the nation's political leadership has the will and capacity to translate the fortuitous opportunity of increased foreign assistance into a better life for ordinary Filipinos.

To sum up, the cautious optimism present at the start of this project has given way to much greater uncertainty and apprehension. However, we believe that these changed circumstances in no way invalidate our fundamental story. The Philippines has no control over international events. But we believe that it can improve the lives of its citizens, or at least ameliorate their hardship during difficult times, by drawing on the analysis and reform agenda laid out in this book. To this end, we hope that our labors will be of interest to Philippine politicians, government officials, business people, journalists, academics, and students, and to all those abroad with an interest in this fascinating and important country.

Contents

List of Figures

List of Tables

List of Contributors

Arsenio M. Balisacan is Professor of Economics at the University of the Philippines School of Economics, Diliman, and President of the Asia-Pacific Policy Center. He has served with the Philippine government as Agriculture Undersecretary and has been a Visiting Fellow at the Australian National University. His recent research has focused on poverty, inequality, agricultural and rural development, and the political economy of policy reforms. His articles have appeared in numerous books and professional journals.

Hal Hill is the H.W. Arndt Professor of Southeast Asian Economies at the Australian National University. His general research interests are the ASEAN economies, especially Indonesia and the Philippines, and industrialization and foreign investment in East Asia. He is the author or editor of 14 books and has written about 110 academic papers and book chapters.

Rahimaisa D. Abdula is a PhD candidate at the University of the Philippines School of Economics, Diliman, and is also pursuing a doctoral degree in Environmental Economics at the University of Gothenburg. She has served as a lecturer at the University of the Philippines-Diliman and as a research specialist at the Philippine Institute for Development Studies. Her research interests include public finance, agriculture, and trade and the environment.

Ma. Joy V. Abrenica is Associate Professor of Economics at the University of the Philippines School of Economics, Diliman. She is also the Executive Director of the Society for the Advancement of Technology Management in the Philippines. Her research interests lie in the fields of industrial organization and international economics.

Romeo Bautista is Visiting Research Fellow at the Philippine Institute for Development Studies. Previously, he was Professor of Economics at the University of the Philippines School of Economics, Diliman and Research Fellow at the Trade and Macroeconomics Division of the International Food Policy Research Institute. His recent research has focused on multisector policy analysis in developing countries.

Dante Canlas is Enrique Virata Professor of Economics at the University of the Philippines School of Economics, Diliman. He was seconded to the national government in January 2001 as Secretary of Socioeconomic Planning and Director-General of the National Economic and Development Authority. He has published articles on macroeconomics, money, and labor.

Shiladitya Chatterjee is an economist with the Asian Development Bank (ADB), and currently the bank's Principal Programs Officer and Country Team Leader for Indonesia. He worked earlier as the ADB's Senior Economist for the Philippines. Before joining the ADB he held, as a member of the Indian Administrative Service, positions at the provincial and central government levels, including Secretary of Finance, Government of Assam; and Director of the Prime Minister's Office.

Ian Coxhead is Associate Professor at the Department of Agricultural and Applied Economics, University of Wisconsin-Madison, where he teaches economic development with special reference to the countries of Southeast Asia. His primary research interests are trade and development, development policy, and the links between trade, development policy, and the management of environmental and natural resources.

Cristina C. David is Research Fellow at the Philippine Institute for Development Studies. She previously served as Agricultural Economist at the International Rice Research Institute and member of the faculty of the University of the Philippines at Los Baños. Her primary research interest is the economics of food and agriculture. Her articles in this area have appeared in numerous books and professional journals.

Emmanuel S. de Dios is Professor of Economics at the University of the Philippines School of Economics, Diliman, where he has taught since 1981 and served as Chair of the Economics Department several times. He maintains an interest in aspects of choice theory and the history of thought, but is using his current sabbatical to develop a number of papers on institutions and economic development and to complete the translation of a work on economic geography.

Maria Socorro Gochoco-Bautista is the Rosa Alvero Professor of Economics and Chair of the Economics Department at the University of the Philippines School of Economics, Diliman. She was previously Assistant Professor of Economics at the University of Hawaii, Manoa. Her latest publication, which appeared in the *Journal of Macroeconomics*, dealt with the stylized facts and leading indicators of currency crises.

Alejandro N. Herrin is Professor of Economics at the University of the Philippines School of Economics, Diliman. He has served as Chair of the Economics Department and Coordinator of the School's Health Economics Program at various times, and as President of the Philippine Economic Society in 1992. His main research interests are population, health and nutrition, and gender and development in the Philippines.

Paul D. Hutchcroft is Associate Professor of Political Science at the University of Wisconsin-Madison. He has written extensively on Philippine politics and political economy, as well as on the politics of corruption. He is the author of *Booty Capitalism: The Politics of Banking in the Philippines* (Cornell University Press, 1998) and *Deciphering Decentralization: Central Authority and Local Bosses in the Philippines and Beyond* (forthcoming, Cambridge University Press).

Sisira Jayasuriya is Director of the Asian Economics Centre at the Department of Economics, University of Melbourne. He has previously held appointments at La Trobe University and the Australian National University in Australia, and at the International Rice Research Institute in the Philippines. His current research interests are economic integration and policy liberalization, resource and environmental issues, and the political economy of South and Southeast Asia.

Gilberto M. Llanto is Deputy Director-General (Undersecretary) of the National Economic and Development Authority and Vice-President (on leave) of the Philippine Institute for Development Studies. He is a member of the editorial board of the Philippine Journal of Development and was a member of the Board of Trustees of the Philippine Economic Society from 1992 to 1995. His main research interests are public economics and fiscal policy.

Rosario G. Manasan is a Research Fellow at the Philippine Institute for Development Studies, where she coordinates the research program on public finance and fiscal policy. She has published numerous articles on taxation, government expenditure, public enterprises, fiscal decentralization, and industrial promotion policies in local and international journals.

Ernesto M. Pernia is Lead Economist at the Economics and Research Department, Asian Development Bank. He was Professor of Economics at the University of the Philippines School of Economics, Diliman, in 1982–85, and President of the Philippine Economic Society in 1988. He co-authored (with M.G. Quibria) a chapter on "Poverty in Developing Countries" in the *Handbook of Regional and Urban Economics*, Vol. 3 (Amsterdam: North Holland, 1999).

Gerardo P. Sicat began his career at the University of the Philippines School of Economics, Diliman and is winding it down there. In past years he has served as Minister of Economic Planning and Director-General of the National Economic and Development Authority, and worked for 13 years at the World Bank.

Gwendolyn Tecson is Professor of Economics at the University of the Philippines School of Economics, Diliman. She served as Director of the Program in Development Economics in 1997–98 and in 1999–2001. She has written extensively on trade policy issues in the Philippines. Her main research interests are international trade and industrial policy.

PART I

Setting the Scene

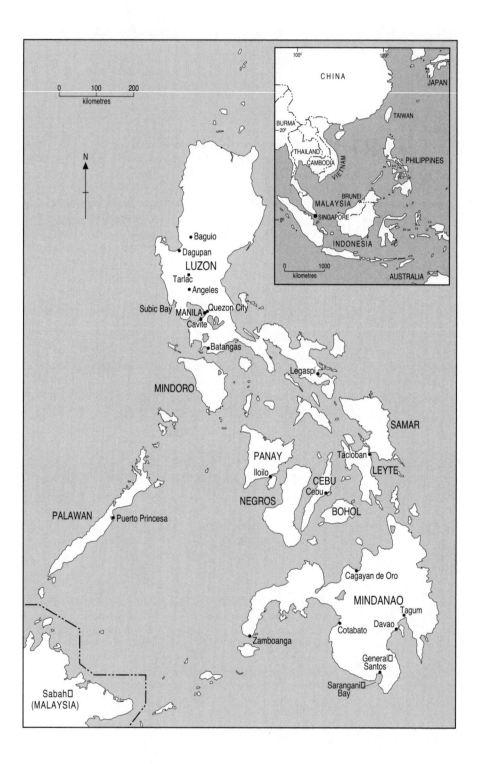

1

An Introduction to the Key Issues

Arsenio M. Balisacan and Hal Hill

1.1 A PUZZLE TO EXPLAIN

The Philippines is one of the world's major development puzzles. In the immediate aftermath of the Pacific war, and despite extensive wartime destruction, it had one of the highest per capita incomes in East Asia: above South Korea and Taiwan, significantly higher than Thailand, Indonesia and China, and below only Japan, the then Malaya, and the city states of Hong Kong and Singapore.

Among newly independent countries, its initial conditions were favorable. American rule from 1898 had been comparatively benign by colonial standards. The transition to formal independence was relatively painless, certainly when compared with the experience of some neighboring countries. Again, unlike some of its neighbors, the Philippines had no really serious communal or ethnic divides. Its educational standards were among the highest in the developing world. By dint of its colonial experience, it had privileged access to the market of the world's largest economy, a facility which continued until the expiration of the Laurel–Langley Agreement in 1974. The country's civil institutions were comparatively well developed, too. It possessed a reasonably democratic political system, albeit of the "winner-takes-all" variety. Its judiciary and legal system were quite well developed and somewhat independent. Its press was open and vigorous. Finally, while not especially resource-rich, the Philippines possessed ample agricultural land to sustain several decades of rapid agricultural growth.

By the mid-1960s, there was still little evidence that things were to go seriously wrong. Indeed, the Philippines was largely free of the major problems then besetting Southeast Asia: the Vietnam War, amid fear of the "domino theory"; Indonesia's campaign of *konfrontasi* against newly formed Malaysia; and the Malaysia–

3

Singapore separation of 1965. As a vote of confidence in Philippine stability and the country's future, the headquarters of the region's major international development institution, the Asian Development Bank, were located in Manila. Even as late as 1980, the Philippines was still regarded by most analysts as belonging to the second generation of the Asian "tiger" economies.

Yet its development outcomes have been disappointing by any yardstick. In 2000, official statistics suggest that its real per capita GDP was about the same as in 1980. Its per capita income was overtaken by Korea and Taiwan in the 1950s, Thailand in the 1970s, Indonesia in the 1980s (though more recently it has fallen behind again), and China in the 1990s. It missed out almost completely on the Asian boom from the late 1970s until the mid-1990s. In particular, the restructuring from the mid-1980s, which witnessed the large-scale migration of labor-intensive industries to China and the lower-wage ASEAN economies, bypassed the Philippines. Especially in the 1980s and early 1990s, the country became an increasingly marginal player in the region's trade and investment flows. In consequence its social indicators stagnated, in marked contrast to the situation in its high-growth neighbors. The Philippines is obviously well endowed with human capital, but an uncomfortably high proportion of its best and brightest aspire to employ their talents abroad, often never to return.

The comparison with Thailand is particularly pertinent. The two countries have much in common apart from their location—a similar population size, land area, resource base, and economic structure, and similar movements in their terms of trade. Yet Thailand, which was significantly poorer in the 1950s, overtook the Philippines in the early 1970s; just before the recent Asian crisis, its per capita income was almost three times higher. If ever there were a case of non-identical twins, this would be it.

A number of caveats need to be attached to this gloomy assessment. First, it is important not to overstate the initial conditions. There was extensive wartime destruction. Many of the apparently well-developed political, legal, and bureaucratic institutions established in the wake of the American colonial era had shallow roots, and could easily be manipulated by powerful political–business oligarchs. This was particularly the case since the country's agrarian structures, which in turn established the parameters of political power, were highly unequal. Moreover, the relationship with the United States, while conferring significant potential commercial advantages, proved to be a troublesome one. It arguably distorted the elite's commercial calculus, and it complicated political and strategic considerations.

The second caveat is that the performance of the Philippines looks deficient partly because it is most often compared with its neighbors. The above comparisons are with economies which, until 1997, were the world's fastest growing. The Philippine record is in fact broadly similar to that of the developing world as a whole. If the comparison were with Latin America (with which the Philippines is sometimes grouped in view of its colonial history), or with South Asia or Africa, it would be about par for the course.

Third, it is important to emphasize that the really pronounced divergence in development performance occurred in the decade and a half from the late 1970s until the early 1990s. Philippine growth rates never matched those of the newly industrializing economies (NIEs), and especially from the late 1960s the country's economy grew more slowly than those of its major ASEAN neighbors. But decennial growth comparisons reveal only a gradual divergence in the 1950s, 1960s, and even the 1970s. The gap became sharply evident only in the 1980s; despite a modest recovery, it continued to widen in the first half of the 1990s. Thus, explanations for the weaker record of the Philippines need to focus on this period, while of course recognizing its historical roots.

The final caveat is that the Philippines weathered the recent economic crisis more successfully than most major Southeast Asian economies. For once, being the "East Asian exception" was good news.

The chapters in this book examine all major facets of the Philippine economy and development policy. The authors attempt to look both backward and forward. They examine and assess trends since the 1980s, in the process synthesizing the relevant specialist literature. They identify the major policy issues and provide a balance sheet of achievements and deficiencies over the past decade and beyond. Finally, they highlight future challenges which need to be addressed if the country is to embark on a sustainable, durable, and equitable growth trajectory.

Drawing on the contributions to this volume, the objective of this introductory chapter is three-fold. First, in section 1.2 we provide a broad overview of the development record since around 1980. Next, we look at the picture in more detail, examining international and macroeconomic dimensions, trends at the sectoral level, and various socioeconomic development indicators. On this basis, we offer an assessment of the achievements and failures of the post-Marcos period. Finally, in section 1.4 we return to the larger question of why the Philippines has often underperformed relative to its obvious potential. As a corollary to this larger question, it is also of interest to explore why the country has not received a larger "reform dividend" from the significant policy achievements of the first three-quarters of the 1990s, and why also it came through the recent Asian crisis relatively unscathed.

Our approaches are variously descriptive, analytical, interpretive, and comparative. The subject of the book is self-evidently important. The Philippines is a large country of more than 75 million people, and the world's second largest archipelagic state. It is often poorly understood abroad, a factor not helped by tired old cliches such as that it is a "Latin American country located in East Asia." It is the least integrated within Southeast Asia of the original ASEAN member countries. With the removal of U.S. bases in 1992, its geostrategic ties with its former colonial master have waned. The country has been off the radar screens of international investors recently, as it was for most of the 1980s. The world takes note of spectacular successes, such as the Asian tigers since the 1960s, and catastrophic failures, such as Indonesia in 1997–98. The Philippines has really been neither, and therefore for much of the past 20 years it has received surprisingly little international attention.

We are therefore approaching the subject as one worthy of study given its inherent importance. But there is clearly much more to the story than this. There are lessons from the Philippines' development experience that are of much general relevance and interest. In particular, there is the question of why it has been an East

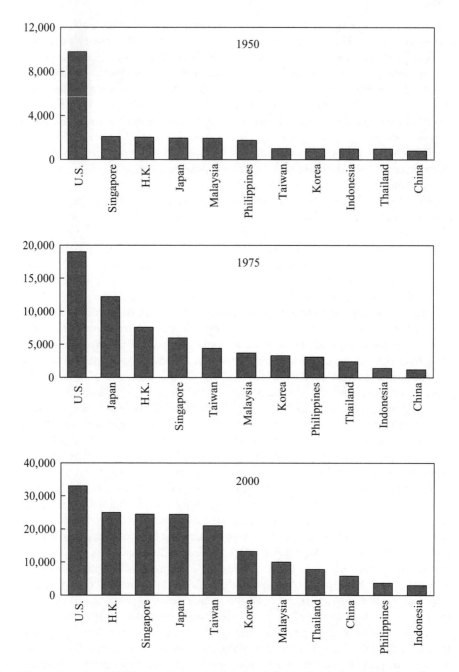

Figure 1.1 Real GDP per Capita in Selected Countries, 1950, 1975, and 2000 ($)

In constant prices based on 1999 purchasing power parity (PPP) exchange rates. *Sources*: IMF, World Economic Outlook database.

Asian outlier—first in the negative and then in the positive sense—for much of the past 30 years. As noted, the comparison with Thailand is especially apposite here. The Philippine record post-Marcos may also, unfortunately, be indicative of what is in store for post-Soeharto Indonesia as it grapples with a difficult mix of abrupt political transition and deep economic crisis, much as Filipinos had to in the second half of the 1980s.

1.2 AN OVERVIEW OF THE RECORD

Figure 1.1 and Table 1.1 locate the Philippine record in comparative East Asian context. In 1950, when most developing countries' national accounts were admittedly rudimentary, per capita GDP in the Philippines, in purchasing power parity (PPP) terms, was midway between that of the richer city states and that of the poorest country in the sample, China. By this measure, some 25 years later it had slipped behind Taiwan and Korea and was similar to Thailand. By 2000 China and for a period Indonesia had overtaken it. As Table 1.1 makes clear, the growth record of the Philippines was comparable to that of its neighbors in the 1960s and 1970s, albeit a percentage point or more lower. The really pronounced divergence occurred in the "lost decade" of the 1980s, when its neighbors averaged about 6% annual growth, in contrast to its 1%. (In per capita terms the differences were larger still, since by the 1980s Philippine population growth rates were significantly higher.) The differences in growth rates narrowed in the 1990s, but for most of the decade the Philippines continued to fall further behind.

Economic Growth

Figures 1.2 and 1.3 document the story on an annual basis from 1970 to 2000. The 1970s were a decade of continuous expansion, with GDP growth averaging 5.8% annually.[1] In every year during that decade, growth in both GDP and per capita GDP

Table 1.1 Average Growth of GDP in Southeast Asia, 1950–2000 (% p.a.)

Country	1950–60	1960–70	1970–80	1980–90	1990–2000
Indonesia	4.0	3.9	7.6	6.1	4.2
Malaysia	3.6	6.5	7.8	5.3	7.0
Philippines	6.5	5.1	6.3	1.0	3.2
Singapore	n.a.	8.8	8.5	6.6	7.8
Thailand	5.7	8.4	7.2	7.6	4.2

Sources: Lim (2001: 38); World Bank (2002), *World Development Report 2002*.

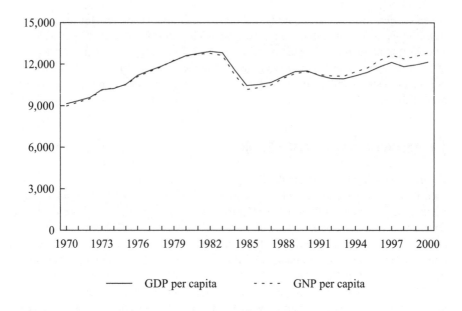

Figure 1.2 Real GDP and GNP per Capita, 1970–2000 (pesos, in 1985 prices)

Source: National Statistical Coordination Board.

was positive, with peaks in excess of 8% GDP growth twice, in 1974 and 1977. However, by the late 1970s growth was more subdued, at less than 6%. It then collapsed in 1984, as a political and an economic crisis set in. The former was triggered by the assassination of former opposition leader Benigno Aquino at Manila International Airport in August 1983. The economic crisis was partly a response to this incident, but its roots lay deeper, in the economic policy settings of the previous decade in particular. Negative external shocks further complicated the situation. These events culminated in a deep economic contraction in 1985–86, in the midst of which Ferdinand Marcos was deposed after 20 years of rule. Per capita GDP plunged by almost 20% over these two years.

Thereafter, a patchy economic recovery got under way, but this proved to be short-lived. By the early 1990s growth had again stalled, and there were two years of contraction. This was a much milder recession than in the mid-1980s, and by 1994 the growth momentum had resumed. In 1998 there was further dislocation, this time caused by the Asian economic crisis in combination with a severe El Niño-induced drought. On this occasion the downturn was very brief. Growth—albeit subdued—was restored the following year.

Figure 1.2 plots the picture in terms of real per capita GDP and GNP in 1985 prices. There is a growing divergence between the two series in the 1990s, reflecting the increasing impact of (probably more accurately measured) overseas remittances. The data suggest that, by 2000, per capita GNP had recovered to the peak

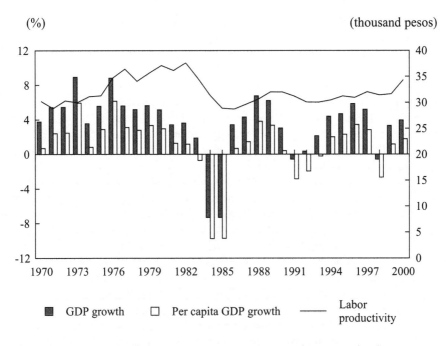

Figure 1.3 GDP Growth (%), per Capita GDP Growth (%), and Labor Productivity (in thousand pesos at 1985 prices), 1970–2000

Source: National Statistical Coordination Board.

year of 1983, but that per capita GDP remained almost 10% below this high point, at about the level achieved in 1980.[2]

The main point to emphasize is that, unlike many of its neighbors, the Philippines has not experienced a sustained period of rapid growth since the 1970s. The 1970s were its best decade, but even then very high rates were a rarity. Moreover, since 1980 the Philippines has not had more than four consecutive years of positive growth in per capita GDP. Finally, what growth there has been has been rather anemic, rarely above 3% (in per capita terms). With so many years of decline, it is easy to understand why progress has been minimal.

Labor productivity broadly followed the trend in real per capita GDP, except that its decline in the mid-1980s was sharper and its recovery thereafter slower. As Herrin and Pernia (Chapter 9) point out, several factors are at work here. Labor productivity typically falls faster than per capita GDP during a recession. In the formal wage sector, both employers and employees adopt various survival strategies, imperfectly recorded since hours worked are not measured accurately. Non-wage employment is elastic, especially in agriculture and the informal sector. Within sectors, too, there have been adjustments. In some cases the decline may have been no bad thing, most notably the shift in manufacturing from protected, capital-intensive activities toward export-oriented, labor-intensive industries.[3]

How might the years since 1970 be classified episodically? Inevitably the divisions are somewhat arbitrary, with different criteria (growth rates, policy emphases, external conditions, administrations) yielding different results.[4] One classification might be as follows.

- *Debt-driven growth, 1970–83.* Growth was quite respectable over this period, but was declining steadily following the 1977 peak. Moreover, it was driven by large overseas borrowings. This strategy was unsustainable since the funds were generally not invested productively, and by the early 1980s the country had essentially hit its borrowing limits.
- *Stagnation, then deep crisis, 1984–86.* Political and economic events together resulted in a very large economic contraction, the largest in the country's post-independence history. President Marcos was finally removed from office in February 1986, through a combination of disputed electoral returns and massive demonstrations along Manila's main arterial route, EDSA.
- *Erratic recovery, 1987–91.* Economic recovery ensued as the political situation stabilized, facilitated also by some return of capital, a competitive peso, mostly positive movements in the terms of trade, and strong regional growth. Toward the end of this period, a serious reform agenda began to be implemented.
- *Mild crisis, 1992–93.* Notwithstanding a pick-up in the momentum for reform, both in the late Aquino period and more decisively under the Ramos administration, the economy slowed. This mild downturn was the result of the conjunction of several negative factors—a succession of coup attempts in the early 1990s, very serious power shortages, some particularly destructive natural disasters (especially the eruption of Mt Pinatubo in 1991), and the removal of U.S. military bases in 1992. (The latter alone were estimated to contribute, directly and indirectly, as much as 5% of GDP.)
- *Recovery and growth, 1994–97.* This was an important period in Philippine economic history. It was an era of decisive reform in which there was a return to moderately good growth rates, peaking at almost 6% in the middle of the decade. There was a clear, if modest, reform dividend. Unfortunately, however, just as the country appeared set to rejoin the East Asian growth club, external factors intervened.
- *Weathering crises, 1998–2001.* The Asian economic crisis affected the Philippines only mildly and briefly (certainly when compared with its neighbors). The period was notable for at least two reasons. First, it was the country's first significant crisis that was clearly not of the government's making, but rather precipitated mainly by external factors—namely the regional economic crisis of 1997–98 and, not much less importantly, a very serious drought. Second, it was the first occasion on which a sharp devaluation of the peso did not trigger either a financial crisis or a generalized economic contraction. Both were significant achievements in the long sweep of post-independence Philippine economic history. From mid-2000 a general political malaise began to set in, owing to widespread disenchantment with the administration of President Estrada. This eventually resulted in his removal from office in January 2001.

Sectoral Expansion and Structural Change

Growth in the principal sectors of the economy has generally followed the aggregate picture, once sector-specific factors are taken into account (Figure 1.4 and Table 1.2). All major sectors grew quite strongly in the 1970s. The momentum of growth fell sharply in the 1980s, and the pick-up in the 1990s was mixed. As would be expected, the sharpest fluctuations have occurred in industry. High levels of protection in manufacturing, the major sector, left it exposed to the contraction of the 1980s (Hill, Chapter 7). Firms were simply unable to switch quickly to exports, notwithstanding the sharp peso depreciation and buoyant international markets. After double-digit growth rates in the 1970s—much of it public sector-dependent—construction activity shrank during the 1980s before it too returned to modest growth in the 1990s.

Agriculture grew strongly in the 1970s, driven in particular by a creditable performance in food crops (David, Chapter 6). For a number of reasons growth petered out in the following decades, and per capita agricultural output actually fell marginally. In contrast to several of its neighbors, the Philippines has not developed a viable export-oriented cash crop sector. Its historically important cash crops, sugar and coconuts, are both in the doldrums. Forestry output has declined continuously, a trend that accelerated in the 1990s, by which time virtually all primary forests had disappeared.

If there has been a sectoral success story, it would be services. It is the only sector to have recorded positive per capita growth in all three decades, as shown in

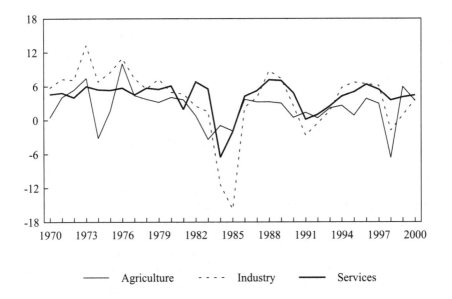

Figure 1.4 Growth by Sector, 1970–2000 (%)

Source: National Statistical Coordination Board.

Table 1.2 Annual Growth by Sector, 1970s, 1980s, and 1990s (%)

Sector	1970s	1980s	1990s
Agriculture, fisheries & forestry	3.7	1.5	1.5
Agriculture	5.8	2.4	2.0
Crops	6.3	1.3	1.3
Livestock & poultry	3.1	5.7	4.7
Fisheries	4.1	4.1	1.7
Forestry	−2.7	−6.0	−13.5
Industry	8.0	0.9	2.5
Mining & quarrying	6.8	3.8	−1.5
Manufacturing	6.6	1.2	2.3
Construction	14.2	−0.7	2.9
Electricity, gas, & water	13.7	5.7	5.3
Services	5.2	3.5	3.7
Transport, communication, storage	7.6	3.7	4.4
Trade	5.9	3.3	3.6
Finance	8.4	3.3	5.6
Occupied dwellings and real estate	1.2	2.7	2.2
Private services	5.0	5.5	3.6
Government services	4.6	3.4	3.6
GDP	5.8	2.0	2.8
GNP	5.9	1.8	3.6

Source: National Statistical Coordination Board.

Table 1.2. Growth has been positive in every year except the two severe recession years of the mid-1980s. The same relatively even pattern has been evident in most of its subsectors; all recorded positive growth during each decade. Whether this resilience can be interpreted positively is a moot point. Clearly, as Abrenica and Llanto (Chapter 8) emphasize, the 1990s reforms propelled growth in several sub-sectors. But growth in the 1980s was very similar to that in the 1990s, suggesting the possibility that, with its highly elastic employment coefficients, services may also have acted as a sector of "last resort" employment.

Trends in real sectoral labor productivity shed a little light on this issue (Table 1.3). In agriculture, productivity bottomed in 1985 and has increased erratically since then. In services, productivity also reached a low point in 1985, and since then has been virtually constant. In industry it peaked in 1980, declined by 30% during the 1980s, and then remained fairly flat in the 1990s. Increases in the 1970s and declines in the first half of the 1980s are easy enough to explain, since they pre-

Table 1.3 Real Value Added per Worker, 1970–2000 (pesos)[a]

Year	Agriculture	Industry	Services
1970	15,884	62,364	36,666
1975	14,961	84,227	38,578
1980	16,791	99,162	39,048
1985	14,472	77,396	32,551
1990	16,046	69,976	33,279
1995	15,391	67,985	32,897
2000	17,151	72,000	32,436

a   Each entry is a three-year average of the year indicated, the previous year, and the succeeding year, using 1985 prices.

Source: National Statistical Coordination Board.

dominantly reflect the effects of the economic cycle. But since 1985 industry has become more labor-intensive, and agriculture less so. In other words, sectoral differences in factor proportions have narrowed. Labor productivity in industry was 5.9 and 2.5 times that of agriculture and services respectively in 1980. By 2000, the ratios had declined to 4.2 and 2.2. This narrowing may be interpreted positively, as presumptive evidence of a more integrated, and less distorted, "dualistic" economy.

Diverging sectoral growth rates of output and employment have resulted in some structural change, though not in the manner customarily expected (Tables 1.4 and 1.5). Because economic growth has generally been slow, the really sharp and rapid structural transformation commonly seen in East Asia is not evident. The share of agriculture in GDP has declined steadily. But whereas the more general pattern is for the share of industry to expand, in the Philippine case it too has shrunk, albeit marginally. The consistent gainer, as implied by the growth rates, has been services. Its share of GDP has risen by an extraordinary 50% since 1980, and during both good times and bad. The employment story has been broadly similar, with the declining agricultural share more or less mirroring the increase in services. In the early 1980s agriculture's share of total employment dipped below 50% for the first time. In the late 1990s services overtook agriculture as the single largest employer of labor, and on present trends is likely to account for half of the total quite soon. Of course, agriculture remains a major employer of labor (39% in 2000). And, especially for rural employment, one should be careful about drawing too sharp a distinction between the sectors.

These trends throw up several pertinent questions. Why is agriculture's share of GDP declining even with slow growth? Why has the industry share—and in particular that of manufacturing—actually declined marginally? And why is the share of services increasing inexorably? Several factors would appear to be relevant.

Table 1.4 Share of Sectors in Current Price GDP, 1970–2000 (%)[a]

Sector	1970	1975	1980	1985	1990	1995	2000
Agriculture, fisheries and forestry	29.9	30.2	25.8	24.4	21.9	21.4	16.5
Agricultural industry	25.7	27.5	23.2	22.6	21.0	21.2	16.4
Crops	16.2	18.5	14.9	13.5	12.0	12.5	10.1
Livestock & poultry	4.9	3.9	3.2	3.3	4.2	4.2	3.4
Fisheries	4.9	5.2	4.7	4.8	3.8	3.5	2.5
Forestry	4.2	2.7	2.6	1.9	0.9	0.2	0.1
Industry	31.5	35.2	38.5	35.9	34.5	32.2	30.9
Mining & quarrying	1.8	1.6	2.1	2.0	1.5	0.9	0.6
Manufacturing	24.5	25.6	25.5	24.8	25.0	23.0	22.1
Construction	4.3	6.7	9.4	6.4	5.7	5.7	5.2
Electricity, gas, & water	0.8	1.4	1.6	2.6	2.2	2.6	2.9
Services	38.6	34.6	35.7	39.7	43.7	46.4	52.6
Transport, communication, storage	3.4	3.8	4.5	5.5	5.2	4.7	5.7
Trade	9.5	10.4	11.9	14.1	14.4	13.7	14.2
Finance	3.0	3.2	3.6	3.1	3.9	4.2	4.6
Occupied dwellings & real estate	8.3	6.3	5.2	5.5	5.8	6.8	6.9
Private services	7.5	5.5	5.5	6.7	7.6	8.9	11.4
Government services	6.8	5.4	5.1	4.9	7.0	8.1	9.8

a   Each entry is a three-year average of the year indicated, the previous year, and the succeeding year.

Source: National Statistical Coordination Board.

Table 1.5 Share of Major Sectors in Employment, 1970–2000 (%)[a]

Year	Agriculture	Industry	Services
1970	52.1	16.1	30.9
1975	54.3	14.7	30.7
1980	51.3	15.1	33.5
1985	49.7	13.9	36.4
1990	44.8	15.6	39.2
1995	43.5	16.0	40.5
2000	38.6	15.8	46.3

a   Each entry is a three-year average of the year indicated, the previous year, and the succeeding year.

Source: National Statistical Coordination Board.

First, agriculture has encountered resource constraints. These are most obvious in forestry and fishing, but more generally the country hit the land frontiers—and hence the limits of extensive agricultural growth—around the 1970s, especially against a backdrop of continuing rapid population growth and slow non-agricultural employment absorption. For the reasons discussed by David (Chapter 6), agricultural yields have increased only slowly since 1980.

The case of industry is particularly interesting and unusual. The share of manufacturing output is now lower than it was in 1970. Is this cause for concern? As Bautista and Tecson (Chapter 5) and Hill (Chapter 7) point out, several factors have been at work. Output growth has been sluggish in some years. It may be that some of the new, export-oriented electronics output is not being counted properly. Protection has fallen steadily, and thus the reported decline is overstated if measured in international prices. (By contrast, the opposite phenomenon has occurred in agriculture, since protection has risen over this period.) An appreciating currency in the mid-1990s, combined with an urban minimum wage appreciably higher than that in competitor countries, may also have impeded growth in what is overwhelmingly a tradable activity. Thus there is no clear answer to the question. The evident decline in labor productivity may be no bad thing, since the sector is now embarked on a more labor-intensive and efficient trajectory. And the overcounting implicit in past protection has been removed. But the fact remains that growth has still been anemic.

There is no clear and obvious explanation for the continuing rise in services. The trend has occurred across virtually all subsectors, public and private, quasi-tradable and non-tradable, substantially and minimally deregulated alike. The increase has occurred both when the real exchange rate has been appreciating and when it has been depreciating, so the relative price of tradables to non-tradables does not seem to have been a decisive factor. The increase has also occurred during periods of high and low growth, so it is difficult to find support for either an "employment of last resort" or "agent of growth" hypothesis. Perhaps the inflow of remittances has in various ways been particularly pro-services, as some have conjectured. It may also simply be that services are what the Philippines is best at, another school of thought which has its adherents. Clearly more research is needed on this subject.

Expenditure and Savings

The slow growth has also been reflected in the expenditure accounts (Table 1.6). The share of personal consumption is high in the Philippines by East Asian standards. It rose sharply in the first half of the 1980s, predictably, as a protective strategy during the economic downturn. However, once ratcheted up to over 70%, it has failed to decline in response to positive growth. The share of government consumption has also picked up appreciably since the mid-1980s recession, rising by about 70% over the period 1985–2000, and now well above the level prevailing during the 1970s. An increase would be expected as the economy recovered; democratic expenditure pressures have no doubt also played a role.

While the rising consumption shares have cushioned living standards during hard times, this has been achieved partly at the cost of falling investment. Since

Table 1.6 Expenditure Shares in Current Price GDP, 1970–2000 (%)[a]

Type of Expenditure	1970	1975	1980	1985	1990	1995	2000
Personal consumption	67.2	62.3	64.2	71.9	71.6	74.0	71.7
Government consumption	9.5	10.5	9.1	7.5	9.9	11.4	13.0
Capital formation	21.6	30.2	29.1	16.6	22.0	23.5	18.3
Fixed capital	18.7	23.6	26.7	18.5	21.3	23.1	18.6
Construction	7.8	11.9	15.2	10.5	10.8	10.0	8.9
Durable equipment	8.8	10.1	9.8	6.5	8.9	11.5	8.3
Breeding stock & orchard							
development	2.1	1.7	1.8	1.6	1.6	1.6	1.4
Changes in stocks	2.9	6.6	2.4	–1.9	0.7	0.4	–0.3
Net exports	–0.8	–4.8	–4.4	1.7	–3.6	–7.7	3.2
Statistical discrepancy	2.5	1.8	2.1	2.3	0.2	–1.21	–6.0

a   Each entry is a three-year average of the year indicated, the previous year, and the succeeding year.

Source: National Statistical Coordination Board.

1990, the share of investment has been around 10 percentage points below that prevailing for much of the 1970s. Both net exports and a puzzlingly large statistical discrepancy have fluctuated considerably. The movement in net exports correlates closely with the overall level of economic activity. Years of high growth (1975, 1980, 1995) result in a negative figure (that is, a current account deficit), while periods of recession or slower growth (1985, 2000) have the opposite effect. There is no obvious explanation for the statistical discrepancy.

The data in Figure 1.5 highlight the proximate cause of slow Philippine growth. The country had something approaching "East Asian" savings and investment rates during much of the 1970s. Both, but particularly investment, declined sharply during the 1980s recession. Investment then recovered somewhat, albeit to levels much below those in other countries in the region, whereas savings remained anemic, at essentially "OECD" levels. With such a low savings rate, and an inability to run much more than a 3–5% current account deficit (anything higher would in any case have been dangerous), Philippine growth has struggled to get above 6%. That the country was able to grow quite vigorously in the mid-1990s—at something approaching the 1970s rate, but with an appreciably lower savings and investment rate—is a creditable achievement, and indicative of the higher post-reform efficiency levels. But a savings rate of 15–18% remains too low for high growth.

Why did savings remain so low, even when growth resumed and financial liberalization ushered in positive real interest rates for savers? One explanation lies in the

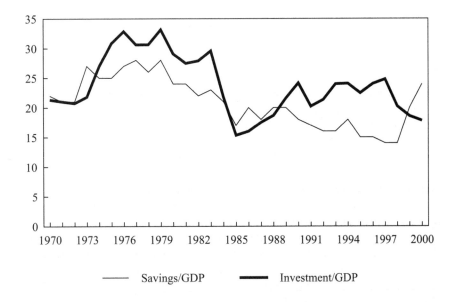

Figure 1.5 Ratio of Savings to GDP and Investment to GDP, 1970–2000 (%)

Savings, investment, and GDP are in current prices. *Source*: World Bank, *World Development Indicators*.

country's chronic fiscal deficits. Unlike the governments of its high-growth neighbors (Malaysia partially excepted), successive Philippine governments have almost always been net dissavers. Partly, of course, this reflects low economic growth. As the East Asian experience illustrates, there is a "virtuous circle" in the sense that it is easier for governments to achieve fiscal balance during periods of high growth, which in turn facilitates good macroeconomic outcomes. (Hence, it is no coincidence that a (small) fiscal surplus was achieved in the years of growth, 1994–96.) Another element of the East Asian growth story is that higher rates of savings invariably follow a period of sustained growth (see, among others, Harrigan 1998). Indonesia and Thailand, for example, both had savings rates closer to the current Philippine levels in the early stages of their long economic booms. So the real problem may simply have been that the country never achieved a long enough period of growth to induce higher rates of savings. Political instability and lack of security (among the Philippine Chinese community, for instance) have no doubt contributed at the margin.

1.3 THE RECORD IN DETAIL

We turn now to a more detailed look at the development record, drawing primarily on the contributions to this volume, and following its general structure. We focus particularly on the post-Marcos period, and therefore do not look in detail at the events leading up to the economic crisis of 1984–86.[5]

The Political Economy Setting

Is the Philippine system of democracy and government conducive to rapid economic development? Democracy is of course an end in itself, but here we are particularly interested in the economic and political interactions.

As de Dios and Hutchcroft emphasize in Chapter 2, this is a complex issue, and the system has notable strengths and weaknesses. The authors survey the post-Marcos period, starting with Aquino's "modest revolution" (1986–92). Forced to grapple with a severe economic crisis, a major political transition, attempted coups, and serious natural disasters, President Aquino was at least able to institute a more open and accountable system of government and, later in her term, initiate some policy reforms. But much of the period was characterized by "stop–go" economic policies, continuing fiscal crises, largely futile attempts to regain the Marcos wealth and manage sequestered corporations, and a cautious and limited social agenda. In the end, de Dios and Hutchcroft conclude that the "Aquino government came to rationalize its role as being limited to that of undoing the Marcos legacy."

The Ramos administration (1992–98) is characterized as one of "building reform momentum." It continued and deepened the macroeconomic and trade reforms of the late Aquino era, began to dismantle cartels in telecommunications, shipping, and civil aviation, achieved a measure of peace in Mindanao, and took steps to overcome the then very serious power shortages. Several factors were significant in this process: the beginnings of reform in the late Aquino period; the global and regional trend toward liberalization; a distrust of elements of the traditional Philippine elite; and a sense of vulnerability in the wake of the removal of the U.S. bases in 1992. The reforms were decisive enough that they delivered a prompt though modest dividend, which saw rising growth by 1995. De Dios and Hutchcroft conclude that the Ramos administration was good at liberalization; made less progress with institutional reform (of the bureaucracy, the tax system, and the judiciary); focused only to a limited extent on redistribution objectives; and had a very limited capacity to deliver on political reforms.[6] But there was an orderly succession of power in 1998, even in the midst of the Asian economic crisis.

Finally, there was the "flawed experiment" of the Estrada administration (1998–2001). This attracted a highly diverse group of supporters, was avowedly pro-poor in its rhetoric (though much less so in practice), and broadly maintained Ramos's macro and trade policy framework. But "palace connections" and cronyism quickly and blatantly became important again, and by the second half of 2000 the whiff of scandal began to engulf the administration. Ultimately, Estrada was tipped out in quasi-constitutional circumstances in January 2001.

In sum, what can be said? The Philippines is now a more democratic society, nationally and (since 1992) locally. Its civil society is undoubtedly stronger. Its economy is more open and diversified. There are considerable checks and balances on government, both from inside and outside. Once a reform has passed into law, there is a reasonable prospect that it will be durable. The country's post-independence economic history has been one of recurring economic crises—in 1949, the early 1960s, 1969, the mid-1980s, and the early 1990s. Policy reforms have been partial at best, and sometimes quickly overturned by powerful vested interests. Perhaps now there is a chance that the boom–bust economic and policy cycle can be more or less permanently overcome, at least in some measure. But there remain notable weak points, putting aside the immediate challenge of bedding down the legitimacy of the young Macapagal-Arroyo administration. Three in particular stand out.

First, the political system is highly personalistic. It can produce competent or inept presidents (such as Ramos and Estrada respectively). This can happen in any country, of course. The particular problem in the Philippines is that regime changes have major consequences since, with its U.S. style of government, they percolate right through the system. In contrast to the situation in most of its neighbors, where the civil service remains largely intact when the regime changes, in the Philippines regime changes affect the top layer of the civil service (at the level of secretary), the next layer (under-secretary), quite often the third tier (assistant secretary), and sometimes even the fourth (at the director level).

This has two immediate implications. One is that it reduces the likelihood of policy consistency. If much of the top leadership of a department turns over every six years, there is a distinct possibility of change of direction. Secretaries want to leave their mark through pet projects. More importantly, investors will calculate that they have policy certainty for no more than six years, and in practice much less, owing to settling-in and "lame duck" periods and to turnover within administrations. Another implication is that, below these senior echelons, there simply is not the pool of high-level talent to anchor policy consistency, since poor salaries and a lack of career structure constitute major deterrents to entry into the civil service.

A more general consequence is that the Philippine system—unlike a system of career public service—makes it more difficult to deeply entrench pro-reform lobbies within the bureaucracy. Within the Philippine setting, the National Economic and Development Authority (NEDA) is perhaps the most reform-oriented—though not the most financially powerful—department. The other major proponent of reform, the Department of Finance, is generally preoccupied with the immediate struggles of fiscal policy, while the central bank has a limited remit in the field of monetary policy and banking. Similar comments apply at the level of agency head, accounting for their variable quality.[7]

A second challenge is that it is often difficult to get reforms through the system, because there are so many points at which progress can be stymied.[8] The bureaucracy, the legislature (both national and regional), the palace itself, and the judiciary can all be employed by lobbyists determined to resist reform. Moreover, different pressure points may be important in different administrations. Under Estrada, it was widely perceived to be the president himself whose so-called "midnight cabinet" of "drinking buddies" could overturn decisions taken by the "daytime cabinet." Ramos had problems with the legislature, while Aquino's cabinets became well known for their policy rifts, particularly in the early years.

A third challenge, systemic in nature, concerns the extent to which deeply entrenched and high levels of inequality impede reform. De Dios and Hutchcroft highlight this factor and implicitly suggest an "Olsonian" explanation for the slow post-Marcos policy reform processes. The Philippines has never experienced a Taiwan-style land reform, nor has there been an administration determined to cater to a poor rural constituency as there was in Malaysia and Indonesia. Thus, powerful land-owning groups and business conglomerates have been a constant feature of the country's history. This does not of course preclude the possibility of effective reformist administrations—as evidenced by Ramos—that can certainly help the poor by accelerating economic growth. But, it is contended, the political system is such that distributionalist objectives will always be difficult to achieve, and reforms may subsequently be overturned.

Macro and International Dimensions

If post-independence Philippine history has been characterized by stop–go economic policy, then macroeconomic and trade policy must surely have been at the heart of the problem. It is therefore not surprising to find that they have been central to reform efforts since the late 1980s. This is one area where the achievements have been significant, arguably constituting the key contributors to improved development outcomes. We consider each topic in turn.

Macroeconomic Policy

Philippine macroeconomic outcomes have traditionally lagged behind those of the high-growth East Asian countries, though by general developing-country standards they have not been disastrous. Inflation has been higher than in Singapore, Malaysia, and Thailand, but these have been the exemplars of the developing world. The Philippine record has not been significantly worse than that of Indonesia and Korea, and it has of course been superior to that of Latin America.

The bases of the country's macroeconomic problems are well known: chronic budget deficits, which were in turn monetized by a politicized central bank that was also attempting to run a quasi-fixed exchange rate regime. The results were moderately high inflation, a black market foreign exchange rate, and periodic balance of payments crises. The reform process that got under way in the late 1980s, and which delivered lower inflation in the 1990s, was therefore a milestone in the country's history.

Exchange Rate and Monetary Policy. Here the main story, as told by Gochoco-Bautista and Canlas (Chapter 3), is a major shift in the policy regime. Until the late 1980s the central bank was grappling with the funding of a chronic fiscal deficit, which was often monetized. The authorities attempted to control too many variables—money supply, interest rates, the exchange rate—with too few instruments. The central bank periodically incurred large losses, operating as it did as a de facto arm of government in a highly politicized atmosphere.

The reform momentum started in the late 1980s. The international capital account was progressively opened, culminating in full peso convertibility in 1992. This was one of the first major economic policy initiatives of the incoming Ramos administration. As part of the reform, a new institution was created in 1993, Bangko Sentral ng Pilipinas (BSP), and the debts of the old central bank were taken off its books. The new regime emphasized inflation targeting and instituted a floating exchange rate within a managed band. The results were immediately obvious: inflation stayed under control throughout the 1990s, remaining in the range of 6–9%. Perhaps more importantly, the peso convertibility removed an endemic source of corruption, both petty and grand, and was fundamental in instigating a more outward-looking mentality among investors.

As Gochoco-Bautista and Canlas stress (see also Rodlauer et al. 2000), the 1990s were a period of learning for the new monetary authorities. They had to manage a new and very different policy regime in the context of a rapidly changing international environment. The latter was an important consideration. The low global inflation of the 1990s facilitated their policy objectives. But opening up to international financial markets was a major challenge, because the country had effectively been closed to private capital until 1992 (owing to its protracted debt crisis), and because short-term capital flows to "emerging markets" were increasing dramatically throughout the decade. There was also some ambivalence about objectives, with a mixture of inflation and exchange rate targets being formally or informally pursued. Finally, banking supervision remained within the BSP's jurisdiction, an issue to which we return below.

Initially the authorities attempted to emulate neighboring countries, running monetary policy with a quasi-fixed exchange rate in the context of an open capital account. Here the familiar Mundell–Flemming problem began to surface, albeit in milder form than in neighboring countries owing to the much smaller volume of capital flows in the Philippines (Rodlauer et al. 2000). For a (fortunately) short period, in fact, Philippine conditions and policy settings were quite similar to those of the soon-to-be crisis economies. The real exchange rate began to appreciate mildly, threatening export competitiveness and also complicating the trade liberalization process then under way. Capital flows were increasingly directed toward non-tradable activities. Local banks became significant international borrowers, a trend hastened by the gap between domestic and international interest rates and by the perception that the authorities would hold the nominal rate more or less constant.

This period was short-lived, as the crisis began to impact by August 1997. The BSP's initial reaction, like that of its counterparts elsewhere, was to defend the peso through higher interest rates. This quickly proved futile. Allowed to float, the peso then fell sharply, approximately halving in value against the U.S. dollar in the next six months. But this was a most unusual balance of payments crisis by Philippine standards. First, the trigger (namely the contagion from Thailand) was mainly external. Second, it did not lead to a general financial crisis, as occurred in Thailand, Malaysia, and Indonesia. Finally, growth was interrupted only mildly.

We return to these issues shortly. The main point to stress here is that the BSP survived its first major challenge quite creditably. In the process, it further refined its monetary policy settings in 2000. It progressively de-emphasized a nominal exchange rate objective and asserted that its primary objective was to achieve inflation outcomes within a targeted band. The political crisis involving the transition from Estrada to Macapagal-Arroyo again tested this framework, but, while obviously intervening in the market, the BSP did let the peso slide considerably.

Thus the new framework appears to have taken root in the system. It is true that this framework will only work if fiscal policy is also cautious—and here problems remain—so that monetary policy does not have to "carry" the major task of macroeconomic management. There also continues to be debate about the advisability of some sort of capital controls, *à la* Malaysia. The major worry would be the feasibility of reintroducing foreign exchange controls given their history of endemic abuse.

Fiscal Policy. There has been major progress in fiscal policy since the 1980s, as outlined by Sicat and Abdula (Chapter 4). Successive Philippine governments have almost always run fiscal deficits. Although there has rarely been a complete loss of fiscal discipline, these deficits have invariably peaked around election time—the years 1969 and 1985 stand out during the long Marcos period. These deficits have typically resulted in difficult fiscal adjustments, and often a sharp depreciation of the peso.

As Sicat and Abdula point out, fiscal policy settings and the role of the government have varied since 1970. The size of the public sector grew significantly in the 1970s. There was a perceived need to accelerate growth through an increase in the supply of public goods, especially infrastructure. It suited President Marcos, too, of course, since large projects constituted a major source of patronage and largesse. By the end of the decade this strategy was no longer sustainable, as many of the projects were unable to generate viable returns and debt service difficulties were exacerbated by several negative external shocks. A painful period of adjustment followed in the first half of the 1980s. Real per capita expenditure almost halved. There were very large cuts in infrastructure expenditure, which arguably laid the basis for later problems. And debt service rose sharply; at one stage interest and debt payments absorbed more than 40% of the budget.

From the late 1980s significant progress occurred. The ratio of government revenue to GDP almost doubled between the recession years of 1983–85 (9.6%) and 1997 (17%), by which time the country's tax effort had nearly caught up with that of Indonesia and Thailand. Faster growth, a simplification of tax scales, and more vigorous collection procedures all contributed to this result. The resumption of growth, combined with some debt workouts, also meant that the debt service burden was progressively lightened over this period.

As Sicat and Abdula show, the fiscal policy stance improved immeasurably from the mid-1980s. The deficit, narrowly defined, peaked at 8.5% of GDP in 1986. The position then improved steadily and for three years (1994–96) a slim surplus was recorded. With the onset of the crisis, however, there was a quick return to deficits.

The authors highlight a key issue in fiscal policy, namely that any assessment of the official budget position is highly sensitive to definitions. The deficits have been either quite modest or veering toward unsustainability depending on whether central government or consolidated government figures are used (Figure 4.11). The latter are of course the relevant indicator. As Sicat and Abdula show, deficits in excess of

5% of GDP were the norm in the 1980s and resurfaced in the late 1990s. The budget was in surplus in 1994–96, however, even according to this broader definition.

The principal difference between the two measures is that the state-owned enterprise (SOE) sector is included in the consolidated measure. In the worst years of the 1980s the losses of this sector were equivalent to over 5% of GDP; during the 1990s they were much smaller, although in 1999 and 2000 they again became large. Financial institutions (the old central bank, the Philippine National Bank, and the Development Bank of the Philippines) accounted for much of the sector's losses, but there were problems also in utilities and trade.

The SOE sector, though small, will pose a continuing challenge to policy-makers. State enterprises are sometimes able to operate outside the normal checks and balances of the government's financial framework. Their financial operations lack transparency and are ostensibly justified by alleged (but often spurious) "social missions." Some cases of asset sales and privatization have been questionable.

To sum up, post-Marcos administrations have inherited a very complex fiscal situation. There has been major progress since the 1980s, especially in the tax effort, the restoration of essential public goods, and the control of the deficit. Against this:

- there was disappointingly little progress in recouping the "crony assets" of the 1980s (although in fairness the international experience anywhere else has not been much better);
- there is still chronic underprovision of key public goods (in infrastructure, education, and health);
- SOE reform and privatization continue to constitute major challenges;
- there is the ever-present danger of crony-related contingent liability, which surfaced again under the Estrada administration in particular; and
- decentralization has been managed quite effectively, though it has not been entirely revenue-neutral.

As Sicat and Abdula point out, the Philippines now has a president who, in her earlier academic writings, had stressed the importance of sound fiscal management. One has to hope that President Macapagal-Arroyo and Professor Macapagal-Arroyo are one and the same person.

International Dimensions

The Philippines has a history of perverse trade policy interventions, which have been extensively documented in earlier studies.[9] Significant progress has been made since the late 1980s, to the point where openness appears to be quite deeply rooted in the polity and in the community at large, and the country now has a reasonably open trade policy regime. Average rates of protection have fallen, the dispersion in these rates is lower, and there is less reliance on non-tariff barriers. Nevertheless, the Philippines is a much less significant international commercial player than most of its neighbors, as a result of past barriers to trade and investment, and an unwelcoming business environment.

Bautista and Tecson (Chapter 5) chart these changes, characterizing the 1970s as a decade of export promotion and flexible exchange rates, the 1980s as a decade of trade liberalization under a foreign exchange rate constraint (with most progress made in 1981–85), and the 1990s as a decade of reform, with an unstable and appreciating exchange rate. The progress made in the early 1980s was interrupted by the economic crisis of 1984–86. The momentum resumed in the late Aquino period and was carried forward under Ramos. During the period of the Estrada administration there was no significant regress, although several highly politicized cases of cronyism attracted attention.

There were two unusual features of the reforms in the 1990s: trade barriers came down notwithstanding an appreciating currency (typically reforms occur after crises, accompanied by a depreciation); and agricultural protection rose, to the point where it now exceeds that for manufacturing. Both require some political economy explanation. Bautista and Tecson attribute the decline in overall protection to decades of intellectual effort, gradually percolating through the bureaucracy and the political process.[10] Much of that work was located at the University of the Philippines and the Philippine Institute of Development Studies. Foreign inputs helped, but the domestic impetus was the critical factor.

The rising level of agricultural protection may be explained by several factors. One is the voice of the rural constituency with the return of democracy. Powerful landlords have played on this factor, together with sentimental notions of food self-sufficiency, to engage in pork barrel politics with Congress. Another explanation is rural–urban income distribution concerns (even if protection is a relatively blunt instrument to achieve this goal). Third, there has been a less intensive intellectual effort on the costs of protection in this sector. Finally, the availability of loopholes in regulating international trade in agricultural products may have meant that the international costs (of scrutiny and, possibly, reciprocity) are lower.

This more open trade regime has been accompanied by other reforms, most notably in opening up more sectors to foreign investment. Consequently, foreign investment flows rose during the 1990s. For a period the services sector became the largest recipient, while in manufacturing there was an impressive shift out of the former concentration in protected activities and into new export-oriented sectors.

Looking at the balance of payments as a whole, a striking feature is the dominance of remittances. They now total about $6 billion, equivalent to 20% of exports (to comprise by far the largest "export" item) and 70% of total service income. Both push and pull factors have been relevant here, including sluggish domestic growth, high levels of human capital across most skill groups, an increasingly open international labor market, and well-established information flows and recruitment channels. We return shortly to some of the pros and cons of these large labor flows.

Notwithstanding the significant achievements made, Bautista and Tecson are careful to highlight the outstanding policy agenda. First, protected sectors remain, particularly in agriculture, but also still in manufacturing. As and when protection is wound back, there will probably need to be some compensating support measures, particularly for poor rural dwellers. Second, the macroeconomic policy environment needs to be supportive of the reform agenda. The large effective depreciation of the peso since 1997 has facilitated trade liberalization, whereas if the appreciation in the mid-1990s had persisted, progress may have been jeopardized. Third, international competitiveness is still a concern, and obstacles ranging from poor infrastructure to a somewhat rigid formal urban labor market need to be addressed. Finally, there is the paradox that, in order to diversify exports, a strategy of industrial promotion was pursued, but—as in some neighboring countries as well—merchandise exports in the Philippines are now more narrowly concentrated (on electronics) than ever before.

The Sectors

As noted above, fortunes at the sectoral level have generally reflected economy-wide conditions. But there are exceptions to this generalization, and an examination of the major sectors provides additional insights into the Philippine development record.

Agriculture

Despite its shrinking share, agriculture remains a key sector, generating about 17% of GDP and employing a little under 40% of the workforce. If a broader definition that encompasses agricultural processing and related activities is adopted, the indirect shares rise to about 40% and 67% respectively. Moreover, some 70% of the poor depend on this sector, and thus its fluctuating fortunes have a direct impact on the nation's welfare.

As David documents in Chapter 6, agriculture's record has been mixed. The sector achieved respectable growth in the 1970s, much of it driven by yield increases in the wake of the Green Revolution of the1960s, and notwithstanding the high levels of manufacturing protection. But since then growth has been sluggish, and has failed to keep up with population growth.

There have been notable differences between subsectors and crops. The livestock and poultry industry has grown quite quickly and appears to be internationally competitive. The Philippines is an efficient producer of a variety of tropical fruits, including pineapples, bananas, and mangoes. But other sectors have lagged. It is striking, for example, that the country has not enjoyed any significant tropical cash-crop export boom over the past 20 years, analogous (for instance) to the boom in rubber in Thailand, palm oil in Indonesia and Malaysia, cocoa in Indonesia, and coffee in Vietnam.

Several factors appear to account for this outcome. The country's natural resource base is inferior to that of several of its ASEAN neighbors (though its population density is similar to that of Vietnam). An additional complication is that the natural area of expansion—the country's frontier zone, Mindanao—has been beset by constant unrest, deterring investors, who necessarily require a secure investment climate for longer-gestation cash crops. The agrarian reform program has introduced uncertainty with regard to property rights, again especially affecting cash crops.[11] The state of the country's rural infrastructure, particularly its roads, has also inhibited competitiveness.

Although rapid population growth is resulting in an inexorable decline in comparative advantage in agriculture, David stresses that government policies have accentuated the trend. Government expenditure on the sector declined sharply during the economic contraction of the 1980s. With growth and renewed emphasis on rural development, by the late 1990s expenditure had been restored to real 1970s levels (though not in per capita terms). However, budgets have continued to be misallocated. The authors argue that there has been too little productivity-enhancing investment, on rural roads (which are often intensely politicized), irrigation, and R&D, and further misallocations of priorities within each of these. By contrast, distributional goals (for example, price interventions and supports, and agrarian reform), often with perverse efficiency and equity outcomes, have been overemphasized.

Philippine agricultural interventions have traditionally favored the well-endowed regions close to the major centers of political power over upland and more remote regions. The case of perverse intervention in sugar—with powerful vested interests clinging to the quota rents implicit in favorable U.S. market access at the expense of the industry's general modernization—has been extensively documented. The once dominant sugar industry has shrunk dramatically, and is now smaller than both bananas (although here too there are restrictions on expansion) and pineapples.

David singles out the National Food Authority (NFA) as a particularly perverse case of costly intervention; its direct and indirect costs are as much as 50 billion pesos per year, most of which does not appear as a formal budget item. The official justification for its continued monopolization of international trade, namely to prevent "exploitation" by private traders, has little analytical basis. It has, rather, introduced major inefficiencies into the country's food-marketing system.

The authors highlight the need for a range of additional policy reforms. One example is the effects of the value added tax on the development of agro-processing industries. There is also a need for bureaucratic reform, including effective decentralization to regional offices of the Department of Agriculture, and removal of the overlap between this department and the Department of Environment and Natural Resources.

As noted above, the protection story has changed significantly. Agricultural protection has increased and now exceeds that for manufacturing. Moreover, although the dispersion in intersectoral rates has declined, that within agriculture has increased. The resultant increase in the (domestic) agricultural terms of trade has thus cushioned farmers from the declining international commodity prices of the 1990s. While desirable on income distribution grounds, protection is a blunt redistributive instrument, and there are more effective means of helping the rural poor. Perhaps there is a political economy dilemma here, in the sense that there are so few alternative instruments available in practice to assist this constituency of rural poor.

Industry
The industrialization record is also mixed. As noted above, the early push for industrialization through high protection resulted in a large but generally inefficient man-

ufacturing sector. The sector has been unable to adjust to a less protected environment, resulting in the curious phenomenon of "deindustrialization" at a low level of economic development.

Nevertheless, there has been progress, as Hill documents in Chapter 7. The country has shifted to a more efficient, export-oriented trajectory. Fewer sectors are heavily protected, and a much higher proportion of output originates with internationally competitive industries. Thus, the observed decline in the share of manufacturing may not be such a cause for concern, since some inefficient activities have been shed, and value added at domestic prices is no longer inflated by high levels of protection.

Not only have effective protection levels declined, but the general liberalization has resulted in lower levels of industrial concentration. As a result of the reforms, there are relatively few industries with a serious competition problem. The past pattern of industries both heavily protected and subject to little domestic competition, in which the dominant players were the politically well connected or foreign owned (or often both), has been discarded.

Moreover, export growth since the early 1990s has been creditable. Electronics has been the major engine of growth, with its exports rising dramatically from about $1 billion in 1985 to $7 billion in 1995 and over $20 billion in 2000. This growth continued during the recent Asian crisis and was a factor in the country's resilience. Together with the smaller (and related) item of machine goods, electronics now constitutes almost 70% of Philippine merchandise exports. In addition, it accounted for the entire expansion of merchandise trade in the 1990s.

With this mixed picture as a background, Hill identifies a number of major challenges for development policy. One is the now very great reliance on electronics, and the puzzle as to why this industry has performed well while others with broadly similar characteristics (such as textiles and garments) have lagged. There is also impatience that backward linkages from electronics exporters have not developed more quickly. The industry's strong growth has been enclave and dualistic in nature, and located entirely in the zones of the Philippine Export Zone Authority (PEZA). Such a pattern has been observed in most early-stage East Asian exporters, and the weak linkages in part reflect industrial infancy. But to the extent that the barriers between these firms and those located outside the zones are regulatory in nature, the obvious solution is to adopt economy-wide reforms. There are also questions concerning the fiscal sustainability of PEZA incentives.

There are other industrial structural imbalances that need to be addressed. The Philippines has missed out on Taiwanese-style dynamism in the small and medium-sized enterprise (SME) sector. The reasons for this are complex, and no doubt reflect mainly economy-wide influences. Poor rural infrastructure, segmented factor markets, weak provision of industrial extension services, and unequal rural income distribution are all elements in this story. The spatial pattern of industrialization is also highly uneven. Almost 80% of value added comes from just the three central regions of Metro Manila, Central Luzon, and Southern Tagalog, which together virtually constitute the country's integrated industrial heartland. Elsewhere, only Cebu has a significant industrial base. Decentralization, better rural infrastructure (and international connections), a more scattered system of industrial zones, and congestion costs around the capital may in time produce a more even spatial distribution. But such a trend is not yet evident.

Services

As noted above, the services sector has shown consistent growth over the past three decades. It is now by far the largest sector and its share is likely to continue to rise. A number of decisive reforms during the 1990s opened up hitherto moribund industries to competition and innovation. It appears increasingly apparent, too, that the Philippines has a stronger comparative advantage in labor-intensive services than in much of the goods sector. The success of the country's labor exports is in effect an indication of this proposition.

As services become increasingly tradable, numerous export opportunities are opening up for the country. It has already carved out a niche in certain areas. With a little over 1% of the world's population, for example, Filipinos constitute about 25% of the world's seafarers. They reportedly comprise as much as half of the non-managerial staff on international cruise lines. Filipinos also dominate Asia's live music and entertainment industry, as well as being the principal source of domestic employment in Hong Kong and Singapore. The country is emerging as a major information technology (IT) center in developing Asia and is competitive in health, education, and a range of other services, all increasingly traded. Business activities as diverse as international call centers and graphic cartoon design are being established. English-language competence, competitively priced labor for a range of middle-level technical skills, familiarity with American cultural norms, and widespread international employment experience all constitute a competitive advantage for the Philippines in these service exports. It is notoriously difficult to measure non-factor service exports such as these, but the available evidence suggests that they have been growing quickly since the late 1980s.

To exploit these advantages, the competitive provision of complementary inputs is also required. Where they are not available, growth has been disappointing. An obvious case in point is tourism, where, in spite of much natural potential, the record has been disappointing. Poor infrastructure and security concerns have held back growth in the tourism sector. Another example, now changing, is IT, where growth has been retarded by an inefficient telecommunications industry.

Abrenica and Llanto (Chapter 8) document the changing face of the services industry with special reference to two case studies, telecommunications and banking. Both are largely positive cases of reform leading to the more efficient provision of a range of services. The authors point out that there were other cases of successful reform in the 1990s, including domestic shipping and civil aviation. But the forward momentum seemed to slow under the Estrada administration, which was responsible for some damaging backtracking on international civil aviation.[12] Progress has also been slow in opening up the retail sector to competition, particularly from overseas, and in the employment of foreigners.[13]

In the first of Abrenica and Llanto's case studies, telecommunications, liberalization was initiated in 1993, while in the second, banking (and insurance), this happened in 1994. Civil aviation and domestic shipping followed a year later.

The reforms in telecommunications were bold, resulting in clear gains for consumers in terms of lower prices, improved services, and rising telephone density. However, the benefits of incumbency for the Philippine Long Distance Telephone Company (PLDT), the former near-monopolist, should not be underestimated. In 1999, for example, the authors estimate that PLDT still accounted for 61%, 55%, and 71% of local connections, cell phones, and international calls respectively. Moreover, there was such a large backlog in telecommunications infrastructure pre-reform that it will be some time before the country's services match those of its more advanced neighbors. Finally, the reforms have been incomplete. The various inter-connection agreements between telecommunications carriers have thus far been left untouched. And foreign equity shares have been limited to 40%, which by current international standards is quite restrictive.

The record on financial services is also largely a positive one. Reform got under way gradually in the 1980s. The Philippines has had a history of tight central bank regulation of banks but weak (and sometimes corrupt) supervision of them. After the central bank itself had been cleaned up and reformed, the government rehabilitated the two large state-owned banks (the Philippine National Bank and the Development Bank of the Philippines), partially privatizing one of them. Some mergers and closures resulted, the regulatory framework was improved, and entry was eased. Several foreign banks entered the market as a result. Abrenica and Llanto show that the banking sector is in consequence more efficient. Bank profits have declined and spreads (between deposit and lending rates) are lower. There has also been an increase in national bank density ratios, although much of it has been concentrated in the three richest central regions of Metro Manila, Southern Tagalog, and Central Luzon. There has been some increase in seller concentration, but the rise has been modest and the ratios are not unduly high; they are well below those in Thailand, for example. Perhaps most important of all, the banks came through the Asian economic crisis intact—in part no doubt fortuitously, since they had not had the opportunity to indulge in the spending spree evident in several neighboring countries.

As with telecommunications, the reform process will have to be an ongoing one. Steps are in place to improve transparency and enforce stricter disclosure requirements. And while the banking sector is now a more efficient financial instrument than it was in the past, the same cannot be said of the Philippine stock exchange, which over the years has proven consistently resistant to attempts to clean it up.

Social and Distributional Issues

Most social indicators have reflected general economic conditions, with stagnation and decline in the 1980s and some hopeful signs in the 1990s. Overall the picture is mixed, with some very worrying problems alongside significant improvements. This is of course a case of complex, two-way causality, with social conditions being determined by, but also shaping, economic progress. We consider in turn each major area: demographics and human resources, poverty and inequality, regional development, and the environment.

Demography and Human Resources

Herrin and Pernia analyze this diverse set of topics in Chapter 9, highlighting the Philippines' daunting demographic challenges, its distinct (though arguably fading) educational advantage, and its labor market conditions.

Demographically, the Philippines is an East Asian outlier. Its population, of 75.3 million in 2000, has doubled since 1970, and most projections suggest that it will at least double again before stabilizing. The population is now growing more slowly: the growth rate fell from about 2.7% annually in the 1970s to 2.3% in the 1980s and 2.2% in the 1990s. The total fertility rate has also fallen, from about six births per woman in 1973 to 3.7 in 1998. These rates of decline are slow compared with those in high-growth neighbors (except Malaysia, owing to complex socioeconomic dynamics), and no doubt reflect both slow economic growth—a key factor in the process of demographic transition—and powerful church-based opposition to contraception. (As Herrin and Pernia point out, contraception options for most Filipinos are both limited and dangerous.) The authors allude to the "waxing and waning" of population policy and argue for an integrated approach to family planning, including measures to safely stem the high level of unwanted pregnancy.

Another factor is that infant mortality rates are still high, and declining only slowly. In 1990 the rate was about 60 deaths per 1,000 live births, and is now probably a little below 50. In addition there are marked regional differences, with poor regions recording rates some two-thirds higher than those in the national capital. Child malnutrition is high, again with substantial regional variation.

In education, the Philippines rates above most countries with similar per capita incomes, and has the additional advantage of widespread English-language fluency. It thus has an edge in activities requiring middle-level human capital inputs. Reflecting an early commitment to public education, about 95% of the population aged 10 years and over has "simple" literacy skills, while about 84% may be said to be functionally literate. Primary school participation is at least 95% of the relevant age group, falling to about 64% for secondary schools. There is no gender bias, and in fact female participation is slightly ahead of that of males. However, the country's lead is slipping as these rates stagnate and other countries catch up. Moreover, it rates poorly in international quality comparisons. For example, it ranked 39 out of 43 in a recent testing of math/science competence; Singapore and South Korea ranked first and second.[14]

Expenditure on both health and education is rising, and is broadly comparable to that in neighboring countries. But Herrin and Pernia worry about targeting and priorities in these sectors. Health expenditure is mostly in the private sector, and therefore highly inequitable. The Department of Health has a bias toward the urban, hospital-based system. Malnutrition also needs more attention. In education, there is a strong case for more funding at the primary school level and greater cost recovery at the tertiary level. The public school system needs more funds for non-salary items.

With rapid population growth and a large backlog of unemployed workers, employment provision is a chronic problem in the Philippines. The labor force is growing by about 2.8% each year, equivalent now to about 800,000 new job entrants.

Absorbing the rising numbers of female workers is another major challenge. Unemployment currently stands at about 10%, with underemployment variously estimated at around 20%. These levels fluctuate with the economic cycle and have predictably distinct age, skill, regional, and gender correlates. The problem of child labor also needs to be addressed.

The inevitable consequence is of course that many people are seeking employment abroad. The number of Overseas Filipino Workers (OFWs), as they are known in-country, has been growing at a phenomenal pace, almost quadrupling between 1980 (about 215,000 persons) and 1999 (around 837,000). The Middle East was a key destination during the 1970s oil boom. Its share has since declined, while that of East Asia has been rising quickly. Now the industry is global. While OFWs are predominantly unskilled and semi-skilled, they encompass all major occupational groups.

Analyses of this phenomenon display an understandable ambivalence. At the micro, household level, it is a sensible poverty alleviation strategy in the face of sluggish domestic employment growth. It accords with the country's comparative advantage across the spectrum of labor-intensive activities. In the neighboring countries that were able to achieve rapid export-oriented industrialization, the jobs migrated to the country concerned. In the Philippines to some extent the reverse has happened, with workers migrating across international boundaries.[15]

But what of the national cost–benefit ratio? Here the picture is more clouded. There is obviously a serious brain drain under way. Set against this, in some cases the migrants are among the less skilled, and thus the loss of human capital is not so significant. There is also a high return rate, often with augmented human capital. (This has been an important and beneficial factor in the case of Taiwan and Korea.) Remittances are a boost to national welfare (even if they may marginally worsen income distribution, to the extent that they are concentrated among better-off households and regions). But there are many workers who do not return, particularly among the more skilled, for whom permanent migration is possible. The option of exit appears to have become so prominent on the horizons of the country's "best and brightest" that one begins to wonder if it is affecting the national psyche, and perhaps in the process diminishing the urgency with which the political leadership tackles the country's pressing development challenges.

Poverty and Inequality
Balisacan's analysis of poverty and inequality (Chapter 10) is central to an understanding of the Philippine development record, both in the aggregate, and at the micro level in explaining variations among households and regions and over time.

The principal macro conclusion—obvious but often poorly understood—is that levels of poverty are highly growth-sensitive; that is, since distribution does not change significantly in the short to medium term, changes in the level of household income, which are affected by aggregate levels of economic activity, are the major proximate determinant of the incidence of poverty. Balisacan's analysis demonstrates this very clearly. The incidence of poverty fell sharply by about one-third (from 41% to 25%) from 1985 to 1997, that is, from the depth of the recession to the peak of the boom, although it rose perceptibly in 2000 due to the lingering effects of the Asian financial crisis and the drought-inducing El Niño phenomenon.[16] Moreover, Balisacan shows that poverty declined fastest during the subperiods of higher growth, 1985–88 and 1994–97. This conclusion requires some qualification, depending as it does on which poverty line is chosen and whether one focuses on the level of poverty or, in addition, on its depth and severity. But overall the principal conclusion is the primacy of growth as the key determinant of poverty reduction.

The poverty picture varies significantly among sectors, regions, and households. Poverty is higher in rural areas and among agricultural workers. About three-quarters of the poor are in agriculture (a similar ratio to that in the 1960s), and so agricultural growth is especially beneficial for the poor. Among regions, Luzon is generally better off, and Metro Manila always records the lowest poverty incidence. Consistently poor regions include Eastern Visayas (about 14 times the incidence of Manila) and Bicol. There has been a good deal of regional re-ranking since the mid-1980s, with some regions, such as Western and Central Mindanao, becoming relatively poorer, while others have progressed faster.

Balisacan then shifts attention to the key variables influencing provincial and household welfare. At the household level, he finds less poverty in male-headed households, with household size exerting a negative influence on welfare. Location is significant, but sector of employment is a minor factor. At the provincial level, he finds that changes in poverty over time depend not only on the rate but also on the type of local economic growth. Put differently, the poor will benefit even more from growth if institutions and policies are reformed to favor them, or are at least made more neutral. His model also shows that, apart from provincial economic growth, other factors exert a direct impact on the welfare of the poor: it highlights the importance of education, infrastructure, price policy regime, agrarian reform, governance, and certain geographic attributes. Schooling, if accompanied by complementary public investments, raises the welfare of the poor, apart from its indirect effect through economic growth. So do the implementation of agrarian reform, investment in land quality improvement, and the removal of price distortions that diminish the profitability of agriculture relative to non-agriculture. Political dynasties do not appear to benefit the poor, because they constrain local economic growth and because they restrict the access of the poor to basic services. High transport costs lead to geographic "poverty traps," as the poor are impeded from taking advantage of economic opportunities elsewhere.

Reverting to the national picture, the distribution of wealth is more unequal in the Philippines than in most of its neighbors. At the outset of independence, the distribution of land ownership from the Spanish colonial period was highly unequal. This inherited legacy seems to have been perpetuated in the modern commercial–industrial sector and, arguably, political structures. There have been no major ameliorating factors, in the form either of agrarian reform (as in Taiwan) or of a national leadership beholden to an initially poor and rural constituency (as in Malaysia). The question then becomes whether growth is a sufficient prerequisite for sustained poverty reduction. (It is clearly a necessary one.) And if distributional policies are pursued, which ones will also simultaneously achieve growth objectives? It is not obvious that agrarian reform has achieved much in aggregate, or that it ever will, although of course individual recipients have benefited. This analysis certainly points to the primacy of national governments focusing on the provision of good-quality, equity-oriented public goods such as primary and secondary education, basic health services, and rural infrastructure. It also highlights the importance of continued domestic and international liberalization, to ensure that the privileged commercial position of the highly concentrated family conglomerates (the so-called "oligarchs") is subjected to greater competitive pressure. As noted above, how and how much this concentrated agrarian and commercial power translates into political power is one of the most intriguing issues in Philippine political economy.

Regional Development

Regional development issues are important in the Philippines. It is the world's second largest archipelagic nation and thus features considerable spatial diversity. Beginning in 1991, a significant decentralization program was initiated to transfer administrative and fiscal functions to the regions. One decade on, an interim assessment of this reform is possible.

In Chapter 11, Manasan and Chatterjee start by tracing the history of regional development policies, taking as a point of departure an earlier major study (Pernia et al. 1983). They draw attention to the challenge of delineating "regions," pointing out that, inevitably, the official definition of regions (of which there were originally 12, now increased to 15) does not necessarily correspond to natural economic zones.

There are significant variations across regions, and social and economic indicators are usually highly correlated. Manila in particular stands out, with a per capita income that is always about twice the national average, and superior social indicators (except for environmental amenities). There have been some re-rankings of regions, as Balisacan also pointed out. For example, relative to the national figure, Southern Tagalog has (surprisingly) been declining, while Central Visayas and West and North Mindanao have been gaining.

Employing convergence methodology, Manasan and Chatterjee find that there has been "alpha" convergence (that is, a decline in overall regional inequality) and also (most of the time) "beta" convergence (that is, the poorer regions catching up to the richer ones). Thus the record is moderately encouraging given past patterns of deeply entrenched inequality, and compares favorably in the East Asian context, where increasing spatial dispersion has been common (as, for example, in China or Thailand). The authors then decompose these economic outcomes into what they term "net differential shift" and "net proportional shift." They are able to show that, in the 1990s, the faster growth of industry and services tended to increase regional inequality because these sectors were unevenly spatially concentrated. (Something similar happened in China and Thailand, too.) By contrast, agricultural growth was faster before 1986, as David showed, and this tended to be spatially equalizing. There is a particularly strong correlation between beta convergence and agricultural growth.

The authors draw attention to the key role of physical infrastructure in shaping regional outcomes. There has been some reallocation of infrastructure expenditure away from the three central regions, though much of it has also been a reallocation from Southern Tagalog and Central Luzon to Manila. In addition, the Mindanao regions have received substantial additional funds.

Turning to the experience with decentralization, the authors observe a gradual freeing up of the system. Alternative growth centers have emerged, although Manila remains pre-eminent. As would be expected in a country with 79 provinces, 84 cities, and 42,000 *barangays* (barrios), the outcomes present a complex picture. In principle, since 1991 the division of funding and functions has been carefully defined, with special additional provisions covering the Autonomous Region of Muslim Mindanao (ARMM), set up in 1989. In practice, of course, the central government agencies remain very powerful. Moreover, local government units (LGUs) still account for only 3.4% of GDP (up from 1.7% in 1985–91). And much of this is concentrated in the major cities of the four largest regional economies (that is, the three central regions plus Central Visayas).

As in all spatially dispersed countries, there are vertical and horizontal fiscal imbalances. With regard to the former, the funding for LGUs is often not commensurate with their expenditure responsibilities. The pattern is uneven, with some LGUs receiving more than they can realistically absorb, and others less. Inevitably, too, there are disparities in revenue-raising capacities, with the "big four" collecting 72% of all local taxes in 1999. Horizontal imbalances also present a challenge. There is some, though rather limited, equalization across regions. In consequence, Manasan and Chatterjee show that total per capita LGU revenue (including both local and central sources) is positively correlated with the per capita income of LGUs.

In any discussion of regions, Mindanao and especially the ARMM must figure prominently. The central government continues to be fiscally generous to this region but, notwithstanding the best of intentions, a culture of dependency has emerged. The local tax effort is poor and the region has little incentive to develop its own revenue base.

Environment and Natural Resources

The state of the environment and natural resource management present serious challenges in the Philippines. This is a general East Asian problem. But at least in the high-growth economies there has been some material compensation for the environmental degradation, and some prospect of improvement through a "Kuznets environmental curve" at work as incomes exceed some threshold level.

Coxhead and Jayasuriya provide a comprehensive stocktake of the challenges and policy issues (Chapter 12). Beginning with forests and uplands, they point to rapid deforestation occurring at one of the fastest rates in East Asia, with the result that forest cover declined from about 70% to less than 20% during the 20th century. This has resulted from commercial exploitation and land clearing for cultivation, propelled in part by inexorable growth in the uplands population, which doubled to 18 million persons between 1960 and 1987. The familiar results have included loss of livelihoods and soil depletion.

In the agricultural croplands the quality of irrigation services has diminished, and around 74–81 million tons of soil is lost annually. There has been a rapid and dangerous increase in the (often uncontrolled) use of fertilizer and pesticides. Since the country has effectively hit the agricultural frontiers, and must therefore shift toward a strategy of agricultural intensification, the slow growth in agricultural productivity gives cause for concern.

With its 7,107 islands, very long coastline, and extensive coastal waters, the Philippines has much potential for environmentally sound marine activities. However, Coxhead and Jayasuriya show that these resources have been degraded and are subject to huge pressures. Fish stocks have been depleted, mangroves and coral destroyed, waterways polluted. Some 95% of reefs have suffered some destruction. Freshwater resources are even more heavily polluted, with the large Laguna Bay adjacent to Manila being among the worst cases.

Urban environmental systems are also under stress, owing to rapidly accumulating industrial and consumer effluents. Air pollution in Metro Manila is obviously very serious, at levels frequently above those recommended by the World Health Organization (WHO). The use of fuel oils is a major source of the problem, particularly given the shift from hydropower to oil as a source of electricity since the 1970s. There are also very serious waste disposal problems in urban areas.

There has as yet been little serious analytical work in the Philippines on the costs of this heavy environmental damage. Some countries have developed a system of "green accounting" that attempts to factor environmental degradation and depletion of non-renewable natural resources explicitly into the national accounts. For the Philippines, this has yet to be undertaken in a comprehensive manner. But these estimates, combined with loss of livelihood in rural and coastal regions and urban disamenity costs from high levels of pollution, would undoubtedly be very high.

There are many explanations for this state of affairs. Economic scale—principally high population growth—is arguably the major factor. Weak enforcement of property rights and corruption in the allocation and management of access to natural resources are additional factors. (The Department of Environment and Natural Resources is the subject of frequent public criticism.) There is no evidence that decentralization has made much difference, although in principle it might have been expected to help. Urbanization and the shift toward more pollution-intensive activities are additional factors.

Coxhead and Jayasuriya place particular emphasis on the interaction between the trade regime and the state of the environment. The past bias against agriculture and in favor of capital-intensive industrialization has resulted in limited employment generation, and pushed workers into environmentally destructive activities such as upland agriculture. (Increased protection for corn, grown mainly in upland areas, has had a similar effect.)

But the situation is not without hope. Manufacturing protection has fallen sharply, resulting in a more labor-intensive growth path and cleaner industry (particularly electronics). There is growing official and community awareness of the gravity of the problems. Several non-government organizations (NGOs) are active in identifying and combating environmental problems. There has been a shift away from the use of leaded petroleum, and some attempts to impose environmental use fees for heavily polluted waterways such as Laguna.

1.4   BACK TO THE PUZZLES

We now return to the puzzles, of which three in particular deserve attention. What explains the Philippines' indifferent long-term growth record? Why did it not receive a larger reform dividend from the significant policy initiatives that got under way in the late 1980s? And why was it able to come through the recent Asian economic crisis relatively unscathed? The answers to these questions are complex, interrelated, and not easily amenable to quantitative analysis. No simple or single theory suffices. We need to develop a coherent story relating outcomes to an array of external and internal factors—some narrowly economic, others broader and embedded in political, historical, and institutional factors.

Surviving the Crisis

Of the three questions, the second and third are arguably more straightforward. As is evident from the analysis above, the Philippines suffered only a mild recession in 1997–98, for two main reasons.[17] First, it did not receive the exceptionally large, private short-term capital flows that went into neighboring high-growth economies (see Gochoco-Bautista and Canlas, Chapter 3). The country was effectively excluded from international capital markets until 1992, except for inflows associated with the debt workouts. Even when the capital account was opened, foreign investors who had lost out in the 1980s approached the country with caution. By the mid-1990s these flows began to increase rapidly, and for a period portfolio investment exceeded foreign direct investment. Also beginning to emerge was the problem common to the crisis economies, of governments attempting to peg to the U.S. dollar, alongside which domestic currency interest rates exceeded those in international markets. With little perceived exchange rate risk, few foreign borrowers took out hedging. Had this continued for several more years, the Philippines may have encountered the same problems as other Asian countries. However, the boom was so short-lived—effectively three to four years—that the magnitudes were quite modest. Thus no (or limited) boom meant no bust.

Second, the Philippine financial sector was in better shape than was the case in neighboring countries. As Abrenica and Llanto show (Chapter 8), the banks were comparatively prudent and cautious, and the central bank's regulatory/supervisory framework had been strengthened since the early 1990s. The level of non-performing loans was modest, and there was not as sharp an appreciation in urban asset prices in the mid-1990s. Neither had there been such reckless banking expansion prior to the crisis. Most of the major banks were well established and had conservative portfolios. Several foreign banks had recently entered the country. The strength of banks is indicated by the fact that they were able to endure a sharp depreciation of the peso in the second half of 1997, a factor that was central to the financial crisis in neighboring countries. Here also, one would not want to overstate the case. If the boom had been of longer duration, the banks would no doubt have been tempted to borrow from abroad on a much larger scale.

There were other contributing factors. The Philippines recorded the strongest export growth of any crisis or near-crisis East Asian economy during 1998. Undoubtedly, the combination of a sharp peso depreciation and an intact banking system contributed to this result. The country was also riding the crest of a wave with its electronics exports, as investments from the mid-1990s onward came on stream. With the United States absorbing a higher percentage of exports from the Philippines than from any other East Asian economy, the connection to the then booming American economy provided a further fillip to export growth.

A Larger Reform Dividend?

It is sometimes argued that the Philippines should have received a larger growth dividend from the reforms that began in the late 1980s. After all, the argument goes, these reforms were significant. Moreover, the Philippines meets practically all the non-economic conditions set out in the so-called Washington consensus, with its very open press, vibrant "civil society," and democratic processes.

It is difficult to answer this question in a rigorous quantitative fashion, and so instead we adopt an inferential approach. It should be noted immediately that there was actually a sizable dividend. As noted, Balisacan (Chapter 10) found that the incidence of poverty declined from 41% in 1985 to 27% in 2000. But the economy struggled to grow faster than 6%, even at the peak of the 1990s boom.

Three factors appear to be particularly relevant. First, the reforms were inevitably partial. As we have seen, inflation was still relatively high by East Asian standards. Trade reform progressed, but there remained a large unfinished agenda. Government spending on infrastructure and social goods was politicized, and priorities suboptimal.

A second explanation is that there was not a prolonged boom. In the high-growth neighbors, growth typically accelerated as reforms attracted additional resources, thus contributing to the so-called "virtuous circle of growth." It takes time for investors, especially foreign firms (and the sometimes vulnerable local ethnic Chinese business community), to feel confident that the policy settings are durable. The Philippine boom was short-lived by these standards, essentially lasting just four years before the Asian crisis hit in mid-1997.

Finally, significant impediments to growth remained. As noted, savings never got much above 15% of GDP. Since the country could not safely run a current account deficit of more than 5% of GDP, investment could not exceed 20% of GDP for any sustained period, whereas in nearby countries it exceeded 30% for two decades or more. Unless the Philippine incremental capital–output ratio was exceptionally low—which historically it has not been—6% growth in GDP was about the upper limit. There were in addition serious supply-side constraints to growth as a result of the 1980s fiscal crisis. Notable among these were the rundown state of physical infrastructure and a public education system starved of resources.

Slower Long-term Growth

Perhaps the central question facing scholars of Philippine economic development is why long-term growth has lagged. Various schools of thought approach the question from different perspectives, and hence provide different answers. Economists focus on conventional policy weaknesses, for example in trade and macroeconomic policy. Political scientists highlight flaws in the structure of government, both during and after the Marcos period. Sociologists draw attention to the power of vested interests, rooted in the highly inequitable colonial past. Others simply point to extraordinary misfortune. These various hypotheses are not necessarily mutually exclusive, of course, and in this subsection we attempt to briefly integrate and assess the arguments.

"Conventional" Growth Explanations

There is a large literature that attempts to explain international variations in long-term rates of economic growth—or growth in total factor productivity (TFP)—with reference to a range of policy and country endowment factors (see, for example, ADB 1997: Ch. 2). A large set of variables is included, but the core typically consists of proxies that measure macroeconomic outcomes, trade policy, human capital, institutional quality, natural resource endowments, proximity to large economies, and initial levels of per capita income (to capture the "catch-up" phenomenon). Many other variables could be added to this list.

We are unaware of any systematic testing of such a relationship against Philippine data. A framework of this type might go some way toward explaining the country's inferior performance. For example, the Philippines has been somewhat more inward looking than most of the high-growth economies, and its macroeconomic outcomes have not been as good. But such a methodology is unlikely to explain all or even a major part of the divergence. The Philippine macroeconomic record (for example, its inflation rate) has not matched that of Singapore, Malaysia, and Thailand, but it has been broadly similar to that of Korea and Indonesia for much of the period since 1970. Similarly, its trade regime has not been as open as that of Singapore, Hong Kong, and Malaysia, but did not differ significantly from that of Indonesia and even Thailand over this period. Its stock of human capital has been better than in almost all of the lower-income East Asian economies, while institutional quality has not been markedly inferior. Other variables, such as proximity to major economies, length of coastline, the incidence of political disturbances, and ethnolinguistic fragmentation, are either irrelevant or would make little difference.

Moreover, the growth determinants framework is particularly useful in explaining long-term growth differentials, and is therefore less relevant in coming to grips with the episodic nature of Philippine growth—which until about 1980 was slower than, but not markedly inferior to, that of most of its neighbors. It was the "lost decade" of the 1980s which really separated the Philippines from East Asia.

Thus, we get some way in explaining the country's slower growth using this methodology. Just how much, precisely, is a separate study in itself, and beyond the scope of this book. But we can assert with confidence that a considerable part of the story remains unexplained.

Bad Luck

One might argue that, at critical junctures in Philippine history, there has been an awful lot of bad luck, or at least unfortunate timing. For example, from the mid-1970s the Marcos administration embarked on a strategy of aggressive overseas borrowing. This was partly to boost its own fortunes, but it needs to be remembered that the international financial institutions were concerned about the rapid build-up of petrodollars in the wake of successive oil shocks, and were concerned that they be recycled. Thus, for very different reasons, the objectives of the international financial institutions and President Marcos coincided. However, shortly after the borrowing commenced, the country experienced a large negative shock in the terms of trade. Sugar prices declined sharply in 1974–75 and coconut prices in 1979–80, while oil prices rose again in 1978–79. Then, in the early 1980s, with the country carrying a much increased external debt, world interest rates rose substantially.

A second instance is that, from 1984, the country experienced a prolonged political and financial crisis, and this occurred just as the massive East Asian restructuring got under way. The resultant regional boom in trade and investment almost completely bypassed the Philippines. Moreover, from the late 1980s the commercial environment was soured by a series of adverse events: several coup attempts, the terrible volcanic eruption of Mt Pinatubo in 1991, chronic and severe power shortages, and the removal of the U.S. bases. Each of these was large enough to trigger one-off decreases in GDP growth of several percentage points.

A third example occurred in the late 1990s when, just as the economy appeared set for a period of sustained progress, the Asian economic crisis and a severe El Niño-induced drought nipped growth in the bud.

Finally, owing to protracted instability, the Philippines has never been able to exploit the opportunities presented by its frontier region, Mindanao. This has not only resulted in reduced agricultural growth but also tarnished the international reputation of the country.

The question is how important these factors were, and how much of the misfortune was really endogenous? Other countries have survived sharp declines in their terms of trade, most notably Thailand in the 1970s and Indonesia in the mid-1980s. For well-managed, prudent economies, such shocks constitute a temporary setback, not a crisis. Much of the problem in the Philippines was not the borrowing strategy per se, but the uneconomic projects for which the funds were used. Similarly, natural disasters are quite common in the region. Taiwan, for example, has had many similar experiences. Finally, while recognizing the deep historical complexities, one could plausibly argue that Mindanao was essentially a home-grown problem. Other countries have been able to manage serious regional insurrections. Thailand and Malaysia immediately come to mind.

Thus, it is difficult to sustain the case that these instances of bad luck and misfortune are the key explanators. They have certainly been very costly, and have often occurred at inopportune moments. But by themselves they cannot explain chronic underperformance.

Institutional and Political Barriers to Good Policy

It is sometimes argued that good economic policy-making in the Philippines has been frustrated by particular social structures or political institutions. There are several strands to the argument, not all of them consistent. It might be tempting simply to assign the ills of the country to the 20-year Marcos rule. Obviously personalities do matter, but can one advance the argument in a somewhat more analytical manner?

One strand of the argument asserts that highly unequal social structures—the "oligarchs'—have infected the political process to the point where serious policy reform, especially if it challenges this group's vested interests, is impossible. While it is true that the distribution of wealth in the Philippines is more unequal than in its neighbors, it does not necessarily follow that growth has to be slower. The record of the Ramos administration in fact constitutes a partial counter to this hypothesis— there were quite significant reforms in trade policy, telecommunications, and inter- island shipping. One might quibble about the scope and pace of these reforms, but they do at least suggest that the sociopolitical system is not so ossified as to be inca- pable of reform.

As an aside, a popular view posits that the "Latin America" model can be employed to explain the poor Philippine record. There are some obvious similari- ties, especially in the colonial legacy of deep agrarian inequality. However, the par- allels should not be overstated. The Philippines has never experienced Latin American-style hyperinflation (except very briefly in the mid-1980s). The planta- tion sector was never quite as dominant. The labor market has generally been more flexible. And, until very recently, there have been consistently positive "neighbor- hood effects" flowing from the proximity of the Philippines to high-growth economies. Thus the Latin America caricature, while helpful, is not a central ele- ment of the explanation.

In the post-Marcos period, it is argued that a different type of political obstacle has emerged. This is the assertion noted above that the political system is no longer able to provide longer-term economic policy predictability. Owing to the country's U.S.-style strong legislature and weak bureaucracy, and its highly personalistic pol- itics, regime changes every six years introduce much commercial uncertainty. Each new administration results in significant turnover at the upper echelons of the bureaucracy, percolating down even to the middle levels. It therefore becomes very difficult to establish "insulated" technocratic policy-making capacities. In conse- quence, investors do not think much beyond a six-year time horizon, and few prob- ably think even this far ahead.

Summing Up

As is usually the case in the search for explanations of complex phenomena, we are left with elements of a case but no grand and all-encompassing answer. All of the above factors are relevant and constitute part of the story. The Philippines failed to grow as quickly as several of its neighbors in the 1960s and 1970s for the reasons adumbrated above. In the second decade of the Marcos administration, the development strategy changed to one of adventurous overseas borrowing. This came unstuck owing to a combination of reckless investments, ever-increasing cronyism and corruption, rising community disaffection (especially in the wake of the 1983 Aquino assassination), and external misfortune. The culmination was a serious political impasse and a deep and prolonged economic crisis that set the country back more than a decade, and from which recovery has been slow and painful.

1.5 CONCLUSION

What would a balance sheet of achievements in the post-Marcos era look like? Recognizing that this is a complex and controversial issue, and at the risk of oversimplification, it might be useful to classify the record into three broad areas: significant accomplishments, a just-adequate record, and major remaining challenges.

The following areas would appear to belong to the first category, of significant accomplishments.

- *The monetary/exchange rate policy framework.* This has resulted in lower inflation, and clearer official objectives and assignment of instruments.
- *Trade reform.* Although areas of concern remain, the country now has much lower and "cleaner" levels of protection.
- *The financial sector.* Banks weathered the Asian crisis fairly successfully, and the supervisory framework is much improved.
- *Export-oriented manufacturing.* Reduced protection, liberalized foreign investment rules, and the system of export-processing zones resulted in strong export growth for most of the 1990s, albeit heavily centered around electronics.
- *Civil society.* The Philippines has one of the region's most active and open presses, together with some good quality thinktanks and NGOs. Whatever may be said of its democratic system, elections are generally orderly and open.

Among areas that are adequate, some only just, the following stand out.

- *The fiscal policy framework.* This is now better managed than in the 1980s, but except in very good years there are chronic though just managable deficits.
- *Decentralization.* This process has proceeded quite smoothly since its start in 1991, while not having a discernible impact on development outcomes at the national level.
- *Social progress.* This has been modest. Although the level of poverty has fallen, it is still high. Educational and health indicators continue to improve slowly.
- *Property rights and the investment climate.* Although there has been progress since the 1980s, the Philippines is still regarded as a relatively risky investment destination, in both a commercial and political sense.
- *Legal and judicial reform.* Elements of the legal system are sophisticated, but the courts cannot be relied upon to protect investors in an impartial manner.

Finally, among the major challenges remaining, the following would appear to be important.

- *Physical infrastructure.* Infrastructure such as roads (especially in rural areas), power, telecommunications, and ports has fallen behind that in neighboring countries. Major issues to do with supply, pricing, and regulation still need to be addressed.
- *Managing highly politicized regime changes.* The country has had four presidents since Marcos. All changeovers occurred without major violence, and two proceeded unambiguously according to the constitution. However, changes at the top lead to major turnover among the senior echelons of the bureaucracy and introduce the possibility of significant policy uncertainty.
- *Demographics.* Although falling slowly, both the population growth rate and the fertility rate are significantly higher in the Philippines than in most neighboring countries.
- *Corporate governance and the stock market.* The stock market is unable to play a role as an efficient instrument of financial intermediation owing to periodic scandals and the perception that the interests of minority shareholders are weakly protected.
- *Environment and the management of natural resources.* The Philippines continues to suffer major environmental degradation and loss of natural resources.
- *Mindanao.* Chronic problems of insecurity and disaffection create a serious problem both in the region itself and for the country's international reputation.

In the early 21st century, looking backward as well as forward, it would be tempting to conclude that the Philippines is at a crossroads, were it not for the fact that such a characterization has a sense of *déjà vu.* The past twenty years have seen very little achieved, but the past decade has demonstrated that the Philippines is not inherently a "non-developmental" state, as some have suggested. Extrapolating from the past to the future, it might be difficult to be optimistic about the country's development prospects. There have been episodes of growth, but they were short-lived and the growth has rarely matched the levels observed elsewhere in East Asia.

The key question is whether the political system can deliver the sort of substantial reforms achieved in the 1990s, in a durable and sustained fashion. The Aquino and Ramos administrations demonstrated that sound economic policy does deliver results, and seemed to suggest a decisive break with the past. But by 2000 it appeared again as though these achievements may have constituted a temporary aberration, as some of the reform progress was undone by a combination of external circumstances and domestic incompetence.

An optimistic scenario would envisage the Macapagal-Arroyo administration returning to something like the good economic management of the Ramos period, which featured sensible, pragmatic reform, and a reasonably secure and predictable policy and investment environment. With her academic and bureaucratic background, President Macapagal-Arroyo obviously understands the importance of sound economic management. She also has the prospect of a nine-year presidency to pursue a coherent economic strategy. Whether this expertise translates into a decade of solid economic development remains to be seen. A decade of 5–6% economic growth would do much to overcome the country's deeply entrenched problems of poverty and social deprivation, and it would consolidate a pro-reform constituency. Conversely, a return to populist and corrupt politics *à la* Estrada would undo the gains of the 1990s and consign the Philippines to a dismal future.

NOTES

1. There is a considerable literature on Philippine economic development in the 1970s, with the most comprehensive being ILO (1974). This was the so-called Ranis Report, named after the report's mission chief, Professor Gustav Ranis of Yale University. (This was also the most acclaimed of the ILO's major country reports of the 1970s.) If the present study has a benchmark against which to look back over the past three decades, this report would be it.

2. This observation is not without controversy. Many seasoned observers believe that the national accounts figures are understated, mainly because new, faster-growing sectors (such as electronics and some services) are probably undercounted and underweighted. The fact that most social indicators are now better than they were in the 1980s lends support to this view. Conversely, it needs to be remembered that there is now probably slightly greater monetization of economic activities, and that allowance needs to be made for the upward bias caused by the consequent overstatement in measured growth rates.

3. Since there was very little growth in aggregate over this 20-year period, it follows that the usual growth-accounting techniques are not particularly relevant. The Philippines has thus been spared the East Asian "inspiration versus perspiration" debate. Not surprisingly, several studies have found TFP growth to be either negligible or negative (see, for example, Austria 1998 and Cororaton et al. 1995). In fact, even during the earlier period of modest growth, very little TFP growth was detected by Hooley (1985), at least for manufacturing.

4. The Philippines has had five presidents since 1970, and one cannot help but observe in passing that, perhaps understandably, members of each administration are inclined toward a somewhat partial assessment of the period in which they were in government. This is becoming a matter of no small consequence since, given the high turnover at senior echelons between (and sometimes within) administrations, practically all of the country's leading economists have served in government at some stage.

5. This episode is already well told by others. See, for example, Remolona, Mangahas and Pante (1986) and Dohner and Intal (1989).

6. The latter is illustrated by the fact that the administration suffered periodic scandals and, to get its reforms through, had to rely on extensive "pork barrel" discretionary funds to legislators totaling nearly $1 billion by 1996.

7. To give just one example from the Estrada administration, PEZA has generally been regarded as well managed, whereas the regulatory authorities have appeared unable to clean up the periodic crises on the Philippine stock exchange.

8. Perhaps this is what long-time Singapore leader Lee Kuan Yew had in mind with his controversial remarks in the early 1990s to the effect that the Philippines needed "discipline" more than it needed "democracy."

9. See, for example, Power and Sicat (1971), Bautista, Power, and Associates (1979), and Medalla et al. (1995/96).

10. In passing, it might be noted that modesty has evidently prevented the authors from mentioning their own significant contribution to this process.

11. More generally, agricultural growth appears to be more rapid, other things being equal, in countries with a "unimodal" structure of ownership than in those with "bimodal," dualistic land distribution structures. Here too the Philippines–Thailand comparison is relevant.

12. The issue was complicated by the close relationship between former President Estrada and the major owner of the national flag carrier, Philippine Airlines. Especially damaging was a protracted civil aviation dispute in 2000 with Taiwan, one of the country's major trading partners and sources of investment.

13. Controls on expatriate employment are puzzling, since the Philippines has depended on open markets abroad for its large-scale labor exports. Moreover, they are probably redundant. In the niches where Philippine workers would not be competitive with foreign labor, it would make sense to allow foreign workers in to facilitate emulation, and thus the rapid diffusion of new technologies.

14. In addition to the chapter by Herrin and Pernia, see ADB/WB (1999) and HDN/UNDP (2000) for recent detailed analyses of social policy issues in the Philippines.

15. For an analysis of these patterns in East Asia, see Athukorala and Manning (1999).

16. One frustration with Philippine household income and expenditure statistics, and hence poverty analysis, is that it is difficult to compare the data for the Marcos and post-Marcos (that is, post-1986) periods.

17. See in addition World Bank (1998a, 2000b), Sicat (1999), and Noland (2000).

2

Political Economy

Emmanuel S. de Dios and Paul D. Hutchcroft

2.1 INTRODUCTION

This chapter provides a brief—and necessarily broad-brush—account of major historical trends in the Philippine political economy. We begin by examining the character of the economic elite that emerged during the country's integration into the world economy in the 19th century, and proceed to show how the American colonial era produced a national oligarchy, dominant in both the economic and the political spheres, that remains enormously influential to this day.[1] The economic interests of this primarily agricultural elite became much more diversified in the early postwar years, in large part through a process of import-substituting industrialization that seemed at the time to be propelling the country toward long-term economic success—within the region, only a handful of economies had a higher standard of living.[2]

Particularly over the past two decades, the Philippines has endured a host of economic difficulties and faced repeated challenges in attempting to convert its rich natural and human resources into developmental success. This chapter focuses particular attention on the period since 1986, and argues that political and institutional factors are central to understanding the uneven and often lagging character of Philippine economic performance. Economic reforms have commonly been promoted in the wake of crisis, but policy reforms alone have continually faced political and institutional constraints. Most recently, the considerable success of economic reform efforts in the mid-1990s encouraged transformation of important sectors of the economy and a stronger pro-market orientation among many leading elements of the business community. Subsequent experience, however, has demon-

45

strated the often weak character of the political and institutional foundations upon which the program of liberalization rested.

Equally glaring has been the failure to ensure that the benefits of economic growth and the costs of economic crisis are shared equitably among the population as a whole—a task made all the more urgent and difficult by the historical absence of any thorough program of land redistribution. Unlike South Korea and Taiwan at similar stages of their industrialization process, the Philippines exhibits a particularly immense gulf in levels of wealth and income between members of the elite and the millions of Filipino workers, urban poor, and peasants below them. Despite the relative success of many recent economic reform initiatives, the lack of attention to issues of redistribution threatens the long-term viability of any program of liberalization. The ultimate goal of political economic reform, it must not be forgotten, is the prosperity of all segments of Philippine society.

2.2 HISTORICAL FOUNDATIONS

The modern Philippine political economy can be traced to a 19th century process of agricultural commercialization led by British and American trading houses, Chinese traders, and an increasingly powerful landed elite consisting predominantly of Filipino-Chinese *mestizos*. The importance of the latter group bears special emphasis: unlike in Thailand and Indonesia, explains Harold Crouch (1985: 10), where "bureaucratic–aristocratic" elites (descending from pre-colonial kingdoms) were strengthened by the 19th century commercialization of agriculture, the same process in the Philippines "gave rise to a new class of ... landowners who were quite separate from the bureaucracy."[3] Their economic base was firmly *outside* the state.

This group of relatively autonomous landowners formed the primary social base for the first Republic of the Philippines, established in 1899. When the United States subsequently began its conquest of the Philippines, American colonials sought to win over these very powerful local forces in a "policy of attraction" intended to undermine widespread support for the struggle for independence. The American colonial government successfully co-opted local *caciques* (powerful landowners) into newly formed political institutions, in the process not only strengthening the *caciques'* power base at the local level, but also extending it upward to both the provincial and the national level (Hutchcroft 2000). The creation of a national assembly in 1907 enabled provincial elites to consolidate their hold on the national state and fostered the creation of "a solid, visible 'national oligarchy'" (Anderson 1988: 11). The oligarchy took advantage of its independent base of power, and came to exercise a powerful—yet particularistic—control over elements of the state apparatus through a spoils system that was already well entrenched at the national level early in the century.

Under the American regime, the oligarchs responded to countless new opportunities for enrichment. One source of largesse came in the form of preferential access for Philippine agricultural products (primarily sugar, coconut, and abaca) in American markets (Hawes 1987). A second source came from the effective manipulation of the growing colonial state apparatus at the national level—most dramatically evidenced by the plundering of the Philippine National Bank between 1916 and 1921 (Stanley 1974). Third, at the local level, effective manipulation of state agencies provided a range of means by which mayors, governors, and legislators could acquire land and obtain favorable access to timber, mineral, and marine resources (Sidel 1999). On the eve of the Pacific War, Philippine elites so enjoyed the arrangements provided by the American colonial regime that they were loathe to make the transition to independence. When independence did come, in 1946, it was accompanied by provisions that were clearly advantageous to the landed oligarchy that controlled the state (most of all, a bilateral trade agreement ensuring continuing dependence on the American market).[4]

In part because the grantor of independence was a rising superpower—not a declining European power, as elsewhere in Southeast Asia—it was especially difficult for the Philippines to emerge as a truly sovereign nation. Throughout the postwar years, oligarchs have needed external support to sustain an unjust, inefficient, and graft-ridden political and economic structure; Washington, in turn, received unrestricted access to two of its most important overseas military installations. The status of the Philippines, first as colony and then as post-colonial client of the United States, effectively insulated it both from the need to guard against external threat and (because of a steady flow of external resources) from the need to develop a self-sustaining economy. Only three years after independence, in 1949, the Philippine state nearly collapsed. Oligarchs plundered rehabilitation assistance to pay for duty-free imports of consumer durables, and the government lacked the means to stem the hemorrhage of foreign exchange (Golay 1961: 71–2, 80).

In a pattern that has repeated itself many times in the postwar years, the challenges of crisis induced major reform. In this case, import and exchange controls were instituted in response to the balance of payments crisis—after which rent-seeking entrepreneurs flooded the halls of the central bank in search of dollar allocations that would enable them to reap windfall profits in producing for a protected domestic market. The result was an ad hoc process of import-substituting industrialization (ISI) that involved both domestic and foreign firms, and that resulted in the increased prominence of manufacturing (which grew from from 10.7% of domestic product in 1948 to 17.9% in 1960). In historical context, the period of controls can be seen as one more source of privilege for an oligarchy whose strategies of capital accumulation had long depended on favorable access to the state apparatus. As one scholar of the Philippines noted in 1959, "business is born, and flourishes or fails, not so much in the market place as in the halls of the legislature or in the administrative offices of government" (McHale 1959: 217). Given the weak capacity of the state apparatus, it is not surprising that the controls were far less a tool of state industrial planning than an object of oligarchic plunder (Golay 1961: 92, 95, 168, 178–9; Hutchcroft 1998: 72–5).

The early years of ISI produced important changes in the economic interests of the Philippine elite (Rivera 1994). By the mid-1950s, there were signs of a significant fissure between agro-exporters (particularly the sugar bloc) and emerging industrial interests. However, the more family conglomerates moved away from an overarching concern with agriculture and toward a more diversified mix of interests (in agriculture, industry, commerce, real estate, and finance), the more consensus existed within the elite on broader issues of economic policy and the less evident were sectoral disputes. Diversified family conglomerates became the leading segment of Philippine capital, and within these conglomerates loyalties to family were stronger than to any single economic sector. There emerged a substantial homogeneity of interests on major issues of economic policy (including, of course, a commitment to prevent genuine land reform), beyond which it was far more advantageous for families to use their influence to gain particularistic favors than to seek generalized policy change favoring the interests of any given sector. Amid this simultaneous process of diversification and homogenization, political battles came to be fought more exclusively over the factional and personal issues that arose in the quest for favorable access to the state machinery (Hutchcroft 1998: 82–4).

The process of decontrol in the early 1960s brought strikingly little sense of direction to the country's economic policy.[5] Economists saw a plethora of contradictions: while the 1962 devaluation boosted agricultural exports—and spurred the growth of raw material exports, especially copper and logs—it was accompanied by tariff measures that provided continuing protection for emerging industries. By 1966, the impact of the devaluation was being eroded by inflation—thus assisting import-dependent manufacturing firms and inhibiting the fuller development of the export sector. Nonetheless, ISI continued to stagnate, and in the late 1960s the government enacted measures to promote export-led growth. But as Manuel Montes explains, these measures were only a "half-hearted flirtation." From an economist's standpoint, the country lacked any clear developmental policy.[6]

From the perspective of a diversified Philippine family conglomerate, however, things probably didn't look so grim, especially if favorable access to the political machinery provided opportunities for a range of particularistic privileges: loans from state banks, special favors for their own banks, logging and mining concessions, preferential tax exemptions, advantageous treatment on tax assessment and payments, special tariff walls or exemptions, favorable arrangements with the Bureau of Customs, and so on. Precisely because the overall policy regime was so lacking in direction, families could move in many directions in pursuit of augmenting their wealth. Exports of sugar, logs, and copper were propelled by devaluation, while manufacturing firms were accommodated by a new form of protection (through tariffs rather than exchange controls). Although incoherent from an economic standpoint, contradictory macroeconomic policies seem to have been a quite coherent means of serving the economic interests of the diversified family conglomerates that dominated the political economy.

In the late 1960s, as exports became sluggish and ISI stagnant, yet another balance of payments crisis sent the economy reeling. The crisis was triggered by one politician's particularly shameless efforts to maintain a grasp on the reins of the political machinery. In order to ensure his re-election in 1969, President Ferdinand Marcos raided the public treasury and thereby hastened the arrival of the young republic's third major balance of payments crisis. As his defeated opponent grumbled, "[We were] out-gooned, out-gunned and out-gold" (Abueva 1970: 62).[7] The post-election balance of payments crisis was followed by a devaluation, which fueled inflation. This, in turn, heightened mass demands for change.[8] Marcos, meanwhile, was determined to extend his tenure beyond the two-term limit prescribed by the 1935 Constitution. Toward that end, in September 1972, he declared martial law.

Even under martial law, development strategies remained incoherent from an economic point of view: there was continued promotion of exports, but at the same time continued protection of ISI firms. Because of the ready availability of external funds, there was never any need to make a comprehensive push for export-oriented industrialization; it was much more expedient to simply adopt the strategy of "debt-driven growth."[9] Understanding Marcos's access to external resources requires one to move beyond the realm of economic policy per se and into the realm of geopolitics. Among postwar Philippine leaders, Marcos displayed a particularly keen insight into the nature of the neocolonial bond—and knew that American strategic needs presented ample opportunity for private gain.[10] Close relations with the United States assisted him in his efforts to cultivate closer relations with the IMF and World Bank, and for a full decade he very adroitly managed to extract enormous quantities of funds from these institutions as well as from bilateral donors and commercial banks.

Marcos increased the stature of technocrats within the government and, through their public rhetoric in favor of policy reform, helped to ensure the continued flow of loans into the country (Fabella 1989). Over time, however, it became increasingly clear that the logic of the regime, like the logic of the earlier Philippine political economy, is much better understood in terms of strategies of accumulation by diversified family conglomerates than in terms of battles among coherent economic strategies or sectors. Marcos and his cronies used access to the political machinery to accumulate wealth, and—like the major families of the pre-martial law years—had little loyalty to any particular sector. The cronyism of the Marcos regime was more obvious than the cronyism of either the pre-1972 period or the post-1986 years, since the regime had more centralized control over the state apparatus and enjoyed much longer tenure in office.[11] But amidst important change in the political economy was a remarkable continuity in the nature of business–government relations; as one of the present authors has previously explained, "the crony phenomenon was no more than a logical extension and culmination of the premartial law process of using the political machinery to accumulate wealth" (de Dios 1990: 114).

Manufactured exports did indeed post major gains in the late 1970s and the 1980s, but the sector's major supporters, the technocrats and the multilateral agencies, were unable to do much more than create one more avenue of diversification for the major family conglomerates to pursue. The "non-traditional exports" were not only dominated by the already established family conglomerates, they were also so highly import-dependent that their existence did not create a clear new constituency demanding an end to the longstanding overvaluation of the peso.[12]

In declaring martial law, Marcos promised reforms that would usher in equality of opportunity and save the country from "an oligarchy that appropriated for itself all power and bounty" (Marcos 1979: 6). But while he did indeed tame selected oligarchs most threatening to his regime, a "new oligarchy" (of Marcos and his relatives and cronies) achieved dominance within many economic sectors. In exchange for the dismantling of democratic institutions, the Filipino people enjoyed only fleeting economic gain. While foreign loans sustained growth in the 1970s, crony abuses brought economic disaster in the early 1980s (de Dios 1984). Most fundamentally, martial law perpetuated important shortcomings of Philippine capitalism, because Marcos was merely expanding earlier patterns of patrimonial plunder. Particularistic demands continued to prevail, the difference being that one ruler now appropriated a much larger proportion of the state apparatus toward the service of his own private ends. As the economic crisis intensified—especially after the 1983 assassination of opposition leader Benigno S. Aquino—the IMF transformed itself from "doting parent" to "vengeful god" and forced a wrenching process of economic stabilization that induced severe recession (Montes 1987: 15). This heightened the regime's unpopularity, assisted the continuing growth of both leftist and moderate resistance throughout the archipelago, and paved the way for the Marcos regime's demise amid the "people power" uprising of February 1986. More thoroughgoing attempts at reform awaited the advent of a new democratic era.

2.3 THE MODEST REVOLUTION: THE AQUINO PERIOD (1986–92)

The economy the Aquino government inherited in 1986 was in the midst of the deepest recession of the postwar period. The collapse of investor confidence in the Marcos regime, the withdrawal of short-term foreign loans, and the enforced contraction of domestic credit had caused GNP to contract by more than 15% in two consecutive years (1984–86). Between 1982 and 1986, per capita GNP had contracted by as much as 19%. The task of restoring investor confidence, however, was even more complex than it seemed.

The accumulation of wealth by the small clique around Marcos had so radically rearranged political and economic institutions that the regime's overthrow created a vacuum that lent an unprecedented opportunity to redefine property rights in favor of previously marginalized groups. The wide-ranging opposition provoked by the regime meant that the political coalition that swept Corazón Aquino to power was likewise broad-ranging in nature. Its elements ranged from the politicized and putsch-oriented factions of the military, the anti-Marcos financial and industrial elite, traditional politicians disenfranchised by the previous regime, the Catholic Church, the articulate urban middle classes, and a plethora of non-government and people's organizations representing the moderate to radical Left. Each of these shared in and felt vindicated by the victory of the 1986 revolution, and therefore felt entitled to press its particular claims under the new regime. In particular, social demands previously associated only with the Left became part of the political mainstream, such as calls for universal land reform, a repudiation of the fraudulent loans contracted under the Marcos regime, the release of political prisoners, and an end to the U.S. military presence in the country. This was due, on the one hand, to the Left taking advantage of "democratic space" to play a more vocal role in mainstream politics.[13] On the other hand, some hitherto mainstream elements had also undergone a form of radicalization during the Marcos period, making demands from the Left appear less daunting and egregious.[14]

A conflict would emerge, then, between the need to maintain the broad basis for the regime's legitimacy and the need to regain the confidence of investors and creditors as soon as possible. A major requirement for the latter was that the government visibly limit the scope for arbitrary action. In the first few years, owing to the rapid fall of the Marcos regime, the Aquino government partook of a revolutionary character, governing largely by decree. The revolutionary basis of government encouraged expectations among the Left that deeper social reforms were indeed possible. This very openness and discretionary power, however, prevented the government from making the credible commitment to domestic and foreign economic interests that was needed to restore investor confidence.

Moreover, the new government confronted a serious threat from putschist elements, who remained unreconciled to the need to share power with a civilian government following the aborted coup of 1986. These elements calculated (wrongly) that the United States would for strategic reasons be open to supporting alternative power arrangements, particularly in the light of the increasing respectability of reform demands by the Left both within and outside the government.[15] The Aquino government needed to forcibly suppress actual threats to its power from these recalcitrant military elements in 1987 and 1989.

Putschist threats and the urgent need to regain creditor and investor confidence were the most important influences on the content of the political and economic agenda under President Aquino. From the viewpoint of making a credible commitment by diffusing authority that had temporarily been concentrated in the executive, it is understandable why the regime sought almost immediately to dilute its revolutionary discretion and create a denser network of institutions. In the process it returned the country to the familiar structures that had formed the basis of elite democracy prior to 1972. The most significant first steps in this process were the expeditious drafting of a new constitution and the holding of elections for legislative and local officials. The 1987 Constitution restored most of the pre-martial-law political institutions (most notably, a presidential system with a bicameral legislature), modified mainly by provisions seeking to prevent a return to dictatorship (for example, limits on the president's term and on the power to declare martial law).

In macroeconomic terms, the administration saw its main job as the relatively straightforward one of reviving the economy, after drastic stabilization in the last years of the Marcos regime had pushed it into a contraction, imposing a brute force solution to the external balance problem. Clearly, however, any pick-up in growth would boost imports and quickly be reflected in an external deficit, since foreign exchange earnings were being pre-empted by debt payments. A debate arose over the course of action to be taken on the debt overhang left by the Marcos regime, which had led to a massive outward resource transfer. The administration devoted a good deal of effort to restoring confidence among foreign creditors and investors, presumably in the expectation that this would be reciprocated by debt restructuring and new lending. One of the most controversial policies under the Aquino government was the decision to continue to service the country's debts fully and unconditionally, instead of declaring a selective moratorium to address the resource transfer issue. This, notwithstanding the widespread suspicion in government circles (not to mention popular clamor) that a number of loans had been attended by fraud.[16] The administration's decision reflected the approach and priorities of key economic officials[17] who were anxious to normalize relations with creditors, as well as strong pressure from the creditor consortium as represented by the IMF.

Another watershed in the changing balance of support for the administration was the issue of agrarian reform. Initially recognizing the historic standing of the issue and its resonance among non-government organizations (NGOs) and people's organizations, the government first called it a "centerpiece program" and placed all agricultural land under reform, regardless of crop cultivated. Subsequent efforts to implement the program decisively faltered, however. By that time, the newly instituted legislature had provided a venue for landlord interests (especially sugar bloc interests as well as those of members of the Aquino family themselves) to undermine the enacted law by allowing various loopholes in implementation. Uneven application, slow adjudication of cases, and the government's inability to finance the compensation to landlords stipulated in the law further hindered progress (Putzel 1992; Riedinger 1995).

Even the immediate issue of disposition of the Marcos assets saw no definitive resolution. Where this simply meant restitution, as in the case of major families (such as the Lopezes and the Osmeñas) whose assets had been seized by Marcos, it was a straightforward matter and readily resolved. The disposition of many other assets whose ownership was in dispute, however, was delayed by the build-up of interest among both old oligarchs and new carpetbaggers, who schemed to skew the disposition in their own favor. Quick disposal was also against the interests of bureaucrats who had been appointed to the boards of "sequestered" corporations as part of largesse. The ownership of these corporations, a number of which were economically important (airlines, banks, oil companies), would remain in the balance for many years. Run inefficiently or milked by government-appointed bureaucrats, and with no new financing or investment forthcoming, the sequestered corporations represented a significant unrelieved drag on the country's economic performance.

The sacrifice of the social agenda to reassure domestic and foreign investors was fraught with its own complications. Politically, the government's inability or unwillingness to provide sufficient financial support for agrarian reform and other social programs showed that decisive changes would not be forthcoming. In addition, the Aquino administration did not seek to mobilize and institutionalize popular support through the creation of a strong and program-oriented political party. These factors placed the government's political support in question and made it vulnerable to challenges from both the Left and the Right. In particular, the coup attempts of 1987 and the more bloody one in 1989 contributed to the ensuing weakness of the economy by 1990.[18]

But the approach that was taken was by no means without its own economic problems. The gamble to regain creditor confidence at all costs yielded only meager returns, since international credit and foreign direct investment were slow to return and a promised major inflow of U.S. support through the Philippine Aid Plan produced few substantial benefits in the end. At the same time, the failure to stem the foreign debt hemorrhage caused a huge drain on the budget and severely limited the government's options. The government resorted to the stopgap measure of heavy domestic borrowing, which created a fiscal treadmill. In a vicious cycle, large deficits pushed up interest rates, increased the internal debt-service requirements, and caused even larger deficits. In the early 1990s, the government's room for maneuver was severely limited and its ability to provide infrastructure and social services hampered (de Dios 1993). Higher oil prices due to the Gulf War, and natural calamities such as earthquakes and later the eruption of Mt Pinatubo, put severe fiscal pressure on government social spending and safety nets. With deficits threatening to get out of hand, the government (with added pressure from the IMF) cut back drastically on spending and imposed extraordinary revenue measures (a specific tax on petroleum and a 10% levy on all imports). This, together with the political instability from the coup attempts, sufficed to tip the economy into recession in 1991.

The fiscal crisis, putsch attempts, and the desire to restore investor confidence thus precluded the undertaking of more ambitious social projects that could have further consolidated support for the government among the masses. Ultimately the government was nudged toward an agenda that was decidedly modest, if not downright conservative. Ideologically, the Aquino government came to rationalize its role as being limited to that of undoing the Marcos legacy. In politics, this largely meant a return to the institutions prevailing before martial law, the world to which Senator Aquino, and President Aquino, were accustomed and in which they had thrived.

In the meantime, of course, society had moved on. Growing urbanization, education, and the very process of resisting and overthrowing the dictatorship had created new forces with no historical equivalent. The dense network of non-government, people's, and church organizations (later to be termed "civil society"), the mass media, and the amorphous, unorganized, but articulate urban middle class (which turned out in large numbers at the February 1986 people power uprising) was a political force that had no precursor in the system under the 1935 Constitution.

In economics, the agenda of self-limited steps—as already discussed—was the key factor in determining the sacrifice of more ambitious social programs to the restoration of investor confidence. In one area, however, this limited agenda fortunately proved adequate, namely *trade reform*. In its latter years, the Marcos regime had favored cronies through its sponsorship of ambitious industrial projects and the monopoly control of trade in important agricultural products (sugar and coconut oil). Part of its measures in the crisis period had also involved the imposition of a large number of import controls on various products. True to its word, then, the Aquino government proceeded to dismantle import controls and the monopolies in agriculture, eschewed favoritism to further large industrial projects, and committed itself to a unilateral, programmed reduction of tariffs, as well as to the process of forming the ASEAN Free Trade Area (AFTA). External support for these reform measures came, of course, from both the IMF and the World Bank, and such measures seemed to be favored by private creditors as well. In addition, they carried social legitimacy as part of the anti-Marcos thrust of the administration. While opposition to trade reforms was evident, even within the Aquino cabinet itself, the relative ease with which tariff measures were carried out is traceable in no small measure to the overall weakness of the economy. The recession and the collapse of the domestic market had simply decimated a large number of import-substituting industries (for example, automobiles). Early in the administration, the prospect of building them up again did not seem promising, and lobbies to revive or protect them had not yet had time to regroup. In the meantime, where industry lobbies were active and influential in government,[19] such as in consumer durables or food processing, accommodation could take the form either of a slower decline in tariffs on their own output, or a faster reduction in tariffs on their inputs, both tending to raise effective protection.

While modest, these liberalization moves sufficed to spur not only the initial recovery of agricultural production, but also the formation of a more conscious and vocal manufactured-export lobby based on small to medium-sized enterprises, gathered in the Philippine Exporters' Confederation (PHILEXPORT). Perhaps more important than the actual policies initiated by the government, however, was the open political framework, which allowed new economic actors to express and lobby for their interests with government, a phenomenon unthinkable in the Marcos period, when policy-making was predominantly controlled by the cronies and other favored groups.

2.4 BUILDING REFORM MOMENTUM: THE RAMOS ADMINISTRATION (1992–98)

The initial movement toward liberalizing reforms in the late Aquino years was greatly accelerated under the administration of Fidel V. Ramos, the former Marcos-era military official who had served as Aquino's defense chief and enjoyed the president's support in the 1992 elections. Under Ramos, new perceptions of the country's place in the world combined with new leadership to produce major goals for the wholesale transformation of the political economy. Indeed, the economic reforms of the Ramos administration represented the first major strategic vision of Philippine political elites since the anti-oligarchic rhetoric of the early Marcos regime (Rocamora 1994: 173).

In undertaking these reforms, Ramos and his advisers were motivated by a number of factors. First, the major economic crises of the previous decade had demonstrated the need for fundamental change. Second, the Philippines was influenced by global trends toward economic liberalization, and the need to make decisions about committing the country to new international forums and free trade associations—notably Asia Pacific Economic Cooperation (APEC), AFTA, and the General Agreement on Tariffs and Trade (GATT). Third, more intangibly but perhaps most importantly, the departure of the U.S. bases in 1992 had left the country feeling both more exposed and more aware of its surroundings. With the American security umbrella no longer providing an extensive overhang, there was suddenly a greater tendency to look around the neighborhood. From the start, Ramos expressed a clear sense of the country's weakness in competing effectively in the international and regional arenas. At his inauguration, the president decried an economic system that "rewards people who do not produce at the expense of those who do, ... [and] enables persons with political influence to extract wealth without effort from the economy." The political dominance of oligarchic groups, he explained a year later, is "the reason why the Philippines has lagged so far behind the East Asian Tigers."[20]

Under the banner of "Philippines 2000"—a rallying cry to join the ranks of the newly industrializing countries by the end of the century—Ramos combined measures of economic liberalization, privatization, and infrastructural development with concerted attacks on "cartels and monopolies." Trade liberalization, long a priority of local technocrats, the IMF, and the World Bank, was given ongoing encouragement by the country's participation in APEC, GATT, and AFTA. Foreign exchange and foreign investment were also liberalized, and major state firms extensively privatized. The Central Bank of the Philippines, after perishing under the weight of $12 billion of accumulated debt, was resurrected as the debt-free Bangko Sentral ng Pilipinas (BSP) in 1993.[21] By 1994, two rival stock exchanges were at last forced to unite in the midst of extraordinary growth in the long-dormant Philippine bourse. Greater political stability emerged in the wake of major agreements with military rebels and Muslim secessionists, and with the decline of the Communist Party. Ramos is also credited with ending the crippling power shortages that had deprived Manila and other areas of electricity for as long as 8–12 hours a day in 1992 and 1993, the very existence of which displayed the woeful neglect of the country's infrastructure in the previous decade.

Perhaps the most dramatic initiative of the new administration, led by presidential security adviser Jose Almonte, was a very public challenge to "cartels and monopolies" and the oligarchic privilege that had nurtured them. The first target was the moribund and inefficient telecommunications industry, which was transformed by new competition and came to serve as the model for thorough reform of other sectors, most clearly airlines and shipping. While other reform efforts—such as the challenge to the banking cartel—were ultimately not very effective, the fact that they were even attempted signaled a new orientation among the political leadership. Thanks to measures liberalizing foreign exchange and foreign investment, many of the new competitive pressures came from a major influx of international investment, which had previously tended to bypass the Philippines.

The success of the Ramos reforms rested on the deft and savvy leadership of the president and his key advisers, especially Almonte (who, like Ramos, was a former military officer). Liberal ideas had been floating around in Philippine policy circles for decades—yet were commonly batted down decisively by those with most to lose from their promulgation and implementation. Ramos and Almonte adopted many liberal ideas, combined them with occasional advocacy of a "strong state" (to combat oligarchic dominance), and pushed through the resulting program with very clever and well-planned maneuvers in the rough and tumble arena of real politics.

Almonte, known as the administration's "chief ideologue," often expressed marked distrust of the Philippine business elite—and showed a clear determination to press measures on a business community that was by no means demanding to be reformed. In 1993, he told business leaders that while reform "may hurt your small finger, it will certainly save your necks."[22] Some viewed the administration's rhetoric as "a cloak for Marcos-style corporate takeovers"; others feared "a military man's anti-business sentiment." The head of the huge Ayala conglomerate, Jaime Zobel de Ayala, spoke for many in the business community when—at the height of the Ramos administration's battle against the telephone monopoly—he denounced "a determined effort, on the part of some officials in sensitive places, to look upon business, particularly large and established ones, as detrimental to the national interest."[23] As the promotion of greater competition came to be associated with renewed growth, however, many business leaders actively sought to sustain the momentum of reforms. Zobel de Ayala, for example, had by 1996 cast aside his earlier criticisms of anti-big business tendencies among top officials, and spoke with great enthusiasm of the Ramos reforms.[24]

Indeed, the Ramos administration was lauded internationally for the fruits of its reform efforts—even as some of the reformers themselves freely admitted their amazement at how far their initiatives had proceeded. Growth resumed at a very respectable pace, far above the rock bottom growth rates experienced in the later years of the Aquino administration, which had been plagued by coup attempts and fiscal crises. Unlike in earlier years, economic expansion was driven not by external debt and aid, but by foreign and domestic investment. Furthermore, the growth extended far beyond Manila to include major new regional centers, including Cebu and General Santos City in the south as well as Subic Bay and other areas near Manila. There were many fresh faces on the business scene, most notably the innovative group of exporters noted above, as well as heightened prominence of Chinese-Filipino conglomerates. After years of frequently stalled reform initiatives, many observers became confident that market-oriented, outward-looking policies had at last emerged "as the unchallenged paradigm of Philippine development" (Magno 1995: 31).

Amid these and similarly triumphal statements, the Philippines displayed some of the same hubris found among other newly emerging markets in the region. In 1992, soon after the elections, the government had decided to eliminate most capital controls as a means to attract foreign investment and ease requirements for exporters.[25] Enough time had passed since the debt crisis that the country was finally able to tap international credit markets once more. The subsequent respectable showing of the economy drew in foreign portfolio flows, as did other countries in the region, creating a stock market and real estate bubble that began in 1995. In view of the capital account liberalization, a large factor contributing to the bubble economy was the central bank's decision at the time to keep the exchange rate virtually fixed in nominal terms since 1995, in what was probably the single most misguided policy under the Ramos administration (see de Dios et al. 1997). One reason for this policy was the central bank's historical insistence on the exchange rate as the anchor for inflation. The exchange rate was a "political variable," large movements in which often served as a focal point for coordinated hikes in the prices of fuel, fares, and wages. Another part of the explanation, however, is thought to have come from a strong banking community lobby to minimize foreign exchange risk while they arbitraged the large differences between domestic and foreign interest rates.

The rigid exchange rate removed virtually all foreign exchange risk to borrowing abroad and to foreign investment in the risky bills and equities markets. As a result foreign debt rode up once more. Unlike in the Marcos period, however, it was private corporations and not the public sector that did most of the borrowing. The stage was set, therefore: the collapse of the Thai baht in 1997 caused a sympathetic abandonment of the peso, leaving huge bankruptcies in banks and other corporations that had borrowed aggressively abroad.

Even in the event of the regional crisis, the Ramos program was credited with the distinct achievement of enabling the Philippine political economy to weather the crisis better than its neighbors. While there is some truth to this claim, it was actually the country's earlier adversity that offered the greatest advantage in dealing with the Asian crisis: the country's very lack of extended periods of high growth inhibited the huge surges in foreign indebtedness—and property and stock values—found elsewhere in the region. Since the Philippines never achieved high peaks, neither did it have as far to fall.[26] This is not to minimize the major accomplishments of the Ramos reformers, who exercised effective and persistent leadership at a propitious crossroads, and who had begun to effect fundamental change. The fact remains, however, that the reformers lacked the political strength to achieve their goal of "leveling the playing field" in the economy as a whole: alongside the successes, there were also initiatives (most notably in the banking sector) that were effectively stifled by those who were supposed to be the targets of reform.[27] In sum, there were marked limits to the degree to which these past efforts could effectively inoculate the country from further economic woes, particularly at a time when the greater openness of the Philippine economy made it all the more susceptible to infirmities across the seas.

In assessing this situation, it is important to recall how the political sustainability of reform was problematic from the start; even in the midst of impressive achievement, many were skeptical about future reform prospects. Most notable are the caveats of Jose Almonte, the leading figure in the Ramos reform effort, who did not hesitate to contradict the more exuberant optimism of his cabinet colleagues. Speaking to the Philippine Economic Society in early 1996, Almonte proclaimed that the hardest reforms—those involving sustained administrative capacity—were yet to come. "If our country is to organize the rational economy that will move us into the mainstream of regional development," he warned, "the State must first free itself from the influence of [the] oligarchy. ... [T]he paradox of market reforms is that they require capable states." Despite the clear impetus for change, he cautioned further, the "rich and powerful families" could still "prove stronger" than the forces of reform (Almonte 1996).

It is useful to expand on this analysis and develop a fuller taxonomy of four major types of effort that fall under the broad label of "reform."[28] First are various measures of *economic liberalization*, accompanied by widespread privatization and aggressive challenges to "cartels and monopolies." Even if more successful in some sectors than others, Ramos and such key advisers as Almonte nonetheless articulated a strategic vision as to how they might defeat obstructive oligarchic forces and promote market reforms as a means of democratizing Philippine society.

The second category of reform goes beyond standard liberal prescriptions, and involves the creation of stronger *institutional* foundations for development. The Ramos reformers did not ignore this element of reform, but, as Almonte acknowledged, such reforms as improving the quality of the bureaucracy and revamping the tax and judicial systems would prove much "harder" than the earlier "easy" tasks of liberalization. As argued further below, a concerted strengthening of institutional foundations is essential to the country's long-term prospects for sustained developmental success.

The third type of reform is *redistributive* in character and includes a range of state-initiated efforts "to transfer claims, access, rights, credit, perhaps food and income, toward poorer people, and to reduce their liabilities, duties, and barriers" (Lipton 1995: 1). Land reform, historically the most widely debated redistributive reform in the Philippines, was not a major priority of the Ramos administration; as under the previous administration, progress was slow and uneven. The administration's "social reform agenda," similarly, was notably ineffective.[29] Despite Ramos's strong rhetorical commitment to reducing poverty, those at the bottom of society generally felt excluded from the benefits of his economic program.

The fourth broad category of reform is *political*, and relates to efforts to reform democratic structures in order to encourage greater participation of, and responsiveness to, those social forces that have long been marginalized. The Ramos administration was proud to demonstrate the compatibility of development and democracy, but consistently had to rely on old-style pork-barrel politics in order to promote new-style economics (Rocamora 1995: 1–3).[30] The price of this dependence has been remarkable: the total cost of discretionary funds granted to legislators had grown to consume nearly $1 billion of the annual budget by 1996, and scandals involving persons appointed by Ramos to satisfy political debts tarnished the administration's reputation.[31] In the absence of any real reform of political structures, there is little hope that Philippine democracy will give much voice to those at the bottom rungs of society—or that economic reform programs will be crafted in ways that address their needs. Parties and the electoral process remain dominated by personalities rather than programs; legislative institutions continue to be the domain of many of the same old political clans and traditional politicians (disparagingly referred to as *trapos*, or dish rags); and the legislative process is still driven by the politics of pork and patronage. A major challenge—*the orderly attainment of which can only come through the long-term cultivation of stronger and more programmatic political parties*—is to insulate structures from particularistic demands (especially from the dominant oligarchy), and open them up to respond more effectively to collective pressures from societal groups whose interests have long been marginalized.

If the reform momentum was tenuous and the reform content uneven during the economic successes of the Ramos administration in the mid-1990s, such problems were enormously exacerbated in subsequent years. One major source of uncertainty, of course, arose from the continuing travails of other economies in the region, the contagion effects of which continued to be felt in the Philippines. As discussed in the next section, another equally important element of uncertainty revolved around the leadership of actor-turned-president Joseph Ejercito Estrada, elected in 1998 and forced to resign from office in January 2001 after massive demonstrations in the capital. As detailed below, through his close and readily apparent ties both to former Marcos-era cronies and to his own new batch of cronies and familial hangers-on, Estrada thoroughly undermined earlier efforts to "level the playing field."

2.5 THE FLAWED EXPERIMENT: THE ESTRADA ADMINISTRATION (1998–2001)

Even as it became embroiled in the Asian crisis, the Philippines was still widely expected to have the best chance of a quick recovery. The country arguably underwent the least sacrifice in terms of growth opportunities. More than this, however, the Philippines—unlike Indonesia, Malaysia, and to some extent even Thailand—was among the few countries that did not confront a problem of political transition or legitimacy, which would have complicated the purely economic and financial aspects of the crisis. Indeed, in the midst of the crisis, the country observed the revolution's centennial, held a constitutionally determined presidential election, and saw the peaceful transition of power from Ramos to Joseph Ejercito Estrada.

The victory of Estrada was less remarkable than it seemed. It was, after all, part of a continuing post-1986 political trend for the electorate to reject the discredited traditional politician, or at least its stereotype.[32] Though possessing a long political career as a local official, the ex-actor Estrada's rise to prominence had bypassed the customary route of obvious patronage and horse trading that typified the *trapo* career at the national level, relying instead on media-driven national name recognition.[33] The demonstrated power of media and of direct national appeal was, of course, a recent qualification to the pre-martial law politics that had been built largely on the foundations of local bailiwicks. As the politics of personality was expressed in new ways, party structures seem to have become even weaker and more marginal to the overall political process: throughout his term, Estrada relied on loose and ill-defined coalitions and did not even bother to form his own political party (see Landé 2001: 89).

During the presidential campaign, Estrada's obvious policy-inexperience, seeming naivete, reputed lightweight intellect, and evident inarticulateness served to cultivate the image of a political "outsider." It was ironically these same qualities, together with Ejercito's obvious celebrity and likelihood of winning, that attracted an odd spectrum of business people (including resurrected Marcos cronies), traditional politicians, and sundry intellectuals (notably including some from the Left) to gravitate around what was essentially an unknown quantity. Part of the conceit or naivete of each was that they thought they could ultimately write their own agenda on a *tabula rasa*. Contributing to the suspended disbelief was the simple, populist, "pro-poor" rhetoric the Estrada campaign had adopted, which appeared to strike a chord among the masses. In the event, the significant accretion of members of the social and intellectual elite endowed the Estrada candidacy and administration with a social legitimacy that sheer celebrity alone could not have achieved.

For all the pro-poor rhetoric and vague redistributive promises made on behalf of those who felt excluded by the economic gains of the Ramos years, the major redistributive benefits of the Estrada administration were extended to those who enjoyed most favorable access to the Palace, most infamously those privileged to join the "midnight cabinet" drinking sessions presided over by Estrada himself (Tordesillas 2000). Estrada's own feeble attempt at an anti-poverty program never took off and easily degenerated into a grab for patronage among local officials and privileged NGOs.

The controversies surrounding the administration, particularly the immediate circle around Estrada, from its earliest days showed poor presidential judgement or attention deficit at best, and the most cynical corruption and cronyism at worst. In a mode that might be termed "primitive accumulation," only the faintest attempts were made to conceal the use of power and prerogative to benefit close associates, immediate families (of which there were several), and large campaign contributors. One of the first controversies was the government's restitution of claims by Eduardo Cojuangco, a major campaign contributor and Marcos crony, to ownership of the country's largest conglomerate, San Miguel Corporation. Political indebtedness also lay behind the reversal of the country's liberal airline policy and the economically disastrous dispute with Taiwan over airline routes, whose sole purpose appears to have been to protect Philippine Air Lines, which was owned by Estrada's largest political contributor, Lucio Tan. The president was also accused of intervening personally with government agencies with a view to exonerating close associates, notably Dante Tan, who was involved in a prominent stock-price manipulation scandal (the BW Resources case), and Lucio Tan, who had a case of tax evasion pending. Exposés of spectacular real-estate acquisition, other unexplained wealth, and failure to divest on the part of the president and his legal and suppositious families also went unrefuted.

The administration's *outré* character in fact exceeded all expectations and revealed an unexpected rogue and criminal element, which finally tipped the scales and changed a business confidence problem into a full-blown political crisis. In October 2000, a provincial governor and long-time associate of Estrada[34] testified that the president was in fact the head of a national syndicate running an illegal numbers game (*jueteng*) and the recipient of regular pay-offs amounting to hundreds of millions of pesos. Testimony was presented showing that the proceeds of earmarked taxes had been hijacked and paid into private accounts meant for the president himself. Estrada also intervened in major corporate takeovers and buy-outs. Through direct influence or mandated stock purchases by public pension funds, he facilitated the takeover of private corporations in order to favor crony interests (for example, PCI-Equitable Bank), or in order to earn commissions on sales of stock (for example, Belle Corporation and PLDT, the Philippine Long Distance Telephone Company). Particularly damning was the testimony of bankers who had personally witnessed Estrada signing documents to open bank accounts under a false name.

Such revelations sparked public outrage among widening circles of "civil society," a phenomenon that encompassed the country's intelligentsia (especially the huge population of students), the religious, the rest of the middle and upper classes, and conscious, politicized sections of the masses, particularly the Left. A legacy of the 1986 revolution (the bellwether being the involvement of Corazón Aquino and Cardinal Sin), the core of civil society consisted of the relatively small membership of NGOs and cause-oriented groups. Yet it could at critical moments draw on a broad but largely unorganized and non-partisan mass of educated and politically informed sections of society.[35] While differing on specific issues, they could unite around the ideal of attaining a modern, democratic, and progressive state, in contrast to the longstanding patrimonial state that had been the perennial target of plunder by a powerful oligarchy. For civil society, Estrada, apart from being an obvious affront to morality and a national embarrassment, was the embodiment of the worst features of a corrupt state, as well as the immediate obstacle to the restoration of normal business conditions and the return of investor confidence in the country.

The brewing political crisis stood in contrast to the country's modest but creditable economic performance in the early phase (1997–98) of the Asian crisis. Not to be neglected in terms of stabilizing business expectations about policy direction and continuity was the administration's appointment of highly regarded and well-qualified individuals to its team of "economic managers" (a latter-day term for "technocrats"). Many of these individuals had consistently enunciated a philosophy of continuing liberal economic reforms in trade, industrial policy, regulatory frameworks, public procurement, franchises, and the financial sector. Aside from running a larger deficit (even here, though, with the assent of the IMF), no major shifts in policy direction were announced, so that the economic managers of the new administration were, at least on paper, sending a signal to investors of wishing to pursue the strategy of liberalization (to the extent of rejecting proposals for re-regulating the capital account, as Malaysia had done).

Indeed, some of the benefits of past liberalization were already being reaped. Among these were the continuing rise of manufactured exports, which now made up the bulk of all export receipts; which showed a small measure of diversification and deepening even within the predominant electronics sector; and which turned in the best (double-digit) performance throughout the Asian crisis. The success of manufactured exports certainly contributed in no small measure to the resilience of incomes in the face of falling domestic demand.

A second sign that past liberalization had seeped in was the muted inflationary impact of devaluation. The peso depreciated by as much as 40% during the Asian crisis. Yet, unlike previous instances, this did not result in runaway inflation in prices and wages. No inflation spike occurred, and the economy ultimately settled at the lowest rate of price change in decades. While no doubt also partly due to weak demand, a substantial part of the explanation for this must be sought in the liberalization of trade in goods, which placed a cap on the ability of domestic producers to raise prices.

Third, the removal of some restrictions on foreign entry into the banking system, the legacy of past government hand-outs to banks, and a somewhat greater emphasis on prudential regulation had minimized (but not eliminated) the incidence of bank and quasi-bank failures that were a key link in the financial debacle in other countries. Also auspicious was the shift in the central bank's policy (after a change in leadership) toward a more benign regard for currency depreciation, and a corresponding abjuration of the "interest rate cure" defense of the currency, which had punished the economy many times in the past.

This picture of macroeconomic stability and policy consistency was swept aside, however, by the wave of scandals and criticism that engulfed the presidency. The credibility of the administration's entire program was undercut by charges and exposés of corruption and cronyism, putting paid to all sanctimonious pronouncements about "leveling the playing field" and "transparency" in doing business. Hence, while no explicit disavowal of liberal and transparent policies and credible reform commitments was ever made, sufficient experience existed to show they were not to be taken too seriously. What was instead conveyed to economic agents was the classic rent-seeking message: that resources may profitably be diverted to change rules in one's favor, to protect oneself from harassment, or to gain entry to the favored activities themselves. This schizophrenia was possibly worse and more demoralizing, in fact, than if the Estrada administration had openly turned its back on liberalization. The disjunction contributed to the political crisis, and partly explains the paradox that a democratic exercise that elected a president with one of the largest majorities in Philippine history should end in the gravest constitutional crisis the country had faced since 1986.

By then the extended political crisis had sapped business confidence and threatened to scuttle a fragile economic recovery. The peso depreciated rapidly from 2000 to early 2001, and the scandal-ridden stock market continuing its downward slide, well out of line with regional trends. Confronted with growing civil society demonstrations,[36] widening exposés of corruption,[37] and increasing demoralization among the business sector, the House of Representatives transmitted the articles of impeachment to the Senate in November 2000—ushering in the first-ever impeachment of a Philippine president—and the Senate began the impeachment trial shortly after. On 16 January 2001, the Senate narrowly voted (11 to 10, along the lines of prior political alliances) to refuse admission of important evidence implicating Estrada. This precipitated the resignation of the Senate president, the withdrawal of the prosecution panel, the loss of confidence in the entire process, and even more massive and sustained demonstrations at the historic EDSA shrine and in other parts of the country, in what came to be known as People Power 2, or EDSA Dos.[38] Sustained popular pressure, the withdrawal of support by key political figures, the resignation of key members of the Estrada cabinet, and, more definitively, the defection of the entire leadership of the armed forces and the police on 19 January 2001 compelled Estrada to abandon Malacañang Palace on the following day—an ambiguous act that the Supreme Court subsequently deemed a de facto resignation.[39] This paved the way for then Vice-President Gloria Macapagal-Arroyo to take her oath as president before the throngs at EDSA.

In many ways, Estrada's brief tenure probed and exposed the structural weaknesses of the country's political and social institutions. It was, of course, nothing new for the politically informed civil society to learn that politicians, the bureaucracy, and the police could be willing parties to corruption (although the involvement of a sitting president in underworld activities admittedly plumbed new depths). In this case, however, even the credibility and transparency of banks, large conglomerates, the financial markets, the legal profession, and academe appeared to hang in the balance, as large parts of these were drawn into the web of corruption and irregularities under Estrada. Finally, as the Senate's vote to exclude damning evidence showed, formal proceedings could be reduced to a sham by the larger social realities of bribery and patronage. The resort to people power to remove the president in January 2001 was thus proximately an indictment of the constitutionally designated impeachment process and its failure as an effective mechanism for recall. But ultimately it was also an indictment of the character of the country's political and social institutions in general.

2.6 PEOPLE POWER AND INSTITUTIONAL REFORM

From the start, the reprise of people power carried the burden of its own ambiguities. In the first place—as foreign commentaries have noted and Estrada's lawyers have used in his defense—People Power 2 confronted an obvious dilemma when it asserted the value of public morality and the rule of law while overriding normal constitutional processes (notably by aborting the impeachment trial itself). Unlike in 1986, when Aquino's supporters never conceded the legitimacy of Marcos's usurpation of power, the legitimacy of the rules by which Estrada had *assumed* the presidency was unquestioned by both sides. Yet the mode of his *removal*, entailed by the same set of rules, was highly disputed. As alluded to above, this dilemma was resolved only by invoking a higher, extra-constitutional logic that recognized that "normal" institutions and other rules had in fact been debauched. Indeed, in justifying the changeover from Estrada to Macapagal-Arroyo, the Supreme Court initially reached deep down to retrieve that most elemental of governance principles, *salus populi suprema lex*, demonstrating that any rationale based on customary subsidiary rules would fail.

A similar dilemma presented itself regarding the extent to which society would actually be reformed in a post-Estrada period. Civil society at EDSA 2 sought to hew as closely as possible to the constitution (which also explains the acclamation for the vice-president and constitutional successor, Gloria Macapagal-Arroyo, even if she was not necessarily the first choice of those demanding the president's resignation).[40] Estrada's removal was thought to be a needed excision to preserve the healthy parts of the political body. With the president extra-constitutionally removed, civil society sought to retreat and allow the normal functioning of institutions to resume. It expected people power to "eventually become a relic of the past, never to be called upon again to resolve divisive political issues" (Bautista 2002: 34).

If the Estrada episode demonstrated anything, it was that institutions themselves were weak, corruptible, and susceptible to capture, *even in their normal state*. This was a condition Estrada and his cohorts did not create, although they recognized it and exploited it well. EDSA 2 was an eloquent protest against the country's fractured institutions, and forcefully asserted popular anger over the blatant corruption of democratic principles and processes. While political confrontation such as this can indeed provide an important basis for the strengthening of political institutions (contrary to those who dismiss EDSA 2 as mere "mob rule"), it must be followed by new rules to suppress the politics that made a president like Estrada possible in the first place. What it attained at most was a return to normal life and business conditions (which was the main concern of the middle classes and business elite), and the *promise* of reform effort and "new politics" from the executive branch now headed by Macapagal-Arroyo and members of her cabinet (a number of whom were picked from the NGOs and people's organizations that had launched People Power 2). Civil society's optimism that there would be political reforms beyond Estrada's removal, however, was overly optimistic, since everywhere else the same socioeconomic structures and clientelistic relations continued to set the tone for social conditions and politics.

The rude awakening from the reverie of People Power 2 came soon enough in the April–May Reaction, also controversially dubbed "People Power 3," when hundreds of thousands of Estrada's supporters, mostly from the urban poor, occupied EDSA for several days in protest over his arrest on charges of plunder. This event culminated in an assault on Malacañang and widespread rioting in Manila. The new administration portrayed these events as part of a rebellious conspiracy hatched by politicians associated with Estrada to take power for themselves, using the pro-Estrada masses as cannon fodder. It was undeniable, however, that entire sections of the population, particularly the otherwise "unorganized" and relatively "unpoliticized" poor, harbored a diametrically opposite assessment of exactly what People Power 2 had accomplished. In their view, it had robbed them of "their" president; they would not believe that the corruption charges against Estrada could be true, or, even if true, that these were exceptional enough to single him out for "persecution." In a surreal role reversal, it was the normally politically inchoate masses who were now (admittedly cued by Estrada's legal defense) demanding that "due constitutional process" be observed and accusing the intelligentsia of mob rule. Of course, in their own paradoxical logic, the April–May demonstrators and their handlers seemed prepared to resort to violence to assert "due process." In the event, this regrouping of pro-Estrada forces contributed significantly to preventing a clean sweep at the polls for the new administration's candidates in the senatorial elections.[41]

The events of April and May revealed a surprisingly wide gap in perceptions of governance between "politicized" civil society and the "amorphous" masses. Estrada's misrule had brought a more radical change—for the worse—in the material and moral conditions of the elite and middle classes. It was they, to begin with, who had the greatest existential contact with and comprehension of government and its actions. A deterioration in the quality of governance on the scale that Estrada represented hit them hardest, and provided the strongest stimulus for them to seek redress and demand better governance and a stricter adherence to the letter of the law.

Against this, one must contrast the political inclinations of the greater number of people, consisting mostly of the unorganized poor.[42] Issues of high governance, especially as these pertain to the workings of the economy, the design of legislation, and the canonical conduct of high public officials, carry much less weight with those who, from the start, have been excluded and are distant from the mainstream economic and social activities potentially affected by these acts.[43] For those who benefit but little from it, government is an abstraction, an alienated entity, whose only palpable dimension is the episodic patronage dispensed by bosses and politicians, which merely reinforces the poor's real condition of dependence. This same alienated condition causes the electorate in many places repeatedly to elect convicted criminals, underworld characters, and known grafters, simply because such behavior is *irrelevant* to the more advantageous local clientist functions those persons discharge, whether this be of a material nature (for example, the local privileges of Ilocandia and Leyte under the Marcoses) or a symbolic one (for example, Estrada's image as champion of the masses). In either case, the same explanation must be adduced:[44] the people's own powers are projected onto a strong, charismatic personality, which then confronts them as a powerful icon to be venerated.

The preceding makes clear the disjunction between perceptions of Estrada's removal by organized civil society on the one hand and by the inchoate masses on the other: what for the former was a step toward rational and impartial government, represents for the latter a return to a heartless dispensation and an affront to the already powerless. Paradoxically, therefore, the alienated masses under the thrall of clientelistic relations may relate to certain middle-class reform impulses as a *conservative* force; and given formal democracy, they are bound to be a substantial force as well. Pushing forward a reform agenda under these conditions is the major challenge that confronts the Macapagal-Arroyo administration.

Ultimately, the perceptual divide in Philippine politics must be traced to the effects of a real class divide in a society where, even if the numbers of poor have officially fallen as a proportion of the population, inequality has nonetheless continuously increased. As already discussed, the roots of inequality and dependence originated in unequal relations in agriculture. The slow pace and ambiguous intent of agrarian reform under various administrations robbed it of its initial promise, earlier on in the past century, of creating a broad and stable middle class with a stake in a new politics and a modern economy. The accretion of incremental gains in agrarian reform over many decades has indeed resulted in a substantial amount of land being redistributed (Borras 2000), although admittedly further progress is possible. But the significance of these gains has diminished with rapid population growth, growing urbanization, and the declining importance of agriculture. These have created new sources of wealth (notably financial capital and real property, which became prominent before the Asian crisis), as well as new bases of inequality and deprivation that even a completion of agrarian reform would likely be unable to redress.

2.7 THE DILEMMA OF NORMALCY: THE MACAPAGAL-ARROYO ADMINISTRATION

The Macapagal-Arroyo administration faced the difficult task of normalizing political and economic conditions after the excesses and inadequacies of the previous Estrada administration. To some degree, the greater professionalism and back-to-business mien of the Macapagal-Arroyo cabinet represented a welcome change. Corruption, even as it persisted, was kept within bounds and did not reach the institutionally disruptive scale experienced under Estrada. In terms of macroeconomic management, the country even appeared to regain a semblance of balance. The first-year budget deficit was kept under control, reversing the past administration's stance of deficit spending. Inflation continued on a downward path to historically low levels of below 5% by the end of 2001, and pressures on the peso abated, allowing interest rates to be reduced in line with worldwide rates.

Economically, however, the most serious challenge was the sharp recession that gripped the United States and most of the world in the wake of the terrorist attacks of September 2001.[45] Philippine exports dropped drastically, and manufacturing shrank. As a result, the strong recovery awaited after Estrada's removal failed to materialize. Even so, the Philippines posted positive growth based on continuing growth in services and agriculture, faring better than more export-dependent neighbors like Malaysia and Singapore. Such elements in themselves were sufficient to reconcile most of the business community to the administration, and by early 2002 a mood of cautious optimism had begun to spread among both domestic and overseas investors.

It was another question—as it had been earlier for Aquino—as to what extent a simple reversion to normalcy would suffice to meet growing cynicism and impatience among the lower classes for concrete improvements in their lives. This disjunction between business perceptions and lower-class expectations was partly manifested in the periodic threats of pro-Estrada forces to launch massive anti-government demonstrations based on the disaffection of the poor, particularly in urban areas. It was clear even to the administration that the manifestly respectable economic growth under the circumstances—of 3.4% GDP growth amid a weakening world economy—would hardly suffice to reduce poverty significantly. Moreover, any further growth acceleration approaching East Asian trends was unlikely unless deeper structural problems were resolved—including low saving, low agricultural productivity, high population growth, inferior infrastructure, property rights issues, industrial concentration, and political underdevelopment, as well as public sector inefficiency and corruption. Since the Aquino and Ramos administrations, the need to craft a national response to globalization and locational competition had provided a rough national reform agenda around which many social groups could rally. The actual experience of growth had rendered that vision at least plausible. The weakening world economy, however, knocked the wind out of the globalization agenda (at least for the moment), depriving the administration of a ready intellectual vehicle for mustering national unity. With avenues for growth receding, the national debate instead came to focus on the distributional gap and a challenge to the political system to redeem longstanding social claims.

The Macapagal-Arroyo administration was also hobbled by the circumstances by which it had come to power. Owing to the need to cement shaky alliances in the face of legal and extra-constitutional challenges to legitimacy, and the prospect of a re-election bid,[46] a number of the president's alliances and appointments were based on political loyalties and quid pro quo rather than (or in addition to) fitness or principle. In particular, the military and the police, whose shift in allegiance had been pivotal in deposing Estrada, were largely left to run their own affairs. The administration seemed unwilling or unable to apply pressure on the military and police to perform, notwithstanding the deterioration in peace and order (as seen in rising cases of kidnapping, drugs, and gambling).

It was in particular the fecklessness of local police and the military in bringing the Abu Sayyaf terror group to justice that ultimately led to a call for U.S. troops to participate in ostensible "war exercises," with the very real objective of decimating the group and freeing its captives. While the United States viewed this as an extension of its global "war on terror," the Macapagal-Arroyo administration used the closer alliance with the United States to strengthen its legitimacy in the face of challenges from pro-Estrada forces, even as the obtrusive and extended presence of American troops reopened old debates about sovereignty and undue foreign influence on policy. The latter widened the split between the administration and the ideologically oriented civil society groups that had initially supported it.

Thus, early in its term the administration confronted the task of meeting popular expectations for a rapid improvement in people's lives, when the only means of doing so involved resolving deep-seated problems that would take years to accomplish. Whether and how to bridge this gap and still ensure its political survival beyond the 2004 elections was the difficult choice the administration needed to make.

2.8 CONCLUSION

The imprint of recent events is too fresh to gain a complete perspective on the future. Yet it is inaccurate and perhaps unfair to conclude that little has changed in Philippine political economy over the past half-century or so. Urbanization, better education, the media, globalization, and the emergence of a civil society with a higher standard of public consciousness and morality have ensured that, even as pre-martial law political institutions have been restored, they have not functioned in the same way. Indeed, the present crisis is testimony to that: in the 1950s, similar political controversies and scandals would have been confined primarily to politicians themselves (perhaps to be turned into political capital in the next election) but would not have reached the extent of spawning a massive outcry and a constitutional crisis.

Similarly, even the economy has been changed by years of deregulation and liberalization in the direction of more diversified activities and more actors in the policy arena, so that it manifests a resilience that has allowed it to tolerate a measure of political turmoil (though not indefinitely and repeatedly). Although large family conglomerates do exist, and at times even dominate, external openness has placed limits on monopolistic power and provided a fairer and more even test for new entrants in activities such as manufactured exports, information technology, and e-businesses. Traditional conglomerates must at times measure themselves against newer forces such as foreign direct investors, or the Chinese-Filipino *taipans*.

Notwithstanding these changes (dare one call them progress?), it will be admitted that the Philippines still has not hit upon the proper combination of political institutions to provide the required responsiveness to public interest on the one hand, and flexibility with respect to changing economic conditions on the other. The crisis provoked by President Estrada demonstrates clearly that progress in the political system has not kept pace with what is required by economic development. Political development has not reached the point where democratic institutions in themselves guarantee that informed public choices will be made that are ultimately responsive to the people's demands and the requirements of the economy. This should be no source of wonder. For a large part of the population, electoral choices remain an abstraction, since government itself, as Corpuz (1965) noted long ago, has historically been distant and unresponsive, while smaller social units such as family, extended kin, or ethnic group are more concrete sources of benefits and social insurance. Simple cost–benefit analysis would suggest that, in this case, even democratic electoral choices are unlikely to be invested with much introspection or investment in information. Indeed, as mentioned previously, the election of Estrada himself— despite the later misgivings—was already in the way of a learned political choice, to the extent that popular sentiment had progressed far enough to reject traditional politics.

Nonetheless, as the same example shows, elections are at present a blunt instrument for the improvement of governance. It might be hoped that in the wake of the recent crisis will come an opportunity to consider creative reform of legislative and electoral institutions, in order that the democratic structures put in place in 1986 become more effective in promoting national goals. In particular, it is of crucial importance to promote the creation of more effective and cohesive political parties, oriented to programmatic rather than particularistic goals, policy rather than pork. Contrary to the currently fashionable rhetoric valorizing civil society and NGOs, there is no substitute for the role that well-institutionalized and programmatic political parties can play in promoting both developmental and democratic goals (Bevis 2001; Montinola 1999). Valuable as it is, civil society's episodic intervention to resolve political crises in 1986 and 2001 falls short of what is needed to build new political institutions. People power cannot be established as an institution, since almost by definition its reappearance is an admission that institutions have failed yet again. "Meaningful social change has been inhibited," argues Montinola (1999: 133), "because political parties have failed to structure political competition to allow for representation of the interests of the poor and marginalized sectors." Fuller political representation in turn will ensure that long-neglected redistributive measures will finally be given sustained attention. Without such representation and measures, the threat will always exist that the demands of the marginalized will continue to be expressed in violent and socially disruptive ways, through rebellion, criminality, or both.

The lack of congruence between political structures and the needs of economic development is most evident when one considers the stringent requirements of an economy that must navigate in a global environment of changing markets, technologies, and institutional arrangements. Even before that, however, the Philippine government had often had difficulty providing even the most basic foundations for a free-market economy—whether it be supplying electricity, safeguarding the process of timber extraction, arbitrating among investors squabbling over the proper site for a petrochemical plant, or providing even-handed regulation of the financial system. Certainly one commonly promoted alternative is to shrink the role of government and promote private sector initiative. Yet that cannot be all, since there is no size of government that is immune to damage from rogue elements thrown up by an unsophisticated political process. More fundamentally, therefore, it is essential to improve the overall performance of government, insulate it from the plunder of oligarchic groups, and promote new *types* of private sector initiative.

Over the long term, a more prosperous Philippine capitalism will require a government apparatus able to provide these foundations. Major institutional hurdles exist in the judicial and law enforcement systems, where extensive corruption and ineffectiveness have provoked widespread public cynicism; as Joseph Estrada himself ironically observed when he was vice-president, these systems are plagued by "hoodlums in robes" and "hoodlums in uniform."[47] It is difficult to instill investor confidence when a high degree of arbitrariness often reigns in the political and legal spheres, and kidnappings undermine the personal security of an important element of the business community. The country's weak fiscal position, moreover, keeps civil servants' salaries at miserable levels, and obstructs the long-term goal of strengthening the civil service and curbing the prevalence of corruption. It is essential to build on substantial talent already present in the Philippine bureaucracy, and to ensure that the hard work of honest civil servants is not dissipated by corruption among those around them.

Sustained economic growth depends upon improving the quality of the bureaucracy—once described by Ramos as the "weak link" in national developmental efforts. Even if the Philippine bureaucracy seems unlikely to achieve the level of coherence and capacity historically found in the highly interventionist "developmental states" of Northeast Asia, incremental measures can nonetheless enhance provision of the basic legal and administrative underpinnings necessary for the functioning of a "free-market" variety of capitalism. Thus far, the most successful economic reform efforts have been those that merely remove restrictions on competition; far more complicated are initiatives requiring sustained administrative capacity. Just as liberalization of the banking sector by no means resolves ongoing deficiencies in regulatory capacity, neither do broader programs of economic reform obviate the need to address other political and institutional problems. It is one thing, for example, to liberalize agricultural imports or remove restrictions on agricultural exports, but quite another to provide the roads, irrigation facilities, extension services, and other infrastructure necessary for farmers to improve their productivity and meet the challenges of international competition. Similarly, it is far easier to open up the economy to foreign investment and imports than to develop sustained programs of export promotion that can assist local entrepreneurs anxious to tap new opportunities in world markets.[48] In any project of institution building, it is particularly important to concentrate on the enhancement of administrative capacity in such key institutions as the new BSP, the Securities and Exchange Commission, and the Bureau of Internal Revenue.

On many fronts, Philippine state institutions have shown themselves to be incapable of providing the necessary political foundations required even by the laissez-faire model of development that the IMF, World Bank, and the former colonial power have long been trying to promote in the country. Overall, it is difficult to instill long-term investor confidence when a high degree of arbitrariness reigns in the political and legal spheres; until there is greater attention to such underlying constraints, economic liberalization initiatives rest on less than secure bases, threatened on the one hand by simmering resentment among the marginalized, who are unable to participate in the mainstream political arena, and on the other by the power of particularistic demands of the oligarchy. No matter how sound the policy agenda promulgated at the national level, there is little hope of coherently sustaining such an agenda without careful and sustained nurturing of the country's institutional and political foundations.

NOTES

The authors would like to express their sincere appreciation to those who provided helpful and insightful comments on earlier drafts of this chapter, in particular Kit Collier.

1. This influence endures in the midst of continuing change in the oligarchy's composition, as new families appear out of nowhere and some of the old families fall by the wayside. Unlike an aristocracy, an oligarchy has little stability in its composition; there is a constant stream of new entrants as new wealth is created. As a system of government, oligarchy is rule "for the benefit of the men of means," not rule for the "common interest." In polities "where men rule because of the possession of wealth, whether their number be large or small, that is oligarchy" (Aristotle 1985: 190, 192; see also 252–60).

2. In 1955, Japan's per capita income was roughly double that of the Philippines; per capita incomes in Malaysia and Taiwan were, respectively, roughly 25% and 10% higher than in the Philippines. There are no 1955 data available for Hong Kong and Singapore, but by 1960 the per capita GDP figures for both were substantially higher than those for the Philippines. See Penn World Data, http://www.bizednet.bris.ac.uk/dataserv/penn.htm.

3. See also Crouch (1985: 10–18). For richly detailed accounts of economic change in the 19th century, see Legarda (1999) and McCoy and de Jesus (1982).

4. Between 1946 and 1974, the Philippines was granted an annual quota for sugar exports to the United States. Guaranteed access to the U.S. market provided little incentive for efficient production, and in 1974 "the Philippines was completely unprepared for its sudden entry into a highly competitive world market" (McCoy 1983: 142–3, quoted here at 143).

5. The most comprehensive account of the decontrol process is found in Baldwin (1975: 50–64). The system of controls depended on American support, but at some point in the late

1950s the United States began to push for a new economic strategy. See Maxfield and Nolt (1990: 62–8), Cuaderno (1964: 71–7), and Payer (1974: 60–61).

6. See Jurado (1976: 274); Montes (1987: 2), and Baldwin (1975: 62). A similar argument is found in Power and Sicat (1971: 42).

7. See Power and Sicat (1971: 50) and de Dios (1990: 111–12). On economic performance in this period, see Bautista, Power, and Associates (1979: 59) and Montes (1989a: 88–9).

8. These demands related both to domestic politics and to ongoing neocolonial ties to the United States. A major focus of contention and uncertainty was the status of American investments in the country, since "parity rights" granted in 1946 were due to expire in 1974. See Shalom (1981).

9. The term "debt-driven growth" comes from Montes (1989a: 90). In an earlier analysis, de Dios has argued that easy access to foreign loans meant that "pressure from the multilaterals to adopt the EOI [export-oriented industrialization] strategy could be effectively deflected," and "the issue of the development strategy could be essentially avoided throughout most of the Marcos regime" (de Dios 1990: 116).

10. Enlightening scholarship on the historical process of tapping American patronage is found in Paredes (1989). For a well-documented account of the history of neocolonialism, see Shalom (1981). Bonner (1987) gives a good sense of how the Marcoses knew how to maneuver in Washington circles.

11. "Crony" is used to describe those whose positions are particularly favored by the current regime, regardless of their origins. An "oligarch" may or may not be a current crony but in either case has already established his or her fortune under earlier dispensations. Under the Marcos regime, both "old oligarchs" and "new men" gained "crony" status, and they were referred to collectively as the "new oligarchy."

12. See Montes (1989b: 71–3), World Bank (1981: 1), and de Dios (1988: 119–20).

13. One of the first acts of the Aquino government was to release political prisoners, including Jose Maria Sison, the leader of the Communist Party, and Bernabe Buscayno, the leader of the New People's Army.

14. Representative of this was the transformation of Senator Benigno Aquino himself in the course of his exile. Similarly, the support of members of the Lopez and Osmeña families for extremist urban terror (the "Light-a-fire" movement) marked a political watershed for the traditional elite.

15. A particular source of uncertainty for the United States was the impending end of the military bases agreement.

16. The classic example was the syndicated loan to finance the nuclear power plant project in Bataan, which was later revealed to be hugely overpriced and attended by corruption.

17. The exception to this view was represented by Solita Collas-Monsod, who served as the first secretary of planning to Corazón Aquino.

18. It is further testimony to the fragility of the regime that the military conspirators who had openly rebelled and done damage to the economy went unpunished. For a comprehensive account, see McCoy (1999).

19. The trade minister at the time, Jose Concepcion, represented business interests opposed to liberalization in principle, but such powerful opposition was ultimately reconciled through particularistic accommodation. The original executive order setting forth the programmed tariff reductions was withdrawn, only to be reissued later to accommodate some interests of specific industries.

20. For a more comprehensive analysis of the motivations behind the reform effort, see Hutchcroft (1998: 241–6).

21. The enormous burden of the former central bank's profligacy, meanwhile, was assumed by the country's taxpayers. See Hutchcroft (1998: 207–12).

22. Speech, Jose Almonte, Asian Institute of Management, Metro Manila, 29 April 1993.

23. *Far Eastern Economic Review* (28 May 1992: 14–15, and 6 May 1993: 44–5). Perceptions that certain Ramos appointments to the board of PLDT were patronage-based did little to dispel doubts about administration motives. See, for example, *Far Eastern Economic Review* (18 October 1993: 30).

24. *Business World* (1 October 1996); see also Magno (1996: 298–9). In praising the reform program, Ayala called it "a breathtaking ride our country has not known since … independence in 1946. … The Philippines is faring better today because we have literally changed the road map to the future."

25. The right to hold on to part of their foreign exchange receipts (needed as working capital for foreign purchases) was a longstanding demand from exporters. While exporter groups were requesting the right to retain only 50%, the administration exceeded their expectations by allowing 100% retention.

26. On the "advantages of lower elevation," see Hutchcroft (1999b).

27. The limitations of banking reform under Ramos are analysed in Hutchcroft (1998: 212–20).

28. This discussion expands upon Lipton (1995: 1–3). For a comparative view, see Hutchcroft (1999a).

29. On the limitations of Ramos's social reform agenda, see Collas-Monsod (1998) and Martinez (1996: 39–40).

30. The term "political reform" can encompass a broad range of processes, from the promotion of political stability (noted above), to the installation and consolidation of democratic institutions (the Philippine experience of which is most ably analyzed in Thompson 1996), to reform of electoral, party, and legislative structures (with the goal of improving the quality of democracy). In this chapter, we are dealing with the latter aspect of the term.

31. On controversy over the discretionary "Countrywide Development Fund" and "Congressional Initiative Allocation" granted legislators, see *Philippine Daily Inquirer* (26 and 27 July 1996, 4 and 18 August 1996).

32. Neither the winner of the 1992 election, Fidel Ramos, nor the close runner-up, Miriam Santiago, were career politicians: Ramos was a former general, Santiago a former judge. The traditional politician Ramon Mitra was a distant third. The prototype of the traditional politician was arguably represented in the 1998 elections by Jose de Venecia, who also lost by a large margin.

33. Estrada's career spanned a long period as mayor of a Metro Manila municipality, then, in quick succession, election as senator, vice-president, and president.

34. Luis (by name Chavit) Singson was governor of the province of Ilocos Sur.

35. In 1997 and 1999, massive civil society demonstrations also intervened to thwart attempts to amend the 1987 Constitution, particularly its provisions regarding limits on the terms of elected officials.

36. Bautista (2002) reports survey results from Pulse Asia suggesting that participants in People Power 2 rallies in Metro Manila consisted of some 18% from the elite, 47% from the middle classes, 31% from the poor, and 4% from the very poor, utilizing the AB-C-D-E socioeconomic classification typically used in such surveys.

37. Investigations into Estrada's unexplained wealth and misuse of power by the Philippine Center for Investigative Journalism and the *Philippine Daily Inquirer* played an especially important role. See, for example, Coronel (2000).

38. The reference is to Epifanio De Los Santos Avenue (EDSA), a principal artery in Metro Manila, the venue of the first people power revolution in 1986, and likewise the scene of the large demonstrations precipitating Estrada's fall. Hence EDSA 1 and EDSA 2, respectively.

39. Estrada would later maintain he had not really resigned his office but had merely "taken leave," a claim dismissed by the Supreme Court.

40. Opinion polls by Pulse Asia showed Macapagal-Arroyo's performance rating actually falling during the impeachment process, particularly among the rich and middle classes, who were among the most articulate participants in EDSA 2. The trend reversed after she was proclaimed president.

41. Of 13 seats at stake in the senatorial elections of 17 May 2001, the new administration's candidates obtained eight, somewhat less than the 10–11 hoped for during the euphoric phase of the campaign. In particular, the opposition managed to win seats for the legal wife of the deposed president and two ex-military men accused of plotting the violent April–May Reaction.

42. The weak level of self-organization is evident in the low rate of membership of trade unions, peasant organizations, and other types of people's organizations.

43. Making the same point, political wags ventured that the election of Estrada was "the revenge of the masses on the elite," since he could certainly pull down the latter, but not those who were already at the bottom of the rung.

44. With apologies to the young Marx.

45. The U.S. economy had been weakening even earlier, however, and the National Bureau of Economic Research backdated the recession to as early as March 2001.

46. Since she was merely serving out Estrada's unexpired term, Macapagal-Arroyo is not covered by the constitutional single-term limit and is qualified to run in the 2004 presidential election.

47. Similarly, Archbishop Jaime Cardinal Sin has denounced the "judicial Judases" found throughout the system, and observed that the study and practice of law in the Philippines are "as different as heaven and hell" (*Philippine Daily Inquirer*, 27 April 1996). A rash of kidnappings and bank robberies (widely thought to involve "law enforcement" officials) highlighted the corruption and incompetence of judicial and police officials. See *Asian Wall Street Journal* (23 May 1997) for a detailed account of corruption in the Supreme Court.

48. Because the country's commitment to liberalization has not been matched by any similar commitment to export promotion, the result has been a kind of reverse mercantilism. The mercantilists of Northeast Asia, it is worth recalling, restricted imports while promoting exports; in the Philippines, on the other hand, the ports have been opened up to a stream of foreign goods without any concomitant effort to promote higher value-added exports. The one success story in Philippine exports, electronics equipment, remains highly dependent on imported inputs.

PART II

Macroeconomic Policy and
International Dimensions

3

Monetary and Exchange Rate Policy

Maria Socorro Gochoco-Bautista and Dante Canlas

3.1 INTRODUCTION

This chapter examines the evolution of monetary policy rules and exchange rate regimes in the Philippines over the past two decades and the resulting macroeconomic performance. In a small open economy, the choice of exchange rate regime cannot be made independently of monetary policy. Failure to appreciate this interdependence can yield undesirable consequences, such as a collapsing exchange rate and balance of payments crisis accompanied by financial market failure. In the wake of the Asian financial crisis, which was triggered by the sharp depreciation of the Thai baht in the second half of 1997, the search is on for an appropriate monetary policy rule the central bank can implement in order to achieve price stability and secure efficient financial intermediation in an environment that is increasingly one of integration with international financial markets.

The start of the 1980s was an inauspicious period for the Philippines. By the time the second oil shock hit in 1979, easy foreign financing, which had fueled debt-driven growth throughout the 1970s, had come to an end. This meant that the country's massive foreign borrowings could neither be rolled over without additional foreign borrowing, nor financed through increased exports because of the deterioration in the terms of trade. The result was an external debt crisis. Adding to the country's problems was the collapse of the commercial paper market in 1981, marking the beginning of a major financial crisis. In 1983, with the assassination of Benigno Aquino and massive capital flight from the Philippines, a moratorium on external debt payments was imposed.

Despite the difficulties of the early 1980s, the government began to implement a package of economic policy reforms aimed at greater integration with the world economy. These reforms included import liberalization and reductions in tariffs, accompanied by liberalization of foreign direct investment and of the financial and foreign exchange markets. As a result of these policy adjustments the Philippine economy undoubtedly became more integrated with the rest of the world, not only in the area of trade in commodities but also in trade in securities and national currencies. A study by Gochoco (1991a) confirms that the economy was quite open, with domestic interest rates largely influenced by the forward premium on foreign exchange even in an era when there were legal controls on capital flows. Given the episodes of profound peso depreciation in 1983, 1990, and 1997, it is clear that the conduct of monetary policy must be consistent with the choice of exchange rate regime.

In 1973 the central bank of the Philippines announced that it would implement a flexible exchange rate system while reserving the right to intervene in the foreign exchange market to avoid unwanted volatility in the value of the peso. The system was essentially a managed float, with the degree of activism of the central bank in the foreign exchange market depending largely on the preferences of the incumbent governor, who concurrently chaired the monetary board, the policy-making body of the central bank.

Over the period 1980–90, the managed float of the peso remained in place. The central bank allowed the nominal exchange rate to vary, but only within a narrow band. Excessive money creation was spurred in no small way by a large public sector deficit; the consolidated public sector deficit as a proportion of GDP amounted to 5.3% in 1982 and 4.8% in 1990. The monetization of such deficits provides an adequate explanation of the peso collapses in 1983 and 1990.

In 1992 the central bank decided to liberalize nearly all capital flows and foreign exchange transactions. An independent central bank was established in 1993, with the maintenance of price stability as its main goal. In 1995, the central bank modified its so-called monetary aggregate targeting framework, apparently to complement this with some form of inflation targeting.

The openness of the economy to internationally mobile capital has given rise to difficulties in the usual conduct of monetary policy. This is because, when capital is mobile, it is difficult (if not entirely impossible) for the authorities to target both the money supply and the exchange rate simultaneously. In attempting to fix the level of the exchange rate against the dollar, for example, the monetary authorities must buy dollars, and hence increase the supply of pesos, at times when there is excess demand for pesos. However, this means that the domestic money supply will increase, *ceteris paribus*. The only way to undo the automatic effect on the money supply of the foreign exchange market intervention is to reduce domestic credit or sterilize the effects of the intervention on the domestic money supply. For various reasons cited by many economists, the effects of sterilization are limited and this technique cannot be used indefinitely.

The collapse of the peso in 1997 when the Asian financial crisis hit highlighted the constraints on monetary policy imposed by international capital mobility and by more integrated goods and financial asset markets. One of the lessons to be learned from the crisis was the importance, under a flexible exchange rate system, of appreciating the theoretical consistency of targeting the growth of monetary aggregates in order to control inflation. Certainly, after the crisis, many policy-makers, including the monetary authorities, stated that they would now allow a greater degree of flexibility in the exchange rate. The search for a post-crisis monetary and financial framework has been launched in earnest. The central bank recently announced that it would adopt inflation targeting starting in 2001.

This chapter is organized as follows. Section 2 discusses the early monetary framework and examines the performance of the economy under exchange rate targeting before the liberalization of the capital account. Section 3 looks at the liberalization of financial and capital markets and discusses the Philippine experience with capital inflows. Section 4 examines the performance of the economy after the Asian crisis. Section 5 raises some important institutional issues and reviews the conduct of monetary policy in the more recent post-crisis period.

3.2 THE MONETARY FRAMEWORK IN THE 1980s AND EARLY 1990s

Under the monetarist framework that forms the basis of the IMF's financial programming approach, including its program with the Philippine government, controlling the growth of the money supply is the key to controlling inflation. This is the basic approach that has been in use in the Philippines since the mid-1980s.[1]

From an operational perspective, a stable and predictable relationship between monetary growth and inflation is assumed to exist. Consider the quantity theory of money (QTM) equation of exchange, $MV = PY$, where M is the stock of money, V is the income velocity of money, P the price level, and Y the level of real income or output. Given target values for the rate of inflation, real GNP growth, and estimates of the income velocity of money, the rate of growth of the money supply can be derived (residually) to ensure equilibrium in the money market.

The choice of the particular monetary aggregate to use is an empirical issue. In theory, a narrower monetary aggregate would be assumed to have a closer link to inflation, as narrow money (M1) is held primarily for transaction purposes whereas broader money measures partly reflect the holding of money as a store of wealth. Some empirical studies have validated the usefulness of targeting a relatively narrow monetary aggregate. Gochoco (1993) found that only M1 was cointegrated with interest rates, output, and the exchange rate. A study by Guinigundo (2000: 11) likewise implied that narrower monetary aggregates were to be preferred as targets, since broader aggregates tended to adjust more slowly toward equilibrium after a shock.

Despite such evidence, Bangko Sentral ng Pilipinas (BSP, the central bank) has used and continues to use total liquidity (M3) as its intermediate target—intermediate because its ultimate target is the rate of inflation. In order to have control over its intermediate target, the central bank must have an operating target with which to affect M3. The BSP's operating target is base money (BM), defined as reserve money (RM) plus reserve-eligible government securities, liquidity reserves, and reserve deficiency.[2] RM represents liabilities of the central bank and consists of currency in circulation and the reserve deposits of banks and other deposit-taking non-bank financial intermediaries. BM is related to M3 via the money multiplier, that is,

$$M3 = \text{money multiplier} \times BM.$$

Once M3 is known, BM can be obtained using the simple QTM equation of exchange. Hence there are two key relationships in attaining the goal of controlling inflation, namely the relationship between the intermediate target (M3) and inflation; and the relationship between the operating target (BM) and the intermediate target (M3).

Casual empiricism suggests that over the period 1980–91, the central bank was not engaged in monetary aggregate targeting; average annual growth in M1 during that period was about 16%, with a standard deviation of about 10.2%. Rather, exchange rate targeting dominated, in conjunction with an output-growth objective. The central bank used its foreign reserves to keep exchange rate movements within a narrow band, which it widened somewhat after 1986.

A formal empirical test showing that the central bank targeted the exchange rate rather than a monetary aggregate in the 1980s is presented in Gochoco (1991b). Generalized autoregressive conditional heteroskedasticity (GARCH) models of the log of the exchange rate, monetary growth, and interest rates are estimated to obtain the conditional variance of each of these variables. If the monetary authorities had attempted to fix the exchange rate, to the degree that they were successful, the conditional variance of the exchange rate would be very low while that of monetary growth and/or interest rates would be quite high. This is because, under exchange rate targeting, the authorities would have to offset shocks to the exchange rate by varying money and/or interest rates. Gochoco finds that—except in 1983 and 1984, when there were large and discrete devaluations of the peso—the exchange rate remained very stable while monetary growth and interest rates exhibited large variability.

Table 3.1 shows time-series, end-of-year data for 1980–2000 on the peso/dollar exchange rate, the central bank's gross foreign reserve assets (consisting largely of gold and foreign exchange holdings, as well as foreign treasury bills and bonds), and the reserve money of the central bank. Under exchange rate targeting, a sharp nominal peso depreciation exceeding 40% occurred in 1983–84, and a depreciation exceeding 20% in 1990. These are to be regarded as episodes of peso collapse. During both episodes, the level of reserve money greatly exceeded the gross foreign reserve assets of the central bank at least a year before the collapse took place, as can be seen from the ratios shown in the last column of Table 3.1.

In 1982, gross foreign reserves exceeded reserve money. The situation reversed in 1983, when reserve money was four times the amount of gross foreign reserves.[3] In that year the peso lost 52.7% of its nominal value against the dollar. Apparently the depreciation was not enough, and in 1984 the peso again shed 41.1% of its value. An appreciation took place in 1985 in spite of the continued high ratio of reserve money to gross foreign reserves, followed by a correction in 1986 as the ratio improved to 1.81. The peso depreciated by 7.9% in 1986, falling back to 1.3% in 1987.

Table 3.1 Foreign Reserve Assets, Reserve Money, and the Exchange Rate, 1980–2000

Year	Exchange Rate (end of period, peso/$)	Nominal Depreciation (end of period, %)	Foreign Reserve Assets (billion pesos)	Reserve Money[a] (billion pesos)	Reserve Money/Foreign Reserve Assets (ratio)
1980	7.6	–	24.7	17.0	0.69
1981	8.2	7.9	22.4	18.6	0.83
1982	9.2	11.8	24.5	19.7	0.80
1983	14.0	52.7	12.1	48.7	4.02
1984	19.8	41.1	17.6	77.2	4.38
1985	19.0	−3.7	20.7	88.9	4.30
1986	20.5	7.9	51.4	93.2	1.81
1987	20.8	1.3	41.9	84.6	2.02
1988	21.3	2.6	45.0	95.0	2.11
1989	22.4	5.2	53.2	119.8	2.25
1990	28.0	24.8	57.6	143.1	2.48
1991	26.7	−4.8	122.4	171.4	1.40
1992	25.1	−5.8	133.5	178.2	1.33
1993	27.7	10.4	164.0	210.3	1.28
1994	24.4	−11.9	173.8	226.9	1.31
1995	26.2	7.4	203.6	255.2	1.25
1996	26.3	0.3	308.8	338.2	1.10
1997	40.0	52.1	349.3	317.6	0.91
1998	39.1	−2.3	422.1	323.8	0.77
1999	40.3	3.2	605.2	442.7	0.73
2000	50.0	24.0	751.3	395.9	0.53

a   Beginning in 1983, the data are based on an improved sectorization of the accounts. From 1993, the data reflect the financial restructuring of the BSP.

Source: IMF, *International Financial Statistics*.

The peso collapsed again in 1990, losing 24.8% of its value against the dollar. High domestic credit creation by the central bank in the preceding years appears to have been responsible. The ratio of reserve money to gross foreign reserves exceeded 2 in 1987 and had climbed to 2.48 by 1990.

The question is why money creation was excessive. It has been said that central bankers do not deliberately create inflation, and that excessive money creation is largely rooted in the need to accommodate government budget deficits. Sooner or later, large and persistent national government deficits will be accommodated by the central bank if the latter is not independent.

This appears to have been the case here. Following the oil price shock of 1979–80, the national government engaged in deficit spending and instituted an expansionary monetary policy in an attempt to counter the expected slowdown in growth. The consolidated public sector deficit amounted to 4.8%, 5.3%, and 3.3% of GDP respectively in 1981, 1982, and 1983, as shown in Table 3.2. These budget deficits resulted in large current account deficits, of 6.0%, 9.3%, and 10.4% of GDP respectively, financed largely by foreign borrowings that were not completely sterilized by the central bank. This led to unwarranted increases in the money supply.

Performance of the Economy under Exchange Rate Targeting

The output and price performance of the economy during the period 1980–91 left much to be desired. Erratic monetary policy produced wild swings in the inflation rate marked by episodes of double-digit inflation lasting two to three years, as shown in Table 3.3. From 1984 to 1985, for instance, inflation was exceedingly high, reaching a peak of about 47% in 1984. Growth in real GDP was also uneven throughout the decade. The recession of 1984–85 was the most serious in the postwar economic history of the Philippines. Double-digit inflation occurred in 1988–89 and again in 1990–91. In 1991 there was another recession, albeit milder than that experienced in the mid 1980s. It seems obvious that erratic monetary policy can be counted on to produce inferior macroeconomic outcomes such as the boom and bust cycles witnessed during this period.

The 1983–84 and 1990 peso collapses were largely the offshoot of erratic and excessive money creation. Under exchange rate targeting, such a monetary policy stance could be expected to bring about a balance of payments crisis sooner or later. Despite the fact that the foreign exchange market remained highly regulated throughout the 1970s and 1980s, the central bank relaxed some foreign capital controls in 1979, in particular to give domestic residents access to dollar loans from the foreign currency deposit units of banks. Coupled with negative real interest rates on domestic lending in 1979 and 1980, and negative real foreign interest rates in the late 1970s, the result was overborrowing from abroad (Intal and Llanto 1998a: 9). This led to mounting short-term external debt.

When world interest rates increased in 1983, and the official reserve assets of the central bank to defend the peso and service the external debt ran out, the government was forced to declare a moratorium on foreign debt servicing. It reached a standby credit arrangement with the IMF for the special drawing rights it needed. In line with the conditional lending policy of the IMF, the peso was devalued.

The collapse of the central bank's defense of the curency, particularly during 1983, was extremely costly to the economy, and the central bank incurred large losses (Gochoco-Bautista 2002: 15). The bank argued that this was inevitable because of the quasi-fiscal functions it was forced to perform, such as providing forward cover on the foreign exchange requirements of oil importers. Between 1983 and 1986, the central bank's losses hampered its ability to conduct monetary policy. The losses were hidden in so-called "suspense accounts" in the books of the central

Table 3.2 Current Account, Consolidated Public Sector Account, and Savings–Investment Gap, 1980–2000 (% of GDP)

Year	Current Account	Consolidated Public Sector Account	Savings– Investment Gap[a]
1980	−5.9	0.5	−6.4
1981	−6.0	−4.8	−1.2
1982	−9.3	−5.3	−4.0
1983	−10.4	−3.3	−7.1
1984	−4.2	−2.5	−1.7
1985	−0.3	−5.9	5.6
1986	3.2	−6.6	9.8
1987	−1.4	−1.8	0.4
1988	−1.0	−3.1	2.1
1989	−3.5	−3.8	0.3
1990	−6.7	−4.8	−1.9
1991	−1.9	−2.1	0.2
1992	−1.6	−1.9	0.3
1993	−5.7	−1.7	−4.0
1994	−4.3	−0.5	−3.8
1995	−4.5	−0.2	−4.3
1996	−4.8	0.3	−5.1
1997	−7.2	−1.0	−6.2
1998	1.9	−3.1	5.0
1999	9.7	−3.4	13.1
2000	13.6	−4.6	18.2

a   The savings–investment gap is taken as a residual.

Source: Bangko Sentral ng Pilipinas, *Selected Philippine Economic Indicators*.

bank. By the end of 1986, the balance on these suspense accounts had reached nearly 170 billion pesos, with counterpart liabilities of a corresponding amount (Paderanga 1996: 2). The servicing of these liabilities implied a continual injection of money into the economy. To meet the monetary targets agreed with the IMF, the injections then had to be mopped up through the flotation of treasury bills, whose proceeds were immediately deposited with the central bank to prevent inflationary effects.

Both the financing of the public sector deficit and the collapse of the peso led to excessive money creation and very high rates of inflation. The inflationary pressures did not come from the demand side alone; given the highly import-dependent nature

Table 3.3 Real GDP Growth, Inflation, and Money Growth, 1980–2000 (%)

Year	Real GDP Growth	Inflation Rate (CPI)	M1 Growth
1980	5.8	18.2	19.6
1981	3.7	13.1	4.4
1982	3.6	9.0	–0.1
1983	1.9	5.3	38.6
1984	–7.3	46.7	3.6
1985	–7.3	23.2	6.4
1986	3.4	–0.3	19.0
1987	4.8	3.0	22.8
1988	6.3	12.2	13.9
1989	6.1	11.4	31.5
1990	2.4	13.2	13.4
1991	–0.2	18.5	13.9
1992	0.3	8.6	10.6
1993	2.1	6.9	19.4
1994	4.4	8.4	13.5
1995	4.8	8.0	21.7
1996	5.8	9.0	20.0
1997	5.2	5.9	16.4
1998	–0.8	9.7	9.0
1999	3.2	6.7	40.0
2000	3.9	4.3	–1.8

Sources: GDP and consumer price index (CPI): National Statistical Coordination Board, *Yearbook of Statistics*; M1: Bangko Sentral ng Pilipinas.

of Philippine industry, there were inflationary pressures from the supply side as well. In addition to currency devaluation, in accordance with the IMF program both fiscal and monetary policy were tightened. The monetary authorities responded by driving domestic interest rates to historically high levels, which led to the recession of 1984–85 (Table 3.3).

The recovery that emerged in 1986 continued until 1990. Output growth peaked in 1988, but in view of the persistent deficits in the budget of the national government, money growth rates tended to be erratic and excessive.

In the early 1990s, the weak macroeconomic fundamentals of the economy were further undermined by more political and economic disasters. The economy went into recession in 1991, but a balance of payments crisis was averted through another standby credit arrangement with the IMF.

3.3 LIBERALIZING ACCESS TO INTERNATIONAL CAPITAL MARKETS

The peso collapsed once again in 1997. However, this episode was different from those that had taken place in 1983–84 and 1990. Whereas observed money growth not commensurate with growth in foreign reserve assets under a fixed or managed exchange rate regime had played a profound role in the earlier collapses, the later collapse occurred even though money growth was not obviously excessive. In contrast to the earlier periods, the ratio of reserve money to gross foreign reserves was approximately unity in 1996, and slightly below that in 1997 (Table 3.1). One important factor in the 1997 collapse may have been the liberalization of the capital account in 1992. Therefore, it is advisable to look at the role played by international financial factors.

The Philippines made a modest re-entry into international capital markets in the mid-1980s after reaching agreement with the Paris Club of official creditors on a series of debt reschedulings to begin in 1985, and the implementation of a debt-to-equity program in the following year.[4] The country also agreed to a further two-year IMF program, to start in 1986. However, only in the early 1990s was the Philippines able to float bonds and some international equity issues, and it has yet to have international credit-rating agencies award it another investment-grade credit rating.

In 1992 the foreign exchange market was liberalized. This entailed the elimination of restrictions on the current account, and greatly diminished restrictions on the inward and outward movement of capital flows. The capital account virtually became open. Foreign exchange earners were now allowed to retain 100% of their earnings. Exporters were given 90 rather than 60 days to remit their foreign exchange receipts to authorized banks, and could avail themselves of loans from the banks' foreign currency deposit units. Limits on the purchase of foreign exchange were removed. Full and immediate repatriation was allowed, without central bank approval, of foreign investments duly registered with the central bank or a custodian bank. In addition, the Foreign Investments Act of 1991 simplified procedures for registration of such investments. The prohibition on on-floor foreign exchange trading was also lifted (Intal and Llanto 1998a: 13).

Unfortunately this liberalization of the foreign exchange market, and the virtual opening of the capital account, was not preceded by adequate strengthening of bank supervision and regulation. For example, the central bank was largely ignorant as to the nature of financial derivatives and how to regulate their trading—regulations on such derivatives were issued only *after* their introduction into the market. Coupled with a domestic currency maintained at what many regarded as an overvalued level, the result was overborrowing from abroad.

Capital Inflows

Whereas the 1970s were characterized by large borrowings from abroad by public enterprises, the capital flows in the 1990s were primarily private. Despite the confidence of policy-makers that the private nature of the flows meant that they would not pose a problem for the country as a whole, in the run-up to the Asian crisis there was a tremendous increase in foreign borrowing that ultimately increased the vulnerability of the financial system when the exchange rate collapsed.[5] The total foreign exchange liabilities of private domestic banks, for example, increased from $715 million in 1990 to $1.7 billion in 1995, then jumped almost five-fold to $5.0 billion in 1996 (BSP, various issues). Those of private non-bank institutions (mainly large private corporations that can issue bonds in international capital markets) rose from $3.2 billion in 1990 to $9.1 billion in 1996, bringing the total foreign exchange liabilities of the private sector, both bank and non-bank, in that year to about $14.1 billion.

There were several reasons for the tremendous increase in foreign borrowing. A major one was that the exchange rate was fixed within a relatively narrow band until the peso collapsed on 11 July 1997, masking the possibility of exchange rate risk. In 1994, for example, the average exchange rate was 26.41 pesos to the dollar, very close to the 1996 rate of 26.34 pesos to the dollar. As interest rates in the domestic market were high relative to those in both developed countries and other ASEAN countries (with the exception of Indonesia), there was a strong incentive to take advantage of interest arbitrage opportunities. In 1996, for instance, the average Philippine treasury bill rate was 12.4%, compared with about 6.4% in Malaysia and 0.9% in Singapore for securities with comparable maturities. The yield on the 31-day bill—the most actively traded type in the Philippines—was much higher than that on long-term U.S. bonds.

Net foreign loans and discounts, an asset item of the banking system, increased from 53% in 1995 to 103.1% in 1996. In other words, a high proportion of the funds sourced abroad was being re-lent locally. Prudential borrowing and lending behavior seems to have all but disappeared with the easy availability of funds from abroad. It is not difficult to see why the stability of the banking system would be imperiled if the peso were to weaken against the dollar, especially as many of the loans appear to have been unhedged against exchange rate risk. In a study of Philippine banks, Deutsche Morgan Grenfell (1998) found that dollar loans constituted an average of 30% ($3.6 billion) of a total loan portfolio of $12 billion. Evidently these were practically all unhedged, as the central bank estimated that unhedged loans as of June 1997 also amounted to $3.6 billion.

Since the peso was apparently overvalued, most of the money sourced abroad was lent to the non-tradable sector, particularly the real estate sector. The central bank has stated that the average share of loans to the real estate sector by the entire commercial banking system was not over 10%. However, it is also true that the ratio was significantly higher for some banks, including some large ones. Many banks or their subsidiaries suffered huge losses because of the collapse of the real estate sector. At least two major commercial banks failed because of overlending to property developers.

The corporate sector also showed signs of overborrowing and declining productivity of investments beginning in 1993, albeit to a lesser extent than in other crisis-hit Asian countries (Saldana 1999: 1). Corporations suffered from weak internal generation of funds and reduced liquidity, which led to the financing of asset growth through incremental borrowing.

Capital flows showed particularly large increases in 1993 and 1994 relative to levels before the capital account liberalization, and rose steeply in 1996, just before the Asian crisis. From 1.2% of GDP in 1988, capital inflows increased to 3.4% in 1989 then to 6.9% in 1991. Inflows surged further to 7.4% of GDP in 1994, and reached 10% of GDP in 1996 before the massive retreat of capital in 1997.[6] In general the capital account was larger and more volatile in the 1990s than in the previous decade. Portfolio inflows in particular increased in the more recent period, after exceeding direct investment flows in the third quarter of 1989 for the first time. It bears emphasizing, however, that the size of capital inflows to the Philippines was smaller than those to countries like Malaysia and Thailand, and also came later.

Both "push" factors, such as low interest rates in the United States, and "pull" factors, such as the economic reform measures undertaken in the Philippines, seem to have played a part in the resurgence of private capital inflows. The country had overcome its debt crisis and regained its financial credibility. Foreign debt service had fallen from almost 36% of total exports of goods and services in 1986 to 17% in 1993. In 1992, the year in which the liberalization of foreign exchange transactions began, net short-term portfolio inflows became almost as large as net foreign investment flows, as shown in Table 3.4.

The current account deficit as a proportion of GDP (Table 3.2) widened from 3.5% in 1989 to 6.7% in 1990, fell back slightly to 5.7% in 1993, and reached 7.2% in 1997, the year the Asian crisis struck. Domestic savings as a proportion of GDP declined in the 1990s and were similar to levels in Latin America. The difference between capital inflows and current account deficits implies an accumulation of official foreign reserve assets. The change in international reserves as a percentage of GDP increased during the periods of high capital inflows—from –0.8% in 1990 to 5.4% in 1991, and from 1.0% in 1993 to 1.9% in 1994.

Effects of Capital Inflows

Capital inflows can be a blessing for capital-scarce countries like the Philippines, helping to finance current account deficits and provide liquidity to the stock market as well as the treasury bill market.[7] However, large capital inflows can also complicate the conduct of monetary policy: the ability to conduct an independent monetary policy tends to be compromised, as the simultaneous targeting of the exchange rate and the money supply is not feasible when capital is mobile.

In such circumstances, central banks typically resort to sterilization in an attempt to regain some degree of control over monetary policy. This is a process that entails the purchase of the capital inflows, and a simultaneous reduction in domestic credit in order to prevent the expansion in the money supply that would occur if the capital inflows were not mopped up. Reductions in domestic credit raise domestic interest rates, acting to dampen aggregate demand. However, high domestic interest rates may also attract further capital inflows, setting up a vicious cycle in which attempts to neutralize the effects of the inflows actually attract more capital inflows. Sterilization also entails quasi-fiscal costs and imperils the central bank's institutional viability, since, in effect, it involves the exchange of high-yielding domestic assets for

Table 3.4 Capital Flows, Net Direct Investment, and Portfolio Inflows, 1980–2000 ($ million)

Year	Net Capital and Financial Flows	Net Direct Investment Inflows	Net Short-term Capital Inflows
1980	1,235	−102	305
1981	1,494	151	11
1982	1,594	−99	145
1983	776	−5	−611
1984	917	−85	524
1985	1,032	−22	−1,733
1986	−3	89	−824
1987	504	265	80
1988	63	885	−303
1989	1,033	741	−89
1990	1,776	480	19
1991	1,878	654	349
1992	1,850	737	660
1993	2,820	812	−148
1994	4,547	1,558	1,002
1995	3,393	1,609	−56
1996	11,075	3,517	540
1997	6,593	762	495
1998	478	1,672	−1,521
1999	−1,816	1,427	−4,617
2000	− 6,469	1,348	-10,518

Source: Bangko Sentral ng Pilipinas.

lower-yielding foreign assets. For numerous reasons, then, sterilization cannot be undertaken indefinitely; and the currency itself may become prone to speculation as to when a policy of sterilization will be abandoned.

Capital inflows in the presence of domestic currency overvaluation tend to favor non-tradable sectors that are not subject to competition from abroad (such as real estate and construction) over tradable sectors that compete against imports in the domestic market or are exportable. Between 1989 and 1995, the composition of capital inflows in the Philippines—in contrast to its Asian neighbors—was biased in favor of consumption over investment. Total consumption as a proportion of GDP averaged 6.1%, whereas total investment averaged only 1.7% (World Bank 1997b). This increased the risk of asset bubbles developing in the non-traded goods sector. The viability and stability of the banking sector and of other sectors with exposure to non-traded goods sectors such as real estate (and/or whose assets, such as loans, are collateralized by real estate) are extremely vulnerable to asset price collapses, as became evident during the Asian financial crisis.

Gochoco-Bautista (1997/2000) examined the effects of capital flows on interest rates and money demand in the Philippines using counterfactual simulations as to what the time paths of these variables would have been in the absence of capital flows. The rationale for this approach was that greater financial integration should have allowed capital flows to have significant effects on important macroeconomic variables (see also Kamin and Wood 1996).

The simulation results showed, first, that domestic nominal interest rates would have been higher in the absence of capital inflows, and second, that real demand for broad money (M2) would have continued its rising trend even in the absence of capital inflows. This suggests that factors other than capital flows per se, such as successful domestic reform measures that lowered inflation, may have been responsible for increased money demand and the expansion of monetary aggregates. The results also suggest that changes in reserves have a structural relationship with interest rates.

Nevertheless, it appears that demand for money was influenced by the capital account, although not primarily by increasing reserves. This seems consistent with data showing that, in the face of large capital inflows, the central bank accumulated considerable reserves without causing any large increases in base money, indicating that these flows were sterilized. There may have been other channels of influence from the capital account to money demand, and the importance of these may have changed over time. They include the return to voluntary capital markets, reductions in the public sector deficit, financial liberalization, and changes in the money multiplier. Gochoco-Bautista (1997/2000) concludes that, while the influence of external factors on domestic macroeconomic performance in an integrated world is heightened by capital flows, the effects of these depend on the degree to which the monetary authorities are able to control the money supply or the availability of credit.

3.4 MACROECONOMIC PERFORMANCE SINCE THE ASIAN CRISIS

After experiencing trade deficits amounting to about 12% of GDP in the years before the Asian crisis, there was a reversal of this historical trend in 1998 owing to the sharp depreciation of the peso. The trade deficit narrowed as a result of the large decline in imports. Export growth remained strong at 17% despite the crisis, as 60% of Philippine exports were destined for countries outside Asia.[8]

As shown in Table 3.4, portfolio investments dropped sharply in 1998 and even more steeply in 1999, mirroring events in other emerging markets. The table also shows that net capital inflows have tended to decline since 1997, never quite matching the level of investments in 1996, before the crisis. Massive capital outflows were experienced in 1999 and 2000.

The peso collapse in 1990 gave rise to a very high total external debt ratio of 77.9%, as shown in Table 3.5. Shortly thereafter the ratio began to decline. With the

Table 3.5 Foreign Exchange Liabilities, 1990–2000 (% of GDP)

Year	Medium and Long-term	Short-term	Total
1990	66.5	11.4	77.9
1991	56.6	10.3	66.9
1992	49.8	9.8	59.6
1993	57.3	9.5	66.8
1994	48.3	7.5	55.8
1995	46.9	7.3	54.1
1996	42.0	8.7	50.7
1997	61.1	13.9	75.0
1998	59.6	10.5	70.2
1999	62.9	7.8	70.7
2000	69.8	9.0	78.8

Source: Bangko Sentral ng Pilipinas.

exception of 1993, when medium and long-term foreign exchange liabilities as a percentage of GDP increased over the previous year's level, short, medium, and long-term foreign exchange liabilities all fell continuously through to 1997. This situation changed with the onset of the Asian crisis. The collapse of the peso in 1997 once again raised the ratio of total foreign exchange liabilities to GDP to over 70%, a worryingly high proportion given the present sluggish world economy. One consolation is that the ratio of short-term debt to GDP is less than 10%.

The large depreciation of the peso in 1997 and the subsequent tightening of liquidity adversely affected the financial sector, the corporate sector, and the rate of economic growth. Bank profitability plunged in 1998 relative to the two previous years. Bank return on equity declined from 16.3% in 1996 to 12.4% in 1997, and to a low but still positive 6.6% at the end of 1998 (Guinigundo 1999: 4). In the corporate sector, large enterprises were the most severely affected. The return on equity of this subsector declined to 3.8% in 1997, compared with a previous low of 12.5% experienced in 1995 (Saldana 1999: 12).

Despite the crisis, most observers assert that the Philippine financial system managed to survive the Asian financial crisis relatively unscathed, noting that the country did not experience a banking crisis.[9] This resilience was due to several factors.

First, beginning in 1996, the central bank had implemented some measures to strengthen the prudential framework for banks, in order to reduce systemic risks, strengthen regulatory oversight, and align domestic banking standards with international "best practice." The banking system was able to weather the Asian crisis relatively well in particular because of its strong capitalization. In March 1998, for example, the capitalization of the commercial banking sector stood at 17.3% of assets (Saldana 1999: 96). Second, the low level of financial intermediation in the Philippines, with a loan to GDP ratio of less than 65%, and the fact that capital inflow surges arrived later and in smaller amounts than in other Asian countries, also insulated the financial system somewhat from greater damage (Goldman Sachs 1999: 17). The financial system was not dependent on external investment and financing flows. In large part this was because the external debt moratorium imposed in 1984 had been lifted only in 1991, delaying the access of the public and private sectors to foreign debt markets. Historically, because of its relatively poor economic performance, foreign investment flows to the country have been low.

3.5 THE CONDUCT OF MONETARY POLICY TODAY

Central Bank Independence

Recent theoretical developments in monetary theory have drawn attention to important institutional issues such as the necessity for the monetary authority to remain independent of the fiscal authority. Excessive growth in money supply and the corresponding emergence of inflation are often rooted in inappropriate fiscal policy.

The policy independence of the Philippine central bank was not instituted until 1993. Before that, the monetary board—the policy-making body of the old central bank—was dominated by cabinet secretaries sitting in an ex officio capacity. Under this arrangement there was an incentive for any budget deficit created by the fiscal authority to be readily accommodated. The arrangement also created an incentive for a strong peso, since government corporations such as electricity and water utilities were financing many of their import-dependent projects through foreign loans. The secretary of trade and industry on the monetary board was protective, too, of the interests of capital-intensive private industries receiving special fiscal incentives; these protected industries wanted a strong peso to help them pay for their imports. All these factors succeeded in producing large and chronic current account deficits in the balance of payments.

In an environment where the fiscal authority dominated the monetary board, policy was based mainly on exchange rate targeting. The targeted exchange rates could not be maintained, however, while there were large and chronic deficits in the budget and current account. The episodes of recurrent peso collapse set the stage for making the central bank independent, to remove the incentive for it to accommodate the deficits created by the fiscal authority, a situation that was compromising monetary growth targets and inflation control.

In 1993, Republic Act (RA) 7653 established a new, independent, central monetary authority, the BSP. The losses of the old central bank were transferred to a board of liquidators so as not to impair the functioning of the new bank. The law provided that the president of the Philippines would appoint a majority of the members of the monetary board from the private sector. Only one member was to be appointed from cabinet to sit in an ex officio capacity, the reason behind this provision being to try to achieve coordination between fiscal and monetary policy.

To reduce the inflationary bias of monetary policy and establish their credibility, central banks usually adopt a monetary policy rule. The key feature of any such rule is the use of a nominal anchor, which can be an effective constraint on the value of domestic money. Exchange rate targeting is one example of a monetary policy rule. However, the painful experience of many countries with exchange rate targeting has been balance of payments and financial crises, diminishing its appeal. Under monetary aggregate targeting to control inflation, the central bank may use the monetary base as an instrument to target a particular monetary aggregate, while relying on the foreign exchange and financial markets to determine exchange and interest rates.

Inflation targeting is another example of a monetary rule. It entails the announcement by the central bank of a numerical inflation target of, say, 2–3% per year. The bank attempts to keep inflation within this band through the use of some instrument, such as the central bank's fund rate, and of optimal control techniques to determine the value of the range of instruments available to it. The central bank is free to change its instruments or respond to what it perceives to be the factors affecting the value of the target variable. Hence, while the objective function of the monetary authorities would be announced to the public, the authorities' reaction function would not necessarily be. In the wake of the Asian financial crisis, the Philippine central bank recently announced that it would adopt inflation targeting starting in 2001.

The Monetary Framework since June 1995

Guinigundo (2000) states that large fluctuations in the velocity of money have weakened and in some cases broken down the relationship between monetary aggregates and the variables that are their ultimate goal.[10] He claims that Philippine financial liberalization has weakened the two key relationships (that between velocity and monetary aggregates, and that between monetary aggregates and variables of interest), citing in particular as a break from the past the deceleration in the rate of inflation from 9% in 1994 to 8.1% in 1995, despite the historically high rates of liquidity growth in 1994–95. He attributes the good inflation performance in part to supply-side factors such as a favorable agricultural harvest in 1994 and the easing of power shortages. Nevertheless, Guinigundo's study seems to belie his own argument.

The author tests the stability of the income velocity of money and finds that the first difference of income velocity is stationary. This means that its growth rate is predictable, even though its level is not, as it contains a unit root. Guinigundo incorrectly interprets the assumption in the QTM equation of exchange of a *stable* income velocity of money in terms of a *constant* income velocity of money (Guinigundo 2000: 8). The results imply that the growth rate of income velocity is stable, and therefore would not potentially pose a problem as far as the reliability of monetary targeting in achieving the goal of price stability is concerned.

Guinigundo finds that the money demand equation remained stable in the period 1986–99 despite financial liberalization and other shocks such as large capital inflows. In particular, all monetary aggregates, with the exception of reserve money, are cointegrated with output and the interest rate. Gochoco (1993) also finds that currency substitution does not make the money demand function unstable.

This means that there is a long-run relationship between money on the one hand and output and interest rates on the other, so that even if there are shocks to the economy, the variables will return to their trend equilibrium levels. Although financial liberalization and economic growth may have led to changes in the money multiplier, for example, this does not mean that the money demand relationship is no longer stable and predictable. The money multiplier began to increase in 1993 following financial liberalization, as the currency to deposit ratio declined in the face of economic growth and technological innovations such as electronic banking.

Under its charter, the mandated duty of the BSP is to maintain price stability. Despite evidence to the contrary, the bank does not claim to have abandoned monetary targeting. Nevertheless, the supposed weakening of the two key relationships underlying the monetary targeting framework led the BSP to adopt what it called a "modified framework" beginning in the second semester of 1995. This modified framework apparently attempts to enhance the effectiveness of monetary policy "by complementing monetary aggregate targeting with some form of inflation targeting, placing greater emphasis on price stability in lieu of rigidly maintaining the intermediate monetary targets" (Guinigundo 2000: 7). This approach evidently "reduces the risk of monetary policy being either too tight or too loose, as may happen with strict adherence to a traditional base money program."

Certain key modifications were introduced into the monetary targeting framework over the next four years, and included in so-called adjustment clauses under the agreement with the IMF. The main change appears to be that the modified framework allows base money levels to go beyond the target as long as the inflation targets are met. As Guinigundo (2000: 7) states:

> As long as inflation adheres to the program monthly path, the base money limits are automatically increased by the amount of the excess of net international reserves over the program targets. This provides an automatic mechanism for the BSP to respond to unexpected increases in the real demand for money coming from improvements in the external sector of the economy ... An excess of one or more percentage points of inflation over the program induces a mopping up operation by the BSP to bring down base money to the previous month's level. If actual inflation exceeds targets for three consecutive months, then the entire monetary program is reviewed.

The question that comes to mind is what the difference really is between this modified framework minus the adjustment clauses, and the original monetary targeting framework. The phrase "complementing monetary aggregate targeting with some form of inflation targeting" is technically incorrect as they are two distinct types of nominal anchors for monetary policy. Marrying these two procedures so that they "complement" each other is difficult to understand.

Under a monetary aggregate targeting framework, the monetary authority fixes money growth in order to reduce expected inflation in long-run equilibrium. In so doing, the authority gives up on affecting output. The optimal growth rate of money sets Ep, where p is the log of the price level, equal to the target value for p, which is zero. This means that the log of the money supply, m, is set at Ey, where y is the log of real output. This is equal to y^*, the log of the natural rate of output, since, in the long run, this is the only level of output consistent with non-accelerating inflation (Frankel 1993: 43).

The price level rule eliminates the effects of demand disturbances. It can be shown that it is likely to dominate the money supply rule if velocity shocks are large and any weight at all is placed on the inflation objective (Frankel 1993). This is precisely because the one-to-one correspondence between money and prices under the QTM equation of exchange formulation, for example, is not likely to hold when the income velocity of money is unpredictable. However, as pointed out earlier, income velocity growth *has* been predictable.

It is unclear what theoretical basis underlies this framework of "monetary aggregate targeting with some form of inflation targeting". Under a monetarist framework, the control of inflation relies on the control of monetary growth. The BSP's modified framework reverses this theory and states that *if* inflation is under control, then monetary growth can be allowed to increase. It is not a monetarist explanation of inflation at all. It seems to allow monetary authorities pleasantly surprised by good inflation figures to passively allow base money to increase. If this is so, it appears that the monetary authorities themselves have all but forgotten that monetary growth is related to the rate of inflation, since excessive monetary growth, whether due to the financing of deficits or to inflows of capital that are not completely sterilized, and with no corresponding increase in output, will produce inflation at some time in the future. When this future inflation will occur is not known with certainty, as money growth is assumed to work with long lags. Monetary policy here is endogenous, reacting passively to good developments on the inflation front. Furthermore, the authorities do not seem to have an alternative explanation as to what drives inflation.

Base money automatically increases when there are capital inflows that tend to raise net international reserves, with no sterilization measures undertaken to reduce the expansionary effect on the money supply. In other words, the authorities do not have to do anything to raise the level of base money when there are capital inflows, because the money supply will automatically increase if no sterilization measures are undertaken. This is what is implied by Guinigundo's statement about "an automatic mechanism for the BSP to respond to unexpected increases in the real demand for money coming from improvements in the external sector of the economy." However, it is not quite correct to say that the BSP "responds" by not countering the natural tendency of money demand to increase when there are capital inflows as long as inflation is below target, since it is the *money supply* that is affected.[11] In other words, the BSP passively adapts to what is happening to the money supply as a result of capital inflows. Perhaps the authorities do not believe this will lead to higher inflation, and that is why they are not countering the expansionary effects on money—a distinctly non-monetarist approach. It is difficult to believe that the authorities are serious about targeting money.

When inflation is higher than the target for three months, however, the authorities go into high gear. They undertake mopping up operations to bring base money down to the previous month's level if there is an excess of one or more percentage points of inflation over the program, and they even review the entire monetary program if actual inflation exceeds targets for three consecutive months (Guinigundo 2000: 7).

It appears that whereas inflation targets are "hard," base money targets are not. One piece of evidence in support of this hypothesis is that average annual M3 growth rates using year-on-year monthly data have consistently been much lower than the annual growth targets for base money. According to information obtained from the BSP website, for example, the base money targets for 1999 and 2000 were 17% and 15% respectively. Yet the actual growth rates for M3 in these two years were only 10.6% and 12.1% respectively, as shown in Table 3.6. This means that actual base money growth rates had to have been very much less than the latter two figures, unless the money multiplier declined by a substantial amount, which is unlikely for the period in question. Thus it appears that the base money growth rates have been set at very high (one could even say incredibly high) levels. They are certain to make the authorities look good, especially in the eyes of the IMF, since both base money and M3 will consistently overperform (be below target) when such ceiling rates are used.

Conversations with monetary officials seem to confirm that the base money targets are not really hard in the monetarist sense, and that the very high ceilings on base money have been set to give the authorities a great deal of leeway. If this is so, then it is difficult to say whether the basic monetary targeting model is used at all, since the actual monetary growth figures do not appear to be consistent with targets even as actual inflation targets are met or are close to being met. It appears either that other rules are governing the conduct of monetary policy and/or that the authorities use a great deal of discretion in their conduct of monetary policy.

The modified framework was revised further to place a limit on the degree of allowable adjustment in the base money ceilings if there was overperformance in the BSP holdings of net international reserves as these intensified beginning in 1994. In particular, the limit would be increased by the full amount of the first $500 million over the international reserves target, translated into pesos at the average exchange rate prevailing in the month concerned, and by one-half of any additional overperformance (Guinigundo 2000: 7). This meant that the authorities would not sterilize capital inflows, but simply raise their base money target and accept the increase in base money in the relevant period. Guinigundo (2000: 7) further states, "Limiting the allowable adjustment in base money ceilings on account of capital inflows was another step towards greater emphasis on reining inflation *through controlling money growth*" [emphasis added].

The peso depreciated continuously against the dollar in the latter half of 1997. Reverse repurchase (RRP) rates—the central bank's borrowing rates for securities— were about 2–3% higher in the last half of the year than they had been prior to July. The interest rate differential between the 91-day Philippine treasury bill rate and the 3-month U.S. treasury bill rate reached 10% in September 1997 and stayed in the double digits until April the following year, reflecting very high Philippine bill rates of 15.4%–17.7% between August and December 1997. In the face of high interest

Table 3.6 Inflation Rates, Peso Depreciation, Monetary Growth, and Interest Rates, 1997–2000 (%, monthly year-on-year)

Month	Actual Inflation	IMF Target Inflation	Rate of Peso Depreciation	Reserve Money Growth	M3 Growth	Term RRP Rate	Overnight RRP Rate	91-day T-Bill Rate	Interest Differential
1997									
January	5.0	6.4	0.6	16.9	14.3	10.8	10.5	10.8	5.8
February	4.4	5.5	0.6	18.8	17.2	10.6	10.5	10.7	5.7
March	4.9	5.8	0.7	8.6	17.3	10.2	10.2	10.1	5.0
April	4.6	5.9	0.8	8.5	17.6	10.1	10.1	10.0	4.8
May	4.2	6.3	0.6	12.3	19.3	11.6	15.8	10.9	5.7
June	4.8	6.4	0.7	5.2	18.9	10.5	14.4	10.5	5.6
July	4.8	6.6	10.5	4.5	24.2	14.6	25.7	12.2	7.1
August	4.4	6.8	15.1	8.4	23.6	12.8	15.6	14.2	9.1
September	5.2	7.3	29.0	11.3	23.5	13.9	12.0	15.3	10.3
October	5.6	7.5	32.9	13.1	23.8	12.7	12.1	16.5	11.6
November	6.4	7.5	31.8	12.3	23.9	12.8	12.0	15.9	10.8
December	6.0	7.1	52.1	9.5	21.0	12.0	11.5	17.7	12.5
Average	5.0	6.6	14.6	10.8	20.4	11.9	13.4	12.9	7.8
1998									
January	6.4	6.4	61.0	13.9	21.4	16.9	12.4	19.1	14.0
February	7.4	7.1	53.3	12.0	17.9	15.8	13.1	17.8	12.7
March	7.3	7.0	40.6	-0.3	17.2	16.1	13.0	16.6	11.6
April	7.8	7.5	51.6	4.7	17.0	14.4	13.0	15.2	10.2
May	9.2	8.4	47.5	-3.0	17.1	14.6	13.4	14.4	9.4
June	9.9	8.2	59.5	-3.0	17.3	14.5	13.1	14.0	9.0
July	10.1	8.6	45.0	0.8	10.2	14.5	13.1	14.7	9.7
August	9.6	9.0	45.5	-12.0	10.8	13.7	16.7	14.1	9.2
September	9.3	8.8	29.3	-14.3	7.8	13.9	16.0	13.8	9.1
October	9.6	11.7	16.9	-2.4	7.5	14.1	13.9	13.5	9.5
November	10.8	11.5	13.9	-4.8	7.2	13.9	13.7	13.5	9.0
December	10.5	11.7	-2.3	-10.0	7.4	13.5	13.4	13.4	9.0
Average	9.0	8.8	38.5	1.5	13.2	14.7	13.7	15.0	10.2

1999

January	11.6	10.1	-8.7	-6.1	6.7	13.1	13.1	13.2	8.9
February	10.0	9.4	-3.1	-8.0	7.7	12.6	12.5	12.7	8.3
March	9.0	9.1	4.5	4.5	7.1	12.2	12.1	12.1	7.7
April	8.3	8.7	-4.9	2.3	7.0	11.2	11.0	10.9	6.6
May	7.0	8.1	-2.1	9.4	8.2	10.1	10.3	10.0	5.5
June	5.9	7.5	-9.7	9.7	8.5	9.5	9.5	9.3	4.7
July	5.7	7.8	-9.0	11.1	10.3	9.0	9.0	8.4	3.8
August	5.8	8.2	-9.6	10.4	11.6	9.1	9.0	8.4	3.6
September	6.1	8.4	-6.2	19.5	13.2	9.1	9.0	8.6	3.9
October	5.7	8.3	-1.7	10.1	12.1	9.1	9.0	8.6	3.7
November	4.2	7.0	3.4	12.6	15.2	8.8	8.8	8.9	3.8
December	4.2	—	3.2	34.2	19.3	8.8	8.8	8.9	3.7
Average	7.0	8.4	3.6	9.1	10.6	10.2	10.2	10.0	5.3

2000

January	2.6	2.6	4.4	11.7	13.6	8.8	8.8	8.9	3.6
February	3.0	3.0	4.4	8.5	11.8	8.8	8.8	8.8	3.2
March	3.3	3.3	6.0	9.9	13.7	8.8	8.8	8.9	3.2
April	3.6	4.3	8.6	12.7	15.2	8.8	8.8	8.8	3.1
May	4.0	5.3	12.4	4.3	10.8	9.6	9.5	8.8	2.9
June	3.8	5.4	13.6	13.0	11.5	10.1	10.0	8.9	3.2
July	4.2	6.0	17.4	8.9	10.4	10.1	10.0	8.9	8.9
August	4.6	6.9	13.7	7.0	9.9	10.1	10.0	8.9	8.9
September	4.5	7.1	12.6	10.8	9.1	10.7	10.8	9.1	9.1
October	5.0	7.1	28.0	5.1	10.7	12.4	13.0	9.4	9.4
November	6.0	7.0	21.1	3.6	8.8	15.1	15.0	15.8	15.8
December	6.6	7.0	24.0	-4.2	4.6	14.0	13.8	13.6	13.6
Average	4.3	5.5	13.9	7.7	10.8	9.4	9.3	9.9	7.1

RRP = reverse repurchase rate; T-bill = treasury bill.

Sources: Bangko Sentral ng Pilipinas; Guinigundo (2000) for the IMF inflation targets.

rates, reserve money was allowed to expand between September and November 1997. M3 grew at higher rates during the last half of 1997 than before the crisis—by over 20% year-on-year on a monthly basis. This seems to have been the only time in the 1997–2000 period that the monetary authorities permitted large increases in the rates of M3 growth, despite the depreciation of the peso. They may have been attempting to cushion the impact of the Asian crisis on the economy while taking into account the overperformance on both the monetary and inflation targets for the year.

In December 1997 the peso depreciated by 52.1% year-on-year, up from 31.8% a month earlier. This was the highest figure ever recorded until that point. Growth in reserve money decelerated to single digits, growing by only 9.5% compared with 12.3% in the previous month. Again, this was despite an inflation rate of 6% in December 1997 and an average rate of inflation for the year of 5.0%, both below the targets set under the IMF program of 7.1% and 6.6% respectively.

In January 1998, the peso rate of depreciation increased to a historically high figure of almost 61%. The BSP responded by hiking the term RRP rate from 12.0% in December to 16.9% in January, with the overnight RRP rate rising slightly from 11.5% to 12.4%. Term RRP rates throughout 1998 were about 4–6% above the pre-crisis levels. The interest rate differential between Philippine and U.S. treasury bills increased further, reaching 14.0% in January 1998 as the Philippine rate touched 19.1%. With the exception of January, February, April, and July, growth in reserve money was negative throughout 1998 (and in the first two months of 1999); the average for the year was –1.54%. The sharply decelerating trend in reserve money growth rates suggests that whatever intention the authorities had to cushion the impact of the Asian crisis by trying to spur aggregate demand was put aside in light of the historically high rates of peso depreciation experienced between December 1997 and February 1998.

Meanwhile, the inflation rate stood at only 6.4% in January 1998, up from about 5% in the previous year, despite the hefty rates of growth in the money supply in the latter half of 1997 (Table 3.6). The low rate of inflation despite high rates of money growth was largely on account of the tremendous slack in the economy. In other words, although inflation had risen, it had not increased nearly enough to justify contracting reserve money growth and raising interest rates to the extent done. In fact, while inflation rates were above target from February to September 1998, only in June and July did they exceed by more than 1% the targets set under the IMF program—whereas interest rate hikes and monetary tightening had begun at the beginning of the year. In October and December 1998, actual inflation rates were below target by 2% and 1% respectively, yet the contraction in reserve money growth continued until the end of the year.

Hence, what appears to have precipitated monetary tightening were the historically high rates of peso depreciation that began in December 1997 and persisted almost until the end of the following year. In August and September 1998, for example, reserve money was not growing: the respective growth rates for these months were –11.99% and –14.31%. From 13.1% in July, overnight RRP rates jumped to 16.7% in August and 16.0% in September. These very large contractions in reserve money growth and steep hikes in BSP borrowing rates coincided with periods of high peso depreciation. They appear to have worked to slow the rate of depreciation, from 45.5% in August to 29.3% in September, and further to 16.9% in October and 13.9% in November. In October 1998, the statutory reserve requirement was raised. Curiously, between November and December, inflation rates, while high, were actually below target, yet reserve money growth continued to *decline* and the rate of depreciation of the peso slowed. In December 1998 the peso actually appreciated for the first time since the crisis, even though inflation stood at 10.5%.

The following year saw a strengthening of the peso. In January 1999 the currency appreciated by 8.7%, then continued on this trend until October. The 10.0% decline in reserve money in December 1998 may have led to the 6% appreciation of the peso in January 1999 over the previous month. It seems almost certain that the appreciation was due to the contraction in reserve money growth that characterized almost all of 1998, particularly the latter half, and that continued into early 1999. The peso appreciation observed from December 1998 through to February 1999 could not have been due to low inflation rates per se, since inflation, although below IMF targets, was above 10% throughout this period.

The monetary authorities increased the rate at which reserve money grew from March 1999, in which month it registered positive growth of 4.5%. This trend of monetary loosening continued for the rest of the year, with the rates hitting double digits from July. M3 also exceeded the 10% mark in July, curiously, following a 9.7% appreciation of the peso in June. RRP rates continued to decline. In June 1999, as the peso appreciation peaked at 9.7%, its highest rate for the year, both overnight and term RRP rates fell below 10% for the first time since 1996. From March, inflation rates were in the single digits and below target.

The peso again began to depreciate in November 1999, and by January 2000, the rate of reserve money growth had decelerated to 11.7% from 34.2% in December.[12] Growth in M3 also slowed in January, to 13.6% compared with 19.3% in the previous month. As the peso depreciated, these lower rates of growth in reserve money and M3 also continued, despite the fact that inflation was very low, in the 2–3% range.

In May 2000 the depreciation rate returned to double digits, and reserve money and M3 growth slowed further to 4.4% and 10.8% respectively (from 12.7% and 15.2% in April). This was despite a low inflation rate of 3.6% in April and 4.0% in May. According to the BSP, this tightening was in response to the U.S. Fed's decision to raise the federal funds rate by 50 basis points.[13] In July, reserve money growth decelerated to 8.9% from 13.0% in the previous month as the rate of peso depreciation increased to 17.4% from 13.6% in June. Overnight and term RRP rates rose to 10% in June 2000 even though inflation remained at 4–5%. In October, reserve money growth again decelerated to 5.1% from 10.8% in the previous month, while the rate of peso depreciation rose from 12.6% in September to 28.0% in October. The inflation rate barely moved.

It is apparent from these figures that, in general, inflation rates were very low—similar to levels prevailing before the Asian crisis—at times when the authorities were reducing reserve money growth and raising interest rates. The only apparent reason for their tightening stance and the timing of their interventions was the higher rates of peso depreciation during these periods.

Some Empirical Tests

Granger causality tests are used to determine the direction of causality between bivariate variables of interest. More precisely, they show the significance of the information contained in lagged values of the independent variable (the "causing" variable) in explaining variations in the dependent variable (the "caused" variable). The following sets of bivariate regressions were estimated based on monthly year-on-year data for the period January 1996 to December 2001:[14]

1. term reverse repurchase rates (TRRP) and the log of CPI/CPI(–12) to see whether TRRP causes inflation and vice versa (where CPI = consumer price index);
2. the log of E/E(–12) and TRRP to see whether policy interest rates cause the exchange rate and vice versa (where E = peso/$ exchange rate);
3. the log of RM/RM(–12) and TRRP to see whether RM causes policy interest rates and vice versa;
4. the log of CPI/CPI(–12) and the log of the peso/$ exchange rate to see whether the exchange rate causes inflation and vice versa;
5. the log of RM/RM(–12) and the log of CPI/CPI(–12) to see whether RM growth causes inflation as posited by the QTM and vice versa;
6. the log of E/E(–12) and the log of RM/RM(–12) to see whether the exchange rate causes RM and vice versa;
7. overnight reverse repurchase rates (ORRP) and the log of CPI/CPI(–12);
8. the log of E/E(–12) and ORRP; and
9. the log of RM/RM(–12) and ORRP.

The final three sets of regressions, (7), (8), and (9), are the same as the first three sets, except that overnight borrowing rates are used instead of term borrowing rates. Lag lengths used ranged between two and six. A summary of the results is given in Table 3.7.[15]

Certain results obtained seem to be robust regardless of the number of lags used. These include the following.

1. TRRP causes inflation. This means that TRRP can be used to influence inflation, presumably by contracting aggregate demand. The converse is not always the case. In only two cases, when the lag lengths used were five or six, could the result be found that inflation causes TRRP, meaning that the authorities react to inflation by changing TRRP.
2. The exchange rate causes inflation. This is statistically the strongest result obtained, as is to be expected in an open economy. When the peso depreciates, demand tends to switch in favor of Philippine goods, adding to demand for the economy's output. Nevertheless, the converse also applies: inflation causes the

Table 3.7 Summary of Granger Causality Tests[a]

	2 lags	3 lags	4 lags	5 lags	6 lags
TRRP → P	√	√	√	√	√
P → TRRP				√	√
E → TRRP	√	√	√	√	
TRRP → E					√
E → P	√	√	√	√	√
P → E	√	√	√	√	√
RM → P	√				
P → RM	√	√	√	√	√
RM → E			√		
E → RM	√	√	√	√	√

TRRP = reverse repurchase rates (term); E = depreciation rate; P = inflation rate; RM = reserve money growth rate; √ denotes significance at the 10% level or higher.
a   Causality test results of overnight RPP rates with other variables are not statistically significant.

exchange rate. As a country's inflation rate exceeds that in the rest of the world, the domestic currency will tend to depreciate. The levels of statistical significance are higher for the proposition that the exchange rate causes inflation than for the converse proposition, however.

3. Inflation causes RM growth. This means that the authorities react to inflation by changing RM, thus making monetary policy endogenous and passive. This is not the relationship posited by the QTM. However, the levels of statistical significance for this proposition are much lower than those for the proposition that the exchange rate causes inflation. The converse hypothesis that RM causes inflation—the monetarist proposition—is not upheld by the results except in the case with two lags.

4. The exchange rate causes RM growth. Again, this means that when the exchange rate is changing, the monetary authorities react by changing RM. This is a more statistically robust result than the proposition that inflation causes RM growth, suggesting that RM reacts more strongly to information contained in exchange rate changes than to information contained in changes in the rate of inflation. Presumably, as seen from the earlier discussion and from Table 3.6, when the peso is depreciating, RM growth decelerates or is reduced. Only when four lags are used is the converse true.

5. TRRP causes the exchange rate only when six lags are used. This implies that raising interest rates to defend the peso generally does not work.

6. ORRP does not exhibit any significant causal relationship either way with the inflation rate, RM growth, or the log of the exchange rate. The implication is the same as in (5) above.

Based on a cursory examination of the data and the results of the Granger tests, the framework currently being used by the monetary authorities cannot be described as monetarist in the tradition of the QTM. The results of the Granger tests, albeit a crude form of empirical testing, tend to support the hypothesis that the basic force driving monetary policy in the Philippines is concerns over the exchange rate. Changes in the exchange rate cause TRRP and RM growth—both under the control of the monetary authorities—to change. It appears that the authorities use monetary growth reactively to set a floor on the rate of peso depreciation, ultimately as a way to control the rate of inflation.

In contrast, using RM growth and policy interest rate changes to affect the depreciation rate of the peso is more the exception than the rule. Hence, it appears that, try as they may, the monetary authorities cannot effectively control the rate of peso depreciation, a result that is not surprising given the openness of the economy.

Even as the authorities are unable to control the rate of peso depreciation, peso depreciation causes the rate of inflation. This result is a very robust one, even though the converse is also true. That the exchange rate has a large role to play in controlling inflation is consistent with the open nature of the economy. Be that as it may, however, it is unclear whether the central bank attempts to prevent peso depreciation as a goal in and of itself, or whether it does so because it recognizes the effect of peso depreciation on inflation. In any case, the penalty that goes with a regime of stabilizing the exchange rate is to be saddled with a monetary policy that destabilizes the overall price level, as has been pointed out elsewhere (Frankel 1993: 32).

The central bank announced that it would resort to inflation targeting starting from 2001. A recent empirical study on the Philippines examines the feasibility of adopting modified instrument rules in an inflation targeting framework (Dakila 2001). In this study, the nominal feedback rules are modified so that the rule adjusts to the forecasted, rather than actual, rate of inflation. This is described as a forward-looking monetary policy, and is justified on the basis of earlier findings of a decreased likelihood of policy-generated instability in the economy when the policy instrument reacts to forecast variables rather than current or actual values. In this particular study, base money reacts to the deviation between the forecasted rate of inflation and the long-term inflation target. The simulation results show that it is feasible to target inflation through forward-looking policy and the use of either reserve money or the RRP rate as an instrument, as there is a reduction in the simulated rate of inflation following the use of such rules.

3.6 CONCLUSION

This chapter has examined the evolution of monetary policy rules and exchange rate regimes in the Philippines since the 1980s. Monetary policy has evolved from exchange rate targeting to a modified monetary aggregate targeting framework with less overt moves to fix the level of the exchange rate. Recently, in the aftermath of the Asian financial crisis, the central bank announced that it would pursue inflation targeting from 2001.

In the past, excessive money creation emanated largely from the need to accommodate the budget deficits of the government. Excessive money creation in a regime of essentially fixed exchange rates undermined the exchange rate target. One indicator of excessive money creation was that the level of reserve money, which represents the liabilities of the central bank, typically exceeded the level of the bank's gross foreign reserve assets for at least one year before an exchange rate collapse. The resulting pressure on the peso led to a series of depreciations exceeding 20% in 1983–1984 and 1990.

From 1991, the monetary authorities were able to maintain about a one-to-one ratio of reserve money to gross foreign assets, in contrast to the earlier period in which this ratio tended to exceed unity. At the same time, reforms were deepened on the financial and trade liberalization fronts. The country overcame its debt crisis, regained its financial credibility, and was able to float bonds and international equity issues in the early 1990s. In 1992, the foreign exchange market was liberalized. In 1993, an independent central bank was created. In 1994, 10 foreign banks were allowed entry into the local banking industry.

Capital inflows grew strongly in 1994–96 following the liberalization of the capital account in 1992. Relative to other Asian countries, capital inflows to the Philippines came later and in much smaller amounts as a ratio of GDP. Both external and domestic factors presumably played a part in the resurgence of private capital flows to the Philippines.

While capital inflows are usually regarded as a blessing for capital-scarce countries like the Philippines, several factors prevented this from being the case. As the exchange rate was still being targeted at the time, the mobility of capital made the conduct of an independent monetary policy extremely difficult; that is, it compromised the simultaneous targeting of the exchange rate and the money supply, thus undermining the attempt to control inflation. The authorities resorted to sterilization, but for several reasons this was only partially successful. There is empirical evidence to show that domestic interest rates would have been higher in the absence of capital inflows, but at the same time, real money demand itself would have been increasing even in the absence of such inflows.

The collapse of the peso in 1997 was not due to the same set of circumstances that had led to the earlier collapses in 1983–84 and 1990: the ratio of reserve money to gross foreign reserve assets of the central bank was about unity, indicating that monetary growth could not be seen as excessive. The later episode occurred in a period of heightened capital mobility that made the simultaneous targeting of the exchange rate and the money supply difficult, if not impossible. In such a setting, targets can be tested and the currency speculated against. People may act on their expectations about both external events, such as the effects of the baht collapse, and internal events, such as possible moves by the central bank to counter speculative pressure. The collapse of the peso in 1997 convinced everyone that it was futile to try to fix the exchange rate in a world where capital was mobile.

The central bank's new policy of inflation targeting requires that the monetary authority be independent from the fiscal authority in its policies and instruments. In his conclusion, Guinigundo (2000: 21) asserts that "adopting inflation targets at the practical level amounts to formalizing the present monetary targeting approach that after all, now places greater emphasis on the ultimate objective of price stability." What this seems to imply is that inflation targeting will not materially change the manner in which the BSP conducts monetary policy. In part this may be because of the absence of any episodes of high inflation over the past decade, in contrast to the experience in 1984–85. In this sense, one can regard the experience with inflation control in the recent period as being successful, although the reasons for this success are less clear.

The results of Granger tests show that peso depreciation causes inflation, and vice versa. It is unclear whether minimizing peso depreciation is a goal in and of itself as it was in the past, or whether there is an attempt to minimize depreciation because of its recognized inflationary effects. In any case, the Granger test results show that it is unlikely that the central bank is allowing the peso to float freely in the post-Asian crisis period or that it intervenes only occasionally as it has publicly stated.

If inflation control is the goal of the monetary authorities, perhaps we can learn much from the experience of New Zealand with respect to inflation targeting. The New Zealand approach to measuring the effect of the exchange rate on prices is encapsulated in a so-called monetary conditions index (Brash 1999: 18). In New Zealand, offsetting increases in interest rates are considered unnecessary when a sharp movement in the exchange rate is due to adverse developments in external markets, as these are assumed to have sufficient disinflationary impact on the economy to offset the inflationary impact of domestic currency depreciation. However, if the exchange rate change reflects some shift in investor preferences, without any underlying justification in the real economy, appropriate adjustments in monetary policy are made. Hence, further studies that enlighten us on why the exchange rate changes will be important.

NOTES

1. This section draws on Gochoco-Bautista (2001).

2. In the balance sheet of the BSP, BM is on the liabilities side. It is equivalent to net foreign assets (NFA) and net domestic assets (NDA) on the assets side of the balance sheet.

3. The figures for reserve money shown in Table 3.1 are taken from the 2000 International Financial Statistics (IFS) tables (IMF 2000), which use revised data from 1983 onward to reflect an "improved sectorization" of the accounts. If data from the 1999 IFS tables were used instead, the ratio of reserve money to foreign reserve assets in 1983 would be 2.4 rather than 4.0. Either way, the trend in the ratio remains the same.

4. This section draws on Gochoco-Bautista (2002).

5. This section draws on Gochoco-Bautista (1999b: 8–10).

6. This section draws on Gochoco-Bautista (1999b: 8–10).

7. This section draws on Gochoco-Bautista (1997/2000).

8. This section draws on Gochoco-Bautista (2002: 3–4).

9. This section draws on Gochoco-Bautista (1999a).

10. This section draws on Gochoco-Bautista (2001).

11. Net foreign assets (NFA) + net domestic assets (NDA) = base money (BM). When there are capital inflows, NFA increases and hence BM automatically increases (via the money multiplier, so does the money supply), unless the monetary authorities reduce NDA through sterilization measures. They can do this by reducing domestic credit through the usual mopping up techniques.

12. Apparently the large growth in reserve money in December 1999 was instigated in anticipation of Y2K-related problems.

13. This information was obtained from the BSP's website (www.bsp.gov.ph). However, we believe that it was not the federal funds rate that the Fed adjusted, since this interest rate is market-determined, being the rate at which banks borrow from each other.

14. Computing annual growth rates in monthly data is equivalent to seasonal differencing of the logarithm of the variables, that is, $\log(x) - \log(x(-12)) = \log(x/x(-12))$.

15. The results are available from the authors upon request.

4

Public Finance

Gerardo P. Sicat and Rahimaisa D. Abdula

4.1 INTRODUCTION

Episodes of macroeconomic turbulence have been part of the two decades of Philippine fiscal history analyzed in this chapter. This turbulence was induced in part by external shocks that took place in the 1970s—namely the oil shocks and the replacement of a fixed with a floating exchange rate regime—and by the rises in world interest rates that marked the early 1980s. But domestic adjustments to those shocks, including political upheavals, resulted in a unique trajectory of development experience.[1]

Political history provides the backdrop to fiscal episodes. Governments and their leaders make the policy decisions on the level and composition of expenditure and taxation. In the Philippines, the long presidency of Ferdinand Marcos began in 1966 and lasted 20 years. The early period of his presidency was marked by a major effort to raise the level of public investment. However, the external shocks of the 1970s—especially the oil shock of 1973—caused a serious external payments problem, ushering in a prolonged period of fiscal adjustment. Marcos's stewardship of "constitutional authoritarianism"—a dictatorship initiated under martial law in 1972—came to an abrupt end in 1986 following a failed presidential election (in which both candidates claimed to have won) and popular disaffection aggravated by serious political and economic turmoil. Corazón Aquino, the other presidential candidate, came to power on a platform of constitutional reform and economic stabilization. By the end of the decade, the major fiscal challenge of her administration was how to restore economic growth in the face of a high external debt service burden. Fidel Ramos, who succeeded Aquino in 1992, hastened the pace of economic liberalization and openness. His presidency ended in 1998, shortly after the onset of the Asian financial crisis in late 1997. The abbreviated presidency of less than three years of Joseph Estrada was characterized by economic mismanagement. Under Estrada, the country's fiscal framework deteriorated far beyond what would have been expected from adjustment to the Asian financial crisis. The legacy of the Estrada years is mentioned only briefly in the concluding section of this chapter. The presidency of Gloria Macapagal-Arroyo, who succeeded Estrada on 21 January 2001, has yet to be tested. The main focus in this chapter, therefore, is on the two decades from 1980 through to 2000.

4.2 THE NATIONAL BUDGET: OPERATIONAL DEFICITS AND FISCAL STABILIZATION

At the start of the 1980s, GDP was growing at 5.5% per year and the national government fiscal deficit stood at 1.4% of GDP. Following a minor financial crisis in 1981–82, an economic crisis of major proportions hit the country in 1983–85, causing a drastic fall in output, a reduction of external credit flows, and high inflation. Severe measures were adopted in an attempt to contain demand through fiscal compression. Figure 4.1 shows the magnitude of the national government's fiscal deficit in 1981–2000 as a proportion of GDP, along with the annual rate of inflation, the real GDP growth rate, and a fourth measure to be discussed later, the net fiscal impulse.

The mid-1960s and early 1970s had seen a consolidation of efforts to raise public investment in the country's poor and inadequate infrastructure. As a net energy importer, however, the Philippines was severely affected by the energy shocks of the 1970s. The government's fiscal response to these external shocks was characterized by volatile macroeconomic adjustments and rising fiscal deficits as it fought to maintain public investment in the face of a tumultuous external situation.

A fiscal deficit of 4.3% of GDP in 1981, accompanied by a growing gap in the balance of payments, the threat of high inflation, and market nervousness, was a sign of the impending problems. In 1983, domestic political events (in particular, the assassination of Benigno Aquino) precipitated an economic crisis already in the making. The serious external debt overhang led to an economic depression. Output fell by an average of 10% for two years in a row. The loss of credit lines, scarcity of imported raw materials, high interest rates, and rapid fall in government revenue all conspired to send the economy into a tailspin.

Aside from the international debt problems of developing countries, which were already creating nervousness in international capital markets, the Marcos government had lost market credibility. With the sudden choking off of international credit and the decline in domestic fiscal resources, public expenditure and domestic investment had to be slashed. With output also falling, the fiscal gap became unsustainable. The debt problem escalated, engendering the graver problem of high inflation. In 1984 the annual inflation rate reached 55%.

A contraction of aggregate demand was achieved through the tightening of monetary and fiscal policy. The introduction of central bank bills carrying high rates of

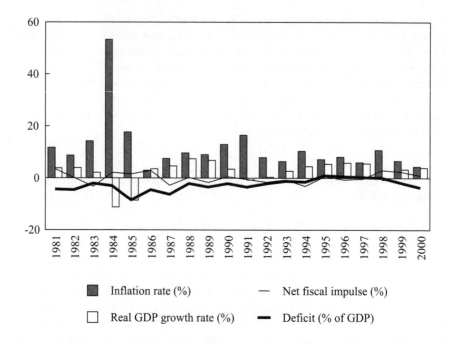

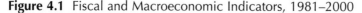

Figure 4.1 Fiscal and Macroeconomic Indicators, 1981–2000

Sources: Bangko Sentral ng Pilipinas; National Statistical Coordination Board; Bureau of the Treasury.

interest helped to mop up private savings at the same time that the government greatly reduced public expenditure. The resulting fiscal stabilization brought the annual rate of inflation down to 3% in 1986. It stayed under 10% for the rest of the 1980s and most of the 1990s.

From 1981 to 1984, the deficit on national government fiscal operations had been less than 5% of GDP. It then rose sharply to peak at 8.5% of GDP in 1985. Since 1988 the deficit has tended to hover at around the 2–3% mark, closing toward fiscal balance in the second half of the 1990s (Figure 4.1).

The fiscal and inflation record outlined above reflects an essentially restrained fiscal stance achieved with the help of strategies mapped out between the Philippine government and the IMF. While helpful in speedily restoring macroeconomic stability, these results were achieved through the sudden compression of aggregate demand, especially during the early stages of the corrective fiscal policies.

Fiscal Stabilization and Net Fiscal Impulse

The net fiscal impulse summarizes the overall influence of budgetary operations on output. Whereas the fiscal impact of public expenditure is to cause output to rise,

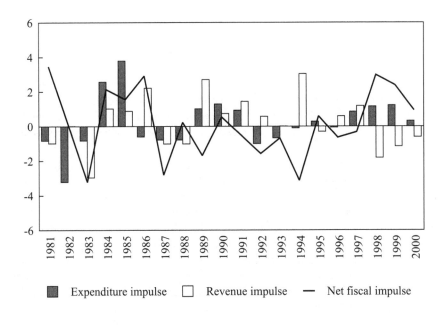

Figure 4.2 Decomposition of Net Fiscal Impulse, 1981–2000 (%)

Sources: Authors' estimates based on Bureau of Treasury data.

taxation restrains output from rising because purchasing power is taken away from the general public. An expansionary outcome with respect to output results when the expenditure effects exceed the taxation effects. This model is based on the premise that potential output is greater in magnitude than actual current output. The existence of unemployed resources opens the way for a further expansion of output, an assumption that is realistic as applied to the Philippines. To derive estimates of potential output, we fitted a trend model of the economy to national income data and calculated an annual series for potential output from the derived structural equation. The model is explained in Appendix 4.1.

The net fiscal impulse is the difference between the change in expenditure and the change in taxation set against, respectively, the expected average level of expenditure and of taxation evaluated at the level of potential output. Figure 4.2 shows the decomposition of the net fiscal impulse into its components. Intuitively, public expenditure would make output expand and taxation would make it contract. But the net fiscal impulse is essentially defined by year-to-year changes in the level of expenditure and taxation (that is, by the size of the fiscal deficit). If tax proceeds are falling, then the tax impulse is expansionary because output is being taxed less. An expanding expenditure program also has an expansionary public expenditure impact. The formula for net fiscal impulse compares the economic expansion caused by an increase in government spending with the contraction caused by the withdrawal of income from the public through higher taxes.

From 1986 the Philippines experienced a strong swing back to fiscal contraction as the new Aquino government sought to stabilize the economy. This proved effective in containing inflation, which fell by almost 15 percentage points between 1985 and 1986, from 18% to just 3%. Despite the improvement in expectations that was an immediate outcome of the euphoria accompanying the change in government, the cost of the contraction in terms of reduced resources for the public sector was significant.

The net fiscal impulse was contractionary for much of the 1990s, with the cost to the country being that fiscal tightening greatly curtailed demand. The most apparent new development was the return to a fiscal deficit in 1998 following the onset of the Asian economic crisis, deteriorating further since then. The resurgence of the deficit was partly due to the effort to counter the fall in aggregate demand expected as a result of the crisis, which thus provided the basis for an anti-cyclical fiscal posture. Under the Estrada administration there was a failure to realize expected revenue as targeted (after adjusting for diminished expectations). The government was slow to implement planned privatizations of government agencies, thereby depriving it of additional, temporary revenue that could have been used to scale back the fiscal deficit. The increased fiscal demand arising from military developments affecting peace and order in Mindanao compounded the fiscal problem. In 2000 the country faced the strong likelihood of a new wave of difficult fiscal adjustments, and a reversal of the gains made in previous years.

The Primary Fiscal Balance

Evidence for a narrowing of the real fiscal deficit comes from an assessment of the primary fiscal balance (Figure 4.3). The primary fiscal balance is equivalent to the normal fiscal balance minus expenditure on interest payments. It therefore indicates the relationship between government expenditure and revenue, after expenditure to service existing debt has been taken into account. If it is zero, it means that no new debt has been incurred. If it is in surplus, it means that tax revenue has exceeded public spending excluding interest payments on debt. And if it is in deficit, it implies that new debt is being incurred.

Starting from a large deficit of 3.5% of GDP in 1981, the primary fiscal balance began to narrow significantly until brought to a halt by the economic and political turmoil of 1986. The primary fiscal balance recorded a surplus of 3.5% of GDP in the following year and remained in positive territory until 1998. A change in the pattern can be observed from 1994, however, when the primary balance—while still positive—began to decline, indicating that new debt was being incurred and that debt service payments were again rising. Even more problematic was the response of the deficits to the Asian crisis: the normal fiscal deficit rose steeply in 1998 and 1999, and the primary balance turned negative for the first time in many years.

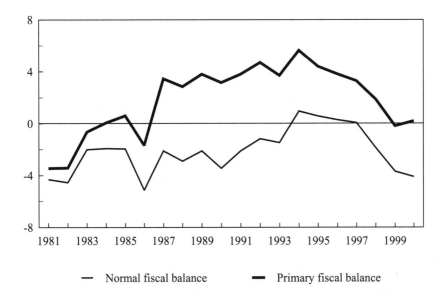

Figure 4.3 Normal Fiscal Balance versus Primary Fiscal Balance, 1981–2000 (% of GDP)

Source: Department of Budget and Management.

4.3 PUBLIC EXPENDITURE

Per Capita Real Public Expenditure

Real public expenditure per head in constant 1985 pesos was running at relatively high levels as the 1980s opened, then fell from 1982 through to 1985 (Figure 4.4). The impact of the crisis of 1983–85 sent real GDP down by more than 10% from its level in 1981, causing a particularly sharp drop in per capita spending in 1984–85. Real per capita expenditure then grew slowly and unevenly over time.[2]

Figure 4.4 shows real government expenditure per capita for the period 1981–2000 in terms of both total per capita spending and spending net of interest payments on debt. By presenting these numbers in the same chart, the per capita cost of servicing the debt becomes clear. The interest payment burden rose sharply in 1987, then was reduced between 1989 and 1995 with the help of the Brady bonds debt reduction scheme (see below).

Sectoral Allocation

The steep decline in GDP between 1984 and 1985 was accompanied by an even sharper drop in total expenditure as a percentage of GDP. Even with the recovery in

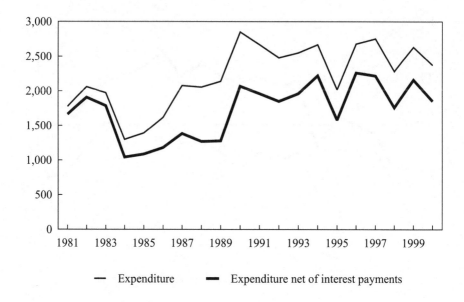

— Expenditure   ▬ Expenditure net of interest payments

Figure 4.4 Real Public Expenditure per Capita, 1981–2000 (constant 1985 pesos)

Sources: National Statistical Coordination Board; Bureau of the Treasury.

the level of expenditure from 1986 onward, the inclusion of a large expense in the form of interest payments took a huge slice of public resources away from government programs.

Public expenditure underwent structural changes in composition between 1981 and 2000, as shown in Figure 4.5. The figure shows the components of total expenditure as a proportion of GDP in the years under review, whereas the following discussion focuses more on the percentage share of each in total expenditure. In 1981, the share of economic services in total expenditure was 45%, with the infrastructure agencies that deliver most economic services (power and energy, water resources and flood control, and public works and communications agencies) accounting for 28.4% of total expenditure in that year. The share of economic services then fell consistently over the next few years as a result of budgetary constraints and reallocations, to average 34.4% in 1981–85. Economic services comprised an average of only 22.5% of total government expenditure in 1992–97, with infrastructure agencies accounting for 10.8% of the total. These reduced shares represented a severe real cut in development expenditure.

The share of expenditure on social services (such as education and health) remained relatively steady from 1981 through to 1997, then began to rise. From an average of 20.7% in 1981–85, the share of social services in total expenditure had risen to 23.6% by 1997.

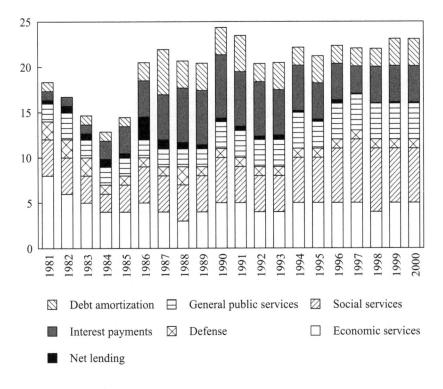

Figure 4.5 Expenditure by Sector, 1981–2000 (% of GDP)

Source: Department of Budget and Management.

Interest payments and debt amortization were a major component of spending, as the mandatory obligation to service the public debt took precedence over discretionary claims. Interest payments as a proportion of total expenditure rose from below 5% in 1981 to account for 15% of the total budget in 1984. The share of interest payment allotments to service debt more than doubled between 1981 and 1985, from 10.9% to 24.8% of total expenditure. In 1988, interest payments reached 27.3% of total expenditure, a peak they would nearly reach again in 1992. Eventually, a decrease in the level of interest payments would benefit social services and make possible other development expenditure.

The interest burden of the debt was particularly heavy immediately following the economic crisis of 1983–85. As well as crowding out allocations for other types of public expenditure, the high external debt made the budget vulnerable to exchange rate fluctuations because a major part of it was denominated in foreign currency. The debt-servicing requirements squeezed out peso resources that could have been used to provide matching funds for foreign-assisted projects. As a result, some projects backed by international and bilateral donor institutions had to be canceled, to clear the way for a rationalization of the use of the remaining peso funds. By the end of the decade it was apparent that some kind of relief was necessary to improve the allocation of budget resources toward more essential expenditure categories.

What could the Philippines do to reduce the immediate interest burden of the public debt and thereby free up resources for development and other discretionary public programs? Debt rescheduling offered one useful route to relieve the country of its immediate external debt burden, but at some point in the future the same large debt would still need to be absorbed. Moreover, rescheduling would involve a long process of negotiation with creditors, accompanied by possible delays and uncertainty of outcome. Debt repudiation as an alternative would have been too radical and self-immolating for the Philippine government to contemplate—this option carried the worst potential consequences because the country would have become isolated from international capital markets.

A partial solution to the problem was offered by the Brady bonds program of the U.S. Treasury, devised to help highly indebted middle-income countries retire some of their commercial debt. The Philippine government used this facility to purchase commercial debt already available at a discount in the commercial debt market, to be swapped for Brady bonds. In this way, the country was able to effectively reduce its external debt by $4.6 billion in 1992 (that is, by about 12% of the $38 billion debt outstanding at the time). As well as freeing up a significant amount of government resources to help finance public expenditure programs, this also, of course, had the effect of reducing the primary fiscal deficit (see Figure 4.3).

The reduction in the external public debt allowed an incremental increase in the allocation of resources to other expenditure needs. Strong and sustained growth in output would also have helped alleviate the debt burden, but this did not eventuate. Despite positive developments in the investment environment, output growth had been hampered by the long delay in instituting trade and industry liberalization. Eventually, the effort was amply rewarded in the early 1990s by a surge in export performance and an improvement in the fiscal picture.[3] But, from a fiscal viewpoint, it was the reduction in the fiscal burden that provided the most direct benefit, in that it enabled the government to allocate resources to areas other than the debt. As already indicated, social services were a clear beneficiary of the reallocation of budgetary resources. By 1997 the sector accounted for 29.5% of total expenditure.

Budget Flexibility: The Wage Bill and Other Mandated Expenditure

Budget flexibility implies the ability of the fiscal branch of government to juggle resources so as to enable the funding of services identified as being important in the scheme of priorities. Figure 4.6 shows the various categories of mandatory claims on the budget by functional classification (in contrast to the sectoral distribution shown in Figure 4.5). The discussion below is based on current operating expenditure rather than total expenditure, to emphasize the more urgent competition for funds in the current period. Of the resources allotted to spending in each year, how much was really discretionary in character?

The mandated expenditures shown in Figure 4.6 include the government wage bill, interest payments, the share of local government units (LGUs), especially fol-

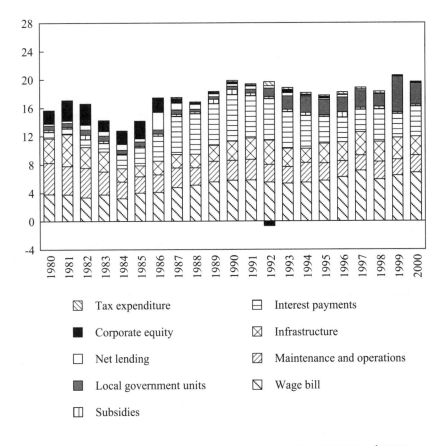

Figure 4.6 Expenditure by Economic Category, 1980–2001 (% of GDP)

Sources: Department of Budget and Management; Bureau of the Treasury.

lowing devolution in 1992, and the cost of subsidies and tax expenditures automatically appropriated by specified agencies (at about one-quarter the cost of allotments to LGUs). All told, mandated expenditures accounted for close to 90% of current expenditure. Even at their lowest level, around 82%, this was a very high share.

The government wage bill has consistently absorbed around 35% of total operational expenses. In 1986 it climbed to 37% of operational costs, but in more recent years has been as low as 33% of total current expenditure. Because the wage bill remains much the same regardless of the level of resources available, at times of reduced overall expenditure it occupies a higher proportion of the budget. As the budget expands, however, part of that pressure is relieved.

Among other mandated expenditures, we have already commented on interest payments. During the difficult years of the debt crisis, interest payments accounted for up to 40% of current operating expenditure (in 1988), with the average for 1987–91 a slightly lower 38%. The fiscal problems of the Aquino administration were prodigious on this count alone, for very little was left over to put toward any other type of expenditure.

The local autonomy law came into effect in 1992. It placed heavier revenue raising obligations on the national government because of the increased proportion of internal revenue reserved for LGUs. Effectively, this involved a transfer of tax revenue (and, in consequence, some public spending obligations) to local governments. In theory this posed no major problem as long as the national government could continue to meet its obligations to the national expenditure program, and as long as there was effective substitution of local for national government services. Although expenditure on interest payments had fallen as a proportion of total current expenditure (to 22% of total current operating expenditure by 1996), the climb in the financial requirements of LGUs took away some room for fiscal flexibility on the national front. Once other mandated claims had been attended to, very little fiscal flexibility was possible.

The big squeeze was put on discretionary expenses related to maintenance and operations, such as the purchase of supplies and upkeep of public facilities. During 1986–2000, the share of the budget allotted to this item ranged from 12% to 24% of total current expenditure. The normal requirements of maintenance and operations should be covered by the current operating budget. But because of the pressure placed on the budget by mandatory expenses, it often ended up in deficit as the government sought to maintain essential maintenance and operations.

The constraints on the budget represented a heavily committed budget with limited budget flexibility. But this situation only emphasized the lack of taxation and other sources of revenue. If government revenues had exceeded mandated expenditures by a good margin, the problem of budgetary inflexibility would have diminished.

4.4 PUBLIC REVENUE MOBILIZATION

The Tax and Revenue Effort

Tax collections have risen over time as a ratio of GDP but remain low in terms of the country's public expenditure requirements. In 1981, the government collected 11.2% of GDP in tax. This fell to 9.6% at the height of the economic crisis in 1983–85, before climbing back over the following decade to reach 17% of GDP in 1997. The tax effort then suffered another sustained drop in 1998–2000 following the Asian financial crisis.

Here, a comparison with other countries in the Asian region may be useful. Statistics on the central government revenue of a number of countries have been published by the Asian Development Bank (ADB 2001: 263, Table A22) (see Table 4.1 for a more general comparison of developing and industrialized economies). Central government revenue is a slightly different concept from pure tax effort, in that it includes both tax and non-tax revenue received by the central government. By and large, Philippine efforts at revenue raising (at 19% of GDP) had caught up with

Table 4.1 Typical Tax Revenue Patterns in the Philippines, Compared with Developing and Industrialized Countries (% of GDP)

Type of Tax	Philippines	Developing Countries	Industrialized Countries
Total tax revenue	19.5	18.0	31.2
Income tax	5.6	5.5	11.0
Corporate	3.3	n.a.	n.a.
Personal	2.3	n.a.	n.a.
Domestic taxes	6.0	5.2	9.4
Commodity tax	4.3	n.a.	n.a.
Sales tax/VAT	2.8	n.a.	n.a.
Excise tax	2.4	n.a.	n.a.
Other domestic taxes	1.6	n.a.	n.a.
Foreign trade taxes	4.4	5.1	0.7
Social security	1.5[a]	1.3	8.9
Wealth and property tax	1.0	0.4	1.1
Other taxes	1.1	n.a.	n.a.
Collections of local governments	1.0	0.4	0.1

a   Authors' estimate.

Sources: Philippine Government; IMF; World Bank.

those of Thailand and surpassed those of Indonesia (17% of GDP) by 1996–97. Other high-growth economies in the region performed significantly better, however: Malaysia raised 23% of GDP, Singapore 37%, and Hong Kong, South Korea, and Taiwan 21%.

Figure 4.7 shows both tax and non-tax revenue for 1980–2000 as a proportion of GDP. During the period under study, non-tax revenue accounted on average for around 2% of GDP. The contribution of the non-tax revenue effort to total revenue could be substantial. The bulge in non-tax revenue in 1994–95, for instance, provided close to 1% of GDP in additional revenues. This significant addition to the public purse was due to the presence of large-ticket privatization items.

The problems related to tax revenue collection in the Philippines are generally similar to those found in other countries. The main obstacle to improving the tax effort remains the poor overall performance of the economy. The modest rate of economic growth in the Philippines relative to other countries in East and Southeast Asia has prevented the tax base from expanding sufficiently to raise the level of tax income.

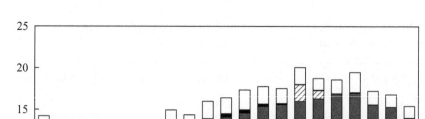
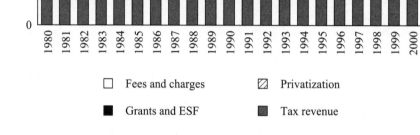
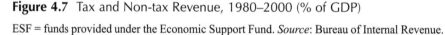

Figure 4.7 Tax and Non-tax Revenue, 1980–2000 (% of GDP)

ESF = funds provided under the Economic Support Fund. *Source*: Bureau of Internal Revenue.

Some taxes already set at relatively low rates have even lower average effective rates because of poor compliance and loopholes. There is room for improvement, for instance, in raising the level of revenue collected from existing commodity and sales taxes. The basic rate of value added tax (VAT), which was introduced in 1988 to replace the existing sales tax system, is 10%. At its inception many goods and services did not attract VAT because of exemptions and zero rating. Bringing services (including a narrow range of financial services) within the ambit of the tax in 1994 went some way toward addressing the problem, by raising its potential coverage. However, there is room for increasing the rate of the VAT, and expanding its coverage further, given that the current rate is generally at the low end of the worldwide scale for taxes of this type.[4] The VAT has not produced as much revenue as the sales taxes it replaced because of difficulties in implementation, and in fact appears to have encouraged more evasion of commodity taxation. Exemptions have also reduced proceeds. This suggests the need to invest more resources in improving the administration of the VAT. Some revenue officials argue, however, that it would be more productive of revenue to revert to the previous sales tax system, even though it is widely accepted that the VAT produces less distortion in economic allocation.

Taxes set at high rates are the main targets of tax exemption, tax evasion, or some other form of leakage. Whereas protected industries and agriculture have benefited from investment incentive schemes, tax exemptions, and tax-like subsidies, high taxes prevailed outside the industrial promotion program. One consequence was to induce smuggling of competing imports. In addition, the imbalances in the system made the tax system more complicated to administer and weakened the revenue effort.

To account for the impact of tax exemptions and other kinds of services based on fees, the government began to track subsidies through tax expenditures. Tax expenditures represent benefits received by specific sectors and are charged automatically as expended (or foregone) taxes, as in the manner of subsidies and fee-based services.

Weak tax administration highlights the inadequacy of the tax collection effort under existing laws. Observers cite corruption—both in the internal revenue service and in the customs service—as a factor in poor tax collections. This is an area of weakness continually identified in IMF and World Bank reports as a major obstacle to resource mobilization (see, for instance, World Bank 1992). In public discussion of the issue, it is commonly noted that the problem lies not in the tax laws themselves, which are sufficient to generate large revenues, but in their implementation.[5] The failure to set an example by bringing tax evaders and corrupt revenue agents before the courts has caused demoralization within these government agencies, further weakening tax administration.[6]

It is clear that improvements in tax administration have a potentially large payoff in terms of compliance and the amount of revenue collected. Partly in response to the weak implementation of income tax laws, the government has instituted a system of final taxes on various transactions, as discussed below. This has simplified the income tax-filing procedures for corporations and (especially) individuals.

Raising Performance

The major impediments to improving the tax effort remain the inadequate level of tax compliance and the existence of fiscal incentives and loopholes that reduce tax receipts. Fiscal incentives supplied as part of the country's industrialization strategy have been tantamount to an exception from income taxes (for a period) and other types of sales taxation.

Of course, if the industries targeted by the nation's industrial and trade policies had succeeded in achieving a sustained improvement in their economic efficiency and competitive position, then the generosity of the government's fiscal incentives would have paid off in a strengthening of the tax base as the economic ventures matured. The economic liberalization program of the 1990s had the effect of reducing high tax barriers and simplifying the tax system. This reduced the effectiveness of fiscal incentives, many of which remained in protected sectors.

Mistakes in industry and trade policy were therefore partly responsible for the low tax effort. The strategy of providing enormous fiscal and other government subsidies to protected domestic industries failed to produce internationally competitive firms. When the government tried to reorient the economy toward greater openness and competition, the same industries became the bulwark of resistance to structural reforms and economic liberalization, because of their dependence on a protected domestic market. When policy changes took place nonetheless—often as a result of adjustments to economic crises—many of these industries became a heavy drag on the adjustment process.[7] Some had borrowed from state financial institutions that had given them preferential access to credit and, because of their poor economic performance, were unable to meet their loan obligations. The expansion in the tax base anticipated from the industrialization program therefore did not eventuate to the extent originally envisioned.

On the other hand, the expansion of new manufacturing exports over the past decade has made it possible to raise the economy's base, even given the expense of initial grants of tax and fiscal advantages to the new firms setting up manufacturing plants. The increase in newly employed workers led to an expansion of payroll-based income taxes and raised domestic demand for output. Moreover, the expansion of export earnings has helped to reduce the external debt service burden.

The recent surge in export industries from the manufacturing sector has been driven by economic liberalization, the reduction in protective barriers, the economic impact on investors of regional preferential tariffs within the ASEAN Free Trade Area (AFTA), and the continuing search by international firms to find lower costs of production for traded manufactures. The track record of electronics export companies established in the Philippines during the previous decade was also instrumental in this (see Bautista and Tecson, Chapter 5).

Tax reform is not a politically popular way of spending public money, especially in a democracy. In the citizen's mind, tax reform implies some increase in the tax burden. In addition, it is difficult to argue the case for reform when the compliance record is weak. Citizens would naturally expect an improvement in the efficiency of collecting existing taxes before agreeing to new ones.

Nevertheless, comprehensive approaches to tax reform have been undertaken in the Philippines to restructure taxation, redistribute the tax burden, and remove inefficiencies in the taxation system. One example is the reform of the sales tax system undertaken in the mid-1980s, under which specific retail and wholesale taxes were replaced by an ad valorem system of taxation that made tax revenues more sensitive to increases in the value of goods. The impetus for the introduction of a VAT was the need to broaden the coverage of the tax system and make it fairer. The VAT did not remove, but supplemented, the existing regime of excise taxes, which were retained on such goods as energy consumption, tobacco, and alcohol. Trade liberalization led to a reduction in import duties, weakening the effect of fiscal subsidies to sheltered industries. When the protective elements in import duties were reduced, these import duties began to produce more revenue.

To help close the gap in compliance created by widespread tax evasion, under-reporting of income, and non-payment of other forms of income tax, in the late 1980s the government introduced a number of taxes based on the time of the transaction, a kind of withholding tax serving as a final tax on the specific transaction involved. This was thus an extension of the system of withholding taxes already being paid on wages, royalty payments, and rental income. The current system is, however, still dominated by taxes that have been in place for decades, such as capital gains tax and tax on bank interest earnings. These are essentially final taxes and, therefore, schedular in character.[8]

Another major tax reform was the simplification of the income tax system in 1986 to reduce the extreme number of progressions in income tax rates and lower the average level of taxation. Introduced in part to improve compliance, this move was also consistent with the need to align Philippine tax rates with those in neighboring countries, as part of the initiative to attract investment and improve the investment regime.

The simplification of the income tax system and the introduction of schedular taxes on other forms of income collected at source have led to an increase in the relative importance of income taxes in overall collections. During the 1990s, revenue from "other income taxes" grew significantly, making it important to itemize these revenue sources more fully. To this day, however, the Bureau of Internal Revenue continues to report such income as a residual group.

The bureau has been trying to reintegrate schedular taxes back into the consolidated income tax framework with the object of making the tax system simpler and fairer. New tax returns allow individuals to enumerate the final taxes they have paid, based on withholding tax schedules, so that these can be included in the calculation of income subject to tax.

Sometimes, the trade-off between revenue creation and efficiency can result in the retention of a harmful tax. For example, the gross receipts tax of 5% on financial transactions has been on the tax books for years. It has been criticized as being harmful to the development of financial instruments and financial institutions, because of the high up-front cost on transactions. But the government—in its pursuit of revenue—has been tardy in finding a more suitable substitute, such as bringing the bulk of financial transactions within the ambit of the VAT.

Changing Composition of Tax Revenues

Over the period under study, there has been a growing reliance on domestic taxation rather than international trade taxes, and, within domestic taxation, on income rather than commodity taxes. This is an indication of the changing structure of taxation, as shown in Figure 4.8.

From 58.4% in 1981, the share of domestic taxes in total tax revenue had increased to 63.8% by 1985, and to 79% by 1999. Income taxes (both individual and corporate, including other forms of profit tax) accounted for a rising share of total tax revenues: from 24.7% in 1982, their share had increased to 43.2% by 1999. As expected, the major reform of income tax rates that took place in 1986 had brought about improved tax compliance and raised the share of income as opposed to commodity and other forms of taxation. The growing importance of income over commodity taxes in the Philippines also confirms an experience in common with other developing economies.

Within commodity taxation, general sales taxation through the VAT is now a more important means of revenue production than excise tax on commodities. Import duties, which comprised 34% of total taxes in 1981, accounted only for

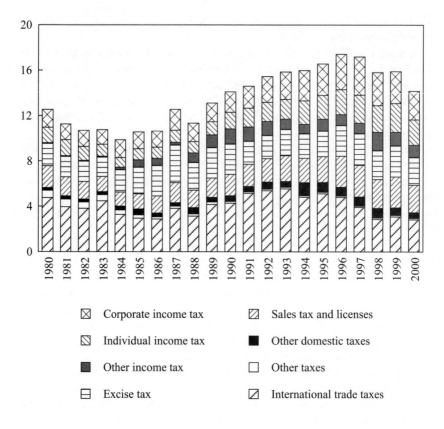

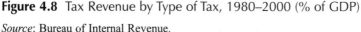

Figure 4.8 Tax Revenue by Type of Tax, 1980–2000 (% of GDP)

Source: Bureau of Internal Revenue.

around 20% of tax revenue in 1999. (The slight bulge in the share of trade taxes at the beginning of the 1990s was due to the introduction in 1989 of a two-year temporary surcharge on crude oil imports.) The relative decline of import taxes as a revenue base is therefore well established.

Non-tax Revenue

Non-tax revenue can make a considerable difference to the level of funds available for public expenditure. Revenue from fee-collecting agencies, income from services sold to the public, and profit contributions are forms of non-tax revenue, as are proceeds from the sale of state-owned assets—in recent years the single most important source of non-tax revenue. Added to these are supplementary revenues from foreign development grants. For instance, until the termination of the military bases agreement, the Economic Support Fund provided a significant channel for revenue from the United States, deemed a quid pro quo for the use of military bases.

Unlike regular taxes, non-tax revenue is often the result of extraordinary and temporary situations. Sales of government property fall into this category. Lumped together as privatization proceeds, these disposals have included the sale of lands formerly used by the military for conversion to commercial, private sector use, the disposal of assets transferred from public financial institutions (including non-performing assets), and the sale of state enterprises to the private sector.

The government set up the Asset Privatization Trust (APT) in the mid-1980s to serve as a central agency to hold and dispose of state-owned assets, especially those transferred from state financial institutions. Another source of privatization revenue was state land, especially land unencumbered by intricate valuation problems, which produced sizable windfalls for the government. Of this type was the extensive and valuable portfolio of urban real estate held by the government, which included former military bases and land acquired through seafront reclamation projects. The sale of Fort Bonifacio produced the highest revenues for the government because of its location in the heart of Metro Manila. The bidding process was transparent and the government was able to extract the best possible price from the bidding entities.[9] Other land sales have been less productive, with some becoming subject to partisan issues of valuation.

The APT has also disposed of a number of privately owned enterprises transferred to it from state financial institutions under bank restructuring agreements. These have included big-ticket items such as a nickel refinery in Nonoc, a copper smelter in Leyte, and a phosphate fertilizer plant. These projects were white elephants of the past caught up in changing circumstances and misjudgments, and their sale yielded minimal cash revenues for the government. The main benefit received from these privatization efforts was to reduce the exposure of the fiscal branch of government to further operational risks (including the risk of incurring new debt), by transferring the liabilities of the enterprises to private parties.

The privatization program was introduced to improve economic efficiency, and not primarily to raise revenue. But it did have a positive revenue-raising impact, even though in all likelihood the price received for the assets was nowhere near their value if they had become successful industrial ventures as originally envisioned when loans were initially made to them. Non-tax revenue from the sale of government assets amounted to 0.18% of GDP in 1987, and reached a peak of 1.77% of GDP in 1994. These were substantial sources of temporary revenues which, for a while, enabled the government to buy time to raise its level of expenditure.

4.5 THE "HIDDEN" DEFICIT FROM QUASI-FISCAL ACTIVITIES

Many institutions are considered to be outside direct budgetary operations, even though they undertake activities that have an impact on the fiscal balance. In recent Philippine experience, the activities of these institutions have added to fiscal instability and placed a large financial burden on the shoulders of taxpayers.

Off-budget institutions are of two kinds. The first is government corporations engaged in the provision of special economic services related to the government's economic and social development policies, such as infrastructure, public utilities, and consumer price stabilization services. The purpose is to give the government a direct market presence to promote price stabilization in essential consumer commodities such as energy products.

The second set is public financial institutions set up by the government as a source of domestic finance for commerce and industry. Foremost among these are the Philippine National Bank and the Development Bank of the Philippines. Before being dissolved in 1993, the former central bank also incurred major financial losses. A fuller examination of government financial institutions would focus as well on the operations of the country's two major pension funds, those of other specialized banks such as the Land Bank and the Export Loan Guarantee Bank, and those of credit programs operated by the private sector but involving government intervention.

This is clearly a large topic, and can be addressed here only in brief. But in short, the hidden fiscal problem of public off-budget agencies is this: many of them have incurred huge losses. So long as the net worth of such institutions remains positive, they do not pose a fiscal problem for the central government. But when their assets are deteriorating in quality at the same time that their liabilities are increasing, a fiscal danger arises. If they continue to make a loss and their net worth is wiped out, the government may be forced to attempt a rescue, with serious implications for the budget.

There are many factors in the poor financial performance of public corporations. The causes overlap, and include inefficiency of operations, overstaffing, lack of true financial autonomy, weak management, and political interference. Even agencies not in imminent danger of financial collapse have in many cases failed to justify the high hopes held for them when the government originally set them up. Their failure to grow to their full potential has also acted as a brake on national economic growth and productivity.

Non-financial State Enterprises

Following the crisis of 1983–85, the Department of Finance placed 14 of the country's largest government non-financial corporations under regular monitoring. This monitoring was designed to install a hard budget constraint in the enterprises and make them financially self-reliant. The government also hoped that by having advance knowledge of their financial and operational position, it would be able to forestall major financial problems that might involve a national remedy.

These 14 corporations carried heavy responsibilities for public investment in public infrastructure, transport, energy, and food price stabilization. They were the Philippine Ports Authority and National Irrigation Administration (NIA) (infrastructure); National Power Corporation (NPC), National Electrification Corporation, Philippine National Oil Company (PNOC), and Manila Gas Corporation (energy); Philippine National Railways, Light Rail Transit, and Metro Manila Transit (transport); Manila Waterworks and Sewerage System (MWSS) and Local Water Utilities Corporation (water); the national postal service and the national telegraph service

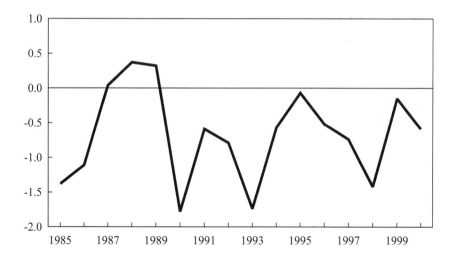

Figure 4.9 Aggregate Deficit of Monitored Government Corporations, 1985–2000 (% of GDP)

Source: Department of Finance.

(communications); and the National Food Authority (NFA) (food price stabilization). Figure 4.9 shows the aggregate deficit of these corporations as a proportion of GDP. Figure 4.10 gives a partial breakdown of Figure 4.9, focusing on the corporations that have contributed most to the size and volatility of the aggregate deficit.

In 1985, the total aggregate deficit of these corporations amounted to 1.4% of GDP. Between 1986 and 1991, this fell to around 0.57% of GDP. The aggregate financial deficit of these corporations in 1992–97 was 0.74% of GDP, rising to 0.76% in 1998–2000. In general, therefore, the overall level of the deficit has remained under control.

The public corporations in the energy sector were the greatest source of volatility, as this sector is the most sensitive in relation to the management of price inflation. Such was the case with the NPC, the state corporation in charge of power generation and distribution, which at times was responsible for 40–60% of the aggregate deficit. The PNOC, which engages in oil exploration and petroleum importing and refining, accounted for another part of the deficit. As the holding company for an energy product retailer, it competes directly with a number of foreign oil companies engaged in the sale and distribution of petroleum products.

These two corporations were the focus of efforts to provide a mechanism to rein in consumer prices in times of international volatility. But as was the case with many such policies involving price controls, the process of intervention became politicized. The tendency was for the fuel subsidy scheme to be adjusted to market developments only after problems had become severe. The system promoted an accumulation of losses borne by the state, by the enterprises, or by both, and even

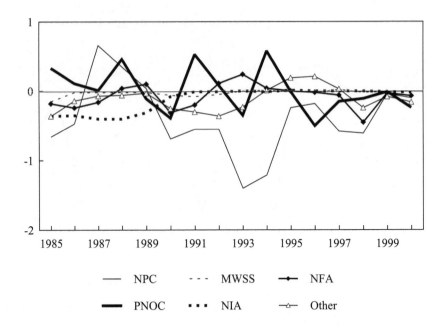

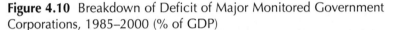

Figure 4.10 Breakdown of Deficit of Major Monitored Government Corporations, 1985–2000 (% of GDP)

MWSS = Manila Waterworks and Sewerage System; NFA = National Food Authority; NIA = National Irrigation Administration; NPC = National Power Corporation; PNOC = Philippine National Oil Company. *Source*: Department of Finance.

added to price volatility because, at times of adjustment, the government tended to overcompensate for future price increases. The fuel subsidy scheme was thus partly responsible for the cycle of macroeconomic booms and busts of the last two decades, hampering the government's efforts to keep the national budget deficit within reasonable bounds.

Under the energy deregulation law crafted in the early 1990s, energy subsidies were removed and the price setting of energy products left to the market. The deregulation was undertaken at the level of both refining and distribution of energy products, permitting new players to enter the field and encouraging greater competition in the market. This removed the worst impact of the fuel subsidy scheme on the budget and opened the way for private sector investment in the sector, which had leveled off since the 1970s because of government intervention. Among the new entrants were a number of foreign enterprises, resulting in an expansion of refining capacity and an opening up of international trade in refined petroleum products.

As part of the reform of the energy sector, the PNOC was partially privatized in 1994. The privatization involved the choice of a strategic partner for PNOC—Saudi Arabia National Oil Company—and the sale of part of the government holding to private investors under an initial public offering.[10] This had the effect of stabilizing the sourcing of supply and limiting the volatility in PNOC's financial deficits.

The NPC is a different matter. This corporation is at the core of electricity provision to the nation. It earns a significant proportion of its income from the sale of electricity, but more importantly, it sets the pace of pricing for all of the country's electricity retailers. The huge annual deficits of the NPC (0.7% of GDP on average in 1990–98, peaking at 1.4% of GDP in 1993) have become unsustainable in relation to the containment of the consolidated fiscal deficit. The high cost of energy—the result of aging plants on the one hand and, on the other, of expensive and inefficient energy generators hurriedly installed during the energy crisis of the late 1980s—is also an obstacle to improving the efficiency of the economy.

The other government corporations suffer from similar problems, although their impact on the national budget is less severe. Nevertheless, they pose a similar dilemma for the government: how to provide essential services without eroding the financial viability of the enterprise or placing too much strain on the national budget. The pricing of services is thus a critical issue for the economic survival of these enterprises. In some cases, their problems include generating a sufficient positive cash flow from their operations to maintain their investment programs.

Public Financial Institutions

The problems of two financial institutions in particular—the Philippine National Bank (PNB), set up in 1916, and the Development Bank of the Philippines (DBP), established shortly after independence—substantially increased the fiscal burden of the central government. The fiscal burden generated by these two banks was the product of a long delay in dealing with the accumulation of non-performing loans that were weighing down their loan portfolios. In past episodes in the history of the banks, an increase in capitalization and a reorganization had been the principal vehicles for restoring them to financial health and operational capacity. But the economic crisis of 1983–85 accelerated their financial insolvency, necessitating major reforms in 1986 to rehabilitate them.

A major cause of the poor lending record of these institutions was that they lent mainly to highly protected economic ventures. The "behest" loans the banks made to political favorites and cronies further sacrificed efficiency criteria in lending and weakened these institutions. Some of the projects underwritten by the banks failed because of unfortunate timing.[11] Others were essentially limited from the start in their scope for success because they had been nurtured under a protectionist industrial policy that discouraged expansion beyond the boundaries set by the size of the protected domestic market.

To reduce the liabilities of the banks, in 1986 approximately 10 billion pesos of non-performing assets were transferred to the newly created APT. With this transfer, the corresponding liabilities were absorbed by the national government. The job of the APT was to sell the assets and/or arrange debt workouts. The revenue the government received for the devalued assets was of course much lower than that implied by their book value.

The financial restructuring of these two public banks reduced their previously dominant position in the credit market. Following the restructuring, the PNB went from being the country's largest bank in terms of assets—a position it had held for many years—to being only its sixth largest. The DBP is unique in being the Philippines' only long-term industrial and development finance bank, but it has been much diminished in size, too.

The financial restructuring of the DBP reduced the worth of its total asset base from 74 billion pesos to 10 billion pesos. In the case of the PNB, the restructuring involved the transfer of 47 billion pesos in assets to the APT and 55 billion pesos in liabilities to the national government, including a write-off of 5 billion pesos in assets. In short, the national government suddenly found itself burdened with new assets of doubtful value, but with a book value of almost 100 billion pesos. The substantial liabilities of the banks were assumed as new debt in the national government's book. To the extent that asset recovery has been made through privatization and other measures (such as swaps of new assets with other parties—including former owners!), the government was able to offset a small fraction of these liabilities. But many of the disposals were in the nature of fire sales.

One only has to examine the recent record of the PNB to discover that the partial privatization of the bank did not extirpate the problems that had beset it over the years. During the 1990s its poor lending practices continued, and its non-performing loans rose once more to alarming proportions. Some of the bank's new problem loans were again in the nature of behest loans that soured quickly as the impact of the Asian financial crisis made itself felt.

The Restructuring of the Central Bank

Over the years, the former Central Bank of the Philippines accumulated losses that can be considered fiscal in nature. These were related to its operations in pursuit of government objectives associated with the promotion of economic development policy. The bank's role in development stood in contrast to its isolated role as a regulator of monetary and exchange rate policy, in which it did not take financial risks.

The philosophy of central banking has changed over the years, and some of the losses incurred by the bank were the outcome of central banking policy implementing what was then received wisdom in the area. The losses it incurred as an enterprise—like the losses of other government enterprises—can be considered fiscal in nature because its operations veered away from the provision of prudent credit and monetary policies that did not involve taking a profit or loss position. When the central bank undertook to pursue state economic development objectives, as in the pursuit of government expenditure policy, then such operations would be deemed to have a fiscal character. New thinking on central banking suggests that the monetary authorities should confine themselves to the objective of dealing with monetary policy and regulating the price level, leaving the pursuit of development and fiscal objectives to the government.

Along with its chief objective of maintaining monetary policy, however, the Central Bank of the Philippines from its inception was expected to facilitate the development of some sectors of the economy. This proactive stance engaged it in peripheral interventionist policies. For instance, it supported credit programs for the development of agriculture; provided preferential interest rates on some types of credit; and encouraged the development of rural banks through the provision of subsidies. The losses arising from these credit subsidies were unrelated to the implementation of the pure central banking objective of using interest rates for monetary management. In the same fashion, the later and more substantial losses incurred by the central bank arose from its efforts to defend the exchange rate and provide guarantees against exchange rate risk for some private sector debt. The central bank as a rule would not assume exchange rate risk but would utilize exchange rate management to effect an orderly adjustment to changes in international monetary conditions.

A World Bank study of the Philippine financial system in 1987 found that the central bank's net assets had failed to take account of the large liabilities arising from losses incurred in the past (World Bank 1988).[12] Essentially, the central bank had become insolvent because of these accumulated losses. Its problems were therefore similar to those of the public banks, which had collapsed under the weight of unrecognized non-performing loans and a high debt repayment bill.

The losses of the Central Bank of the Philippines were estimated at 5% of GDP in 1984 and close to 1.6% of GDP in 1992. In 1993, under a major reform initiative, it was renamed Bangko Sentral ng Pilipinas (BSP) and made much slimmer as an institution. Its functions were more narrowly confined to monetary and exchange rate policy, and excluded developmental objectives. Some of its assets were transferred to the national government, which also absorbed the losses on its books. In short, the final net fiscal burden fell on the taxpayers. The BSP was recapitalized, with the government initially providing a fresh injection of 10 billion pesos in funds.

Consolidating the Fiscal Deficit

The conventional fiscal deficit of the central government was the focus of discussion in the earlier part of this chapter. This concept does not include the quasi-fiscal deficits of public enterprises operating outside the government budget, namely the off-budget agencies. As shown above, their fiscal operations constituted an important element of the overall fiscal burden borne by the government, particularly as many of them play a large role in the total economy. The conventional deficit would be an adequate measure of the actual deficit if off-budget enterprises operated at a profit (and if they did not declare their profits or remit them to the government), or if their operations did not imply a contingent claim on the national budget. On the contrary, however, these enterprises made persistent losses that were eventually absorbed by the fiscal branch of government.

The financial deficits of off-budget enterprises are captured only partially in the budget, as "net lending." This item records financial transfers—such as equity injections, subsidies, and special loans—from the central budget to all government subentities. The entry is net of profit remittances and other reverse transfers from enterprises to the national government. A profit remittance or financial surplus would of course be a rarity, since most enterprises incurred at least intermittent losses, but in any case the financial surpluses of those that did make a slim profit were used to fund capital expenditure or were retained as reserves. Meanwhile, the losses of the majority of enterprises continued to accumulate, and their liabilities to increase, until their coffers were replenished anew from the budget.

The deficits of off-budget agencies raised the level of aggregate demand more than was suggested by the national government deficit as reported. The quasi-deficits of financial institutions probably provided a bulwark against a contraction in output since, at best, they were incurred in part to finance or refinance projects that were midway through implementation. They therefore extended the period during which borrowing entities could continue to operate, fending off their immediate collapse. In more normal circumstances, the tightening of loan collections would have called for major loan accounts to be restructured or written off, thereby reducing aggregate demand.

One gauge of the fiscal deficits of financial institutions is the magnitude of growth in their loan liabilities, which has swamped the size of the conventional fiscal deficit. The IMF calculated, for instance, that annual changes in the foreign debt of the DBP and PNB (converted into pesos) would have at least doubled the size of the conventional deficit during the period 1981–85. During the financial crisis of 1983–85 the change in borrowings in relation to the fiscal deficit was estimated to be 3.5:1 (Liviatan 1994). Such measurements may exaggerate the size of the total consolidated deficit. Nevertheless, they bring home the important point that a potentially large financial deficit arising from the operations of government enterprises can loom behind central budgetary fiscal operations, when the houses of these enterprises are not in order.

Figure 4.11 reconstructs the national fiscal deficit to take account of the fiscal deficits of financial and non-financial government corporations. Throughout the period under consideration, the consolidated fiscal deficit has been much larger than the conventional deficit. Its size demonstrates that the operational deficit of government corporations is larger than the conventional budget—a statistic that should concern fiscal and economic managers and underline the need to develop more sophisticated measures of the state of the nation's fiscal health.

4.6 CONCLUSION

The experience under review covers a period of two decades. In some years the government's dominant fiscal problems were caused, at least initially, by external economic shocks. Fiscal strategy was influenced for the most part by the need to rein in domestic expenditure to match the level of available fiscal resources. By and large, this strategy was successful in removing the threat of double-digit inflation and in constraining the expansion of the fiscal sector to keep spending within the limits of growth in public revenue.

The net fiscal impulse is the most important indicator of the degree of fiscal stabilization. Over the period under study the net fiscal impulse of central government fiscal operations has been relatively contractionary, especially during crisis periods.

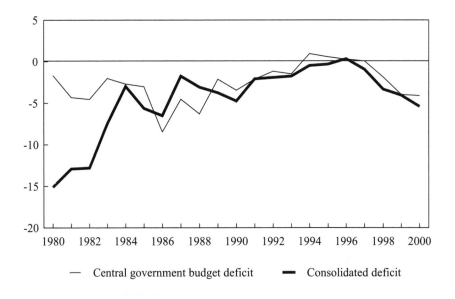

Figure 4.11 Consolidated Deficit Compared with the Central Government Budget Deficit, 1980–2000 (% of GDP)

Thus the record of fiscal management has been to remove the inflationary influence on public fiscal operations, although the strong contractionary role played by the fiscal sector was less helpful in facilitating output growth during some critical periods.

Growth in public expenditure has largely been constrained by the scarcity of fiscal resources. Until a deal could be struck to reduce the debt burden (through the conclusion of the Brady bonds scheme), it was not possible to raise significantly the real level of expenditure on government programs. The lack of flexibility in government expenditure commitments with regard to most economic and social sector spending implied that—during the most difficult times when economic expansion was constrained—these sectors of government were also hit by a steep cut in spending. By and large, however, the social sector was a net beneficiary in the allocation of expenditure.

Even though the bulk of expenditure has shifted away from economic development services, this happened partly as a result of the shift in the financing of public investments away from public resources and to the private sector. Innovative financing mechanisms such as the build–operate–transfer (BOT) schemes developed to finance new projects during the 1990s made it possible to commit future resources to services that had previously been reserved for the public sector, such as electricity generation, transport, and telecommunications. However, this trend would require a complementary streamlining of expenditure in economic development services within the budget, partly to complement new regulatory requirements and partly to strengthen the remaining services.

The changing composition of sources of taxation indicates a maturing process. The change in the tax structure can be discerned by viewing the relative contribution of domestic and international trade taxes in the economy. Another view can be obtained by comparing the relative contribution of income and commodity taxation. And a third view is given by the expansion of the taxation network across a wider set of tax bases, especially with the extension of the VAT to cover some services. In spite of these trends, the question of how to strengthen tax administration remains a sticking point. Non-revenue resources such as privatization proceeds and the sale of state assets such as real estate are only temporary measures to bridge the expenditure gap.

In closing, it may be useful to address current fiscal issues stemming from the Asian financial crisis of 1997–98. The crisis coincided with the abbreviated presidency of Estrada, which lasted almost three years. It brought about an alarming reversal of the major gains in fiscal management made over the two decades discussed in this chapter. Fiscal management worsened. The fiscal deficit increased, partly as a result of the exigencies of sustaining economic activity during the Asian financial crisis, and more importantly because of the weak leadership shown in economic matters. With projected expenditure that was too great to be met from government resources, the revenue effort was anchored on the sustained collection of targeted revenue and a strong push to continue the privatization program. But these revenue targets were off the mark, and the privatization effort achieved negligible results (as is clear, for example, from the data for 1997–2000 shown in Figure 4.7). Although the Asian financial crisis made economic conditions difficult, the Philippines was in a good position to take advantage of potential gains from the opportunity to install deeper economic reforms. However, the Estrada administration plunged the country into further, self-inflicted, pain through numerous mistakes that served to undermine investment confidence.[13]

The government needed to take measures that would show its commitment to stronger tax administration and the privatization program, but these were not vigorously pursued. Tax collections were eroded by import smuggling and by the decision not to pursue a high-profile tax evasion case involving a presidential crony, which sent the wrong message both to the public and to the tax collection machinery. Scheduled privatizations of government corporations were put on hold, but in the meantime their financial position continued to deteriorate. Legislation required to implement the privatization of the energy-generating sector and the restructuring of the NPC, for instance, stalled in Congress. The government also vacillated on the privatization of the NFA, even though this was already part of announced policy. The accumulated losses of public enterprises thus continued to be a source of pressure on the fiscal side.

Perhaps, in the long haul, the weakening of fiscal management since 1997 will prove to be a historical aberration, and not a disturbing new trend. With the accession of the Macapagal-Arroyo government in January 2001, fiscal and economic management has again become a central aspect of the policy framework.[14] It is to be hoped that the present government will be able to correct the failures of the previous regime.

APPENDIX 4.1

Data

The data used in this study were derived from a number of government sources. These include *Philippine Statistics*, compiled by the National Statistical Coordination Board (NSCB), which contains a compendium of varied statistics on prices, income, and the public sector accounts; the very useful *Statistical Yearbook* published by the National Census and Statistics Office; and the *Statistical Bulletin* published by the BSP. The Department of Finance and its offices (such as the Bureau of the Treasury and the Bureau of Internal Revenue) proved very helpful in filling in the gaps, in particular by providing information updates. We thank Dr Rosario G. Manasan of the Philippine Institute for Development Studies for guiding us toward useful data sources.

Fiscal Impulse Estimation

Fiscal impulse assesses the annual outcome for aggregate demand of budgetary action on public expenditure and taxation—expansionary, contractionary, or neutral. It is used to test actual changes in the budget deficit against a normative neutral change as given by movement in the cyclically neutral budget. If the actual change in the budget deficit is larger than the normative change, the fiscal impulse is viewed as expansionary. This could arise from excessive growth in expenditure, inadequate growth in revenue, or some combination of these. Computed as a percentage of previous GDP, it is treated as a growth rate, exacting the initial fiscal contribution to growth in aggregate demand.

The net fiscal impulse measure has a number of limitations. However, it is sufficient for our purpose, which is mainly to illustrate the implications of central government budgetary actions for aggregate demand. The limitations of the approach include the following.

1. It includes the effect of structural changes in the economy.
2. It suffers from the balanced budget multiplier.
3. It ignores effects on prices, interest rates, and the exchange rate.
4. As used in this chapter, it is applied against parameters obtained only from the central government budget balance.

Our study provides estimates of the net fiscal impulse for the period 1980–98, following the methodology employed by Heller, Haas, and Mansur (1986). The net fiscal impulse is measured as follows:

$$\text{Net fiscal impulse} = ([\Delta G - g_0 \Delta YP] - [\Delta T - t_0 \Delta Y])/Y_{-1}$$

where
Δ = the year-to-year operator;
G = government expenditure;

YP = potential output;

$g_0 = G_0/YP$, where 0 corresponds to the base year 1980;

T = revenue;

$t_0 = T_0/Y$;

Y = actual output; and

Y_{-1} = actual output in the previous year.

Potential output is a trend path of GDP, indicating the path it would take at full capacity utilization. It is unthinkable to equate it with full employment GDP, given labor market conditions in the Philippines. Potential output is estimated for the entire period using the following equation:

$$YP_t = 41{,}961 + 0.82 \text{ Consumption}_t + 0.32 \text{ Investment}_t + 2.22 \text{ Government Consumption}_t$$
$$\quad (4.55) \quad (11.05) \qquad\qquad (1.34) \qquad\qquad (2.98)$$

$$+ 0.44 \text{ Exports}_t - 0.45 \text{ Imports}_t + 9{,}996.96 \text{ Time}_t$$
$$\quad (1.52) \qquad\qquad (-1.86) \qquad\quad (2.53)$$

The adjusted R^2 = 0.99; DW = 1.98; and Prob(F-statistic) = 0.0000. Figures in parentheses are t-statistics; those in italics are t-statistics significant at the 5% level.

NOTES

1. First, the energy shock of the 1970s caused a serious external payments problem which extended beyond the decade because of the high dependence of the Philippines on energy. The next shock was the institution of floating exchange rates in world currencies, brought about by the collapse of the Bretton Woods system of fixed exchange rates. A new era of uncertainty in exchange rate anchors for weak currencies like the peso ensued. This ended with the sudden interest rate shocks of the 1980s, which brought about a crisis in international debt for countries already heavily indebted because of the energy shocks. The Philippines was among the countries drawn into this trap.

2. A GDP deflator was used to derive the real level of government expenditure. It would be misleading to use sectoral deflators to deflate the components of expenditure, as many of the relevant services rendered by government within each sector would involve a basket of services composed of government projects, personnel services, and consumption of materials.

3. The debt service burden also eased from a balance of payments viewpoint. Improved export earnings, especially in the 1990s, became a major factor in the evolution of trade performance as the industrial sector became more proficient in producing semiconductors and other electronics exports.

4. The average rate across developed countries would be above 15%.

5. Manasan (1997) estimated the level of tax evasion in 1992–96 at between 53% and 63% for domestic sales taxes, and between 48% and 55% for import taxes. For the same period, she estimated non-payment of taxes on salaries at between 24% and 43%, and on professional income at between 65% and 83%. These results probably represent a combination of deliberate evasion and avoidance as well as weakness and inefficiencies in the tax collection system. The estimates are of course, sensitive to the author's particular assumptions. But

the principal message of such calculations is to call to mind the failure of the tax system to collect all the taxes due under existing tax laws.

6. Consider, for example, the celebrated affair of Lucio Tan, who was accused during the Ramos period of evading taxes initially assessed at 27 billion pesos. The case has been politically charged, since Tan was widely known to be a benefactor of and large political/financial contributor to the ruling party. Despite the early efforts of the Bureau of Internal Revenue to build a case against Tan, enthusiasm to pursue the case waned following the installation of the Estrada government. Probably taking its cue from the Secretary of Finance, Edgardo Espiritu, who remarked during a press interview that the case against Tan was weak, the Bureau of Internal Revenue (an agency under the Department of Finance) announced it would not pursue the case. (Later, as a witness for the prosecution at the Estrada impeachment trial, Espiritu would say that corruption in the revenue service was rampant.) When the Justice Department decided to pursue the case in the Court of Appeals without the support of the Bureau of Internal Revenue, an adverse ruling against the government was inevitable. The Macapagal-Arroyo government has since announced that it will appeal the case in the Supreme Court. High-profile cases like this one have an impact on the way both the tax-paying public and the tax collection machinery perceive the seriousness of compliance.

7. The average nominal tariff rate fell from 23.4% in 1993 to 10% in 1999. Prior to 1974, when tariff reform began in earnest, nominal tariffs had ranged from zero to 259%, with the average nominal tariff leaning heavily on the high side (up to 100%) and the number of tariff rates many and widely dispersed. See Manasan and Pineda (1999).

8. For a review of the issues associated with schedular taxation, see Sicat (1994: 64–82).

9. Ayala Land, the developer of Makati, was outbid by a new group headed by a consortium from Hong Kong.

10. The privatization therefore had the secondary effect of increasing market activity in the stock market.

11. The best example of this was a nickel refinery conceived in the late 1960s. After it had been completed, the project was caught out by changes in the fundamentals of energy pricing. Another example was the country's nuclear power plant project, which became embroiled in national politics and the international politics of environmental safety.

12. These assets included an item called "revaluation of international reserves," which were losses incurred in swap transactions (13.2 billion pesos) and in forward cover operations (22.4 billion pesos). Accumulated interest expenses and costs related to the issuance and servicing of central bank securities and open market instruments (such as central bank bills and reverse repurchase agreements), as well as the cost of printing and minting currency, were itemized in the "monetary adjustment account." If these items were netted from the share of the central bank in financial system assets, the central bank would have accounted for only 28% of the financial system, rather than 43% (World Bank 1988: 20).

13. Estrada's weak economic leadership is analyzed in Sicat (2000: 4).

14. The new president, an economist by training, published a paper in 1987 in which she concluded that government expenditure could have the effect of crowding out private economic activity (Macapagal-Arroyo 1987). See also Sicat (2002), which speculates as to whether economic management, especially fiscal management, will improve under her stewardship.

5

International Dimensions

Romeo Bautista and Gwendolyn Tecson

5.1 INTRODUCTION

The collective experience of developing countries in the past half-century strongly suggests that economic openness matters. According to World Bank data, countries that adopted less restrictive policies on foreign trade and investment not only registered higher growth rates for exports and imports but also achieved significantly more rapid GDP growth and higher levels of per capita GDP. Indeed, there is overwhelming evidence of faster growth among more open economies, based on country studies and cross-country regression analyses (see, for example, Dollar 1992). Among Asian countries, the post-1965 record demonstrates the superiority of development performance in terms of both growth and equity where output mixes, technology choices, and patterns of trade "roughly conform to the country's initial factor endowment and evolving comparative advantage" in international trade (Bautista 1992: 51). In the Philippine case, more appropriate trade policies "than the inward-looking policy of import substitution" of the 1950s and 1960s "might have resulted in faster growth [during that period] ... and almost certainly would have set the basis for a higher development rate" subsequently (Baldwin 1975: 150).

This chapter is an interpretive essay examining the related influences of foreign trade and trade policy on income growth and distribution in the Philippines, based on existing studies and findings. Additionally, we analyze other types of international economic transactions—foreign investment and remittances—to tease out their contribution in helping to advance the twin objectives of economic growth and equity. The premise is that sustained growth of the Philippine economy can be achieved only if there is a wider sharing of the benefits of growth, arguably a necessary but not sufficient condition.

International trade represents an alternative "technology" to domestic production. For any given resource endowment, a country that has no monopoly power in foreign trade can achieve a static welfare optimum, according to standard trade theory, by allocating resources such that the marginal rate of transformation in domestic production between any pair of commodities, represented by the slope of the transformation curve, is equal to the inverse of their price ratio in foreign trade. Autarky and restricted trade give rise to deviations from the optimality condition, and to lower real income and consumption levels relative to free trade in a static sense.

More importantly, international trade has significant dynamic effects that can provide a strong stimulus to economic growth. It improves a developing country's access to new production technologies, to international capital, and to labor skills (including management)—leading to an outward shift of the production possibility frontier. Moreover, foreign trade overcomes the limitations of a small domestic market, enabling the country to take advantage of specialization and scale economies. It helps promote the growth of national income without being subject to a binding demand constraint.

Various arguments for restricting trade, and their assessment in the context of developing economies, have appeared in the literature.[1] The most prominent invoke a presumed dynamic income gain from import protection, in that it will over time alter the relationship between the domestic marginal rate of transformation and the international price ratio by allowing cost reductions (for example, as the necessary skills are learned) that enable domestic "infant industries" to compete eventually with foreign suppliers. This line of argument has provided a major analytical underpinning for the adoption of industrial import substitution as an economic development strategy for many developing countries, especially in the post-World War II period. But it is now widely agreed that, at least with respect to the growth objective, protection is an inferior policy to one of production subsidies, and that the subsidies should be directed to the source of the income gain—the upgrading of worker skills, for example, or the acquisition of improved technologies.

There are of course other objectives that motivate the policy choices of developing country governments apart from overall income (or GDP) growth. In the Philippines, given the persistence of large income disparities among various population groups, improving equity warrants inclusion as a major policy objective, as indeed past and present national development plans and policy documents have generally acknowledged (see Balisacan, Chapter 10).

The next section of this chapter describes the evolution of Philippine trade and exchange rate policies since the early 1970s and examines their effects on sectoral incentives. We then discuss the growth and changing structure of Philippine foreign trade in section 5.3, relating them to the nature of domestic policies adopted. The further repercussions of trade and exchange rate policies on overall income growth and distribution are analyzed in section 5.4. Section 5.5 turns to other international economic transactions—foreign investment, portfolio investment, and remittances—discussing their role in the promotion of economic growth with equity and how they have been influenced by government policies. Some relevant issues concerning recent domestic and international developments that bear directly on the country's trade regime are addressed in section 5.6.

5.2 PHILIPPINE TRADE AND EXCHANGE RATE POLICIES AND THEIR INCENTIVE EFFECTS

The Early Period

In 1970 the Philippines had already had two decades of industrial import substitution policies and attendant high costs of manufacturing production. As has been well documented (Power and Sicat 1971; Baldwin 1975), the introduction of comprehensive controls on imports and foreign exchange in 1949–50 and the maintenance of a highly overvalued exchange rate mainly benefited the producers of import-competing final consumer goods. Large rents were created, encouraging rent seeking over more socially productive activities.

Decontrol and devaluation in the early 1960s did not much change the biases in the production incentive structure. A highly protective tariff system, introduced in 1957 but made redundant at the time by import and foreign exchange controls, preserved the incentive structure favoring consumer goods industries producing import substitutes, to the detriment of export production. Tariff escalation, making import duties higher on semi-finished products and higher still on finished products, encouraged assembly and packing operations that depended heavily on imported materials and machinery, at the expense of backward integration.

After the "easy stage" of import substitution, manufacturing value added increased very little, and industrial employment even less. Consequently, the manufacturing share in total employment remained nearly constant at about 12% through the late 1960s. GDP growth (averaging 4.5% during 1957–69) was slow by East Asian standards, and household income distribution remained heavily skewed (as reflected in an observed Gini coefficient of about 0.50 in the survey years of 1956, 1961, and 1971). All this was related to the failure to expand labor-intensive production in areas of the country's comparative advantage, and to the accompanying decline in total exports as a proportion of GDP (Baldwin 1975: 11).

Export Promotion and Flexible Exchange Rates in the 1970s

The enactment of the Export Incentives Act of 1970 following the floating of the Philippine peso earlier in the year (which had resulted in a de facto devaluation of more than 60%) signaled a policy shift toward a more outward-looking industrial development strategy. In addition to the tax exemptions and other fiscal incentives provided by the Board of Investments (BOI), the government offered export producers, on a selective basis—which turned out to favor large capital-intensive enterprises—various forms of financial and infrastructure support. These included the chance to locate their operations in export-processing zones, the provision of marketing services, and the simplification of export procedures and documentation.

All this served to compensate only in part for the still pervasive bias of the incentive system against exporting. The country's highly protective tariff system constituted the primary source of this bias, but no attempt was made to deal with it directly as part of the industrial export promotion program of the 1970s. Furthermore, there was a marked rise in the number of imported products subject to quantitative restrictions, their share in the total number of Philippine Standard Industrial Classification (PSIC) seven-digit product categories doubling from 26% in 1970 to 52% in 1980.

Agriculture was subjected to increased government intervention throughout the decade (see David, Chapter 6), ostensibly aimed at shielding the sector from the pronounced instability of the international economy. Government monopoly of foreign trade in the principal food grains (rice, corn, and wheat) was the primary means of regulating their domestic price levels. This was supplemented in the 1970s by direct price controls, which effectively lowered the domestic prices of food crops relative to world prices. Trade in coconut and sugar—the dominant export crops—was heavily restricted. An export quota was in operation for sugar, and sugar trading in both domestic and foreign markets was a monopoly of state corporations. A production tax was placed on coconut in 1973, at rates averaging about 20% of the border price of copra. From 1970 a 6% export tax was levied on copra and sugar; other agricultural exports were taxed at rates ranging from 4% to 10%. Export premium duties imposed on agricultural products in 1973 served in part to siphon off the gains from the world commodity boom.

These policy measures had the effect of artificially depressing the domestic prices of agricultural products. Nominal protection rates, representing the excess of the domestic price of a product over its international price, were estimated to be negative (at –6% and –16% on average for food and export crops respectively) for the 1970s (Bautista 1986a). Indeed, with the exception of poultry, meat, and eggs, negative protection characterized all agricultural products.

Government intervention in agricultural input markets reinforced the policy bias against agriculture, raising domestic input prices relative to their social opportunity cost. Estimated implicit tariff rates, indicating the excess of the domestic price of an input over its international price, for the 1970s were 10% for fertilizer, 23% for other agricultural chemicals, 10% for four-wheeled tractors, 33% for hand tractors, and 30% for irrigation pumps (David 1983).

As a measure of relative incentives, effective protection rates (EPRs)—the rates of protection of value added by domestic factors, indicating the proportionate difference between domestic and foreign value added—are more meaningful than either nominal protection rates or implicit tariff rates. This is because EPRs include both the subsidy to domestic producers from the protection of output and the penalty from the protection of inputs. A study of effective protection in the Philippines, based on tariffs and indirect taxes in the mid-1970s (Tan 1979), finds the weighted average EPR for manufacturing industries to have been 44%, compared with only 9% for the primary sectors (agriculture and mining). Export-oriented sectors had an EPR of 4%, versus 61% for non-exporting industries. The other findings of this study indicate the persistence of a strong bias in the tariff structure and the indirect tax system in favor of consumer goods, at the expense of intermediate products and capital goods.

The effective subsidy arising from the fiscal incentives accorded to BOI-registered export producers has been observed to be relatively large for *firms* that actually received the tax benefits, but for BOI-subsidized *industries* the average EPR in 1974 rose by only about 5%. This reflected the inability of many firms, especially the smaller ones, to gain access to BOI export incentives.

Despite the large nominal devaluation of the peso in February 1970 and subsequent "managed float" of the Philippine peso, the real exchange rate (RER) remained highly overvalued throughout the decade, indicating a strong incentive bias against tradable goods production. The average RER overvaluation has been estimated at 24% for the period 1970–74 and as much as 32% for 1975–79 (Intal and Power 1990), the latter resulting from the reliance on foreign credits following the 1973–74 oil shock (Bautista 1988).[2] Based on the comparisons given in Bautista (1990: 122), these rates are much higher than those derived for Thailand (16% in 1970–74 and 24% in 1975–79) and Malaysia (less than 3% in both periods) using the same estimation methodology.

The price incentive effect of exchange rate policy for export producers can be represented by the purchasing power parity–effective exchange rate (PPP–EER) of the Philippine peso, obtained by multiplying the effective exchange rate (indicating the units of domestic currency per U.S. dollar actually received by exporters) by the export unit value index, and dividing by the general wholesale price index. PPP–EER estimates for traditional and non-traditional exports in 1970–71 indicate increases of 40% and 65% respectively over the 1967–69 averages (Baldwin 1975), implying that the policy measures adopted in the early 1970s significantly enhanced the attractiveness of production for export *vis-à-vis* domestic sales. After 1974, however, the PPP–EER of the peso dropped sharply, and by 1979 it was about 30% lower than the 1974 value. This reflected the failure to sustain the real devaluation and improved relative export profitability achieved earlier.

Trade Liberalization under Foreign Exchange Constraint in the 1980s

By the late 1970s policy-makers were acutely aware that the country needed to improve the international competitiveness of its domestic industry—a government study found domestic industry to be more heavily protected in the Philippines than in other Southeast Asian market economies (Philippine Tariff Commission 1979). With technical and financial support from the World Bank, a program of industrial structural adjustment was launched in 1981. It included measures to significantly liberalize the trade regime through tariff reform and the easing of import restrictions. However, the program was overtaken by the foreign exchange crisis that began in August 1983, and some of its components were superseded by policy actions intended to deal with short-term contingencies.

What remained relatively unaffected was the tariff rationalization scheme. Peak tariff rates of 100% and 70% were lowered to 50% in two stages.[3] Very low tariff rates, on the other hand, were increased to at least 10% by 1985, which further reduced the degree of dispersion of tariff rates. Overall, the average tariff rate dropped from 43% in 1980 to 28% in 1985.

To complement the tariff reform, import licensing was also gradually to be relaxed. From the original list of 1,300 import items banned or requiring prior approval by the central bank and other government agencies, 264 were removed in 1981. Another 610 were taken off the list in early 1982, and the plan was to do away with the rest by year-end 1983. Owing to the foreign exchange crisis, however, this did not happen.

Instead, comprehensive controls on foreign exchange and imports were introduced in October 1983, signaling an emergency retreat from the trade liberalization program. The central bank required all commercial banks to turn in their foreign exchange receipts so that priority imports and other payments could be made. As a revenue measure, and also to discourage imports, a 5% general import tax was imposed in November. This was raised to 8% in April 1984 and then to 10% two months later. Additional export duties ranging from 2% to 5% were levied on traditional export products from November 1983 through to December 1984, and an economic stabilization tax of 30% was imposed on all exports in June–September 1984. To curtail imports and capital outflows, the peso was devalued three times— by 7.8% in June 1983 to 11 pesos/dollar, then in October to 14 pesos/dollar, and in June 1984 to 18 pesos/dollar. In October 1984 the exchange rate was allowed to float. It is also worth noting that tax reforms during 1983–85 gradually unified sales taxes on imports and import substitutes, removing one source of import protection; moreover, the mark-up rate (which increases the tax base for imports) on essential and semi-essential goods was reduced to a uniform 25% in 1985, and removed altogether in 1986.

In the second half of the 1980s the new government of President Corazón Aquino abolished export taxes (except on logs) and accelerated the import liberalization process. About half of the 951 import items liberalized in 1986 were manufactured goods (such as textiles, leather, rubber, and paper products). Quantitative restrictions on 170 products were removed in 1987, and on another 209 products in 1988. The remaining 673 restricted import items were classified into three lists. Those under list A were scheduled for immediate liberalization, and 94 of them were liberalized by year-end 1989; those under list B were scheduled for further review; and those under list C, numbering 114 items, continued to be restricted for national security or health reasons.

Sectoral EPRs for 1983, 1985, 1986, and 1988 estimated by Tan (1995: 173) indicate a significantly declining trend for importables and somewhat erratic changes for exportables. Within the manufacturing sector, the average EPR for import-competing industries fell from 108% in 1983 to 75% in 1988, while that for export-oriented industries increased slightly from 3.1% to 3.8% (assuming that exporters obtained the full benefit of duty drawbacks). The incentive bias persisted not only against export production but also against agriculture: even as the average EPR declined for all manufacturing from 79.2% in 1983 to 55.5% in 1988, that for agriculture also fell—from 10.3% to 5.2%. Thus, while changes in trade policy in the 1980s represented a general movement toward incentive neutrality, the biases against agriculture and export-oriented industries remained significant.

The trend of the RER in the 1980s was favorable to the production of tradable goods relative to non-tradables. The trade-weighted real effective exchange rate (REER), based on IMF (1999) data,[4] depreciated at an average annual rate of 2.7% from 1980 to 1989. Actual RER changes cannot of course be attributed solely to the country's trade and macroeconomic policies. Among other possible influences, the deterioration in the country's external terms of trade during the decade would likely have contributed to the observed depreciation of the RER.

Trade Policy Reform but Unstable Real Exchange Rates in the 1990s

In July 1991 the government launched the country's second most important tariff reform (after the 1981–85 tariff changes). Executive Order (EO) 470 aimed to significantly reduce the number of commodity lines[5] carrying high tariff rates and increase the number of commodity lines with low tariffs over a five-year period. Thus, the 1,177 lines carrying a 50% tariff rate in 1991 were to be reduced to 208 by 1995; the 480 lines with a 40% rate were to be reduced to zero. By the end of 1995, the minimum tariff rate of 3% applied to 35% of all tariff lines; another 62% had duties of 10%, 20%, or 30%; and less than 3% lines were subject to duties of over 30%. The average nominal tariff rate decreased from 33.3% in 1990 to 26.8% in 1995.

Further tariff cuts were forthcoming. EO 189 reduced tariff rates on capital equipment to 10%, and on spare parts for machinery to 3%. It was followed by EO 264 and EO 288, which lowered tariffs on some industrial and agricultural products respectively, to put 76.7% of total commodity lines in the 0–10% tariff band by 2000. More comprehensive tariff adjustments took effect in January 1998 under EO 265 and in July 1998 under EO 486. The average nominal tariff rate had fallen to 19.5% by 2000. The declared goal of the government is to reach a uniform level of 5% for all products (except "sensitive" agricultural products) by 2004.

In what were announced as temporary adjustments to alleviate the difficulties faced by domestic producers during the Asian economic crisis, in 1999 import duties were increased on 720 tariff lines involving textile and garment products, petrochemicals, and iron and steel products. The economic rationale for the preferential treatment accorded those industries has not been made clear. It is obviously a departure from the earlier trend of tariff reductions aimed at making the incentive structure more neutral.

The lifting of import restrictions continued in the early 1990s. In total, 190 commodity lines were liberalized during 1990–92. In 1992, 113 previously restricted lines were tariffied under EO 8, issued in July 1992 by the new Ramos administration. In general, the adjusted tariff rates under EO 8 were much higher than those applicable under EO 470, but the scheduled reductions in subsequent years would lead to comparable rates by 1995. Most quantitative restrictions had been lifted by the end of 2000, an important exception being rice imports, which continued to be under the control of the National Food Authority (NFA). The motor vehicle industry remained heavily protected, with parts and components as well as used motor vehicles being subject to import licensing.

The effect of the EO 470 tariff reductions was to decrease the average EPR from 30% to 24%, and the standard deviation from 42% to 32% (Tan 1995: 201). Based on a comparison of domestic and border prices for 169 commodities (incorporating the effects of quantitative restrictions), Manasan and Querubin (1997) calculated that the average EPR would decline from 29.4% in 1990 to 18% in 2000. The reduction would be more pronounced for manufactured than agricultural commodities, so that in the second half of the decade, relatively higher protection, on average, would be accorded agriculture than manufacturing. Despite the substantial liberalization, the trade regime would continue to overprotect importables relative to exportables.

The RER of the Philippine peso was highly unstable during the 1990s. There was a markedly appreciating trend until the advent of the Asian financial crisis in 1997, and a substantial overall depreciation subsequently (Figure 5.4). By 2001 the REER index had fallen well below the 1990–91 levels, indicating that the real depreciation since 1997 had more than fully offset the extent of the REER appreciation earlier in the decade. Thus, the exchange rate change improved the relative profitability of both import-competing and export industries. At the same time, trade liberalization was significantly lowering effective protection of importables and, to a lesser extent, that of exportables. As Hill (Chapter 7) points out, this recent evolution of the incentive structure represents "a major boost in competitiveness for tradable goods industries" and improves the ability of domestic producers to exploit their comparative advantage.

Political Economy Considerations

As indicated above, the government gave increased attention to the promotion of industrial exports beginning in the early 1970s. This arose in part from the observed favorable experiences of some East Asian economies, in particular Taiwan and South Korea, which had registered exceptionally rapid economic growth, employment generation, and improvement in income distribution following the shift to export-led industrial development in the 1960s. Government policy was also influenced by contemporary academic discussion about the penalties being imposed on export-oriented industries by import substitution policies (Power and Sicat 1971; Bautista, Power, and Associates 1979).

Indeed, since the mid-1960s the number of senior government officials with strong academic backgrounds (including postgraduate degrees from leading U.S. universities) has increased markedly. These "technocrats," possessing an international perspective on economic and development issues, were generally sympathetic to the idea of outward-oriented industrialization. They became the de facto political representatives of export producers—especially producers of non-traditional labor-intensive manufactured goods, in which the country was thought to have comparative advantage. Export producers comprised a very small group of industrial entrepreneurs at the time relative to other producer groups being favored by the protectionist trade regime.

The technocrats were successful, especially during the first half of the 1970s, in implementing policies that reduced the incentive bias against export production, including selective subsidies to producers of labor-intensive industrial exports. However, these fell far short of the penalties imposed by existing import restrictions and the indirect tax system. As noted, the attempt in the early 1980s to liberalize the foreign trade regime with World Bank assistance was derailed by the external debt-related foreign exchange crisis of 1983–85, lending support to the argument that trade liberalization without macroeconomic stabilization is not viable.

Subsequently, the Aquino and Ramos governments were able to lower trade barriers gradually and significantly. Implementation of trade policy reforms was delayed at times by strong opposition from producer interests in the affected industries, with whom some key government officials were known to be associated. The February 1986 revolution did not bring to power a new ruling class that could quickly do away with economic corruption. But along with the stimulus provided by a free press, it helped that policy analysis and monitoring continued to be carried out competently and objectively, most notably at the University of the Philippines School of Economics and the Philippine Institute for Development Studies (Fabella 1991). Also, under President Ramos, substantial progress in macroeconomic stabilization, including the country's return to creditworthiness, was achieved.

Barely had the Ramos reforms begun to produce tangible results than the Asian financial crisis struck. Although the Philippines was initially less badly affected than its Asian neighbors, it suffered nevertheless from the "contagion effect" of the crisis. Moreover, it began to face what was probably a more formidable problem on the domestic front, namely the growing pessimism over economic prospects given the increasingly untenable political environment under the Estrada administration. The problems of poor governance and allegations of economic corruption at the highest levels of government began to spill over into the economic sphere, dampening both domestic and foreign investment. With the subsequent impeachment of President Estrada and the installation of the Macapagal-Arroyo administration came the hope of a return to the serious business of tackling the deep social, economic, and political problems confronting the Philippines.

5.3 GROWTH AND STRUCTURAL CHANGE IN FOREIGN TRADE

Philippine exports in current (dollar) prices have been growing since the 1970s at double-digit rates, except during the economic recession of the early 1980s (Table 5.1). With the resumption in earnest of the trade reform policy in 1986, and the progressive dismantling of the anti-export bias of the prevailing protectionist regime, there has been a continuous acceleration of export growth through to the present. Not even the most recent regional crisis was able to restrain the growth of exports. Imports, on the other hand, outpaced exports during most periods, but proved more vulnerable to domestic economic slowdown as well as to the regional crisis.

Table 5.1 Average Annual Growth of Export and Import Values in Current Dollars, 1970–2000 (%)

	1970–75	1976–80	1981–85	1986–90	1991–95	1996–2000
Exports	18.5	20.7	–4.0	12.3	16.6	17.0
Imports	28.2	17.8	–7.5	19.6	17.1	4.3

Source: National Economic and Development Authority (various years), *Philippine Statistical Yearbook*.

In absolute terms, the country's imports have consistently exceeded its exports since the 1970s. Thus the trade balance remained negative throughout 1977–98 (Figure 5.1), a trend that became even more pronounced during the 1990s. Toward the end of the decade, as economic growth decelerated, the negative trade balance began to shrink. Indeed, with declining imports coupled with growing exports as the decade drew to a close, the trade balance turned positive.

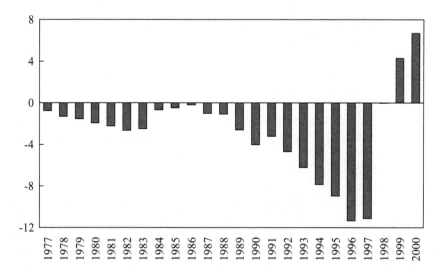

Figure 5.1 Trade Balance of the Philippines, 1977–2000 ($ billion)

Source: Bangko Sentral ng Pilipinas (various years), *Selected Philippine Economic Indicators*.

Table 5.2 Composition of Philippine Imports, 1970–2000 (%)

Import Type	1970	1980	1990	2000
Capital goods	36.7	24.6	25.6	39.1
Raw materials &				
intermediate goods	42.8	38.9	47.6	38.3
Mineral fuels, lubricants	10.9	29.1	15.1	11.9
Consumer goods	9.1	5.2	8.7	8.1
Special transactions	0.5	2.2	3.0	2.5
Total	100.0	100.0	100.0	100.0

Source: Bangko Sentral ng Pilipinas (various years), *Selected Philippine Economic Indicators*.

Structural Change in Foreign Trade

Imports, unlike exports, have shown very little compositional change over time. About 80% of the country's import bill is still made up of capital goods as well as raw materials and intermediate goods (Table 5.2). The share of consumer goods, of only about 9% of total imports, has hardly changed over time, in spite of the trade reform policy, which drastically reduced both tariffs and non-tariff barriers on imports of most consumer goods. This reflects the degree of import substitution that had been achieved in consumption goods, where tariff protection was strongest before liberalization. However, second-stage import substitution has failed to take place in any meaningful way. With the tariff and tax structures generally biased against the domestic production of capital and intermediate goods, the country remains dependent on imported sources after four decades of industrialization, a classic case of import-dependent import substitution.

In contrast to imports, a structural change in exports can readily be observed, reflecting the shifting pattern of the country's competitiveness (Figure 5.2). There is a clear shift from primary sector exports to exports of manufactured goods: from about one-third in 1970, the share of manufactured exports had risen to over four-fifths of total exports by 2000.[6] Among manufactured exports, there was likewise a rapid decline in the country's dependence on natural resource-based manufactures such as processed food, beverages, and wood products (Table 5.3). And while the share of labor-intensive manufactures (for example, apparel) initially showed a rising trend, their relative importance began to decline in the 1990s. In contrast, capital/technology-intensive exports continued to increase in importance, with their share rising from about half of total manufactured exports in 1980 to around four-fifths in 2000. This category mainly comprises semiconductors, electrical and electronic equipment, parts and components, and telecommunication products destined for the developed markets of the "triad" (the United States, the European Union, and

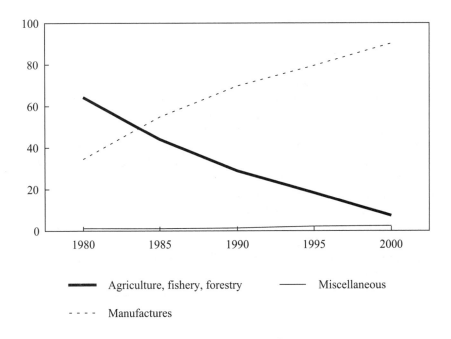

Figure 5.2 Distribution of Philippine Exports, 1980–2000 (%)

Source: Bangko Sentral ng Pilipinas (various years), *Selected Philippine Economic Indicators*.

Table 5.3 Sectoral Shares of Manufactured Exports, 1980–2000 (%)

Export Type	1980	1985	1990	1995	2000
Processed food & beverages	4.6	4.2	3.6	2.1	0.8
Wood, resource-based exports	8.6	7.2	7.6	3.9	2.2
Labor-intensive exports	34.3	29.0	36.6	24.0	9.7
Capital & technology-intensive exports	45.9	51.2	44.0	62.4	83.7
Miscellaneous manufactures, n.e.s.	2.9	2.5	2.3	1.4	0.7
Other	3.7	5.9	5.9	6.2	2.9
Total	100.0	100.0	100.0	100.0	100.0

Source: Bangko Sentral ng Pilipinas (1997), *Selected Philippine Economic Indicators*.

Japan) (see Hill, Chapter 7). They are intensive in the utilization of semi-skilled and technical labor, with which the Philippines is relatively well endowed. The growth of these exports is, however, very much linked to resource-seeking foreign direct investment (FDI) by multinational enterprises, utilizing the Philippines as an export base for technology-intensive products destined for developed country markets.

The observed structural change in the country's export trade reflects the shift in the pattern of its comparative advantage over time. A simple measure of a country's pattern of specialization is given by the index of revealed comparative advantage (RCA) originally developed by Balassa (1965).[7] A country is said to be specializing in a category of exports—presumably where it has a "revealed" comparative advantage—more than the rest of the world if the RCA index for exports assumes a value of 1 or greater than 1. Changes in the country's pattern of specialization over time can likewise be deduced from the decline in the RCA index in some categories and its rise in others. Figure 5.3 presents the trend in the RCA index for the Philippines over time for various categories of exports.

The Philippines has traditionally specialized in agriculture-based exports, especially processed food. However, starting in 1975, such specialization shows a rapid

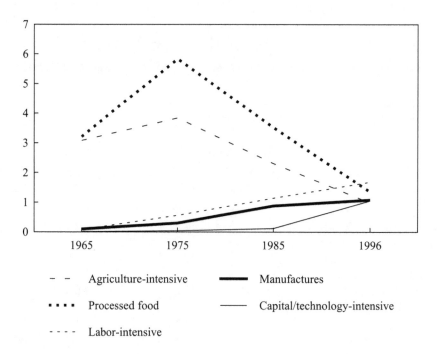

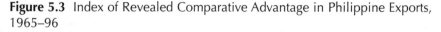

Figure 5.3 Index of Revealed Comparative Advantage in Philippine Exports, 1965–96

Source: Tan (2000).

decline, with the RCA index for agriculture-intensive exports dipping below 1 in 1996. In contrast, one can observe a rising trend for manufactured exports, especially exports of labor-intensive goods, which eventually surpassed even processed food in their degree of specialization. By 1996, an emerging upward trend can also be observed for capital and technology-intensive exports.

These trends are indicative of the underlying shift in the country's comparative advantage from agriculture to manufactures, and, within manufactured exports, to labor-intensive and capital/technology-intensive exports.[8] Worth noting is that the shift becomes most pronounced after 1985, that is, after the country embarked in earnest on its trade reform policy. Whereas manufactured exports were penalized by the protective structure of the economy during the pre-reform period, the penalties began to ease with the progressive dismantling of tariff and non-tariff barriers to imports.

Trade Liberalization and Efficiency in the Manufacturing Sector

Underlying the shift in the structure of the country's export competitiveness was the improvement in resource allocation that accompanied the trade reform policy. Table 5.4 shows manufacturing industries classified according to their measured efficiency levels. In 1992, six years after the resumption of the trade reform policy, 73% of all industries in the manufacturing sector could be classified as at least only mildly inefficient, compared with 48% in 1983. The share of highly inefficient industries shrank from 40% to 18% over the same period. Efficient industries were likewise found to have grown more rapidly than inefficient ones (Sachs et al. 1998).

Currency Appreciation and Trade

These improvements in efficiency were not accompanied by the expected improvements in the relative importance of the manufacturing sector or its employment-generating capability. Contrary to expectations, a decline in the share of the manufacturing sector in GDP can be observed (see Balisacan and Hill, Chapter 1)—this in spite of the remarkable growth in manufactured exports noted above. Although the highly protected import-substituting industries contracted with the reduction in import barriers over time, a more than proportionate expansion of export industries seems not to have occurred. Export growth accelerated, consistent with trade policy reform, but this growth does not seem to have been strong enough to generate a sufficient expansion of manufacturing sector value added. To a great extent, this can be traced to the very low levels of value added in the sectors in which export growth could be observed, particularly semiconductors and other electronic products.

Moreover, with the declining share of the manufacturing sector in GDP, its share of employment in total employment also declined, from 12% during the pre-liberalization years to 10% in the 1990s. In contrast, employment generated by the services sector had been rising faster than that in all sectors (see Balisacan and Hill, Chapter 1).

Table 5.4 Resource Allocation in Philippine Manufacturing, 1983, 1988, and 1992 (%)[a]

Efficiency Classification	Share in Value of Production		
	1983	1988	1992
Highly efficient	18.8	39.5	43.9
Mildly inefficient to efficient	28.8	22.9	29.5
Inefficient	12.3	14.7	8.4
Highly inefficient	39.6	21.8	18.1
Negative foreign exchange earner/saver	0.5	1.2	0.1

a Four-digit SITC industries are classified according to whether their ratios of domestic resource cost (DRC) to shadow exchange rate (SER) exceed or fall below various levels of efficiency. The DRC measure represents the peso cost in shadow prices of domestic resources used in earning or saving a net unit of foreign exchange. The ratio of an industry's DRC to the weighted average of the DRCs of manufacturing industries—which is equivalent to the manufacturing sector's SER—provides an indicator of that industry's efficiency relative to that of the manufacturing sector as a whole.

Industries are classified as follows: highly inefficient, $0 < DRC/SER < 1.0$; mildly inefficient to efficient, $1.0 < DRC/SER < 1.5$; inefficient, $1.5 < DRC/SER < 2.0$; highly inefficient, $DRC/SER > 2.0$; negative foreign exchange earner/saver, $DRC/SER < 0$.

Sources: Medalla et al. (1995/96); Pineda (1997).

What can explain the above observations? An important part of the explanation lies in the fact that the continuing program of trade liberalization instituted in the 1980s and 1990s was not accompanied by a consistently depreciating peso in real terms. Based on the IMF REER index, the Philippine peso was appreciating in real terms until the onset of the Asian financial crisis—at an average rate of 5% annually in 1990–96 (Figure 5.4). Even though there was a substantial REER depreciation in 1998, the index rose again in the following year.[9] Such peso appreciation was not conducive to tradable goods production, to which can be attributed (at least in part) the observed relative expansion of the non-tradables (services) sector. The subsequent decline in the REER in 2000 and 2001, if sustained, augurs well for tradables.

The country's experience with trade liberalization thus seems to differ from episodes of "successful" liberalization in other developing countries (Michaely, Papengiorgiou, and Choksi 1991). In the latter, large real depreciations of the local currency accompanied the liberalization process. The result was typically a rising share of the manufacturing sector in both output and employment, fueled by growth in manufactured export production that made up for the contraction in the import-substituting sector.

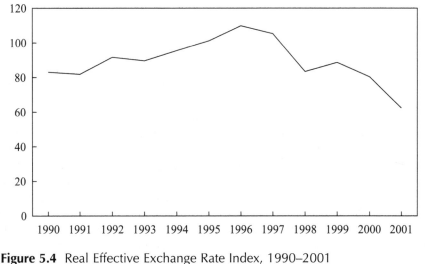

Figure 5.4 Real Effective Exchange Rate Index, 1990–2001

Base year = 1980. *Source*: Bangko Sentral ng Pilipinas, www.pids.gov.ph.

5.4 EFFECTS ON GROWTH AND INCOME DISTRIBUTION

The trade policy biases against agriculture (except, recently, the "sensitive" commodities) and exports would have had unfavorable repercussions on income growth and equity. In the Philippine context, not only are the macro linkages of agricultural growth significant, but the rural sector, in which agriculture is the primary means of livelihood, accounts for a large majority of the poor (see Balisacan, Chapter 10). Discriminating against export production, on the other hand, only serves to inhibit the expansion of labor-intensive industries that could realize the country's comparative advantage in producing for the world market. Labor is the only important income-generating asset of the poor; hence any policy that hinders labor use represents an impediment to improved equity.

Trade Policy and Agriculture

There is wide agreement in the development literature that sustained economic growth in heavily agricultural countries is not likely to be achieved without them first—or concurrently—developing their agricultural sectors. Indeed, the strong association between agricultural growth and overall economic growth is a firmly established empirical generalization in development economics (Timmer 1988). Where poverty is predominantly rural, rapid expansion of agricultural production can also lead to a significant improvement in income distribution. A critical determinant of the latter outcome is the structure of agricultural growth and its linkages to the rest of the economy. These in turn are influenced by domestic policies, including the trade regime.

It has been argued that rapid agricultural growth in the Philippines during the Green Revolution period (1965–80) did not provide a strong impetus to overall economic growth, in part because the agricultural income gains were not widely shared (Bautista 1995).[10] The benefits from the dramatic productivity increases in rice production, for example, effectively bypassed the large segment of the farm population that had little or no access to irrigation water, including small-scale and upland farms. Although there was widespread adoption of modern seed varieties, the new technology was notably much less effective in raising yields on farms where water levels could not be strictly regulated. Also contributing to the bias against small farmers was the greater access of large producers to credit and fertilizer subsidies as well as to infrastructure investments (electricity and roads). Because agricultural growth was not broadly based, the pattern and growth of rural consumption demand favored capital-intensive products and imported goods over labor-intensive, locally produced goods and services. The weak "consumption linkage effect" of agricultural growth would have contributed to the disappointingly low GDP growth rate and persistence of severe income inequality and poverty from 1965 to 1980.

On the supply side, the inability to translate rapid agricultural growth into rapid overall growth of the Philippine economy can be attributed in part to inappropriate domestic policies that weakened the non-agricultural production response to the demand stimulus generated by increased rural incomes. In particular, the highly restrictive trade regime that had promoted industrial import substitution since the early 1950s would have had adverse incentive and output effects, discriminating heavily against small-scale, labor-intensive industries and against enterprises located outside Metro Manila (Bautista, Power, and Associates 1979). This policy-induced supply constraint served to further weaken the linkage between agricultural growth and the rest of the economy.

The economy-wide income and equity effects of crop productivity growth during the Green Revolution period are examined quantitatively under alternative foreign trade regimes in Bautista and Robinson (1997), using an agriculture-focused computable general equilibrium (CGE) model of the Philippine economy that distinguishes among five household groups (Metro Manila, other urban, small-farm, large-farm, and other rural). Under the historical policy regime, real GDP and the income of all household groups increase; however, large-farm households are found to receive proportionately larger income gains than small-farm households, suggesting a negative equity effect of the Green Revolution. Under a counterfactual policy scenario, trade liberalization generally increases the sectoral income benefits from crop productivity growth, especially for the trade-oriented sectors. Small-farm households are the biggest gainers among the five household groups, while Metro Manila households are the biggest losers. The effect on real GDP is also significantly positive, so that the movement toward unrestricted trade does not involve a trade-off between the twin objectives of growth and equity. These results from CGE analysis support the conclusion that a substantial liberalization of the trade regime during the Green Revolution period would have enhanced the contribution of agricultural productivity growth to the achievement of more rapid and egalitarian growth in the Philippines.

Trade Policy Reform, Economic Growth, and Equity

Historically, import protection policies in developing countries have resulted in a significant bias against export production, not only causing a misallocation of scarce domestic resources, but also reducing the country's capacity to benefit from potential learning experiences and develop the competitive (as opposed to rent-seeking) behavior that arises from participation in contestable foreign markets. It is not surprising, therefore, that the total factor productivity (TFP) and international competitiveness of domestic industries are adversely affected by a restrictive trade regime (Chenery, Robinson, and Syrquin 1986), lowering the rate of economic growth. TFP growth is found to increase significantly as trade policy based on import substitution shifts toward export-oriented policies, other things remaining the same. Moreover, a positive long-run relationship is often observed in developing countries between export and GDP growth rates.[11] These considerations contribute to the empirical justification for liberalizing the trade regime and promoting more export-oriented economic growth.

After examining 36 episodes of trade liberalization involving 19 countries, Michaely, Papengiorgiou, and Choksi (1991) concluded that in general economic growth does not suffer even in the short run. Because pre-reform policy typically discriminates against agriculture, liberalization leads quickly to an improvement in agricultural growth performance. The protected manufacturing sector is observed to slow down soon after the policy reform, but growth returns to the pre-liberalization rate within about a year.

In the Philippine context, a number of studies provide abundant evidence that the country's protracted import substitution policies effectively held back output growth in the industrial sector and in the national economy.[12] It has also been shown that export orientation is a significant determinant of manufacturing productivity growth; other things being the same, the larger the export share in industry output, the higher is the TFP growth rate (Hooley 1985).

Capital equipment and machinery were considered "essential" producer goods, and as such were allowed to be imported more liberally than other product categories. This was the case under the earlier regime of direct import and foreign exchange controls, and was subsequently also the case under the highly distorted tariff structure that served to perpetuate the low nominal protection on capital goods. Moreover, the fiscal incentives package and preferential access to low-interest credit given to BOI-registered enterprises had a capital-cheapening effect. All this, combined with the prevailing exchange rate overvaluation, led to a substantial capital-use bias in the structure of industrial growth. Not only were capital-intensive industries favored, but within these industries the choice of technology was skewed toward the use of capital, and against labor employment. The large capital requirements of import-substituting industrialization in the Philippines, reflected in the incremental capital–output ratios for the manufacturing sector and the national economy (which were high by developing country standards), "undermined the efficiency of translating a high level of investment into growth" (Power 1983: 27).

Despite the labor surplus character of the Philippine economy, the contribution of labor-intensive manufactured products to total exports was insignificant throughout the 1950s and 1960s. It may seem paradoxical—but can be attributed to the nature of the economic policies adopted—that export industries with a lower (direct and indirect) labor content increased their share in total exports relative to the more labor-using sectors (Bautista 1975). While labor-intensive manufactured exports began to expand in the 1970s, the incentive structure favored heavy reliance on imported inputs, reducing the possibilities for intersectoral backward linkages. Had the foreign trade regime been more neutral, labor employment and the use of locally produced inputs in export production would have been greater. This would have increased the utilization of the unskilled labor force and, because the poor comprised the bulk of the unemployed and underemployed, reduced poverty and income inequality.

Poverty has been and continues to be widespread among the rural population (see Balisacan, Chapter 10). Rural poverty is attributable to the low agricultural productivity and related lack of employment opportunities in rural areas, and to the inability of the industrial sector to expand labor demand rapidly enough (Balisacan 1992). The large size of the rural labor force and high degree of its underutilization argue strongly for the need to generate productive employment within the rural sector. This did not happen in the past, owing in part to policy biases against agriculture in the form of price disincentives and inadequate infrastructure investments (see David, Chapter 6).

Because agricultural output in the Philippines has a high degree of tradability, the RER overvaluation arising from the restrictive trade regime and at times imprudent macroeconomic policies effectively lowered the relative domestic prices of agricultural products, output levels, and farm incomes. The latter effects are found generally to have been significant—as calculated in an empirical study using a single-crop partial equilibrium framework (Intal and Power 1990). Agricultural exports were more heavily penalized than import-competing food products, taking into account both product price disincentives and input subsidies. Based on a model of the agricultural sector incorporating the food export crop trade-off in production, it has been estimated that, in the absence of trade policy-induced domestic price distortions, agricultural crop income in the Philippines would have been higher by as much as 31% during the 1970s (Bautista 1986a).

An economy-wide input–output framework, in which sectoral output is determined only by its effective price (hence, by the sectoral EPR) and the own-price supply elasticity (that is, no cross-price effects), was used to investigate the effects of the removal of export taxes in 1986 (PIDS/TC 1986), of tariff reform in 1981–85 (Medalla 1986), and of the tariff rate changes under EO 470 and import liberalization in 1991–95 (Tan 1995). The induced changes in sectoral output are assumed to affect national income, sectoral demand, exports and imports, and government revenue in a recursive fashion. Alternative scenarios of fixed and flexible real exchange rates are examined, significant differences being indicated in the corresponding results. Thus, in Tan's study, total output is calculated to increase by 3.8% in the flexible RER case but only by 0.5% under a fixed RER; production of exportables goes up by 11.5% and production of importables by 4.0% under a flexible RER, compared with 5.6 and –2.8% respectively in the fixed RER scenario. These results point to the need for a depreciation of the real exchange rate to ensure the effectiveness of trade policy reform.

In examining quantitatively the income and equity effects of trade and exchange rate policies, general equilibrium modeling is preferable to the partial equilibrium and multi-market approaches—which abstract from many important factors operating simultaneously and interactively. In the Philippines, for example, agriculture has strong linkages to the rest of the economy, especially on the demand side, that need to be taken into account.[13] Empirical models of the CGE type give emphasis to the consistency of intersectoral linkages in production, consumption, and trade, as well as the endogenous determination of relative prices subject to relevant macroeconomic and institutional constraints. Evaluation of the economy-wide effects of policy changes is based on comparisons of the model's counterfactual equilibrium solutions and the base period values.

Clarete and Roumasset (1987), employing a CGE model of the Philippine economy with seven production sectors, find that complete trade liberalization would shift capital and labor resources largely from the more capital-intensive, import-substituting sector to the production of cash crops, agricultural food, and industrial exportables. The former sector would suffer a 39% reduction in income, whereas the latter sectors would gain by 31%, 24%, and 27% respectively. National income would increase by 3.4%, and the wage–rental ratio by 9%—suggesting a positive redistribution effect (in the absence of a household disaggregation in the model). These are considered long-run effects, since the model adopts the neoclassical assumption of equalizing factor prices, including rental rates to capital, across sectors.

Based on a 10-sector CGE model that distinguishes between rural and urban households (Bautista 1986b), adoption of a uniform tariff rate of 10% and removal of agricultural export taxes are found to result in a 2.8% increase in national income, with the distribution of income gains favoring rural households (3.4%) over urban households (1.6%). Since there is a greater concentration of low-income households in rural areas, a likely favorable impact of trade policy reform on income distribution is suggested by the above findings. Notably, agricultural crop income increases significantly (by 6.2%), but there is a decline in government income (of 12.8%), implying that the revenue loss from the reduced trade tax rate exceeds the revenue gain from the larger trade tax base and from the higher incomes of households and enterprises.

The economy-wide effects of the 1991–95 tariff cuts under EO 470 are investigated in Manasan (1991), using a 14-sector CGE model (developed earlier by Habito 1987) that differentiates among 10 household groups by income size. The results show higher total output, exports, and imports but a lower wage–rental ratio. Aggregate household income in real terms increases by 1.4%, the middle-income household groups receiving relatively larger income gains. The latter findings suggest that the tariff liberalization undertaken in the first half of the 1990s had very little impact on poverty and income inequality.

While the qualitative outcomes conform to expectations, these simulation results of trade policy reform, especially the aggregate income and equity effects, are relatively modest. This is due in part to the use of static CGE models based on a fixed sectoral allocation of capital as observed in the base period. In a dynamic context, additional income gains (in the aggregate) would be generated by intersectoral capital flows arising from the changing relative profitabilities induced by the shift in trade policy. Also, there would be improvements in overall productivity at the sectoral level, since greater openness, as indicated above, is conducive to increased competition, better economies of scale, and more rapid adoption of labor skills and new technologies. Moreover, there are positive intertemporal income benefits implied by the larger domestic savings made possible by the observed rise in national income that would finance additional investments.

The aforementioned studies seek to evaluate the effects of trade policy reform, hypothetical or actually implemented, in isolation from other policy changes and other influences on economic performance. The effectiveness of policy reforms may also be evaluated in terms of the observed changes in indicators of economic performance during the reform period. The appropriateness of this analytical approach depends on whether or not other determining factors have exerted a significant influence during the period. In Medalla et al. (1995/96), actual changes in the manufacturing sector and some specific industries between 1983 and 1988 are examined with a view to assessing the impact of trade policy reform on industrial performance. Clearly, those changes represent only a partial response to the trade policy reforms, which spanned the entire decade of the 1980s and are indeed still continuing. The choice of the two end-years was dictated by the availability of plant-level data from the 1983 and 1988 manufacturing censuses.

In terms of output performance, the manufacturing sector (as well as the national economy) exhibited a U-shaped pattern for the 1983–88 period. There was negative growth in the 1984–85 crisis years and a slow recovery in the following three years, attributable more to the fiscal and monetary policies adopted and the change in political leadership than to the trade liberalization measures implemented. While the latter may not have significantly influenced manufacturing output performance in the aggregate, the study finds that there were visible changes in industrial structure and efficiency between 1983 and 1988 associated with the increased incentive neutrality arising from trade policy reform. More specifically, there was:

- increased availability of imports, indicated by the ratio of imports to GNP;
- increased export orientation of the economy, indicated by the ratio of exports to GDP;
- reduced concentration of manufacturing industries, indicated by the value added concentration ratio (four-plant, three-digit);
- a compositional shift toward smaller plants, indicated by the average employment size of manufacturing plants;

- greater regional dispersal of industries, indicated by the share of Metro Manila in total manufacturing output; and
- increased efficiency of resource use among manufacturing plants, indicated by the ratio of *domestic resource cost* to the *shadow exchange rate*.

An extension of this study undertaken by Pineda (1997) confirms the above results for 1992, indicating sustainability of results from continued trade policy reform. These findings lend support to various hypotheses concerning the favorable effects of policy reform toward a more open trade regime in the Philippines. The further effects on overall income growth and equity are presumably positive, but cannot be verified from a simple comparison of observed values in 1983 and 1988 given the more dominant influence of other factors.

Trade Policy Reform Alone Is Not Enough

That Philippine economic growth was neither rapid nor stable over the past two decades of significant trade liberalization would seem to imply that trade policy reform did not provide a sufficient basis for sustained growth. Indeed, apart from the negative effects of non-economic factors on the country's economic performance (domestic political turmoil in the 1980s and natural disasters in the early 1990s), bouts of macroeconomic instability would have impaired the effectiveness of a more liberalized trade regime during the period.

Trade policy reform works best under stable macroeconomic conditions (Rodrik 1992: 88–9); otherwise, it is difficult to sustain the improvements in the price incentive structure and sectoral allocation of scarce resources that trade liberalization is meant to achieve. It is not surprising, therefore, that there was an acceleration of annual GDP growth beginning in 1991 and continuing until 1996 (up to the Asian crisis), a period of recovery from natural disasters, political instability, and macroeconomic imbalances. Moreover, the Ramos administration undertook to improve substantially what can be referred to collectively as competition policies (Bautista and Lamberte 1996). Apart from the significant reduction in trade barriers, the government adopted various economic liberalization measures to lower barriers to entry for foreign investors, deregulate many service industries, and increase private sector participation in infrastructure projects (see Abrenica and Llanto, Chapter 8).

A history of inward-looking trade policy has been at the root of the long-term sluggishness of the Philippine economy. An important lesson from recent experience, however, is that trade policy reform is not a panacea for sustained growth. Trade liberalization can contribute to a policy environment supportive of broadly based employment and income expansion; as argued above, this is necessary to sustain the overall growth process. Its effectiveness in promoting the twin objectives of economic growth and equity depends on whether other, so-called complementary, policies are undertaken concurrently. In the past, significant reform efforts toward a more open trade regime had been undermined by RER appreciation, fiscal imbalances, and external debt problems, not to mention political instability, under which all growth-promoting policy efforts would likely be unproductive.

In a sense there has been an asymmetry in the historical influence of trade policy on Philippine economic performance. The heavily protectionist trade regime was a major contributor to the country's economic disarray and income inequity for three decades in the postwar period—which trade policy reform during the 1980s and 1990s did not substantially alleviate. One can say, however, that the shift in trade policy resulted in an improved "enabling environment" for equitable growth, to which complementary reforms in other policies also need to contribute. In this context, the recent signs of a retreat from trade liberalization (see below) are disturbing. Reverting to the bad old ways of domestic protectionism would undo past efforts to deal with a major impediment to sustained growth of the Philippine economy.

5.5 OTHER INTERNATIONAL ECONOMIC TRANSACTIONS

Foreign Direct Investment

Very much linked to the performance of the export sector are inflows of of FDI. Long-term capital inflows have been rising at double-digit rates since 1980, except during 1986–90 (Table 5.5), a time of great political and economic uncertainty following the period of martial law under President Marcos.[14] The liberalization of existing regulations on FDI following the passage of the Foreign Investments Act of 1991, which allowed foreign equity participation of up to 100% in all investment areas not on the Foreign Investment Negative List (see Abrenica and Llanto, Chapter 8), the easing of political tensions in the early 1990s, as well as the perceived resolve to pursue trade liberalization and deregulation, all contributed to improving the FDI climate from the mid-1990s until the outbreak of the Asian crisis. However, relative to other ASEAN countries, the Philippines is a veritable laggard in terms of attracting FDI (Figure 5.5).

Traditionally, the main source of Philippine FDI has been the triad of the United States, the European Union, and Japan, which in 1997 accounted for about two-thirds of the total. The United States has emerged as the country's most important source of FDI in recent years, due mainly to the continued strong growth of the American economy (whereas Japan has been floundering since 1990). However, overall dependence on the triad has gone down since 1980, when it accounted for four-fifths of total FDI. In contrast, the share of the NIEs rose from 6% in 1980 to 25% in 2000.

In terms of its sectoral distribution, FDI has been concentrated in the manufacturing sector (Figure 5.6). However, with the policy of deregulation and privatization adopted under the Ramos administration especially (1992–98), FDI began to flow steadily into the services sector in the 1990s. For instance, the deregulation of major utility sectors (water, communications, transport) led to a marked increase in the share of public utilities in FDI, from 5% in 1980 to 30% in 2000. Liberalization in the financial sector continued to draw capital inflows from foreign sources during the second half of the 1990s.

Manufacturing has been the most attractive host sector for FDI, in large part because of the protected nature of the domestic market as well as the regulatory con-

Table 5.5 Inward Stock of Foreign Direct Investment, 1980–2000

	1980	1985	1990	1995	2000
Total FDI ($ million)	1,280.9	2,600.6	3,267.9	6,085.9	12,688.0
Average annual growth rate of FDI stock (%)		15.4	4.7	13.3	16.0
Average annual world inflation (%)[a]		12.8	16.7	16.4	5.5
Average annual real growth rate of FDI stock (%)		2.6	–12.0	–3.1	10.5

a   Producer price index: 1995 = 100.

Sources: Bangko Sentral ng Pilipinas (1997), *Selected Philippine Economic Indicators*; UNCTAD (2000); IMF (2001).

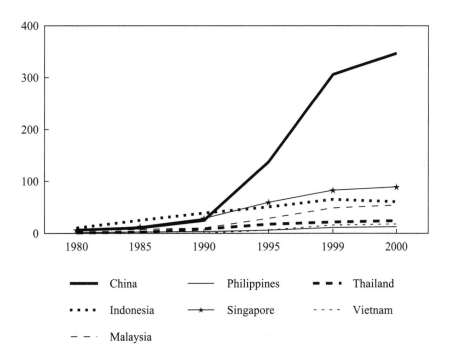

Figure 5.5 Inward Stock of Foreign Direct Investment in Selected Asian Countries, 1980–2000 ($ billion)

Source: United Nations (2001), *World Investment Report 2001*.

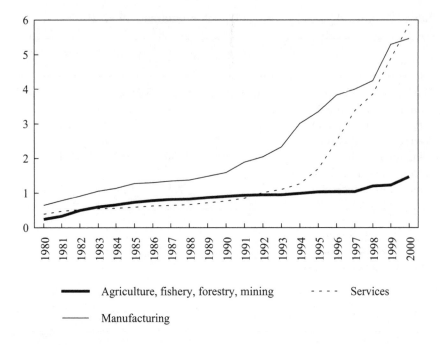

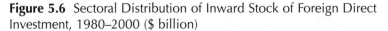

Figure 5.6 Sectoral Distribution of Inward Stock of Foreign Direct Investment, 1980–2000 ($ billion)

Source: Bangko Sentral ng Pilipinas (2000, 2001), *Selected Philippine Economic Indicators.*

trol of government over the services sector in the past. With trade liberalization being pursued vigorously in the 1990s, the import-substituting manufacturing sector lost some of its atttraction. Table 5.6 shows the marked shift in FDI toward export-oriented industries, primarily resulting from the rise in the share of electronics (part of the machinery, apparatus, and appliances industry group) in 1995.[15] The shift of investment registrations to the export-processing zones—with a lower level of dependence on the tax exemptions, subsidized credit, and other fiscal incentives offered by the BOI—also attests to the growing outward orientation of new investments. Foreign multinationals began to take stock of the country's commitment to a more open trading policy and its relatively abundant supply of semi-skilled/technical labor. The possibilities for "splicing the value chain" through flexible manufacturing and assigning the stage of value adding according to the country's relatively abundant factor have fostered greater complementarity between trade and FDI. The exporting activity of the multinationals is behind much of the recent impressive growth in microelectronic exports (semiconductors, computer parts and components, telecommunications equipment), which have emerged as the country's top exports.

FDI represents a supplementary source of savings to help raise total investment and enhance output and employment growth. Its direct linkage to the world market,

Table 5.6 Distribution of Manufacturing Foreign Direct Investment, 1973–2000 (%)

Manufacturing Industry	1973	1980	1985	1990	1995	2000
Import-substituting	69.9	73.8	78.4	72.9	52.4	87.5
Food	6.1	13.7	22.1	19.6	3.1	46.0
Chemicals & chemical products	9.3	29.2	26.5	27.0	10.7	34.4
Petroleum	41.8	4.6	6.2	5.2	12.9	0.0
Metal & metal products	3.5	15.8	13.1	10.8	6.9	3.3
Non-metallic mineral products	3.2	2.1	2.6	3.1	3.1	0.0
Transport equipment	5.9	8.5	7.9	7.3	15.7	3.8
Export-oriented	15.4	11.6	10.1	14.8	43.1	10.9
Textiles & garments	12.7	5.6	4.4	5.1	3.7	0.3
Machinery, apparatus, appliances	2.7	6.0	5.7	9.8	39.3	10.5
Other	14.7	14.5	11.5	12.2	4.5	1.6
Total	100.0	100.0	100.0	100.0	100.0	100.0

Source: Bangko Sentral ng Pilipinas (various years), *Selected Philippine Economic Indicators*.

in terms of access to both output and inputs as well as to improved technologies and management practices, also makes the encouragement of FDI economically desirable. However, these advantages of FDI do not warrant government policies biased toward foreign investors, or the provision of more liberal fiscal incentives than are available in neighboring Asian countries competing for foreign capital. As pointed out in Medalla et al. (1995/96: 53):

> A good climate for investment, both the domestic and foreign, and an expectation of stability and consistency in the economic policy regime can be of greater importance than tax exemptions and credits … Moreover, favorable conditions regarding repatriation of earnings and capital, as well as employment of foreign nationals in key positions, may be more politically acceptable than discriminatory fiscal incentives.

Indeed, regression analysis of the determinants of FDI in the Philippines finds that the fiscal incentive system is not a significant explanatory variable (Mercado-Aldaba 1995). However, the effective protection rate is found to be a significant determinant, and this is consistent with the observed shift of foreign investments toward increased export orientation as the trade regime became more open from the mid-1980s. In producing along the lines of the country's comparative advantage, export-oriented foreign enterprises contribute to a higher growth rate of domestic output, to an improved utilization of the labor force, and presumably also to the reduction of income inequality.

Portfolio Investments

A sharp increase in portfolio investment inflows can be observed in the mid-1990s, particularly from the world's monetary centers, namely the United Kingdom (which surpassed Hong Kong during the second half of the 1990s), the United States, and Singapore. These capital inflows were triggered by the capital liberalization policy of 1992, which allowed generally unhindered movement of short-term capital into and out of the country. In 1995 and 1996 as well as in 1999, the value of portfolio investments surpassed even that of net FDI (Figure 5.7).

Over time, there have been considerable changes in the distribution of portfolio investments in the Philippines. The traditional mainstays (banks, commerce/industry, finance, mining), which in 1990 accounted for 98% of portfolio investments, saw their share decline with the rise in share of the "new" sectors (communications, power/energy, holding firms, property). In other words, like FDI, portfolio investments flowed into the newly deregulated service sectors of the economy.

The opening up of the capital market certainly made foreign exchange management more complex than before. It is very likely that the relatively large net inflows of both short and long-term capital, especially in the mid-1990s, were partly responsible for the tendency of the peso to appreciate during the period immediately preceding the regional crisis. The currency appreciation in turn made exports less competitive than they would otherwise have been. It likewise cheapened imports, exacerbating the pressure on the trade balance following the lowering of import barriers. The strong peso—and the expectation of continued appreciation—emboldened investors to accumulate dollar-denominated debts for lending in local currency. This eventually led to the accumulation of non-performing loans and insolvency of many banks following the steep depreciation of the peso in the wake of the regional crisis.

Any form of capital inflow helps to augment domestic savings and accommodate current account deficits—which in the Philippine context is an important consideration. The volatility of portfolio investments is, however, a source of policy concern. The sudden reversal in financial flows during 1994–98 shown in Figure 5.7 (in contrast to the relative stability of net FDI) is intimately related to the systemic instability of short-term capital flows that arguably was the primary cause of the Asian crisis (Radelet and Sachs 1998). Even so, a stronger domestic financial sector and better prudential controls would reduce any country's vulnerability to the intrinsic volatility of global investment funds. In the process of strengthening the financial system, protection from surges in capital inflows can be provided by restrictions on short-term liabilities, such as unremunerated reserve requirements and minimum holding periods that make capital inflows more costly the shorter the maturity (Asian Policy Forum 2000).

Remittances

Remittances from overseas Filipino workers (OFWs) have emerged as another important source of foreign exchange inflows, becoming more so throughout the 1990s (see Herrin and Pernia, Chapter 9). In 1997, remittances that passed through

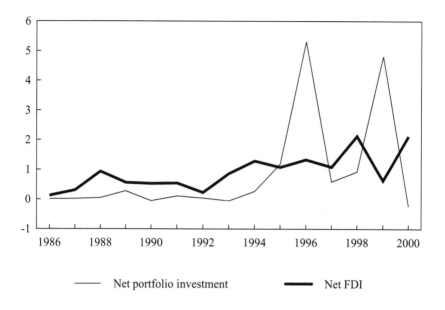

Figure 5.7 Net Portfolio Investments and Net Foreign Direct Investment, 1986–2000 ($ billion)

Source: IMF (2001), *International Financial Statistics*.

the banking system amounted to some $5.7 billion. In terms of their relative importance, they constituted about 20% and 70% of the country's export earnings and services income, respectively.

The overwhelming reason for the outflow of workers is the failure of the country's labor markets to generate enough (sufficiently lucrative) employment for its nationals. Nominal wages have risen in spite of widespread unemployment, leading to a gradual loss of comparative advantage in labor-intensive production to countries like China, Vietnam, and Indonesia. On the other hand, real wages have generally stayed flat, because the growth in nominal wages was eaten up by inflation.

OFWs were attracted to the Middle East during the oil and subsequent construction boom of the 1970s. With the discovery of alternative sources of energy and the slump in oil prices since the early 1990s, the tide of OFWs to the Middle East began to ebb. They began to shift to other destinations, particularly booming Asian economies such as Singapore, Malaysia, Thailand, and Indonesia. One can glean the structure of foreign demand for Filipino workers from the distribution of OFWs by type of occupation (Table 5.7). About 80% are in service and production-related fields, with professional and technical workers making up another 12%.

The economic and social benefits and costs of international migration from the Philippines are examined in Rodriguez (1998). Direct economic benefits come in the form of the increased incomes of households through remittances. Estimates of net benefits in 1991 amount to between 2.4% and 4.5% of GDP.[16] These gains

Table 5.7 Distribution of Overseas Filipino Workers by Occupation, 1991 and 1996 (%)

Type of Occupation	1991	1996
Professional, technical, related	12.7	12.0
Administrative, executive, managerial	0.4	0.4
Clerical and sales	5.0	4.1
Service	37.1	41.3
Agricultural, animal husbandry, forestry, fishing, hunting	0.5	1.3
Production and related workers, transport equipment workers, laborers	44.4	40.0
Workers not classified elsewhere by profession	–	0.9

Source: Bureau of Labor and Employment Statistics, Department of Labor and Employment (1999), *Yearbook of Labor Statistics*.

decline to between 1.2% and 2.6% of GDP after correction for the loss in positive externalities resulting from the emigration of skilled migrants. Other economic benefits flow from the alleviation of financial constraints and urban unemployment, as well as the technological transfer that can result from Filipinos working overseas. On the social cost side must be reckoned the occurrences of broken families, illness (including AIDS and psychological disturbances), and incarceration (or even the death penalty) while the Filipino worker is abroad, and possibly increased income inequality.

The income distributional effects of migration are less well understood. It is readily taken for granted that because remittances augment incomes, and since there is a large number of beneficiaries as well as increasing participation by rural families, international migration must automatically contribute to an improvement in income distribution. However, the literature on the subject yields ambiguous results. In the Philippines, casual evidence indicates that migrants come from better-educated, wealthier, urban households. Based on Rodriguez (1998), income distribution apparently worsens when overseas remittances are factored into household incomes, with the Gini coefficient rising more for rural than for urban households.

5.6 EMERGING ISSUES

The Backlash of Protectionism

While the policy of unilateral trade liberalization has succeeded in bringing down tariff and non-tariff barriers, there have been attempts in certain quarters to hold back the liberalization effort. Unfortunately, the difficulties of recovery from the recent crisis have provided a convenient excuse for such protectionist moves. The clamor for a slowing of or halt to liberalization, or even a reversal of previous modifications to the tariff schedule, seems to have mounted. In early 1999, EO 63 adjusted tariff modifications upward for six industries: textiles and apparel, iron and steel, pulp and paper, petrochemicals, batteries, and pocket lighters. The petrochemicals industry demanded that the average tariff on its products of 15% in 2000 be maintained until 2010. Moreover, a *modus vivendi* has been forged with downstream industries to ask for higher tariff rates on plastic products in order to accommodate the 15% tariff on imports of petrochemicals. This could lead to other industries claiming similar protection. A snowballing of protectionism could ultimately lead to a suspension, if not the scrapping, of the uniform tariff policy slated for 2004.

Even on the regional front, the action of Malaysia in asking for automobiles to be returned to the temporary exclusion list has emboldened the Philippine government (read: the Department of Trade and Industry) to ask for a similar concession for petrochemicals. Likewise, the Philippines, together with a number of other developing countries, has asked the World Trade Organization (WTO) for a postponement of the deadline for the scrapping of the domestic content requirements for automobiles. One can thus expect at least a standstill in protection policy—if not an increase in protection on automobile assembly and auto parts—given the alleged acquiescence of the WTO in this request for postponement. Such reversals in liberalization policy, especially with regard to agricultural products, may run counter to the country's commitments under the ASEAN Free Trade Area (AFTA).

Agricultural protection is a problematic point in the liberalization effort. In 1996, in line with the country's commitment to the WTO, the government eased restrictions on imports of agricultural products (with the exception of rice) and tariffied them under Republic Act (RA) 8178 and EO 313. Two rates were set for products with a minimum access volume (MAV): a lower duty for imports within the MAV (in-quota rates) and a higher duty for those in excess of the MAV (out-quota rates). The latter could initially be set at a maximum of 100% for some products, but had to be reduced over five years. Such tariffication explains the resulting dispersion of tariff rates in 1996 beyond the maximum 50% rate. Moreover, within the manufacturing sector, EPRs are currently highest for food products. Obtained under the WTO, the high and binding tariffs on these products and the exemption of rice from coverage have already escalated into demands for greater protection. The protection accorded corn (of 65% for corn, whole grains, as of 2000), on the grounds that trade liberalization would displace poor small corn producers, has led to increases in protection obtained against imports of hogs and poultry (45–60% as of 2000) and processed meat (65%). The intention, of course, is to compensate producers for the high tariff on corn. A similar 65% (out-quota) tariff rate has been obtained for raw sugar, 60% for coffee, 65% for extracts, essence and concentrates of coffee, and 60% for onions and garlic. Even the implementation guidelines of the MAV are said to have ensured that quantitative restrictions will remain operative, in spite of the tariffication (David 1997).

The Imperative of Competitiveness

During the decade before the Asian crisis, Philippine economic growth had been less rapid than that of most other economies in the Asian region, investment flows among the lowest, and inflation rates among the highest (World Bank 1997a). The country's protracted history of import substitution hardly helped to provide the right environment for the emergence of a culture of world class competitiveness among entrepreneurs and workers, so crucial in the present globalization era. A sense of urgency to become and remain competitive must be gained if industries and firms are to survive the cold, rough winds of international competition. For this, a truly outward-oriented macro and microeconomic environment must be fostered—hence the need to sustain the drive toward liberalization and increasing openness to both trade and foreign investment.

Due to its relatively higher labor costs, the Philippines has already begun to lose its comparative advantage in unskilled labor-intensive production to countries such as China, Vietnam, and Indonesia. Fortunately, its history of educating a relatively high proportion of its people, and the large pool of teachable workers still possessing the skill to speak—or at least comprehend—the English language give it some comparative edge in simple, semi-skilled labor-intensive goods in flexible manufacturing, such as back-end semiconductors and computer parts. However, such an advantage risks being a temporary one, given the rapid pace of development in the region. The Philippines must ensure—at the very least—that it *maintains* that edge through sustained investments in human capital. This implies continual investments in human resource development and skills training relevant to the needs of the market. Moreover, other complementary capital is required, such as investments in competitively priced, good-quality infrastructure, power, transport, communications, and industrial locations. In addition, since the cost of doing business in the country is often raised unduly by poor governance, attention will have to be paid to minimizing, if not eradicating, corruption at all levels and to providing a better-quality public service.

Trade Liberalization and the Environment

Given the dire statistics on the extent of environmental degradation in the country, it is legitimate to ask to what extent economic activity in general and foreign trade in particular have impacted on the environment. Intal (1996) has noted that, due to the incentive system created by the macroeconomic and industrial policies of the 1960s and 1970s, the industrial sector failed to evolve according to the country's comparative advantage in unskilled labor-intensive goods, forcing reliance on resource-intensive exports to generate the needed foreign exchange. Coupled with the underpricing of natural resource extraction and the poor implementation of resource protection measures, this meant "mining" of the country's renewable resources (especially, forests and fisheries) beyond sustainable levels. Thus, even in the context of slow economic growth, the failure to internalize environmental costs and manage resources adequately has led to many of the present ecological problems in the Philippines.

The production of specific traded goods is associated with some amount of environmental stress. Examples are shrimp production, which has led to a substantial decline in the hectarage of mangrove forests as these were transformed into aquaculture farms, and electronics production, which is a major source of highly toxic substances. Thus trade liberalization, to the extent that it causes a shift of resources to environment-intensive (or pollution-intensive) exports, may bring about more environmental damage.

A static simulation model linking trade liberalization to resource allocation in the Philippines suggests a possible trade-off between the implied gains in efficiency from trade opening and the cost of environmental degradation (Intal 1996). Trade liberalization appears to raise the national average pollution intensity of production due to the reallocation of resources to industries with large off-site environmental damages (logging, mining, agriculture), as well as to manufacturing industries with higher pollution intensities (food processing, beverages, wood products). However, the model does not capture the dynamic effects of the trade reform process, namely that increased trade brings about higher income, which in turn is associated with reduced environmental damage. In a two-equation model applied to provincial China, Dean (1999) finds a positive terms of trade effect of trade liberalization—but a negative and significant effect of income growth—on emissions growth.

It cannot be denied that the Philippines would benefit immensely from a balanced approach toward outward orientation that went hand in hand with stronger domestic environmental management. To this end, in-depth studies are needed to determine the extent and nature of the trade-off between efficiency and sustainable development in order to arrive at rational and effective macro and microeconomic policy approaches. Coxhead and Jayasuriya (Chapter 12) is a useful road map to the issues involved in such studies.

Regional and Multilateral Trading Arrangements

The Philippines has undertaken a program of trade liberalization that is both wide (that is, covering all manufactured goods) and deep. It aims ambitiously for a uniform 5% tariff by 2004. Unilateral liberalization, at least for the moment, goes farther than all the country's commitments to the multilateral and regional arrangements to which it is a party. Being unilateral, this reduction in trade barriers does not require reciprocity in terms of market access. It is therefore in the interest of the Philippines to keep markets open worldwide, on both the multilateral and regional fronts. The country is actively engaged in regional integration arrangements with its Southeast Asian neighbors (through ASEAN) and with countries in the Asia Pacific (through the Asia Pacific Economic Cooperation (APEC) process), and is a member of the WTO. As an AFTA participant, the Philippines has studied the possibility of forming a free trade area with Australia and New Zealand, while engaging Northeast Asian countries—Japan, Korea, and China—in periodic dialogues, as in the ASEAN Plus Three ministerial meetings. In particular, the economic cooperation being forged between ASEAN and China promises to lead to closer integration between them.

Various explanations have been offered for the recent interest in regional integration arrangements (Frankel 1997). Whatever the motivations, regional blocs have mushroomed. More than 80 such regional agreements were set up in the 1990s, in contrast to the 75 or so established in the previous four decades. Moreover, a number of characteristics set these agreements apart from those formed earlier, namely their generally outward-oriented approach; the forging of agreements along North–South lines; their extension beyond trade-related agreements ("shallow integration") to deeper forms of integration that include investment liberalization and policy harmonization (competition policy, intellectual property rights, mutual recognition arrangements, and so on); and the geographic reach of such agreements to encompass even countries belonging to different continents—for example, Mercosur with the European Union, or the North American Free Trade Area (NAFTA) with the European Union and APEC.

Given the overwhelming trend toward regional bloc formation, which is in essence discriminatory to non-members, the question becomes whether it is in the interest of the Philippines to remain outside these blocs (and concentrate on multilateral trade liberalization efforts) or be actively engaged in their formation. A difficulty with multilateral agreements is that the large number of negotiating countries can weaken the pressure for substantial reductions in trade barriers. For instance, the trade concessions made by the Philippines under the WTO are actually much smaller than those it is undertaking for manufactured goods under its unilateral trade liberalization policy. Moreover, WTO agreements on tariffication of existing quantitative restrictions have actually raised tariffs on certain agricultural products way beyond the levels envisioned by Philippine trade policy reform. Whatever the response, the motivation has to be the expansion of export opportunities and investment flows, and not losing the momentum toward increasing openness, in order to help accelerate Philippine economic growth and make it sustainable.

In the context of a future agenda for negotiation within the WTO system, an emerging issue meriting close attention concerns the relationship between international trade and environmental and labor standards. Anxiety about degradation of the environment and human rights abuses in the workplace has ostensibly motivated influential groups in some developed countries to advance proposals linking trade and social standards—in essence, using trade-restrictive measures to achieve environmental and labor objectives. Understandably, the response from some developing countries has been negative, with them branding such efforts as disguised protectionism that could undermine their export competitiveness and slow their economic growth. Indeed, low environmental and labor standards in developing countries in part reflect existing resource endowments and social preferences. As such, they represent "a legitimate source of comparative advantage" (Anderson 1998: 250) that can only be undercut by trade-restrictive measures. At earlier stages of their development, now-industrialized countries also had lower labor standards, and surely their contribution to global environmental problems is vastly greater than that of developing countries.

Social standards will improve over time as incomes increase, and this process can be facilitated by unrestricted trade. The first-best policy would be to address the source of the problem directly, and threats of trade sanctions do not do this. Income transfers to bring about improvements in environmental and labor standards (which have to be financed in some way), along with other non-trade measures, might be feasible. Empirical analyses need to flesh out the abstract arguments and assess the effectiveness of alternative approaches. It is in the interest of the Philippines to examine the possible repercussions on the domestic economy arising from various scenarios dealing with the "linkage issue," a matter that is likely to command attention in any future multilateral trade negotiations.

5.7 CONCLUSION

The international dimensions of Philippine economic development appear to have improved, if rather haltingly, over the past half-century. The evolution of the trade regime mirrors the general experience of developing countries that were slow to exploit the potentially large static and dynamic gains from foreign trade. The severity and protracted nature of import protection policies adopted in the Philippines during the 1950s and 1960s led to a heavy bias against export production, penalizing agriculture and labor-intensive industries, in which the country had a comparative advantage. In the 1970s, selective export promotion not only favored large enterprises, the adoption of capital-intensive technologies, and heavy reliance on imported inputs, but also failed to compensate fully for the pervasive bias against exporting in the incentive system. The primary source of this bias was the highly protective tariff and import-licensing system, which was first addressed only in the early 1980s.

Unfortunately, the major attempt at trade liberalization initiated in 1981 was thwarted by the foreign exchange crisis that began in August 1983 and that resulted in significantly negative growth of the Philippine economy in the following two years. Although political turmoil and massive capital flight precipitated the foreign exchange crisis, rapid growth of the country's external debt and the sustained trade deficits that it required could have been avoided had macroeconomic policy been more prudent. The expansionary macroeconomic policy and heavy foreign borrowing in the wake of the 1973–74 and 1979–80 oil price hikes had led to a rapid increase in imports. This was not matched by a commensurate expansion of exports, largely because of the relative non-competitiveness of domestic industry. The latter can in turn be attributed to market price distortions arising from trade and exchange rate policies that prevented more rapid export growth and reduced the efficiency of investment. Not only would growth have been more sustainable had the foreign trade regime been more neutral, but labor employment and the use of locally produced inputs would have been greater. The choice of products and production technology would have favored increased utilization of the unskilled labor force and—because the poor account heavily for the unemployed and the underemployed—greater participation of the poor in the growth process.

An important consequence of trade liberalization during the 1980s and 1990s has been the observed shift in FDI in the direction of increasing export orientation. Previous import substitution policies had effectively encouraged foreign capital to enter the domestic market with capital-intensive technologies and exploit the Philippine consumer with high-cost production behind the heavy protection provided by tariff and non-tariff barriers. A more open trade regime proved less attractive to that kind of investment. Instead, foreign capital became more adaptable to the factor supply situation in the Philippines, producing more efficiently to provide low-cost goods to domestic consumers and compete effectively in the world market.

Developments since the early 1990s illuminate the need for a combination of enabling factors—including political stability, reduced macroeconomic imbalances, and, arising from trade liberalization and other "competition policy" reform measures, improved microeconomic efficiency—in achieving rapid economic growth. That significant equity improvement needs to accompany accelerated growth, in order to sustain it, is also given empirical support. A major challenge for Philippine policy-makers is to continue moving toward economic openness while ensuring that complementary macro and sectoral policies conducive to broad-based income growth are in place.

NOTES

1. See, among others, Corden (1965) and Bhagwati and Srinivasan (1979) for systematic discussion. More recently, it has been argued that in oligopolistic international markets, tariff protection can influence the market outcome and result in a net domestic welfare gain despite the attendant costs (Krugman 1987). The relevance of such a "strategic trade policy" for developing countries is questionable, considering the difficulty of identifying industries to be targeted for protection, the relative absence of active participants among less developed countries in international oligopoly markets, and the risk of provoking retaliation from the country's trade partners.

2. Derivation of RER overvaluation is based on an equilibrium RER under current account balance and no trade restrictions.

3. This reduction did not apply to 14 "strategic" industries that were subject to their own sectoral plans.

4. The IMF index is calculated using the consumer price index (CPI) as the price indicator for both the focus country (Philippines) and trade partners. Using the wholesale price index (WPI) for the trade partners (which better reflects the general level of traded goods prices) yields an average annual RER increase of 2.4% for 1980–89 (Bautista 1993: 356).

5. Under the eight-digit Harmonized System Code.

6. "Miscellaneous exports," making up about 1–3% of total exports, refer mainly to "articles of apparel and clothing accessories" and other miscellaneous manufactured articles (for example, toys, sporting goods).

7. A country j's RCA index in commodity i is measured as follows:

$$RCA_{ij} = (X_{ij}/X_j)/(X_{iw}/X_w)$$

where X_{ij}/X_j is the ratio of the export value of commodity i in country j to the total export value of j; and X_{iw}/X_w is the ratio of the export value of commodity i of the world to the total value of world exports.

8. It has been claimed that the classification of developing country exports into labor-intensive and capital/technology-intensive exports is becoming increasingly irrelevant due to the dominance of electronics exports, which in developing countries are mainly the back-end operations of multinational corporations utilizing cheap labor. While this is to a certain extent true, it cannot be denied that such exports (semiconductor packaging, assembly of computer-related components, and so on) are much more intensive in semi-skilled and technical labor as well as engineering services than traditional labor-intensive exports such as apparel and footwear. Tecson (2000) showed that the ratio of skilled to unskilled labor utilized in the electrical and electronics industry is almost double that in the textiles, apparel, and footwear industries. Moreover, comparative data show that general labor is clearly more expensive in the Philippines than in other countries in the region (China, Indonesia, Vietnam), but that the relative cost disadvantage becomes less obvious in the case of mid-level engineers and managers.

9. As suggested by Prema-Chandra Athukolara in a written comment on an earlier draft of this chapter, the alternative real exchange rate index represented by the ratio of domestic WPI to domestic CPI showed a continuing trend of appreciation even in 1998–99.

10. Not only rice but also other crops experienced substantial yield improvements during that period.

11. See, among others, Michaely (1977), Balassa (1978), and Ram (1985).

12. See Power and Sicat (1971), ILO (1974), Baldwin (1975), and Bautista, Power, and Associates (1979).

13. As reflected in the comparatively large income multipliers for agriculture derived from conventional social accounting matrix (SAM) analysis (Bautista 1997).

14. Given high average annual world inflation in the 1986–95 period, real FDI inflows into the country during this period may have been negative.

15. The steep decline in FDI inflows to export-oriented industries in 2000, particularly to machinery, apparatus, and appliances, reflects the worldwide slowdown in the electronics industry and lies outside the trend of the immediately preceding years.

16. The range is due to two scenarios considered by the author. The first assumes a labor surplus (that is, where marginal labor productivity is zero), so that the net benefits of migration are defined by the sum of the increase in incomes resulting from the average contribution of migrants and the increase in average savings resulting from the reduction in consumption after migration. The second assumes no labor surplus and that the average wages represent the loss of output due to migration.

PART III

The Sectors

6

Agriculture

Cristina C. David

6.1 INTRODUCTION

The nature and pace of agricultural growth is of strategic importance to the Philippines' overall economic development, food security, environmental sustainability, and poverty alleviation efforts. Agriculture continues to be a major source of income and employment, accounting for nearly half of the total labor force and contributing about 20% of GDP. When all economic activities related to agro-processing and the supply of non-farm agricultural inputs are included, the agricultural sector, broadly defined, accounts for about two-thirds of the labor force and 40% of GDP. Moreover, the sector has strong growth linkage effects on the rest of the economy as a source of supply of food and raw materials, and as a source of demand for non-agricultural inputs and consumer goods and services.

With almost 70% of the poor based in the rural sector and depending directly on agriculture-related economic activities for their major source of livelihood (see Balisacan, Chapter 10), the attainment of food security and alleviation of poverty requires rapid, sustainable, and equitable agricultural growth. In contrast to the political objective of food self-sufficiency, food security means ensuring that household incomes, especially those of the poor, are sufficient to purchase adequate food— whether imported or locally produced—at reasonable prices. However, many of the activities that accompany agricultural development—more extensive and intensive land cultivation, the expansion of fisheries and aquaculture, livestock and poultry production, and irrigation networks, as well as the use of pesticides, fertilizers, and other modern inputs—can also threaten the sustainability of the production environment and harm the health of the population.

Philippine agricultural growth has been erratic and slow since the 1980s. The sector performed well relative to other developing Asian countries in the 1970s because of the early advent of the Green Revolution in rice and the boom in world commodity prices. Over the past two decades, however, the Philippines has had one of the lowest average growth rates in gross value added (GVA) in agriculture and agricultural exports in South and Southeast Asia (Table 6.1). The sharp drop in world commodity prices in the 1980s undoubtedly contributed to the fall in growth rates, but the effects appear to have been much less pronounced in other countries. Indeed, agricultural growth accelerated throughout South Asia and in Indonesia in the 1980s with the spread of the Green Revolution, then in transition economies such as China and Vietnam following their shift to a more market-based economy.

This chapter argues that the poor performance of the Philippines in agriculture has been due more to weaknesses in the policy and institutional frameworks governing the sector than to real domestic and external market factors. Government policies distorted economic incentives; the choice of policy instruments promoted rent seeking and raised the economic cost of government interventions. The faulty design and implementation of public expenditure programs to provide public goods lowered the social rate of return on these investments. Similarly, the inadequate design and enforcement of regulatory instruments limited the government's effectiveness in addressing externalities. Weaknesses in the institutional structure of property rights and in land reform policies led to inefficiencies in land market operations and contributed to the degradation of natural resources. Likewise, problems in the institutional structure of the agricultural bureaucracy lowered the efficiency and effectiveness of government efforts to correct market failures.

Section 6.2 briefly describes the growth patterns of agricultural GVA, foreign trade, measures of comparative advantage, and labor and land productivity. The next two sections examine how price interventions and the public expenditure program failed to promote rapid growth of the sector. The fourth section focuses on institutional issues, specifically weaknesses in the property rights structure and the agricultural bureaucracy. The final section explores political economy explanations as to why the policy and institutional structures evolved in the way they did, and suggests directions for reform.

6.2 AGRICULTURAL PERFORMANCE

Gross Value Added

Table 6.2 shows average annual growth in GVA for major commodities over the past four decades. With the exception of livestock and poultry, the growth rates of all commodities have been decelerating over time, and have been below the population growth rate since the 1980s.

GVA in forestry in real terms has declined—by as much as 22% in the 1990s—reflecting the unsustainability of past forest management policies. From an average

Table 6.1 Average Growth Rates of Agricultural Gross Value Added and
Agricultural Exports in Selected Asian Countries, 1970–2000 (%)

Country	1970–80 GVA	1970–80 Exports	1980–90 GVA	1980–90 Exports	1990–2000 GVA	1990–2000 Exports[a]
Philippines[b]	4.9	14.6	1.0	–4.6	1.8	6.1
	(6.0)		(1.8)		(2.0)	
Indonesia	2.0	20.0	4.9	4.7	2.5	11.6
Malaysia	6.5	19.3	3.8	3.1	1.6	9.8
Thailand	4.2	21.2	3.9	4.9	1.2	6.7
China	2.7	13.1	5.6	2.7	6.4	3.9
India	1.8	14.6	3.2	0.8	3.0	12.5
Pakistan	3.0	13.8	4.3	3.2	4.6	–0.5
Nepal	0.8	–2.9	2.7	0.7	2.6	0.9
Bangladesh	1.4	2.6	1.9	–1.5	2.7	–2.8
Sri Lanka	1.8	9.7	2.1	0.03	2.3	0.1

GVA = gross value added.
a   Data refer to 1990–98.
b   Figures in parentheses refer to gross value added in agriculture less forestry.

Source: Asian Development Bank (various issues), *ADB Key Indicators*.

contribution of about 15% of GVA in the early 1960s, forestry's share has dwindled
to just 1% in recent years (Table 6.3).

Although the growth rate for fisheries has also been decreasing, it was higher than
the overall average for most of the period, raising the subsector's share in GVA to
15% in 2000. Whereas value added of municipal fisheries has declined, with its contribution dropping from half of the subsector's share in GVA in the 1960s to only one-
third at present, that of aquaculture and commercial fisheries has become relatively
more important. Aquaculture grew most rapidly, although the scarcity of milkfish fry,
diseases affecting shrimp culture, and red tide episodes have slowed its growth in
recent years. The modest but steady growth rate of commercial fisheries was led by
higher catches of tuna for export. Resource depletion caused by overfishing, destructive fishing methods, degradation of mangroves, and the pollution of major rivers and
lakes largely explains the weakening of the fisheries sector over time. It is evident
that the government has failed to enforce fishery and environmental regulations and
market-based policy instruments to achieve the sustainable management of fishery
and water resources. In addition, public research and extension support to prevent
and control the spread of disease has clearly been inadequate.

Table 6.2 Growth Rates of Gross Value Added of Agriculture by Commodity at 1985 prices, 1960–2000 (%)

Commodity	1960–70	1970–80	1980–90	1990–2000
Total	4.2	3.9	1.0	1.6
Crops	3.9	6.8	0.6	1.2
Palay	4.5	4.7	2.7	1.8
Corn	5.3	5.9	3.5	−1.4
Coconut	2.3	4.9	−4.9	0.6
Sugar	4.8	2.9	−5.3	0.6
Bananas	5.5	15.6	−3.0	2.1
Other	3.6	9.5	1.1	1.7
Livestock and poultry	3.2	3.0	4.7	4.8
Livestock	3.1	0.5	4.9	4.3
Poultry	3.7	9.2	4.4	5.6
Fisheries	6.9	4.5	2.4	1.4
Forestry	5.1	−4.4	−7.0	−21.5

Sources: National Statistical Coordination Board; Bureau of Agricultural Statistics.

A marked slowdown in the GVA growth rate for crops can be observed across commodities since the 1980s. The poorest performers were the major export crops, namely coconut, sugar, and even bananas, which became a major export only in the late 1960s. The high growth rates for a few non-traditional export crops such as mangoes could not overcome the diminishing rates of many other traditional export crops such as tobacco and abaca. The main staple crops—rice and corn—increased at a relatively rapid pace until the late 1980s. Corn production then fell in the 1990s as the area planted to white corn fell sharply in the marginal areas of Visayas and Mindanao. The growth rate for rice, though positive, was below the population growth rate.

The growth rate for livestock and poultry has accelerated since 1980, with its contribution to GVA rising from 13% to 22%. Note, though, that this has simply returned its contribution to the level prevailing in the early 1960s. The remarkable performance in the 1980s and 1990s was due to increasing domestic demand, as well as to productivity gains from the shift to larger-scale operations and adoption of new technologies embedded in imported breeds, veterinary medicines, and feed ingredients.

Table 6.3 Distribution of Gross Value Added in Agriculture by Commodity at Current Prices, 1960–2000 (%)ᵃ

Commodity	1960	1970	1980	1990	2000
Crops	49	54	60	58	59
Palay	15	13	11	15	17
Corn	4	4	5	7	5
Coconut	10	8	9	6	4
Sugar	5	6	4	3	3
Banana	1	2	2	2	3
Other	14	20	28	24	28
Livestock and poultry	22	18	13	20	22
Livestock	17	14	8	13	14
Poultry	5	4	5	7	8
Fisheries	13	15	17	18	15
Forestry	17	14	10	4	1

a   Years represent a three-year average centered on the year shown.

Source: National Statistical Coordination Board.

Agricultural Trade and Trade Openness

Agriculture was historically a net foreign exchange earner, contributing nearly two-thirds of total exports and accounting for only about 20% of total imports (including imports of manufactured agricultural inputs such as fertilizers) in the 1960s (Table 6.4). The agricultural sector's share in total exports decreased much more rapidly than its share in total imports, and by the early 1990s it had ceased to be a net earner of foreign exchange. Agricultural imports rose from about 30% of agricultural exports in the 1960s and 1970s to more than 150% by the late 1990s. The relatively high growth of exports in the 1970s was due mainly to the world commodity boom and the expansion of non-traditional commodities such as bananas, pineapples, and fishery products. But world commodity prices fell sharply in the 1980s and have remained low since then, while the growth of non-traditional agricultural exports leveled off in the 1990s. In sharp contrast to neighboring countries, which experienced a major export boom in cash crops—rubber in Thailand, palm oil in Malaysia and Indonesia, and cocoa in Indonesia—even after the 1980s, the Philippines has failed to recover from these shocks.

Over the last 30 years, the composition of agricultural exports has changed. Coconut products continue to be the top foreign exchange earner, although their

Table 6.4 Agriculture's Share in Total Imports and Exports, Ratio of Agricultural Imports to Exports, and Measures of Trade Openness, 1960–2000 (%)[a]

Year	Share in Total		Ratio of Imports to Exports	Trade Openness		
	Imports	Exports		Agri-cultural Imports/ GVA	Agri-cultural Exports/ GVA	Agricultural Imports plus Exports/ GVA
1960	19	64	31	9	33	42
				(9)	(9)	(18)
1965	21	63	36	16	37	52
				(16)	(14)	(30)
1970	14	44	34	12	44	56
				(19)	(17)	(36)
1975	10	54	26	14	28	42
				(25)	(15)	(41)
1980	8	35	31	12	26	38
				(26)	(18)	(43)
1985	9	26	46	12	18	30
				(18)	(15)	(33)
1990	10	15	96	15	14	30
				(29)	(18)	(48)
1995	9	11	126	19	15	34
				(38)	(23)	(61)
1996	9	9	159	20	12	32
				(42)	(25)	(67)
1997	8	8	161	24	15	38
				(47)	(31)	(78)
1998	10	7	151	29	20	49
				(48)	(45)	(94)
1999	9	5	185	24	13	36
				(42)	(46)	(88)
2000	9	5	168	26	15	41
				(45)	(51)	(96)

a   Agricultural imports include inputs such as agricultural chemicals, machinery, and fertilizer. Figures in parentheses refer to the trade openness of the whole economy.

Sources: Food and Agriculture Organization (various issues), *FAO Trade Yearbook*; National Statistical Coordination Board.

share had decreased from nearly 70% of agricultural exports in 1970 to less than 40% by the end of the 1990s. The contribution to agricultural exports of sugar, which, at 30%, was second only to that of coconut in the 1970s, is now only 5%. The export value of bananas alone is about double that of sugar; and it has also been exceeded by exports of pineapples since the 1990s. Fruit and vegetables account for more than 20% of agricultural exports. Fishery products contribute nearly as much, despite significant decreases in earnings from exports of shrimps since the mid-1990s as a result of infestation and lower world prices. Tuna has become the leading export among fishery products.

The rapid growth of agricultural imports stems from several factors. First, economic development has increased the demand for food products with higher income elasticities. Many of these, such as wheat, milk and other dairy products, and beef, are commodities in which the country does not have inherent comparative advantage in production. Others, such as livestock and poultry, require agricultural inputs (soybean meal, corn, fishmeal) that are cheaper to import than produce domestically. Second, declining competitive advantage in the domestic production of food has led to increased imports and lower self-sufficiency ratios in crops such as rice, corn, and sugar. Third, agricultural modernization has induced greater reliance on mainly imported manufactured inputs such as fertilizer, agricultural chemicals, farm and agro-processing machinery, feed, and veterinary medicines. Finally, trade liberalization has led to a rise in the imports of previously highly protected agricultural commodities and inputs, such as fruit, cattle, and so forth.

Table 6.4 also indicates an apparent decrease in the trade openness of agriculture (that is, imports plus exports as a ratio of GVA). While agriculture was relatively more open than the rest of the economy in 1970, the reverse was the case by the 1990s. This was due not so much to the reduction in import ratios to GVA, as these increased for both agriculture and non-agricultural sectors, but rather to the decrease in the export ratios for agriculture in contrast to the steadily rising trend for the rest of the economy. The declining trend in agricultural trade openness in the 1970s and 1980s gradually reversed in the 1990s, but the rate of increase in the import ratios continued to be higher than that for the export ratios.

Comparative Advantage and Productivity Growth

Comparative Advantage

The slower growth of agriculture in the Philippines than in other developing Asian countries and the stagnation of agricultural exports suggest that the country has been losing its comparative advantage in the sector. Indeed, measures of revealed comparative advantage have decreased sharply both for agriculture as a whole and for all major agricultural exports (Table 6.5). The country's share of the world market in coconut products has fallen. Sugar began to be imported, as exports to the preferential U.S. market garnered higher than world market prices. Even for non-traditional exports such as bananas and pineapples, Philippine shares have declined since the mid-1980s.

Table 6.5 Trends in Revealed Comparative Advantage in Agriculture and Selected Major Agricultural Exports, 1960–98 [a]

Year	Agriculture [b]	Coconut	Sugar [c]	Bananas	Pineapple	
					(canned)	(fresh)
1960	3.0	–	–	–	–	–
1965	2.7	131.8	15.3	–	–	–
1970	2.6	145.0	21.4	–	–	–
1975	3.8	211.2	22.0	29.3	–	–
1980	2.9	224.1	12.1	30.4	82.2	48.9
1985	2.4	212.3	7.6	31.2	91.6	59.7
1990	1.6	212.4	3.8	23.4	70.2	54.6
1995	1.1	153.5	2.0	14.1	41.5	23.6
1998	0.8	105.3	1.4	8.8	33.2	11.5

a   Estimated as the ratio of the share of a commodity group in a country's exports to that commodity group's share of world exports. Except for 1960 and 1998, years represent a three-year average centered on the year shown.
b   Includes fisheries.
c   Sugar has historically been exported to the United States at a premium price. Hence a value greater than unity does not reveal comparative advantage in this case. However, the sharp declining trend may still be interpreted as a rapid deterioration in comparative advantage.

Source: Food and Agriculture Organization (various isses), *FAO Trade Yearbook*.

Labor and Land Productivity

The apparent loss in comparative advantage in agriculture is consistent with the observed trends in labor and land productivity. Figure 6.1 portrays the trends in GVA in agriculture, agricultural labor employment, cultivated and crop area, and measures of labor and land productivity.

Both labor and land productivity were increasing up to the late 1970s, particularly during the Green Revolution period in rice. Whereas labor productivity for agriculture as a whole rose moderately after dropping sharply in the early 1980s, it stagnated for the crop subsector. Measures of land productivity also leveled off during the recent period. Growth in productivity appears to have occurred primarily in the livestock and poultry sector, where international technology transfer, the greater scale of operations, and other management-related innovations have increased production efficiencies significantly.

Among crops, yields per hectare of traditional exports generally remained constant or even declined throughout the post-war period, as no major technological change was observed in the production of these commodities. Relatively high growth rates in yields can be observed in rice, corn, and non-traditional exports such as (index, 1960 = 100)   (%)

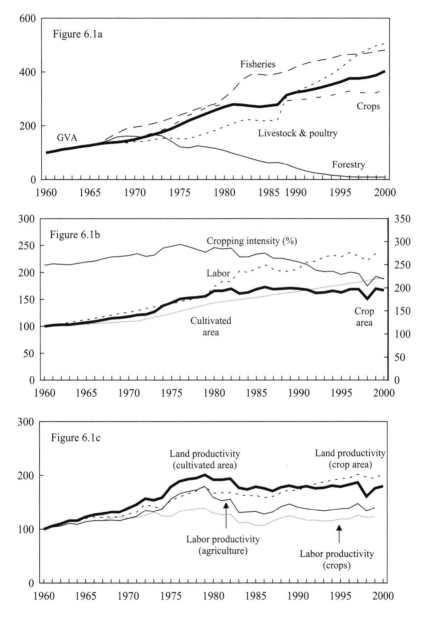

Figure 6.1 Trends in Gross Value Added in Agriculture, Agricultural Labor, Cultivated Land, Crop Area, Cropping Intensity, and Labor and Land Productivity in Real Terms, 1960–2000 (3-year moving average)

Indices of land productivity refer to gross value added of crops per hectare of cultivated area (a) and per hectare of crop area (c). *Source*: National Statistical Coordination Board.

bananas, mangoes, and pineapples. Adoption of modern varieties, increased fertilizer use, and the expansion of irrigation systems largely explain yield increases in rice up to the early 1980s, although that growth leveled off in the 1990s. Growth in corn yields has been due mainly to the spread of hybrid yellow corn for use as feed, coupled with the concentration of production in areas where corn does best, and the decline in the area under white corn in the marginal areas of Visayas and Mindanao where corn is grown as a subsistence crop. Improvements in banana and pineapple yields started on larger plantations with access to international knowhow and gradually spread to smallholder farms. The introduction of chemical spraying to induce flowering promoted the rapid expansion of the mango industry, and growth in yields.

The question remains, what are the underlying causes of the poor performance of Philippine agriculture? In a comparative study of the performance of agriculture in the Philippines, Thailand, and Indonesia, Hayami (2000) highlighted the importance of differences in agrarian structure as determined by agro-ecological conditions and the historical evolution of land ownership patterns. The Philippines and Indonesia have a dualistic agrarian structure of small family farms in lowland areas and plantations specializing in tropical export crops in upland areas, whereas Thailand has a unimodal distribution of relatively small family farms. Despite the relatively larger endowment of crop land per capita in Thailand, the proportion of farm land with an average operational farm size of above five hectares is less than 1% in Thailand, compared with 14% in Indonesia and the Philippines. The proportion of tenanted area is also highest in the Philippines and lowest in Thailand.

Hayami (2000) reasoned that as land frontiers closed, the initial advantage of the plantation mode of operation in opening the hinterland of tropical rainforest—which required high capital outlays for land development and infrastructure—began to be outweighed by the higher cost of monitoring hired labor in the Philippines and Indonesia.[1] Thailand's agrarian structure of mainly small, family-managed farms with much lower supervision costs then became more competitive, as evidenced by its growing share of world markets for agricultural exports in which the Philippines and Indonesia had once had a comparative advantage. In the case of the Philippines, the problem was exacerbated by the regulatory conditions accompanying land reform programs to transfer ownership of farmland to the tillers. The resulting inactivity in land markets brought about major distortions in resource allocation.[2] Because land ownership was far less skewed and the incidence of tenancy much lower, this problem did not occur in Thailand and Indonesia. Plantations in Indonesia were either government-owned or leased on a long-term basis.

In the following sections we examine how price and trade policy interventions, public expenditure programs, and institutional issues, including the land reform programs, may also explain the poor performance of Philippine agriculture.

6.3 PRICE INTERVENTION POLICIES

Past studies have amply demonstrated the fact that until the early 1980s price intervention policies, both economy-wide and commodity-specific, created an incentive structure that was significantly biased against agriculture (David 1983; Bautista 1987; Intal and Power 1991). That bias was primarily evident in the overvaluation of the peso due to industrial protection and other economy-wide policies to defend an unsustainable deficit in the balance of payments.

Economy-wide Policies

Since the early 1980s, the government has adopted various structural adjustment and stabilization measures to correct fundamental distortions in economic incentives and address imbalances in the external and public sector accounts. These measures have included trade policy reforms to remove quantitative restrictions (QRs) on trade and reduce the level and dispersion of tariffs, and liberalization of the foreign exchange market. Consequently, the overvaluation of the peso, which was in the order of 20–30% from 1960 up to the mid-1980s, had dropped to 20% by 1992 (see Bautista and Tecson, Chapter 5). The rate of overvaluation remained sizable, imposing a substantial penalty on agricultural profitability, particularly exportable agricultural commodities.

Furthermore, real effective exchange rates appreciated sharply (by 30%) between 1992 and 1996, which tended to lower the relative prices of tradable agricultural products. This unfavorable trend was caused by several factors. First, trade liberalization, which should have reduced distortions in the exchange rate, was not accompanied by nominal exchange rate adjustments and other appropriate macroeconomics policies (Medalla et al. 1995/96). Second, short-term foreign capital inflows—attracted by high interest rates caused by a tight monetary regime—accommodated an increase in the current account deficit, causing the real exchange rate to appreciate (de Dios and Associates 1993; Lamberte 1995). And finally, domestic inflation rates were higher than those of the country's trading partners, particularly in 1995, when sharp increases in food prices led to double-digit inflation. With the substantial devaluation of the peso in late 1997 and the curbing of inflation, the real effective exchange rate began to increase. By early 1998 it had risen by over 40%, benefiting the tradable goods sector, including exportables and potentially also import-competing agricultural commodities as their competitive advantage increased. Relative prices of these commodities are expected to rise as market demand expands.

Commodity-specific Policies

A wide variety of policy instruments affect agricultural output and input prices. Although import tariffs are generally levied on all agricultural products and inputs, in effect they are more common on commodities that are not produced locally in any significant quantity. Tariff protection is essentially redundant on exportable and non-tradable commodities. Until 1995, QRs, import prohibitions, price controls, and government monopoly control of international trade were important policy interventions affecting import-competing agricultural products.

The government, through the National Food Authority (NFA), has monopoly control of international trade in rice and corn and engages in domestic marketing operations to stabilize prices and narrow geographic price dispersion. Even with the imposition of the tariff structure in 1958, import licensing was widely used. In addition, specific laws were passed prohibiting the import of onion, garlic, potatoes, and cabbage in 1955 (under RA 1296), coffee in 1960 (under RA2712), and tobacco/cigarettes unless for blending purposes in 1964 (under RA4155 and other Presidential Decrees).

Except in the early to mid-1970s, there have been few attempts to intervene in the production and trade of exportable agricultural products. Export taxes of 4–6% were imposed on major agricultural exports as a stabilization measure to accompany the floating of the exchange rate in 1970, and additional export premium duties were collected temporarily to siphon off gains from higher world commodity prices in the mid-1970s. A portion of the funds raised through a levy imposed on coconut in 1973 was used to purchase 80% of the coconut oil-milling industry and establish United Coconut Mills, Inc. (UNICOM). UNICOM operations and a copra export ban further lowered farm prices of coconut by more than 20% (Clarete and Roumasset 1983).

With world commodity prices high in the early 1970s, government monopoly control over food commodities under the NFA was extended beyond rice and corn to allow tariff-free importation of wheat, corn, soybeans, soybean meal, ruminant livestock, and beef. The domestic wholesale and international marketing of sugar was also nationalized.

In the late 1970s world commodity prices began to fall. However, the policies and institutions established to cope with high prices persisted, in part because they had proved to be a convenient means of raising revenues, but even more so because of the private interests involved and because of bureaucratic inefficiencies. It was not until 1986 under a new government that several of these direct government price and market regulations were dismantled. Export taxes, including the copra export ban, were abolished. Government monopoly control over international trade in coconut oil, corn, soybean meal, and wheat, and over the marketing of sugar, were removed. QRs on fertilizer were lifted and tariffs on major agricultural inputs lowered substantially. Rice became the sole subject of government monopoly control over international trade; as the NFA's financial support now had to come mainly from budgetary allocations rather than profits from imports, domestic marketing operations were also reduced.

In spite of trade liberalization efforts in the late 1980s, most major importable agricultural commodities that are produced in significant quantities domestically remain subject to QRs. Efforts to remove such restrictions were pre-empted by the passage in 1991 of the Magna Carta for Small Farmers (RA 7606), which provided blanket authority for restricting the import of agricultural products that might compete with domestic production. It also made the process of implementing QRs more cumbersome, by requiring advance government consultation with farmers and those in other affected sectors. Another such law was the Seed Law (RA 7308), which regulates the import of seeds and planting materials.

Philippine ratification of the Uruguay Round of the General Agreement on Tariffs and Trade (GATT–UR) in 1995 promised to set a decisive path toward trade liberalization by replacing all QRs with tariffs, imposing a ceiling on tariff rates, and reducing tariff protection over time. Unfortunately, the specific agreements reached and the manner of their implementation ensured that most of these objectives would not be attained.

First, rice, one of the most heavily regulated commodities, was exempted from tariffication until 2004, similar to the case of Japan and South Korea.

Second, while QRs were lifted in April 1996, they were replaced, under Executive Order (EO) 313, with applied tariffs that were equal to the high binding tariffs, the maximum tariffs that the Philippines was committed to under the World Trade Organization (WTO). As Table 6.6 shows, these binding tariffs, mostly of 100%, are typically higher than the average nominal protection rates implied by QRs in 1990–94. They are also higher than the book tariff rates set under EO 470, which programmed unilateral tariff reductions on a wide range of agricultural and industrial goods. Furthermore, tariffs were raised on a number of imported agricultural products considered close substitutes for commodities where QRs were to be lifted, such as feed wheat and barley as substitutes for corn. Despite the reductions in applied tariffs scheduled to take effect by 2004, these will at best only be about equal to the tariff rates set back in 1995 under EO 470. And they will definitely be far higher than the target average tariff of 5% for all products by the end of that period.

Third, the manner in which the minimum access volume (MAV) provision of the agreement is being administered for major import-competing commodities has in effect simply replaced QRs with a tariff quota system. A certain volume of a commodity subject to a MAV may be imported at a relatively low (in-quota) tariff rate, while imports beyond that are subject to a higher (out-quota) tariff rate. Since the MAV is not fixed, but may be increased to prevent domestic prices from rising sharply whenever production shortfalls occur, it is operationally no different from QRs. Most MAV volumes are set much lower than import demand at the in-quota tariff. The right to import the full volume is seldom auctioned, thus creating large quota rents.

Nominal Protection Rates

Trends in the nominal protection rate (NPR) for major agricultural commodities based on price comparisons are shown in Table 6.7. The patterns show wide and growing dispersion across commodities as the overall average protection rate increased over time. As would be expected, tariff protection on exportable crops (coconut products, bananas) is redundant. In fact, major exportable crops were penalized in the 1970s by negative NPRs ranging from –4% to –28%, to protect consumers and agro-processors from high domestic prices caused by the devaluation of the peso and subsequent boom in world commodity prices. Taxes on such crops were not lifted until the late 1980s even though world prices had fallen steeply way back in the late 1970s. Not only was the government unable to protect farmers from falling world prices, it was unwilling to immediately abandon policies that had outlived their original purpose, because of the vested interests that had been created.

Table 6.6 Nominal Protection Rates, Book Tariff Rates, GATT Binding Tariff Rates, and Minimum Access Volumes (%)

Com-modity	NPR 1990–94	EO 47 1995	Binding Tariff		Minimum Access Volume		
			1995	2005	Tariff	Quantity (thousand tonnes)	
						1995	2004
Rice	19	50	n.a.	n.a.	50	59.7	238.9
Corn	76	20	100	50	35	130.2	216.9
Sugar	80	50	100	50	50	38.4	103.4
Coffee		50	50	45	50	0.1	0.1
Garlic		30	100	60			
Onions		30	100	60	30	1.6	2.7
Potatoes		30	100	45	50	930.0	1,550.0
Cabbage		30	100	60	30	2.1	3.5
Pork	31	30	100	60	30	32.5	54.2
Chicken	74	50	100	60	50	14.1	23.5
Beef		30	60	45	30	4.0	5.6
						(thousand head)	
Live hogs		30	60	45	30	2,570.0	2,570.0
Live poultry		30	80	50	5	5,708.1	9,513.5
Cattle		30	40	35	30	12.2	20.3

NPR = nominal protection rate; EO = Executive Order.

Source: David (1994).

Although fluctuations in the NPR have to some extent reflected government attempts to stabilize domestic prices, it is clear that the rates are rising, particularly among the major import-competing crops listed in Table 6.7. Sugar has historically been the most highly protected crop, even in the 1970s when it was still exportable. This was initially due to the economic rents conferred by the premium prices obtained under the U.S. sugar quota, and the concomitant implicit tax on consumers due to import restrictions. The plantation-based sugar sector has traditionally been a strong political force that was able to lobby for greater protection even after the quantity and price premium set under the U.S. sugar quota diminished significantly.

Until the late 1980s, the domestic price of rice was on average just equal to the border price converted at the official exchange rate. The Green Revolution in rice and the accompanying expansion of irrigation increased the country's comparative

Table 6.7 Trends in Nominal Protection Rates for Major Agricultural Commodities, 1970–2000 (%)[a]

Commodity	1970–79	1980–84	1985–89	1990–94	1995–2000
Rice	−4	−13	16	19	71
Corn	24	26	67	76	87
Sugar[b]	5	42	154	81	106
Coconut products					
Copra	−17	−28	−6	0	0
Coconut oil	−4	−4	7	18	0
Desiccated coconut,					
copra cake & meal	−4	−4	0	0	0
Bananas, pineapple,					
tobacco, abaca	−4	−4	0	0	0
Pork	6	−9	43	31	29
Chicken	34	46	39	74	45

a   The nominal protection rate (NPR) is the percentage difference between the domestic wholesale price and the border price converted at the official exchange rate. The border price is an FOB export unit value for exportable products and a CIF import unit value for importable products. The CIF import unit value is approximated by the world price, adjusted upward by 15% to cover freight and insurance. In the case of pork and chicken, the Singaporean CIF import unit value was used.

b   Weighted average of NPR on sugar exported to the United States (ratio of export unit value to the border price) and NPR on sugar for domestic use (ratio of domestic whole-sale price to border price). The border price is the FOB world price of sugar adjusted by 15% to obtain the CIF price.

Sources: World Bank; National Statistics Office; Food and Agriculture Organization (various issues), *FAO Trade Yearbook*.

advantage in rice production, turning it from a net importer to being self-sufficient, and reducing the domestic price in real terms. With the drop in the world price of rice, sharp fall in investment in irrigation, and stagnation of the yield potential of newer modern varieties, growth in demand for rice has increased faster than production since the late 1980s. The government began to import rice again, but, to protect farmers' income, only at levels that would not induce further reductions in the real rice price. The increasing trend in the NPR for rice, despite more being imported than ever before, reflects the country's declining comparative advantage in rice production.

The NPR for corn has risen steadily over time, from about 25% in the late 1970s and early 1980s to nearly 90% by the late 1990s. Throughout this period, the penalty imposed on the hog industry by the QRs on corn was greater than the NPR on its own output. The same has been true of poultry since the late 1980s. Despite this, both sectors have grown relatively quickly. The much higher book tariff rates applied on these products compared with the actual NPR based on a price comparison seems to indicate that hogs and poultry have achieved a better productivity performance than most of the major crops.

Trends in the Terms of Trade

Increases in NPRs have been sufficiently high to counter the declining trend in the price of agriculture relative to non-agricultural products in the world market and the appreciation in the real effective exchange rate in the 1990s, as evidenced by the more gradual decline in the domestic terms of trade of agriculture since the 1980s (Figure 6.2). Many major import-competing agricultural products received positive net nominal protection even after accounting for the indirect negative effects of the overvaluation of the peso. In the case of corn, sugar, and chicken, net price protection still exceeds 50%, even higher than the rate for most manufacturing industries. Similarly, the rice sector had become highly protected by 1995.

On the other hand, exportable agricultural commodities continue to be penalized by the overvaluation of the exchange rate, which worsened in the 1990s due to the steep appreciation in the real exchange rate. Although the recent devaluation raised the real effective exchange rate, the domestic terms of trade in agriculture declined slightly in 1997 and 1998, reflecting the government's decision to increase the number of imports that were effectively subject to QRs.

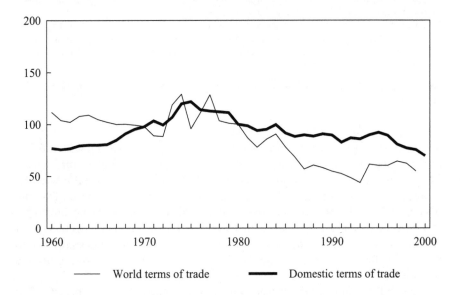

Figure 6.2 Trends in the World and Domestic Terms of Trade (1980 = 100)

Source: National Statistical Coordination Board.

Effective Protection Rates

Resource allocation is affected by effective rates of protection, which measure not only the effect of policies on output prices, but also their effect on intermediate input prices. For agricultural crops, the proportion of the cost of intermediate inputs to the value of output is relatively low, and so trends in nominal and effective rates of protection may not differ significantly. Given the decline in implicit tariffs on crop inputs (Table 6.8), effective protection rates would have risen even faster than nominal rates. In the case of livestock and poultry, effective protection rates may not have increased as much as nominal rates because the implicit tariff on corn, the most important ingredient in animal feed, rose at a higher rate.

While the dispersion of protection rates within the agricultural sector has widened, the difference in the estimated average effective protection rate between agriculture and manufacturing has narrowed (Table 6.9). During the 1970s and 1980s, estimates of effective protection rates for manufacturing ranged from 44% to

Table 6.8 Trends in Implicit Tariffs on Agricultural Inputs, 1970–2000 (%)

Year	Fertilizer[a]		Pesticide[b]	Tractors[b]		Threshers[b,c]	Water Pumps
	Urea	Ammophos		2-wheel	4-wheel		
1970–74	−13	−9	29	21	21	24	46
1975–79	28	54	35	46	24	24	46
1980–84	21	19	35	46	24	24	46
1985–89	11	15	20	30	10	30	30
1990–94	5	12	16	28	10	22	24
1995	5	n.a.	3(10)[d]	10	10	20	10
1996	3	3	3(10)[d]	10	10	10	10
1997	3	3	3(10)[d]	10	10	10	10
1998	3	3	3	10	10	8[e]	10
1999	3	3	3	10	10	8	10
2000	3	3	3	10	10	8	10

a   Based on price comparisons, that is, the percentage difference between the ex-warehouse price and the CIF import unit value.
b   Based on book rates. Implicit tariff for 1960–84 includes the import tariff and advance sales tax (10% and 25% mark-up respectively). The advance sales tax was abolished in 1986 and hence the implicit tariff from 1985 onward includes only the tariff rate.
c   Includes other farm implements produced domestically.
d   The figure in parentheses of 10% refers to insecticides, and that of 3% to herbicides, fungicides and other agricultural chemicals.
e   Changed to 5% effective from 10 July 1998 by EO 486.

Sources: National Statistics Office; Tariff Code; World Bank

Table 6.9 Estimates of Effective Protection Rates, by Major Economic Sector, 1974–2000 (%)[a]

Year	Agriculture, Fisheries, and Forestry	Manufacturing	All Sectors
Tan			
1974	9.0	44.0	36.0
Medalla et al.			
1983	10.3	79.2	52.8
1985	9.2	74.1	49.3
1986	5.0	61.2	39.8
1988	5.2	55.5	36.3
Manasan			
1993–95	24.4 (28.1)	29.1	26.7
2000	19.1 (25.9)	19.2	18.4

a   Figures in parentheses refer to crops and livestock only.

Sources: Tan (1979); Medalla et al. (1995/96); Manasan and Querubin (1997).

79%, much higher than those for agriculture (5–10%) (Tan 1979; Medalla et. al. 1995). By the mid-1990s, the average rate for agriculture and for manufacturing was about equal (Manasan and Querubin 1997). This was primarily due to the decline in effective protection rates for manufacturing, including agricultural inputs, the increase in rates for major import-competing agricultural products, and the decrease in the share of exportable agricultural commodities. Projected estimates of effective rates of protection suggest that the agricultural sector will have higher rates relative to manufacturing given the scheduled reductions in tariff rates up to the year 2000.

The NFA

Because of the political significance of rice as a staple food and as the single most important crop grown by farmers, government policy aims to achieve the inherently conflicting objectives of ensuring low and stable prices for the benefit of consumers and sufficiently high and stable prices for the benefit of farmers. Food security is often interpreted as the achievement of rice self-sufficiency, in part due to the mistaken belief that the world rice price is highly volatile. The common misconception that private traders extract monopoly profits from farmers during the harvest season, especially in the more remote areas, and from consumers when rice is scarce, has been used to justify the NFA's continued monopoly control over international trade in rice and domestic marketing operations, to minimize seasonal and geographical price margins. The trends in the NPR of rice discussed earlier indicate that the twin objectives of low consumer and high producer prices cannot be attained simultaneously. By the late 1990s, NFA trade policies were implicitly taxing the consumer to protect the producer. The inefficient management of rice-importing and buffer stock operations often led to abnormal seasonal price fluctuations (Bouis 1982; David 1996). Umali (1990) also found that the NFA's domestic market operations widened, rather than narrowed, regional price differences; that regional rice markets were intertemporally price-efficient; that paddy-trading and retail-level markets were competitive; and that the structure of the milling industry and government policy created barriers to entry that worked against competition at the mill level.

Roumasset (2000) showed that the economic cost imposed on the economy by NFA operations far outweighed the direct benefits obtained by rice producers and/or consumers. Figure 6.3 illustrates the economic cost to rice consumers, farmers, and taxpayers in general of government market interventions, based on rice production, consumption, and price estimates for 1999. Production was estimated at 7 million tons at a producer price of 14.5 pesos per kilogram (including the conversion of palay to rice, and marketing costs up to the wholesale in situ warehouse point). Consumption was estimated at 7.8 million tons, corresponding to a consumer price of 18 pesos per kilogram, which is 64% above the border price of 11 pesos per kilogram. If this level of price protection were achieved by an import quota of 0.8 million tons, the resulting equilibrium domestic price would be 15.63 pesos per kilogram, with both rice consumers and "producers" (including the marketing sector) facing the same domestic price. In practice, consumers are paying substantially more and producers receiving somewhat less, due to inefficiencies and non-competitive elements in rice marketing caused by current government policies. The consumer price, at least before the 1999 wet season harvest, was in the neighborhood of 18 pesos per kilogram. But the producer price, marked up according to efficient margins, was approximately 14.5 pesos per kilogram. This result could have been obtained by the combination of a tariff sufficient to limit imports to 0.8 million tons (resulting in a domestic price of 15.63 pesos per kilogram) and consumer and producer taxes sufficient to further raise and lower the consumer and producer prices, respectively. The cost to the taxpayers of failing to obtain these revenues was 3.7 billion pesos in foregone tariff revenue, 18.49 billion pesos in foregone consumer tax revenue, and 7.91 billion pesos in foregone producer tax revenue, for a combined total of 30.1 billion pesos in losses. To this, one can add the excess burden of unnecessarily high marginal production costs and the consumer benefits denied by restricting imports, giving a total estimated cost of almost 49 billion pesos.

Rather than gaining from NFA operations, taxpayers have in fact been losing. The cost to taxpayers includes not only the budget subsidies paid to NFA, but the increase in debt (which obligates future tax payments) and the net infusions of new government equity after subtracting the value of new assets. Table 6.10 shows that financial subsidies to the NFA in 1998 (when data were available) appear to have been in excess of 6 billion pesos, even when the increase in rice stocks is valued at

(pesos/kilogram)

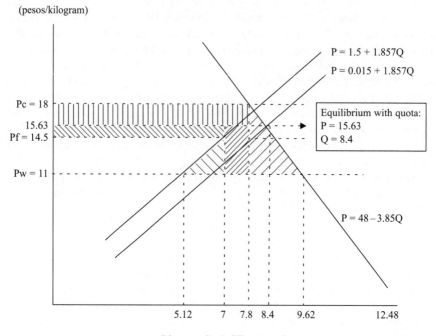

Rice quantity (million tonnes)

(billion pesos)

▨	Foregone tariff revenue = (15.63 – 11) pesos/kg × (7.8 – 7) billion kg	3.70
⊞	Foregone consumer tax revenue = (18 – 15.63) pesos/kg × (7.8) billion kg	18.49
◩	Foregone producer tax revenue = (15.63 – 14.5) pesos/kg × (7) billion kg	7.91
	Tax friction = 0.3 (3.70 + 18.49 + 7.91) billion pesos	9.03
▨	Excess burden for consumer = (1/2) × (18 – 11) pesos/kg × (9.62 – 7.8) billion kg	6.37
◩	Excess burden for producer = (1/2) × (14.5 – 11) pesos/kg × (7 – 5.12) billion kg	3.29

Total cost of rice policy not including financial subsidies to NFA   48.79
Demand as function of price: Q = 12.48 – 0.26 pesos
Supply as function of price: Q = 0.54 pesos – 0.81

Figure 6.3 The Excess Burden of Price Controls on Rice, 1999

Source: Roumasset (2000).

Table 6.10 Financial Cost of NFA Operations, 1998 (billion pesos)

Operational subsidy (budget)	1.2
Equity infusion	0.2
Increase in debt	8.8
Less: increase in value of rice stock	−3.9
Total	6.3

Source: National Food Authority.

almost 4 billion pesos. If financial subsidies for 1999 were roughly half those in 1998, that would still make a total cost for the rice policy of almost 52 billion pesos. Note that most of that cost is not apparent to the general public. Even from the point of view of the government, only the 1.39 billion pesos budgetary outlay and equity infusion is explicitly recorded in the budget. Yet, the financial cost alone of the NFA is about five times that amount.

WTO Agreement

The country's membership of the WTO could have set a decisive path toward an efficient price policy framework for Philippine agriculture, while improving the market access and world prices of agricultural exports. Instead, the specific agreements reached and the manner of their implementation facilitated an increase in tariff protection of major import-competing commodities. The implementation guidelines for the MAV on selected commodities in effect ensured the continuation of QRs despite tariffication because the volume could be increased temporarily whenever there were domestic supply shortages. Not only was rice exempted from tariffication, but the NFA's direct involvement in importation was extended to other commodities that were also subject to an MAV provision, such as sugar and corn.

Recent overall analyses of the Agriculture Agreement (Hathaway and Ingco 1995; Winters 1995; Ingco and Ng 1998) have concluded that any expansion of market access and improvement in world prices will be very limited because of widespread "dirty" tariffication, the concentration of tariff reductions on commodities where tariffs are already low, unusually high tariff equivalents due to low world prices in the base year, the exemption of rice from coverage in several countries, and the continued monopoly power of government marketing/trading agencies. Current rules on the reduction of aggregate measures of support and the elimination of export subsidies will not significantly affect world prices because they apply to aggregate and not individual commodities, allowing some major traded products to retain high domestic support and export subsidies. Unilateral reductions adopted after the base period of 1986–88 already form the major part, if not all, of the country's obligations under the agreement.

Other Policies

At least three other sets of policies retard agricultural growth. The first relates to sugar policies associated with distributing the rents from preferential access to the U.S. premium sugar market The present system, which allocates sugar to the U.S., domestic, and world markets, as well as to reserves, in a fixed proportion, lowers the incentive to increase production and invest in yield-increasing technology, because higher production reduces gross revenues. Furthermore, because exports are allocated to the United States in a fixed ratio, there is no incentive to improve the milling quality of sugar for export, because this would be unlikely to increase net returns. Also reducing the incentive for both growers and millers to raise productivity is the sugar-sharing arrangement instituted under RA 809 to allow millers to share in the benefits of price protection. This is because the arrangement allows growers to receive only 60–70% of the benefits of productivity-enhancing investments (depending on the recovery rate), and millers to receive only 30–40%.

Second are policies limiting competition. One important example is the banana hectarage limitation law (Letter of Instruction 58 and 790), which prevents newcomers from entering the banana export industry and allows existing banana growers to determine among themselves the hectarage under bananas for export. This policy was based on the misconception that the Philippines had a monopoly position in the Japanese market. Blaxall and Lenagham (1994) have shown that the banana cartel promoted by the law has discouraged productivity growth. And in fact the Philippine share of the world market for bananas has declined.

The third set of growth-retarding policies relates to the bias in the value added tax (VAT) structure against the agro-processing sector. Agricultural products are exempt from VAT, and thus the tax base applicable to agro-processing industries is larger by the cost of agricultural raw material inputs. In effect, agro-processing industries pay a higher rate of VAT on true value added than other manufacturing industries, lowering their profitability and, correspondingly, the demand for agricultural raw materials.

6.4 THE PUBLIC EXPENDITURE PROGRAM

Because of the unique features of agriculture, market failures are pervasive in the sector. The private sector will underinvest in key factors that could accelerate agricultural growth, such as modern technology, irrigation, and market infrastructure, which are generally characterized by public good attributes, strong economies of scale and scope, and a long gestation period. Land cultivation, logging, fisheries and aquaculture, irrigation, as well as the use of agricultural chemicals and other modern inputs, often generate externalities that necessitate regulation, market-based policy instruments, and/or public support for resource rehabilitation in order to protect the environment and people's health.

Agricultural production is inherently risky while world commodity markets are perceived to be unstable. It has also become increasingly more capital-intensive with

modernization. Yet credit markets are imperfect and the market for insurance to minimize risk and uncertainty in agriculture has not proven viable, due to asymmetric
information, moral hazard problems, and covariance of risks. The highly unequal
distribution of land ownership and access to natural resources, together with imperfect credit markets and the lack of an insurance market, has tended to exacerbate
income inequalities.

To address market failures, alleviate poverty, and achieve other developmental
and social goals in the sector, the public sector finances the design, implementation,
monitoring, and evaluation of a wide variety of public investments, regulations,
institutional mechanisms, and other policy instruments. In this section, we argue that
the relevant issue has not so much been one of *underspending* on the sector as a
whole, but rather one of inefficiencies in budgetary allocations within the sector
accompanied by low economic returns on, or the doubtful cost-effectiveness of,
many government projects and programs. After all, the opportunity cost of public
expenditure is high. Public investment in other social and economic services, such
as roads and other market infrastructure, education, and health, could have a greater
pay-off for agriculture and overall economic growth than is the case at present, as
well as alleviating poverty in the rural sector. Moreover, permissive policies with
respect to fiscal management typically lead to unstable funding of rural programs.
Equally important, fiscal imbalances often cause the appreciation of the real
exchange rate, since deficits in the current account generate an offsetting capital
inflow, hurting the competitiveness of the agricultural sector.

Aggregate Trends, Strategic Directions, and Priorities

Over the past three and a half decades, public expenditure on agriculture in real
terms and as a ratio of GVA and total government expenditure has fluctuated widely
(Figure 6.4).[3] It increased sharply between 1973 and 1983 in response to high world
commodity prices, shortfalls in rice production in 1973–74, and the introduction of
the modern rice varieties in the late 1960s. In the early 1980s agriculture bore the
brunt of the government's contractionary policies, but expenditure on the sector
recovered quickly in the late 1980s. After reaching another peak in 1991, public
spending again dropped, followed in 1993 by another cycle of sharp rises and falls.
By the late 1990s, public expenditure in real terms and as a ratio of GVA was already
above the high levels of the 1970s. It constituted about 8% of total public expenditure (11% of total public expenditure net of debt service) and represented about 8%
of GVA in agriculture.

The strategic directions and priorities of the government may be inferred from
an examination of the pattern of budgetary allocations by policy instrument, commodity, and region. The distribution of public expenditure across these variables is
interrelated. At the Department of Agriculture and to some extent at the Department
of Agrarian Reform as well, strategic directions tend to be identified by commodity, which in turn affects regional budgetary distribution and the choice of policy
instrument.

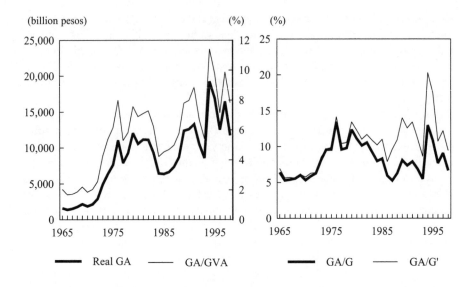

Figure 6.4 Real Government Expenditure on Agriculture (GA) and Its Ratio to Gross Value Added in Agriculture (GVA), Total Government Expenditure (G), and Total Government Expenditure less Debt Service (G')

Real government expenditure on agriculture is in billion pesos in 1985 prices. Totals include state colleges and universities. *Sources*: National Statistical Coordination Board; Department of Budget and Management.

Allocation of Expenditure by Policy Instrument

Figure 6.5 shows that the sharp increase in public expenditure in the 1970s and early 1980s was due mainly to public investment in irrigation as modern rice varieties and high world prices raised its social profitability (Hayami and Kikuchi 1978; Kikuchi et al. 2000). Irrigation accounted for close to half of agricultural spending and 20% of the total infrastructure budget in this period. The recovery in public expenditure in the late 1980s was initially allocated to the strengthening of natural resource and environmental management and the rehabilitation of forest and fishery resources. Increased spending was also directed toward redistributive purposes, namely the agrarian reform program and rice price stabilization, and much less toward productivity-enhancing investments.[4] Investment in irrigation had fallen sharply by the mid-1980s, while remaining the single largest item of public expenditure. Public expenditure on agriculture increased in 1996 and 1997 to support "safety net" programs in the aftermath of the ratification of the GATT-UR Agriculture Agreement. Spending on irrigation also rose, but a higher proportion went to the "other" category, which includes subsidies for credit, post-harvest facilities, farm machinery, seed, and other agricultural inputs.

Table 6.11 presents a more detailed disaggregation of public expenditure on agriculture and natural resources by policy instrument. Public resources devoted to

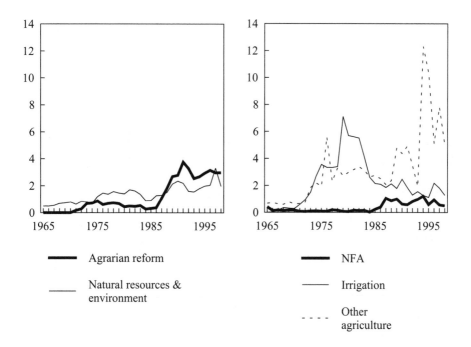

Figure 6.5 Trends in Real Government Expenditure on Agriculture by Policy Instrument (billion pesos at 1985 prices)

Source: Department of Budget and Management.

price stabilization and irrigation are in practice significantly higher once other sources of revenue are added in. In the case of irrigation, about 1 billion pesos is generated from service fee collections, interest earnings, equipment rental, and other sources, raising total irrigation expenditure by another 20%. Adding just the estimated foregone tariff revenue from the government monopoly on rice importation (3.7 billion pesos) to the direct budgetary allocation to the NFA makes rice price stabilization the top item of public expenditure in recent years, followed by irrigation, natural resource and environmental management, and land redistribution. Budgetary allocations for extension and production support—including the distribution of seed and planting materials, animal and fingerling dispersal, and the provision of post-harvest equipment and facilities—were also significant, with each accounting for more than 10% of the total.

It should be noted that a large proportion of public expenditure has been redistributive in nature, financing what are essentially private goods and services, such as foreign and domestic grain trading, and the provision of seeds and planting materials, animals, agro-processing factories, tubewell irrigation, post-harvest equipment and facilities, credit, and so on. Although there has been no systematic evaluation of these production support services, the overpricing of government procurement, the underutilization of farm and post-harvest equipment and facilities, and the poor

Table 6.11 Distribution of Public Expenditure by Policy Instrument, Average 1994–98

	Distribution	
	(million pesos)	(%)
Natural resources & environmental management	4,976	18
Land acquisition & distribution	4,575	17
Price stabilization	1,441	5
Production support[a]	2,940	11
Credit/insurance	844	3
Irrigation	4,661	17
Extension	3,552	13
R&D	2,027	7
Roads	1,170	4
Other[b]	1,038	4
Total	27,224	100

a   Comprises seed and planting materials, animal and fingerling dispersal, post-harvest equipment, and facilities.
b   Includes economic policy and planning, regulatory functions, market promotion, statistical service.

Source: Department of Budget and Management.

quality and late delivery of seed and planting materials have been widely observed. Credit programs, especially those directly administered by non-financial institutions, have been unsustainable due to the low repayment rates and high transaction costs (Lamberte, Casuga, and Erge 1997; Llanto, Geron, and Tang 2000).

Less than 50% of public spending on agriculture has been devoted to productivity-enhancing, public-good type expenditures. The budget allocated to the performance of regulatory functions, statistical data collection, policy analysis and planning, and market development—4% of the total—is clearly inadequate. In the case of irrigation, R&D, and extension, public sector programs are characterized by underinvestment, poor-quality design and implementation, and organizational issues.

Irrigation. Despite the sharp drop in public expenditure on irrigation in the early 1980s, it continues to be the single largest productivity-enhancing public investment. Various studies have shown that the performance of publicly funded national and communal gravity irrigation systems is not as good as projected; that they typically fail to distribute water efficiently and equitably; and that irrigation systems are rapidly falling into disrepair. Ferguson's (1987) study of a sample of national irrigation systems reported that the actual maximum irrigated area averaged only 75%

of the designed service area, and that this ratio was lower for large than for smaller systems. What was even more disturbing was the rapid decline in the ratio over time; those built after 1972 reached only 56% of the designed area, compared with a high of 94% for those constructed before 1965.

Performance indicators for 14 selected World Bank and ADB-funded national irrigation systems were not favorable (World Bank 1991). Time overruns averaged 60% and cost overruns about 50%. About half of the sample projects had estimated economic rates of return (ERR) of below 10% at their completion date. For two projects evaluated a few years after completion, the estimated rates of return were even lower, in part because of the drop in world rice prices since the 1980s.

The performance of communal irrigation systems in terms of proportion of service area actually irrigated is no better than that of the national irrigation systems. De los Reyes and Jopillo (1986) reported the ratio to be higher for those based on a participatory system of management (74%) than for those that were not (64%). Of the 10 new communal construction and rehabilitation projects evaluated by Dy (1990), about half were found to have estimated economic rates of return of 10% or less.

It appears that the design and operation of Philippine gravity irrigation systems may be inappropriate for growing high-value crops. In the case of Taiwan, public investment in the development of highly reticulated irrigation schemes that permitted rotational irrigation at the 10-hectare level, along with improved water management and land consolidation, accelerated agricultural diversification toward higher-value crops. Philippine attempts to follow Taiwan's example were unsuccessful, owing to the lack of appropriate system design and management capacity. A consensus seems to have been reached that design problems and inadequate watershed and system management are behind the low performance of the country's gravity irrigation projects.

With world rice prices low and the cost per hectare of constructing new irrigation systems rising sharply, the government has increasingly funded rehabilitation projects and small-scale irrigation systems such as small water-impounding projects, diversion dams, and shallow tubewells. While investments in rehabilitation may show a reasonable rate of return, the trade-off between improved operation and maintenance and the periodic rehabilitation necessary to address poor or delayed maintenance has not been fully evaluated. Too little attention has been devoted to the institutional strengthening of irrigators' associations, which would be able to undertake the operation and maintenance of national irrigation systems more cheaply and effectively, or to raising the collection rate for irrigation fees to recover at least the cost of operation and maintenance.

Whereas there are few areas suitable for expanding the coverage of small water-impounding projects and diversion dams, substantial private sector investments have been made in tubewell irrigation. However, the government has not been geared up to assume the appropriate public sector role in the regulation of groundwater extraction and monitoring of water pollution to ensure the sustainability of the quantity and quality of groundwater; in the coordination of concurrent surface and groundwater use, in aquifer characterization, and so forth. Growing scarcity of water and increasing demand from domestic and industrial users has raised the opportunity cost of water for agriculture. Yet an appropriate policy, regulatory, and institutional framework for the efficient, equitable, and sustainable allocation and management of competing water uses across sectors has not been developed. No concerted effort is being made to increase the efficiency of water provision and use at the system and farmer level through R&D, extension, and other means.

Research and Development. Agricultural research, including technology generation, has been severely underfunded. Public expenditure on R&D represents only 0.4% of GVA in agriculture, in contrast to an average of 1% among developing countries and 2–3% among developed countries (Pardey, Roseboom, and Anderson 1991). The opportunity cost of underinvestment in agricultural R&D is high; estimates of the social rate of return on agricultural research worldwide are reportedly in the order of 40–60% (Alston et al. 2000). But the problem lies not just in the low level of public expenditure. Equally important are inefficiencies caused by the misallocation of research resources within the sector (for example, across research program areas and ecological regions) and weaknesses in the institutional framework of the research system (including poor organizational structure, lack of accountability, research fragmentation, incentive problems, and weak linkages between research and extension).

The allocation of research expenditure across commodities and regions has been highly incongruent with the relative economic importance of commodities in terms of their GVA contribution to total agriculture (Table 6.12). Estimated research intensity ratios range from 0.05% for corn and 0.15% for cattle, hogs, and chicken as a group to an extremely high ratio of 3.6% for carabao and 25% for cotton. In general, minor commodities in which the country has no historical comparative advantage tend to attract relatively higher budgets that are not commensurate with their economic contribution—nor is there any clear indication of their greater scientific potential or any strong future comparative advantage or market potential. Among major crops corn has been the most neglected, attracting less than 10 million pesos per year in research expenditure in the 1990s. While the private sector does conduct corn research, this is limited to hybrid corn suited primarily to favorable production environments that would comprise no more that 30–40% of the total area under corn.

Fishery research, with a research intensity ratio of only 0.35%, is also significantly underfunded, especially if the country's international funding commitment to the Southeast Asia Fisheries Development Center–Aquaculture Department (SEAFDEC–AQD) is excluded (0.12%). With the exception of carabao, livestock and poultry has also been very much underfunded. Meanwhile, demand for carabao as a draft animal may be expected to decline as the increasing scarcity of labor and water and the introduction of more intensive cropping techniques raise the profitability of farm mechanization. Neither does the future competitiveness of carabao as meat seem promising given the market preference for beef as per capita income increases and the faster rate of technical change in cattle production in developed countries.

The highest research intensity ratios are found among fiber crops. Significant research resources have been devoted to cotton and sericulture, where the country

Table 6.12 Indicative Estimates of Research Intensity by Commodity, 1994–96 (%)

	Research Intensity Ratio
Overall	
(excluding SEAFDEC)	0.41
(including SEAFDEC)	0.45
Rice	0.25
Corn	0.05
Sugar	0.5
Coconut	0.3
Fiber crops	2.5–3.0
Cotton	25
Abaca	1
Tobacco	1.1
Livestock	0.15
Carabao	3.6
Other livestock	0.02
Fisheries	
(excluding SEAFDEC)	0.12
(including SEAFDEC)	0.35
Forestry	3.5

SEAFDEC = Southeast Asia Fisheries Development Center.

Source: David et al. (1998).

has no inherent (or potential for developing) comparative advantage as evidenced by a negligible level of domestic production. By contrast, the research intensity ratio for abaca is much lower—despite its historical importance as an agricultural export, growing world market demand for abaca, and its suitability for cultivation in high-rainfall, typhoon-prone, and economically depressed areas.

Market Infrastructure. Because of the nature of agricultural commodities (bulky, perishable, and tied to specific production locations),[5] the efficiency of the transport system is a major determinant of the performance of the commercialized agricultural sector. The government has a critical role to play in the provision and management of the physical market infrastructure, as well as in the design and enforcement of regulatory instruments to control possible monopoly profits, ensure safety, and address environmental concerns. Although governance of the transport sector is not agriculture-specific and does not fall under the purview of the agricultural bureaucracy, it is instructive to review the status of the market infrastructure and other transport policy issues affecting the agricultural sector. Inadequate physical infrastructure, poor management of port facilities, monopoly elements in the shipping industry, and counterproductive regulations and policies are among those things commonly listed as the most important constraints to the competitiveness of Philippine agriculture in world markets.

Roads. Road density as measured by the ratio of road length to land area (0.63 kilometers per square kilometer) compares well with that in other ASEAN countries (where it ranges from 0.19 in Indonesia to 0.42 in Thailand). The problem relates rather to the poor quality of Philippine roads in terms of their surface condition, width, functional design, and so on. The proportion of paved roads, for example, is only about 20%, in contrast to 47% in Indonesia and up to 82% in Thailand (Tolentino 2000). The actual carrying capacity of the road network is 72 vehicles per kilometer for surfaced roads and 14 for all roads in the Philippines, compared with 433 vehicles per kilometer in Malaysia (World Bank 1995).

A recent assessment of the transport sector has argued that the road network is in fact still very rough and undeveloped in some major regions, including parts of Northern Luzon, Eastern Mindanao, and Western Mindanao, and the interior of medium-sized islands in the Visayas (Halcrow Fox 1999). There may be earth tracks in these places, but most are inaccessible or very difficult to reach, effectively frustrating development in these areas.

While acknowledging funding constraints, Halcrow Fox also emphasizes a number of allocation, design, and implementation problems that have significantly lowered the cost-effectiveness of public expenditure on road provision and maintenance. Construction standards are kept low to reduce costs and raise the estimated rate of return, but the resulting underdesign eventually increases maintenance costs and lowers the life of roads. With the drop in expenditure on road maintenance in real terms during the 1990s, road conditions have deteriorated. In general the road system is not routinely maintained; but instead allowed to deteriorate until rehabilitation becomes an absolute necessity. In the long-run this is an inefficient and costly way of maintaining the system.

It appears that the country's national roads were designed to be all-purpose, with little consideration given to the need for a hierarchy of functions in which the main roads would carry the principal (line haul) flows of through-traffic while supporting networks would perform the collection and distribution function. Apart from the expressways—of which there are less than 200 kilometers in Luzon—national roads are characterized by ribbon development, that is, uncontrolled building along the edges of the road. This has occurred in default of effective land-use planning, including the construction of adequate secondary roads. As a consequence national roads fail to perform efficiently: their carrying capacity is greatly reduced, needless traffic is generated, and the accident level is unnecessarily high.

Perhaps the most destructive cause of inefficiencies in the planning and implementation of road construction and maintenance is pervasive political interference. Halcrow Fox observes that the actual program of roadwork seems inconsistent with the preceding feasibility analysis and evaluation of road projects. The widespread occurrence of serious faults and failures in road construction is indicative of corruption in the system of design, competitive bidding, contracting, and supervision. While poor road maintenance may be attributed partly to a lack of funds, it is also due to the inefficient and improper use of funds and to the limited understanding of maintenance objectives and processes.

Water Transport. Poor cargo-handling services and high effective shipping costs are the issues most commonly cited in relation to the shipping of agricultural products. Increased competition and longer contracts introduced over the past decade have led to some modernization and improvement of cargo-handling facilities. In 1994, EO 185 was issued to liberalize domestic shipping, break up monopoly positions, and ease the entry of new operators. The subsequent passage of EO 213 deregulated domestic shipping rates, but not rates for basic commodities or fares for third class passengers. In practice the entry of new operators continues to be regulated by the government, which subjects applications to an evaluation of the proposed expansion of the shipping service (routes, itinerary, tariffs, duration of business) in terms of its own judgments about market demand. Tariffs also continue to be regulated, under a provision that rates of return should not exceed 12%. The system of cross-subsidies to favor agricultural products ultimately increases their effective shipping costs, as they receive low priority from shipping operators.

Allocation of Expenditure by Commodity

The overriding historical concern for food security, commonly understood as rice self-sufficiency, has led to a disproportionate share of public expenditure (about one-half) being allocated to the rice sector, which presently accounts for about 15% of GVA of the agricultural sector (Table 6.13). The expenditure share of rice would be even higher if public spending on the agrarian reform program related to rice were taken into account. Aside from the budgetary allocation for irrigation and price stabilization, rice dominates spending on extension, credit programs, and subsidies for seed, farm machinery, and post-harvest facilities. It should be pointed out that the transition problems encountered with the introduction of modern rice technology in the late 1960s and the implementation of land reform in rice in the mid-1970s—which would have justified such subsidies—are long gone. In the meantime, traders, millers, and input dealers have successfully replaced landowners and rural banks as the major sources of credit for rice production.

Budgetary allocations for exportable crops have been meager. One exception is the coconut industry, where a major effort has been made to address falling productivity under a fertilization and replanting project funded by the World Bank. There is no clear evidence that the fertilization component of the program has led to long-term productivity growth, however, and hardly any progress has been made on the replanting component where public support is most needed. Landowners hesitate to make long-term investments; instead, trees are cut to facilitate the conversion of land to non-agricultural purposes, to put it out of reach of the land reform program.

There has been very little publicly supported effort thus far to address the problem of the declining competitive advantage of major import-competing commodities—particularly corn and sugar—through productivity-enhancing public

Table 6.13 Estimated Distribution of New Appropriation for the Department of Agriculture by Commodity (million pesos)[a]

	1990[b]	1995	1998
Rice	1,247	5,189	8,692
	(35)	(57)	(55)
Non-rice	1,360	2,131	3,657
	(38)	(23)	(23)
Livestock	642	849	1,685
	(18)	(9)	(11)
Fisheries	212	630	628
	(6)	(7)	(4)
Other	153	292	1,266
	(4)	(3)	(8)
Total	3,614	9,091	15,928

a   Figures in parentheses are percentage shares in total appropriations. The budgets of agencies handling all crops or commodities were allocated across this grouping.
b   Three-year average centered on the year shown.

expenditure programs. As mentioned earlier, national and communal gravity irrigation systems are unsuitable for high-value, non-rice crops such as corn, sugar, and vegetables. Technology generation in sugar and corn has clearly been underfunded. The budgetary allocation for sugar research has only been about 0.5% of its contribution to GVA; the figure for corn is even lower. Public expenditure on extension and other production support services for non-rice agricultural commodities has also been disproportionately low. The sugar sector has started to fund R&D and technology transfer privately, establishing the Philippine Sugar Institute in the mid-1990s.

The Regional Distribution of Expenditure

The distribution of public expenditure across regions may reflect both the priority accorded a region directly and that accorded it indirectly through the importance conferred on commodities and such objectives as environmental protection. It may also be influenced by differences in the cost of providing support services on the supply side, and by the potential benefits of these on the demand side.

In general, the regional allocation of budgetary resources, whether relative to the region's agricultural GVA or as a ratio of the rural population, has varied widely across regions (Table 6.14). Spending by local government units (LGUs) in relative terms has tended to vary less than that of national government departments, the exception being regional expenditure by the Department of Agriculture as a ratio of rural population. As might be expected, the allocations of the Department of Envi-

Table 6.14 Ratio of Public Expenditure on Agriculture to Gross Value Added and to the Rural Population, by Region and Agency, 1998 (%)

Region	Ratio of Gross Value Added					Ratio of Rural Population (pesos/person)				
	Total	LGU	DA[a]	DAR	DENR	Total	LGU	DA	DAR	DENR
Ilocos	2.38	0.78	0.57	0.31	0.73	232	76	55	30	71
CAR	5.91	1.51	0.99	0.52	2.88	597	153	100	53	291
Cagayan Valley	3.45	0.97	0.90	0.32	1.26	379	107	99	35	138
Central Luzon	2.37	0.83	0.46	0.47	0.61	231	81	45	46	60
Southern Tagalog	1.59	0.56	0.35	0.16	0.52	245	86	54	25	80
Bicol	3.19	1.13	0.75	0.33	0.98	202	71	47	21	62
WesternVisayas	1.75	0.59	0.36	0.29	0.51	215	72	45	35	63
Central Visayas	3.71	1.17	0.91	0.44	1.19	213	67	52	25	68
Eastern Visayas	3.84	1.35	0.87	0.43	1.19	270	95	61	30	84
Western & Central Mindanao/ARMM	2.06	0.58	0.54	0.26	0.68	216	61	56	27	71
Northern & Southern Mindanao/Caraga	1.87	0.60	0.41	0.15	0.71	339	109	74	27	128
Total	2.30	0.74	0.52	0.27	0.77	257	83	58	30	86

DA = Department of Agriculture; DAR = Department of Agrarian Reform; DENR = Department of Environment and Natural Resources; CAR = Cordillera Administrative Region; ARMM = Autonomous Region of Muslim Mindanao.
a Based on the agency's total regional expenditure.

ronment and Natural Resources are significantly more unequal, although the differences do not seem to be related to regional variations in forests, minerals, and other natural resources.

In nearly all cases, the Cordilleras (CAR) received the highest budgetary allocations in relative terms, due in part to economies of scale in public service provision. The CAR as a region makes the lowest contribution to GVA and has the smallest rural population, but as a region it would necessarily have the minimum number of local and nationally funded personnel as well as the corresponding physical facilities and operational budget. Moreover, because it is a mountainous region with poor infrastructure and widely dispersed farming communities, the cost of government operations in the CAR is very high.

Budgetary allocations are consistently relatively higher than average in the CAR, Cagayan Valley, and Bicol, and have tended to be lower than average in Southern Tagalog, Western Visayas, and the Mindanao regions. Regional allocations to Central Luzon and Ilocos are close to the average. But if public expenditure on irrigation is included, the "rice bowls" of Central Luzon and Cagayan Valley have actually been highly favored in terms of public support. The relatively low allocations directed toward Southern Tagalog and Western Visayas may reflect economies of scale, because they are the two largest contributors to GVA. However, regional patterns of budgetary allocation clearly indicate that the agricultural sector of Mindanao has generally been neglected.

6.5 INSTITUTIONAL ISSUES

Efficiency in resource allocation, sustainability of the production environment, and equity in the distribution of economic rents from natural resources have all been adversely affected by weaknesses in the property rights structure and associated land reform policies. The efficiency and effectiveness of government efforts to address market failures have in turn been constrained by weaknesses in the institutional structure of governance.

Weak Property Rights Structure

As land and other agricultural resources become increasingly scarce relative to the size of the population, securing private property rights becomes a critical instrument for promoting the sustainable and efficient long-term use of resources. Under a common property regime, the "tragedy of the commons" will prevail and agricultural resources will tend to be overexploited. The use of regulatory instruments alone is insufficient to prevent this, because of the prohibitive cost of enforcement. On the other hand, secure private property rights provide an incentive for long-term investment in land and other capital development, and for the adoption of sustainable management practices. Private property also serves as collateral for credit, increasing the availability and lowering the cost of long-term investment funds. By facilitating market exchange, secure property rights promote the efficient use of agricultural resources. It should be emphasized, however, that the initial distribution and terms and conditions of property rights greatly influences income distribution and long-term efficiency in the management of agricultural resources.

Uplands and Other Publicly Held Natural Resources

With population growth outpacing labor absorption in the industrial sector, surplus labor has increasingly depended on coastal and upland resources as a means of livelihood. These resources continue to be treated largely as common property. Faulty policy and program design and the weak enforcement of regulations have led to excessive logging and fishing, while inappropriate farming practices have degraded forestry, fishery, water, and land resources in the uplands, lowering agricultural productivity and threatening the sustainability of the production environment.

A variety of user rights arrangements have been instituted in the uplands, including the Certificate of Stewardship Contract, the Community Forest Management Arrangement, the Industrial Forestry Management Arrangement, and pasture leases. The area covered by such arrangements is, however, still relatively small. Furthermore, because of their limited tenure and non-transferability, user rights do not confer an adequate incentive for the adoption of sustainable management practices, nor can they serve as loan collateral to lower the cost of capital for long-term investments in tree crops and other land management structures. In the case of pasture leases, minimal rental fees have led to excess demand, and consequently to the inequitable allocation of leases in favor of politically powerful families and to the inefficient management of the leased land.

Agricultural Land

The highly skewed distribution of land ownership dating from the Spanish colonial era, coupled with the perceived injustice of share tenancy arrangements, generated widespread social unrest in the agricultural sector. A series of land reform programs were instituted to address rural poverty and agrarian unrest, starting with the 1963 law (RA 3844) to fix the produce shares of tenants and landlords in a particular ratio. Presidential Decree 27 signed in 1972 mandated the transfer to tillers of the ownership of land in rice and corn-growing areas. In 1987, RA 6675, or the Comprehensive Agrarian Reform Program (CARP), was passed to effect the redistribution of all agricultural land to the tillers while providing fair compensation to the owners. The program went beyond land redistribution to include the provision of support services for beneficiaries. Ostensibly to prevent any further concentration of land ownership and any future oppression by landlords, further legislation prohibited private land sales as well as share tenancy arrangements.

As Presidential Decree 27 was instituted under martial law, and as rice was mainly grown on small landholdings operated under share tenancy arrangements, land reform was implemented quite rapidly in rice-growing areas. In addition, expanded irrigation and the widespread adoption of modern rice varieties significantly increased the returns to land, strengthening tenant farmers' demands for the implementation of land reform (Otsuka 1991). In contrast, implementation of the CARP, which was legislated under a democratic regime and targeted a much wider

area (including plantation-based landholdings), has been slow. Due to inherent political difficulties and the high cost of implementing the land transfer program, only
about 60% of the original target of 4.9 million hectares of public and private land
had been redistributed by the time the program ended in 1998. Redistributing the
remaining private agricultural land is expected to be more difficult, in part because
of strong resistance from plantation landowners. Furthermore, the now landlord-
dominated Congress is less willing to allocate further budgetary resources to land
acquisition and transfer.

A number of studies of land reform in rice indicate that the transfer of land ownership significantly increased the welfare of beneficiaries directly, and also indirectly through the accumulation of physical as well as human capital over time
(Otsuka 1991; Deininger et al. 2000). However, the prohibition on the transfer of
land except to the heirs of beneficiaries and the threat of land reform in areas where
implementation has not been completed have prevented land markets from functioning efficiently and discouraged long-term agricultural investment. This has also
eroded the value of land as collateral, limiting the availability and/or raising the cost
of agricultural investments. Conversion of farm land to non-agricultural uses accelerated to facilitate private land sales or avoid the land reform process altogether. The
analysis of Deininger et al. suggests that the economic cost of the malfunctioning of
land markets due to restrictions on land ownership is probably greater than the direct
benefits of land reform.

The prohibition on share tenancy arrangements has also generated inefficiencies
in the operation of rural labor and land markets, by limiting the use of cost-effective
contractual arrangements and constraining adjustments in farm size in response to
changing factor prices. The common belief that tenancy is exploitative and inefficient has been convincingly negated in the literature. Share tenancy is said to mitigate both the labor-shirking disadvantages of wage contracts and the perverse
risk-bearing of rent contracts (Otsuka, Chuma, and Hayami 1992). According to
Roumasset (1995), share tenancy is simply a contractual arrangement that maxi-
mizes the benefits from specialization and in which the tenants are able to receive a
share of the residual profit from their day-to-day production decisions. Its prohibition prevents landless laborers from sharing in that residual profit and rising up the
agricultural ladder to become leaseholders and perhaps eventually owner-cultiva-
tors. In a Laguna village, Hayami and Kikuchi (2000) found that the size distribution of operational landholdings among farmers had changed relatively little since
the 1960s; while the number of landless agricultural laborers had increased sharply
relative to the number of farmers. In a study of four rice-growing villages conducted
from 1989 to 1998, Deininger et al (2000) reported that in the wake of the CARP
legislation, the ability of poor landless workers to gain access to land through the
established market had worsened significantly.

Weaknesses in the Bureaucratic Structure

The efficiency and effectiveness of government policies and expenditure programs
have been adversely affected by weaknesses in the institutional structure of gover-

nance. These include problems of (a) overcentralization, (b) overlapping and fragmentation of responsibilities across agencies, (c) a commodity-based organizational structure, and (d) inadequacies in the incentive structure and qualifications of staff, and instability in leadership positions.

Overcentralization

Agricultural activities are widely dispersed geographically and the problems of the sector are highly location-specific. Meanwhile, public support is required largely in the form of services, not goods. The efficient and effective provision of public services such as irrigation, research, extension, and so forth depends on the participation of both providers and recipients from the project design stage through to the implementation and evaluation stages (Siamwalla et al. 2000). Hence, the effective governance of the sector requires a high degree of decentralization to facilitate stakeholder participation.

The problem of overcentralization of the bureaucracy has long been recognized. By 1987 the national government had completed the decentralization of its operations down to the regional field units. In 1992, the Local Government Code devolved the provision of frontline services in agriculture and natural resources to the LGUs. The provincial and municipal governments became responsible for agricultural extension, regulation enforcement, communal irrigation, and certain areas of natural resource management.

Despite these organizational changes, the government has been unsuccessful in institutionalizing a genuinely participatory approach to planning and operations. First, the devolution was not complete. The extension force of the commodity-based agencies—those combining all regulatory and developmental functions pertaining to a particular commodity within one agency—was not devolved, and devolution of the personnel and functions of the Department of Environment and Natural Resources was very limited. More importantly, most programs and projects continue to be designed largely at the central level. The existing mechanisms for local and regional feedback to influence program design at the national level are few and mainly ineffective. The allocation of public expenditure according to levels of governance clearly shows that central offices continue to dominate budgetary resources. Before devolution, about 80% of total available appropriations was held by central offices, with the remainder going directly to regional offices. By 1998 the share of the central government had decreased only slightly to 75% of total available appropriations; that of regional offices had fallen to 15%, and LGUs accounted for 9%.

Not surprisingly, the impact of the devolution was most apparent in the regional budget of the Department of Agriculture, which was cut to one-third the previous year's level in 1993 and by 1998 was about half of its 1992 level. Interestingly, total available appropriations of the whole Department of Agriculture had fully recovered in real terms by 1995, just two years after devolution. Most of the budgetary increases were provided as lump sum allocations to broad commodity programs under the control of the Office of the Secretary at the central office. Although part would ultimately be disbursed by the Department of Agriculture's regional offices or selected LGUs, the central office retains control of program design and budgetary allocations. Most of the regular core budget of the regional offices, as well as expenditure on agricultural services by LGUs, is spent on personnel services. Thus the ability of LGUs and regional offices to influence strategic directions and program design at the central level has been extremely limited.

It should be pointed out that, in general, the shift in budgetary allocation to the LGUs has been less than commensurate with the responsibilities devolved (Manasan 1995). The problem has been exacerbated by the bias in fund allocation toward cities and *barangays* and urbanized LGUs, to the detriment of the poorer rural provinces and municipalities that carry the bulk of responsibility related to agriculture and natural resources. Poorer regions, despite having a greater proportion of the population dependent on agriculture, were observed to have lower total budgetary allocations. They also had relatively fewer devolved personnel owing to the continuation of the bias apparent in the original allocation of personnel to the regional offices of the Department of Agriculture (Cabanilla 1995). Finally, the mechanisms by which LGUs would be able to manage foreign-funded projects directly have not been fully developed. In summary, the ability of LGUs to carry out their responsibilities effectively in the agricultural sector has been limited by funding constraints.

Overlapping and Fragmentation

There is an overlap in the functions of the Department of Environment and Natural Resources and the Department of Agriculture in promoting sustainable development in upland areas. Now largely under cultivation and grazing, the upland areas fall under the jurisdiction of the Department of Environment and Natural Resources, which does not have the comparative advantage to effectively provide the necessary support services. The Department of Agriculture has historically focused on lowland agriculture, although it has developed ad hoc cooperative arrangements with the Department of Environment and Natural Resources to undertake upland development projects whenever foreign funding has been available.

The involvement of the Department of Agrarian Reform in the delivery of support services for agrarian reform beneficiaries has meant an overlap with the Department of Agriculture's overall responsibility for agricultural development. About one-half of the agrarian reform budget between 1987 and 1994 was allocated to support services. While only one-third of this was administered directly by the Department of Agrarian Reform, the fragmentation of the budgetary process and the linkage of support service allocations to land reform, rather than to technological and market opportunities, reduced the cost-effectiveness and increased the transaction cost of such expenditure.

The fragmentation of the agricultural research and extension system is one of the most serious weaknesses in the institutional structure of the agricultural sector. Whereas the Department of Agriculture assumes overall responsibility for agricultural development and the Department of Environment and Natural Resources for the sustainable management of natural resources and the environment, the mandate, the authority, and the budget for technology generation are spread across several departments, the state colleges and universities, and the LGUs.

Recent attempts by the Department of Agriculture's Bureau of Agricultural Research to provide leadership may strengthen the R&D effort, but no similar initiative has been proposed to address the fragmentation of the extension system. Although the national government continues to provide the bulk of the budget for extension support, so far it has failed to develop an effective institutional structure to provide overall leadership and coordination of the various extension-related activities conducted by numerous units of the Department of Agriculture. Without strong and coherent support, both technical and financial, from the national government for R&D and extension, most LGUs are unable to provide efficient and effective support services for their agricultural constituents. After all, except in a few provinces and cities, about 90% of the budget for agricultural support services simply covers salaries and wages, leaving little to spare for operational expenses.

Commodity-based Structure
The current organizational structure reflects the proliferation in the 1960s and the 1970s of commodity-based agencies, a number of which were established independently of the Department of Agriculture. Although brought under the department in 1986, they have remained largely intact as attached agencies, retaining weakened controls and accountability in their bureaucracies and constraining the coordination of research and extension.

The commodity-based structure of the Department of Agriculture has led to the fragmentation of the agricultural bureaucracy, contributing to departmental instability and inflexibility. The proliferation of agencies around specific commodities—coconut, sugar, tobacco, fiber crops, cotton—has been motivated in part by political economy factors. The commodity-based structure tends to favor the development of regulations over growth-enhancing activities with a longer-term pay-off such as research and extension. Regulations are easy to implement, have a short-term impact, and generate resources for the agency and rents for those involved in the allocation of permits and issuing of licenses. In contrast, well-documented records are needed to raise budgetary support for productivity-enhancing activities. An additional factor is that the heads of commodity-based agencies are typically non-technical persons who may not fully appreciate the potential contribution of technological change and the scientific skills and different type of management style required for productive research.

Other Concerns
A critical institutional issue that weakens governance of the sector concerns human resource management and the capability of the bureaucracy. Within a span of 14 years from 1994, the position of Secretary of the Department of Agriculture was held by seven different people. With each change of secretary, most of the undersecretaries and assistant secretaries were also replaced. The organizational structure of the department is frequently modified based on the preferred management style and/or expertise of the second and third-tier leaders. With every change of president, the turnover of leadership positions reaches right down to the level of director. A rea-

sonable rate of turnover of leadership and of staff may be advantageous, but the very frequent changes over the past decade have been disruptive and demoralizing for the regular staff.

Limited technical expertise in many parts of the agricultural bureaucracy has greatly hampered efficiency in the design and implementation of policies and programs. The proportion of staff with an advanced degree is too small to effectively carry out technology generation, policy and program formulation, monitoring and evaluation, and so forth. Outside local and foreign consultants have supplemented the department's expertise, but without a minimum level of technical competence within the department, their contribution must be limited and unsustainable.

The incentive structure fails to attract, motivate, and retain the more qualified staff. Aside from the low level of financial compensation, which characterizes the whole bureaucracy, the pervasive influence of political factors in promotion and appointments discourages the more able and qualified employees from joining, then staying in, the bureaucracy.

6.6 CONCLUDING REMARKS

The policy and institutional frameworks governing the agricultural sector have not provided the incentive structure, enabling environment, and level and quality of public goods and support services necessary to promote an efficient and sustainable growth path. While price intervention policies became more favorable to agriculture in the 1990s, this was achieved by increasing protection on major import-competing commodities and lowering implicit tariffs on inputs, rather than by reducing the disincentives on exportable commodities caused by exchange rate distortions. Thus, improvements in agricultural incentives have occurred at the cost of inefficiencies in resource allocation arising from increased price distortions within agriculture and between agriculture and agro-processing.

Artificially raising the profitability of major import-competing commodities increases the cost of land for other crops, thus indirectly reducing the competitive advantage of exportable agricultural products in world markets. The policy of maintaining high corn prices lowers the international competitiveness of the hog industry, in which the Philippines has a comparative advantage (Gonzales and Perez 1991). Very high protection for sugar hurts not only consumers but also the food-processing industry, which accounts for over 20% of value added and employment in manufacturing. The excessively high protection accorded major food commodities reduces the welfare of landless rural and poor urban households and puts pressure on wages, making labor-intensive manufacturing industries less competitive relative to low-wage, cheap food economies like Vietnam and China.

In general, countries switch from taxing to subsidizing their agricultural sectors in the course of economic development due primarily to political economy factors (Anderson, Hayami, et al. 1986; Lindert 1991).[6] It should be emphasized that in the Philippine case, the shift from taxing to assisting agriculture directly through price interventions has occurred at a much lower level of economic development than is usually the case. In a country that would be self-sufficient in food in a world of free agricultural trade, that shift would be expected to occur when per capita income reached 2.6 times the global average (Tyers and Anderson 1992; Anderson 1994). For a country that would be only 65% self-sufficient under free trade, the shift would occur when per capita income reached the global average (of $4,300 in 1992). In the late 1990s, per capita income in the Philippines was only about $1,200. Clearly the country can ill afford the cost of inefficiencies incurred under a highly distorted incentive structure.

Why did the switch toward higher agricultural protection occur so early in the Philippines? The explanation lies in a set of unique historical events, political economy factors, and the political system, facilitated by strong nationalist sentiment for food self-sufficiency, especially in the case of rice. As discussed earlier, the highly skewed distribution of land ownership and dualistic agrarian structure arising from colonial land policies and agro-ecological conditions created a constituency of large landowners and plantation operators who could lobby effectively for their vested interests. These families have historically made up the leadership of Congress and occupied strategic positions in the national and local executive branches of government. The landed oligarchs extended their activities to business, successfully pushing for the industrial protection policy that has biased incentives against agriculture (Yoshihara 1994). As international pressure for trade liberalization mounted, it proved easy to resist the opening of domestic markets to food staples by playing on nationalist sentiment for food self-sufficiency. Political pressure to increase the level of agricultural protection was strengthened by the expanded lobby groups consisting of farmer organizations, large landowners, and agri-business firms.

There has been little resistance to the high prices of white corn because it is grown primarily as a subsistence crop. The livestock and poultry producers and feed millers, who rely mainly on yellow corn, have chosen to lobby for higher output protection to offset the high corn prices rather than for a more rational corn–livestock policy. Objections to the highly restrictive corn import policy have been addressed by allocating imports at a lower tariff to the larger, more organized, and more vocal sector of the feed, poultry, and hog industries. In addition, many large feed mills and livestock and poultry producers own flour mills, and are able to substitute low-grade wheat—which is subject to a tariff of only 10%—for the artificially high-priced corn. Such a policy structure gives large-scale feed, livestock, and poultry producers a cost advantage over smaller ones, who have to rely on the domestic market for their corn supplies.

Apart from the large size of its farms and mills, the sugar sector has historically had strong political influence because of its close relationship and common interest with the government in lobbying for protection of the country's share in the U.S. premium market. In contrast, the share of sugar in household expenditure is very small, so consumers have generally tolerated the high sugar prices. Resistance to high sugar prices from the food-processing sector was mitigated by granting the larger, more vocal food processors some tariff-free sugar import privileges.

The economic waste caused by price intervention policies is magnified by the continued use of quantitative trade restrictions rather than tariffs. In particular, the government monopoly on rice imports and domestic marketing operations has been extremely costly—without achieving the conflicting objectives of lowering food prices to consumers, raising producer prices, and stabilizing prices. The use of quantitative trade restrictions promotes rent seeking, reduces government revenue, incurs a significant bureaucratic cost, and worsens price uncertainties. Unfortunately, recent policy changes in response to the WTO agreement seem to have exacerbated rather than mitigated such problems: nominal protection rates for major import-competing commodities were not only raised but the scope of NFA operations inadvertently expanded. Rice market interventions and the use of quantitative trade restrictions have persisted because the economic cost and even some portion of the financial cost are not readily apparent to the general public. Meanwhile, the bureaucracy has become used to receiving commissions, bribes, and other rents typically involved in government procurement and import licensing, making it even more difficult to effect trade liberalization.

Attempts to redistribute land ownership and promote small family-operated farming through land reform policies were accompanied by restrictions on land transfer by beneficiaries and a prohibition on share tenancy arrangements. These distorted land and labor market operations and eroded the value of land as collateral. In the meantime, the slow and uncertain implementation of land reform accelerated land conversion from agricultural to industrial and residential uses and discouraged long-term investments in land development. Moreover, the lack of an appropriate property rights structure for public land and water resources, which are already characterized by scarcity relative to the population, makes it extremely difficult to achieve sustainable management of these resources.

Public expenditure on agriculture recovered in the late 1980s. However, much of the increase was directed toward redistributive purposes (agrarian reform and input subsidies) and the strengthening of natural resource and environmental management rather than long-term productivity-enhancing investments in public-good type support services to reverse the declining competitive advantage of the agricultural sector. In particular agricultural research has been severely underfunded. Budgetary allocations have continued to favor rice, with very meager amounts going to other major commodities such as corn. Regional allocations of public expenditure indicate relative neglect of Mindanao.

The issue is not just the level of public expenditure and its allocation. Equally important are the inefficiencies caused by the faulty design and implementation of irrigation and other developmental projects and programs. This and the inadequate enforcement of regulatory instruments has limited the government's effectiveness in addressing externalities. The efficiency and effectiveness of governance have been constrained by weaknesses in the institutional structure of the agricultural bureaucracy, including overcentralization, overlapping and fragmentation of functions; the commodity-based structure of the sector; inadequate incentives and technical competence; and instability of leadership.

To improve the economic performance of the agricultural sector and contribute to raising the overall level of people's welfare, strong political commitment will be crucial in meeting the following key challenges:

- removing distortionary policies affecting agricultural output and input markets;
- limiting the role of government to correcting market failures, and minimizing the use of agriculture-specific policy instruments for redistributive purposes;
- replacing regulatory instruments embedded in trade, land, and other policies with more transparent, market-based policy instruments such as tariffs (variable import tariffs in the case of rice) and progressive land taxation;
- streamlining the bureaucracy, professionalizing the civil service, and strengthening government audit and evaluation procedures to improve the efficiency of governance of the sector; and
- easing the burden of structural adjustment away from agriculture in the course of development, through greater public support for education, health, and market infrastructure in rural areas rather than increased agricultural protection.

NOTES

1. Contrary to popular belief, economies of scale are not inherently strong in crop production, mainly because of the difficulty of monitoring the work of hired wage laborers over spatially dispersed and ecologically variable farm operations (Binswanger and Rosenzweig 1986). In the case of bananas, black tea, and sugar, they may be present in the post-harvest processing and marketing stages but could be achieved just as easily through contract farming and improved coordination between production and processing. In land-scarce and labor-abundant situations, the plantation system of operation tends to be less efficient because it is more capital-intensive, substituting machinery for labor to minimize supervision costs and other labor problems. Land is less intensively cultivated under this system, and monoculture preferred over more complex farming systems requiring a greater number of management inputs.

2. The Spanish colonial policy of granting private ownership of large tracts of land to conquistadors and friars, along with the country's relatively free land market and minimal land tax regime, led to a highly skewed distribution of land ownership, the prevalence of shared tenancy arrangements, and an increase in the number of landless households. By contrast, Thailand has traditionally granted its citizens the right to take as much land from the state as the family could cultivate, to an upper limit of about eight hectares. Some large land concessions were granted to private canal builders in Chao Phya Delta in the Central Plains. Shared tenancy arrangements have become common there, but are still of minor importance for the country as a whole. The policy of the Dutch colonial rulers in Indonesia was to preserve traditional village institutions. Dutch plantation owners were therefore restricted to long-term (20-year) leases of virgin public land and holdings of up to one-third of village land. To prevent planters from gaining permanent rights over village land, crops had to be rotated across three pieces of village land over three crop seasons. As a consequence, social stratification in rural areas has been much less severe. Tenancy is much more in the nature of land/labor market arrangements for efficiency reasons than a means of organizing the cultivation of large landholdings, as evidenced by the prevalence in Indonesia of owner cultivator cum landlords and of owner cum tenant cultivators.

3. In the late 1990s the Department of Agriculture, together with its attached agencies and corporations, spent the largest amount, accounting for about 55% of total public expenditure on the sector. This was followed by the Department of Environment and Natural Resources

with 16% of the total. When budgetary allocations to the Land Bank of the Philippines, which manages the financing of land distribution and some credit programs, are added to the expenditure of the Department of Agrarian Reform, the total is comparable to the expenditure of the Department of Environment and Natural Resources. The other national government agencies, including the Department of Science and Technology, state colleges and universities, and the Philippine Crop Insurance Corporation, received only 3–4% of the total budgetary outlay. The contribution of LGUs to total public expenditure on agriculture has grown steadily since devolution, to reach 11% by 1998.

4. The rise in public expenditure on rice price stabilization since the late 1980s was due to greater reliance on direct budgetary allocations to support the operations of the NFA, which had lost its right to import corn and wheat.

5. The geographical distribution of consumers is very different from that of the producers, which will depend importantly on agro-ecological conditions.

6. Cross-country comparisons also show that developed countries tend to overvalue and developing countries to underprice their agricultural products (Bale and Lutz 1981; Johnson 1991; Bautista and Valdez 1993). As economies develop, comparative advantage in agriculture declines; the share of agriculture in GDP and total employment, as well as the absolute size of the agricultural labor force, decreases; and demand for agricultural protection increases. With the smaller number of farm households, the ability to organize and lobby for greater protection becomes stronger. On the other hand, with food occupying a smaller share of the household budget at higher income levels, consumer resistance to higher food prices diminishes.

7

Industry

Hal Hill

7.1 INTRODUCTION

Except in unusual circumstances, or instances of rapid loss of comparative advantage, a sector's fortunes generally follow those of the economy in aggregate. This has certainly been the story of Philippine industrialization. Both the country and the industrial sector were early leaders in East Asia, but neither has lived up to initial expectations. A quite sophisticated manufacturing sector emerged in the 1950s and 1960s, spurred on by protection and a well-developed human capital base. In the late 1960s, there also seemed to be some prospect of a transition to export-oriented industrialization, following the path of the Asian newly industrializing economies (NIEs). However, with some notable exceptions that were mainly to do with the 1990s reforms, during the past 30 years the record has been disappointing: manufacturing output has grown slowly, little structural change has occurred, exports have become very narrowly concentrated in one product group (electronics), and export growth has until recently been disappointing.

The explanations for this poor performance lie principally outside the sector, and are therefore beyond the scope of this chapter. However, in microcosm the manufacturing sector does capture some of the ills that have beset the Philippine economy more generally, including costly and misguided interventions, a sporadically developed international orientation, a tendency to focus on rents rather than efficiency, poor support facilities (especially physical infrastructure), and an uncompetitive cost structure.

This chapter has three main objectives: to provide a descriptive–analytic overview of the record of Philippine industrialization, with special reference to the period since 1980; to identify some of the factors that have retarded efficient industrial growth; and to examine some of the key industrial policy debates and challenges.

The empirical and analytical foundations underpinning this study have both notable strengths and notable deficiencies. A strength is the very rich collection of high-quality literature on the subject.[1] In this respect, the Philippines is an East Asian leader. Few other countries in the region—certainly in Southeast Asia—can match it. The prime deficiencies are the country's weak industrial database, and the absence—apart from within the limited resources of the National Economic and Development Authority (NEDA)—of an institutionalized public sector capacity to sustain the case for a coherent, efficiency-oriented industrial reform program. These strengths and weaknesses will be illustrated throughout this chapter.

The chapter is organized as follows. Section 7.2 reviews basic trends in output, employment, and productivity. This is followed by an examination of broad structural changes within industry, and of export performance. Sections 7.5–7.8 investigate additional aspects of industrial structure and intervention, including ownership and concentration, the size distribution of small and medium-sized enterprises (SMEs), spatial patterns, and import protection. The chapter concludes with a forward-looking assessment of major policy challenges.

7.2 TRENDS IN OUTPUT, EMPLOYMENT, AND PRODUCTIVITY

Philippine industrialization has been characterized by a persistent "boom–bust" pattern, reflecting both the country's general economic fortunes and the fact that, until recently, the manufacturing sector was predominantly inward looking and therefore dependent for its growth primarily on domestic demand. This cyclical pattern continued into the early 1970s, with a sharp decline in 1971–72 followed briefly by strong growth, and modest expansion for the rest of the decade (Figure 7.1). From the late 1970s growth began to decline, followed by an economy-wide collapse in 1983–86. Thereafter a short recovery ensued in the early Aquino period, before another, albeit milder, contraction in the early 1990s. Several years of positive growth occurred during the period of the Ramos presidency, until the Asian crisis brought about yet another setback. On this occasion, however, the industrial recession was short-lived, and growth had resumed by 1999. Employment growth mirrored these trends for some periods, although there have been divergences which are not easily explainable (for example, in the mid-1970s and mid-1980s).[2]

Reflecting its comparatively high initial income per capita and early push for industrialization, the Philippines had one of the highest shares of manufacturing in Asia during the 1960s. For the next 20 years, 1970–90, the share remained fairly constant at around 25% of GDP (Figure 7.2). During the 1990s it declined steadily, and is now a little over 20%. The share of employment has generally mirrored these trends and is now about 10%, indicating also that manufacturing productivity has been about double the economy-wide average throughout this period.

Thus, there are two unusual features of the country's industrialization experience since 1970, certainly in an East Asian comparative context: the absence of rapid

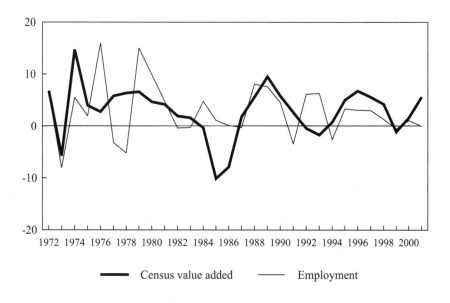

Figure 7.1 Growth of Census Value Added and Employment, 1972–2001 (%)

Source: National Statistical Coordination Board.

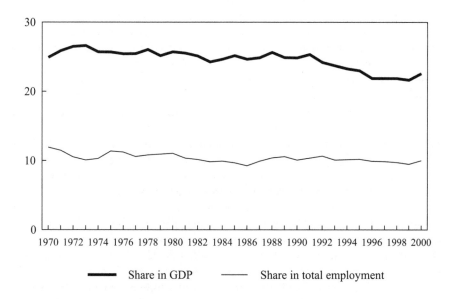

Figure 7.2 Share of Manufacturing in GDP and Total Employment, 1970–2000 (%)

Source: National Statistical Coordination Board.

structural change, and an apparent process of "de-industrialization" occurring at a low per capita income. The first is easily explainable, no doubt reflecting the general lack of economic dynamism. The second is more difficult to understand.

Three sets of explanations appear relevant. The first, and arguably the most important, is the trade liberalization that got under way in the 1980s and that accelerated in the 1990s. Traditionally, manufacturing received above-average protection, but by the late 1990s average nominal protection rates in agriculture exceeded those in manufacturing (see Bautista and Tecson, Chapter 5, and World Bank 2000b). Following the trade reforms, the industrial sector has evidently embarked on a more labor-intensive path: as Figure 7.2 documents, the share of value added declined significantly during the 1990s whereas the employment share was broadly constant. A second factor was the real appreciation of the peso through the 1990s until halted by the Asian financial crisis (see Gochoco-Bautista and Canlas, Chapter 3), which reduced the competitiveness of tradable goods activities, that is, virtually all of manufacturing. This appreciation resulted from a small nominal appreciation in some years, combined with higher inflation than the country's major trading partners in most years. Finally, tightened labor market regulations in the post-Marcos period pushed up wages in the formal sector. Relative wage levels are now high compared with those in neighboring countries, affecting competitiveness in tradable goods industries.[3]

Is this shrinking share a cause for concern? In one sense, no. The higher share in earlier years was in part a statistical artifact, a distortion that inflated the share of manufacturing output as measured in domestic (but not international) prices. The liberalization reforms have resulted in a more efficient manufacturing sector, and one that is better able to exploit its comparative advantage in labor-intensive activities. Nevertheless, it remains a puzzle that the manufacturing sector accounts for little more than 20% of GDP, and less than 10% of employment, and that the liberal reforms and respectable growth experienced during most of the 1990s did not trigger a rising share of manufacturing employment. Is there possibly some truth in the notion that the Philippines has a stronger comparative advantage in the production of services as compared to manufacturing? Another possible explanation is that supply-side constraints have held back manufacturing, particularly exports. Perhaps, too, decades of very large international remittances have resulted in a services sector (particularly trade, construction, and personal services) that is larger than would otherwise be the case. We return to these issues later in the chapter.

The record on growth in manufacturing productivity has been disappointing (Figure 7.3). It has displayed the same boom–bust pattern as manufacturing output. If anything, the cycles have been more pronounced, owing in part to the lack of synchronization between output and employment trends. There is also no evidence to suggest that liberalization has spurred labor productivity growth, as the record in the 1990s reveals several years of negative growth and little aggregate improvement. Some of the decline may of course reflect a reallocation of labor from high-productivity but inefficient activities toward labor-intensive but efficient sectors. To this extent, the decline need not necessarily be regarded with alarm.

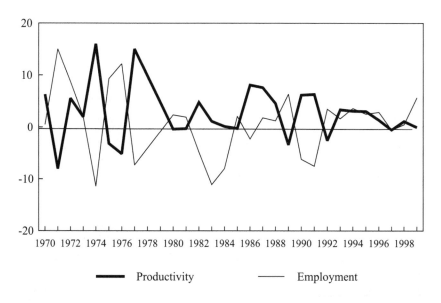

Figure 7.3 Growth in Manufacturing Productivity and Employment, 1970–99 (%)

Source: National Statistical Coordination Board.

Estimates of the growth of total factor productivity (TFP) broadly mirror this record of sluggish growth. The first detailed set of estimates for the manufacturing sector for the period 1956–80, prepared by Hooley (1985), found that the average annual growth rate was –0.15%, with modest growth over the first 15 years replaced by accelerating negative growth during the 1970s. Adjusting for improved labor quality resulted in yet lower growth. Subsequent estimates through to 1992 prepared by Cororaton et al. (1995) show that the situation deteriorated still further in the 1980s. More recently, economy-wide estimates produced by Austria (1998) show an encouraging improvement from the late 1980s, with positive growth during most of the period from 1990 to 1996. No sectoral disaggregation is given, but it is proba-ble that, with its post-reform, more labor-intensive and export-oriented trajectory, manufacturing would have shared in this growth. These latter numbers more or less accord with a priori expectations. Even in high-growth East Asian economies, annual TFP growth has generally been little more than 2%. With its slow growth, rapid labor force expansion, and moderate investment rates, it would be surprising if the Philippine numbers were positive. Perhaps the only encouraging element of these very approximate estimates is the reform-induced pick-up since the late 1980s.

A comparison of factor proportions among major industrial sectors reveals no major surprises. Here, following the work of Lary (1968), the relevant issue is how Philippine industries are ranked, that is, each industry's factor intensities relative to the all-industry average. Table 7.1 presents four standard measures: value added per

Table 7.1 Factor Proportions in Manufacturing, 1995 (% of all-manufacturing average)[a]

Code	Industry	VA/L	W/L	K/L	Skilled Labor
311	Food processing	106	94	91	112
312	Food processing	_[b]	_[b]	83	115
313	Beverages	304	161	283	106
314	Tobacco	384	108	43	76
321	Textiles	51	80	81	87
322	Garments	30	70	11	51
313	Leather products	21	64	12	71
314	Footwear	17	54	10	63
331	Wood products	28	58	34	74
332	Furniture	22	56	15	81
341	Paper products	97	108	190	140
342	Printing & publishing	55	101	50	181
351	Industrial chemicals	187	157	333	259
352	Other chemicals	259	246	129	224
353	Petroleum refining	3,579	568	3,509	618
354	Misc. petroleum	165	158	77	221
355	Rubber products	60	87	55	97
356	Plastic products	67	92	94	113
361	Ceramics	39	93	43	60
362	Glass products	171	145	285	109
363	Cement	313	182	869	187
369	Other non-metals	64	92	93	144
371	Iron & steel	142	115	341	109
372	Non-ferrous metals	360	151	728	200
381	Fabricated metals	42	77	45	99
382	Machinery	65	96	51	107
383	Electronics	79	106	82	68
384	Transport equipment	145	124	87	101
385	Professional equip, etc	33	101	30	66
386	Metal furniture	25	54	32	71
39	Miscellaneous	33	75	22	69
3	**Total**	100	100	100	100
	(thousand pesos or %)	(436)	(84)	(348)	(6.8%)

VA/L = value added per worker; W/L = wages per worker; K/L = (book value of) fixed capital per worker.

a   The data refer respectively to value added per worker (VA/L), wages per worker (W/L), (book value of) fixed capital per worker (K/L), and percentage of managerial and supervisory labor in total employment (skilled); all as a percentage of the manufacturing averages.

b   Included in 311 data.

Source: National Statistics Office, *Annual Survey of Establishments, 1995*.

worker, an overall measure of capital intensity, broadly defined; wages per worker and the proportion of skilled workers in total employment, both indicators of skill intensity; and fixed capital per worker, a measure of physical capital intensity.[4] Data are also available on R&D intensity (that is, R&D as a percentage of total expenditure), but the figure is so small (less than 0.1% for the all-industry average) as to render any comparisons meaningless.[5] In each case, data are presented as a percentage of the all-industry average.

Food-processing industries are close to the industry averages in most respects. Beverages are generally more capital and skill-intensive. In the case of tobacco products, the higher figure for value added is presumably explained mostly by product differentiation, as its skill and physical capital intensity indicators are both below average.

The ratios for textiles, garments, leather products, and footwear are uniformly low, especially for the latter three, as would be expected. Similar comments apply to other labor-intensive activities, including wood products, printing, and publishing, ceramics, metal goods, electronics, and miscellaneous industries. Some of these industries appear to be substantially more skill-intensive than physical capital-intensive. Examples include electronics, machinery, and fabricated metals. Almost all of the so-called "capital goods" industries (ISIC 38) are in reality quite labor-intensive, the principal exception being the transport equipment industry. The processing industries, ISIC 341, 35–7, are mostly above average in their factor intensities. This is most obviously the case for petroleum refining, but it also applies to paper products, chemicals, glass, cement, and basic metals. There are, however, some labor-intensive segments, including rubber and plastic products, and ceramics.

How does Philippine industrialization look in comparative international perspective? It is not obvious which countries are the Philippines' natural comparators, but any East Asian comparisons inevitably draw attention to its indifferent record. For illustration, Table 7.2 summarizes some key indicators for the country alongside those of three of its ASEAN neighbors, Indonesia, Malaysia, and Thailand, all industrial latecomers compared with the Philippines.

The results are as would be expected. The Philippine industrial sector is quite small, less than half the size of Indonesia's and Thailand's sectors, and about two-thirds that of Malaysia. Industrial growth has been much slower, especially in the 1980s but also in the 1990s. The country's shares of output and employment are well below those of its neighbors, and, in contrast to their strong growth (including a doubling in the Indonesian output share), the Philippine shares are declining. Relative capital intensities are broadly similar, except for the much lower Malaysian figure, which is explained by the dominance of labor-intensive electronics. Philippine industrial exports still exceed those of Indonesia, which also made the switch to export orientation quite recently, but are much smaller than those of Malaysia and Thailand. On a per capita basis these differences are magnified. The proportion of exports earned by "high-tech" industries is high—similar to that in Malaysia—but this figure is misleading since it reflects more than anything else a Philippine specialization in "low-tech" electronics activities. The share of manufactures in merchandise exports is the highest in the Philippines, as it was in 1983, owing to the absence of any significant

Table 7.2 Philippine Industry in Comparative Perspective[a]

Indicator	Philippines	Indonesia	Malaysia	Thailand
Total manufacturing value added ($ billion, 1999)	16.1	35.6	25.3	39.8
Share of GDP (%)				
1980	26	13	21	22
1999	21	25	32	32
Share of employment (%)				
1981	10.4	8.0	15.6	7.1
1999	9.6	13.0	22.5	13.7
Capital intensity (%)	219	192	142	234
Output growth (%)				
1980–90	–0.9	6.5	7.2	9.8
1990–99	3.2	9.9	8.8	5.7
Manufactured exports				
Total ($ billion, 1999)	32.2	26.3	67.6	43.2
Per capita ($, 1998)	433	127	2976	718
Share of high-tech (%, 1997)	59	10	59	32
Share of total exports (%)				
1983	88	54	80	74
1999	52	6	25	31
FDI/GDP (%)				
1997	10.2	28.6	38.1	8.5
1980	3.8	14.2	21.1	1.3

a   "Capital intensity" refers to manufacturing value added per worker as a percentage of the country's GDP per worker. "Output growth" refers to industry (not manufacturing). "High-tech exports" refers to the percentage of exports originating in industries characterized by high R&D intensity. "FDI/GDP" refers to the stock of FDI as a percentage of GDP.

Sources: World Bank (2001), *World Development Indicators 2001*; Asian Development Bank (2001), *Key Indicators of Developing Asian and Pacific Countries 2001*; United Nations (1999), *World Investment Report 1999*.

agricultural and resource exports. Foreign investment is of intermediate ranking, above Thailand but below the two resource-rich economies.[6]

7.3 INDUSTRY STRUCTURE AND MAJOR SECTORS

As with the intersectoral picture, there has been a general absence of structural change within manufacturing since 1970 (Tables 7.3 and 7.4). Food processing, beverages, and tobacco products continue to dominate manufacturing, with about 50% of value added and 22–25% of employment. Moreover, contrary to the more usual trends, their share of output appears if anything to be increasing slightly, certainly when compared with the 1970s.

The output shares of labor-intensive and heavy industry are similar, although as a source of employment the former dominates.[7] One would expect the share of labor-intensive activities to have risen since the late 1980s in the wake of the liberalizing reforms, and that of heavy industry, once highly protected, to have declined. This is broadly true in the case of output shares, but there is no clear picture in employment patterns. In any case, the expansion of the labor-intensive group has merely restored its share to that prevailing around 1980. Moreover, almost all of the incremental expansion in the output share of labor-intensive industries since the mid-1980s is accounted for by electronics. This industry has been the best performer, its share of output trebling since the mid-1980s, and it is now the third largest employer after food processing and garments. The share of "non-electronics labor-intensive industries" has been virtually constant since the mid-1980s.

Apart from electronics, the record is very mixed. Garments and footwear have continued to expand their share of employment, to about 18% in the mid-1990s, though their output share has been sluggish. Miscellaneous industries (including a diverse range of export-oriented labor-intensive industries such as sporting goods, toys, and musical instruments) have also performed well. Textiles, by contrast, has been disappointing, its share of both output and employment halving since the 1970s. The shares of wood products and furniture have fallen sharply, especially that of the former, presumably owing to supply constraints in the face of the country's depleted forest reserves. Metal goods and machinery have also declined in importance, in part because their fortunes are linked to the struggling transport equipment industry.

The record of heavy industries is also mixed. These industries generally consist either of "home goods" (petroleum refining, cement), whose fortunes are tied to domestic demand, or of industries once significantly protected as part of earlier, failed, attempts at industry policy, but now struggling to adjust to trade liberalization. Thus the share of petroleum refining, other chemical industries, and non-metal minerals (cement, glass, building products) has not changed markedly since the 1970s. By contrast, the output share of the transport equipment industry fell with the collapse in domestic demand in the mid-1980s and has not recovered. The sector has been unable to adjust to the new, less protected commercial environment.

Table 7.3 The Structure of Manufacturing Output, 1970–2000 (% of total manufacturing value added)[a]

Code	Industry	1970	1980	1985	1990	1995	2000
311–2	Food processing	38.5	34.9	44.8	41.8	40.2	42.6
313	Beverages	3.0	3.6	4.5	4.6	4.7	4.4
314	Tobacco	2.9	3.2	3.5	3.0	2.4	2.1
321	Textiles	4.2	5.5	3.7	3.4	2.5	1.6
322+4	Garments + footwear	4.2	5.5	4.0	6.3	6.9	5.4
323	Leather products	0.1	0.1	0.1	0.1	0.1	0.1
331	Wood products	4.0	4.3	2.0	2.1	1.3	0.8
332	Furniture	3.8	2.4	1.2	1.7	1.6	1.6
341	Paper products	1.0	1.8	1.0	1.1	0.9	0.8
342	Printing & publishing	1.5	1.2	1.0	1.2	1.3	1.0
351–2	Chemicals	7.1	9.2	7.4	7.6	8.1	7.1
353–4	Petroleum products	5.1	10.3	12.6	9.8	8.4	8.9
355	Rubber products	2.5	1.7	1.3	1.3	1.0	0.7
36	Non-metal minerals	3.2	3.3	1.9	2.8	3.9	2.7
37	Basic metals	2.0	1.9	3.0	3.2	3.0	1.6
381	Metal goods	4.8	2.7	2.0	2.4	2.2	1.7
382	Machinery	2.0	1.1	0.9	1.0	1.2	1.3
383	Electronics	4.4	3.1	3.3	3.7	6.4	11.6
384	Transport equipment	4.7	3.2	0.6	1.1	1.7	1.1
39	Miscellaneous	1.0	1.0	1.4	1.9	2.1	3.0
3	**Total**	100.0	100.0	100.0	100.0	100.0	100.0
	(billion pesos)	(10)	(63)	(143)	(267)	(438)	(745)
Major groups:							
	Food, beverages, tobacco	44.4	41.7	52.8	49.4	47.3	49.1
	Labor-intensive	30.0	26.9	19.6	23.8	25.6	28.0
	Heavy industry	25.6	31.4	27.8	26.9	27.0	22.8

a   Shares are based on current prices. The following ISIC codes apply to the major groups: food, beverages, tobacco: 31; labor-intensive: 32, 33, 342, 381–3, 39; heavy industry: 341, 35, 36, 37, 384.

Source: National Statistical Coordination Board.

Table 7.4 The Structure of Manufacturing Employment, 1975–97 (% of total employment)[a]

Code	Industry	1975	1983	1988	1994	1997[b]
311–2	Food processing	19.6	18.7	18.8	18.1	17.8
313	Beverages	5.5	4.0	3.5	2.8	2.8
314	Tobacco	4.0	2.6	1.7	1.3	1.0
321	Textiles	14.2	12.3	10.4	7.1	5.1
322	Garments	6.4	10.8	16.6	16.3	14.5
323	Leather products	0.4	0.5	0.6	0.7	3.7
324	Footwear	0.7	1.2	1.1	1.7	–
331	Wood products	8.5	8.5	6.6	2.7	2.6
332	Furniture	2.1	2.8	4.8	2.7	3.0
341	Paper products	2.1	1.9	1.8	2.0	2.1
342	Printing & publishing	2.4	2.2	2.4	2.5	2.8
351	Industrial chemicals	1.5	1.5	1.3	1.3	1.7
352	Other chemicals	3.9	3.5	3.5	3.5	3.7
353–4	Petroleum	0.3	0.3	0.3	0.3	0.2
355	Rubber products	1.9	2.5	3.1	2.7	0.9
356	Plastic products	2.9	2.4	2.1	2.9	3.1
361	Ceramics	0.5	0.3	0.6	1.2	0.6
362	Glass products	1.2	1.0	0.9	0.6	–
363	Cement	n.a.	1.0	0.7	0.8	0.7
369	Other non-metals	2.6	1.7	1.3	1.6	–
37	Iron & steel	2.0	3.0	2.1	2.8	2.8
381	Fabricated metals	4.4	2.8	2.5	3.3	3.5
382	Machinery	3.1	2.4	2.2	2.4	3.0
383	Electronics	4.2	7.5	6.4	12.1	13.9
384	Transport equipment	3.9	3.2	1.6	2.7	3.3
385	Professional equipment	0.3	0.1	0.4	0.7	1.3
386	Metal furniture	0.2	0.1	0.1	0.2	0.3
39	Miscellaneous	1.4	1.3	2.9	3.0	5.6
3	**Total**	100	100	100	100	100
	(thousands)	(512)	(701)	(857)	(895)	(1,110)
Major groups:						
	Food, beverages, tobacco	29.1	25.3	24.0	22.2	21.6
	Labor-intensive	48.3	52.5	57.0	55.4	59.3
	Heavy industry	22.8	22.3	19.3	22.4	19.1

a   Data refer to firms with 10 or more workers and are taken from *Census of Establishments*, except for 1997, which uses the *Annual Survey*. There are minor differences between the two series. The following ISIC codes apply to the major groups: food, beverages, tobacco: 31; labor-intensive: 32, 33, 342, 381–3, 385–6, 39; heavy industry: 341, 35, 36, 37, 384.
b   A dash denotes that the share is included in the preceding total.

Source: National Statistics Office.

Having surveyed the general trends, let us look more closely at the record of a few key industries. The major success story of Philippine manufacturing since the late 1980s has been electronics (see Austria 2000; Tecson 1999). Electronics exports have grown exceptionally quickly over this period, as shown below, and the share of electronics in Philippine exports is the highest among East Asian economies. The country now registers on international markets, supplying about 2% of global exports. This is a classic case of regulatory reform unleashing the Philippines' strong comparative advantage in both unskilled and semi-skilled labor. There are significant spatial agglomeration trends, with much of the industry locating south of Manila in export zones, together with smaller concentrations in Subic, Cebu, and elsewhere. As would be expected, foreign participation in the industry is very high. Semiconductors are by far the largest export item and constitute a higher share of electronics than is the case in any other East Asian country. This is quintessentially an import–export operation: local value added is thin, backward linkages are not yet well developed, the local R&D base is negligible, and the industry is weakly connected to consumer electronics (which, by contrast, has largely languished). There are emerging infrastructure challenges; linkages need to be developed by reducing barriers between the export zones and the rest of the economy; and the zones' fiscal incentives may not be sustainable in the medium term. But there appears to be sufficient momentum and "country reputation" to be able to sustain the industry's growth, albeit not at the spectacular rates registered in the 1990s, and providing of course that international demand recovers.

Performance elsewhere has been indifferent. The automotive industry is a classic case of high-cost, unsuccessful state intervention. In the late 1960s the government sought to promote the industry through its Progressive Car Manufacturing Plan, which from 1973 onward envisaged up to five local assemblers operating behind high tariff barriers and steadily increasing their local content through subcontracting arrangements (Ybanez 1983). The program was doomed to failure from the beginning: production runs were uneconomic; the foreign parties did not supply the anticipated technology; the envisaged subcontracting networks failed to proliferate (Hill 1985); and powerful vested interests developed to maintain the protection. Takacs (1994), for example, estimated that the cost to consumers of this protection in 1990 was equivalent to about 40% of the value of motor vehicle sales in that year.[8] The economic crisis of the 1980s simply exposed the inefficient nature of the industry more quickly than would otherwise have been the case.

Liberalization commenced in the early 1990s, but by then the investment climate was not conducive to foreign capital, and Thailand was reforming more decisively, in the process becoming Southeast Asia's leading automotive nation. Despite its early lead in the industry, by the mid-1990s Philippine auto production was about one-third that of Indonesia and one-quarter that of Thailand. Exports were negligible (Abrenica 1998).

The record of the textiles and garments industry has also been disappointing (Austria 1996). In spite of a strong potential comparative advantage (in garments especially), based on relative labor costs, a competitive exchange rate, and self-evident design skills, the Philippine industry has been overshadowed by that of its neighbors. In 1997, for example, Philippine exports were about 45% those of Thailand and half those of Indonesia. The contrast is particularly stark in the case of textiles, where exports were less than one-sixth those of neighboring countries. The record is somewhat better for garments, in which exports totaled 62% and 80% those of Thailand and Indonesia respectively. The textiles industry constitutes another case of a failure to adjust from a protected to an outward-looking environment. Production runs and scale are uneconomic, quality control is poor, and vertically integrated facilities are not well developed. The garments industry has not been able to free itself from the tyranny of a high-cost supplier industry and, surprisingly, has not located in the proliferating export zones to the extent that might have been expected.

7.4 EXPORT STRUCTURE AND PERFORMANCE

As noted, Philippine industrial export performance was indifferent for most of the 1970s and 1980s, and generally lagged behind that of its neighbors. In the 1990s, however, growth accelerated significantly, mainly owing to the infusion of foreign-owned electronics investments in export zones. The record during the 1990s is impressive: the total value of exports, in nominal U.S. dollars, rose five-fold from $7.8 billion to $38.1 billion. Moreover, and crucially, the growth momentum was maintained during the second half of the decade, one of the major factors explaining why the country weathered the Asian economic crisis more successfully than any other crisis-affected economy. For example, exports rose 17% in 1998 and 21% in 1999 (again in nominal U.S. dollars).

As Table 7.5 shows, electronics now dominates Philippine merchandise exports. This sector and the related machinery products industry now account for nearly three-quarters of the total. In fact, they account almost entirely (94%) for the expansion in the country's exports since 1990. Over the period 1990–2000, total exports increased by $30.3 billion; manufactured exports rose by $28.2 billion while electronics and machinery rose by $28.5 billion. In other words, non-manufacturing exports—now a very small percentage (10%) of the total—were largely constant, and non-electronics manufacturing exports actually declined slightly. Within manufacturing, nothing else is of much significance apart from garments, which accounted for 7–9% of these exports in 1998–2000.

It is clear that foreign-owned electronics firms located in the country's export-processing zones have largely driven the 1990s export growth. According to estimates by the Philippine Economic Zone Authority (PEZA), over the period 1994–99 manufactured exports from these zones rose from 22% to 50% of the country's total. Electronics accounted for 51% of total PEZA investments in 1995–99, while machinery and equipment constituted a further 39%. Although the zones are open to both foreign and domestic firms, 85% of the exports originated from multinational corporations (MNCs)—46% from Japanese firms alone.

There are significant interindustry variations in export intensity within Philippine manufacturing (Table 7.6, column 2). The country's comparative advantage lies

Table 7.5 Manufactured Exports, 1985–2000

	1985	1990	1995	1996	1997	1998	1999	2000
Total exports								
($ million)	4,629	7,821	17,447	20,543	25,228	29,496	35,037	38,079
Non-traditional (%)	70.7	84.8	86.5	88.7	89.2	90.9	92.3	92.2
Manufactures (%)	59.7	76.7	81.5	84.7	86.1	88.4	90.1	89.9
Manufactured exports								
($ million)	2,765	5,995	14,224	17,409	21,712	26,080	31,562	34,242
of which (%):								
Electronics	38.2	32.8	52.1	57.3	60.0	65.8	67.1	64.8
Machinery	1.1	2.5	5.2	7.4	12.4	12.7	15.7	17.3
Garments	22.5	26.3	18.1	13.9	10.8	9.0	7.2	7.5
Textiles	1.4	1.5	1.5	1.4	1.4	0.9	0.7	0.7

Source: National Statistical Coordination Board (various years), *Philippine Statistical Year-book*.

unambiguously in labor-intensive activities. Its earlier advantage in resource-based activities has now almost completely disappeared. Thus, one would expect a high correlation between the percentage of output that is exported and labor intensity. Since foreign firms are critical to successful export orientation, export shares and foreign ownership are also likely to be highly correlated. Highly export-oriented industries (those exporting at least 70% of their output) include garments, machinery, professional equipment, and non-ferrous metals, while in leather, footwear, furniture, and miscellaneous industries more than half of output is exported. Significant export shares (30–50%) are recorded for textiles, wood products, rubber products, and ceramics. With the exception of non-ferrous metals, all these results are readily understood.

Returning to the story depicted in Table 7.5, it needs to be emphasized that these gross export data overstate the magnitude of the export expansion. The figures are dominated by electronics, in which local value added constitutes just a small share. Indeed, one of the major challenges facing Philippine industry is the need to diversify away from a narrow reliance on labor-intensive electronics exports. Ironically, in seeking to move away from an earlier period of heavy reliance on a small range of commodity exports, the structure of exports has since become more—not less—concentrated in a narrow range of products.

Is this heavy reliance on electronics exports a cause for concern? Which view is more appropriate: an optimistic assessment emphasizing export success based on the rapid growth in recent years; or a more negative judgement that focuses on vulnerability (to fluctuations in one industry) and low value added, and allegations that this is a "dead-end" industry?

There is clearly some truth in both assessments, but on balance this is a positive story. The success in electronics indicates that the country is internationally competitive in a large and expanding industry in which international trade barriers (at least in the segments of immediate interest to the Philippines) are negligible. Electronics is a labor-intensive activity providing much-needed employment. The success in this area also helps to establish a "country reputation" for the Philippines among MNCs and international buying groups. This constitutes an important positive externality as a country's early-stage export drive develops momentum, a point emphasized in the East Asian context by Wells (1994).

It is sometimes argued that electronics is an inherently risky activity that does not provide the basis for sustained, broad-based industrialization. It is alleged that the industry is enclave in nature, characterized by "shallow" linkages with the rest of the economy (both in a spatial and interindustry sense), and that it is prone to international migration as soon as real labor costs begin to rise or fiscal incentives expire. These arguments are greatly overstated. Electronics exhibits factor proportions across the entire spectrum, from labor-intensive to highly skill and research-intensive. As industrialization progresses, the nature of the industry obviously changes as it sheds its initial labor-intensive characteristics. Such a trend is clearly evident, for example, in Singapore and to a lesser extent Malaysia over the past 20 years (McKendrick, Doner, and Haggard 2000; Hobday 2001). The industry has remained highly significant in both countries, but its product ranges and ancillary services have changed significantly.

Similarly, the linkages argument does not constitute a major limitation. Initially, local suppliers are typically unable to meet the demanding specifications of the MNC entrants. But over time this changes, both as the corporations themselves induce supplier firms to relocate and as local firms develop sufficient competence. It also needs to be noted that the enclave nature of the industry is not infrequently exacerbated by host country restrictions on the trading activities of firms in export-processing zones.

Notwithstanding this positive assessment, there are some concerns. High export concentration is risky, as the country is heavily exposed to the fluctuating fortunes of just one industry. It is, moreover, puzzling that there are so few other strong export performers in Philippine manufacturing.

The more common pattern of outward-oriented industrialization in East Asia is a broadening base of export growth over time, but the Philippines has moved in the opposite direction. Unlike its better-endowed ASEAN neighbors, the country has lost its comparative advantage in most resource-based industries. But the record in other labor-intensive industries is also disappointing, raising the question of why the Philippines has succeeded in one (electronics) but failed in others. The answer appears to lie in the dualistic nature of the export policy regime. Electronics succeeds because of the very liberal provisions applying to the export-processing zones. Firms in these zones are protected from the general constraints holding back firms in the rest of the economy: there are no ownership restrictions, bureaucratic obstacles are minimal, fiscal incentives are available, utility supplies are adequate, and there is quick and unhindered access to international markets. Firms in the zones are able to tap into the country's prime comparative advantage—competitively priced unskilled and semi-skilled labor. If export success can be achieved here, there is no reason why it cannot be replicated elsewhere, given appropriate regulatory reform.

Upgrading and diversification within the industry will not occur automatically. One of the key lessons from the success of neighboring countries is that governments need to ensure that barriers to backward integration are not inhibited by trade restrictions or by regulations affecting the spatial location decisions of firms. As simple labor-intensive activities are shed—which is still some way off in the case of the Philippines—proactive measures are needed to ensure that the requisite skill base is in place.

The above analysis should not be construed as a criticism of the PEZA concept or of its operations. There are serious questions about its fiscal incentives, their cost, and their sustainability, especially in view of the chronic national fiscal imbalances. But, unlike earlier, largely unsuccessful attempts to promote export zones,[9] the PEZA is illustrative of how trade and regulatory reform, and private sector provision of infrastructure, can "unshackle" the country's exporters and enable them to compete effectively in international markets. The real policy challenge is to broaden the base of its operations, to in effect create a sort of "nationwide PEZA."

One corollary of the country's export structure is that conventional measures of indices of revealed comparative advantage are quite misleading. The results depend entirely on how the electronics sector is classified. Several studies estimating the factor proportions content of Philippine exports have concluded that the country has one of the highest concentrations of capital/research intensity in the developing world (see, for example, Lall 2000). This is a result of the very high share of electronics in the total, and the fact that these factor proportion exercises assume that electronics is an activity with high value added. The latter proposition does apply in advanced industrialized economies, but in the Philippines, as in other low-wage economies, the industry comprises primarily labor-intensive assembly activities. It is true that the Philippines is intensively engaged in an industry which in other locations exhibits high capital intensity. But very little of the local industry or its segments could be so classified.

7.5 OWNERSHIP PATTERNS AND CONCENTRATION

Foreign Ownership

Ownership patterns reflect the interplay of a range of historical, institutional, and policy factors. As observed in Table 7.2, foreign investment in the Philippine economy is quite modest by East Asian norms, although it has increased substantially since the early 1980s. Two obvious factors explain the historically low shares: foreigners' reluctance to invest in the country, and domestic political opposition to a large foreign presence. Until the early 1980s, the Philippine foreign investment regime placed significant restrictions on foreign equity shares and sectors of activity, while a complex regulatory regime and foreign exchange licensing acted as a further deterrent (Lindsey and Valencia 1981). There were exemptions to these restrictions, principally for export-oriented industries, but such sectors were small in aggregate. From the early 1980s through to the mid-1990s, the country largely missed out on East Asia's foreign investment boom, owing to political instability, economic crisis, and ongoing disputes with international creditors (Dobson and Chia 1997). There has therefore been only a relatively short period in the nation's history of large equity capital inflows.

State ownership has never been a major feature of Philippine industry, except occasionally by default, and so we concentrate here on interindustry patterns of foreign ownership (Table 7.6, column 1). Foreign-owned firms generated quite a high percentage of manufacturing output in 1995, of about 57%.[10] Since there are relatively few industry-specific regulatory barriers to entry of foreign firms in the Philippines, interindustry variations in foreign ownership are likely to follow the pattern predicted by standard industrial organization theory;[11] that is, foreign ownership would be expected to be above average in industries characterized by international R&D intensity, product differentiation, high export orientation, and large absolute capital requirements.

This is largely the case. Foreign firms are dominant (contributing more than 80% of industry value added) in petroleum refining, non-ferrous metals, and electronics. They are also very important (accounting for 50–80% of value added) in chemicals, machinery, transport equipment, rubber products, and miscellaneous industries, and relatively unimportant in industries such as textiles, wood products, furniture, printing and publishing, and metal goods. As is always the case, however, it is important to note that there are departures from the theoretical prediction, reflecting country or even firm-specific factors. Often these occur in small industries where one or two sizable foreign firms assume considerable importance. Examples of this sort in the Philippines include leather products and ceramics, both labor-intensive activities characterized by low economies of scale, and not normally dominated by foreign firms.

Seller Concentration and Competition Policy

There are significant interindustry variations in seller concentration, defined as the share of the four largest firms in each industry's output (Table 7.7). Here also, industrial organization theory provides some guidance in understanding these patterns. Putting aside the effects of the regulatory regime, high concentration is likely in industries characterized by significant barriers to entry, including scale economies, product differentiation, and absolute capital requirements. This is broadly the case for the most recent data available (1995), with very high concentration (at least 70%) evident in petroleum refining, tobacco products, glass products, and non-ferrous metals. High levels are also found in professional equipment, footwear, ceramics, machinery, metal furniture, and transport equipment. Some of these—for example, professional equipment, footwear, ceramics, and metal furniture—are not normally associated with high concentration, and the figures are probably the result of a few large firms operating in a relatively small industry.

Table 7.6 Key Features of the Manufacturing Sector, 1995[a]

Code	Industry	% Foreign	% Exported	EPR
311	Food processing	36.2	27.5	14.5
312	Food processing	37.5	4.9	50.3
313	Beverages	35.3	0.1	44.0
314	Tobacco	42.9	1.3	53.4
321	Textiles	27.2	47.1	1.9
322	Garments	45.3	73.8	4.6
323	Leather products	67.5	68.9	8.0
324	Footwear	38.7	52.2	0.2
331	Wood products	12.2	33.8	7.5
332	Furniture	13.3	67.6	-0.1
341	Paper products	48.3	10.0	19.9
342	Printing & pubs	5.1	5.0	13.6
351	Industrial chemicals	68.6	27.1	3.0
352	Other chemicals	59.0	2.3	29.1
353	Petroleum refining	100	1.4	20.1
354	Misc. petroleum	41.1	0.1	−10.1
355	Rubber products	73.9	30.9	17.3
356	Plastic products	45.8	10.4	17.9
361	Ceramics	77.4	41.8	3.6
362	Glass products	71.8	9.4	20.2
363	Cement	22.8	0	19.5
369	Other non-metals	46.7	14.4	18.4
371	Iron & steel	44.2	5.6	9.1
372	Non-ferrous metals	89.8	77.4	−1.2
381	Fabricated metals	15.6	22.2	28.7
382	Machinery	69.9	78.7	0.4
383	Electronics	84.1	70.8	4.7
384	Transport equipment	71.1	4.5	57.3
385	Professional equipment	n.a.	78.2	1.1
386	Metal furniture	n.a.	79.2	−4.5
39	Miscellaneous	69.1	64.8	−0.8
3	**Total**	56.6	24.6	19.2

a   "% foreign" refers to the percentage of output in each industry produced by firms with foreign equity; "% exported" refers to the percentage of industry output that is exported; "EPR" refers to the effective rate of protection in 1994.

Sources: Columns 1–2: National Statistics Office, *Annual Survey of Establishments, 1995*; EPR: Medalla (1998).

Table 7.7 Seller Concentration, 1983, 1988, and 1995 (4-firm concentration ratio, %)[a]

Code	Industry	1983	1988	1995
311	Food processing	82	59	16
312	Food processing	48	53	22
313	Beverages	64	72	34
314	Tobacco	96	96	96
321	Textiles	37	29	15
322	Garments	26	18	11
323	Leather products	73	52	45
324	Footwear	66	34	56
331	Wood products	35	38	34
332	Furniture	30	18	25
341	Paper products	74	57	40
342	Printing & pubs	52	43	26
351	Industrial chemicals	65	72	41
352	Other chemicals	61	55	37
353	Petroleum refining	100	100	100
354	Misc. petroleum	96	76	55
355	Rubber products	82	69	43
356	Plastic products	32	24	22
361	Ceramics	97	75	61
362	Glass products	73	80	77
363	Cement	43	39	43
369	Other non-metals	65	56	31
371	Iron & steel	75	65	40
372	Non-ferrous metals	84	100	98
381	Fabricated metals	59	58	29
382	Machinery	50	66	59
383	Electronics	65	57	30
384	Transport equipment	79	80	63
385	Professional equipment	98	100	76
386	Metal furniture	58	57	63
39	Miscellaneous	72	54	23
3	**Average**	70	63	

a   "Seller concentration" refers to the output share of the four largest firms in each industry.

Sources: Unpublished data from National Statistics Office, *Annual Survey of Establishments, 1995*—special tabulations; data for 1983 and 1988: Tecson (1996: 23–4).

A most encouraging piece of evidence is that seller concentration appears to have been declining consistently and significantly for all major industry groups since the early 1980s. There were signs of declining concentration between 1983 and 1988, but much more significant trends are evident between 1988 and 1995. The sharpest decline of all occurred in food-processing industries (311–312), and was presumably related to the liberalization of several major agricultural processing industries. Most of the chemicals industries also exhibited a substantial decline, except for petroleum refining, which remained at 100%. The general pattern holds for steel, metal goods, and miscellaneous manufactures. Only in a few minor and unimportant cases (for example, footwear) is any sizable increase evident. Assuming that the ratios have been measured consistently, this suggests that Philippine manufacturers face much stronger competitive pressures than was the case in the 1980s. Moreover, in the wake of successive rounds of trade liberalization, it can be assumed that concentration ratios adjusted for import penetration would have declined still further, although we lack reliable estimates over time.[12]

Several studies of Philippine industry since the 1960s have drawn attention to the undesirable consequences of high levels of seller concentration. Most of this work has been conducted using the standard structure–conduct–performance framework of the industrial organization literature.[13] The general conclusions are consistent with a priori expectations: industry profitability (proxied by price–cost margins) is positively associated with concentration, capital intensity, and foreign ownership, and negatively associated with imports, defined either as import shares or as foreign competition (as measured by levels of protection). It is possible, of course, that high profitability and concentration could reflect "Schumpeterian efficiency." But the persistence of these econometric results, combined with long-established patterns of lobbying for regulatory and price barriers to competition, suggests otherwise.

Running parallel to this industrial concentration analysis is a broader literature in the Philippines which has consistently pointed to very high levels of corporate concentration centered around the country's dominant commercial families, both over time and in comparative international perspective.[14] The two phenomena are not necessarily connected. For example, concentration is usually measured at the firm or even plant level, whereas the literature on corporate conglomerates paints on a much wider canvas, to include extensive multi-plant ownership, often also extending to control backward to the financial sector and forward to wholesale and retail chains. I am not aware of any study that has attempted to systematically link these two sets of literature in the case of the Philippines, and perhaps the empirical obstacles—for example, matching firms and owners to the manufacturing statistics of the National Statistics Office (NSO)—render such an exercise infeasible. But it can safely be concluded that the seller concentration data considerably understate the effective degree of market power in much of Philippine manufacturing.

There continue to be calls for some sort of competition policy, directed in particular at the allegedly uncompetitive industrial sector. While superficially attractive, it needs to be recognized that a competition commission could be both costly and ineffective. The first point to emphasize is that practically all of the manufacturing sector consists of tradable goods industries, and so, providing import and domestic distribution channels operate competitively, the most effective anti-monopoly policy is an open trade regime. Here, as we shall see below, the Philippines has made considerable progress over the past decade, although there is a significant unfinished agenda. The more general question is whether the country has the bureaucratic capacity to implement the sophisticated and complex institutional structure implicit in calls for such a commission. Given the poor regulatory record of the Philippine stock exchange, and the powerful, well-developed legal industry, it is quite likely that, however well intentioned, such an institution would quickly be captured by vested interests and could instead simply become an additional layer of bureaucracy with which firms would have to negotiate. There may well be a case for a government agency to monitor obviously non-tradable sectors such as utilities and telecommunications,[15] but for tradable goods the case is unpersuasive.

7.6 SMALL AND MEDIUM-SIZED ENTERPRISES AND SIZE DISTRIBUTION

A strong and vibrant SME sector is an important element of successful industrialization. It provides a base for major industries such as electronics and automobiles. It constitutes a source of industrial resilience and flexibility. And arguably it contributes to broader development objectives of equity and inclusion. Taiwan exemplifies these advantages perhaps better than any other economy, certainly in East Asia.

There has been virtually no change in the size distribution of Philippine manufacturing industry since the 1970s. Distinguishing among three major size groups of firms—those with 10–99, 100–199, and 200+ employees—we find that the shares of each group in terms of employment and value added were practically identical in 1978 and 1995, although there were some minor changes during the 1980s (Table 7.8). Large firms dominate the manufacturing sector, generating about three-quarters of value added and two-thirds of employment. Middle-sized firms appear to be quite unimportant, while smaller firms make up about one-quarter of employment and one-eighth of value added. One needs to treat these figures with caution, of course. They undoubtedly mask a good deal of firm mobility among the size groups. There are no reliable data on this phenomenon for the Philippines, but there is no reason to believe that it would be any different from other countries for which better data exist (Berry, Rodriguez, and Sandee 1999). The data also exclude very small and cottage industries (firms with fewer than 10 employees), for which reliable time series data are not available.

As would be expected, there is considerable interindustry variation in the size distribution of firms, and the Philippine pattern broadly accords with expected norms. Consistent with industrial organization theory, small firms are relatively more important in industries that are more labor-intensive, and in which economies of scale in the production or marketing processes are less significant. Thus, as documented in Table 7.9, the share of small firms is more than double the industry-wide average in textiles, footwear, wood products, furniture, printing and publishing, industrial chemicals, bricks and tiles (the major part of ISIC 369), fabricated metals,

Table 7.8 The Size Distribution of Philippine Manufacturing, 1978–95 (%)[a]

Establishment Size	1978	1983	1988	1995
10–99 employees				
Share of firms	83	78	84	83
Share of employment	22	18	24	24
Share of value added	15	11	12	12
100–199 employees				
Share of firms	7	9	7	8
Share of employment	10	10	12	11
Share of value added	12	8	11	11
200+ employees				
Share of firms	10	13	9	9
Share of employment	68	72	64	65
Share of value added	74	81	77	76

a   Refers to firms with 10 or more employees.

Source: National Statistics Office (various years), *Annual Survey of Establishments*.

and machinery. It is also high, as would be expected, in some food-processing industries, garments, and miscellaneous manufactures. At the other end of the spectrum, large-scale firms dominate in the technology and capital-intensive sectors, such as petroleum refining, some chemicals, basic metals, transport equipment, and glass products. There are also examples of industries which, while not especially scale-intensive, are dominated by larger firms owing to a major MNC presence, the imperative of export markets, or significant product differentiation. Examples include electronics and tobacco products.

There is little reliable evidence on SME exports. According to Hayami, Kikuchi, and Marciano (1998), there are numerous small and cottage firms clustered to the southeast of Manila that supply city-based buyers with a range of products, some of which are exported directly to retail outlets in the United States and elsewhere. Examples include garments and metalcraft. Among the smaller firms, it is not uncommon to find several tiers in these marketing chains. It is likely that such exports are not fully recorded in the data presented in Table 7.6.

Similarly, the evidence on the SME response to the recent Asian economic crisis is ambiguous. It is probably the case that, as in other countries, size was not the key determinant of outcomes. Rather, export orientation, degree of foreign ownership, exposure to unhedged foreign currency borrowings, and industry location were more important. Lamberte et al. (1999) show that the first and last of these factors

Table 7.9 The Size Distribution of Manufacturing Output, 1995 (% of each industry's value added)

Code	Industry	Small (10–99)	Medium (100–199)	Large (200–999)	Very Large[a] (1,000+)
311	Food processing	22.1	16.3	42.4	19.2
312	Food processing	13.6	17.9	47.5	21.0
313	Beverages	0.5	10.0	68.6	21.0
314	Tobacco	0.0	2.7	97.3	–
321	Textiles	26.0	12.6	40.0	21.4
322	Garments	21.6	10.4	47.0	20.9
323	Leather products	18.1	7.4	74.5	0
324	Footwear	31.2	13.4	55.5	–
331	Wood products	26.6	19.5	28.5	25.4
332	Furniture	43.7	15.0	41.3	–[a]
341	Paper products	9.7	12.8	77.5	–
342	Printing & publishing	35.1	10.7	54.2	0
351	Industrial chemicals	29.7	28.1	42.2	–
352	Other chemicals	16.4	13.3	38.5	31.7
353	Petroleum refining	0.0	0.0	100.0	–
354	Misc. petroleum	100.0	0.0	0.0	0
355	Rubber products	13.4	12.2	74.3	–
356	Plastic products	21.2	18.4	60.4	0
361	Ceramics	6.7	2.2	91.1	–
362	Glass products	2.8	16.3	80.9	–
363	Cement	0.0	0.0	100.0	0
369	Other non-metals	34.8	16.0	49.1	0
371	Iron & steel	11.4	25.9	62.6	–
372	Non-ferrous metal	2.4	0.0	97.6	–
381	Fabricated metals	48.4	9.5	28.5	13.7
382	Machinery	32.4	26.9	10.0	30.7
383	Electronics	3.5	2.5	29.0	64.9
384	Transport equipment	5.8	9.0	34.5	50.7
385	Professional equipment	11.1	11.9	77.1	–
386	Metal furniture	30.6	0.0	69.4	0
39	Miscellaneous	21.4	18.3	60.3	0
3	**Total**	12.5	11.3	42.7	33.6

a   A dash denotes that the share is included in the figure for "large" firms.

Source: National Statistics Office, *Annual Survey of Establishments, 1995.*

were significant determinants of survival. This analysis does suggest that smaller firms fared worse than larger ones, but this is almost certainly due to the factors mentioned above. Electronics performed well throughout the crisis period, for example, and this industry consists almost entirely of larger firms.

So far there is nothing unusual about the Philippine experience with SMEs. However, although the database is weak, various pieces of evidence suggest that the size structure of firms is characterized by considerable segmentation, that something of a "missing middle" is evident, and that Taiwan-style SME dynamism is not present.

The latter proposition would not be much of a surprise, since the manufacturing sector overall has not been growing quickly for most of the past two decades.[16] But the first and second statements, if correct, are cause for concern. Together, they suggest that Philippine manufacturing has something of a bimodal size distribution, featuring both large and small firms but not as many in the middle-sized group as might be expected. This in turns suggests a lack of mobility and a somewhat "unintegrated" industrial sector. Internationally comparable data to test these propositions are not readily available, but some evidence is at least suggestive. For example, a comparison of relative factor proportions across size groups for five Southeast Asian economies, using 1980s data, indicates disproportionate differences in the Philippines; that is, large firms appear to be many times more capital-intensive than small firms, relative to other countries.[17]

Why is this so? One might hypothesize that the historical policy regime and segmented factor markets are plausible explanatory factors. Many large firms owe their existence directly or indirectly to government intervention. One set of examples, reflecting the negative correlation between protection and average firm size, includes the traditionally protected industries such as automobiles, from which SMEs were excluded either by regulatory or economic barriers to entry. More recently, it appears that SMEs have not participated significantly in the new, high-growth, export-oriented electronics sector, both because this is an MNC-intensive activity and because SMEs are constrained in their capacity to locate in the export zones.

A second general set of explanations relates to the interconnected influences of factor markets and government regulations (see, for instance, World Bank 1998b). For example, there appear to be positive inducements for small firms *not* to grow beyond a certain size, in order to avoid a range of regulatory provisions such as minimum wage regulations (including the prohibition on "labor-only contracting") and taxation obligations. The relative wage data presented in note 3 certainly suggest that there are incentives for firms to remain outside the regulated labor market. Access to the formal financial sector has reportedly also acted as a constraint, not least because, before the financial reforms of 1989–92, interest rate ceilings prevented banks from recouping the higher transaction costs that are a feature of small-scale client business. It is probably also the case that poorly functioning land markets and titling (including uncertainty over the implementation of agrarian reform) inhibited the use of land as collateral—and therefore the functioning of rural credit markets—in the manner described by Feder et al. (1988) in their case study for Thailand.

Finally, infrastructure constraints are likely to have held back the growth of small firms, particularly in the more remote agrarian provinces where they are disproportionately located.

These are at best hypotheses, of course, and the situation may have improved in the wake of the financial reforms introduced a decade ago (Berry, Rodriguez, and Sandee 1999). More research on this topic, and a much improved database, are clearly necessary.

7.7 SPATIAL PATTERNS OF INDUSTRIALIZATION

The Philippines is one of the world's largest archipelagic states, with significant interregional diversity in its relative resource endowments (see Manasan and Chatterjee, Chapter 11). In addition, for much of its post-independence history there has been extensive intersectoral policy intervention. Therefore, one would expect to find considerable regional diversity in the extent and nature of industrialization. Footloose export-oriented activities would be expected to locate near international gateways (especially as domestic infrastructure is so congested), in places where high-quality physical infrastructure is available and labor plentiful. Footloose domestic market-oriented industries would be expected to locate near major markets, which essentially means Greater Manila. The capital region would, in addition, be attractive to rent-seeking protected industries. Resource-based activities would generally be expected to locate close to sources of major raw materials, especially if motivated by the economics of on-site processing or transport cost savings.

How do actual patterns of industrialization conform to these a priori expectations? Luzon has always dominated Philippine manufacturing, generating around 80% of value added and a similar share of employment (Table 7.10). The Visayas and Mindanao have similar shares of the remainder, the latter gradually expanding its share, although with considerable fluctuations. There are no major differences in factor endowments across the three island groupings, suggesting, in aggregate at least, the general absence of highly capital-intensive enclave manufacturing. In 1995, for example, manufacturing in Luzon and Mindanao was slightly more capital-intensive than the national average, while in the Visayas it was a little below average. Interestingly, the capital intensity of manufacturing in the regions containing the nation's two largest cities (that is, the National Capital Region (NCR) and Central Visayas) is below average, a point to which we shall return shortly.

Among the major regions, a clear pattern of industrialization emerges. The greater Manila region, defined to include the capital itself and the two surrounding regions of Central Luzon and Southern Tagalog, is absolutely dominant: in 1995 its shares of value added and employment were 78.5% and 77.4% respectively. Both shares appear to be rising steadily over time. Some decline in the share of the national capital is evident during the 1990s, but this has been more than compensated for by the growth in the adjacent region of Southern Tagalog. A combination of regulatory pressures and lower production costs (particularly lower land costs) presumably explains the spillover from the national capital. This trend is likely to

Table 7.10 The Spatial Structure of Manufacturing Output, 1975–95 (% of total manufacturing)

Region	(A) Value Added				(B) Employment			
	1975	1983	1990	1995	1975	1983	1990	1995
Luzon	77.0	78.3	81.6	81.3	77.9	78.1	80.2	79.6
NCR	48.3	48.9	55.7	44.0	58.1	55.5	55.2	49.3
CAR	n.a.	n.a.	0.8	0.9	n.a.	n.a.	0.7	0.5
Ilocos	1.0	0.8	0.6	1.0	1.7	1.5	0.8	0.8
Cagayan Valley	0.5	0.4	0.3	0.2	2.2	1.5	0.7	0.3
Central Luzon	13.2	6.8	7.8	7.5	6.4	7.1	7.4	7.0
Southern Tagalog	13.5	20.9	16.2	27.0	8.3	11.7	14.9	21.1
Bicol	0.5	0.5	0.2	0.7	1.2	0.8	0.5	0.6
Visayas	15.7	7.5	10.9	9.2	12.1	10.4	10.5	12.1
Western Visayas	9.4	2.5	4.0	2.2	6.0	4.4	3.1	2.9
Central Visayas	5.4	4.7	4.9	5.0	5.6	5.6	6.9	8.7
Eastern Visayas	0.9	0.3	2.0	2.0	0.5	0.4	0.5	0.5
Mindanao	7.4	14.2	7.4	10.5	10.2	11.6	9.3	8.4
Western Mindanao	0.5	1.0	0.6	0.5	0.9	1.1	1.2	0.8
Northern Mindanao	2.5	4.1	2.1	3.4	3.0	3.6	3.0	2.2
Southern Mindanao	2.1	3.5	3.0	3.1	4.1	4.7	3.7	3.1
Central Mindanao	2.3	5.6	1.7	1.5	2.2	2.2	1.4	0.8
ARMM	n.a.	n.a.	n.a.	1.2	n.a.	n.a.	n.a.	0.4
Caraga	n.a.	n.a.	n.a.	0.8	n.a.	n.a.	n.a.	1.1

NCR = National Capital Region; CAR = Cordillera Administrative Region; ARMM = Autonomous Region of Muslim Mindanao.
a   Data refer to firms with 10 or more employees.

Source: National Statistical Coordination Board.

have accelerated in recent years with the proliferation of export zones beyond the southeastern boundaries of Manila.

Beyond Manila and its surrounds, there is very little modern-sector industrial activity in the north and south of Luzon, the Eastern Visayas, and Central and Western Mindanao. Indeed, the general impression is that the country's rural industrialization has stagnated as compared to that in, for example, parts of China and Indonesia. The major industrial zone beyond the greater capital region is centered on Cebu in the Central Visayas. Although accounting for just 5% of national value added, it employs almost 9% of the manufacturing workforce, a proportion that has been rising since the 1980s. It is also the most labor-intensive manufacturing region, a feature derived from its reliance on electronics and other export-oriented labor-intensive manufacturing. The share of Western Visayas has fallen considerably since the 1970s, reflecting the declining fortunes of its once dominant sugar industry. Smaller industrial clusters are found in Mindanao, especially around the larger cities in Southern and Northern Mindanao, such as Davao.

The regional manufacturing profiles also broadly confirm a priori expectations of spatial patterns of comparative advantage. The more industrialized regions exhibit a more diversified industrial structure and include a mix of both footloose and export-oriented activities. Less industrialized regions, by contrast, feature a heavier reliance on resource-based processing industries and simple consumer goods, and have little industrial diversity. Table 7.11 summarizes the picture for 1995. In the four most industrialized regions (NCR, Central Luzon, Southern Tagalog, and Central Visayas), the three largest industries together account for 50% or less of industrial output. With one exception (Caraga), the figure elsewhere is at least 80%, and in several it is over 90%. The largest industry in both Central Luzon and Southern Tagalog is petroleum refining, while in Manila it is chemicals. Electronics is the largest industry in Cebu and the second largest in Manila and Southern Tagalog. Its importance would almost certainly have increased in more recent years. By contrast, food processing and beverages is the largest single activity in nine of the remaining 12 regions; in several it practically constitutes the entire industrial sector. A few exceptions to the general pattern include a small steel industry in Central Mindanao, paper and wood processing in Caraga, and metal goods in the Cordillera (the latter reflecting investments in the Baguio export-processing zone).

These patterns of spatial concentration are likely to continue into the future. It might be hypothesized that Manila's share of manufacturing will start to decline as its share of the national economy tapers off in response to the 1990s decentralization initiatives, and possibly in response to some urban disamenity costs. However, the economies of scale and scope are such that Greater Manila will always be the most attractive location for market-seeking manufacturing investments, and these benefits will generally outweigh its higher land, labor, and congestion costs. Industries that require access to middle-level technical and scientific labor, such as the burgeoning information technology and electronics sectors, will also be attracted by the city's stock of skilled labor. Over time its manufacturing base will continue to expand well beyond its current boundaries, with locational decisions significantly shaped by the availability of transport networks and utilities. For footloose export-oriented activities, alternative international gateways outside Manila (for example, Subic and Cebu) may become increasingly attractive, especially if reliable and cost-effective infrastructure is available, and if Manila's relative costs continue to rise. Cebu in particular will probably consolidate its position as the nation's second largest manufacturing center, with a diversified range of export and domestic market industries, although it too is beginning to experience infrastructure (especially

Table 7.11 Major Manufacturing Industries by Region, 1995 (% of each region's manufacturing value added)[a]

Region	Industry 1	Industry 2	Industry 3	Top 3
NCR	352: 18.1	383: 12.1	314: 10.5	40.7
CAR	38: 94.7	39: (2.5)	n.a.	97.2
Ilocos	313: 48.8	363: (28.1)	314: 7.2	84.1
Cagayan Valley	313: 67.6	311: 14.4	312: 9.6	91.6
Central Luzon	353: (21.5)	313: 16.2	312: 11.5	49.2
Southern Tagalog	353: (27.9)	383: 12.3	311: 7.7	47.9
Bicol	311: 65.7	313: 16.1	312: 6.3	88.1
Western Visayas	312: 62.8	313: 27.8	311: 4.6	95.2
Central Visayas	383: 23.0	313: 20.0	312: 7.1	50.1
Eastern Visayas	313: n.a.	351: n.a.	372: n.a.	95.5
Western Mindanao	311: 71.5	313: 18.2	355: 3.6	93.3
Northern Mindanao	312: 41.0	311: 31.3	363: (8.6)	80.9
Southern Mindanao	311: 44.8	313: 30.8	363: (9.3)	84.9
Central Mindanao	371: n.a.	311: 15.9	351: n.a.	86.3
ARMM	312: 60.4	322: n.a.	331: n.a.	99.1
Caraga	341: (31.5)	331: 29.2	311: 11.0	71.7

NCR = National Capital Region; CAR = Cordillera Administrative Region; ARMM = Autonomous Region of Muslim Mindanao.

a   For definitions of industries, see Table 7.3. "Top 3" refers to the share of the three largest industries in the region's value added. Where no figure is recorded, data have been suppressed for reasons of confidentiality. Figures in parentheses are estimates. For regions where data are not available (denoted "n.a."), the share of the top three industries is also an estimate. Only two-digit data are recorded for the CAR region.

Source: National Statistical Coordination Board.

land and water) constraints. Mindanao could become a major producer of resource-based manufacturing if peace and clear land tenure were established.

It might be noted in passing that the government's successful export zone strategy has if anything reinforced the concentration of industrial activity on Luzon, and especially around Manila. In 1999, for example, 92% of exports from these zones came from Luzon. Among the dominant private zones, which produce about two-thirds of the zones' total exports, the concentration on Luzon is even greater, at 96% of total exports. This is not necessarily a criticism of the zones, of course. Partial reforms of this type are almost certainly desirable, and over time the zones may reach more distant parts of the country. But the zones can and do have unintended spatial implications, and in this case it is clear that they have operated contrary to the government's expressed preference for spatial deconcentration.

7.8 IMPORT PROTECTION

Had this chapter been written a decade or more ago, the incentives regime would have warranted major attention. However, by the end of the 1990s the Philippines had a reasonably clean and undistorted trade regime (see Bautista and Tecson, Chapter 5, and Medalla 1998): average tariff levels are now quite modest; there are comparatively few non-tariff barriers in existence; and interindustry variations in effective rates of protection are moderate. Moreover, whereas traditionally there was a major bias in favor of manufacturing, average nominal protection rates for agriculture now exceed those in manufacturing, and arguably the most serious non-tariff barriers are also located in agriculture. This is a signal achievement. It highlights the importance of the high-quality intellectual effort over 25 years in exposing the costs of extensive trade policy intervention (see especially the references in note 1), and the work of courageous policy reformers in the late Aquino and Ramos administrations in implementing the reforms. At the margin, foreign technical assistance and leverage have been of some use, but first and foremost this has been a process driven by Philippine researchers and officials.[18]

As is evident from Table 7.6 (3rd column), interindustry variations in effective protection have certainly not disappeared. The vestiges of past interventions remain, including high protection for transport equipment (about three times the all-industry average), tobacco products, beverages, and chemical products. As Tan (1986) and others have shown, historically there was the usual "cascading" structure of protection, which accorded the highest assistance to finished consumer goods and minimal protection to inputs and some capital goods.[19] Because the most protected industries are generally above average in their capital intensity and located disproportionately in major urban centers, there is in consequence the familiar bias against employment and rural development. By contrast, most of the major export-oriented, labor-intensive industries—electronics, garments, footwear, miscellaneous industries, furniture, textiles—receive very low (and in some cases marginally negative) effective protection. Of course, there are some exceptions to this generalization concerning the positive correlation between effective protection and capital intensity; for example, protection for industrial chemicals and basic metals is well below average. Moreover, to the extent that firms in these labor-intensive industries locate in export zones, they effectively operate on a free trade footing and are therefore able to escape the cost penalties of high upstream protection.

High and variable protection is always of concern, but it is particularly worrying if it coincides with other industry characteristics. Two in particular deserve mention: foreign ownership and concentration. In the case of the former, the coincidence raises the possibility of "immiserizing industrial growth," in which foreign firms extract rents from internationally inefficient industries, with little resultant benefit for the national economy. The latter conjunction points to a potentially serious competition problem, since competitive pressures from both domestic and international sources are muted.

How serious are these problems in Philippine manufacturing? The EPR–FDI correlate is modest. Most of the industries receiving significant protection (at least

50% above the industry average) feature a sizable foreign presence. That *bête noir* of economists working on Southeast Asia, the auto industry, again stands out clearly in this respect. In all the other major protected industries—food processing, beverages, tobacco, chemical products—foreign-owned firms produce at least one-third of industry output. But equally, there are quite a few FDI-intensive industries receiving below-average protection, and so the correlation is not overwhelming.

There is no clear correlation between effective protection and concentration. There are a few instances where the two coexist: autos again stands out, as does tobacco manufacturing and, to a lesser extent, petroleum refining and glass products. These are the most obvious cases where the country has a "competition problem," and where trade and domestic regulatory reforms are the most urgent. There are numerous industries where high concentration is found alongside low or even negative effective protection; examples include basic metals, ceramics, footwear, and professional equipment. In these industries there are no a priori grounds for the introduction of special competitive measures since they are subject to the discipline of import competition (providing of course there are no industry-specific anti-competitive features of import and/or domestic distribution channels).

7.9 LOOKING FORWARD: KEY POLICY CHALLENGES

The industrialization record in sum is rather mixed. The country's early advantages have not been converted into sustained and rapid industrialization. With just a few exceptions, for most of the past two decades manufacturing has performed poorly according to almost all criteria: growth, export performance, employment generation, spatial distribution, and SME dynamism. This record of industrialization has thus, in microcosm, represented the broader story of Philippine development. That is, slow growth has been a general, economy-wide phenomenon. Sluggish employment growth and the absence of much dynamism in the SME sector have contributed to continuing high poverty incidence. The mixed record on exports—with the exception of electronics—has reflected the failure to embed a deep-seated commitment to international orientation, on the part of both the business sector and the bureaucratic–political elite. The stagnation in rural industry outside the greater Metro Manila region has been a factor in the indifferent record of spatial development. The limited adoption of modern technology has held back the fuller utilization of the country's human capital capabilities.

How can the past record of indifferent industrial growth be reversed, and the improved growth record of the 1990s be converted into strong and durable expansion? Rapid economic and industrial growth are of course largely determined by the same set of factors: good macroeconomic management, openness, sound and predictable institutions, an efficient financial sector, a reasonable measure of equity, good physical infrastructure, and a supportive external environment. Unless one can make a case that there are large positive externalities associated with the industrial sector, there is nothing special about manufacturing; that is, a peso of value added in manufacturing, measured at international prices, is equivalent to that generated in any other sector of the economy. Thus policies to promote rapid industrial expansion should be part of, and consistent with, an overall strategy of accelerated, equitable growth. With this caveat in mind, are there any industry-specific measures that warrant attention? It may be useful to conclude this chapter with brief reference to three general sets of industry policy issues.

The Incentive Regime

The agenda here is analytically straightforward, though no doubt politically sensitive. The forward reform momentum needs to be maintained, with continued lowering and unification of tariffs and the removal of remaining non-tariff barriers. Notwithstanding the progress made since the late 1980s, the policy battles have not been won decisively. The country has a history of backtracking on reforms, and the recent Asian crisis has triggered widespread calls for special "temporary" assistance. In the last year of the Estrada administration, the perception intensified that favored treatment was available for the politically well connected. Although the administration held the line on protection for manufacturing, the general policy reform atmosphere was in consequence soured.

Nevertheless, the large real depreciation of the peso since 1997 has been sustained. Providing the Macapagal-Arroyo administration renews the commitment to reform, these exchange rate movements should facilitate the liberalization process, owing to the major boost in competitiveness for tradable goods industries. Structural adjustment measures for affected industries and workers may have to be provided, but such assistance should be strictly time-bound and completely transparent. Compensating fiscal measures may be required to cover any loss of revenue from import duties.

Trade liberalization is the most effective means of ensuring that Philippine manufacturers operate in a competitive environment. Additional regulatory reform and bureaucratic simplification will constitute an important complementary element of these reforms. It is doubtful that a competition commission would do much more than simply add an additional layer of bureaucracy with which firms would have to cope. But some sort of institutional mechanism which ensures that the country's institutions and bureaucratic processes are corruption-free and up to world standards is important.

The export zones are an important institutional innovation facilitating export growth in the 1990s. As domestic trade barriers decline, they become much less important as a means of enabling exporters to escape the cost penalties of protected input industries. It is also desirable that the zones' fiscal incentives be reduced over time and integrated into a general package of fiscal reform and simplification. But the zones remain useful, not only because both these processes will take time, but also because the regulations under which the PEZA operates will put pressure on government regulators and other providers of infrastructure to match their standards.

Given its current structure of exports, Philippine manufacturers do not face serious problems of international market access. The electronics industry is MNC-dominated, and trade barriers for its lower-end products are not significant. The

Multi-Fibre Agreement, which affects international trade in textiles and garments, is gradually being incorporated within general World Trade Organization (WTO) principles. Footwear, furniture, sporting goods, and other labor-intensive manufactures are generally not highly protected industries in OECD markets. The Philippines will have continuing obligations under the ASEAN Free Trade Area (AFTA) and the Asia Pacific Economic Cooperation (APEC) process, but these are not especially onerous, and the country is ahead of most timetables in its reforms. As in the past, it makes sense for the Philippines to immediately multilateralize its AFTA commitments. On both political economy and commercial grounds, there is, moreover, no case for attempting to employ reciprocity as a tool in the reform process.

Innovation and Diffusion Issues

The principal challenge is to maximize innovation and diffusion capacities, consistent with the country exploiting its comparative advantage in unskilled and semi-skilled labor-intensive industries. The Philippines is still at least a decade—and probably a good deal more—away from the "turning point" at which, as in Malaysia in the mid-1990s, rising real wages will force it to begin to shed its labor-intensive activities. It therefore has the luxury of being a "technological borrower." This implies that the principal role of the government's science and technology policies should be to remove barriers to inflows of technology and knowhow, and to ensure that there is sufficient absorptive capacity for these inflows to be utilized by local firms and workers.

One element of such a strategy is an open policy toward the inflow of FDI and skilled labor. A second is a stronger commitment to a high-quality public education system, particularly at the primary and junior secondary levels. Governments may need to play a catalytic role in developing specialist vocational skills where these are not well developed, but in general much of this can be left to private suppliers. Third, there may be a case for the government to support some R&D activities, but the more important strategy is encouraging domestic diffusion of public domain technologies. Thus the country's very low R&D expenditure (currently 0.1–0.2% of GDP) is no great cause for concern, but the underdeveloped state of industrial extension services is. That is, the government does have a role to play in assisting firms to minimize the costs of acquiring information about new technologies, new products, and market channels and trends. International buyers and investors can provide much of this, but, especially for smaller firms, there is evidence that governments can play a useful connecting role.

There is impatience that most of the Philippine export zone activity consists of technologically simple processes with very limited backward linkages. Such an output mix is not surprising, for at least three reasons: it is consistent with the country's comparative advantage; most of the investors are recent arrivals, and it takes time for both international and domestic investors to discern commercial opportunities; and firms moving out of the zones immediately confront significant fiscal and regulatory impediments. Thus the response to this expressed impatience is partly that the issue is not important, partly that it takes time to develop these linkages, and partly that government reforms are necessary to reduce the "enclave" nature of the zones.

Constraints to Industrial Growth

The most important contribution that the Philippine government can make to firms' capacity to compete with international producers both at home and abroad is to ensure that the price, availability, and quality of the requisite services are internationally competitive. These include domestic and international telecommunications services, domestic and international shipping and civil aviation, airports and harbors, the domestic road network, financial services, the taxation regime, import–export procedures, and the general regulatory/licensing regime.

An assessment of these services is beyond the scope of this chapter, but it is readily apparent that there are departures from international norms of best practice. There have been some notable improvements in the past decade, including deregulation of interisland passenger shipping, domestic civil aviation, and cellular phones (see Abrenica and Llanto, Chapter 8). There is also increased private provision of physical infrastructure, including export zones and toll roads. The banking sector is now reasonably competitive, while the removal of interest rate ceilings has enabled SMEs to better access the formal financial sector. However, significant challenges remain. The country's road network is poorer than those of its more developed ASEAN neighbors (for example, Indonesia, Malaysia, and Thailand). The landline telephone network remains deficient, particularly outside major urban centers. Electricity prices are high, partly as a result of the severe shortages of a decade ago, and the crash program of acquiring high-cost, small-scale generators. Utilities in the export zones are expensive by international standards. Interisland shipping freight has been only partially deregulated. Port and customs procedures remain slow and complex.

NOTES

I am indebted to Melody Garcia for excellent research assistance in accessing and compiling much of the data presented in the chapter, and to the head of the Manufacturing Industry Division of the National Statistics Office, Ms L. Homecillo, for kindly providing access to unpublished statistical series. Conference participants provided much useful feedback. I am particularly grateful to my discussant, Romy Bautista, for incisive and comprehensive comments.

1. These include Power and Sicat (1971), Bautista, Power, and Associates (1979), and Medalla et al. (1995/96). In addition, there have been numerous important papers published in the country's main economics/development journals, some of which are referred to in this chapter. The School of Economics at the University of the Philippines and the Philippine Institute for Development Studies have been the key intellectual forces behind these major studies.

2. Employment, both in total and especially in full-time equivalents, is measured only approximately in the cottage industry sector. Indeed, manufacturing employment data in general appear to be rather approximate.

3. One should not overstate the importance of this factor, since there has traditionally been a quite active trade union movement in the Philippines and some labor market regulations. However, since the late 1980s these pressures have intensified, with the result that minimum wages are now high relative to the country's per capita GDP. As World Bank (2000b: 15) shows, the ratio of minimum wages to (PPP) per capita GDP in the Philippines was about double that of Thailand and quadruple that of Indonesia over the period 1995–99.

4. This is not the place to discuss in detail the well-known limitations associated with such measures. For example: value added measures incorporate business cycle effects along with factor intensities; the wage indicator will be affected by labor market imperfections; capital data are often poorly measured; and supervisory labor may not be highly skilled. Nevertheless, numerous studies have shown these ratios to be reasonably robust factor intensity indicators.

5. It might be noted in passing that the percentage for electronics (ISIC 383) is even lower, a further illustration of how misleading it is to characterize the industry in the Philippines as "high-tech."

6. The latter data are not disaggregated for manufacturing, and so need to be interpreted as a more general, economy-wide indicator of openness to foreign investment.

7. The classification of industries by factor intensities follows general rankings, with some modifications introduced for local conditions, and is based in part on the ratios presented in Table 7.1. The resource-based category is not employed because the domestic natural-resource component in Philippine manufacturing is now very small. Similarly, categories such as "human capital"-intensive and "technology"-intensive do not make much analytical sense, for the reasons set out in the text.

8. According to her (plausible) estimates, consumers were unambiguous losers and component producers the unambiguous winners. Assemblers benefited from the higher prices, but lost out from higher component prices. Deadweight costs were equivalent to about 10% of the value of industry sales.

9. See Warr (1989), who compared the performance of export-processing zones in the Philippines, Malaysia, Indonesia, and Korea, concluding that the Philippines had the poorest social rate of return from such investments.

10. Note that the definition of foreign ownership here is a broad one: any firm with foreign equity is regarded as "foreign-owned." The census definition separately identifies the share of output from firms with at least 10% foreign equity. The two series differ little, however, and the broader definition seems justified on the grounds that equity shares invariably understate effective foreign control, through licensing agreements, proprietary brand names, and control of technology.

11. In other words, in seeking an explanation for interindustry variations, one does not have to take specific account of the presence of a large state enterprise sector or a complex foreign investment regulatory environment. This contrasts with the case of Indonesia, for example, where quantitative analysis has demonstrated the importance of the policy regime as a significant determinant of these variations (see Aswicahyono and Hill 1993).

12. For a detailed analysis of trends in industrial concentration in a neighboring country, Indonesia, including also the impact of trade liberalization, see Bird (1999).

13. Examples include Go, Kamerschen, and Delorne (1999), Imbat and Tanlapco (1993), and Lindsey (1977).

14. See, for example, Claessens, Djankov, and Lang (2000), Saldana (1999), Tan (1993), and Ungarte and Sullivan (2000).

15. Even in these cases, such an agency would be no guarantee that uncompetitive practices would not occur. This is so because in many cases it is government decrees that are the source of the problem (for example, PAL's privileged treatment at Manila airport).

16. Ranis and Stewart (1999), for example, draw together an array of empirical evidence to suggest that the urban informal sector, including manufacturing, has tended to operate as a sector of "last resort employment" rather than as a source of dynamism.

17. The comparative data are presented in Hill (1995), which for its Philippine data draws on Alonzo, de Dios, and Tecson (1992).

18. See Alburo (1993) for a political economy analysis of four of the country's major reform episodes, 1962, 1970, 1980, and post-1986.

19. Tan's (1986) regression analysis also detected some of the variables usually associated with high protection, including capital intensity and low import shares, although as is common with such studies the explanatory power is rather weak.

8

Services

Ma. Joy V. Abrenica and Gilberto M. Llanto

8.1 INTRODUCTION

New technologies have instigated profound changes in the services sector. One major change has been the elimination of geographic factors in the provision and use of many services. Whereas, in the past, the co-location of provider and user was required to effect a service transaction, digitization and internet technologies have made feasible the "virtual" delivery of services. This has allowed the cross-border supply of a number of services that were previously considered non-tradable. Internet banking (financial services), e-commerce (distribution services), distance learning (education services), and telediagnosis (health services) are cases in point.

Another major change concerns the feasibility of delivering different types of services over a common platform, a development known as convergence. Historically, such services were differentiated by their technologies and infrastructure. With convergence has come a blurring of industry boundaries, as when broadcasting, information, and electricity services invade the traditional domain of telecommunications.

However, even as networks converge, service offerings are becoming increasingly stratified. Thus a single service offering may involve several layers of activities by different enterprises, not all of which are visible to the user. In telecommunications, for example, the international traffic of messages involves a number of entities engaged in the provision of high-capacity facilities, large-scale traffic aggregation, wholesale and retail marketing, bandwidth management, and value adding (ITU 1999a)—yet users interact only with the carriers to which they are directly linked. The emergence of these new activities has created market opportunities for new players, leading to an expansion of the services sector.

Technology-driven changes have set the stage for the liberalization of trade and investment in services. Although the initiative has come from developed economies, where the services sector already accounts for as much as 70% of GDP and 60% of employment, support from developing economies has not been lacking. In fact, a review of the General Agreement on Trade in Services (GATS) reveals that the commitments made by developing economies to all four modes of service supply do not fall short of those made by developed economies (Adlung 2000). The four modes of supply identified in the GATS are: (1) cross-border supply, which is akin to the movement of goods; (2) consumption abroad, pertaining to the use of services by nationals of one member economy in the territory of another; (3) commercial presence, whereby a foreign service provider establishes a presence in a member's market; and (4) movement of natural persons, whereby foreign individuals (as opposed to establishments) supply services in the territory of a member economy.

What explains this liberal posture? For many developing economies, the impetus for reform originates in the high cost and poor quality of services, which have impinged on the competitiveness of their industrial sectors. The clamor for more efficient services is often strongest among producers of tradable goods exposed to competition in the global or domestic market, with business users thus comprising the main constituency for reform of the services sector.

A related issue is the increasing cost of infrastructure. Most service industries were previously closed to private capital, both domestic and foreign, because of "national security" or "public service" concerns, as in the case of electricity supply or air transport services. When governments ran into difficulties in meeting the investment and management requirements of such industries, they were compelled to turn them over to the private sector. In the Philippines, the campaign to attract the participation of the private sector in infrastructure development took off in the early 1990s, with the government providing financial guarantees to mitigate the investment risks.

As with the goods sector, the full market opening of the services sector may be stymied by institutional rigidities. In services, the impediments to opening commonly take two forms: market access barriers (discrimination against new suppliers in favor of incumbents); and national treatment barriers (discrimination against foreign suppliers in favor of domestic suppliers).[1] In the Philippines, market access restrictions, manifested in terms of limitations on the number of service suppliers and on foreign equity participation, are prevalent in banking and other financial sectors as well as in some segments of the telecommunications industry. Examples of national treatment impediments can be found in financial services, where foreign suppliers are required to have a Filipino understudy in the firm to facilitate the transfer of technology, and education, where foreign providers are subjected to an economic needs test.

An even more potent impediment to market reform is posed by a regulatory regime that is unable to cope with the demands of a new market environment. Innovations in products and processes are challenging the rationales upon which traditional forms of regulation are based. A regulatory system that is not attuned to the new environment may fail to engender effective competition and promote efficiency, even if explicit market access and national treatment barriers are removed. Weak regulation can therefore undermine the value of an economy's commitment to reform.

This chapter examines regulations that distort trade in services.[2] These are barriers that elude the discipline of multilateral agreements such as the GATS and hinder the market from reaping the full benefits of liberalization.[3] The discussion focuses on two of the most technologically dynamic sectors: telecommunications and banking. More reforms have been implemented in these two sectors than in any other branch of services. Their regulatory experience is therefore replete with lessons of relevance for other service sectors.

8.2   REFORMS IN THE SERVICES SECTOR

In the Philippines, a movement of labor from agriculture and industry to services has been observed since the early 1980s (see Balisacan and Hill, Chapter 1). The services sector has become an important contributor to employment and national output, its robust performance compensating both for the slump in agriculture from 1994 to 1997 and for the sluggish performance of industry during years of economic downturn. In 1999 services accounted for 44% of employment and 45% of GDP.

The composition of services in the Philippine national income accounts is shown in Table 8.1. Excluded from the accounts are construction and the distribution of energy and water, which are classified under industry. Over the past three decades trade has consistently accounted for about one-third of gross value added in services. Finance grew faster than other sectors in the 1970s and 1990s but was severely affected by the economic crisis of the 1980s. It was in this decade (specifically, 1981–87) that a major banking crisis occurred, whose cost to the economy was estimated to be equivalent to 3% of GDP (Caprio and Klingebiel 1996).

Despite the expansion of the sector, the value of trade in services remains insignificant compared with that of trade in goods. Exports of services in 2001, for example, were only one-tenth those of goods (Table 8.2). Nevertheless, until 1997 a positive trade balance in services compensated for a widening trade deficit in goods. There have been reversals in the trade balance since 1998, with a slowdown in economic activity depressing imports of goods, but not of services, and a depreciation in the exchange rate helping exports of goods, but not of services. Thus services trade has recently been in deficit and goods trade in surplus.

It should be noted that the trade in services detailed in Tables 8.2 and 8.3 does not include services supplied through mode 3 (commercial presence) or mode 4 (movement of natural persons). Thus far, the only comprehensive source of information on services trade is the IMF's annual *Balance of Payments Statistics Yearbook*, which does not fully cover trade by foreign affiliates or adequately capture transactions by natural persons.[4] The implications vary by sector, but distribution and financial services are likely to be the most affected. Apart from these shortcomings, there is a lack of concordance between the IMF categories for services and those in the Philippine national income accounts. Moreover, the GATS maintains its

Table 8.1 Composition of Services, 1970–2001 (%)

Component	Share of Gross Value Added				Growth Rate			
	1970–79	1980–89	1990–2000	2001	1970–79	1980–89	1990–2000	2001
Transportation, communication, & storage	12.7	13.6	14.1	16.4	8.4	3.1	5.0	8.9
Trade	34.7	35.7	35.3	35.6	5.7	2.3	3.7	5.6
Finance	9.0	9.0	10.3	10.4	9.3	0.6	5.1	0.6
Ownership of dwellings & real estate	17.4	13.9	12.4	10.6	1.1	1.7	2.0	-0.3
Private services	13.8	16.2	16.1	16.3	5.3	4.2	3.7	4.4
Government services	12.3	11.7	11.8	10.8	4.1	2.5	3.4	1.8
Total	100.0	100.0	100.0	100.0	5.3	2.5	3.8	3.4

Source: National Statistical Coordination Board.

own sectoral classification list, which is far more disaggregated than that of the IMF. These data constraints have hindered detailed quantitative assessment of trade in services.

Few would refute that the growth in Philippine services trade in recent years owes a great deal to the market reforms initiated in the first half of the 1990s. During this period structural reforms were introduced in historically sheltered industries such as telecommunications, banking, shipping, and air transport services. The impact of the reforms has been uneven—they were more successful in communications and finance than in transportation.

As there was considerable domestic momentum for reform even before the GATS, it is not surprising to find the Philippine record of external policy commitments to be almost as broad in coverage as that of advanced economies such as Australia, the European Union and the United States (WTO 1999, cited in Adlung 2000). Interestingly, the country's commitments go beyond those made by Singapore and Indonesia but have not been quite as far-reaching as those made by Thailand and Malaysia.

The reform of Philippine services began in 1993 with the adoption of two major laws liberalizing major segments of the telecommunications sector. In the following year, banking and insurance services were opened to foreign suppliers. Air transport services and domestic shipping were liberalized in 1995, paving the way for entry of new local operators. A new national policy issued in 1998 deregulated the use of

Table 8.2 Value and Growth of Trade in Goods and Services, 1985–2001

Component	Value ($ billion)									Growth Rate (%)			
	1985	1990	1995	1997	1998	1999	2000	2001		1985–90	1991–95	1996–2001	1991–2001
Goods													
Exports	4.6	8.2	17.4	25.2	29.5	35.0	38.1	32.1		13.7	16.6	11.6	13.8
Imports	5.1	12.2	26.4	35.7	29.7	30.7	31.4	29.6		21.1	17.1	2.7	9.2
Balance	−0.5	−4.0	−9.0	−10.5	−0.2	4.3	6.7	2.6					
Services													
Exports	3.3	4.8	14.4	22.8	13.9	4.8	4.0	3.2		11.5	25.2	−15.0	3.3
Imports	3.3	4.1	9.6	17.1	13.2	7.5	6.1	5.1		3.3	19.7	−5.7	5.9
Balance	0.0	0.7	4.8	5.7	0.7	−2.7	−2.1	−1.9					

Source: IMF (various years), *Balance of Payments Statistics Yearbook*; Bangko Sentral ng Pilipinas; National Statistics Office.

Table 8.3 Composition of Trade in Services, 2001

Component	Exports		Imports		Net Trade
	Value ($ million)	Share (%)	Value ($ million)	Share (%)	Value ($ million)
Transportation	659	20.9	2,325	45.7	−1,666
Travel	1,723	54.7	1,224	24.0	499
Communication	330	10.5	215	4.2	115
Construction	64	2.0	298	5.9	−234
Insurance	48	1.5	116	2.3	−68
Finance	34	1.1	75	1.5	-41
Computer & information	22	0.7	83	1.6	−61
Royalties & license fees	1	0.0	158	3.1	−157
Other business services	219	7.0	537	10.6	−318
Personal, cultural & recreational	15	0.5	57	1.1	−42
Government	36	1.1	2	0.0	34
Total	3,151	100.0	5,090	100.0	−1,939

Source: IMF (2002), *Balance of Payments Statistics Yearbook 2001*.

international satellite communications. Major changes were made to the regulation of securities in February 2000 and to banking regulation in May 2000.

At least four major amendments to the Foreign Investment Act of 1991 (Republic Act (RA) 7042) have had a direct impact on the services sector. RA 8179 granted foreign investors full access to all tourism-related activities except transport. RA 8366, also known as the Investment Houses Law of 1997, increased the foreign equity cap for an investment house from 40% to 60% of the voting stock. RA 8556, or the Financing Company Act of 1998, raised the allowable limit for foreign equity participation in a financing company to 60% of the voting stock. And in August 1998, private domestic construction contracts were de-listed from the foreign investment negative list, removing all limits to foreign equity participation in construction services.

The Retail Trade Liberalization Act of 2000 replaced a half-century-old law restricting the right to engage in retail distribution to Philippine citizens, thus opening the door to entry of foreign investment in specified areas of retail trade. In the same year the government passed the E-Commerce Law (RA 8792), which provided for legal recognition of electronically transmitted messages, documents, and signatures. The intent of the law was to facilitate and encourage domestic and international transactions conducted over the internet.

Notwithstanding these initiatives, significant impediments related to market access and national treatment continue to prevail in the services sector. Many of these are stipulated in the Philippine constitution and hence are difficult to reform. For example, franchises on all modes of transport services can be awarded only to Philippine citizens, or to corporations or associations organized under Philippine law and at least 60% owned by Philippine nationals. The law on cabotage reserves all coastal trade for national vessels crewed by Filipinos.[5] No cross-ownership of telecommunications and broadcasting is permitted. Foreign investors can lease but not own land.[6] Although the Retail Trade Liberalization Act has opened retail trade to foreign investors, the Philippines still has the highest minimum capital requirement for foreign retailers of any Asian economy.[7] Moreover, retail enterprises with a paid-up capital of up to $2.5 million are still reserved entirely for Philippine citizens.

The trading conditions for mode 4 supply of services (movement of natural persons) are also restrictive. Before a non-resident alien is allowed to supply a service, it must be established that no Philippine national is able and willing to supply that same service. An alien who is permitted to hold a technical position in an enterprise can do so only within the first five years of its operation, and must have at least two Filipino understudies. In the case of activities reserved expressly by law for Philippine nationals, all executive and managerial positions must be held by Filipinos, although foreign investors can participate in governance in proportion to their share of capital in the organization. These restrictions apply even in the tourism sector, which tends to be treated liberally in most countries. Thus, only Filipinos can be employed in tourism-oriented establishments, with some leeway given to hotels and resorts.

These impediments render the Philippine services market restrictive when compared with those of other Asia-Pacific economies. Table 8.4 finds supports for this position based on comparative studies on trade restrictions in services undertaken by the Australian National University and the Australian Productivity Commission (Findlay 2001). Following Hoekman's (1995) methodology of ranking a sector's trade restrictiveness based on a count of the frequency of impediments, in Table 8.4 a value close to zero suggests market openness whereas a value close to 1 indicates restrictiveness. Separate indices are calculated for domestic and foreign suppliers. For all sectors except engineering, the Philippine values for foreign suppliers are higher than the average for selected APEC economies. Compared with the average for ASEAN economies, the Philippine values are lower only for telecommunications. The sector is indeed ripe for market reform.

Two other observations are suggested by these indices. First, although the Philippines has instituted more reforms in telecommunications and banking than in other service sectors, the values for these sectors are no lower than those of sectors in which fewer reforms have been introduced, for example distribution. Second, national treatment impediments are pervasive in all sectors and for all economies, as suggested by the consistently lower values for domestic than for foreign suppliers. In the case of the Philippines, the gap between the domestic and foreign supplier indices is widest in telecommunications, banking, maritime services, and legal services.

Table 8.4 Index of Trade Restrictiveness in Services

Component	Philippines		Average for ASEAN-5[a]		Average for APEC-14[b]	
	Domestic Suppliers	Foreign Suppliers	Domestic Suppliers	Foreign Suppliers	Domestic Suppliers	Foreign Suppliers
Banking	0.1	0.5	0.1	0.5	0.1	0.3
Telecommunications	0.1	0.5	0.3	0.6	0.2	0.4
Maritime services	0.2	0.6	0.2	0.5	0.2	0.5
Distribution	0.1	0.4	0.1	0.3	0.1	0.2
Engineering	0.0	0.2	0.0	0.2	0.1	0.2
Architecture	0.1	0.3	0.0	0.2	0.1	0.2
Accountancy	0.3	0.6	0.2	0.5	0.2	0.4
Legal	0.1	0.5	0.1	0.5	0.2	0.5

a   Comprises the Philippines, Thailand, Indonesia, Malaysia, and Singapore.
b   Comprises the ASEAN-5 plus the United States, Australia, New Zealand, Japan, Chile, Hong Kong, Canada, Mexico, and South Korea.

Sources: Kalirajan (2000), McGuire, Schuele, and Smith (2000), McGuire and Schuele (2000), Kalirajan et al. (2000), Nguyen-Hong (2000), and Warren (2000), as cited in Findlay (2001).

How costly are these barriers? Findlay (2001) has reported the estimated divergence between domestic and world prices resulting from the imposition of restrictions on local and foreign suppliers for a wide cross-section of countries. As might be expected, the cost of impediments is almost nil for the highest-income group of countries (reflected in a divergence of 7% for banking and 2% for telecommunications) but overwhelming for the lowest-income group of countries (with a divergence of 52% for banking and 138% for telecommunications). Specific calculations for ASEAN economies are shown in Table 8.5. It can be seen that, in the case of the Philippines, the price wedge is as high as 11–47% for banking and 21–73% for telecommunications.

Warren (2000) shows further that in the telecommunications sector, trade impediments have retarded investments in the fixed and mobile telecommunications networks. A strong positive relationship is found between market liberalization and telephone penetration rates, despite variation in the elasticity of penetration for each of the countries studied. Unsurprisingly, the values are lower for advanced countries with an already high telephone density ratio than for developing economies where the scope for investment is much greater given their existing low penetration rates. Thus, whereas the elasticity is 2.8–4.8% for Singapore, it is 110–267% for China. This suggests that developing economies in particular stand to benefit from liberalizing their telecommunications markets.

Table 8.5 Price Impact on Banking and Telecommunications of Trade Impediments (%)

Country	Banking		Telecommunications	
	Domestic Suppliers	Foreign Suppliers	Domestic Suppliers	Foreign Suppliers
Philippines	11	47	21	73
Singapore	8	31	2	3
Malaysia	22	61	7	16
Thailand	0	33	30	55
Indonesia	5	49	71	138

Source: Productivity Commission (1999), as cited in Findlay (2001).

It is worth noting that these estimates of the impact of trade impediments, while already high, are based only on market access restrictions and discrimination against foreign suppliers (national treatment barriers). They exclude penalties from regulatory inefficiencies, which are less transparent and hence more difficult to quantify— let alone compare across economies. Yet the trade impediments created by the regulatory regime are often more serious and more difficult to rectify. Worse, they can stall the implementation of external policy commitments to the removal of market access and national treatment barriers, as the following discussion highlights for the cases of telecommunications and banking.

8.3 THE TELECOMMUNICATIONS INDUSTRY

The Philippines joined the league of early reformers of the telecommunications market in 1993. It was among the first 11 countries to permit competition in basic telecommunications services (the local loop), and among the first 14 to de-monopolize the provision of international telephone services.

Market Structure

The imperative to liberalize came on the heels of complaints over the inadequate supply and poor quality of telephone services in the Philippines.[8] For close to two decades telephone density had hovered at 1%, with consumers waiting an average of five and a half years to obtain a connection.[9] Even then, the quality of the service was so poor that on average complaints were made about 17 per 100 phone lines per month in 1988, compared with seven in Thailand and nine in Indonesia (DOTC 1993: A-13).

The local telephone service was at the time a de facto monopoly of the Philippine Long Distance Telephone Company (PLDT), a private company with the sole national franchise. PLDT controlled 94% of local exchanges, with the rest owned by the government and small private carriers. It also controlled the long-distance network by virtue of its ownership of the only nationwide backbone transmission network. PLDT dominated the international service, facing only minimal competition from two other international record carriers. The mobile telephone market was a duopoly dominated by a PLDT subsidiary.

Many countries elect to introduce competition in some market segments—usually the local loop—while retaining others (such as national long-distance and international services) as a monopoly.[10] The rationale for this is that higher prices and profits in the segments run as a monopoly will generate funds that can be invested in the segments where competition has been introduced. Unfortunately, this strategy of service segment cross-subsidy has failed to spur the expansion of the telecommunications network in most developing economies (ITU 1999b: 16).

The Philippine regulator broke with tradition by introducing competition in *all* market segments in 1993, under the Universal Telephone Service Policy. This policy underpins the Service Area Scheme (SAS), a network development program based on a division of the country into 11 service or franchise areas. These service areas were assigned to nine new carriers such that, in each area, one or two new carriers had to compete with the incumbent, PLDT, in the provision of basic services (Table 8.6). The new carriers were cellular operators and/or international carriers. Their licenses obligated them to invest in telephone lines—by installing at least 400,000 lines within three years of being awarded a license in the case of the cellular operators, and 300,000 lines in the case of the international carriers. The SAS was ostensibly designed to hasten network development. Telephone density did indeed rise dramatically, from 1.2 % in 1992 to 9.1% in 2000, which translates to 6.9 million telephone lines for a population of 76.3 million people. Interestingly, only 3.06 million of the lines (44% of total installed lines) were subscribed.

Some observers regarded the SAS as an ingenious scheme for averting cherry picking, or the overconcentration of investment in profitable segments that happens when entry barriers are removed simultaneously in all markets. The service obligations attached to the licenses of the new carriers ensured that some investment would be channeled to network development and that network coverage would expand to include unserved areas, some of them deemed unviable. Yet the ostensible logic of the scheme did not spare it from the criticism that it had been designed more as a political maneuver to accommodate competing interests than as an economic solution to the problem of underinvestment in telecommunications infrastructure. It could be argued that, by turning a blind eye to the need for scale economies, the regulator had eluded responsibility for selecting the suppliers with the most efficient and viable plans for network development. Rather, all those interested in riding the euphoria of market liberalization were accommodated through the designation of service areas.

Notwithstanding its political flavor, the scheme delivered a good number of tangible benefits. It compelled PLDT to double the size of its network, built over

Table 8.6 Structure of the Philippine Telecommunications Market

Company	Foreign Partner	Market Share (%)		
		Local[a]	International[b]	Cellular[c]
PLDT		55.6	71.4	
SMART[d]	NTT (Japan), First Pacific (Hong Kong)	3.8	2.3	44.3
PILTEL[d]		1.9		10.2
Globe Telecom	Singapore Telecom (Singapore)	5.2	3.3	39.7
Islacom	Deutsche Telekom (Germany), Shinawatra (Thailand)	4.9	1.0	2.8
Digitel	Telia (Sweden), Jasmine International (Thailand)	11.3	4.1	
BayanTel	Bell Atlantic (United States)	7.2	4.1	
PT&T/Capwire	Korea Telecom (Korea)	1.7	1.7	
Philcom		1.3	6.4	
ETPI	Cable and Wireless (United Kingdom)	0.7	5.8	
Other		6.2		3.0[e]
Total		100.0	100.0	100.0

a   Based on subscribed lines as of 31 December 2000.
b   Based on incoming and outgoing international traffic in 1997.
c   Based on subscribed lines as of 31 December 2000.
d   Subsidiary of PLDT.
e   Share of Extelcom.

Source: NTC (2001); ITU (1998).

almost half a century, within just four years. Whereas in 1992 the network had reached only 19% of total districts in the country, by 1999 54% of cities/municipalities had access to a telephone service. By December 2000, only 93 of 1,600 cities/municipalities had no fixed lines, public calling office, or cellular mobile telephone service.[11] Improvements were realized not only in supply but also in service quality. The waiting time for a telephone connection fell from 5.5 years in 1994 to 2.1 years in 1998, and the digitization of the network accelerated from 64% in 1994 to 92% in 1998 and 95% in 2000 (ITU 1999b).

The rapid growth of the network was impelled by the entry of new service providers, backed by huge pent-up demand. There are at present 12 major local exchange carriers, 11 international gateway facility (IGF) operators (that is, international service providers), five cellular mobile telephone operators, 15 paging companies, and 10 trunked mobile radio operators. In short, market access has been liberalized in all telecommunications services—local, national long-distance, international, mobile cellular, data, telex, leased line, paging, cable TV, and satellite.

Few developing economies have been as bold as the Philippines in its telecommunications market reforms. Thailand and Indonesia, for example, have yet to allow competition in local services, while Singapore has only recently ended the monopoly of the state-owned carrier, Singapore Telecom (SingTel).[12] ITU (1999b) reveals that, as of 1999, only 32% of countries in Asia allowed some competition in local services, and an even smaller proportion, 24%, in national long-distance and international services.

The legislative seal to the reforms initiated under the Universal Telephone Service Policy came with the passage of RA 7925, also known as the Public Telecommunications Act of 1995. However, it contained important stipulations that continue to bind the regulatory regime. For example, the act:

- made the provision of a universal service the centerpiece of telecommunications development; [13]
- mandated that IGF operators, cellular mobile phone operators, and interexchange carriers should cross-subsidize local exchange operations through payment of an access charge;
- institutionalized bilateral negotiation between carriers as a means of forging interconnection contracts;
- prohibited single entities from engaging in both telecommunications and broadcasting, either over the airwaves or by cable; and
- placed a foreign equity cap of 40% on telecommunications entities and retained the cap of zero for broadcasting entities.

The design of the SAS, combined with the above provisions, has restrained competition, which in turn has hampered trade in telecommunications services. Notwithstanding a seemingly liberal policy, the expansion of the market power of the incumbent and the inability of the regulator to clip its powers has posed an impenetrable barrier to trade.

Flaws in Regulatory Design and the Market Power of the Incumbent

That PLDT remains dominant despite the entry of new carriers may be attributed to the design of the regulatory system. The geographical segmentation of the market prevents the new carriers from achieving scale and scope economies and network externalities. Since they are restricted to operating within their assigned franchise areas, their networks are too small for them to compete effectively against the incumbent. Individually, they have weak bargaining leverage against PLDT, as manifested in their negotiations for interconnection contracts. In 1999 PLDT retained control of 61% of local connections (the combined market share of PLDT, SMART, and PILTEL), 55% of cellular mobile phone subscriptions (the combined market share of SMART and PILTEL), and 71% of international traffic (Table 8.6).

The incumbent's dominant market position is sustained by its ability to squeeze the margins of new entrants through interconnection fees. The SAS allows scope for this practice in the following manner. An important feature of the scheme is the cross-subsidization of local exchanges by the mobile, national long-distance, and international markets through access charges paid by the new carriers to the incumbent. The access charge (a universal service subsidy to the network owner for assuming the social responsibility for building and maintaining the infrastructure) is bundled with the interconnection fee (a payment to the network owner for providing access to its facilities). The lack of transparency inherent in this arrangement allows the incumbent to charge high interconnection fees while preventing new carriers from undercutting its prices. To add to the new carriers' difficulties, tariffs in the competitive markets are regulated; for example, IGF operators are permitted to offer special promotions for a limited period of only 60 days (ITU 1998).[14]

No doubt the squeeze on new carriers could have been averted had the Philippine regulator adopted a less light-handed approach to regulating interconnection. The Public Telecommunications Act stipulates that interconnection agreements should be the outcome of commercial negotiations between private parties. Although in most countries the telecommunications regulator prefers to let carriers negotiate the terms of interconnection agreements for themselves rather than prescribe them, this does not mean that it abstains entirely from intervening. In countries where the inherent conflicts that arise in this area are well managed, the regulator assumes responsibility for enforcing non-discriminatory, timely, and sufficient interconnection arrangements.[15] This is done by defining pricing principles (whether cost-based or revenue sharing, for example), setting a timetable for the completion of negotiations, and approving and supervising the agreements that have been negotiated. In order to curb the power of the incumbent to discriminate against newcomers, many regulators require the incumbent to disclose its costs or publish interconnection charges. This is the case even when interconnection agreements are treated as commercial contracts.

The role of the regulator in forging interconnection agreements becomes crucial when carriers have uneven bargaining positions, as in the Philippines. Yet the Philippine regulator leaves many of the critical issues—such as the pricing structure of interconnection agreements and the location of interconnection points—to the contracting parties to decide. This allows considerable room for bargaining, with the outcome often favoring the incumbent. Moreover, interconnection agreements remain confidential to the contracting parties, making it difficult to check whether there has been discrimination by the incumbent against newcomers.

Nor has the regulator acted decisively on the complaints of new operators that the incumbent is refusing to provide them with sufficient interconnection points, leading to traffic congestion on their networks and impairing the quality of their service. They have also complained about the incumbent's policy against co-location of facilities,[16] failure to supply sufficient interconnection trunks, and propensity to let disputes over revenue and charges drag on.[17]

The regulator could have tempered the market power of the incumbent by allowing competition to flourish across market segments, but here again it is bound to safeguard the market environment created under the SAS. A clear illustration is found in the regulator's handling of internet telephony. Traditional, circuit-switched telecommunications carriers are now facing competition from internet protocol (IP) based networks that can provide voice, data, and video services. There used to be a clear delineation of functions between telecommunications carriers, which provided only basic voice services, and value added operators, which provided additional services (such as computing and data storage using IP networks) over voice lines. New technology now allows value added operators—in particular internet service providers (ISPs)—to provide services that compete directly with those offered by the traditional carriers, such as long-distance telephony. IP telephony remains prohibited in the Philippines on the grounds that if ISPs were allowed to provide IP telephony services, the resulting competitive pressures in the national long-distance and international markets would undermine cross-subsidy flows.[18] The same reasoning explains the ban on call-back, refiling, and international simple resale (ISR) services. Elsewhere, these innovations have led to steep falls in the prices of international calls.

Barriers to Trade in Telecommunications Services

Trade in telecommunications services is dominated by two modes of supply: cross-border and commercial presence. The cross-border supply of international telephone calls is more prevalent than supply through commercial presence, which generally takes the form of entry of foreign suppliers through direct investments.

Until recently, many economies were reluctant to relinquish national control over basic telecommunications services for reasons of national security or the public interest. But attitudes toward foreign equity in basic services have been changing, spurred by demand for investments to keep pace with the rapid modernization of basic telecommunications infrastructure. In Malaysia, for instance, in April 1998 the regulator raised the foreign equity cap on basic telecommunications services from 49% to 61%, to support new carriers facing bankruptcy (Abrenica and de Dios 2000). In April 2000 Singapore removed all restrictions on foreign entry in basic services to boost its infrastructure modernization program.[19] And even China has announced that it will allow up to 49% foreign equity in basic services within the next four years. Meanwhile, the Philippine regulator is bound by legislation (RA 7925 and RA 7042) to restrict foreign equity participation in basic telecommunications services to 40%.[20] In addition, the provision of value added services and the operation of cable TV and other forms of broadcasting remain the express preserve of Philippine nationals.

The imminent restructuring of the telecommunications industry that is being prompted by technological convergence continues to be stalled by foreign equity restrictions. Unexpectedly, opposition to the proposed Convergence Bill, which would have allowed cross-sector ownership and service provision, came from cable operators. Although the bill would have enabled them to deploy their excess cable capacity in the lucrative telephony business, they argued that they would face unfairly tough competition from telecommunications carriers (who are not bound by a 100% Philippine ownership rule).

There can be no doubt that the current foreign equity limits should be reconsidered in light of the pace of technological development. Yet, in terms of attracting foreign capital, this may be less significant than the need to level the playing field. From what has just been described, the exercise of market dominance by the incumbent, sanctioned by regulatory deficiencies, forecloses opportunities for profitable entry.

This profit squeeze is perhaps most severe in the international telephone services sector. The high access charge imposed by the incumbent is not only threatening the viability of IGF operators but, more importantly, it is undermining the regulatory intention to use revenues from international services to subsidize basic telephone services. New carriers point out that at the start of their local exchange rollout in 1996, as provided for under the SAS, the accounting rate—which traditionally forms the basis for international revenue settlements among national carriers—was $1.20 and PLDT's access charge $0.35, leaving them with a margin of $0.25 per minute to finance the rollout.[21] During the last five years, the accounting rate has fallen by 40% (to $0.72 in 2000), but the incumbent has reduced its access charge by only 20% (to $0.28) (Figure 8.1). This translates to a 68% drop in the margins of IGF operators (that is, from $0.25 to $0.08 per minute of international traffic).

The issue is not just the behavior of the incumbent but also the fact that competition and technology are advancing more rapidly in international services than in other telecommunications sectors. Consequently, the accounting rate is being eroded in various ways.[22] Many multinational corporations are now transporting their traffic over leased lines and private networks that bypass the accounting rate system. Where the resale and refiling of traffic are permitted, carriers are able to exploit pricing disparities in the accounting rate system to reduce their costs. And increasingly, traffic is being routed over networks (such as internet telephony networks) that do not use accounting rates at all.

Apart from facilitating the efforts of developed economies to drive down the accounting rate, new technologies are increasing bandwidth capacity and reducing the costs of transmission. As more transoceanic cables are laid and as more satellites come on stream over the next few years, current capacity is expected to multiply. In the immediate future, a new, cost-based pricing structure for international traffic is likely to emerge, in which the individual components of the call are priced separately.

Therefore, the more urgent issue confronting the Philippine regulator is whether it can preserve the present system of service segment cross-subsidy in an increasingly competitive environment. It is evident that the accounting rate system is nearing its end. Of course, the regulator may choose to continue to maintain international calls at artificially high prices, but this would be at the expense of users, primarily the business sector. Moreover, as new technologies make it easier to bypass the traditional telecommunications network, revenue from international call services can be expected to shrink, thus diminishing the funds available for network development.

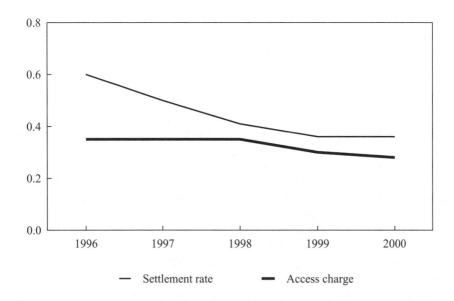

Figure 8.1 Settlement and Access Rates for International Telephone Services, 1996–2000 ($)

If cross-subsidies cannot be depended on to finance future network development, then the only logical option will be to rely increasingly on foreign capital. Yet this will not be forthcoming unless barriers to foreign entry are removed, and, more importantly, unless the regulatory regime nurtures a competitive market environment.

8.4 THE BANKING INDUSTRY

The pressure for regulatory reform is no less palpable in financial services than in telecommunications.[23] Over the past decade, the international financial market has grown more rapidly than the Philippine domestic market. New modes of financial intermediation have emerged; the era of derivatives trading and internet-based banking has arrived. Technology is indeed changing the scope and character of financial services—a fact that regulators are only now beginning to grapple with.

Added pressure comes from the nexus between financial services and the macroeconomy. Of all services, the financial sector, especially its banking component, has the closest links to the economy at large. Prudent financial regulation and supervision underpin macroeconomic stability. Conversely, macroeconomic stability permits the exercise of prudence in the regulation and supervision of the financial system. The depth of the financial system has also been linked with per capita income growth (Berthelemy and Varoudakis 1996; Levine 1994; Haustmann and Gavin 1996). Thus, the stakes are high in ensuring the integrity and stability of the system, as well as its efficiency in mobilizing savings and pooling resources for economic activities. This section examines the impact of a liberal trade regime on the Philippine financial sector, focusing in particular on banking, which comprises 75% of the sector.[24]

Market Structure

The Philippine banking sector consists of commercial banks, thrift banks, specialized government banks, and rural banks.[25] The volume of its assets—equivalent to about 101% of GDP and 82% of total assets in the financial system as of the end of 1999—attests to its dominant position in the financial system. The second largest segment of the financial system pales by comparison: the contractual savings sector, composed of public and private pension funds, pre-need plans, and life insurance companies, has total assets equivalent to only 20% of GDP (World Bank 2000b).

Commercial banks dominate the banking sector, their share in total bank assets rising from less than three-quarters in the early 1980s to nearly five-sixths in the early 1990s. The latest inventory (December 2000) reveals that 45 commercial banks account for 91% of total banking sector assets and 56% of the country's 7,553 banking offices. Table 8.7 traces the growth of commercial banks by ownership type.

Financial Sector Reforms

The rapid growth of the banking sector owes a great deal to the deregulation of financial markets and liberalization of bank entry and branching in the 1990s.[26] However, the liberalization of trade in financial services was preceded by a protracted series of reforms beginning as far back as the 1970s.

In 1971, the IMF and the Philippine Central Bank Survey Commission conducted a joint review of the Philippine banking system, resulting in a redefinition of the various types of financial institutions. Responsibility for maintaining monetary stability remained within the ambit of authority of the Central Bank of the Philippines, which also took over supervision of the entire financial and credit system in view of the rapid growth of non-bank financial intermediaries.[27] As part of the structural adjustment program agreed between the Philippines and its international creditors, the government built a financial liberalization and deregulation program into its economic development plan. It was designed to foster competition in the country's financial markets, as a means of promoting efficiency and increasing the availability of long-term funds for the expansion of the real sector.

The financial sector reforms of the 1980s included changes to the structure of the banking system, deregulation of interest rates,[28] adoption of universal banking, and an increase in the minimum capitalization requirements for banking institutions. However, the reforms failed to adequately address the structural weaknesses in the banking system. The central bank maintained a restrictive policy on bank entry and a discretionary policy on bank branching, which, in tandem with limits imposed on foreign equity participation in domestic banks, restrained competition. The absence

Table 8.7 Commercial Banks by Type of Ownership, 1980–2001 (no.)

Type	1980	1985	1990	1995	1996	1997	1998	1999	2000	Sept 2001
Private domestic banks	27	25	25	30	31	33	32	30	23	23
Foreign bank branches	4	4	4	14	14	14	13	13	13	13
Foreign bank subsidiaries						4	5	6	6	5
Government banks	1	1	1	2	4	3	3	3	3	3
Total	32	30	30	46	49	54	53	52	45	44

Source: Bangko Sentral ng Pilipinas.

of effective competition kept the spreads between lending and deposit rates wide open and depressed the quality of bank services.

It did not help that the central bank was lax in its regulation and supervision of banks. Self-lending, particularly to directors, officers, stockholders, and related interests, was gravely abused; and banks maintained more risky portfolios than they would have done if adequately supervised. The eventual result was bank failures, magnified by a balance of payments crisis and political instability in 1983 (Lamberte 1985).

Policy changes were introduced in 1986 to strengthen the regulatory and supervisory framework of the banking system. They included the strengthening of supervisory procedures and prudential regulations, and new rules governing the establishment of banks and bank branches. The prudential regulations provided for higher minimum capitalization requirements; compliance with a minimum risk–asset ratio; limits on loans to directors, officers, stockholders, and related interests; and stricter auditing and reporting requirements. A major policy pronouncement was that weak banks would no longer be sustained, except in times of general financial emergency or when the bank concerned faced a liquidity (rather than solvency) crisis.

Yet bolder reforms were implemented in the 1990s. The decade saw the creation of a new, independent central bank;[29] the rehabilitation and strengthening of two major government financial institutions, namely the Development Bank of the Philippines and the Philippine National Bank;[30] a spate of closures, consolidations, and mergers among private commercial banks; and a liberalization of foreign bank entry and scope of operations. The New Central Bank Act of 1993 (RA 7653) created an independent central monetary authority called Bangko Sentral ng Pilipinas (BSP). As opposed to the former Central Bank of the Philippines, which also had a development mandate, the BSP was charged solely with maintaining monetary and price stability and safeguarding the convertibility of the peso. The creation of the BSP was deemed an essential prerequisite for the envisaged greater participation of the Philippines in the global financial market.

During this period, the conditions for mode 3 (commercial presence) supply of financial services were also liberalized, under RA 7721 of 1994, to permit the entry of up to 10 foreign banks. Until the passage of this law, banking had been reserved expressly for Philippine nationals, with the exception of the four foreign banks already operating in the country before the passage of the General Banking Act of 1948.[31] Section 2 of RA 7721 prescribed three modes of entry for foreign banks, namely: "(1) by acquiring, purchasing or owning up to 60% of the voting stock of an existing bank; (2) by investing in up to 60% of the voting stock of a new banking subsidiary incorporated under the laws of the Philippines, or (3) by establishing branches with full banking authority." Since 1995 at least nine foreign banks and seven subsidiaries of foreign banks have established a presence in the country.

While it signaled a cautious attempt to introduce greater competition in the financial market, RA 7721 stipulated that "in allowing increased foreign participation in the financial system, it shall be the policy of the State that the financial system remains effectively controlled by Filipinos" (Section 1) and provided that "the Monetary Board shall adopt such measures as may be necessary to ensure that at all times the control of 70% of the resources or assets of the entire banking system is held by domestic banks which are at least majority-owned by Filipinos" (section 3).

The General Banking Law of 2000 (RA 8791) permitted the monetary board to authorize the acquisition by a foreign bank of up to 100% of the voting stock of one bank organized under the laws of the Republic of the Philippines, subject to the guidelines set out under RA 7721. As well as improving market access, the General Banking Law upgraded the rules governing the operation of the BSP to conform to international standards. The aim was "to promote and maintain a stable and efficient banking and financial system that is globally competitive, dynamic, and responsive to the demands of a developing economy." Other salient provisions of the law included:

- establishment of a strong legal basis for consolidated banking supervision;
- adoption of a "fit and proper" rule for individuals appointed or elected as bank directors or officers;
- a requirement that banks have at least two independent directors on their boards;
- adoption of a risk-based capital requirement following the recommendation of the Basle Committee;
- stronger safeguards against connected lending;
- more comprehensive coverage of a single borrower's limit to include guarantees;
- liberalization to permit up to 100% foreign bank ownership of domestic banks during a seven-year window of opportunity;
- establishment of a legal basis for the formulation of standards setting out sound and unsound practices by banks, quasi-banks, and trusts; and

- introduction of rules to ensure greater transparency of banking operations and stricter information disclosure requirements for banks.

It is apparent that the thrust of reform has been toward tighter prudential regulation and closer supervision of banks. To the extent that they prescribe new, higher standards of banking practice, rules to encourage "good" banking should be encouraged. But such rules are only as effective as their implementors. It remains to be seen whether the BSP does in fact develop a strong capacity to monitor and enforce standards.

Impact of Trade Liberalization

The liberalization of entry of foreign banks, albeit partial, has irrevocably changed the structure of the domestic financial market. The larger domestic banks now have some level of foreign equity; and more are willing to accommodate foreign capital in order to comply with the higher minimum capitalization requirements set by the BSP. However, while the share of foreign banks in domestic banking activities has been increasing steadily since 1995, this has not been sufficient to dislodge the domestic commercial banks from their dominant position in the market. As Table 8.8 shows, more than four-fifths of assets, deposits, and loans remain under the control of the domestic banks.

As shown in Table 8.9, there has been a marked decline in the overall profitability of commercial banks in the post-liberalization period, and a narrowing of the spread between lending and deposit rates. This suggests that the entry of foreign banks has provided the impetus to improve the efficiency of the domestic banking system, with some of the benefits flowing back to consumers.[32]

At this point competition among banks is limited to deposit mobilization, with clients being offered new banking technologies and a wider menu of financial instruments.[33] But competition has not significantly reduced the deposit concentration ratio. Intal and Llanto (1998b) report that, as of the third quarter of 1997, the five largest commercial banks retained 49.9% of total deposits—an insignificant decline from the figure of 52% recorded in 1994.

If market competition can be nurtured, then the next stage will see banks chasing borrowers—tailoring their financial packages to meet the specific needs of clients. That future remains outside the current purview of banks, which still continue to ration loans to a select few.

Barriers to Trade in Financial Services

It is possible that bank competition will not advance much beyond its present level, despite the Philippine commitment under the GATS to pursue "progressive levels of liberalization." In August 1999, the BSP issued Monetary Board Resolution 1224 declaring a moratorium on the granting of new banking licenses and on branch expansion by existing banks. This was formalized under the General Banking Law

Table 8.8 Distribution of Assets, Deposits, and Loans between Domestic and Foreign Commercial Banks, 1990–2001

	1990	1995	1996	1997	1998	1999	2000	2001
Total assets (billion pesos)	488.9	1,386.4	1,885.6	2,581.1	2,638.6	2,744.1	2996.5	3,015.3
Domestic commercial banks (%)	88.6	91.3	87.3	82.5	84.4	83.6	82.6	81.4
Foreign commercial banks (%)	11.4	8.7	12.7	17.5	15.6	16.4	17.4	18.6
Total deposits (billion pesos)	306.1	898.0	1,249.5	1,476.4	1,652.2	1,767.3	1,903.0	1,922.0
Domestic commercial banks (%)	92.5	95.2	95.4	91.8	90.6	87.3	84.9	84.9
Foreign commercial banks (%)	7.5	4.8	4.6	8.2	9.4	12.7	15.1	15.1
Total loans (billion pesos)	181.8	810.0	1,122.6	1,366.0	1,369.1	1,269.9	1,628.2	1,625.0
Domestic commercial banks (%)	91.4	92.8	91.7	88.4	88.7	86.6	83.5	82.4
Foreign commercial banks (%)	8.6	7.2	8.3	11.6	11.3	13.4	16.5	17.6

Source: Bangko Sentral ng Pilipinas.

Table 8.9 Average Spreads and Rates of Return for Commercial Banks (%)

	Spread[a]	Rate of Return	
		on Assets	on Equity
Pre-liberalization (1987–94)	4.7	2.5	25.7
Post-liberalization (1995–97)	4.3	2.2	18.8
Crisis period (1998–2000)[b]	5.5	0.6	4.7

a The spread is the difference between lending and deposit rates, adjusted for the gross receipts tax and changes in required reserves.
b Data for 2000 are as of June only.

Source: 1987–97: Lamberte (1999); crisis period: authors' computations.

of 2000, which placed a three-year moratorium on the establishment of new banks. Although the moratorium did not extend to foreign banks, under RA 7721 they were in any case restricted to a maximum of six new branches. This effectively limits the options of foreign banks interested in entering the market to acquiring existing domestic banks.

To be sure, the moratorium is within the scope of prudential regulation allowed under the GATS, which recognizes the necessity for governments to implement measures to preserve the stability of the financial sector and, ultimately, the economy. Typical prudential measures of this type would include capital adequacy ratios, controls on market risk, minimum capitalization requirements, and disclosure and reporting requirements. Since the moratorium is not expressly designed to discriminate against foreign suppliers, it cannot be construed as a market access or national treatment barrier. Nor can it be deemed avoidance by the Philippines of its commitments under the GATS, since it will apply only for a limited period. Yet undeniably, the moratorium gives incumbents a reprieve from foreign competition.

Arguably, the intent of the moratorium is to curb the perceived problem of "overbanking," although it is not clear that the policy can avert the imminent failure of small and vulnerable banks. The stability of the banking system will continue to hang in the balance unless an orderly exit of inefficient banks can be arranged. It has been suggested that the financial market has become overcrowded to the extent that the viability even of efficient financial institutions is threatened. Although evidence for this claim is wanting, the rationale for the moratorium has hardly been questioned.

If the problem of overbanking is indeed real, then a less distortive response than trade protectionism is appropriate. One such response would be to raise the required level of bank capitalization. This would likely facilitate the consolidation of domestic banks, thereby helping to address concerns about the viability of individual institutions. Consolidation strengthens the competitiveness of domestic banks but does not necessarily diminish competition if there is a real and pervasive threat of foreign competition. Thus the solution is not to foreclose entry, but to combine prudential regulation with a liberal trade regime.

8.5 A REGULATORY IMPASSE

The challenges in telecommunications and banking may appear different, but the regulators in the two sectors are in a common bind that can rightly be said to be ubiquitous in services. One hurdle is to shake off the old policy paradigm reserving service sector activities for nationals. Apart from national sentiment in favor of protectionism, it should be understood that this paradigm was congenial to the nature of services in the past, when suppliers and consumers had to be in one place to effect a transaction. The technological impossibility of providing a service without a commercial presence lent some legitimacy to the paradigm. In banking, for instance, traditional regulation assumed the geographical location in the country of the financial institution offering the saving, loan, or investment service. Allowing a foreign bank to offer such services would have meant permitting a non-citizen to operate on national territory. In telecommunications, voice signals had to be transmitted over land-based infrastructure. If a foreign carrier had been allowed in, it would have been necessary to give it rights over the use of land. Consequently, the issue of accommodating foreign suppliers became a question of preserving the national patrimony.

When it became technically feasible to deliver services independently of geographic location, it also became impractical to continue to reserve their supply to nationals. It should have been a matter of course that old policy paradigms would be replaced by new ones more attuned to social and market conditions. But, in the case of services, the old paradigm was embodied in laws that could only be rewritten after a social consensus on the necessity for change had been reached.

To be sure, the Philippine government, through its commitments to the GATS, has made some progress in this direction. The allowable limits on foreign equity participation in telecommunications, banking, distribution, and insurance have been adjusted to allow some room for entry, although market opening has yet to be extended to such sectors as transport, business services, broadcasting, and education. Despite the progress that has been made, the policy of ensuring that majority control of services remains in the hands of Philippine nationals can still be found in new legislation.

Obtaining the social consensus required to amend laws that foreclose market access to foreign suppliers will be just as challenging as dealing with the market power of incumbents. With technological change, it is now possible to provide competitively many of the services that were supplied monopolistically in the past. Service regulators are caught in the dilemma of whether to give full play to new technologies at the risk of undermining the viability of incumbents.

In telecommunications, the regulator's decision on the extent to which it will allow the use of IP telephony will determine the fate of the incumbent. Liberalization will mean entry of non-facilities-based carriers, hence lower call charges for consumers. But IP telephony will also facilitate the bypassing of the accounting rate, which serves as a funding source for PLDT. The choice between the incumbent's viability and consumer welfare would be straightforward if it were not for the fact that PLDT has been charged with the obligation of extending services to the poor.

The banking regulator faces a similar quandary. Should it allow cross-border supply of banking services without requiring a commercial presence? A potent technology that may undermine the present market domination of domestic banks is internet banking. The OECD (1999, cited in Orbeta 2000) estimates that the savings to consumers from using internet banking could be as much as 89%. But here again the issue arises as to how much competitive pressure can be placed on incumbents without compromising the stability of the financial system.

This leads to a final point concerning the choice of liberalization strategy. Notwithstanding the provision in the GATS on pursuing progressive liberalization, decisions about the speed of reform are left to individual member economies. In the Philippines, such determinations are made at the sectoral level to ensure that a consensus can be built among constituents. Public acceptance of reforms is deemed critical. There is, however, a downside to this protracted, sectoral approach to liberalization as opposed to the more general approach of introducing reforms simultaneously in all sectors. Delays in introducing reforms in one sector can prevent another from reaping the benefits of liberalization. A case in point is the delay in introducing air transport reforms, which is perceived to be dragging down growth in the tourism sector.

There is also the issue of the unequal preparedness for reform of different regulators. The inability of some to deal with the internationalized and complex structure of their sectors is slowing down the pace of reform. Regulators may insist on postponing reforms until the sector's institutions have built up the capacity to handle a liberalized environment; worse, the regulatory framework may be so poorly designed that the potential benefits of reform remain unrealized. When regulators are given a reprieve, however, the difficulty lies in distinguishing between a real constraint on the readiness to pursue liberalization on the one hand, and a contrived excuse to delay reform on the other.

In Philippine telecommunications and banking, there is a compelling case for the regulators to focus on the task of catching up with the demands of a global network economy. Old development strategies (cross-subsidies in telecommunications) and traditional instruments for influencing economic behavior (pricing and licensing in banking) must be re-examined; the relevance of the regulatory framework must be checked constantly against a fast-changing global market. One can only hope that the regulators in these two core industries will be able to spark positive reforms in other service sectors.

NOTES

1. The GATS defines limitations on market access in services as: (1) limitations on the number of service suppliers; (2) limitations on the total value of service transactions or assets; (3) limitations on the number of service operations or on the total quantity of service output; (4) limitations on the total number of natural persons that may be employed in a service sector or that a service supplier may employ; (5) restrictions or requirements concerning the types of legal entities or joint ventures permitted; and (6) limitations on the participation of foreign capital.

2. Distortionary domestic regulations that are removed from the context of trade liberalization are not dealt with in this chapter. Examples include interest rate controls in the case of financial services and universal service obligations in the case of telecommunications.

3. The main constraint is imposed by the subsidiarity principle embraced by the World Trade Organization (WTO) community. This principle provides that regulatory decisions are to be made at the lowest level of governance so that they can be designed to take account of social goals (Feketekuty 2000).

4. Only transactions between residents and non-residents are recorded in the balance of payments. By convention, factors of production that have stayed in a country for more than one year are regarded as resident. Thus, the transactions of a foreign affiliate in the domestic market are not registered as trade flows if the affiliate has been in the country for more than one year. In similar vein, only transactions by natural persons during their first year of stay are included in the balance of payments.

5. The law allows a foreign ship to transport goods between two local ports only if no suitable domestic ship is available.

6. The long-term lease of private land to foreign investors is allowed, however, for a maximum period of 75 years.

7. China, Taiwan, Pakistan, South Korea, and Indonesia are among the countries with a nil minimum capital requirement.

8. This section draws on Abrenica (1999a, 1999b, 2000).

9. Telephone density or teledensity refers to the number of main telephone lines per 100 inhabitants.

10. As of 1999, of the 188 member states of the International Telecommunications Union (ITU), 32% had introduced competition in basic services. Only 26% had opened their national long-distance and international service markets to competition (ITU 1999a).

11. This information was provided by infrastructure staff at the National Economic and Development Authority, Manila.

12. In May 2000, a year ahead of schedule, Singapore sanctioned the entry of a new carrier, StarHub, in local services.

13. A universal service has the social goal of extending access to the telecommunications network to all members of society. It therefore calls for the building of a network that offers nationwide coverage, widespread affordability, and non-discriminatory access (ITU 1998).

14. The Malaysian regulator, Jabatan Telekom Malaysia, was caught in the same dilemma of having to preserve the cross-subsidy when introducing competition in national long-distance and international services. To safeguard the subsidy, the new long-distance operators were prevented from offering discounts of more than 20% of current tariffs.

15. Philippine law defines the principle of "timely and sufficient interconnection" as having points of interconnection that are "required, within [a] reasonable time frame, and in sufficient capacity and number to meet all traffic demands for conveyance of messages" (EO 59).

16. This refers to the practice of allowing competing operators to install transmission and switching equipment within the incumbent's switching centers.

17. These issues are raised in the position papers on interconnection issues submitted by new carriers to the regulator in 1998.

18. A draft bill on voice over IP prescribes that only telecommunications carriers should be allowed to offer IP-based services.

19. Singapore was initially scheduled to liberalize its basic telecommunications services in April 2002. Until recently foreign equity in the sector was capped at 49%, with StarHub and SingTel holding exclusive licenses to deliver basic services until 31 May 2002. The government was forced to compensate the incumbents for their rollout, capital expenditure, and losses following the early termination of these licenses. One may view Singapore's accelerated liberalization as a strategic move to ensure its lead over rival Hong Kong in the race to earn the title of regional communications hub. Hong Kong permits 100% foreign equity.

20. RA 7042 lists the investment areas reserved for Philippine nationals, among them basic telecommunications services. The maximum allowable foreign equity for investments on the foreign investment negative list is 40%.

21. The cost of an international telephone call is determined by three basic elements: the international gateway switch (located in the country in which the call originates), the international transmission link (submarine cable or satellite link), and the onward extension to the end user (located in the country in which the call is received). These charges are aggregated into an accounting rate negotiated bilaterally between national carriers. The value of traffic in each direction is multiplied by the mutually agreed tariff or accounting rate to yield revenue that is divided (usually on a 50/50 basis) between the two international carriers. The share of the local carrier, also called the settlement rate, is one-half of the accounting rate; in this case, $0.60.

22. The accounting system works well when the balance of traffic flow is within an acceptable range and international services are supplied monopolistically by both parties, but it is now under pressure. In a given settlement period, the carrier that receives more traffic than it sends receives compensation from the other carrier. The large traffic disparity in favor of developing economies has prompted developed economies such as the United States to bring down the settlement prices. Moreover, since some of the facilities and services required to complete an international call are now being supplied competitively, a carrier with access to a competitive market would want to purchase these services from a supplier other than the carrier to which the end user is connected.

23. The GATS defines a financial service as any service of a financial nature, broadly classified as insurance and insurance-related services and all banking and other financial services.

24. The section draws on Intal and Llanto (1998b).

25. Commercial banks are composed of universal banks and regular commercial banks; thrift banks consist of savings banks, private development banks, and stock savings and loan associations. Universal banks are commercial banks with expanded functions. They may perform the functions of an investment house, invest in non-allied enterprises, and own up to 100% of the equity of a thrift bank, rural bank, or allied financial or non-financial enterprise. Publicly listed universal banks are allowed to own up to 100% of the voting stock of only one other universal or commercial bank.

26. The reform experience is discussed extensively in Intal and Llanto (1998b), Llanto and Lamberte (1998), Lamberte and Llanto (1995), and Lamberte (1993).

27. The central bank and the government shared responsibility for achieving the objective of promoting economic growth.

28. McKinnon (1973) and Shaw (1973) had challenged the repressive financial policies (such as interest rate controls) thought critical to spurring investment and growth in the post-World War II era. They argued that financial liberalization would promote growth by stimulating greater efficiency in financial resource allocation and greater mobilization of savings.

29. The former Central Bank of the Philippines had sustained huge losses arising from its quasi-fiscal responsibilities. Under the 1986 debt-restructuring program introduced in the aftermath of the balance of payments and financial crises of 1983, the central bank was forced to assume the foreign exchange liabilities of a number of public and private firms. Massive losses in forward and swap transactions contributed to a severe weakening of the financial position of the bank.

30. The Philippine National Bank is now a private bank with a minority government shareholding.

31. These were Citibank, N.A., Hongkong and Shanghai Banking Corporation, and Standard Chartered Bank, which opened branches in 1945, and the Bank of America, which established a presence in the Philippines in 1947.

32. In their study of the impact of foreign bank entry into the domestic banking markets of 80 countries, Claessens, Demirguc-Kunt, and Huizinga (1998) observed that high margins and profits reflected an absence of competition, while high overhead costs indicated a less efficient management and organizational structure. Amel and Liang (1997) reported similar results for their study of local banking markets in the United States.

33. These include savings deposits in tandem with life insurance, NOW accounts, and, more recently, COMBO accounts. NOW accounts are interest-bearing demand deposits which can be withdrawn by means of a negotiable order of withdrawal (NOW). COMBO accounts combine the yield of a savings account with the payment efficiency of a demand deposit or current account. The demand deposit account is automatically replenished from the savings account whenever the balance falls below the required minimum balance.

PART IV

Social Dimensions

9

Population, Human Resources, and Employment

Alejandro N. Herrin and Ernesto M. Pernia

9.1 INTRODUCTION

Population growth in the Philippines has diminished only slowly over the last three decades and remains rapid by Asian standards. Over the same period the economy has not performed well. Poor economic performance—caused in part by rapid population growth—has led to persistently high unemployment and poverty rates, feeding back into high fertility rates.

The contrast with other East Asian countries is stark. Remarkable demographic transition, fostered by strong population policy, supported these countries' economic dynamism. The swift decline in fertility resulted in a population age structure that was favorable to increased savings rates, higher investment in both physical and human capital, and early achievement of full employment. This is referred to in the literature as the "demographic bonus."

In the Philippines, while there has been firm support for policies to promote economic recovery and human resource development, a consensus on the critical importance of public policy to slow population growth has been sorely lacking. As a consequence, the country has missed out on the early demographic bonus experienced in other parts of Asia. The challenge in coming years will be for the Philippines to deal with its "demographic onus" while trying to telescope the time taken to gain a demographic bonus.

This chapter reviews critical aspects of Philippine development, particularly population growth, fertility, human resource development, and employment. It identifies key issues and suggests suitable policy directions. A framework is offered for the design of a national population policy based on an analysis of the potential sources of population growth. This underscores the multiple policy responses that are called for.

9.2 POPULATION GROWTH AND FERTILITY TRANSITION

Population Growth

The Philippine population grew by 2.7% annually in the 1970s. Growth slowed to 2.3% in the 1980s and remained at this rate in the 1990s. The 2000 census counted 76.5 million people, more than double the number in 1970 (Table 9.1). South Korea, Thailand, and Indonesia, which like the Philippines had high population growth rates in the 1960s and 1970s, succeeded in reducing their rates to 0.9%, 1.0%, and 1.3% respectively in the 1990s (ESCAP 2000).

Government projections based on data to 1995 suggest that the Philippine population will rise to 98.8 million by 2020 and 114.3 million by 2040 (NSO 1997). This assumes that fertility will decline to replacement level (about two children per woman) by 2010—which seems overly optimistic unless suitable policy measures are quickly put in place.

Fertility

The principal source of rapid population growth is continuing high fertility. In 1973, the total fertility rate (TFR) was 6.0 births per woman, declining to 5.1 in 1983, 4.1 in 1993, and 3.7 in 1998. This fertility rate is among the highest in Asia. By the early 1990s, for instance, Thailand and Indonesia had already achieved much lower fertility rates, at 1.9 and 2.9 births per woman respectively (ESCAP 1998).

The 1998 National Demographic and Health Survey reveals a number of important findings (Table 9.2). First, the actual TFR of 3.7 births per woman is higher than the wanted TFR of 2.7, implying that women are not able to achieve their desired fertility.[1] Second, half of currently married women say they want no more children. Third, of births during the five years before the survey, 27% were to women who would have preferred to delay childbearing and another 18% to women who had not wanted any more children. Fourth, there is an unmet need for family planning: about 9% of currently married women not practicing contraception would like to space births by two or more years, and another 11% want no more children.

Contraceptive Use

A proximate cause of high (unwanted) fertility is the low level of contraceptive use among currently married women. The prevalence rate for all methods of contraception rose from 17% in 1973 to 32% in 1983, climbing further to 40% in 1993 and 47% in 1998 (Table 9.3). However, only about 30% of current contraceptive use is accounted for by modern methods. By contrast, the contraceptive prevalence rate

Table 9.1 Selected Demographic Indicators, 1970–2000

Indicator	1970	1980	1990	2000
Population (million)	36.7	48.1	60.7	76.5
Density (population/sq km)	122	160	202	255
Urban population (%)	31.8	37.3	48.7	n.a.
Rate of annual increase (%)	3.08	2.71	2.35	2.31
Population doubling time (years)	23	26	30	30
Total fertility rate (births/woman)	6.0	5.1	4.1	3.7
Infant mortality rate (deaths/1,000 live births)				
Males	93.8	65.2	59.9	53.2
Females	83.2	59.4	53.4	48.4
Life expectancy at birth				
Males	57.3	59.7	62.2	62.7
Females	61.5	65.1	67.5	67.9

Sources: Population: National Statistical Coordination Board (1999, 2001), *Philippine Statistical Yearbook*, Manila; total fertility rate: 1973, 1983, and 1993 rounds of the National Demographic Survey, 1998 National Demographic and Health Survey, as reported in NSO, DOH, and MI (1999); infant mortality and life expectancy: Flieger and Cabigon (1994) for 1970, 1980 and 1990; Cabigon and Flieger (1999) for last column (data are for 1995).

Table 9.2 Selected Indicators of Fertility and Fertility Preferences, 1998

Total fertility rate (births per woman)	3.7
Total wanted fertility rate (births per woman)	2.7
Currently married women who want no more children (%)	51.4
Of births in the five years preceding the survey (%)	
Wanted then	54.2
Wanted later	26.9
Not wanted	18.2
Of currently married women with unmet need for family planning (%)	
Want to space births	8.6
Want no more children	11.2
Total	19.8

Source: 1998 National Demographic and Health Survey, as reported in NSO, DOH, and MI (1999).

Table 9.3 Currently Married Women Using Modern and Traditional Contraceptive Methods, 1968–2001 (%)[a]

Year	Survey	Modern Method	Traditional Method	Total
1968	National Demographic Survey	2.9	12.5	15.4
1973	National Demographic Survey	10.7	6.7	17.4
1978	Republic of the Philippines Fertility Survey	17.2	21.3	38.5
1983	National Demographic Survey	18.9	13.1	32.0
1988	National Demographic Survey	21.6	14.5	36.1
1993	National Demographic Survey	24.9	15.1	40.0
1998	National Demographic and Health Survey	28.2	18.3	46.5
1995	Family Planning Survey	25.5	25.2	50.7
1996	Family Planning Survey	30.2	17.9	48.1
1997	Family Planning Survey	30.9	16.1	47.0
1999	Family Planning Survey	32.4	16.9	49.3
2000	Family Planning Survey	32.3	14.7	47.0
2001	Family Planning Survey	33.0	16.8	49.8

a   Based on currently married women aged 15–44 years for 1968–88 surveys, and 15–49 years thereafter.

Sources: National Statistics Office, Family Planning Surveys; NSO, DOH, and MI (1999: Table 9.5).

had reached 55% in Indonesia by the early 1990s and 74% in Thailand, with modern methods accounting for most of this.

An explanation for the low level of contraceptive use in the Philippines can be gleaned from the National Demographic Surveys undertaken since 1968. Women who wanted no more children often cited "fear of side effects" and "health concerns" as reasons for not using contraceptives. It thus appears that lack of information on contraceptive methods and limited access to high-quality family planning services are holding back contraceptive use. In other words, the low level of contraceptive use appears to be a supply-side problem—a failure of public policy.[2]

9.3 HUMAN RESOURCE FORMATION

Critical to an economy's productive capacity and ability to provide higher living standards for its growing population is adequate investment in human capital. In the Philippines, recent human resource indicators give cause for concern.

Child Survival, Nutrition, and Basic Education

Infant Mortality

The decline in infant mortality slowed considerably during the 1980s, such that the rate for 1990 was still high when compared with that of countries in the region at similar levels of socioeconomic development. For males, the infant mortality rate of 93.8 deaths per 1,000 live births in 1970 declined to 65.2 in 1980, 59.9 in 1990, and 53.2 in 1995 (Table 9.1). By comparison, Thailand, which had a slightly higher rate of infant mortality than the Philippines in the 1960s, now has a markedly lower rate. According to ESCAP (2000), the infant mortality rate stands at 22 in Thailand, compared with 33 in the Philippines.

The infant mortality rate exhibits large differences by region and province. In 1995, the male infant mortality rate ranged from 38 in the National Capital Region (NCR) to 71 in the Autonomous Region of Muslim Mindanao (ARMM).[3] At the provincial level, the infant mortality rate for males ranged from a low of 43 in Bulacan to a high of 73 in Sulu, putting Sulu about two decades behind Bulacan in terms of progress in this area.

Child Nutrition

Recent data on nutrition are provided by the 1987, 1993, and 1998 National Nutrition Surveys conducted by the Food and Nutrition Research Institute (FNRI), and by the 1989–90, 1992, and 1996 updates. The latter are limited to anthropometric measurements of children aged 10 years and under but use larger sample sizes than the regular surveys. Along with anthropometric data, the National Nutrition Surveys collect information on food consumption and micronutrient deficiencies. The anthropometric measurements of the 1998 survey are nevertheless considered representative at the provincial level.

Child malnutrition remains high. Although some progress was achieved between 1987 and 1993, this appears to have reversed by 1998 (Figure 9.1). The prevalence rate for underweight children aged 0–6 years declined from 9.9% in 1987 to 8.4% in 1993, and from 8.2% to 5.6% for stunted children. However, over the same period the rate of wasting observed in children in this age group rose from 5.5% to 6.2%. The prevalence rate for underweight children aged 0–5 years then increased from 8.2% to 9.2% between 1993 and 1998, while the rate of wasting rose from 5.9% to 7.2%. Large provincial and regional differentials persisted up to 1998.

Micronutrient deficiencies, particularly of iron and iodine, remain high among children and among pregnant and lactating women. Whereas the prevalence of iron deficiency anemia in the general population declined from 37.2% in 1987 to 28.9% in 1993 before rising slightly to 30.6% in 1998, between 1993 and 1998 the rate for infants aged 6–12 months rose from 49.2% to 56.6%, the rate for pregnant women from 43.6% to 50.7%, and the rate for lactating women from 43.0% to 45.7% (Quizon et al. 1994; Madriaga et al. 1999a). These increases may have reflected the adverse effects of the Asian economic crisis.

There was an increase in the prevalence of iodine deficiency disorders (goiter) among the population aged seven years and older, from 3.5% in 1987 to 6.9% in

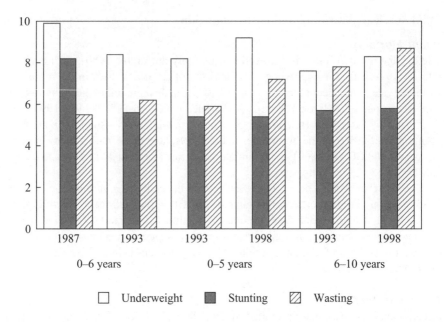

Figure 9.1 Malnutrition Rates among Children Aged 0–10 Years, 1987–98 (%)
Sources: FNRI (1988, 1994, 1999).

1993. The condition mainly affected females, particularly pregnant women (around 25%) and lactating women (21%) (Velandria et al. 1994). In 1998, 12.3% of children aged 6–12 years had an iodine deficiency disorder characterized as "severe" (Madriaga et al. 1999b).

Basic Education

Indicators on the performance of basic education include literacy (simple and functional) and schooling outcomes such as participation, survival, and achievement. While literacy rates have improved, little progress has been made in other schooling outcomes, particularly cohort survival rates and learning achievement.

Data from the 1989 and 1994 Functional Literacy, Education, and Mass Media Surveys show that simple literacy rose from 90% in 1989 to 95% in 1994 while functional literacy (the ability to read, write, and compute) rose from 73% to 84% (NSO 1989, 1994). As would be expected, rates of both simple and functional literacy are lower in rural than in urban areas. There is no significant gap between the sexes; if anything, the female literacy rate tends to be slightly higher than the male rate.

Primary and secondary school participation stood at 96% and 72% respectively in the 2000/01 school year. However, cohort survival rates remained low at 67% for primary schools and 73% for secondary schools (NSCB 2001).[4] Indeed, these rates

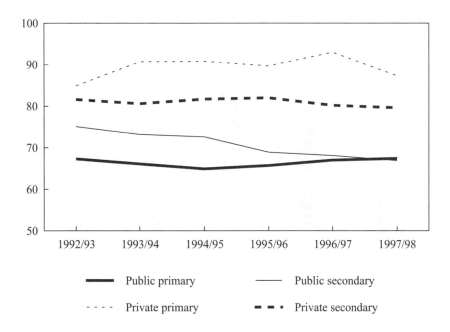

Figure 9.2 Cohort Survival Rates in Public and Private Primary and Secondary Schools, 1992/93–1997/98 (%)

Source: Maglen and Manasan (1999: Table A.10), based on Department of Education, Culture, and Sports (various years), *Statistical Bulletin*.

had barely risen over 20 years; in the 1981/82 school year the cohort survival rates were 66% and 71% respectively (NSCB 1990). As seen in Figure 9.2, based on limited data for the 1992/93–1997/98 school years, the cohort survival rate appears to have been higher in private schools than in public schools.

Achievement levels in schools, as measured by the National Elementary Assessment Test (NEAT) and the National Secondary Assessment Test (NSAT), were only 50% for public primary schools and 46% for public secondary schools in the 1997/98 school year (Figure 9.3). In the Third International Mathematics and Science Test administered to 13-year old children in 1995, the Philippines ranked 39th (fourth from the bottom), whereas Singapore and South Korea ranked first and second respectively.

Human Resource Investment and Long-term Productivity

The critical role of education and training in raising levels of productivity is well known. Ogawa, Jones, and Williamson (1993: 5), for example, state that "human resource development made an important contribution to the spectacular growth observed along the Pacific Rim over the 1960s to 1980s, and it will make an impor-

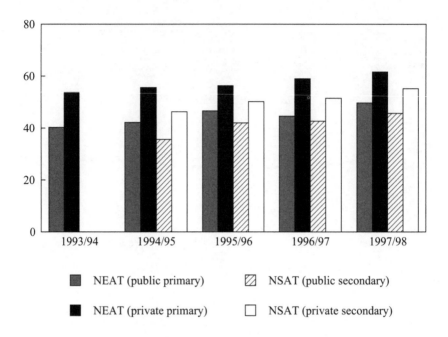

Figure 9.3 Achievement Levels in Public and Private Primary and Secondary Schools, 1993/94–1997/98 (%)

Source: Maglen and Manasan (1999: Table A.13), from National Education Testing and Research Center: National Elementary Assessment Test; National Secondary Assessment Test.

tant contribution in the 1990s and beyond as well." Other studies also highlight the impact on productivity of nutrition and health.[5] They conclude, among other things, that:

1. chronic nutrient deficiency leading to physical stunting in childhood affects future economic performance, and, conversely, that improvements in the nutritional status of children resulting in greater adult height can have substantial long-term pay-offs in terms of increased agricultural productivity and earnings;
2. improved nutritional status affects children's early abilities, subsequent schooling performance, and future productivity as adults; and
3. adequate nutrition at early ages significantly influences the productivity of investments in education and health.

Fertility, Population Growth, and Human Resource Development

High fertility has an independent impact on human resource formation. Micro-level studies for the Philippines reveal the adverse effects of high fertility on child survival, nutrition, and educational outcomes, after controlling for a number of socio-economic variables. A higher risk of infant and child mortality is associated with birth order and the age of the mother—the risk associated with the first birth is high, declining during the second and third births and usually rising rapidly thereafter, and risk is higher among the children of mothers aged under 20 or over 35 years at the time of the birth.

High fertility, as indicated by birth interval, the number of younger siblings, or birth order, adversely affects the nutritional status of preschoolers, as Bouis and Haddad (1990) have shown for Bukidnon; Horton (1988) for Bicol; Garcia and Pin-strup-Andersen (1987) for Abra, Antique, and South Cotabato; and Battad (1978) for Laguna. The number of siblings also has a negative impact on schooling outcomes, especially among children of high school age and among boys. Data for a sample of households in Misamis Oriental province show that for children aged 13–17 years (though not for children aged 7–12), family size significantly reduces school partic-ipation and increases participation in wage employment. The upshot is lower schooling attainment among children with many siblings (Herrin 1993). The data also show that boys in both age groups tend to participate less in school and have lower schooling attainment than girls in the same age groups.

In another study based on data from the 1983 Bicol Multipurpose Survey, DeGraff, Bilsborrow, and Herrin (1996) find that boys' participation in education is negatively affected by high fertility regardless of the birth position of the child. High fertility has a negative effect on the school enrollment of girls only if the child is an older sibling. The conclusion is that in general the education of boys is more likely to be negatively affected by high fertility than that of girls.

Studies using national data sets set out similar findings. Based on the 1982 Household and School Matching Survey, Paqueo (1985) finds that, after controlling for household economic resources and the social characteristics of parents and chil-dren, the number of siblings is negatively related to the educational attainment of children aged 7–12 years. The study also finds that the educational attainment of boys in this age group is lower than that of girls.

At the aggregate level, high fertility and rapid population growth adversely affect the capacity of the economy to mobilize resources for human capital invest-ment, particularly in basic education (Jha, Deolalikar, and Pernia 1993; Orbeta and Pernia 1999). Although a number of interacting factors are responsible for the unfa-vorable trends in cohort survival rates and quality of basic education, rapid popula-tion growth has been flagged as the "most fundamental problem" (Gonzalez 2000). High fertility translates into rapid growth in the numbers of school-age children. This places a severe strain on the capacity of the basic education sector to accom-modate them, let alone its ability to improve the quality of the education provided. The low cohort survival rates and poor achievement levels noted earlier are testi-mony to this predicament.

The potential impact of rapid fertility decline (hence, slower growth in the num-ber of school-age children) versus slow fertility decline on resource requirements for improving educational outcomes has been illustrated by Herrin (1990b).[6] During the 1970–85 period, the actual number of primary and high school-age children grew by

3.2 million. The number was projected to grow by 1.8 million between 1985 and 2000 under a scenario of rapid fertility decline, compared with 3.9 million under a scenario of slow fertility decline. Between 2000 and 2015, the number of school children would decline by almost 2.0 million under a scenario of rapid fertility decline, compared with an increase of 2.1 million under slow fertility decline. In short, had the Philippines succeeded in reducing fertility as swiftly as other countries in Southeast Asia since the 1970s, there would clearly have been much less pressure on available resources, thereby leading to better educational outcomes.

Indeed, the experience of East Asia provides a stark contrast to that of the Philippines. Analysis by the World Bank (1993) shows that, during the 1980s, the growth of the school-age population (children aged 6–11 years) was very slow in East Asia; the absolute number of school children actually declined in Korea, Singapore, and Thailand. The implication is that in these countries the increases in educational expenditure could be used to raise participation rates or improve pedagogic quality through substantial increments in per pupil investment.

9.4 THE EMPLOYMENT PROBLEM

Employment has posed a persistent challenge in the Philippines, both historically and in the broader context of comparison with the rest of East Asia. Despite the bold promises of successive political administrations to address this problem squarely, it appears to be getting worse rather than better. There are two principal, self-explanatory, reasons for the country's poor employment performance, namely weak economic growth and rapid population growth. Intertemporal and comparative data on GDP and population growth indicate that the Philippines has been lagging in both respects (Figure 9.4).

The problem has been exacerbated by the legacy of capital-intensive industrialization, as discussed in other chapters in this volume, and by legislation that has induced labor market distortions (for example, periodic minimum wage increases often unsupported by increases in productivity). A common escape from the regulated formal-sector labor market has been subcontracting in small and medium-sized enterprises. These firms largely operate in the informal sector and are characterized by instability and low productivity.

Labor Force Growth

The working age population grew by 2.6% annually in 1981–89, accelerating to 2.6% in 1990–2000. This translates to an average of 761,000 new entrants and re-entrants into the labor force each year in the 1980s, rising to 738,000 in the 1990s. Thus the labor force, which numbered 17.3 million in 1980, had nearly doubled to 32.2 million by 2000.

The rapid increase in the size of the labor force can be attributed not only to high population growth but also to the steady increase in the participation of women in the workforce. The total labor force participation rate rose from 49% in 1970 to 60%

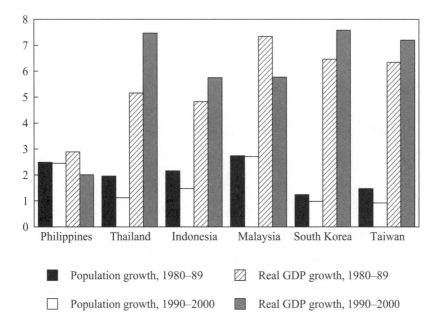

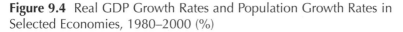

Figure 9.4 Real GDP Growth Rates and Population Growth Rates in Selected Economies, 1980–2000 (%)

Source: Asian Development Bank (1995, 2001), *ADB Key Indicators*.

in 1980, and then to 65% in 2000. Male participation increased from 78% in 1980 to 82% in 2000, while female participation climbed faster—from 42% to 49%—over the same period. The upward trend in the total labor force participation rate was observed in both urban and rural areas, but with a faster rise in urban areas.

Unfortunately, employment opportunities have failed to keep up with the rapid growth in the labor force. The consequence has been unemployment and underemployment rates that are persistently high by East Asian standards. Open unemployment rates have hovered just below the double-digit mark, typically hitting double digits during periods of low or negative economic growth. Unemployment stood at about 8% in 1980, peaked at 12.6% in 1985—the trough of the 1980s economic recession—and rose above 10% again in 1991 and 1998 (which were also recession years) (Figure 9.5). The total number of unemployed persons rose from 1.3 million in 1980 to 3.6 million in 2000—or 11.2% of the workforce. In earlier decades unemployment rates had been markedly lower (Tidalgo and Esguerra 1984). The highest unemployment rate of the 1970s, for example, was 6.3%, recorded in 1972.

Underemployment has always been much greater than unemployment, remaining above 20% during the 1980s and 1990s and peaking at about 33% in 1983–84. The total number of underemployed persons swelled from 3.6 million in 1980 to 6.3

Unemployment   GDP

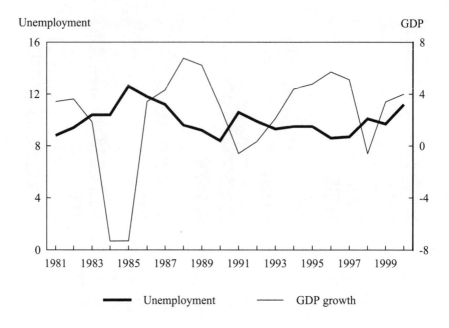

Figure 9.5 GDP Growth and Unemployment, 1981–2000 (%)

Source: BLES–DOLE (1984, 1990, 1998), *Yearbook of Labor Statistics*; BLES–DOLE (2000, 2001), *Current Labor Statistics*; Asian Development Bank (1995, 2001), *ADB Key Indicators*.

million in 2000. Underemployment cuts across all age groups and educational backgrounds and has serious implications for the adequacy of incomes. It can take the form either of a lack of full-time employment (visible underemployment) or of a mismatch between occupation and educational background or training (invisible underemployment) (Esguerra 1995). Underemployment is particularly pervasive in rural areas, where farm work is irregular and seasonal and off-farm employment opportunities few and far between. In 1999, rural underemployment was estimated at 25%, compared with the overall rate of 19.5% (BLES–DOLE 2000).

Unemployment has typically been higher in urban than in rural areas, reflecting rural to urban migration. For most of the 1980s and 1990s urban unemployment rates were above 10%, with the typical peaks during the recession years. Rural unemployment rates also tended to rise during recession years, with a particularly sharp upswing in 1998 when an El Niño drought coincided with the Asian economic crisis.

Unemployment among young and educated workers is a common phenomenon in the Philippines. In the 1970s and early 1980s, most unemployed were in the 15–24-year age group and had been educated to the primary or secondary level (Reyes, Milan, and Sanchez 1989). However, an increasing proportion of the unemployed now possess a tertiary education. The percentage of total unemployed with at least some college education increased from 27.4% in 1980 to 33% in 2000. Even more telling was the proportion with a college degree, which rose from 8.5% in 1980 to 14.8% in 2000. This trend could reflect the "choosy youth" phenomenon (Manning 2000) or the overseas worker phenomenon, which tends to raise the reservation wage. Nevertheless, it implies a serious waste of resources.

Coping with the Employment Problem

Women in the Workforce

The adequacy of incomes, under pressure from unemployment or underemployment, influences decisions on whether to enter the labor market. To augment household income, members of the family increase their supply of labor by working longer hours or by joining the labor market. This trend—referred to in the literature as the "additional worker phenomenon"—is partly borne out by the increasing participation of women in the labor force. In the Philippines, females currently account for close to two-fifths of the workforce.

Unemployment tends to be higher among females than among males. Women also receive lower wages than men. This can in part be explained by the types of work women are engaged in. The services sector has been the major employer of women, accounting for 55% of all employed women in 1999. The increased absorption of female labor can be attributed to the opening up of several export-processing zones specializing in garments and electronics exports in the late 1980s, as well as to the expansion of the services sector in the 1990s. In turn, this explains the dominance of females in migration flows to major urban centers (Engracia and Herrin 1984; Pernia and Israel 1994).

In general women have a higher employment share than men in manufacturing; wholesale and retail trade; finance, insurance, real estate, and business services; and community, social, and personal services.[7] By broad occupational group, women are more likely to work as professional, technical, and related workers; clerical workers; sales workers; and service workers. The share of female workers classified as unpaid family labor has been consistently about double that of males. From 29% in 1980, it had declined to 16.5% by 1999.

The wage differential between female and male workers, especially in manufacturing firms, cuts across educational levels and is more pronounced among white-collar workers (Aganon 2000). This observation is supported by the finding that women employed in export-processing zones, which are largely labor-intensive, are worse off than women employed in firms outside the zones. Women in the zones tend to be paid lower wages and are required to work longer hours. Nor do they have job security: their employment is usually terminated after six months, making them ineligible to receive the benefits that regular workers are entitled to.[8]

Non-regular Workers

Non-regular workers generally do not have security of tenure and are often excluded from receiving non-wage benefits (BLES–DOLE 1998). They comprise contractual, casual, and part-time workers, and constituted 20–25% of total establishment employment during the period 1992–96. In 1996, the construction sector employed the highest proportion of non-regular workers (68%). Contractual workers contributed the largest share to total establishment employment (12% in 1996), and comprised the single largest group (51%) of non-regular workers hired annually. Contractual workers are mainly employed in construction, finance, manufacturing, and community, social, and personal services.

Child Labor

Another critical manifestation of the employment problem is child labor. A national survey on working children conducted in 1995 by the National Statistics Office (NSO) and the International Labor Organization (ILO) showed that of a total of 22.4 million Filipino children aged 5–17 years (that is, comprising one-third of the total population), 3.7 million (16%) were working at one time or another.

Working children are predominantly male (65.5%) and from rural areas (68.9%). A large majority (69%) work unpaid for family farms or businesses, and another 24.7% work in private establishments. Female working children are in similar types of employment, but many also work in private households. In general, such children start working at very young ages; do not attend school; have no days off; are exposed to hazardous environments; and experience work-related problems of exhaustion, stress, risk, injury, and illness. While a number of laws relating to child labor already exist, enforcement has been patchy.

Overseas Labor Migration

The high level of unemployment in the Philippines has naturally made overseas employment an attractive option. The government encourages labor migration by providing services to protect overseas Filipino workers (OFWs) from fraudulent placement agencies and work-related risks. Two such bodies are the Philippine Overseas Employment Administration and the Overseas Workers Welfare Administration.

The growth in the number of OFWs has been tremendous. From 214,590 in 1980, the number of OFWs had more than tripled to 841,628 by 2000. The Middle East continues to be the dominant destination, although OFW flows to this region have declined sharply since 1985, with the slack being picked up by Asia. Although the total stock of OFWs remains large, new hires are declining. The fall-off in demand can be attributed to the financial crisis and to the changing character of Middle Eastern economies. The social and economic transformation experienced in the Middle East has led to a need for a better-educated workforce, more sophisticated technology, and improved institutional and physical infrastructure (Tan 2000).

The changing structure of labor demand in the Philippines is also evident in the flow of remittances. The proportion of remittances coming from North America—traditionally the destination not of contract workers but of migrants—increased from 71% in 1995 to 81% in 1998 before tapering off to 70% in 2000. By contrast, the share of remittances coming from the Middle East, Hong Kong, and Singapore has diminished.[9] Thus, although the number of deployed workers is increasing, remittances from OFWs would appear to be shrinking.

Table 9.4 Sectoral Employment Shares in Selected East Asian Countries, 2000 (%)

Sector	Philippines	Thailand	Indonesia	Malaysia	Taiwan	South Korea
Agriculture	38.30	44.52	45.28	18.36	7.80	10.86
Manufacturing	9.53	15.92	12.96	22.80	27.97	20.15
Mining	0.39	0.14	0.58	0.29	0.12	0.09
Other	51.78	39.42	41.18	58.54	64.11	68.90
Total	100.00	100.00	100.00	100.00	100.00	100.00

Sources: BLES–DOLE (1999, 2000), *Current Labor Statistics*; Asian Development Bank (2000), *Key Economic Indicators*.

9.5 SLOW TRANSFORMATION OF THE ECONOMY

The sluggish transformation of the economy means that the agricultural sector continues to account for a substantial share of total employment (see Balisacan and Hill, Chapter 1). The share of agriculture in total employment fell gradually from 51% in 1980 to 38% in 2000. The current share is lower than in Indonesia and Thailand, but much higher than in Malaysia, South Korea, and Taiwan (Table 9.4). It is also noteworthy that in the Philippines, workers leaving the agricultural sector tend to be absorbed not by industry but by services. The expansion of the services sector is mainly attributable to the growth of traditional activities such as wholesale and retail trade, and community, social, and personal services. The sector, which not unlike agriculture is typically characterized by short hours of work, instability, and low productivity and earnings, now accounts for more than 44% of total employment.

The share of the industrial sector in total employment has been stagnant since the 1970s, remaining at around 14–16%. The share of manufacturing, the most dynamic part of the industrial sector, fell from about 12% in 1970 to 11% in 1980, then declined further to 9.5% in 2000—the lowest level among East Asian countries. The dismal performance of industry underscores the unfavorable effects of the trade and industrialization policies pursued in the 1960s and 1970s (see Bautista and Tecson, Chapter 5, and Hill, Chapter 7). The capital-intensive nature of industrialization, the bias against backward integration, and the heavy dependence on imported raw materials and intermediate inputs have greatly constrained the growth of industry, including exports. Moreover, the country's trade and industry policies effectively penalized agriculture, which consequently failed to experience sustained increases in productivity that could form the basis of improvements in rural livelihoods. This largely explains the persistence of high levels of poverty in rural areas (see Balisacan, Chapter 10).

Far from signaling modern economic transformation, the increase in the share of service sector employment merely points to the growth of the informal sector.[10] Moreover, to the extent that the output of the services sector is mostly non-tradable, the sector's expansion is limited by the development of the domestic economy. This constraint means that, in the absence of significant increases in income and employment in the rest of the economy, especially industry, further rises in the employment share of the services sector will tend only to perpetuate underemployment and low-wage, low-productivity employment (Esguerra 1995).

Declining Labor Productivity

Increases in labor productivity stem from improvements in the capital–labor ratio via investments in physical capital (including infrastructure and equipment) and/or human capital (education, training, and health). Labor productivity (real output per unit of labor input) in the Philippines has been declining. The fall has been virtually continuous over the past two decades, from 38,002 pesos in 1981 to 33,301 pesos in 2000, with the dips coinciding with upswings in employment growth (Figure 9.6). This downward trend implies any or all of the following:

1. firms have failed to invest in state of the art technology and implement best practice;
2. the population has been unable to maintain the required investments in human capital;
3. the figures reflect the relatively rapid expansion of employment in the low-productivity services sector.

Given the twin adverse phenomena of weak economic growth and rapid population growth, the deterioration in labor productivity can probably be attributed to all three factors.

With labor productivity declining and nominal wages increasing (though real wages have been largely stagnant), the international competitiveness of the economy has been seriously eroded. The Philippines has been losing out to other Asian countries with respect to labor-intensive exports (see Bautista and Tecson, Chapter 5). If not reversed soon, eroding competitiveness could next adversely affect electronics exports, which have been the heart and soul of the export sector.

9.6 POPULATION POLICY

The Waxing and Waning of Population Policy

Population policy had a strong start during the early years of the Marcos regime. A national population program with emphasis on family planning was installed in 1969. It was designed to reduce fertility, but no specific limits were placed on family size and no distinction was made between wanted and unwanted fertility. In the

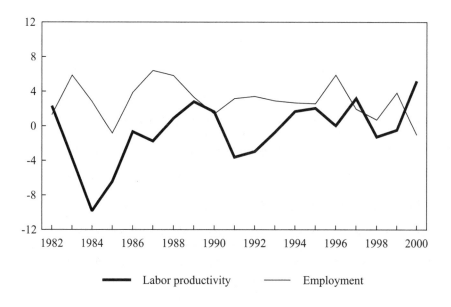

Figure 9.6 Labor Productivity Growth and Employment Growth, 1982–2000 (%)

Source: Lim (2000); BLES–DOLE (1984, 1990, 1998), *Yearbook of Labor Statistics*; BLES–DOLE (2000, 2001), *Current Labor Statistics*.

latter part of the 1970s the vigor of the program waned considerably, following changes in the leadership of the National Economic and Development Authority and the Commission on Population (Orbeta and Pernia 1999).

The policy climate changed again in the latter part of the 1980s under the Aquino administration. It "tolerated de facto cessation of public sector family planning service delivery" owing to "Catholic Church representations on matters regarding public policies on population" (RP/UNFPA 1999). In 1988, authority for the national family planning program was transferred from the Commission on Population to the Department of Health, which emphasized the health rationale for family planning.

Under the Ramos administration, population policy shifted from population control to population management, with family planning being subsumed under a population–resources–environment framework. Family planning was subsequently placed under the rubric of reproductive health.

Under the Estrada administration, population policy focused on the role of the government in assisting married couples to achieve their fertility goals, by helping them to reduce unwanted fertility and by responding to the unmet need for contraception (POPCOM 2000). In addition, the government began to consider expanding the resources available for family planning through budget appropriations for the purchase of contraceptives, which had previously been provided almost totally by international donors. This effort has not prospered, given the Catholic Church hierarchy's opposition to artificial contraception and, hence, the use of government funds for that purpose.

In support of the church's position, some civil society groups have argued that decisions on fertility are the sole prerogative of couples and that the government should therefore stay out of this area. Others argue for a more explicit and stronger population policy, citing the economic and social benefits of slower population growth, as evidenced in other East Asian countries. Under the Macapagal-Arroyo administration, population policy has barely changed and public debate on the issue remains muted.

A Framework for Population Policy

We propose a policy framework based on a decomposition of future population growth in terms of its main sources—namely unwanted fertility, the preference for large family size, and population momentum (Herrin and Costello 1998).[11] The three distinct policy instruments called for are discussed below.

Reducing Unwanted Fertility
The family planning program should focus on reducing unwanted fertility ("unwanted" as defined by the couples themselves). Given that a large part of the unmet need for family planning is due to fear of side effects or health concerns, greater attention must be paid to quality in the provision of family planning services. "Quality" includes such aspects as expanding the range of contraceptive choices available, providing better information on the risks and potential side effects of contraception (and how to avoid these), improving the technical competence of providers, establishing friendlier relations with clients, and offering a broader range of services, particularly with regard to reproductive health and safety (Population Council 1994).

Changing Family Size Preference
Wanted fertility (as distinguished from unwanted fertility) remains higher than is necessary to achieve population replacement level. This suggests the need for a wider array of policy instruments to modify fertility preferences. Investment in human development, in areas such as child health, nutrition, and education, would not only directly promote well-being but also create the necessary incentives for lowering the demand for children.

Reducing Population Momentum
Population momentum is by far the most significant source of future population growth. It can be slowed by increasing the length of generations. This might involve raising the marriage age or the age at which women begin to bear children, as well as promoting wider birth spacing. Investment in education and increased employment opportunities for women are associated with later age at marriage, while a

more responsive family planning program would make wider birth spacing more feasible and effective.

Age at marriage has been increasing for both sexes over several decades, to reach 26.3 years for men and 23.8 years for women in 1990. Judging from the experience of countries in the region that have achieved rapid demographic transition, such as Korea and Singapore, there is still room for the age at marriage to rise further. This could be achieved by encouraging primary and high school-age children—especially those from low-income families—to remain at school longer rather than going out to work. There is also a need to promote non-traditional roles for women, both through formal schooling and through entrepreneurship programs.

9.7 HEALTH, NUTRITION AND EDUCATION

Health Sector Reforms

An analysis of the national health accounts for the period 1991–2000 reveals several noteworthy points (NSCB 2002).

1. Total health expenditure has been increasing in real per capita terms. It has also grown faster than GNP, rising from 2.9% of GNP in 1991 to 3.3% in 2000.
2. Households pay the largest share of the country's health care costs out of their own pockets (41–48% in 1991–2000) (Table 9.5). This places a heavy financial burden on individual families and makes access to health care highly inequitable. The share of the national health insurance program in total expenditure has been small, at around 5% for most of the period. In 1995, a new National Health Insurance Law was enacted to expand the coverage and expenditure share of the national health insurance program. The new law also created a public corporation to manage the system in place of the Medicare Commission. In 1998 Philippine Health Insurance Corporation (PhilHealth) formally took over all activities formerly performed by the Medicare Commission. Delays in processing of claims during that year caused a dip in the share of the national health insurance program in total expeniditures. Having caught up with the backlog of claims, PhilHealth was able to restore its share of total health spending in 1999, and increase it to 7.1% in 2000, partly as a result of an increase in health benefits.
3. Central government spending on health is accounted for mainly by the Department of Health. Its budget decreased immediately following the devolution of much responsibility for health to local government units (LGUs) in 1994, but rose rapidly thereafter to reach 19.6 billion pesos in 2000—compared with its pre-devolution budget of around 4.4 billion pesos.
4. While local government spending on health has increased beyond what is needed to maintain the devolved health functions, it has been noted that local efforts remain uncoordinated. The devolution of administrative powers has also led to technical fragmentation in the delivery of basic health services (Solon et al. 1999).

Table 9.5 Total Health Care Expenditure by Source of Funds, 1991–2000 (%)

Source	1991	1992	1993	1994	1995	1996	1997	1998	1999	2000
National government	34.7	30.8	24.1	21.3	19.3	19.9	20.5	21.0	21.0	21.5
Local government	3.9	4.4	12.5	16.0	16.0	16.4	17.8	18.5	18.7	19.6
National health insurance	5.4	6.0	6.4	5.7	4.5	5.1	5.1	3.8	5.1	7.1
Households	47.7	49.6	47.8	47.5	50.4	48.7	46.9	46.8	43.9	41.0
Private insurance/ Health Maintenance Organization	4.1	4.1	3.8	3.7	3.8	4.0	4.4	5.0	6.2	5.9
Other private	4.2	5.1	5.5	5.9	6.0	6.0	5.3	4.9	5.1	4.9
Total										
(%)	100.0	100.0	100.0	100.0	100.0	100.0	100.0	100.0	100.0	100.0
(billion pesos)	35.9	39.6	47.4	54.6	65.2	76.2	87.1	93.5	103.4	113.5

Source: NSCB (2002: Tables D.1 and D.2).

5. Whereas the share of spending on public health care rose from 8.1% in 1991 to 10.0% in 2000, the share of spending on personal health care services fell from 80% to 73.4% (Table 9.6).

The above findings point to the need for change in the sourcing and use of funds. First, the financial burden on families needs to be shifted to societal risk pools, in particular the national health insurance program. Second, there is a clear need to spend more on public health care and administration, funded especially from government sources. In 2000 the Department of Health formulated a policy program for implementing change, called the Health Sector Reform Agenda. It lists five major reforms needed to improve the way health care is delivered, regulated, and financed. These are summarized below.

1. Government hospitals should be given greater fiscal autonomy. They would be allowed to collect socialized user fees, which would reduce their dependence on government subsidies. The government resources thereby freed up could be used to increase financing of critical public health programs.
2. Priority public health care programs should be given secure funding through multi-year budgets. Investments would be undertaken to address emerging health concerns and to advance health promotion and prevention programs. To ensure that such investments are utilized effectively, the management capacity and infrastructure of public health care programs should be upgraded.

Table 9.6 Total Health Care Expenditure by Use of Funds, 1991–2000

	Personal Health Care		Public Health Care		Other		Total	
	(billion pesos)	(%)	(billion pesos)	(%)	(billion pesos)	(%)	(billion pesos)	(%)
1991	28.7	80.0	2.9	8.1	4.3	12.0	24.4	100.0
1992	32.8	82.9	2.8	7.2	4.0	10.0	21.1	100.0
1993	36.1	76.3	5.9	12.4	5.3	11.3	29.0	100.0
1994	42.4	77.7	6.6	12.1	5.6	10.2	27.9	100.0
1995	50.5	77.5	7.7	11.8	7.0	10.8	29.5	100.0
1996	59.1	77.6	9.5	12.5	7.6	9.9	30.0	100.0
1997	64.8	74.4	11.8	13.5	10.5	12.1	36.1	100.0
1998	70.8	75.8	12.5	13.4	10.2	10.9	34.4	100.0
1999	77.8	75.2	13.3	12.9	12.3	11.9	37.1	100.0
2000	83.8	73.9	15.9	14.0	13.8	12.2	40.0	100.0

Source: NSCB (2002: Table E).

3. Under the present devolution arrangement, local health care systems should be developed that will ensure the effective and efficient delivery of basic services. LGUs should be encouraged to enter into cooperative and cost-sharing arrangements among themselves as well as with the private sector. To promote the development of local health care systems, funds would be secured to upgrade local facilities and build local human resource capacities.
4. The capacity of health regulatory agencies to provide safe, good-quality, accessible, and affordable health services and products should be strengthened. This would include upgrading facilities and human resource capability in such areas as standards development, technology assessment, and enforcement.
5. The coverage of the national health insurance program needs to be expanded to provide especially for the needs of the poor. This would mean, in particular, securing adequate funding for premium subsidies, so that the poor can afford to participate. The benefits of health insurance should also be enhanced to make the program more attractive to the rest of the population, including groups not yet covered by the program such as the self-employed.

The Department of Health views these five reform areas as interdependent and complementary, and therefore believes they should be implemented as a package. Implementation of the Health Sector Reform Agenda will require public funding estimated at 112 billion pesos over the next five years. The success of the reforms will depend not only on the availability of resources but also on the patience and persistence of the department's leadership in overcoming the barriers to health sector reforms. These include bureaucratic inertia, especially in the reorganization of personnel, and pressure from special interest groups.

National Nutrition Interventions

Nutrition interventions adopted by the government have included food assistance programs; micronutrient supplementation and fortification; growth monitoring and promotion programs and nutrition education; home and community food production schemes; and credit assistance schemes aimed at raising household income. However, there has been little systematic assessment of the impact and cost-effectiveness of each (or any combination) of these interventions, and many programs have been criticized as being too complex. Below are key findings from the few assessments made thus far (see, for example, Heaver and Hunt 1995; GOP/UNICEF 1997). They point to the need for more methodical assessments to determine which interventions are cost-effective, which can be adequately funded, and which can be implemented properly.

Heaver and Hunt (1995) conclude that design problems are constraining the effectiveness of food assistance programs. The problems they identify include: (1) poor targeting, such that much of the food provided goes to older children rather than those at the peak ages at which wasting occurs; (2) leakages, such that much of the food is distributed on a "take home" basis, with the result that a large proportion may be consumed by older family members; and (3) periods of participation in the feeding program that are longer than necessary (that is, more than 12 months).

Micronutrient supplementation is considered difficult to sustain over long periods owing to problems of supply and the varying ability of LGUs to deliver services. While vitamin A and iodine supplements can be provided through national campaigns such as those conducted on National Immunization Day (Araw ng Sangkap Pinoy), iron supplements are more difficult to deliver through a campaign approach and must rely on systems of routine health delivery.

It is generally believed that the fortification of dietary staples with micronutrients can help maintain the gains from supplementation and accelerate the reduction of micronutrient deficiencies. However, survey data reveal that knowledge among the population about fortified staples does not readily translate into consumption of such staples. For example, while awareness of the importance of iodized salt is high, the 1996 Multiple Indicator Cluster Survey conducted by UNICEF revealed that only 15% of people had iodized salt in their homes. Another issue concerns the capacity of the government to test fortified products and monitor manufacturers' compliance with standards, to protect consumers and ensure the desired nutritional impact.

Growth monitoring and promotion programs require careful design, training, and supervisory support in order to be effective. An assessment of current programs— the Under Six Clinic Program and Operation Timbang—indicates that these are not working well (Heaver and Hunt 1995). In the case of the Under Six Clinic Program, mothers are encouraged to bring their children to a government health center for monthly weighing and other services. However, the children most in need of the program often fail to appear regularly. Under Operation Timbang, children's growth is monitored once a year—usually on a campaign basis—with the help of rural health midwives, *barangay* (barrio) nutrition scholars, and *barangay* health workers. One annual intervention is deemed too infrequent to catch most children in nutritional trouble, and cannot educate parents in the importance of nutrition by demonstrating monthly weight gains.

An outreach approach has been suggested that would involve monthly monitoring and counseling carried out in the *barangay*. It would target children aged 24–36 months, the peak period at which wasting occurs, with older preschoolers being monitored quarterly. The outreach approach is, however, quite staff-intensive, and its cost-effectiveness, affordability, and sustainability have yet to be demonstrated in the rural setting.

Schemes to promote dietary change through the cultivation and consumption of micronutrient-rich foods in home and community gardens are considered very hard to implement and sustain (Florentino et al. 1993). Maintaining a home garden is expensive, as basic inputs such as seed and water can be costly. Often, access to adequate land and water may simply not be available. Moreover, cultivation is intensive of a mother's time, involving possible trade-offs with the quality of care a child receives while the mother is working. As a result, sustaining commitment and enthusiasm for such activities, on the part of both households and program agencies, has been found to be difficult.

Studies indicate that the resources provided under credit assistance schemes often end up in the hands of the non-poor or go to unintended recipients. Moreover, the direct impact on nutrition of livelihood programs of the type envisioned by a credit assistance program is likely to be small. A study conducted in Bukidnon found that a doubling of incomes was needed to effect a 5% change in a child's nutritional status (Bouis 1989).

Education Sector Reforms

Recent studies on the education sector have been carried out by the Asian Development Bank and World Bank (ADB/WB 1999) and by the Human Development Network and United Nations Development Program (HDN/UNDP 2000).

As with the health sector, total (government and private) expenditure on education has increased in real terms over the last 15 years. As a proportion of GNP, total spending on education rose from 4.9% in 1986 to 5.6% in 1994, and to 6.9% in 1997 (Table 9.7). Although this is comparable with other countries in the region, the share of government (as opposed to private) spending on education, at 2–4% of GNP, is lower than in many other countries.

The increased spending on education has financed larger enrollments at the primary and secondary levels, catering to the rapid growth in the numbers of school-age children. However, this has been achieved at the expense of quality, as manifested in low survival rates and low achievement levels. The question is, then,

Table 9.7 Expenditure on Education by Level of Schooling and Source of Financing, 1986, 1994, and 1997

Expenditure	1986				1994				1997			
	Central Govt	Local Govt	Private Households	Total	Central Govt	Local Govt	Private Households	Total	Central Govt	Local Govt	Private Households	Total
By level of schooling (%)												
Primary	68.4	77.0	33.6	52.1	58.8	63.5	34.6	46.7	60.8	62.8	34.5	49.6
Secondary	11.5	18.1	32.3	21.8	19.3	20.1	29.3	24.4	19.8	19.8	26.0	22.4
Tertiary	19.7	1.6	34.1	25.9	21.0	1.1	36.0	27.9	18.7	1.1	39.5	26.8
Total	100.0	100.0	100.0	100.0	100.0	100.0	100.0	100.0	100.0	100.0	100.0	100.0
By source of financing (%)												
Primary	62.8	6.2	31.0	100.0	56.6	5.6	37.7	100.0	64.8	5.5	29.7	100.0
Secondary	25.4	3.5	71.1	100.0	35.5	3.4	61.1	100.0	46.6	3.9	49.5	100.0
Tertiary	36.5	0.3	63.3	100.0	34.0	0.2	65.9	100.0	36.9	0.2	62.9	100.0
Total	47.8	4.2	48.0	100.0	45.0	4.1	50.9	100.0	52.9	4.4	42.7	100.0

a   Total central government and total local government expenditure include expenditure on technical/vocational schools, preschools, and the Department of Education's non-formal education programs.

Source: Maglen and Manasan (1999), Table B.7.

whether the education sector would be able to obtain better results from the available resources.

Recent analysis suggests there has been some serious misallocation of public resources. First, with respect to public versus private spending on education, one would expect the central government—the main source of government funding—to contribute the largest share of expenditure on primary schooling, based on the externality argument. However, as Table 9.7 shows, its share actually fell between 1986 and 1994 from 63% to 57%, with private sources (mainly households) picking up the shortfall. By 1997, however, the share of central government spending had recovered to 65%.

Second, as a share of total spending on education, central government spending on primary schooling dropped from 68% in 1986 to 59% in 1994, recovering somewhat to 61% in 1997. Its role in secondary and tertiary education, meanwhile, became relatively more important. Spending on secondary education rose from 12% in 1986 to 20% in 1997, with spending on tertiary education remaining at around 20% during this period.

Third, with respect to input mix, the Department of Education's budget for personal services rose from 74% in 1990 to 88% in 1999, attributable in part to an increase in teachers' salaries, while the share of maintenance and operations fell from 17% to 9% (Table 9.8). This has resulted in a deterioration in school buildings, severe shortages of desks and teaching materials, particularly textbooks, and a backlog in the provision of much-needed teacher training (ADB/WB 1999).

The above analysis suggests broad directions for the allocation of public resources. First, the government needs to play a larger role in primary education relative to the private sector. Second, a higher proportion of government spending on education should be invested in primary schooling relative to the other levels, particularly the tertiary level. And third, a higher proportion of spending should be directed toward non-salary recurrent items relative to personal services. This will entail a number of reforms, including reduced government subsidies and increased cost recovery for public tertiary education, to release resources for primary and secondary education. While various analysts and donor agencies have made recommendations on policy reforms, the Department of Education will still need to come up with a coherent reform agenda that it can call its own, as the Department of Health has done.

9.8 CONCLUSION

It seems clear that feeble economic growth and transformation, exacerbated by rapid population growth, have been responsible for the Philippines' poor performance in human resource development and employment over the past two to three decades. Slow economic growth has generated only meager resources for investment in health, nutrition, and education, where demand has been expanding fast owing to high fertility. The legacy of capital-intensive industrialization has meant fewer jobs being created than are required by the country's rapidly expanding labor force.

Table 9.8 Budget of the Department of Education by Expenditure Category, 1990–99

Category	1990	1991	1992	1993	1994	1995	1996	1997	1998	1999
Personal services										
million pesos	20,788	18,515	25,968	26,581	32,089	40,849	49,640	64,898	74,345	78,859
(%)	(74.3)	(68.2)	(82.3)	(82.6)	(87.4)	(79.3)	(81.7)	(84.0)	(87.9)	(87.7)
Maintenance and operations										
million pesos	4,611	5,363	4,588	4,842	4,336	5,211	5,455	6,687	7,345	7,957
(%)	(16.5)	(19.8)	(14.5)	(15.1)	(11.8)	(10.1)	(9.0)	(8.7)	(8.7)	(8.8)
Capital outlay										
million pesos	2,563	3,263	1,009	744	269	5,426	5,643	5,714	2,891	3,117
(%)	(9.2)	(12.0)	(3.2)	(2.3)	(0.7)	(10.5)	(9.3)	(7.4)	(3.4)	(3.5)
Total										
million pesos	27,963	27,141	31,566	32,167	36,695	51,486	60,738	77,299	84,582	89,933
(%)	(100.0)	(100.0)	(100.0)	(100.0)	(100.0)	(100.0)	(100.0)	(100.0)	(100.0)	(100.0)

Source: Maglen and Manasan (1999: Table B.3).

Moreover, within the social sectors, there has been misallocation of the limited resources available.

There is an evident need to address the population problem vigorously while dealing relentlessly with the structural weaknesses in the economy. Population growth must be slowed: first, by reducing the level of unwanted fertility through a stronger national family planning program; second, by changing the preference for a large family size through an incentive structure that raises investment per child and reduces the demand for children; and third, by reducing population momentum through later age at marriage, later childbearing, and wider birth spacing, made possible by a more responsive family planning program. These need to be backed up by appropriate policy reforms in the social sectors.

The key challenge—coming to grips with the country's demographic onus while trying to telescope time to achieve some kind of demographic bonus—is becoming increasingly daunting. A strong population policy must be made an integral part of the development strategy of the Philippines.

NOTES

The authors would like to thank Pilipinas F. Quising for very able technical and research assistance.

1. Demographers estimate "wanted fertility" based on household surveys asking mothers whether births had been planned or wanted at the time of birth. Economists adopt the Easterlin framework to estimate the demand for and supply of children. Using data from the 1983 National Demographic Survey, Boulier and Mankiw (1986) estimated demand for children in the Philippines at 3.12 children per woman and the potential supply of children at 7.98. Since actual fertility was 6.23, the implied excess supply was 3.11 children.

2. As opposed to a demand-side problem, namely that women (or couples) are averse to practicing contraception on account of their religious beliefs. Hence, the problem seems to be more that the government has not instituted a strong family planning program (supplying both relevant information and reliable contraceptive methods) for fear of incurring the wrath of the Catholic Church hierarchy.

3. In the interest of space, the breakdown by region is not shown. This information is available from the authors upon request.

4. Based on limited data for the 1992/93 to 1997/98 school years, the cohort survival rate is higher in private schools than in public schools, as seen in Figure 9.2.

5. See, for example, Behrman, Deolalikar, and Wolfe (1988), Deolalikar (1988), Haddad and Bouis (1991), Jamison (1986), and Herrin (1990a).

6. Under the rapid fertility decline scenario replacement fertility is reached by 2000, whereas under the slow fertility decline scenario it is not reached until 2020.

7. Based on data from the *Philippine Statistical Yearbook* published by the National Statistics Office, and Lim (2000).

8. This is commonly referred to as the "5–6" employment arrangement (named after a usurious loan system), under which workers are employed and then laid off after five or six months so that the company is not forced, as the law mandates, to make them regular work-

ers. This arrangement also prevails in wholesale and retail trade, where many women are employed (Aganon 2000).

9. This might be a statistical artifact, however. According to central bank sources, official remittances made through U.S. banks are generally recorded as coming from the United States regardless of their true origin.

10. Tidalgo and Esguerra (1984) note that in the wholesale and retail trade sector, the major sources of employment are hawking and peddling, and *sari-sari* stores (micro retail outlets).

11. Their analysis shows that: (1) by 2020, of the increase in population from the 1995 level of 37.1 million, 5.8 million will be due to unwanted fertility, 6.7 million to preference for large family size, and 24.6 million to population momentum; and (2) by 2040, of the increase in population over 1995 of 57.8 million, 9.3 million will be due to unwanted fertility, 10.9 million to preference for large family size, and 37.6 million to population momentum.

10

Poverty and Inequality

Arsenio M. Balisacan

10.1 INTRODUCTION

A peculiar aspect of Philippine development in recent decades is the rather slow pace of poverty reduction and the persistently high level of economic inequality. Among the major East Asian economies, the Philippines has had the slowest rate of poverty reduction during the last three decades and, at the turn of the present century, had the highest incidence of absolute poverty. Yet only three decades ago, by Asian standards, the country had comparatively low levels of absolute poverty. Even in other dimensions of human underdevelopment, such as illiteracy and infant mortality, the Philippines had favorable initial conditions compared with its neighbors, especially Thailand and Indonesia (see Balisacan and Hill, Chapter 1, and Herrin and Pernia, Chapter 9). What has gone wrong?

This chapter examines the nature, pattern, characteristics, and causes of poverty and inequality in the Philippines over the last quarter-century. Specifically, this study aims to:

- distill the implications of development strategies and policy regimes for the evolution of poverty and income (consumption) inequality;
- provide comparable estimates of average welfare, inequality, and poverty over time and across geographic areas (provinces, regions, urban and rural areas) and sectors of the economy;
- examine the composition of poverty and inequality, the contribution of growth and inequality change to the evolution of poverty, and the impact of sectoral composition of growth on nationwide rates of poverty and inequality changes;

- assess the importance of initial conditions (related to rural infrastructure, human capital, agrarian structure, and geographic and political attributes) and time-varying factors in accounting for spatial differences in poverty reduction;
- identify the channels by which the poor respond to adverse economic and weather-related shocks and examine what these imply for public policy; and
- identify key policy handles for reducing poverty in the light of limited fiscal resources.

The chapter starts with an overview of the past half-century *vis-à-vis* development planning and approaches to poverty reduction. It then uses comparable household data for 1985–2000 to examine the nature, characteristics, and sources of poverty and inequality, including factors explaining the provincial differences in the evolution of the welfare of the poor. It concludes with policy suggestions for winning the war against poverty in the Philippines.

Poverty Reduction and Postwar Development Planning

Economic reconstruction was the singular concern of development planning immediately after World War II. The Hibben Plan of 1947 focused on the investment requirements of the war-torn economy over the next five years (1947–51). Successive development plans up to 1962—seven comprehensive five-year plans, a three-year plan, annually updated five-year fiscal plans, and specialized electric power and agricultural development plans—increasingly emphasized industrial development and social investment in power and transportation facilities.[1]

All these plans recognized the fact that, given the severity and magnitude of unemployment and underemployment, as well as the attendant poverty problem, the only sure way to reduce poverty and improve the quality of life of the poor would be to increase the overall size of the economic pie. The Five-year Economic and Social Development Program for funding years 1957–61, for example, states:

> A higher standard of living of the people is the core of economic growth. To attain this end, aggregate production has to be increased and the low-income groups must be particularly benefited. Unemployment and under-employment must be … significantly reduced (p. 12).

Similarly, the introduction of the Five-year Economic Development Program for funding years 1955–59 bears President Ramon Magsaysay's State of the Nation Address, which calls for a development plan that would particularly benefit the rural population:

> What we need above all is a coordinated plan theoretically sound and practically feasible to increase national production and income opportunities for more jobs and higher income for our people *particularly in the rural areas* [emphasis added].

Thus, the commonplace claim frequently made in the literature, that poverty reduction as a central element of the development effort is a "new" development of the 1970s and 1980s, is not entirely correct. The plans provided a strategy of rapid growth that was thought, rightly or not, to be the only reliable way of making a sustained, rather than a one-shot, impact on poverty. However, as noted above, planned public investments, particularly for rural areas, were never realized. On the other hand, macroeconomic policies, including trade and exchange rate policies, effectively promoted local production of industrial goods, particularly finished consumer goods. As discussed by Bautista and Tecson (see Chapter 5), the comprehensive system of direct controls on imports and foreign exchange, along with the severe overvaluation of the domestic currency in the 1950s and the highly protective tariff structure in the early 1960s, effectively stimulated the production of import-substituting industrial consumer goods, but penalized exports, agricultural production, and backward integration. When the potential for growth offered by the import substitution of finished consumer goods was exhausted in the late 1950s, import substitution expanded to include intermediate consumer goods and capital goods. Import controls were gradually lifted in the early 1960s, but the quantitative nature of industrial protection remained the same. That is, the highly protective tariff system introduced in the second half of the 1950s, but made redundant at the time by direct import and foreign exchange controls, became applicable.

Industrial development continued to be a general development thrust in much of the 1960s and throughout the 1970s, as evidenced by the official pronouncements of top government officials, and by successive development plans.[2] In contrast to previous plans, the development plans of this period, beginning with the Philippine Economic Program of 1967, explicitly set out the policy measures to be adopted, as well as the investments required in priority areas. The policy measures were aimed at dealing with the basic problems that the plans identified, including chronic unemployment and underemployment, high population growth, inadequate infrastructure, and a tight balance of payments situation. In addition, income inequality, a low standard of living, and—partly in the wake of the oil shock in the early 1970s—rising prices became major policy concerns in the 1970s. Thus, while the development plans of the 1950s and most of the 1960s saw rapid economic growth through industrial development as the central thrust of efforts to reduce poverty and raise the quality of life of the poor on a sustained basis, those of the 1970s moved beyond this to emphasize, as well, the adoption of *direct* policy measures aimed at "sharing the fruits of development" with a broad section of the populace.

The overall development policy regime remained substantially biased in favor of industrial import substitution, although to a lesser extent than in the 1950s and early 1960s (Bautista and Tecson, Chapter 5). The overvalued peso and the fiscal and credit incentives offered to preferred industries also encouraged capital-intensive production, thereby inhibiting the expansion of employment opportunities for the rapidly expanding labor force.

The chaotic events of the late 1970s and early 1980s—deep recession in the world economy, sharp falls in the world prices of the country's traditional exports, internal political turmoil punctuated by the assassination of Benigno Aquino, Jr. in August 1983—revealed the inherent fragility of the economic base that the heavily import-dependent industrialization strategy had hitherto promoted. While the newly revised development plan for 1984–87 identified sustained economic growth, equitable distribution of income, and development of human resources as goals, the government's immediate concern was political survival and putting in place a recovery program focused on loan restructuring, economic stabilization, and expanded structural adjustment. Unlike the development plans of the 1970s, the plan identified only policy concerns, without specifying the policy tools to be used to achieve its goals.

The economic crisis of 1984–85 and the Marcos regime's loss of political credibility propelled to power in February 1986 a new government headed by President Corazón Aquino. The new government's development program primarily stressed the alleviation of poverty, the generation of more productive employment opportunities, and the promotion of equity and social justice. The strategy adopted to achieve these goals was, however, quite distinct from previous ones in emphasizing a market-based development strategy rather than unrestricted government interventions in the marketplace. Unlike previous programs, which had emphasized import-substituting industrial development, the new program called for the removal of policy biases against agriculture and the rural sector and, thus, for the improved profitability of labor-intensive and agriculture-based non-traditional exports. In short, the new program embraced an employment-oriented, rural-based development strategy that had its origin in the work led by Yale University professor Gustav Ranis in the early 1970s.

Serving as the centerpiece of the Aquino administration's economic and social development program was the Comprehensive Agrarian Reform Program (CARP). Started in the second half of the 1980s, the CARP departed from all previous legislation by including all agricultural lands, and by going beyond tenancy to include alternative production arrangements such as production or profit-sharing, labor administration, and distribution of stock shares. The program prescribed the acquisition and distribution of lands within a period of 10 years. However, its overly ambitious design, as well as its failure to take account of budgetary constraints, stood in the way of its successful implementation. By the close of the 1990s, hardly one-half of its original target for acquisition and distribution had been achieved. In the meantime, because the program severely limited land transferability, the attraction of land as collateral was greatly diminished. This discouraged credit flows to agriculture, thereby contributing to the sluggish performance of the rural economy throughout the 1990s (Balisacan, Debuque, and Fuwa 2001).

While the Aquino administration's central theme for poverty alleviation was rural development, it failed to address the single most important constraint to sustained rural development, namely the poor state of rural infrastructure, particularly transport, electricity, and water, including irrigation. Indeed, during most of the second half of the 1980s and in the early 1990s, real public investment in agriculture and rural areas fell not only in relation to the total government budget but also in absolute terms (see David, Chapter 6).

The Ramos administration (1992–98) de-emphasized agrarian reform as the key to poverty reduction and focused instead on accelerating the pace of economic growth, by building the international competitiveness of domestic industries, reforming regulation in services and industry (mainly in commercial banking, transportation, and telecommunications), and investing in basic infrastructure. But it also had a Social Reform Agenda (SRA) for achieving its human development targets. A package of government interventions organized around "flagship programs" for the country's 20 "poorest" provinces, the SRA is considered to be the first effort of the Philippine public administrative system to organize the various sectors of government toward securing so-called minimum basic needs before attending to other demands of priority sectors.

Indeed, overall economic growth accelerated under the Ramos administration, and, as shown in the next section, the welfare of the poor did respond respectably to this growth. The SRA suffered, however, from policy implementation problems, namely lack of focus and inadequate budgetary support (Collas-Monsod and Monsod 1999: 90–91).

The Estrada administration (1998–2001) came to power with a lavish pro-poor agenda. It recognized the imperative of broad-based rural development to win the war against poverty. Its Medium-term Philippine Development Plan for 1999–2004 identified the main elements of the development strategies required to spur growth and achieve sustainable development in rural areas. The plan envisioned, for example, an aggressive delivery of basic social development services, removal of policy and regulatory distortions inhibiting resource allocation efficiency and equitable outcomes, sustained development of rural infrastructure, improvement in governance, and macroeconomic stability.

On the ground, the Estrada administration's flagship program for poverty alleviation was Lingap Para sa Mahihirap (Looking after the Poor). The Lingap program involved the identification of the 100 poorest families in each province and city. They would be provided with a package of assistance, including livelihood development, price support for staple foods, medical assistance, socialized housing, and a rural waterworks system. Tasked with formulating and coordinating the program was the newly created National Anti-Poverty Commission. In practice, the Lingap budgets were largely pork barrels. But even if resources had reached the intended beneficiaries, the poverty outcomes would still have been inferior to those of other schemes tried in the recent past, including the SRA (Balisacan et al. 2000).[3] Indeed, the poverty alleviation program of the entire Estrada administration did not go far beyond rhetoric.

The ascension to power of the Macapagal-Arroyo administration (in 2001) following the exit of the disgraced President Estrada gave birth to a new program for direct poverty alleviation. Dubbed KALAHI (Kapit-Bisig Laban sa Kahirapan, or Joining Hands against Poverty), the program covers asset reform, provision of human development services, creation of employment and livelihood opportunities, participation of so-called basic sectors in governance, and social protection and security against violence. While it is—at the time of writing—premature to assess its effectiveness, the program's lack of focus, especially in view of the country's tight fiscal bind, casts doubt on what it will achieve. Moreover, it gives priority to major urban centers, especially Metro Manila, rather than rural areas where, as shown below, nearly two-thirds of the poor live.[4] However, like the Ramos administration, the present administration recognizes the urgency of generating sustained, rapid economic growth as the vehicle for poverty reduction in the medium to long term.

In summary, the thrust and the zeal to achieve sustainable poverty reduction as well as economic growth have certainly been present during the postwar period. By and large, only the emphasis and the strategy to achieve these goals have changed over the years, at least as indicated by development plans and official policy statements. The 1950s and a large part of the 1960s saw rapid economic growth through import-substituting industrial development as the central focus of efforts to improve living standards. The 1970s and 1980s increasingly emphasized direct poverty reduction schemes, including land reforms, along with strategies to achieve economic growth. During most of the 1990s, the emphasis shifted back to growth, though this time fueled by exports and foreign investment. The late 1990s and turn of the 21st century witnessed a lavish pro-poor agenda centered on rural development. Development plans are, of course, one matter; development records are another.

10.2 AGGREGATE POVERTY, INEQUALITY, AND WELFARE

An almost regular pattern of boom and bust has characterized the Philippine economy over the last three decades. Bust and stagnation soon followed each episode of boom, fueled largely by massive foreign borrowing and capital-intensive import-substituting industrialization. The period also saw heavy government regulation of the market economy, as well as political instability, natural disasters, and major shocks in global trade and finance. For these reasons, for most of the 1980s and early 1990s, the country had the unenviable reputation of being Asia's "sick man." However, the growth episodes in the second half of the 1980s and in the 1990s, notwithstanding the interruption in 1998 owing to the combined impact of the Asian financial crisis and the El Niño phenomenon, appear to have a fundamentally different character from previous ones. The growth took place in an environment of political stability, economic deregulation, and institutional reform. While policy coordination problems (for example, in public investment) persisted, it could not be denied that the country at the end of the millennium was closer to a market economy than it had ever been in the past. One could ask: how far have the poor benefited from the growth process?

Data and Measurement

The data sources for poverty and inequality comparisons are mainly the various Family Income and Expenditure Survey (FIES) rounds from 1985 to 2000. Conducted every three years, these surveys are undertaken by the government's primary statistical agency, the National Statistics Office (NSO). While earlier surveys covering the 1960s and early 1970s are available, I have excluded them because they are either beset by serious technical problems (1975 and 1979 surveys) or available only in published form (1961, 1965, and 1971), whereas unit record data are available for the 1985–2000 surveys.[5]

As its name suggests, the FIES provides data on the two popular broad indicators of household welfare: current income and current consumption expenditure. On both conceptual and practical grounds, I have chosen the latter. Standard arguments in microeconomic theory suggest that since welfare level is determined by "life-cycle" or "permanent" income, and since current consumption is a good approximation of this income, current consumption is an appropriate measure not only of current welfare level but also of *long-term* average well-being. Indeed, measured consumption is invariably less variable than measured income (Deaton 2001). From a practical viewpoint, the difficulty of acquiring accurate information proves to be less severe for consumption than for income, especially in developing countries where governance infrastructure is weak and local markets either nascent or simply absent (Deaton 1997; Ravallion and Chen 1997).

The national income accounts are another distinct source of data on the country's *average* welfare, as given, for example, by the level of per capita GDP or—even closer to a measure of households' command over resources—by per capita personal consumption expenditure. The data from the two sources do not necessarily agree in their measurements of the level or growth rate of welfare, largely because of differences in definition, method, and coverage. Fortuitously, in the Philippine case, they do agree at least in so far as trends in the 1980s and 1990s are concerned (Figure 10.1). Henceforth, average welfare pertains to average expenditure based on the FIES, unless otherwise stated.

The chosen indicator of household welfare has to be adjusted for spatial cost-of-living differences, because prices vary significantly across provinces and regions of the country. I employ the 1997 provincial cost-of-living indices reported in Balisacan (2001b). The reference province is Metro Manila (that is, the cost-of-living index for this province is 100), although any other province could serve the same purpose. Since I wish to make welfare comparisons over time, I have updated these indices to reflect nominal price movements during the 1985–2000 period. This was done by applying the regional consumer price index (CPI) to the provincial cost-of-living indices.[6]

Official poverty estimates are available but are not used in this chapter. The official approach to poverty measurement does not capture well the changes in the welfare of the poor. This is because it uses current income as the welfare indicator and applies poverty lines that are inconsistent across space and time in terms of the living standards they imply. As shown in Balisacan (2001a), the poverty lines applied for the various regions, areas, and years imply different levels of living standards that tend to systematically underestimate (overestimate) the reduction (increase) in absolute poverty in economically more progressive (backward) regions or sectors, or during periods when the overall economy is expanding (contracting). The problem arises because of the use of a region-specific (and, within regions, an area-specific) poverty line based on the prevailing consumption pattern of that region (area).

In this chapter, I employ the consistency-conforming provincial poverty lines given in Balisacan (2001b). The construction involves fixing the standard of living used for provincial comparison, but not the composition of goods used in each

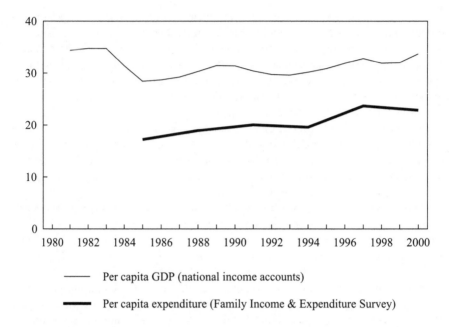

Figure 10.1 Average Welfare: Per Capita GDP versus per Capita Household Expenditure, 1980–2000 (thousand pesos at 1997 prices)

province. The underlying assumption is that the main objective of development policy is to reduce absolute poverty across space and over time. A poverty indicator and monitoring system must therefore be capable of adequately capturing comparative performance in terms of the *changes* over time, or *differences* across space, in absolute poverty.

Aggregate Trends

Four distinct phases characterize the growth process during the last 15 years. The first is a brief period of economic growth (1986–89) following a sharp contraction in 1984 and 1985, when per capita GDP shrank by an average of 10% per year (Figure 10.1). Based on the FIES, average expenditure in 1988 was 10% higher than in 1985, although arguably still much lower than the level prevailing at the turn of the decade.

Political instability, natural disasters, and macroeconomic mismanagement caused overall economic growth to falter in the succeeding four years (1990–93). Nonetheless, mean expenditure in 1991 managed to rise by approximately 6% over that in 1988. Per capita GDP growth, albeit very modest, resumed in 1994, but the combined impact of the contraction in the previous two years caused average per capita expenditure in 1994 to dip 2% below that in 1991. Following the restoration of political stability and deepening of policy and institutional reforms, GDP growth accelerated in the following three years (1995–97). Mean expenditure was approximately 21% higher in 1997 than in 1994, the highest three-year growth achieved since the mid-1980s. However, owing to the combined impact of the Asian financial crisis, the El Niño phenomenon in 1998, and political uncertainty, the overall growth rate again slowed to just a little over the population growth rate in the following three years (1998–2000). Mean expenditure in 2000 was, in fact, 3% lower than in 1997. Overall, per capita GDP (and possibly average welfare) at the turn of the millennium was no higher than in 1980.

Table 10.1 provides estimates of three dimensions of poverty—incidence, depth, and severity—from 1985 to 2000.[7] All the poverty indices show significant reductions during periods of relatively rapid growth of mean expenditure (1985–88 and 1994–97). The highest three-year poverty reduction was achieved during the "economic boom" of 1994–97, when real per capita expenditure rose by 21%. But poverty also fell when the growth of mean expenditure was negative (1991–94). Surprisingly, too, poverty depth and severity increased even when the growth of mean expenditure was positive (1988–91), though at a comparatively low rate. It thus appears that the observed poverty changes are related to the growth (and stagnation) of real mean consumption, while obviously also influenced by other factors. Indeed, as Table 10.1 indicates, another proximate cause for poverty changes may well be the evolution in expenditure distribution. After falling slightly to 0.40 in 1988 from 0.41 in 1985, the expenditure Gini rose to 0.43 in 1991. It fell back to its 1988 level in 1994, only to rise to 0.43 in 1997 and 0.45 in 2000. The same pattern

Table 10.1 Average Welfare, Poverty, and Inequality, 1985–2000 (%)

	1985	1988	1991	1994	1997	2000
Average per capita expenditure (pesos, in 1997 prices)[a]	17,197	18,926	20,049	19,600	23,694	22,865
Dimension of poverty						
Incidence	40.9	34.4	34.3	32.1	25.0	27.5
Depth	13.2	10.1	10.6	8.7	6.4	7.2
Severity	5.8	4.2	4.5	3.4	2.3	2.7
Inequality						
Gini	0.41	0.40	0.43	0.40	0.43	0.45
Share of richest 10%	26.2	24.2	26.9	24.9	28.4	28.2
Share of poorest 20%	8.6	9.1	8.4	9.7	8.8	8.8

a   Adjusted for provincial cost-of-living differences. The reference province is Metro Manila.

Source: Author's estimates, based on FIES data.

emerged for two other simple inequality indicators—the share of the richest 10% and poorest 20% of the population in total expenditure. While these changes are not spectacular, they could have a considerable impact on aggregate poverty, as will be shown below.

The evolution of average welfare, poverty, and inequality in the 1980s and 1990s may well be related also to movements in price levels. Inflation averaged 25% in 1983–85. The rate dropped from 18% in 1985 to 9% in 1988, possibly benefiting the majority of the poor, who tended to be fixed income earners or self-employed workers in rural areas. Inflation surged once more to an average of 15% per year at the end of the decade. This was accompanied by an increase in inequality. Inflation decelerated to only 7.9% per year during 1992–94, 7.7% during 1995–97, and 6.9% during 1998–2000. As shown elsewhere (Balisacan 1995), high inflation during a period of low growth increases aggregate poverty.[8] Particularly vulnerable to commodity (particularly food) price increases are the numerically large small-scale agricultural producers and landless workers who are net buyers of food.

Are the conclusions about changes in poverty over time robust? A comparison of the cumulative distributions (CDs) of per capita expenditure adjusted for provincial cost-of-living differences, shown in Figure 10.2, proves useful here. As shown by Foster and Shorrocks (1988), two non-intersecting CD curves suggest that the direction of poverty change is unambiguous for all plausible poverty indices—including the headcount—that satisfy certain appealing properties of a desirable poverty measure. Such is the case for the adjacent 1985 and 1997 CD curves, as well as the 1994 and 1997 CD curves and the 1997 and 2000 CD curves. Thus, poverty fell unambiguously, regardless of the assumed (but plausible) poverty norm and the chosen poverty index, during the 1985–87 and 1994–97 periods, while it increased during the 1997–2000 period.

The possibility of disagreement about the direction of poverty change applies to the 1988–91 and 1991–94 periods, where the CD curves intersect. Indeed, the poverty estimates in Table 10.1 indicate an inconsistent ranking of 1988 and 1991 by the three poverty indices. It is also apparent in Figure 10.2 that employing some other poverty lines much higher than those applied here would be consistent with rising—not falling—poverty incidence during 1991–94, when mean expenditure contracted by about 2%. It thus appears that conclusions drawn about poverty change during periods of low or negative growth depend partly on the choice of poverty norm and aggregation procedure. For this reason, care must be exercised in interpreting poverty changes in the recent history of the Philippine economy. In the rest of this section, I focus on the 1985–88, 1994–97, and 1997–2000 periods, when poverty change was unambiguous.

As shown above, both growth and redistribution influenced the pattern of poverty reduction during the 1985–88, 1994–97, and 1997–2000 periods. It is possible to determine the relative importance of these two factors to the observed changes in poverty measures through some simple counterfactual experiments. One such experiment would be: what would the change in poverty have been during a given period if all consumption groups had shared equally in the growth that occurred? Another would be: how much further would poverty have increased

(% of population)

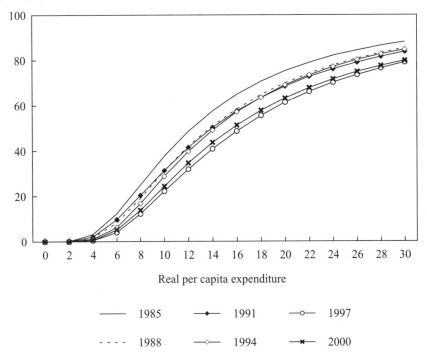

Figure 10.2 Cumulative Distribution of Real per Capita Consumption, 1985–2000 (thousand pesos in 1997 prices)

(decreased) during the period if not for the growth (decline) that did occur? The latter experiment requires simulating the poverty measures that would have been observed in the end-year of the period if mean consumption did not change but inequality did as actually observed.

The two experiments correspond to components of a poverty change, that is, the growth and the redistribution components of observed changes in the poverty measures employed in this chapter.[9] Put differently, the growth component is the change in the poverty measure due to a change in mean consumption per capita while holding the consumption distribution constant at some reference level. The redistribution component, on the other hand, is simply the change in poverty due to a change in consumption distribution while keeping the mean consumption constant at some reference level.

Table 10.2 shows the decomposition of national poverty for the three periods. Clearly, in periods when poverty reduction was comparatively large (1985–88 and 1994–97), the growth component contributes the bulk of the observed poverty change. If growth was distributionally neutral in 1994–97, poverty incidence would have fallen from 32% to 22% instead of 25%; that is, the increase in inequality

Table 10.2 Simulated Poverty Measures, 1985–2000 (%)[a]

	Incidence	Depth	Severity
1985–88			
1985 (actual)	40.9	13.2	5.8
1988 (actual)	34.4	10.1	4.2
1988 (with no change in inequality)	35.0	10.7	4.5
	(−5.9)	(−2.5)	(−1.3)
1988 (with no growth in living standards)	40.2	12.6	5.4
	(−0.7)	(−0.6)	(−0.4)
Change in poverty (actual)	−6.5	−3.1	−1.6
1994–97			
1994 (actual)	32.1	8.7	3.4
1997 (actual)	25.0	6.4	2.3
1997 (with no change in inequality)	21.7	4.9	1.6
	(−10.4)	(−3.8)	(−1.8)
1997 (with no growth in living standards)	35.4	10.7	4.5
	(3.3)	(2.0)	(1.1)
Change in poverty (actual)	−7.1	−2.3	−1.1
1997–2000			
1997 (actual)	25.0	6.4	2.3
2000 (actual)	27.5	7.2	2.7
2000 (with no change in inequality)	26.9	7.1	2.6
	(1.9)	(0.7)	(0.3)
2000 (with no growth in living standards)	30.6	8.9	3.6
	(5.6)	(2.5)	(1.3)
Change in poverty (actual)	2.5	0.8	0.4
1985–2000			
1985 (actual)	40.9	13.2	5.8
2000 (actual)	27.5	7.2	2.7
2000 (with no change in inequality)	24.5	6.6	2.6
	(−16.4)	(−6.6)	(−3.2)
2000 (with no growth in living standards)	47.0	17.2	8.2
	6.1	4.0	2.4
Change in poverty (actual)	(−13.4)	(−6.0)	(−3.1)

a   Figures in parentheses show the share in total (actual) poverty change. The sum of the shares does not add up to total poverty change since the decomposition also involves a residual component (not reported in the table).

Source: Author's estimates.

blunted the impact of growth on poverty by three percentage points. On the other hand, if the distribution of consumption did not change in 1985–88, poverty reduction would have been lower than actually observed. Inequality actually fell during this period, thereby augmenting the impact on poverty of mean consumption growth. Note, however, that the growth component contributes the bulk (over 70%) of the observed change in any of the poverty measures. For the entire 1985–2000 period, the increase in inequality reduced the impact of growth on poverty, but this effect was proportionately small relative to the reduction attributable to consumption growth.

It is thus the changes in real mean consumption, rather than changes in its distribution, that have mainly contributed to the observed changes in poverty in recent years. This result runs counter to the common claim in policy dialogues that recent episodes of growth have largely benefited the non-poor.

10.3 SPATIAL AND SECTORAL DIMENSIONS

A widely held view on the Philippines is that development policy has favored Luzon and discriminated against Visayas and (especially) Mindanao. Moreover, the poor performance of the Philippine economy over the last three decades has been attributed partly to the relatively large variation in access to infrastructure and social services between the major urban centers and rural areas (see, for example, Ranis and Stewart 1993; Balisacan 1996; Bautista 1997). Spatial variation in certain summary measures of human development is also evident (UNDP 1996, 2000).

If indeed spatial income disparities are at the core of the poverty problem in the Philippines, then policy reforms aimed at reducing these disparities have to be central elements of the country's poverty reduction program. This may also promote efficiency goals: important dynamic externalities can arise from targeting by area or according to sector-specific characteristics (Bardhan 1996; Ravallion and Jalan 1996). Investment in physical infrastructure (such as roads, communications, and irrigation) in backward areas, or in the rural sector in general, may improve the productivity of private investment, influence fertility through its effect on labor allocation and educational investment decisions, promote the development of intangible "social capital" (in the form of social networks, peer group effects, role models, and so on), and mitigate erosion in the quality of life in urban areas through its effect on rural–urban migration decisions.

However, if disparity in incomes and human achievement *within* each of the regions or areas of the country were itself the major problem, a different approach to poverty reduction would have to be found. It is possible, for example, that systematic differences in levels of human capital between low and high-income groups within a geographic area translate into considerable differences in earning opportunities. In this case, the policy prescription to reduce overall income inequality and poverty would have to involve expanding the access of low-income groups to basic social services, technology, and infrastructure.

Table 10.3 shows population shares and mean expenditure for selected spatial characteristics (locality, region, and the employment sector of the household head). Clearly, average welfare varies substantially between urban and rural areas, as well as across regions. Metro Manila, which accounts for about 14% of the population, has the highest mean living standard. In 2000, its mean expenditure was nearly twice the national average or about three times the mean living standard for Bicol and Western Mindanao, the poorest regions of the country. Except for Bicol and Cagayan, mean expenditure for the Luzon regions is higher than for most of the regions in Visayas and Mindanao. Note, however, that the ranking of most regions changed between 1985 and 2000, as noted above. Only Metro Manila maintained its relative position during the period.

An even greater disparity in welfare exists among the various employment sectors. As can be expected, agriculture, which employs roughly 40% of the labor force, has consistently had the lowest mean expenditure among all sectors. Manufacturing and trade have almost twice agriculture's mean expenditure, utilities and services more than twice, and finance, the richest sector, four times agriculture's mean expenditure.

Table 10.4 summarizes poverty and inequality estimates for both the urban and the rural sector.[10] High mean consumption disparity between urban and rural areas is apparent. Mean consumption in urban areas is nearly twice that in rural areas, rising significantly during the high-growth periods of 1985–88 and 1994–97 for both sectors. Correspondingly, all poverty indices declined significantly during both periods. The direction of inequality for both sectors also generally followed the overall pattern reported in Table 10.2. Clearly, poverty reduction during high-growth periods was quite broadly based, that is, taking place in both urban and rural areas.

Table 10.5 shows the extent of poverty across regions of the country from 1985 to 2000, as well as the importance of each region in national poverty. Considerable variation exists, but with Metro Manila consistently having the lowest poverty, and Bicol, Western Mindanao, and the Visayas the highest. In 2000, poverty incidence was nine times higher in Bicol than in Metro Manila. Some significant re-rankings also occurred, such as Central Mindanao becoming the fourth poorest region in 2000 when it was only the ninth poorest in 1985. Even more significant is the differential evolution of poverty over time. In two regions, Central and Western Mindanao, poverty—in all three dimensions—was higher in 2000 than in 1985.[11] Toward the close of the 1990s, these two regions, particularly Western Mindanao, were at the center of violent confrontations between the military and armed dissidents.

The evolution of poverty in each sector of the economy is shown in Table 10.6. Relative poverty rankings were virtually unchanged over the years—the highest poverty (all indices) being in agriculture and the lowest in finance. As in the 1960s (see Balisacan 1993), agriculture continues to account for the lion's share (roughly three-quarters, based on the severity index) of total poverty.

The additive decomposability of the poverty measures employed in this chapter can be exploited to explore the proximate factors underlying the observed changes in aggregate poverty during the period of interest. In doing this, I use the household's region of residence and the household head's sector of employment as the

Table 10.3 Average Welfare by Locality, Region, and Sector, 1985–2000 (%)

	Population Share		Average Welfare[a]					
	1985	2000	1985	1988	1991	1994	1997	2000
Philippines (1997=100)	100.0	100.0	72.6	79.9	84.6	82.7	100.0	96.5
Locality (urban 1997=100)								
Urban	38.7	49.0	76.1	83.0	82.8	79.3	100.0	95.5
Rural	61.3	51.0	40.6	45.5	43.8	44.7	52.0	49.9
Region (Metro Manila 1997=100)								
Metro Manila	14.0	14.2	64.7	69.4	79.5	77.4	100.0	93.9
Ilocos	7.2	6.5	41.0	41.9	45.1	42.7	53.5	52.4
Cagayan	4.6	4.0	35.3	36.8	37.9	40.7	44.3	45.4
Central Luzon	9.9	9.9	53.6	56.7	61.0	44.8	54.2	51.1
Southern Luzon	12.5	14.5	43.1	47.3	53.9	46.8	55.3	57.3
Bicol	6.8	7.5	26.2	29.3	27.9	33.6	38.5	35.8
Western Visayas	8.9	8.0	38.3	42.4	45.0	44.1	52.8	50.8
Central Visayas	7.6	7.1	27.2	33.8	36.2	38.8	46.7	43.3
Eastern Visayas	5.4	4.7	27.4	31.5	32.2	31.0	35.5	39.2
Western Mindanao	5.1	5.2	30.6	36.2	33.8	32.2	39.7	33.4
Northern Mindanao	6.1	5.7	32.5	39.4	34.1	41.1	52.9	48.2
Southern Mindanao	7.3	7.4	30.9	36.0	32.6	47.6	50.8	51.4
Central Mindanao	4.5	5.3	37.4	42.3	36.9	38.0	42.0	38.8
Sector (agriculture 1997=100)								
Agriculture	47.3	36.8	79.5	86.7	86.6	87.6	100.0	94.7
Mining	0.8	1.1	109.7	105.9	114.4	137.2	133.6	103.5
Manufacturing	7.0	7.2	136.2	151.7	163.8	170.3	194.2	174.0
Utilities	0.5	0.5	167.8	229.0	187.7	190.7	251.5	235.4
Construction	4.9	7.1	103.3	111.7	126.1	106.0	138.0	120.2
Trade	8.0	10.4	145.2	161.5	176.1	171.2	199.0	179.6
Transportation	6.1	9.2	129.4	131.4	143.6	140.9	163.6	155.4
Finance	1.8	2.1	235.4	257.4	293.1	258.2	394.6	403.3
Services	12.1	11.1	160.9	182.5	192.0	184.6	229.7	227.8
Unemployed	11.4	14.4	160.2	170.1	184.7	172.0	201.7	197.5

a   Per capita consumption expenditure adjusted for provincial differences in the cost of living. Mean welfare in 1997 for the Philippines, urban areas, Metro Manila, and agriculture is 23,694 pesos, 31,657 pesos, 42,367 pesos, and 14,886 pesos respectively.

Source: Author's estimates, based on FIES data.

Table 10.4 Average Welfare, Poverty, and Inequality in Urban and Rural Areas, 1985–2000 (%)[a]

	1985	1988	1991	1994	1997	2000
Urban						
Dimension of poverty						
Incidence	21.7	16	20.1	18.6	11.9	13.2
Depth	5.9	3.8	5.7	4.4	2.6	3.0
Severity	2.3	1.4	2.3	1.5	0.9	1.0
Inequality						
Gini	0.41	0.39	0.42	0.39	0.43	0.41
Share of richest 10%	26.9	24.5	28.0	25.7	31.1	30.7
Share of poorest 20%	7.5	8.0	7.0	8.2	6.7	7.0
Rural						
Dimension of poverty						
Incidence	53.1	45.7	48.6	45.4	36.9	41.3
Depth	17.8	14	15.6	13	9.8	11.3
Severity	8.0	5.9	6.8	5.2	3.6	4.3
Inequality						
Gini	0.35	0.35	0.36	0.34	0.35	0.41
Share of richest 10%	23.2	23.1	23.9	23.1	24.3	24.3
Share of poorest 20%	9.6	9.7	9.8	10.7	10.3	10.7

a   Poverty and inequality estimates are based on per capita consumption expenditure adjusted for provincial cost-of-living differences. Poverty lines employed to calculate poverty indices are fixed in terms of living standards.

Source: Author's estimates.

basis for disaggregating the population. Then, the change in observed aggregate poverty can be expressed as the sum of (a) intraregional (intrasectoral) effects, (b) population shifts, and (c) interaction effects. The intraregional (intrasectoral) effects are simply the contribution of the gains of the poor within each region to the change in aggregate poverty, controlling for the population share of the poor during the base period. The population shifts are the contribution of changes in the distribution of the population across regions (sectors) during the period. The residuals, or the interaction effects, arise from the possible correlation between population shifts and intraregional (intrasectoral) changes in poverty.

Table 10.7 summarizes these decompositions for the periods in which the poverty change is robust, that is, 1985–87, 1994–97, and 1997–2000. The figures shown are averages of the components for the three periods and for two household attributes, namely the region in which the household is located and the household head's sector

Table 10.5 Poverty by Region, 1985–2000 (%)[a]

	1985	1988	1991	1994	1997	2000	Contribution to Total Poverty, 2000
Incidence							
NCR	11.6	9.5	5.9	5.6	3.5	5.5	2.9
Ilocos	33.1	27.6	27.3	26.5	21.0	19.4	4.6
Cagayan Valley	44.9	39.7	42.2	39.8	29.5	29.7	4.4
C. Luzon	19.1	15.3	15.4	24.3	13.2	16.1	5.8
S. Luzon	35.4	31.7	22.9	28.6	19.6	19.5	10.3
Bicol	67.0	60.9	62.2	50.2	45.6	53.3	14.4
W. Visayas	49.4	34.4	31.6	34.5	21.8	28.1	8.1
C. Visayas	66.5	55.2	53.2	42.8	35.2	39.4	10.2
E. Visayas	59.3	53.7	54.4	51.5	50.6	46.8	8.0
W. Mindanao	52.5	43.8	44.0	53.7	44.6	56.0	10.5
N. Mindanao	52.6	41.4	54.2	37.9	29.9	30.1	6.2
S. Mindanao	51.8	43.7	53.9	30.7	27.8	25.8	7.0
C. Mindanao	35.8	30.1	42.3	39.8	32.9	39.9	7.6
Depth							
NCR	2.3	1.9	1.0	0.9	0.6	0.9	1.8
Ilocos	8.0	5.9	6.4	5.8	4.2	4.0	3.6
Cagayan Valley	13.0	11.3	13.5	10.5	7.1	6.8	3.8
C. Luzon	5.1	3.6	3.9	5.8	2.5	3.1	4.2
S. Luzon	10.0	8.6	5.6	7.0	4.5	4.8	9.6
Bicol	24.8	20.2	21.9	16.4	12.6	15.8	16.3
W. Visayas	14.5	8.3	8.5	8.1	4.7	6.4	7.0
C. Visayas	27.7	21.6	20.2	13.1	10.3	11.8	11.7
E. Visayas	22.0	16.5	18.2	15.6	16.0	14.2	9.2
W. Mindanao	16.8	12.8	12.8	18.1	12.5	18.7	13.3
N. Mindanao	17.9	12.1	18.6	10.3	7.6	7.6	6.0
S. Mindanao	17.6	14.5	18.6	8.1	7.1	6.4	6.6
C. Mindanao	8.9	7.1	11.5	10.0	8.4	9.6	7.0

NCR = National Capital Region.

a　The regional classification of provinces and cities is kept fixed to that existing in 1985.

Source: Author's estimates.

of employment. Clearly, the observed changes in poverty for the entire period are attributable mainly to intraregional (intrasectoral) changes in consumption.

As noted above, the large income disparity between Luzon and the rest of the country, as well as between urban and rural areas, has attracted much attention in policy discussions. The common theme emerging from these discussions is that the

Table 10.6 Poverty by Sector of Employment, 1985–2000 (%)

	1985	1988	1991	1994	1997	2000	Contribution to Total Poverty, 2000
Incidence							
Agriculture	57.7	51.2	51.9	49.9	42.3	45.9	61.3
Mining	46.4	34.4	44.7	37.1	30.0	58.4	2.4
Manufacturing	31.4	21.9	20.9	16.5	13.5	16.1	4.2
Utilities	17.5	10.8	12.5	9.5	9.5	6.7	0.1
Construction	39.6	33.8	33.8	34.5	23.1	29.8	7.7
Trade	27.3	18.6	21.3	17.8	13.5	15.4	5.8
Transportation	27.8	24.1	22.5	21.2	13.7	18.2	6.1
Finance	13.2	8.5	6.9	7.1	3.0	9.1	0.7
Services	20.0	15.4	15.2	12.7	9.9	10.5	4.3
Unemployed	21.5	18.3	16.8	17.1	12.1	14.0	7.3
Depth							
Agriculture	20.0	15.9	16.9	14.5	11.5	12.8	65.0
Mining	13.8	8.9	12.5	7.4	10.0	20.9	3.3
Manufacturing	9.3	6.0	6.3	3.8	2.7	3.9	3.9
Utilities	4.3	3.0	3.8	2.3	2.4	0.9	0.1
Construction	11.7	9.2	9.9	8.9	5.0	7.1	7.0
Trade	6.9	4.7	5.6	4.0	2.9	3.3	4.8
Transportation	7.0	5.4	6.0	4.7	2.8	4.1	5.2
Finance	2.4	1.6	1.9	0.9	0.5	2.6	0.8
Services	5.2	4.0	4.0	2.8	2.2	2.4	3.7
Unemployed	6.1	4.9	4.5	4.1	2.9	3.2	6.4

Source: Author's estimates, based on FIES data.

disparity is largely responsible for the high income inequality in the country, implying that much of the inequality would be reduced by policy reforms aimed at closing the income gap between regions and between rural and urban areas.

Figure 10.3 suggests that this claim is grossly inaccurate. While regional differences in average expenditure are substantial, the contribution of the between-group component to overall inequality is rather small (no more than 18%).[12] This implies that removing between-group inequality by equalizing all regional mean incomes (but keeping within-group inequality constant by equiproportionately changing the incomes of all members of that region) will reduce overall inequality by at most 18%. Conversely, removing within-region inequality by making everyone's income within a region equal to the mean for that region would reduce overall inequality by at least 82%.

Table 10.7 Sources of Change in Aggregate Poverty during the 1980s and 1990s (%)

Source	Incidence	Depth	Severity
Regional decomposition			
Intraregional effects	100.6	100.2	100.1
Population shifts	−0.7	−0.5	−0.4
Interaction effects	0.1	0.3	0.3
Total	100.0	100.0	100.0
Sectoral decomposition			
Intrasectoral effects	90.8	92.0	93.0
Population shifts	8.9	9.0	8.7
Interaction effects	0.3	−1.0	−1.7
Total	100.0	100.0	100.0

Source: Author's estimates, based on FIES data.

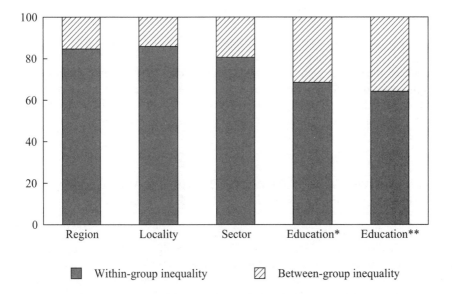

   Within-group inequality    Between-group inequality

Figure 10.3 Within-group and Between-group Inequality (%)

The welfare indicator is per capita consumption expenditure, except for decomposition by education of household head, when household expenditure is used. * is education of household head; ** is level of human capital in the household, measured as the ratio of total school years to total potential school years of household members.

Inequality arising from large differences in mean expenditure between urban and rural areas also accounts for no more than 20%. Again, this contradicts the widely accepted view that urban–rural disparity accounts for a very large part of the existing inequality in the Philippines. What Figure 10.3 suggests is that potentially larger gains in terms of a reduction in overall inequality will be achieved if efforts are focused on reducing inequality within both urban and rural areas. Decomposition by sector of employment gives similar results: it is inequality within sectors, not between sectors, that accounts for the bulk of the observed national inequality.

Clearly, disparity in incomes and human achievement within each of the regions or areas of the country is the major problem, not disparity between regions, between urban and rural areas, or between agriculture and industry. Within-region inequality arises from differences in possession of (or access to) both physical and human assets, including public goods. Differences in educational attainment alone raise the contribution of between-group inequality to one-third of the observed national inequality. Unfortunately, while the distribution of human and physical assets is within the influence of government policy, public investments have fallen short of creating a highly favorable environment for asset formation, especially among the poor.

The recent changes in overall inequality (Table 10.1), albeit small, are also accounted for largely by changes in relative expenditure *within* geographic boundaries, and not from changes in relative mean incomes among regions or areas of the country.[13] This observation suggests a crucial point: it is how the economic and institutional environment affects rewards to owners of factors of production—which are distributed highly unevenly within a region or location—that largely determines the country's performance in inequality reduction.

In sum, income inequality at any point in time has come mainly from differences within geographic boundaries and sectors, not from differences in mean incomes between boundaries and sectors. Similarly, the changes in inequality in recent years have come mainly from changes within geographic boundaries and sectors, not from changes in mean-group incomes.

10.4 RELATIVE CONTRIBUTION OF LOCATION AND HOUSEHOLD ATTRIBUTES TO DIFFERENCES IN HOUSEHOLD WELFARE

The above decomposition approach provides at best an indication of the contribution of a set of factors—location and household-specific attributes—to poverty and inequality. The approach is, however, rather cumbersome in cases where many of these factors have to be treated jointly rather than individually. More importantly, the *relative* contribution of each of the factors in explaining the level of inequality (poverty) is sensitive to the inequality (poverty) measure employed. Also, the approach does not provide any explicit policy handle for addressing the inequality issue.

An alternative approach is to use a parametric procedure to explore systematically the contribution of each of these factors to the observed variation in household

Table 10.8 Relative Contribution of Household and Spatial Attributes to Variance of Household Welfare (%) [a]

Attribute	Contribution to Explained Variance
Household head	30.1
Age	0.4
Male	0.6
Married	–0.6
Education	29.7
Household composition	24.2
Family size	10.6
Child dependency	10.9
Household members employed	2.6
Economic attributes	7.8
Economic sector	6.2
Class of worker	1.2
Status of employment	0.3
Infrastructure	21.6
Electricity	21.6
Location	16.8
Urban	5.5
Region	11.3
Total	100.0
Variance explained by model (average)	55.5

a The figures shown are averages of estimates obtained from regression results, based on FIES data in the 1980s and 1990s.

Source: Author's estimates.

welfare. Specifically, one could estimate a standard set of earnings regressions and use the parameter estimates to calculate the relative contribution of each factor to the differences in household welfare. Table 10.8 summarizes the results of such an exercise, giving the shares accounted for by the location and household-specific attributes in the total variance explained by the estimated model.[14]

Household composition and the household head's attributes, most especially educational attainment, account for one-half of the variance explained by the model. Infrastructure, represented by access to electricity, accounts for another quarter, while location of the household represents one-sixth. Employment sector contributes only a relatively small proportion (less than 10%) of the explained variance. This suggests that it is differences in welfare levels within a sector, rather than differences in mean welfare levels between sectors, that accounts for a significant proportion of the variation in household welfare nationally.

10.5 WHAT EXPLAINS DIFFERENCES IN POVERTY REDUCTION ACROSS PROVINCES?

Recent research employing cross-national comparisons shows that the incomes of the poor move one-for-one with overall average incomes, suggesting that poverty reduction requires nothing much more than promoting rapid economic growth (Dollar and Kraay 2001). In the Philippines, cross-province comparison likewise appears to lend support for this finding. In Figure 10.4, province-level data covering the five FIES surveys in the 1980s and 1990s (a total of 360 observations) show a positive correlation between province-level average incomes and the average living standard of the poor, here defined to comprise the bottom 20% of the population (based on a ranking by per capita expenditure). The slope of the fitted line—obtained by simply regressing the average living standard of the poor against overall mean income— indicates a "growth elasticity" of 0.7; that is, a 10% increase in the overall mean income raises the living standards of the poor by 7%.

The story, however, is not as straightforward as it seems. Other variables that have a direct impact on the well-being of the poor may be correlated with the growth variable; if these variables are omitted from the analysis, their impact would be wrongly attributed to growth. For example, local infrastructure, institutions (for example, social capital), and agrarian structure vary considerably across provinces and correlate strongly with provincial mean incomes. Put differently, these factors may affect the welfare of the poor either indirectly, through overall income growth, or directly, through redistribution, or both. Not surprisingly, changes in the average welfare of the poor during the 1980s and 1990s vary widely across provinces.

Further, there is the possibility that the welfare level of the poor and overall mean incomes are jointly determined. Recent theory and evidence show a link running from inequality (hence, the incomes of the poor) to subsequent overall income growth. One strand of the literature suggests that income (or asset) inequality inhibits subsequent overall income growth (Alesina 1997; Deininger and Squire 1998), while another strand says the reverse (Forbes 2000; Li and Zou 1998).

Balisacan and Pernia (2001) have exploited the longitudinal nature of the provincial data (1980s and 1990s) to examine empirically the link between the welfare of the poor on the one hand, and overall income growth and other factors on the other. The dependent variable is average per capita expenditure for the bottom 20% of the provincial population. The impact of overall provincial income growth on poverty reduction is distinguished from the direct impact of certain economic and institutional factors. The explanatory variables are categorized into two groups, namely initial condition variables and time-varying variables. Included in the first group are province-specific human capital endowment, farm and land characteristics, social

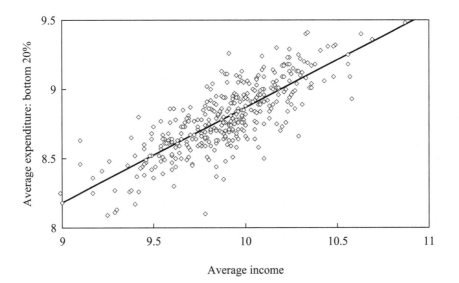

Figure 10.4 Average Welfare of the Poor versus Overall Average Income, 1980s and 1990s

capital, geographic attributes, and political economy characteristics. The time-varying variables include relative price incentives (terms of trade), road access and electricity, agrarian reform, and overall average per capita income. The estimation takes into account the possibility of a reverse causation in the poverty–growth relationship. The regression results are summarized in Table 10.9.

The response of the average welfare of the poor (bottom 20%) to overall average income growth is far lower than is suggested by cross-country studies. The growth elasticity is only slightly higher than 0.5, suggesting that a 10% increase in overall per capita income raises the average per capita expenditure of the poor by about 5%. This result suggests that the quality or type—not just speed—of growth matters for poverty reduction. It further implies that the same growth brings about disproportionately higher welfare gains for some of the other quintiles of the population.[15]

The agrarian reform variable, defined as the proportion of cumulative agrarian reform accomplishments out of total potential land reform area under the CARP, is significant in one of the two variants of the model. Interestingly, the estimated coefficient is positive and highly significant when the specification allows for the possibility that agrarian reform is itself endogenous—that is, it is influenced by poverty, among other factors.

By itself (apart from its direct impact on overall mean income), schooling does not seem to have a direct impact on the well-being of the poor. The schooling coefficient is not significantly different from zero in both variants of the regression model. However, when schooling interacts with the roads variable, which is a proxy for access to markets and social services, the coefficient is positive and significant.

Table 10.9 Determinants of the Average Welfare of the Poor (bottom 20%)[a]

Explanatory Variable	Model 1		Model 2	
	Coefficient	Standard Error	Coefficient	Standard Error
Initial conditions				
Schooling	−0.072	0.091	−0.010	0.094
Local dynasty	−0.101	0.029***	−0.104	0.030***
Political party	0.026	0.015*	0.029	0.015**
Landlocked	−0.062	0.019***	−0.067	0.019***
Typhoon	−0.042	0.017**	−0.064	0.019***
Irrigation	0.309	0.039***	0.233	0.046***
Farm size	0.008	0.018	0.010	0.019
Time-varying variables				
Per capita income (Y)	0.602	0.044***	0.544	0.047***
Terms of trade (Pa/Pna)	0.118	0.042***	0.140	0.043***
Roads	−0.208	0.095**	−0.212	0.096**
Electricity ($\times$ 100)	0.051	0.086	0.049	0.086
Agrarian reform	−0.005	0.010	0.041	0.017**
Interactions				
Schooling*roads	0.109	0.051**	0.110	0.051**
Schooling*electricity ($\times$ 100)	0.016	0.037	0.007	0.038
Intercept	2.865	0.385***	3.324	0.406***
R^2	0.771, 0.394		0.758, 0.385	

a   Estimation is by three-stage least squares. Instruments are actual values of schooling, roads, electricity, political economy, and geographic variables, agrarian reform (except for variant 2), terms of trade, and lagged values of the other variables, including the twice-lagged value of average income growth. For model 2, two additional instruments are lagged land inequality and tenancy. Data are for provincial panel covering the 1980s and 1990s. The R^2 values apply to the level and the difference form of the estimated log (per capita expenditure) function. ***, **, and * denote significance at the 1%, 5%, and 10% levels respectively.

Source: Balisacan and Pernia (2001).

This suggests that complementarities are important, and that returns to schooling are dependent on the availability of complementary factors.

The coefficient for roads is significant but, surprisingly, has a negative sign, implying that, by itself, access to markets and information may not necessarily improve the plight of the poor. It appears that roads do not typically reach the areas where most of the poor live and, where they do, they may exert an adverse impact on the poor through factor market, political economy, and other processes. Nevertheless, as pointed out above, road access can improve the well-being of the poor provided they have sufficient human capital to take advantage of it. Indeed, the results indicate that the incremental impact of roads on the welfare of the poor rises with schooling level.

Electricity, which serves as a proxy for access to technology and information, is not significant. This result is quite puzzling, considering the importance often attributed to access to technology as a factor in poverty reduction. It is possible that this variable, which is defined simply as the (lagged) proportion of households with electricity, is a poor proxy for access to technology and information.

As expected, the terms of trade variable is positive and significant, indicating that changes in the price of agriculture relative to the price prevailing in other sectors of the local economy have a profound impact on poverty reduction.[16] This result reflects the favorable effects on the poor of the trade and exchange rate reforms of the 1990s. These reforms have effectively reduced the degree of overvaluation of the local currency, thereby improving the price incentives for tradables relative to nontradables. Since agriculture is more tradable than either industry or services, the policy shift would have improved the relative profitability of agriculture. Further, since agriculture is more labor-intensive than industry, the reforms would have benefited labor, especially of the poor.[17]

Initial farm size is not significant, but irrigation (defined as the ratio of irrigated land to total farm area) is, suggesting that it is land quality, not farm size per se, that tends to positively influence the living standards of the poor. This result conforms to the common view that investment in productivity-enhancing land improvement, such as irrigation and drainage, is an important policy measure for poverty reduction in land-scarce, labor-abundant developing countries.

Interestingly, the local political dynasty variable is highly significant and has a negative sign, indicating that the welfare of the poor tends to be lower in provinces governed by political dynasties than in provinces characterized by competitive politics, other things being equal.[18] This is consistent with the view that dynasty in local politics inhibits economic performance—through its negative effects on economic efficiency—and restricts the access of the poor to basic services. The other political economy variable—political party affiliation of local chief executives—is likewise significant, suggesting that resources for employment generation and poverty reduction tend to flow more toward local governments run by administrators with direct ties to the country's ruling political party (or president).

Two geographic attributes—frequency of typhoons hitting the province and a dummy variable indicating whether or not the province is landlocked—are intended to capture geographic "poverty traps." A number of observers have noted that the areas most frequently hit by typhoons are among the poorest in the country. Using cross-country regressions, Gallup and Sachs (1998) find that the geographic location of a country tends to influence the speed of its economic growth, noting in particular that landlocked countries tend to grow more slowly than those with direct access to sea transport. In the case in point, both variables are consistently negative and highly significant, suggesting that typhoons and high transport costs tend to depress the average living standards of the poor.

In sum, provincial panel data suggest that the response of poverty to overall average income growth is far more subdued than is suggested by cross-country analyses. It seems clear that changes in poverty over time depend not only on the *rate* but also on the *type* of economic growth. Put differently, the poor benefit from growth, but they benefit even more from it if institutions and policies are reformed to favor them, or are at least made more neutral. Schooling, if accompanied by complementary public investments, raises the welfare of the poor, apart from its indirect effect through economic growth. And so do the implementation of agrarian reform, investment in land quality improvement, and removal of price distortions that diminish the profitability of agriculture relative to non-agriculture. Political dynasties are bad for the poor, as they not only constrain local economic growth but also restrict the access of the poor to basic services. High transport costs lead to geographic "poverty traps," as the poor are impeded from taking advantage of economic opportunities elsewhere.

10.6 POVERTY DURING CRISES

How do the living standards of the poor evolve during an adverse economic shock, such as the Asian financial crisis, or at times when natural calamities, such as drought, hit rural areas? How do the poor respond to these shocks? How should public safety nets be designed to effectively mitigate the adverse consequences of such shocks on the poor?

The Asian financial crisis is over, but its full impact on various social and economic groups will continue to linger for years to come. Some useful lessons for policy can be learned from the crisis, but only if its causes and consequences have been adequately understood. A number of reports describing its impact on Philippine households have appeared since the crisis erupted in late 1997 (for example, Lim 1999; Reyes et al. 1999; Datt and Hoogeveen 2000). Discussion in these studies has, however, been limited by the lack (or inadequacy) of nationwide household data that could be used to describe changes in the economic well-being of various household groups: their economic conditions before the crisis, changes in these conditions during the crisis, and the impact of government policies and programs implemented to address the crisis. Also, with the exception of Alba (2001), none of these studies has systematically explored the factors that make some households more vulnerable than others to macroeconomic shocks of this type.

In the Philippine case, what has complicated the analysis of the impact of the crisis on the poor was the concurrent onset of severe drought—the El Niño phenomenon—in many parts of the country. Extrapolating household survey data for 1998, Datt and Hoogeveen (2000) estimated the combined impact of the two shocks to be in the order of a 5% reduction in average living standards and a 9% increase in the incidence of poverty. Their exercise suggests that the El Niño shock accounted for the largest share of the overall impact.

In an earlier paper (Balisacan 2001a), I exploited the substantial sample overlap of two nationwide surveys covering the crisis period, that is, the 1997 FIES and the 1998 Annual Poverty Indicator Survey, to deepen our understanding of household adjustment to shocks. This overlap allowed the formation of panel or longitudinal data on households, thereby permitting examination of the influence of pre-crisis living standards and certain household characteristics on the impact of, and household responses to, the crisis, as subjectively reported by survey respondents (in the 1998 Annual Poverty Indicator Survey).

One key finding was that households that had reported experiencing the adverse effects of the crisis (increased prices, reduced earnings), as well as the El Niño phenomenon (at least for some regions), came disproportionately from the poorer households. Loss of domestic jobs affected the middle deciles of the expenditure distribution more, while loss of overseas jobs was more likely to affect the upper expenditure deciles.

Households responded differently to the crisis and to the El Niño phenomenon depending on their household attributes, most importantly pre-crisis living standards and location. The panel data suggest that the probability of households changing their eating patterns, taking children out of school, or increasing their working hours was inversely related to their pre-crisis living standard. It thus appears that a macroeconomic shock like the Asian crisis tends to systematically hit hardest the poorest groups in society. On the other hand, the probability of receiving assistance/relief from the public sector or from other households was not significantly related to pre-crisis living standards. This suggests that, during an economy-wide crisis, social safety nets, whether from formal or informal sources, do not have a pro-poor bias. It is, of course, possible that the amount of income transfers received by the poor was higher (in absolute terms or as a proportion of their pre-transfer incomes) than that received by the non-poor. Unfortunately, the data do not contain information on the type and amount of income transfers received from either the public or the private sector.

Migration as a household response to the crisis was found to be positively related to pre-crisis living standards: the richer the crisis-affected household, the more able it was to smooth consumption through migration. This may suggest that there are fixed costs of migration and that, for the poor, financing these costs through credit channels during a crisis could be extremely difficult.

To succeed, a public policy aiming to provide safety nets for the poorest groups of society during an economic crisis must be informed by a clear understanding of the sources of household vulnerability to shocks, the channels through which a crisis affects the economic well-being of the various population groups, and their responses to the shock. The above results contribute to building that information.

10.7 CONCLUDING REMARKS

Success in winning the war against poverty in the Philippines depends on having a good understanding of the interaction between growth and poverty, as well as the policy handles required to influence household welfare and income distribution. Such understanding should underpin the identification of what works and what does not. It is thus imperative to examine recent data, assess the robustness of conclusions about the link between growth and poverty in the Philippines, and use this evidence to inform policy choices *vis-à-vis* poverty reduction and equity goals. This chapter is a modest contribution to that goal.

Contrary to recent claims, poverty reduction as a central development goal is not a new invention of either the 1970s or the late 1990s. The thrust and the zeal to achieve sustainable poverty reduction, as well as economic growth, have been present throughout the postwar period. By and large, only the emphasis and the strategy used have changed over the years, at least as indicated by development plans and official policy statements. The 1950s and a large part of the 1960s saw rapid economic growth through import-substituting industrial development as the central focus of efforts to improve living standards. The 1970s and 1980s increasingly emphasized direct poverty reduction schemes, along with strategies to achieve economic growth. The late 1980s and the first half of the 1990s re-emphasized economic growth, but this time led by exports. The late 1990s stressed rural growth as the main vehicle for reducing poverty. Finally, the turn of the new millennium underscored the urgency of efficiency and global competitiveness—and hence economic growth—as the key strategy for winning the war against poverty. But development plans are one matter, and the economic record, as the various chapters of this volume show, another.

There is no question that overall economic growth benefits the poor and that it is crucial to poverty reduction in both the short and the long term. Indeed, no country has ever won the war against absolute poverty without first getting its economy to sustain growth at rates higher than its population growth rate over a reasonably long period of time. The key to success in poverty reduction in the major East Asian countries was their rapid economic growth—averaging 6–9% a year—sustained over two to three decades. Seen from this perspective, the main reason for the high level of absolute poverty in the Philippines is primarily the short duration, and the slowness, of economic growth.

While growth in recent years has benefited the poor, the response of poverty to growth has not been good enough, at least in comparison with similar responses observed for major East Asian countries. Moreover, the response varies quite remarkably across geographic areas (regions, provinces) and population groups.

Newly constructed provincial panel data spanning the 1980s and 1990s reveal substantial differences in the evolution of poverty across provinces. These data suggest that the growth elasticity of poverty is, on average, just above 0.5, indicating that income growth alone does not translate into one-for-one changes in the welfare of the poor. It seems clear that changes in poverty over time depend not only on the rate but also on the type of economic growth. Put differently, the poor will benefit even more from growth if institutions and policies are reformed to favor them, or are at least made more neutral.

Apart from economic growth, other factors exert a direct impact on the welfare of the poor (as well as on that of the non-poor). This chapter has highlighted the importance of education, infrastructure, terms of trade, agrarian reform, governance, and certain geographic attributes. Schooling, if accompanied by complementary public investments, raises the welfare of the poor, apart from its indirect effect through economic growth. So do the implementation of agrarian reform, investment in land quality improvement, and removal of price distortions that diminish the profitability of agriculture relative to non-agriculture. Political dynasties do not benefit the poor, because they constrain local economic growth and restrict the access of the poor to basic services. High transport costs lead to geographic "poverty traps," as the poor are impeded from taking advantage of economic opportunities elsewhere.

Fiscal resources are scarce. Generous budgets for direct poverty reduction programs may come at the expense of funding for other development needs, especially ones that will enhance the capacity of the economy to grow on a sustained basis. Clearly, the national government has to focus its limited resources on areas where they will make the biggest dent on poverty. What areas should the national government spend more on, and what areas should it spend less on?

Lessons from recent experience, both in the Philippines and in numerous other developing countries, suggest that the following areas should be afforded high spending priority: rural infrastructure, especially transport, power, and communications; irrigation, especially small-scale systems; primary education, especially quality enhancement; technical education and skills development; basic health care and family planning services, especially in rural areas; targeted supplementary feeding programs; R&D for agriculture and for small and medium-scale enterprises; and capability building for local government units (LGUs) and microfinance providers. The same lessons suggest that the national government should spend less in the following areas: tertiary education (by implementing cost recovery); general food price and credit subsidies; livelihood and public-works equipment programs, except for short-term disaster relief; post-harvest facilities; and export-processing zones. Spending in these areas is a blunt instrument for achieving poverty reduction goals.

NOTES

The author is grateful to Sharon Faye Piza for very able research assistance. The usual disclaimer applies.

1. The Cuaderno Plan of 1948 and the Yulo Plan of 1950 were exceptions to the above generalization. These two plans emphasized agricultural development more strongly, both for domestic consumption and for export.

2. See Sakai (1989) for an informative survey of development plans from the 1960s to the 1980s.

3. This would be so since poverty is not uniformly distributed across provinces and cities. Put differently, because some areas have higher shares in national poverty, prioritizing the budgets for poverty reduction to those areas should lead to better outcomes.

4. The immediate objective is apparently to endear the urban poor who still support the former president.

5. See Balisacan (1994, 2001a) for a discussion of the comparability of the FIES data. Of special note here is the problem posed by the periodic regrouping (and sometimes splitting) of provinces into regions, which makes the published tables unsuitable for spatial comparison of poverty reduction performance. In this chapter, the unit record data of the FIES were used to reconstruct *spatially comparable* poverty profiles; that is, the geographical boundaries of the provinces were kept constant throughout the period of interest.

6. Provincial CPIs are not available.

7. In this chapter, the incidence, depth, and severity dimensions of poverty are characterized by the headcount index, poverty gap index, and the distribution-sensitive Foster–Greer–Thorbecke measure, respectively. The headcount index is simply the proportionate number of the population deemed poor. The poverty gap index is defined by the mean distance below the poverty line as a proportion of that line (where the non-poor are counted as having a zero poverty gap). The distribution-sensitive Foster–Greer–Thorbecke measure is defined as the mean of the squared proportionate poverty gaps. This index incorporates a society's "moderate" aversion to poverty (see Foster, Greer, and Thorbecke 1984). While other poverty indices have been suggested in the literature, the above indices are the more commonly used owing to their appealing empirical properties (Ravallion 1994).

8. Self-rated poverty indicators are likewise sensitive to inflation (see Mangahas 1995).

9. On this sort of decomposition, see Datt and Ravallion (1992).

10. Rural poverty indicators constructed from the FIES for the 1980s are not comparable with those for the 1990s owing to the urban–rural reclassification problem. The classification into urban or rural areas is based on population density and the presence and quantity of public infrastructure, facilities, and establishments. As the population grows and/or economic activity expands, an initially rural area will be classified as urban, sooner or later. While this may not be problematic for purposes of measuring, say, urbanization trends, it tends to create a systematic upward (downward) bias on urban (rural) performance indicators. Substantial reclassification of villages occurred between the 1980 and 1990 population censuses, though not between the 1990 and 1995 censuses. Thus, when disaggregating by urban area, the only strictly comparable FIES years are 1985 with 1988, 1991 with 1994, and 1997 with 2000, since, for each pair, the classification (that is, the sampling frame used) is based on the same census.

11. Owing to space considerations, estimates of the severity index are not shown in Tables 10.5 and 10.6 but are available from the author upon request.

12. I have employed the Theil L and T inequality indices, both of which are decomposable exactly into between-group and within-group components. The two components shown in Figure 10.3 are averages of the respective components of the two measures.

13. The results of the decomposition of inequality change are not shown but are available upon request.

14. The regression is of the Mincerian form

$$\ln y_{it} = \alpha_t + \beta_t X + \varepsilon_{it},$$

where the subscript *i* refers to the household, *t* refers to year, *y* is welfare level (defined as per capita household expenditure adjusted for provincial cost-of-living differences), and *X* is a vector of explanatory variables. This is a standard formulation of the earnings function in the human capital literature (see Mincer 1974; Atkinson 1983). Following Fields (2002), the relative contribution of each factor to the differences in household living standards can then be estimated as:

$$s_j = \text{cov}[a_t Z_t, Y] / \sigma^2(Y) = a_t * \sigma(z_t) * cor[Z_t, Y] / \sigma(Y),$$

where a is the vector of coefficients (α, β), Z is the vector of explanatory variables plus a constant (1, X_i), and Y is log y. See Balisacan (2001a) for details of the parameter estimates.

15. See Balisacan and Pernia (2001) for estimates of the differential responses of the various quintiles to local economic growth (and other factors).

16. As shown above (section 10.2), income poverty in the Philippines is a largely rural phenomenon, regardless of the poverty norm employed. Of the rural poor, nearly two-thirds are dependent on agriculture for employment and income. As such, improvement in the terms of trade in provinces where agriculture is a dominant component of the local economy tends to raise the welfare levels of the poor.

17. The severe overvaluation of the peso in the 1970s and 1980s disproportionately penalized agriculture and the export-oriented manufacturing sector (see Bautista and Tecson, Chapter 5).

18. "Political dynasty" is defined as the proportion of local officials, related to each other by blood or by marriage, occupying the total number of elective positions. Local governance by political dynasty may make feasible the concentration of economic power and control in a few hands, thereby leading to (perpetuating) high income inequality. High income inequality, in turn, may inhibit subsequent growth in the local economy, as suggested by recent development literature. Moreover, such a governance structure may make public services that directly benefit the poor less accessible to them.

11

Regional Development

Rosario G. Manasan and Shiladitya Chatterjee

11.1 INTRODUCTION

The Philippines, the second largest archipelagic state in the world, is characterized by considerable spatial diversity in levels and rates of change of development and socioeconomic progress. As such, regional development is viewed both as an end in itself and as a means toward overall development.

Taken as a goal, balanced regional development refers to the minimization of regional socioeconomic disparities. It has been argued that large inequalities among individuals as well as across regions give rise to a breakdown in the social fabric and may weaken social cohesiveness. This argument gains special meaning in countries where a regional income divide coincides with a religious or ethnic divide, as is the case in the Muslim regions of the Philippines.

As a strategy, regional development is viewed as a means to promote the overall development of the economy. It is anchored in the premise that sustainable economic development can be achieved by enhancing the status of needy regions relative to others to effect a balance in development levels across regions, while taking into account the growth potential of each region (Lawas 1990). This is accomplished by providing all regions, on the basis of their comparative advantages, with opportunities to expand their contribution to equitable growth, while widening the access of their populations to productive resources, social services, and physical facilities to enable them to exploit and benefit from emerging economic opportunities (NEDA 1993).

Regional development has been a major policy thrust in the Philippines since the 1960s, as articulated in the 1963 Integrated Socioeconomic Plan and 1967 Industrial

Incentives Act (Lamberte et al. 1993). In 1972, the Integrated Reorganization Plan (Presidential Decree 1) established an institutional framework for regional development through the creation of 12 administrative regions. Since then, the principle of regional development both as a development strategy and as a goal for national development has become firmly established as part of the mainstream policy framework. The focus of policy and the strategies adopted have differed, though, from one medium-term development plan to the next.

Under the Integrated Area Development (IAD) approach adopted in the 1974–77 plan, areas were identified where priority development planning and infrastructure development assistance would be provided. The 1978–82 plan expanded the number of IAD program areas and placed more emphasis on the lagging regions. The 1983–87 plan continued the strategy of earlier plans while focusing more on potentially dynamic cities. Thus, increased infrastructure investments were made in Cebu, Iloilo, Bacolod, Cagayan de Oro, and Davao with a view to encouraging industries to locate in these areas. The plan was later updated to emphasize balanced agro-industrial development, thereby promoting the development of agro-based or agriculturally linked industries.

Much along the lines of the preceding plan, Aquino's 1987–92 plan adopted an employment-based rural development strategy as its principal means of achieving regional balance. Focusing in particular on small and medium-sized cities in the regions, the plan identified a number of regional agro-industrial centers (RAICs) as a way of strengthening the linkages between rural resource areas and urban centers.

As part of the move toward greater democratization, the Local Government Code enacted in 1991 provided the framework for the increased autonomy of local government units (LGUs). The code included far-reaching provisions on the assignment of functions across different levels of government; revenue-sharing arrangements between the central government and the LGUs; the resource generation and utilization powers of LGUs; and the participation of civil society in various aspects of local governance.

In its 1993–98 plan, the Ramos administration instituted its vision of the Philippines as a "newly industrializing economy" while also adapting the agro-industrial development strategy of the previous government. The plan encouraged the development of regional growth networks linking two or more RAICs, both by providing its own priority development scheme and by encouraging substantive private sector participation in the financing of infrastructure development. The plan also strengthened the shift toward greater fiscal decentralization.

It should be emphasized here that national macroeconomic policies, including trade and exchange rate policies, do affect regional balance. Pernia et al. (1983: 139) document the fact that many policies have unintended regional effects, pointing out that "firms respond to some economic policies which, although not designed to effect a particular spatial configuration in the economy, nevertheless reinforced the operation of those market forces favoring a specific location for economic activity." They found, for example, that the concentration of manufacturing activity in and around Metro Manila was positively associated both with the import content of manufacturing industries (reflecting the locational advantages enjoyed by Manila, such as ease of access to imported machinery and raw materials, and proximity to government offices) and with effective protection rates (which are directly related to the trade policy regime). Manufacturing concentration was also found to have a direct relationship with firm size and capital intensity, variables that have been intertwined with industrial and trade policies in the postwar years.

This chapter attempts to evaluate the progress that has been made to date in reducing spatial inequality. More specifically, it aims to evaluate the pattern of regional economic development from 1975 to 1999; assess the gains, if any, in reducing regional disparities; and evaluate the extent to which government policies have contributed to regional convergence.

11.2 PATTERNS OF REGIONAL DEVELOPMENT

This study primarily uses per capita gross regional domestic product (GRDP) as an indicator of regional development, while acknowledging the well-known shortcomings of this measure in assessing overall economic welfare and progress in human development in the regions. The weakness of GRDP in tracking economic welfare stems from the fact that it does not include factor incomes derived by residents from other regions, while including factor incomes derived by non-residents from within the region. In this sense, per capita household income—which can be obtained from the Family Income and Expenditure Survey (FIES) conducted periodically by the National Statistics Office (NSO)—may be a better indicator of economic welfare in the regions.

Nonetheless, Table 11.1 shows that per capita GRDP is closely associated not only with per capita FIES income, but also with broader measures of social well-being such as poverty incidence and the Human Development Index (HDI) developed by the United Nations. Correlation analysis reveals a positive relationship between per capita GRDP and the functional literacy rate in 1980–2000. In like manner, a strong inverse relationship is evident between per capita GRDP on the one hand and infant mortality and poverty incidence on the other. It cannot be denied, however, that interregional inequality accounts for only a small portion of inequality among individuals. Balisacan (1998) finds, for instance, that inequality *within* regions is much higher than inequality *between* regions.

It should be stressed that the discussion that follows adheres to the administratively defined regional boundaries. The Philippines was initially divided into 12 regions, the number of which has grown over the years to 15. Note, however, that some analysts have indicated that these boundaries do not divide the country into natural economic zones. Pernia et al. (1983), for instance, partition the country into four zones: Metro Manila or the National Capital Region (NCR); the metropolitan periphery comprising Central Luzon and Southern Tagalog; the traditional agricultural regions of Ilocos, Bicol, Eastern Visayas, Western Visayas, and Central Visayas; and the frontier region composed of Cagayan Valley and all of the Mindanao regions.

The National Capital Region

Table 11.2 presents indices of per capita GRDP for the period 1975–2000.[1] It shows the NCR persistently dominating all other regions, with a per capita GRDP that is more than twice the national average. The NCR lost considerable ground between 1975 and 1986, as indicated by a decline in its per capita GRDP index from 255 in 1975 to a low of 219 in 1986. Although it has not been able to fully regain its former position, its GRDP index had risen nonetheless to 240 by 2000. Whereas in 1975 the NCR's per capita GRDP was 2.1 times that of the second richest region (Southern Tagalog) and 5.6 times that of the poorest (Bicol), by 2000 it was just 1.8 times that of the second richest region (the Cordillera Administrative Region, or CAR) and 5.4 times that of the poorest (Bicol). This came about because the NCR's per capita GRDP in real terms rose at a slower pace (0.2% per year) than the national average (0.5%) between 1975 and 2000.

This development was more the result of the high rate of population growth in the NCR than of poor economic performance per se. The capital's average GRDP growth rate in 1975–2000 was slightly higher than the national average (Table 11.3), and its contribution to national GDP consequently fairly stable at around 30% during the period (Table 11.4). In contrast, the NCR's rate of population growth was 2.8%, more than 16% higher than the national average of 2.4% (Table 11.3).

Luzon

In Luzon, the per capita GRDP index for Southern Tagalog fell markedly from 119.2 in 1975 to 98.2 in 2000, while that of the CAR rose steeply from 97.8 in 1987 to 130.8 in 2000 (Table 11.2). The growth of both GRDP as well as per capita GRDP in the CAR was the highest in the entire country in 1987–2000 (Tables 11.2 and 11.3). In contrast, Southern Tagalog's per capita GRDP decreased by 0.3% per year on average between 1975 and 2000. Like the NCR, Southern Tagalog was burdened by a high rate of population increase which in effect negated the positive effects on welfare of its creditable rate of GRDP growth.

Ilocos and Cagayan Valley showed moderate improvements in their per capita GRDP indices, from 53.7 and 59.1 respectively in 1975 to 57.8 and 61.5 in 2000. While the per capita GRDP index of Bicol stagnated at around 45 throughout 1975–2000, that of Central Luzon actually declined from 93.2 to 84.6. In these four regions, changes in the indices were driven largely by the relative growth in their GRDP.

Visayas

Central Visayas exhibited exemplary gains in economic development, with its per capita GRDP index surging from 80.9 in 1975 to 91.3 in 2000 (Table 11.2). It posted the third fastest rate of annual real per capita GRDP growth (0.9%) among all regions in 1975–2000 (after Northern Mindanao and Western Mindanao), because of its higher than average rate of real GRDP growth and lower than average rate of

Table 11.1 Relationship between per Capita Gross Regional Domestic Product and Social Development Indicators, 1980–2000[a]

| | 1980 | | | | | 1988 | | | | |
	Per Capita GRDP (pesos)	Per Capita Income[b] (pesos)	Literacy Rate	Infant Mortality Rate	Poverty Incidence[b]	Per Capita GRDP (pesos)	Per Capita Income (pesos)	Functional Literacy Rate[c]	Infant Mortality Rate[d]	Poverty Incidence
NCR	32,202	10,797	97.2	48	27.2	26,090	11,826	90.6	46	25.2
CAR	–	–	–	–	–	11,066	5,140	73.7	63	50.7
Ilocos	6,892	5,733	84.5	58	43.5	5,675	5,236	75.1	56	51.7
Cagayan Valley	8,189	5,030	79.4	66	42.7	5,942	5,130	72.0	62	44.6
C. Luzon	12,271	6,808	88.7	43	32.2	10,546	7,543	84.1	45	33.8
S. Tagalog	15,150	5,514	85.8	60	45.7	12,784	5,451	79.8	53	46.6
Bicol	6,166	3,446	85.1	67	67.6	4,789	3,937	68.8	64	61.4
W. Visayas	10,787	4,295	81.8	60	66.5	8,586	4,470	71.3	61	56.6
C. Visayas	11,653	3,878	76.3	51	61.9	9,696	4,337	70.6	55	52.1
E. Visayas	6,228	3,281	79.2	77	65.2	5,334	3,748	65.5	76	54.7
W. Mindanao	8,061	4,110	65.7	56	60.0	6,393	4,671	57.7	64	43.7
N. Mindanao	11,059	4,874	84.6	67	56.7	10,356	5,320	76.5	57	50.2
S. Mindanao	12,325	5,190	81.1	51	49.7	11,784	5,390	74.1	56	48.9
C. Mindanao	10,087	4,088	64.1	80	56.3	8,800	5,085	63.1	56	41.0
ARMM									74	
Correlation coefficient with per capita GRDP	0.8823	0.5728	-0.4810	-0.6449		0.8978	0.7455	-0.6538	-0.7198	

346

	1998					2000				
	Per Capita GRDP	Per Capita Income[e]	Functional Literacy Rate[f]	Infant Mortality Rate	Poverty Incidence[e]	Per Capita GRDP	Per Capita Income	Functional Literacy Rate[f]	Infant Mortality Rate[g]	Poverty Incidence
NCR	27,198	18,472	92.4	41.5	8.5	29,835	16,643	92.4	41.5	12.7
CAR	15,295	8,442	78.6	37.1	55.8	16,269	8,241	78.6	37.1	43.9
Ilocos	6,983	6,821	86.4	28.7	44.1	7,194	6,941	86.4	28.7	43.5
Cagayan Valley	6,441	6,772	86.6	35.3	38.0	7,650	6,622	86.6	35.3	36.3
C. Luzon	10,962	11,088	87.3	31.4	18.5	10,525	9,867	87.3	31.4	22.9
S. Tagalog	12,924	10,072	88.0	26.0	30.0	12,220	9,792	88.0	26.0	31.7
Bicol	5,574	6,034	82.8	23.6	57.0	5,529	6,031	82.8	23.6	62.8
W. Visayas	10,159	7,075	80.9	60.8	45.9	10,764	6,628	80.9	60.8	51.2
C. Visayas	11,417	6,375	80.8	44.6	38.9	11,355	5,553	80.8	44.6	43.9
E. Visayas	5,891	4,698	79.7	41.0	48.5	6,342	5,237	79.7	41.0	50.5
W. Mindanao	8,391	6,705	75.4	40.9	45.5	8,703	5,461	75.4	40.9	53.0
N. Mindanao	11,400	5,026	83.4	48.4	52.7	10,736	5,948	83.4	48.4	52.2
S. Mindanao	9,712	5,945	79.4	55.1	44.3	11,263	6,775	79.4	55.1	46.3
C. Mindanao	9,416	5,344	77.4	53.2	50.1	9,865	5,330	77.4	53.2	57.9
ARMM	4,120	4,374	61.2	55.1	62.5	3,781	3,703	61.2	55.1	73.9
Correlation coefficient with per capita GRDP	0.8738	0.5340	−0.0102	−0.6854		0.8808	0.5254	0.0213	−0.7275	

NCR = National Capital Region; CAR = Cordillera Administrative Region; ARMM = Autonomous Region of Muslim Mindanao.

a Per capita GRDP and income are in pesos. Infant mortality is infant deaths per 1,000 live births. Poverty incidence is the proportion of the population whose family income cannot provide basic food and non-food requirements.

b Uses 1985 data.   c Uses 1985 data.   d Uses 1990 data.   e Uses 1997 data.   f Uses 1994 data.   g Uses 1998 data.

Source: National Statistical Coordination Board.

Table 11.2 Per Capita Gross Regional Domestic Product Index, 1975–2000 (based on GRDP in 1985 prices)

Region	1975	1980	1986	1987	1992	1997	2000
NCR	255.2	245.1	219.1	228.3	237.5	227.0	239.8
CAR				97.8	107.4	121.4	130.8
Ilocos	53.7	52.5	66.6	51.1	52.4	54.3	57.8
Cagayan Valley	59.1	62.3	56.4	53.0	54.3	56.0	61.5
C. Luzon	93.2	93.4	90.7	93.3	102.5	94.0	84.6
S. Tagalog	119.2	115.3	120.6	113.0	119.8	106.2	98.2
Bicol	45.6	46.9	46.2	42.8	50.5	46.8	44.4
W. Visayas	88.4	82.1	71.3	78.4	90.4	83.1	86.5
C. Visayas	80.9	88.7	89.5	84.5	93.0	91.1	91.3
E. Visayas	52.3	47.4	47.6	47.2	50.6	48.6	51.0
W. Mindanao	52.2	61.4	68.5	59.6	49.1	61.8	60.5
N. Mindanao	76.9	84.2	94.2	95.4	69.4	97.6	86.3
S. Mindanao	107.2	93.8	107.3	111.6	88.9	78.6	90.5
C. Mindanao	66.2	76.8	82.2	80.3	50.5	61.0	61.8
Philippines	100.0	100.0	100.0	100.0	100.0	100.0	100.0

NCR = National Capital Region; CAR = Cordillera Administrative Region; ARMM = Autonomous Region of Muslim Mindanao.

Source: National Statistical Coordination Board.

population increase (Table 11.3). Note, however, that its share in national GDP remained fairly stable at around 6.5% throughout the period (Table 11.4).

In contrast, the GRDP of both Western and Eastern Visayas registered sluggish growth in real terms in 1975–2000 (Table 11.3). Despite their low rates of population increase, per capita GRDP in both regions rose by only 0.4% per annum on average, one of the lowest rates of regional growth during the period. Consequently, the contribution of Eastern and Western Visayas to national GDP contracted, respectively, from 3.2% and 8.7% in 1975 to 2.4% and 7.0% in 2000 (Table 11.4), while their respective per capita GRDP indices went from 52.3 and 88.4 in 1975 to 51.0 and 86.5 in 2000 (Table 11.2).

In both cases, the slump was particularly severe in 1975–86.[2] However, whereas in Eastern Visayas per capita GRDP continued to stagnate in 1987–2000, in Western Visayas it recovered somewhat, but not enough to regain its 1975 level.

Mindanao

Western and Northern Mindanao showed tangible gains in their per capita GRDP indices between 1975 and 2000—from 52.2 to 60.5 in the case of Western Mindanao

Table 11.3 Rate of Growth of Gross Regional Domestic Product and Population, 1975–2000 (%)

Region	GRDP			Population		
	1975–86	1987–2000	1975–2000	1975–86	1987–2000	1975–2000
NCR	1.9	3.9	3.0	3.4	2.4	2.8
CAR		5.3			1.9	
Ilocos	3.8	4.0	1.8	1.8	1.8	1.0
Cagayan Valley	2.2	3.9	2.2	2.7	1.6	1.5
C. Luzon	2.4	3.1	2.7	2.6	2.7	2.6
S. Tagalog	3.2	3.7	3.0	3.1	3.6	3.3
Bicol	2.2	2.5	1.9	2.1	1.0	1.6
W. Visayas	0.1	3.1	2.0	2.1	1.2	1.6
C. Visayas	3.1	3.9	3.1	2.2	2.1	2.1
E. Visayas	0.8	2.7	1.7	1.7	1.0	1.3
W. Mindanao	5.9	3.6	3.8	3.3	2.4	2.8
N. Mindanao	5.1	2.4	3.5	3.2	2.0	2.6
S. Mindanao	3.4	2.2	2.8	3.4	2.7	3.0
C. Mindanao	4.3	2.2	2.9	2.3	3.1	2.8
Philippines	2.6	3.4	2.9	2.6	2.3	2.4

NCR = National Capital Region; CAR = Cordillera Administrative Region; ARMM = Autonomous Region of Muslim Mindanao.

Source: National Statistical Coordination Board.

and from 76.9 to 86.3 in the case of Northern Mindanao (Table 11.2). Although the population of both regions was growing at a higher rate than the national average, their per capita GRDP indices improved markedly between 1975 and 1986 because of their creditable GRDP growth rates: these regions registered the highest rates of growth in GRDP among all regions in the country during this period (Table 11.3). Their per capita GRDP indices then declined somewhat between 1986 and 2000 because of the relatively slower growth in their economies even as population growth remained high.

The per capita GRDP indices of both Southern Mindanao and Central Mindanao deteriorated between 1975 and 2000, from 107.2 to 90.5 in the case of Southern Mindanao and from 66.2 to 61.8 in the case of Central Mindanao (Table 11.2). The mediocre performance of these two regions in terms of GRDP growth, coupled with high rates of population increase, largely explains the lackluster development in their per capita GRDP.

Table 11.4 Regional Shares of Output, 1975–2000 (%, based on GRDP in 1985 prices)

Region	1975	1980	1986	1987	1992	2000
NCR	30.1	30.2	28.0	29.3	30.0	31.1
CAR				1.8	1.9	2.3
Ilocos	4.2	3.9	4.7	3.0	2.8	3.2
Cagayan Valley	2.7	2.9	2.6	2.1	1.9	2.3
C. Luzon	9.3	9.3	9.1	9.3	9.8	8.9
S. Tagalog	14.8	14.7	15.7	14.8	15.8	15.2
Bicol	3.5	3.4	3.3	3.1	3.1	2.7
W. Visayas	8.7	7.7	6.6	7.3	7.4	7.0
C. Visayas	6.5	7.0	6.8	6.4	6.6	6.8
E. Visayas	3.2	2.8	2.7	2.6	2.4	2.4
W. Mindanao	2.5	3.2	3.6	3.1	3.0	3.2
N. Mindanao	4.2	4.8	5.5	5.6	5.2	4.9
S. Mindanao	6.9	6.5	7.5	7.8	6.8	6.7
C. Mindanao	3.3	3.6	3.9	3.8	3.4	3.3
Philippines	100.0	100.0	100.0	100.0	100.0	100.0

Source: National Statistical Coordination Board.

11.3 REGIONAL CONVERGENCE ANALYSIS

The previous discussion shows that marked disparities among regions persisted throughout 1975–2000. This section examines whether these disparities narrowed or widened over time and attempts to determine the rate of convergence (or divergence) during the period under study.[3]

Convergence Indicators

We adopt the classical approach to convergence analysis introduced by Sala-i-Martin (1996) to examine the dispersion of per capita income across regions. Two convergence models are used in this study: σ-convergence and β-convergence.

A group of economies (or regions) is said to be converging in the sense of σ if the dispersion of their real per capita GDP levels is tending to decrease over time. The relationship is defined by:

$$\sigma_{t+T} < \sigma_t, \tag{1}$$

where σ_t is the time t standard deviation of log $(y_{i,t})$, which is the logarithm of region i's GDP per capita at time t.

On the other hand, absolute β-convergence is said to exist if poor economies (regions) are tending to grow faster than rich ones. Specifically, in the following regression equation, β > 0 indicates absolute β-convergence:

$$\gamma_{i,t,t+T} = \alpha - \beta \log (y_{i,t}) + \varepsilon_{i,t}, \tag{2}$$

where $\gamma_{i,t,t+T} \equiv \log (y_{i,t+T}/y_{i,t})/T$, region i's annualized growth rate of GDP per capita between t and $t + T$.[4]

Sala-i-Martin points out that β-convergence is a necessary but not a sufficient condition for σ-convergence. He notes that these two concepts may not always show up together because they capture different aspects of convergence: σ-convergence relates to whether or not the cross-regional distribution of national income is shrinking over time, whereas β-convergence relates to the mobility of different regional economies within the given distribution of national income.

σ-convergence

Figure 11.1 plots the dispersion of the log of per capita GRDP across 14 regions for the period 1975–2000. Overall, σ-convergence is evident for the entire 25-year span, although there are significant variations within subperiods. Cross-regional dispersion of per capita income fell continuously from 0.202 in 1975 to 0.179 in 1985. It then rose sharply, peaking at 0.199 in 1989. It dipped to 0.187 in 1990 but shot back up to 0.199 in 1991 and 0.200 in 1992. It declined to 0.181 in 1995, then slowly inched upward to 0.187 in 2000.

The process of σ-convergence in real per capita GRDP for the Philippine regions compares favorably with that in most other Asian countries. Figure 11.2 presents the

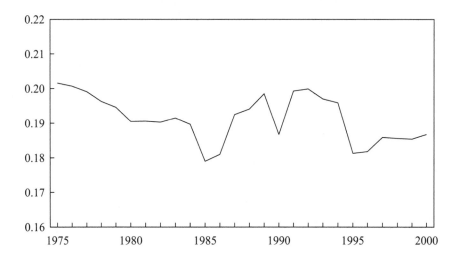

Figure 11.1 σ-convergence Estimates: Dispersion of Log of per Capita GRDP, 1975–2000

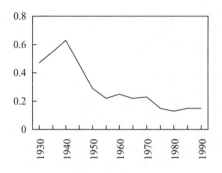

Figure 11.2a Japan: Dispersion of per Capita Personal Income, 1930–90

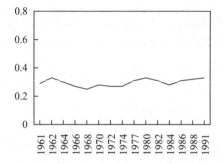

Figure 11.2b India: Dispersion of per Capita Net Domestic Product, 1961–91

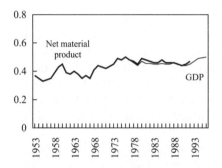

Figure 11.2c China: Dispersion of per Capita Net Material Product and Gross Domestic Product, 1953–96

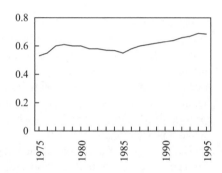

Figure 11.2d Thailand: Dispersion of per Capita Gross Provincial Product, 1975–95

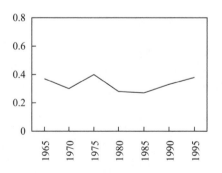

Figure 11.2e Malaysia: Dispersion of per Capita Gross Provincial Product, 1965–95

Sources: Japan: Barro and Sala-i-Martin (1993, 1995); India: Cashin and Sahay (1996); China: Garbaccio and La Croix (1998); Thailand: Southichak and La Croix (1998); Malaysia: La Croix (1998), all as cited in La Croix, Garbaccio, and Southichak (1998).

most recent σ-convergence estimates available for Japan, India, China, Thailand, and Malaysia.

Barro and Sala-i-Martin (1993) found regional σ-convergence in Japan's 47 prefectures during the post-World War II period; the standard deviation of the logarithm of per capita personal income fell from a wartime high of 0.63 in 1940 to 0.15 in 1987 (Figure 11.2a). In contrast, σ-divergence was observed in the regional economies of India, China, and Thailand, while Malaysia was fairly stable.

Cashin and Sahay (1996) reported σ-divergence in 25 Indian states, where the standard deviation of the log of per capita net domestic product rose from 0.29 in 1961 to 0.33 in 1991 (Figure 11.2b). Similarly, a study by Garbaccio and La Croix (1998) revealed σ-divergence in the 29 provinces of China in 1953–78 (the Maoist period) and σ-stagnation in 1978–96 (the reform period). In the Maoist period, the standard deviation of the log of per capita net material product increased from 0.37 in 1953 to 0.48 in 1978. In the reform period, it rose almost imperceptibly from 0.48 in 1978 to 0.49 in 1996 (Figure 11.2c).

Southichak and La Croix (1998) documented the rise in the standard deviation of the log of real per capita gross provincial product (GPP) in Thailand's 71 provinces, from 0.53 in 1975 to 0.69 in 1994 (Figure 11.2d). In the 12 provinces of Malaysia, meanwhile, the standard deviation fluctuated around the 0.35 mark throughout 1965–95 (La Croix 1998) (Figure 11.2e).

β-convergence

Regressing equation (2) with Philippine data for the period 1975–2000 provides some evidence for β-convergence. The β-coefficient was estimated to be 0.0044 and was found to be statistically different from zero at the 5% level of significance. However, the speed of convergence was found to be faster in 1975–86 (β = 0.0137) than in 1987–2000 (β = 0.0067). Not only was the β-coefficient for the later period weaker, it was also statistically insignificant, unlike that for the earlier period.

The estimated speed of convergence for the Philippines between 1975 and 2000 is considerably lower than that observed in developed countries, where it has been found to cluster at around 2% per year, that is, β = 0.02 (Cashin and Sahay 1996). However, unlike in other developing Asian countries, in the Philippines the estimated β-coefficient is positive (indicating β-convergence) and statistically significant (Table 11.5). Although India, Malaysia, and China (in 1978–96) all yielded positive β-coefficients, the estimates were found to be statistically insignificant; Thailand and China (in 1953–78) had negative β-coefficients (La Croix 1998). The analysis that follows indicates that the quality of GDP growth affects not only β-convergence, but also σ-convergence.

11.4 SHIFT ANALYSIS

This section attempts to explain the variation in regional economic performance using shift analysis. The analysis puts emphasis on differences in the economic structure of regions to clarify why some grow faster than others. Shift analysis is a

Table 11.5 β-convergence in Selected Asian Economies[a]

Country/Period	β	R^2
Philippines		
1975–2000	0.0044	0.23
	(0.0025)	
1975–1986	0.0137	0.21
	(0.0054)	
1987–2000	0.0067	0.07
	(0.0073)	
Japan		
1955–90	0.0191	0.59
	(0.00035)	
India		
1961–91	0.0027	0.65
	(0.0057)	
China		
1953–78	−0.003	0.01
	(0.005)	
1978–96	0.008	0.05
	(0.007)	
Malaysia		
1965–95	0.020	0.18
	(0.016)	
Thailand		
1975–95	−0.0077	0.05
	(0.004)	

a   Figures in parentheses are standard error values.

Sources: Philippines (this study); Japan, India, China, Malaysia and Thailand: La Croix et al. (1998).

method of quantifying the differences in regional growth by comparing the performance of each region with the national average. Actual regional development is compared with what would have happened had the region grown at the national GRDP growth rate. The difference between the actual and the estimated GRDP of region j, if its economy had grown at a rate equal to the national average, is called total net shift (TNS). If the TNS value of region j is positive (negative), its development is above (below) the national average.

TNS can be divided into two components: net differential shift (NDS) and net proportional shift (NPS). NDS is the difference between actual regional performance and the development that would have occurred if the region's sectors had each grown at the national average sectoral growth rate. Thus, if the growth of specific sectors within a region is higher (lower) than the national average, NDS values will be positive (negative), indicating that the region possesses localization advantages (disadvantages) that are favoring (hindering) the development of specific sectors (Lamberte et al. 1993).

NPS is the difference between TNS and NDS, and refers to the structural composition of the regional economy. High (low) NPS values indicate structural advantages (disadvantages) for a region. For instance, if aggregate regional growth is higher than the national average for GRDP (positive TNS) but the growth rate of some regional sectors is lower than the national average for sectoral growth (negative NDS), the fast-growing sectors of the region will have a greater impact on the regional economy (positive NPS) than on the national economy (Lamberte et al. 1993).

The 1975–86 Period

The Philippine economy grew by 2.6% per annum on average in 1975–86. From positive growth of over 6.2% in 1975–80, the economy contracted by 0.3% in 1980–86, primarily because of the recession in developed countries in the early 1980s combined with economic and political turmoil on the domestic front.

In the first half of the 11-year subperiod under study, the vibrant performance of the economy was spurred by the industrial sector, which expanded by 7.3% per year on average. Also notable were the gains in the services and agricultural sectors, which registered annual rates of growth of 5.8% and 5.3% respectively. The recession of 1984–85 caused serious dislocation in all sectors, particularly industry, which contracted by 2.7% annually over 1980–86. While the services sector was fairly stagnant during the subperiod (posting 0.1% average annual growth), the agricultural sector proved more resilient to the external and domestic shocks (with 2.4% annual growth).

Consequently, over the entire 1975–86 period, the primary sector (agriculture, fisheries, and forestry) registered the highest rate of growth (3.7%). In contrast, industry grew by only 1.8% annually and the services sector by 2.7%. The structure of the economy thus shifted from industry to agriculture. The share in GDP of agriculture, fisheries, and forestry expanded from 24.1% in 1975 to 27.0% in 1986, while that of industry contracted from 34.7% to 31.7%. The share of the services sector remained constant at 41.3%.

Not surprisingly, shift analysis shows high positive TNS and NDS values for the regions that are largely dominated by the agricultural sector, specifically all the Mindanao regions and Ilocos (Figure 11.3). However, Southern Tagalog and Central Visayas also managed to register positive TNS during the period despite their small agricultural base. This may be due to the smaller impact of the economic contraction of 1984–85 on the industrial sectors (Southern Tagalog) and/or services sectors (Southern Tagalog and Central Visayas) of these regions. Thus, unlike in the NCR,

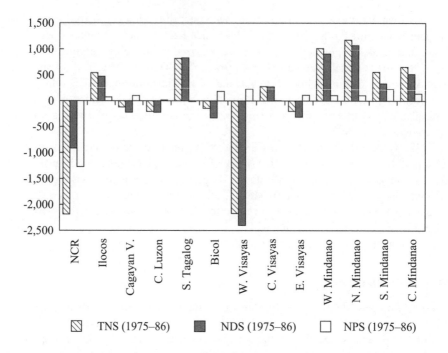

Figure 11.3 Shift Analysis of Gross Regional Domestic Product, 1975–86 (computed using real GDRP in 1972 prices)

the recession was not enough to wipe out the gains made in 1975–82 in these two regions.

Southern Tagalog's economy grew at a rate above the national average, primarily because of the strong growth of its services sector during the entire period under study. It also benefited from the fact that its industrial sector was relatively shielded from the ill effects of the economic crisis of 1984–85, perhaps because of the smaller exposure of its industries to the export market. The region's proximity to the NCR and the consequent inflow of both public and private investment appear to have given it some advantage in industry and services, as indicated by a high NDS value. Note that a ban on industry within a 50-kilometer radius of the capital, which was implemented starting in 1973, provided the impetus for economic activities to cluster on the periphery of the NCR.

Similarly, Central Visayas and Ilocos outperformed the overall economy in 1975–86 on account of the better than average performance of their industrial and services sectors. While the industrial sector of Central Visayas proved vulnerable to the 1984–85 crisis because of its stronger links to the international market, the recession was not enough to wipe out the gains made in the earlier subperiod. The region was also able to exploit its structural advantage in services (accounting for 51.1% of the regional economy), which led growth in the region in 1975–86. The region is the financial, commercial, and educational hub of the Visayas and, to some extent, of the Mindanao regions as well.

Ilocos benefited from the high annual growth of 5.9% in its agricultural sector (spurred by crops, livestock, and poultry production); the share of agriculture in GRDP increased from 33.3% in 1975 to 41.6% in 1986. In addition, the industrial sector, particularly manufacturing and utilities, grew at a faster pace (2.9%) than the national average (1.8%) during the period.

All of the Mindanao regions experienced overall GRDP growth rates well in excess of the national average. Although led by agriculture, GRDP growth in the industrial sectors of these regions was also remarkable.

Northern Mindanao's GRDP growth rate of 5.1% was the result of better than average performance across all three sectors, especially agriculture. Annual growth in agriculture of 6.1% led to the expansion of the sector's share in GRDP from 38.4% in 1975 to 42.8% in 1986. In like manner, the respectable performance of its industrial sector, particularly in 1975–80, increased the contribution of industry from 20.1% in 1975 to 21.3% in 1986. The region's agricultural sector was dominated by crop production and its industrial sector by mining/quarrying and construction.

Developments in Western, Southern, and Central Mindanao closely mirrored those in Northern Mindanao. Agriculture and industry spurred growth in these regions during 1975–86, resulting in an expansion of their contribution to GRDP. However, the services sector did not do as well in Western and Central Mindanao as in the other two Mindanao regions.

In contrast, the analysis shows that the NCR and Cagayan Valley, Central Luzon, Bicol, Western Visayas, and Eastern Visayas performed sluggishly in 1975–86. Agriculture made a substantial contribution to the regional economies of Cagayan Valley, Bicol, Western Visayas, and Eastern Visayas but failed to perform as well as the national average. The agricultural sector in Central Luzon likewise registered lackluster growth during this period. Together with a similarly lethargic performance by services, this was enough to reverse the gains made in the industrial sector in this region. The NCR, meanwhile, had to deal with the structural disadvantage of having a production base that was primarily industrial; the 1984–85 recession hit this sector badly.

The 1987–2000 Period

The period 1987–2000 witnessed a slowdown of agriculture and a recovery in the industrial and services sectors. The economy grew by 3.4% annually on average, compared with 2.6% over the previous decade. Services expanded by 4.3% annually and industry by 3.4%, whereas the primary sector rose by a mere 1.8%.

As a result of these developments, the economy's structure became increasingly oriented toward the services sector. The share of agriculture, fisheries, and forestry in GRDP declined from 24.4% in 1987 to 20.0% in 2000. In comparison, the share of services rose from 41.0% to 45.6% while that of the industrial sector remained constant at 34.5%.

The slowdown in the agricultural sector was partly due to major natural disasters (earthquake, volcanic eruption, the El Niño effect). Problems and slippages in the implementation of agricultural programs and infrastructure projects also played a part. The latter included difficulties in allocating water from multipurpose dams to power generation and irrigation, irrigation system breakdowns, the poor condition of farm-to-market roads, and the slow implementation of the Gintong Ani Program following the devolution of agricultural extension to the LGUs.[5] In turn, the shift from agriculture to services adversely affected economic development in those regions that depended heavily on agriculture.

Shift analysis shows the slower than average growth (and, consequently, negative TNS values) in most of the agriculture-based regions in 1987–2000, including Bicol, Western Visayas, Eastern Visayas, Northern Mindanao, Southern Mindanao, and Central Mindanao (Figure 11.4). Conversely, high positive TNS and NDS values were found for regions having large industrial and/or service sector bases, including the NCR, the CAR, Southern Tagalog, and Central Visayas. However, Ilocos, Cagayan Valley, and Western Mindanao all overcame lower than average growth in services to achieve positive TNS values during the period. This was largely on account of the commendable performance of their agricultural and industrial sectors, which grew by some 4% and 5% per year respectively.

The growth of the industrial sector in Ilocos is partly attributable to the post-earthquake reconstruction activities of both the government and the private sector.

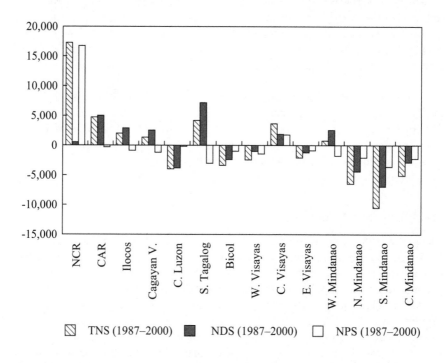

Figure 11.4 Shift Analysis of Gross Regional Domestic Product, 1987–2000

However, it has also been due to the inflow of private investments to the region's industrial sector, especially since 1992; as Table 11.6 shows, for instance, Ilocos captured substantial investments from enterprises registered with the Board of Investments (BOI) in 1986–2000. Infrastructure development and the investment activities under the North West Luzon Growth Quadrangle may also have stimulated the region's growth; new investment flows were notable in the food-processing and wood products subsectors. Consequently, the industrial sector improved its share in the regional economy, particularly in 1992–97, when its contribution to GRDP rose from 12.8% to 17.2%. Industrial growth in Cagayan Valley and Western Mindanao, meanwhile, was based largely on agriculture: forestry-based in the former case and marine-based (seaweed/carrageenan processing) in the latter.

The creditable performance of the agricultural sector in Ilocos, Cagayan Valley, and Western Mindanao in 1987–2000 cannot be overemphasized. Together with positive developments in their industrial sectors, this resulted in positive NDS values for these regions during this period. Their negative NPS values, meanwhile, reflect the small industrial base of these regions.

The NCR exhibited the highest positive TNS value. The regional economy grew by 3.9% per year in 1987–2000. Rapid growth in GRDP in 1987–97 was fueled by large public sector investments in urban infrastructure and the continued inflow of

Table 11.6 Regional Shares of Project Cost of BOI-registered Firms, 1986–2000 (%)

Region	1986–2000	1986–92	1993–2000
NCR	10.2	18.9	8.8
CAR	0.4	0.4	0.4
Ilocos	4.1	5.0	4.0
Cagayan Valley	1.2	0.1	1.3
C. Luzon	11.9	7.3	12.6
S. Tagalog	16.5	31.6	14.0
Bicol	1.1	0.6	1.2
W. Visayas	1.3	1.5	1.3
C. Visayas	4.6	6.0	4.4
E. Visayas	1.8	4.2	1.3
W. Mindanao	1.2	0.3	1.4
N. Mindanao	4.1	15.9	2.2
S. Mindanao	1.5	2.1	1.4
C. Mindanao	0.8	0.8	0.8
No definite site	32.6	2.8	37.5
Not indicated	6.8	2.5	7.5
Philippines	100.0	100.0	100.0

Source: Board of Investments.

private sector investments. However, the NCR was more severely affected by the Asian financial crisis than other regions, and so did not do as well as the national economy in terms of overall growth in 1997–2000.

The NCR's low NDS value for 1987–2000 was due to slower than average industrial growth, indicating perhaps that agglomeration diseconomies have started to creep in. On the other hand, high positive NPS was indicative of the region's strong structural advantage in the services sector. The share of services in the NCR's GRDP expanded from 55.6% in 1987 to 61.1% in 2000, whereas that of the industrial sector contracted from 44.4% to 38.9%.

The CAR posted the highest rate of growth in GRDP (5.8%) during the period, accounting for the region's positive TNS. It also registered positive NDS, as its industrial and services sectors grew at a more rapid pace than the national average. The share of industry in the CAR's economy increased from 53.9% in 1987 to 64.4% in 2000. Construction contributed significantly to the expansion of the sector, due to the rebuilding and rehabilitation of facilities damaged by the 1990 earthquake. In 1994, public investment in the CAR hit an all-time high with the rehabilitation of the Binga Dam. The Baguio export-processing zone turned in a noteworthy performance, making a substantial contribution in terms of export value. Significant investment inflows outside of the special economic zone enclave were also registered during the period. In 1995, following the enactment of a new Mining Code, a larger portion of private investment in the CAR was directed toward mining exploration and development. These investments were brought about by the vigorous marketing efforts of the North West Luzon Growth Quadrangle, of which the group of cities known collectively as BLIST (Baguio, La Trinidad, Itogon, Sablan, and Tuba) is one of the growth areas.

Given its proximity to the capital and the continued thrust to disperse industries to areas outside Metro Manila, Southern Tagalog has become a very desirable location for investors. Unsurprisingly, then, the region recorded the second highest TNS value, next only to that of the NCR. Its GRDP grew by 3.7%, with all sectors consistently outperforming the average. Southern Tagalog's positive NDS has been led largely by growth in services and industry, which grew by an average of 4.6% and 4.0% per annum respectively in 1987–2000. The share of the agricultural sector in total regional output decreased from 29.7% in 1987 to 24.1% in 2000, while those of industry and services increased from 39.6% and 30.7% respectively in 1987 to 41.5% and 34.1% in 2000.

The structural advantage of Southern Tagalog in industry is evident in the presence of numerous industrial estates and a major government-operated export-processing zone. The CALABARZON area (encompassing Cavite, Laguna, Batangas, Rizal, and Quezon) has continued to receive the greatest share of investments in its industrial parks and export-processing zones (Table 11.7). These zones also contribute significantly to exports. Similarly, the region's share in the investments of BOI-registered enterprises during the period has been substantial (Table 11.6). However, its structural disadvantage in services, as indicated by the sector's relatively small contribution to the regional economy, helps to explain its negative NPS in 1987–2000.

Table 11.7 Distribution of Investments, Exports, and Employment of PEZA Enterprises, 1995–99 (%)

Region	Investments	Employment	Exports
NCR	0.2	0.5	0.2
CAR	0.5	2.1	14.4
C. Luzon	6.1	14.6	5.2
S. Tagalog	88.6	61.3	63.5
C. Visayas	4.6	19.5	12.1
E. Visayas	–	2.0	4.7
Total[a]	196,844,824	924,653	50,488

NCR = National Capital Region; CAR = Cordillera Administrative Region.
a   Investments: million pesos; emploment: number employed; exports: million dollars.

Source: Philippine Economic Zone Authority.

The GRDP of Central Visayas expanded at an average annual rate of 3.9% in 1987–2000, with the services sector leading the way. Because the share of services in the regional economy was large (51.1% in 1987), the sector's strong growth also had a considerable impact on the region's overall performance. Tourism was a major reason for the better than average performance of the services sector. An influx of tourists to the region followed the expansion there of airline and hotel facilities and services.

Growth in industry, on the other hand, was low in 1987–92 (1.2%), due to the decline in the output of the manufacturing subsector in the early 1990s and the deceleration of growth in the mining and quarrying subsector. Although the industrial sector began to recover from 1993 as investment surged in the region's industrial estates (Mactan Export Processing Zone II, Naga Township, Balamban, and Cebu Light Industrial Park in Mactan), this was not sufficient to make up for the contraction in the earlier subperiod.

Although Central Luzon's GRDP grew at a notable rate of 4.2% per year in 1987–92 (underpinned largely by growth in industry and agriculture, which expanded by 5.4% and 4.6% respectively), toward the end of this period the region was devastated by two major natural disasters: the 1990 earthquake and the 1991 Mt Pinatubo eruption. The withdrawal from the American bases in 1991 also exacted a toll on investment and employment. To make matters worse, the adverse effects of the Mt Pinatubo eruption were longlasting in nature, and were not confined solely to the industrial sector but extended to other sectors as well. The industrial development programs pursued in Pampanga, Zambales, and Bulacan—such as the Subic Bay Freeport Zone, Clark Special Economic Zone, and Bataan Export Processing Zone—have been slow to take off and appear to have weak linkages to the rest of the region. Thus, if one looks at the whole of 1987–2000, it is apparent that services and industry in Central Luzon have failed to grow in tandem with the national economy, giving rise to the region's negative TNS during this period.

Negative TNS values in 1987–2000 for Bicol, Western and Eastern Visayas, and Northern, Southern, and Central Mindanao can be attributed largely to the poor performance of the services sector in these regions. Agriculture, which accounted for some 35–50% of the economy in these regions, exhibited lackluster performance. In addition, the regional pattern of budgetary allocations for agriculture indicates that the Mindanao regions have generally been neglected (see David, Chapter 6).

The poor performance of agriculture was the result of various natural disasters in all regions except Central Visayas. Typhoons and flash floods caused production setbacks in Bicol. Following the 1990 drought, which affected the production of major crops such as palay, coconut, sugarcane, corn, banana, and mango, Western Visayas was hit by a typhoon in December 1993. The 1990 drought and the devastating typhoons of 1994 and 1996 accounted for the poor performance of the agricultural sector in Eastern Visayas. In 1995, excessive rainfall in Southern Mindanao, particularly in Sarangani province, and flash floods in South Cotabato affected the region's standing crops. The problem was further aggravated by the Lake Maughan tragedy. These critical events contributed to a 23% decline in Southern Mindanao's corn production. The creditable growth of the industrial sector in all regions except Southern and Central Mindanao failed to make a perceptible impact on their overall rate of economic growth because of the low share of industry in these regions.

11.5 CONVERGENCE AND SHIFT ANALYSIS: A SYNTHESIS

In this section, the results of the convergence and shift analysis discussed above are seen to be complementary and integral. Indeed, regional convergence relates significantly to the critical alterations or shifts in the growth and structure of the economy of the various regions over time.

σ-convergence and Overall GDP Growth

A comparison of σ-convergence and national GDP growth reveals that changes in σ-dispersion are closely correlated to changes in the country's overall GDP growth (Figure 11.5). At the same time, this relationship appears to be characterized by a one-year lag, with the latter leading the former.

Figure 11.5 also indicates that the relation between σ-convergence and overall GDP growth tended to be positive in 1985–90 and negative in 1991–2000. The Philippine experience in the latter period is consistent with that of other Asian countries, including Thailand and Malaysia, where a positive relationship was found between increasing regional dispersion (in the sense of σ-dispersion) and the growth rate of GDP (La Croix 1998). In these economies, high rates of economic growth were driven largely by export-led industrialization. Because exports in Thailand and, to a lesser extent, Malaysia have tended to be concentrated in special economic zones or regions adjacent to major ports, this type of growth has tended to increase regional

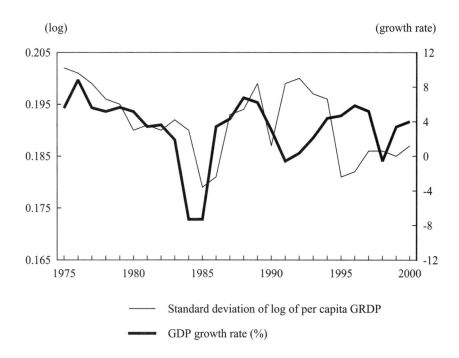

Figure 11.5 σ-convergence and GDP Growth Rate, 1975–2000

inequality. In like manner, Philippine GDP growth in 1991–2000, a period character-ized by high growth in industry and services, tended to increase regional inequality precisely because industry was concentrated in the NCR, the metropolitan periphery (Southern Tagalog and Central Luzon), and Cebu. In contrast, the GDP growth driven by the agricultural sector in 1975–86 tended to be more equalizing.

This finding highlights the possibility that σ-convergence varies not so much with GDP growth per se, but with the *quality* of GDP growth, a point that will be echoed in the next subsection.

β-convergence and Agricultural Growth

Table 11.8 establishes the link between the speed of convergence and the growth of the agricultural sector. It suggests that the speed of convergence is relatively high (as in 1975–86) when growth is led by agriculture. Conversely, when overall growth is being propelled by industry or services, the speed of convergence is relatively slow (as in 1987–2000). This is not surprising considering that most of the regions with a relatively low income are also those that are predominantly agricultural. Thus, when regions with a large agricultural base grow at a faster rate than the rest of the economy, there is a tendency for regional disparities to narrow.[6]

The analysis in the previous section shows, though, that not all of the poor regions that had a large agricultural base were able to benefit from the compara-

Table 11.8 Regional Convergence and Growth of Agriculture and Industry Sectors, 1975–2000

Year	β-coefficient	Agriculture Growth Rate (%)	Industry Growth Rate (%)
1975–86	0.0137	3.7	1.8
1987–2000	0.0067	1.8	3.4

tively rapid growth of the agricultural sector in 1975–86. During this period, the agricultural sector in Cagayan Valley, Bicol, Western Visayas, and Eastern Visayas lagged behind the rest of the country, causing stagnation or a deterioration in their per capita GRDP rankings (Table 11.2). This points to the need to look in depth at some of the structural constraints confronting these regions.

In much the same way, not all of the regions with a large agricultural base were left behind by the industry/services-led growth of 1987–2000. As noted, Ilocos, Cagayan Valley, and Western Mindanao all registered positive TNS in 1987–2000 despite having economic structures that were skewed in favor of agriculture. This came about primarily because industry grew side by side with agriculture in these regions.

In a sense these findings validate the agro-industrial approach to regional development adopted by the Aquino and Ramos administrations, which was premised on the enhancement of linkages between agriculture and industry. What appears to have been missing, however, was an overall strategy to improve productivity in the agricultural sector (see David, Chapter 6), quite apart from the impetus that greater forward linkages and market access bring.

11.6 OUTSTANDING ISSUES IN REGIONAL DEVELOPMENT

Structural Constraints

Structural constraints refer to the geographic characteristics or natural endowments that affect a region's development and growth, such as climate, water resources, topography, and soil types. Because they are inflexible, these constraints may be viewed as binding (Lamberte et al. 1993). A review of the physical endowments of the Philippine regions shows that some of those that have consistently lagged behind are predominantly agricultural but vulnerable to typhoons and other natural calamities. These regions are Cagayan Valley, Bicol, and Eastern Visayas.

In more recent years, especially in 1987–2000, changes in climatic conditions have been observed such that some regions that were not formerly prone to natural disasters have been affected by El Niño and La Niña episodes. The occurrence of these abnormal weather conditions has wrought havoc, especially in the Visayas and Mindanao. Without timely government intervention to help avert the worst effects of El Niño and La Niña, these regions failed to grow in tandem with others even during periods when the agricultural sector was buoyant.

All this points to the need for the redesign of regional development strategies to take into account the specific constraints stemming from each region's topographical characteristics. In this light, it is critical to realize that the present emphasis on a sector-based approach to regional development may need to be tempered by a spatially based approach. It also indicates the inappropriateness of one-size-fits-all programs, say in agriculture, that tend to suit conditions only in the traditional agricultural regions. For instance, in place of the traditional emphasis on rice and corn production, it may make better sense for farmers living in regions in the typhoon belt to raise livestock while also cultivating typhoon-resilient crops.

Agricultural Productivity

The strong link between regional convergence and agricultural growth highlights the need to improve agricultural productivity. The decline in productivity due to distortionary price intervention policy and weaknesses in the design and implementation of public expenditure programs is well documented (David 1999; see also David, Chapter 6).[7]

Increasing price distortions in the agricultural sector have had a detrimental effect on growth of employment in the sector. The drift toward increasing protection of agriculture, despite Philippine membership of the World Trade Organization (WTO), has arisen because of high binding tariffs. Moreover, the existing mechanism for distributing the minimum access volumes to be imported at lower tariffs has effectively resulted in rent seeking and price uncertainties (David 1999). Because of this, increases in nominal protection rates have been more than enough to counter the declining trend in the relative price of agricultural products in the world market and the appreciation of the real effective exchange rate in the 1990s. Many import-competing agricultural products continue to garner high effective protection rates, whereas exportable agricultural commodities have persistently been penalized by the overvaluation of the exchange rate. For instance, the high rates of protection on corn, livestock, and poultry have tended to work against small growers, who have become less competitive *vis-à-vis* large hog and poultry producers with access to lower-cost corn imports (David 1999).

Poor infrastructure has also held back the growth of the agricultural sector. Not only did public expenditure on irrigation fall sharply in the 1980s, but the design and operation of gravity irrigation systems left much to be desired. The road transport system is inadequate and the water transport system poorly managed and regulated. Although the country's road density is comparable with that in other ASEAN countries, Philippine roads are worse in terms of their surface conditions, road width, and functional design. At the same time, poor cargo-handling services and high shipping costs have hurt the marketing of agricultural products. While the deregulation of the domestic shipping industry got under way in the mid-1990s, the government continues to regulate the entry of new shipping operators, shipping rates for basic commodities, and third-class passenger fares. Consequently, the system of cross-subsidies that is meant to favor agriculture ultimately makes the effective shipping costs of agricultural products higher, as they are given low priority.

These shortcomings will need to be addressed—possibly through an intensified implementation of the Agriculture and Fisheries Modernization Act—if the future performance and incomes of agriculture-based regions are to improve.

Infrastructure Development

Uneven economic progress and wide income disparities among regions have always been blamed, in part at least, on regional differences in the level of infrastructure development (Lamberte et al. 1993; Basilio and Gundaya 1997). Table 11.9 shows the strong correlation between TNS values and major infrastructure development indicators for roads, power/energy, irrigation, and telecommunications for the period 1987–2000. At the same time, it appears that government investment has crowded out private investment in eight of the 13 regions. These findings lend support for the recurring call to improve the regional allocation of infrastructure investment so that lagging regions have the opportunity to catch up and increase their growth potential.

Table 11.10 indicates that some redistribution of government construction away from the central industrial region (the NCR plus the metropolitan periphery consisting of Central Luzon and Southern Tagalog) was effected in 1987–2000. However, this came largely at the expense of the periphery; the share of the NCR itself in total government construction expenditure actually increased in 1987–2000.

Table 11.9 Rank Correlation Coefficients: Total Net Shift Values and Infrastructure Development Indicators, 1987–2000 [a]

Infrastructure Development Indicator	Spearman Rank Correlation Coefficient
Road density	0.47
Percent electrified	0.40
Percent irrigated	0.69
Telephone density	0.53

a   "Percent electrified" refers to the ratio of actual energy connections to potential energy connections; "percent irrigated" is the ratio of irrigated area to potential irrigable area.

Sources: Roads: Department of Public Works and Highways; other data: National Statistical Coordination Board *Philippine Statistical Yearbook*.

Table 11.10 Regional Shares of Government and Private Sector in Construction Expenditure, 1975–99 (%)

Region	1975–85	1975–80	1981–85	1988–99	1988–92	1993–99
Government						
NCR	13.0	13.2	12.9	16.3	17.9	15.5
CAR	–	–	–	4.0	5.4	3.4
Ilocos	3.3	3.3	3.4	5.8	8.2	4.7
Cagayan Valley	12.5	14.0	11.1	5.9	7.1	5.3
C. Luzon	19.1	17.3	20.9	14.3	20.2	11.4
S. Tagalog	18.0	15.9	19.9	11.8	10.1	12.6
Bicol	6.2	7.2	5.3	6.0	5.3	6.4
W. Visayas	3.2	3.6	2.9	5.0	3.6	5.6
C. Visayas	4.2	4.3	4.2	5.7	3.9	6.5
E. Visayas	4.9	5.8	4.0	4.8	2.1	6.1
W. Mindanao	2.6	2.6	2.6	4.8	3.1	5.6
N. Mindanao	3.9	3.9	3.9	4.7	2.9	5.7
S. Mindanao	4.4	5.4	3.4	5.6	3.9	6.5
C. Mindanao	4.8	3.7	5.8	5.3	6.3	4.8
Philippines	100.0	100.0	100.0	100.0	100.0	100.0
Private						
NCR	49.1	50.0	48.2	40.9	47.8	37.0
CAR	–	–	–	1.7	1.8	1.6
Ilocos	3.0	2.8	3.3	4.1	3.2	4.6
Cagayan Valley	1.6	1.6	1.6	1.2	1.3	1.2
C. Luzon	6.2	5.9	6.6	8.1	6.7	9.0
S. Tagalog	13.3	13.4	13.2	17.1	13.6	19.0
Bicol	2.6	2.8	2.5	2.4	2.7	2.1
W. Visayas	4.9	4.5	5.3	4.1	4.6	3.9
C. Visayas	5.5	5.4	5.5	6.9	6.4	7.2
E. Visayas	1.6	1.6	1.6	1.5	1.6	1.4
W. Mindanao	1.8	1.7	1.8	1.3	1.4	1.3
N. Mindanao	4.3	4.2	4.4	4.0	2.8	4.7
S. Mindanao	4.5	4.7	4.4	5.2	4.5	5.6
C. Mindanao	1.6	1.6	1.6	1.6	1.7	1.6
Philippines	100.0	100.0	100.0	100.0	100.0	100.0

NCR = National Capital Region; CAR = Cordillera Administrative Region.

Source: National Statistical Coordination Board, *Gross Regional Domestic Expenditures*.

The major beneficiaries of this reallocation were the Mindanao regions, whose shares expanded, particularly in 1993–99. This appears to have had some positive effect on these regions, as indicated by positive TNS values for Western Mindanao, Southern Mindanao, and the ARMM in 1997–2000 (Figure 11.6).

Decentralization

The Philippines has a unitary form of government with a multi-tiered structure. At the top is the central government operating through some 20 departments/agencies. The country is divided into 15 administrative regions, with most departments maintaining regional offices. In addition, there is one autonomous region, the Autonomous Region of Muslim Mindanao (ARMM). It should be emphasized, however, that with the exception of the ARMM, the regions are simply administrative subdivisions, and not regional governments with elected regional representatives.

The second tier of government is composed of the LGUs. The local government structure has three layers. Provinces and highly urbanized cities comprise the first layer. The provinces are divided into municipalities and component cities, each of which is further subdivided into *barangays* (barrios), the smallest political unit. Highly urbanized cities exist at the same level as provinces—that is, they share the same functions and authority—but are partitioned directly into *barangays*. At present there are 79 provinces, 84 cities, 1,525 municipalities, and some 42,000 *barangays*. Each LGU is headed by an elected chief executive (governor, mayor or *barangay* captain) and has a legislative body, or Sanggunian, composed of an elected vice-governor or vice-mayor and council members.

The Philippines has a long history of highly centralized government administration dating back to the days of Spanish colonial rule. Decentralization initiatives first surfaced in the 1950s as part of the counterinsurgency response to the Huk rebellion. With the declaration of martial law in 1972, decentralization flourished more in form than in substance. However, the people power revolution that installed the Aquino administration set the stage for a radical departure from the centralist tendencies of the previous regime. A major shift toward political and fiscal devolution was ushered in with the enactment in 1989 of the Organic Act for Muslim Mindanao (which created the ARMM) and in 1991 of the Local Government Code. Together they aimed to build national solidarity through local autonomy.[8]

These two pieces of legislation jointly define central–local relations in the country. They mandate the transfer of principal responsibility for the delivery of basic services and operation of facilities from the central government to the ARMM regional government or the LGUs. These devolved services included agricultural extension, social forestry, environmental management and pollution control, primary health care, hospitals, social welfare, municipal services, and the repair and maintenance of public works such as local roads, bridges, water supply systems, and communal irrigation systems. The devolution was substantial not only in terms of the sheer number of functions that were shifted, but more so in terms of the number of personnel transferred.

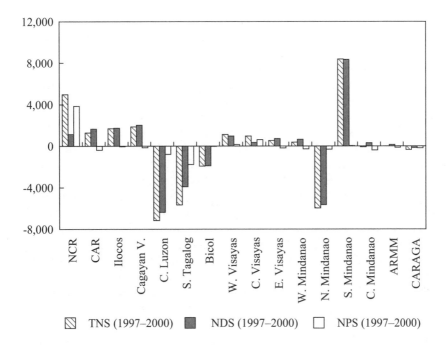

Figure 11.6 Shift Analysis of Gross Regional Domestic Product, 1997–2000

The devolution of expenditure responsibilities to LGUs and the ARMM is, with a few exceptions, consistent with the decentralization theorem. For the most part, the services the local governments provide are suited to low levels of government. Their activities have few important spillovers to a broader community to indicate that they should be provided by higher levels of government, except perhaps in the case of environmental management and primary health care. At the same time, expenditure assignments are generally clear and well understood by LGUs and the ARMM regional government. Indeed, the Local Government Code provides an explicit and clear delineation of functions across levels of government, with the exception of environment and natural resource management and public works.[9] However, a continuing source of irritation between the central government and the LGUs is the propensity for some central government agencies to exercise undue influence on the LGUs with regard to how they should conduct their expenditure responsibilities.

The Organic Act for Muslim Mindanao and the Local Government Code pre-scribed that the regional government and LGUs would receive a higher share of internal revenue taxes (through the internal revenue allotment, or IRA). This is transferred to them as a block grant from the central government. Apart from their share in national tax revenues, they are also allowed to levy local taxes and borrow from both public and commercial sources.

More than a decade after the creation of the ARMM, and almost 10 years after the implementation of the Local Government Code, the more decentralized arrangement has not been able to generate the momentum for development expected of it or contribute significantly to more balanced regional development despite evidence of some efficiency gains.[10] The numbers indicate that the development content of local government expenditure has, on the whole, tended to stagnate since 1992.

Table 11.11 shows that whereas aggregate LGU expenditure rose from an average of 1.6% of GNP in 1985–91 to 3.6% of GNP in 1993–2000, the combined share of the economic and social services sectors in total LGU spending remained fairly constant at its pre-code level of around half. This was because most of the increment in total LGU spending went to social services,[11] with a corresponding contraction in the expenditure share of economic services (especially transport and communications). Moreover, the share of capital expenditure in total LGU expenditure actually contracted, from 22.4% in 1991 to 19.5% in 2000.

The distribution of local government capital expenditure is highly skewed across regions, with the less well-off regions hardly able to incur any significant capital expenditure.[12] Over two-thirds of all capital expenditure by cities in 2000 was incurred by cities in just four regions: Metro Manila, Central Luzon, Southern Tagalog, and Central Visayas. Similarly, over one-half of capital expenditure by provinces in 2000 was incurred by provinces in the regions of Ilocos, Central Luzon, Southern Tagalog, and Western Visayas.

Table 11.12 shows that cities have in general fared better over time than provinces in terms of capital expenditure, particularly in the early years of the implementation of the Local Government Code. For instance, the share of capital expenditure in total LGU expenditure in cities increased from 24.2% in 1991 to 31.4% in 1994 before decreasing to 27.1% in 1997 and 25.3% in 2000. In contrast, the share in provinces declined from 23.3% in 1991 to 15.3% in 1994 before expanding to 17.4% in 1997 and 18.1% in 2000. While both started out in 1991 with fairly similar shares of personnel spending in total LGU expenditure, cities, but not provinces, have been able to reduce this share.

Among the principal causes of the deterioration in quality of LGU development expenditures, and increased skew in their distribution, the most crucial relates to the failure of the decentralization process to give local governments adequate financial capacity to carry out their developmental function. This failure arises from a number of factors: vertical and horizontal imbalances, the absence of intergovernmental transfers to equalize revenue-raising capacity, and the resulting fiscal inefficiencies.

Vertical/Horizontal Imbalance

As indicated earlier, the implementation of the Local Government Code resulted in significant increases in the IRA share of LGUs, with *barangays* and cities receiving the largest proportional rate of increase. Despite this, there is a widespread perception that a vertical imbalance exists, in the sense that the LGUs' prevailing share in national taxes is insufficient to cover the cost both of devolved functions and of the so-called unfunded mandates. The latter include salary increases under the Salary

Table 11.11 Consolidated LGU Budgets, 1985–2000 (%)

Item	1985–91	1993–2000	1991	1993	1997	2000
SHARE OF GNP						
Total receipts	1.7	3.6	1.9	3.0	3.7	4.0
Local sources	0.8	1.2	0.8	1.2	1.3	1.2
of which:						
Local tax revenues	0.5	0.9	0.6	0.9	1.0	0.9
External sources	0.9	2.4	1.1	1.8	2.4	2.7
of which:						
IRA	0.6	2.2	0.8	1.7	2.2	2.5
Total expenditure	1.6	3.6	1.9	2.7	3.8	3.9
By sector						
Economic services	0.5	0.9	0.7	0.7	1.0	1.0
Social services	0.3	1.0	0.3	0.8	1.0	1.0
General public services	0.7	1.4	0.8	1.5	1.5	1.6
By type						
Current expenditure	1.3	2.9	1.5	2.2	3.0	3.2
Capital expenditure	0.3	0.7	0.4	0.5	0.7	0.8
DISTRIBUTION						
Total receipts	100.0	100.0	100.0	100.0	100.0	100.0
Local sources	48.0	33.4	44.1	39.1	35.2	30.7
of which:						
Local tax revenues	31.9	25.0	29.2	30.2	26.0	23.2
External sources	52.0	66.6	55.9	60.9	64.8	69.3
of which:						
IRA	36.4	61.7	39.8	56.5	60.2	64.4
Total expenditure	100.0	100.0	100.0	100.0	100.0	100.0
By sector						
Economic services	32.9	25.6	35.8	25.5	26.0	25.0
Social services	20.5	26.7	15.4	27.9	26.8	25.6
General public services	42.8	39.8	44.5	40.8	39.2	40.4
By type						
Current expenditure	83.6	81.1	77.6	81.1	80.3	80.5
Capital expenditure	16.4	18.9	22.4	18.9	19.8	19.5

Source: Commission on Audit (various years), *Annual Financial Report of Local Government Units.*

Table 11.12 Capital and Current Expenditure in Total Expenditure of Local Governments, 1991–2000 (%)

	1991		1994		1997		2000	
	A	B	A	B	A	B	A	B
All provinces	23.3	41.6	15.3	47.5	17.4	48.8	18.1	45.7
All cities	24.2	45.8	31.4	34.7	27.1	38.4	25.3	36.6

a   Column A refers to the share of LGU capital expenditure in total LGU expenditure. Column B refers to the share of LGU expenditure on personnel services in total LGU expenditure.

Source: Annual Financial Report of Local Government Units, Commission on Audit, various years.

Standardization Law and the provision of additional personnel benefits under the Magna Carta for Health Workers. Analysis shows that while these concerns were unfounded in aggregate in the early years of the code's implementation (1993, 1994, and 1995), this was not the case in 1996, 1997, and 1998, when salary adjustments under the Salary Standardization Law were so hefty that increases in the IRA were not able to keep up. The situation has since improved, however. A matching of aggregate IRA levels with LGU expenditure responsibilities (including devolved functions) in 1999 shows that the natural increase in the IRA arising from the implementation of the code is now sufficient to cover the inflation and population growth-adjusted cost of devolved functions and unfunded mandates (Manasan 2001).

In the case of the ARMM, there has been a mismatch between the expenditure responsibilities transferred to the regional government and its means of revenue raising, resulting in a severe vertical fiscal imbalance. The regional government's share in national taxes is equivalent only to about 3% of the cost of the devolved functions, not nearly enough to cover the expenditure responsibilities assigned to it. This occurs largely because the ARMM's share in national taxes is computed on the basis of point of collection (that is, where the tax is actually collected)—but precisely because the ARMM is a less developed region, its tax base is smaller than the average tax base for the country in its entirety. An additional factor is that all of the responsibilities devolved by the central government were shifted to the regional government, with none being assigned to the LGUs in the area.

As a result, the ARMM regional government is dependent on yearly allocations from central government general appropriations to carry out its mandate. It has very little control over the size and composition of this funding, competing for central government resources along with other central government agencies. The allocation of transfers to various uses is also determined by the central government, under line items in the General Appropriations Act. The regional government is therefore reduced to an administrative arm of the central government, simply implementing its plans and programs.

It should be pointed out that since 1992 central government transfers to the ARMM regional government have grown at a faster pace than if adjustments had simply been made for inflation and population growth. In fact, central government allotments for the regular operations of the ARMM are now about double what they used to be. Perhaps this is the central government's way of making up for its past neglect of the region.

In contrast, LGUs in the ARMM have access to resources but are not burdened with expenditure responsibilities. They are entitled not only to their share of national taxes as provided for by the Local Government Code but also to a share of the ARMM's internal revenue collections as mandated by the Organic Act for Muslim Mindanao. Consequently, the aggregate intergovernmental transfers accruing to the LGUs are more than 20 times those accruing to the regional government itself.

Quite apart from the issue of vertical balance is the related issue of horizontal balance. Provinces absorbed 45.6% of the total cost of devolved functions, munici-palities 47.4%, cities 7.0%, and *barangays* 0%. Contrast this with the mandated share of LGUs in the IRA—provinces 23%, cities 23%, municipalities 34%, and *barangays* 20%—and it becomes clear that there is a mismatch in the resources transferred and the expenditure responsibilities devolved to the different levels of local government.

In addition to the horizontal imbalance across levels of local government, an imbalance also exists across LGUs *within* each level. Thus, while the IRA share of some LGUs is not enough to finance the functions devolved to them, others have received resources beyond their requirements. For instance, in 1993 the per capita net resource transfer was negative in 37 of the 66 provinces for which data were available.[13] By 1994 this number had dropped to three. However, the situation has worsened since then given the blowout in unfunded mandates. Thus, in 2000, 15 of 79 provinces, 295 of 1,525 municipalities, and three of 83 cities suffered negative net resource transfers. Clearly there is a need to improve the IRA distribution for-mula so that the expenditure needs of the various levels of local government, and of the different LGUs within each level, are taken into account.

Disparities in Revenue-raising Capacity

There are large differences in the revenue-raising capacity of the various types of LGUs. In 2000, for instance, close to 72% of all local taxes collected by LGUs came from just four regions: Metro Manila, Central Luzon, Southern Tagalog, and Cen-tral Visayas. Cities have contributed much more than other categories of local gov-ernment in local revenue generation. Thus, while the locally sourced revenues of all cities in aggregate rose by 63% in real terms per capita between 1991 and 2000, those of provinces and municipalities increased by only 14%. In principle, inter-governmental transfers are expected to address this problem of disparities among LGUs in income and economic opportunities.

Simple regression analysis between per capita IRA on the one hand and per capita household income on the other reveals that these two variables are negatively

Table 11.13 Regression of per Capita IRA and per Capita Total LGU Revenue with per Capita Household Income, 1999 (provincial level)[a]

Dependent Variable	log(PC IRA)	log (PC LGU Rev)
Constant	3.46	−5.16
	(12.89)	(−9.69)
Per capita household income	−0.65	2.97
	(−5.60)	(12.94)
Adjusted R^2	0.20	0.59

IRA = internal revenue allotment; LGU = local government unit.
a   Numbers in parentheses refer to *t*-statistics. Per capita household income is derived from the FIES.

related to one another; that is, LGUs with lower per capita household income tend to receive higher per capita IRA (Table 11.13). This result suggests that the IRA distribution formula is equalizing. However, the analysis also indicates that the equalizing effect of the IRA is not sufficient to compensate for the inherent disparities in the tax base. Thus, per capita total LGU revenue (that is, the sum of locally sourced LGU revenue and IRA) is found to be positively related to per capita personal income. This apparent weakness of the IRA distribution formula in equalizing the fiscal capacity of LGUs may in turn explain the skew in the distribution of LGU capital expenditure in favor of cities and the more developed LGUs, exacerbating existing disparities.

Augmentation Funds and Externalities

The augmentation fund provision (section 17c) of the Local Government Code presents a logical opening for the operation of a matching grants program for devolved activities with significant externalities and spillover of benefits (such as environmental projects or basic social programs). It does this by providing the basis for the continued involvement of central government agencies in functions that are primarily assigned to LGUs.[14] Although the Investment Coordinating Committee of the National Economic and Development Authority (NEDA) Board offers guidelines on cost-sharing arrangements for big-ticket government investments in regional projects, the code and its implementing rules and regulations fail, for the most part, to define the mechanisms by which the central government can direct such assistance to LGUs. For instance, Executive Order (EO) 53 allows national government agencies to retain management control of all foreign-assisted projects and/or nationally funded projects even if they involve devolved activities. At the same time, because many of the "devolved" national government agencies are made accountable for the overall outcome in their respective areas, they deem it their responsibility to direct

LGU behavior in support of the national objective.[15] Congressmen are enamored of section 17 of the Local Government Code because it gives them easy access to pork barrel funds through the simple act of inserting a special provision in the General Appropriations Act to ordain that monies from the augmentation funds can only be released for "projects identified by members of Congress."[16] Consequently, the prevailing regulatory framework effectively permits, even encourages, the existence of a two-track delivery system whereby both national government agencies and LGUs are able to initiate devolved activities without either having to take primary responsibility for the final outcome, thereby weakening accountability at both levels (Gonzalez 1996).

Fiscal Inefficiencies

The existing state of intergovernmental relations has prevented the ARMM regional government from capturing the expected efficiency gains from fiscal decentralization. First, although the regional government is vested with sufficient taxing authority, it has chosen not to make full use of its powers. Since the regional government is assured that the central government will directly fund the cost of devolved functions, it has little incentive to raise its own revenues locally. This situation has effectively severed the link between expenditure decisions and local taxation, with implications for the accountability of local officials to their constituents.

Second, the regional government has not been able to alter at will the expenditure mix in the ARMM to better correspond to local preferences, for two reasons. As discussed above, it is the central government that determines how much is spent, and on what, when it provides the ARMM with its line budget under the General Appropriations Act. In addition, by retaining all of the responsibilities devolved to it rather than passing some of them on to the LGUs in its jurisdiction, the regional government is not able to maximize the allocative efficiency that arises when subnational governments reallocate their resources to match the needs of the local people. Many of the functions that now rest with the regional government would be better assigned to LGUs. These include the construction and maintenance of local roads and other infrastructure, the operation of rural health units and hospitals, the delivery of social welfare services, and the provision of agricultural extension. Outside the ARMM, LGUs already hold primary responsibility for these functions.

The contribution of LGUs outside the ARMM to the total tax revenues of the general government remains low (at 5%), despite an increase in the ratio of aggregate local tax revenues to GNP from an average of 0.5% in the pre-code era to 0.9% in the post-code period. This is indicative of the low local tax effort. The collection efficiency for the real property tax has actually deteriorated in the post-code period (Manasan 1999), and there is anecdotal evidence to suggest that many local officials shy away from the task of imposing and collecting local taxes.

The IRA is by far the largest source of revenue for most LGUs and, indeed, in most cases more than covers the cost of devolved expenditures. If local revenue raising comes at a considerable cost for LGUs, then it is logical that they would rely upon the IRA for revenue and not exert a vigorous local tax effort.[17] Empirical evidence supports this view. Regression analysis shows that whereas intergovernmental transfers had a neutral effect on local revenue performance in 1985 (before the code), it substituted for local tax revenue at all levels of local government in 1992 and 1993 (Manasan 1995).

Using panel data for provinces, cities, and municipalities in 1995–98, we conducted a regression analysis of per capita local tax revenue on per capita household income (as a proxy for the local tax base or local ability to pay) and per capita IRA (as a way of checking whether intergovernmental grants stimulate or substitute for local government revenue effort).[18] The results validated the disincentive effect of the IRA on local tax effort, showing that the LGUs that were net winners in fiscal decentralization tended to have lower per capita local tax revenue. This was indicated by the negative and statistically significant coefficient of the product of the dummy variable for per capita net resource transfer and per capita IRA in the local business tax equation of cities, and in both the local business tax and real property tax equations of municipalities.[19] Similarly, the coefficient of per capita IRA was itself negative and statistically significant in the real property tax equation of provinces. These findings suggest that LGUs receiving more resources than expenditure responsibilities tend to be lax in their tax effort. Thus, there appears to be a need to alter the IRA distribution formula so as to provide incentives for local tax effort.

As expected, the analysis also showed that per capita local tax revenue is positively and significantly related to per capita household income for both real property tax and local business tax for cities, municipalities, and provinces alike in all three years (Table 11.14). This finding confirms that local tax effort is largely determined by the ability to pay. Given the wide disparities in the size of the local tax base across regions, this result further highlights the potential for increased regional inequality with greater fiscal decentralization.

Regional Disparities in Access to Commercial Sources of Finance

In principle, commercial sources of finance should be able to augment public sources, both national and local, to constitute an important source of additional funding for regional development. The access of LGUs to the banking system has generally been minimal. Given the state of local government finances, banks, particularly private banks, have generally shied away from lending to them. An important factor behind the lack of lending by private banks is the requirement by the Commission of Audit that LGUs maintain their deposits at government-owned banks. However, despite their advantage of monopoly over LGU deposits, lending to LGUs in the total loan portfolios of government financial institutions has been very small—less than 13 million pesos through to 1999.

It is also possible for LGUs to borrow on commercial terms from the central government-administered Municipal Development Fund (MDF), basically for projects financed through foreign bilateral or multilateral assistance.[20] However, MDF operations have been small and ineffective, with total loans to LGUs amounting to less than 5 billion pesos through to 1999. Although the MDF provides long-term finance (typically around 15 years, compared with an average of five years or less for banks), it has concentrated mainly on loans to the better-off class I and class II

Table 11.14 Linear Regression of per Capita Tax Revenue of LGUs[a]

	Provinces		Cities[b]		Municipalities[c]	
	PC LBT[b]	PC RPT[c]	PC LBT	PC RPT	PC LBT	PC RPT
Constant	−10.5267	−19.8245	−6.2778	−4.8622	−17.5335	−18.0570
	(−4.422)	(−2.728)	(−4.047)	(−3.191)	(−4.931)	(−4.329)
Density	0.2353	−0.0014	0.2496	0.1745	0.0949	0.1024
	(1.063)**	(−0.407)	(2.933)**	(2.131)**	(12.390)**	(10.539)**
PC FIESY	0.6611	0.0029	0.9352	0.8799	0.0001	−0.0004
	(2.098)**	(6.497)**	(6.926)**	(6.674)**	(0.488)	(−2.195)**
PC IRA	0.2925	−0.0138	−0.0349	−0.0410	0.0413	0.0621
	(1.101)	(−2.329)**	(−0.187)*	(−0.237)	(21.130)**	(29.993)**
D1*PC IRA	−0.0188	0.0036	−0.0097	−0.0149		
	(−1.630)*	(0.315)	(−3.379)**	(−4.895)**		
X^2 (Chi-square)	15.78	46.85	128.37	99.82	604.72	999.98

PC = per capita; LBT = local business tax; RPT = real property tax; FIESY = household income; IRA = internal revenue allotment. * denotes statistically significant at the 10% level; ** denotes statistically significant at the 5% level.
a   Numbers in parentheses refer to z-statistics.
b   Follows double log specification.
c   Follows linear specification.

municipalities. LGUs have little discretion over the choice of projects to be funded, as this is dictated by the foreign loan covenant between the national government and the international donor. The processing of subloans has been subjected to drawn-out bureaucratic processes, and the lending terms of the MDF have on the whole been less attractive than those offered by government financial institutions.

Due to the undeveloped nature of the Philippine bond market, local governments have had only limited access to long-term bonds. Very few municipal and local bonds have been issued so far (less than 15 by 1999). The reasons are not hard to find. Interviews with capital market participants and experts in the Philippines reveal that bond offerings by LGUs suffer from a general perception of high credit risk, which works against even the financially better-off LGUs.[21] This is compounded by the political risk of lending to LGUs: with changes in administration occurring every three years, investors fear that succeeding administrations may not honour the credit obligations of the previous ones.

As a result of all these supply-side factors, combined with the low development and revenue-generating orientation of LGU expenditures, borrowing makes up a very small portion of their total income. In 1997, for instance, the total borrowing of all LGUs comprised only 3.4% of their total income.

Even when unable to do so directly as a result of their weak finances or borrowing capacity, local governments can assist local development by actively encouraging private commercial involvement in revenue-generating investment projects in their areas. The government, with assistance from the Asian Development Bank (ADB), recently launched a major effort to generate private sector participation in infrastructure creation through build–operate–transfer (BOT) arrangements. Although a promising avenue, actual involvement by the private sector has so far been minimal. By 1999, only two BOT-type projects had been completed at a total cost of 1.4 billion pesos. Another seven projects worth 1 billion pesos are either under construction or under tender. A major obstacle to the success of the BOT process has been the inability of LGUs to develop projects for consideration by private sponsors. To address this problem, the national government recently took the step of setting up a loan facility with the Development Bank of the Philippines to provide technical assistance to LGUs in developing project feasibility studies.[22]

The basic problem facing BOT projects remains the willingness and ability of the public to pay for infrastructure services, to allow viable and potentially profitable projects to get off the ground. This is likely to restrict the implementation of such projects to metropolitan regions, at least in the near future.

Given the crisis in local development funding, there is an urgent need to create a mechanism that would give LGUs access to stable and predictable resources for development, while ensuring that they would be made available strictly on the basis of demonstrated effective and sound utilization. One possibility would be an arrangement whereby development resources would be channeled to LGUs under terms graded according to the level of development in the region.[23] This would help to address directly the equity issue in regional development.

NOTES

1. The per capita GRDP index is defined as the ratio of regional per capita GRDP to the national average for per capita GRDP. Thus, a per capita GRDP ratio of below 100 implies that a region's per capita GRDP is below the national average, while a ratio above 100 implies that its per capita GRDP is above the national average.

2. In Western Visayas, the slowdown during this period followed the collapse of the sugar industry.

3. This section and the next draw heavily from updates in Manasan and Mercado (1999).

4. Absolute β-convergence assumes that the only difference between regions lies in their initial levels of per capita output. In other words, the different regions share not only the same steady-state per capita output and the same rate of technological progress but also the same stock of governance institutions and technologies of production and organization. In contrast, conditional β-convergence may be more relevant if the regional economies do not share the same rate of technological progress and/or steady-state per capita output.

5. The Gintong Ani Program is the flagship program for agricultural development. It envisions a modernized and productive agricultural and fisheries sector and the provision of food

to the needy at affordable prices. It is targeted especially at marginalized sectors, which will eventually be empowered as the benefits from responsive support services flow through to them.

6. In this regard, it is interesting to note the finding by Balisacan (1997) that despite its sluggish growth, the agricultural sector had the most pronounced effect on poverty alleviation in the 1980s and early 1990s.

7. The Philippines had had one of the lowest growth rates of agricultural gross value added and exports among developing Asian countries.

8. Widening income disparities, the growing number of poor people, and the repressive political environment of the 1960s, 1970s, and 1980s fueled both leftist sentiment and separatist armed resistance in the country. However, it cannot be denied that the underlying motivation of the people of Mindanao in their pursuit of self-determination went beyond the need to address the substandard income levels and poor human development outcomes prevalent in their region. It was deeply rooted in their desire to preserve their unique and distinct heritage, culture, and religion, and to re-establish their inherent right to their ancestral land. Put another way, Tanggol (1990: 23) has said that the quest for autonomy has

a dual significance to Muslim Mindanao. One concerns the imperative for an effective public administration where goods and services are efficiently delivered to the poor. Here, these two communities are similarly situated with the rest of rural and poverty-stricken Philippines. The second concerns the need to preserve the uniqueness of Muslim culture, religion and way of life. Here, these communities are not similarly situated with the other Filipinos, the dominant majority.

9. For instance, the Local Government Code gives municipalities implementing responsibility over community-based forestry and watershed projects but allows the Department of Environment and Natural Resources to retain supervision and control over such projects. Similarly, LGUs have primary responsibility for the construction and maintenance of local roads but the Department of Public Works and Highways may continue to undertake similar activities with funding from the national budget.

10. Case studies have shown that LGUs tend to do things cheaper. This is certainly true in the case of the construction of roads, school buildings, and other local facilities (Loehr and Manasan 1999).

11. The increase in expenditure on health services (primarily because the cost of devolved health functions accounted for more than half of the total cost of all devolved functions) was the main cause of the expansion in the share of social services in the LGU budget.

12. A positive correlation (of 0.47) is found between per family capital expenditure by provinces and cities combined and the regional average family income in 1997

13. The per capita net resource transfer for 1993 is defined as per capita 1993 IRA less per capita 1992 IRA less the per capita cost of devolved functions (adjusted for inflation).

14. Section 17c of the Local Government Code allows central government agencies to implement "public works and infrastructure projects and other facilities, programs and services *funded by the national government under the annual General Appropriations Act, other special laws, pertinent executive orders, and those wholly or partially funded from foreign sources*" [emphasis added].

15. For instance, the Department of Health is accountable for the overall health status of the country in the same way that the Department of Environment and Natural Resources is accountable for overall environmental and natural resource management results.

16. Thus, it has come about that the budgets of devolved central government agencies have grown disproportionately relative to the IRA: whereas the IRA grew by 15% per year

on average between 1994 and 1997, the budget of the Department of Agriculture expanded by 48%, that of the Department of Health by 25%, and that of the Department of Social Welfare and Development by 22%. Although this trend has reversed in more recent years, the practice whereby congressmen identify the type and location of projects financed from augmentation funds continues. This continues to be a major source of discord between Congress and LGU officials, as it violates the spirit of local autonomy.

17. Interviews with local government officials invariably indicate that they equate an increased tax effort with a lower chance of winning the next election.

18. Specifically, a random effects model was estimated using the generalized least squares approach. Personal income data from the FIES were used to calculate per capita household income.

19. In the regression analysis, a dummy variable that takes a value of 1 if the LGU has a positive per capita net resource transfer due to fiscal decentralization (and zero otherwise) was introduced to check whether net winners behaved differently from net losers. Note that net resource transfer is defined as the difference between the increment in the IRA and the cost of devolved functions and unfunded mandates.

20. The MDF started operations in 1984.

21. Staff of the Asian Development Bank conducted detailed discussions on this matter with market participants, LGUs, and financial experts when setting up the bank's LGU Private Infrastructure Project Development Facility.

22. This has been done under the LGU Private Infrastructure Project Development Facility, mentioned in the previous note.

23. Such an arrangement—called the Local Government Units' Development Fund (LGUDF)—has in fact been proposed under an ADB technical assistance project.

12

Environment and Natural Resources

Ian Coxhead and Sisira Jayasuriya

12.1 INTRODUCTION

What is the state of the Philippine environment, and what are the links between environment and development in the Philippine setting? In this chapter we first review the available data on environmental quality and natural resource degradation in the Philippines. We consider trends over time and compare the Philippine case with those of its Asian regional neighbors. Second, we present a brief review of theoretical links between environmental quality, resource depletion, and development strategies and outcomes, and consider the Philippine data in light of this theory. Third, we discuss recent economic trends and policy initiatives having a bearing on environment and development, and present some simulation results indicating likely trends in economic and environmental variables under alternative policy regimes. Finally, we ask what past experience and current trends might indicate for the future of the Philippine environment.

The "environment" can only be discussed meaningfully in terms of its component parts. As identified in official Philippine documents, these include natural resource stocks such as forests, minerals, water, biodiversity, and soils, as well as air and water quality in specific locations and at specific times. Since these categories are sometimes difficult to identify separately, it is convenient to group them as a set of *ecosystems*—forests and uplands, lowland agriculture, urban-industrial, coastal/marine, freshwater—and a set of *resources* (that are of course components of ecosystems): forests, fisheries, soils, minerals, and biodiversity. We examine the data and some analytical evidence on each of these, but concentrate in the second half of the chapter on some case studies of specific ecosystem and natural resource issues.

12.2 THE STATE OF THE PHILIPPINE ENVIRONMENT

The Philippine environment and natural resource sector is generally classified as comprising five major interlinked, and sometimes overlapping, ecosystems: (1) the forest and uplands ecosystem; (2) the agricultural/cropland ecosystem; (3) the freshwater ecosystem; (4) the coastal and marine ecosystem; and (5) the urban ecosystem.[1] Some of these ecosystems include significant mineral and other natural resources; others also host a rich variety of flora and fauna (Table 12.1). The Philippines is home to 5% of the world's flora species, 6% of its birds, and 4% of its mammals; 67% of the species in the major groups of animals and plants are not found anywhere else in the world. The country's coral reefs are second only to Australia's Great Barrier Reef in terms of the diversity of coral and fish species, and it has the second highest number of seagrass species in the world. However, each of these ecosystems faces significant, often severe, problems of environmental degradation, both from the depletion of resource stocks and from the production of polluting emissions.

Forests and Uplands

The forest and uplands ecosystem covers around 45% of total land area, and its resources directly support about 30% of the population, including some of the poorest in the country. It is experiencing severe pressure of a variety of kinds, the most prominent of which is rapid deforestation. Deforestation reduces biodiversity through its destructive impact on plant and animal habitats, alters the hydrological properties of soils, and adversely affects watershed functions. Further, a large proportion of the uplands have steep slopes which, once cleared of their permanent cover, are prone to severe land degradation, particularly soil erosion, unless adequate conservation measures are implemented.[2]

Estimates of actual forested area and rates of deforestation vary, reflecting different definitions as well as severe data deficiencies, but there is general agreement that continuing rapid tree cutting has greatly shrunk the area of forested land in recent decades. According to Kummer (1992), between 1900 and 1950 national forest cover fell from around 70% of total land to 50%, and by the end of the 1980s had fallen further to less than 25%. With deforestation proceeding at an average annual rate of 2.9% even according to Philippine government sources, by the late 1990s forest cover was less than 19%.[3] Table 12.2 provides a regional perspective, showing the Philippine deforestation rate to be well in excess of rates in neighboring countries—even those, like Vietnam, in which initial forest stocks are not especially large.

The two main causes of deforestation are land clearance for agriculture and commercial exploitation of forests for logs, lumber, fuel (including charcoal), and pulpwood. The relative importance of these two activities is a matter of dispute, but commercial logging, both legal and illegal, appears to bear primary responsibility for the depletion of old-growth *dipterocarp* forests containing valuable timber, with conversion to agricultural uses accounting for much of the deforestation of degraded, secondary, or residual forest lands.[4]

Table 12.1 Flora and Fauna in the Philippines

Species	Approximate Number
Plants	13,500
Animals	170,000
Pteridopytes, broyophytes, fungi, algae. and lichens	4,000
Terrestrial vertebrate	1,090
Birds	558
Mammals	185
Amphibians	95
Reptiles	252
Marine	3,088
Corals	488
Fish	2,400
Algae	69
Protozoans	125
Seagrasses	6

Source: Republic of the Philippines (1998).

In upland areas, increases in agricultural production have traditionally come to a great extent from expansion at the cultivated margin rather than through improvements in the efficiency with which existing land resources are utilized. Between 1960 and 1987, the upland population more than doubled to an estimated 18 million, and the area devoted to upland agriculture increased six-fold, coinciding with a rapid decline in forest cover (Bee 1987; World Bank 1989; Cruz et al. 1992; WRI 1999). In upland agriculture, the highest fraction of land is planted with upland rice and corn, with smaller amounts given over to vegetables, tree crops, pasture, and other uses. Since 1990 the national planted area of major upland and rainfed crops such as corn has declined somewhat, but this is due more to the conversion of land to other crops and non-agricultural uses than to a contraction at the land frontier.

Deforestation has both direct and tangible economic effects as well as environmental impacts whose economic costs are less immediately visible. In the recent past, Philippine timber and processed wood products were major sources of foreign exchange, accounting for as much as one-third of all exports during the late 1960s. They now account for only 0.2%—or 1.15% if the gross value of finished wood products is included (NSCB 1995). Similarly, gross value added in forestry and wood products fell in absolute terms throughout the 1970s and 1980s. In relative terms, the GDP share of forestry and wood industries fell from 2.5% in 1975 to just 0.3% by 1994. A large part of the population, particularly in rural areas, depends on charcoal and fuelwood for household energy, and deforestation threatens future fuelwood supplies. The potential for irreversible changes in the stock of biodiversity,

Table 12.2 Forest Cover and Deforestation in Asian Developing Countries, 1980–2000

Country	Forest Area (thousand km^2)			Forest Area/ Land Area (%)	Average Annual Change in Forest Area (%)	
	1980	1990	2000	2000	1980–90[a]	1990–2000
China	126,398	145,417	163,480	17.5	0.6	1.2
Indonesia	124,476	118,110	104,986	58.0	−0.8	−1.2
India	58,259	63,732	64,113	21.6	1.1	0.1
Myanmar	32,901	39,588	34,419	52.3	−1.2	−1.4
Malaysia	21,564	21,661	19,292	58.7	−2.1	−1.2
Thailand	18,123	15,886	14,762	28.9	−3.1	−0.7
Lao PDR	14,470	13,088	12,561	54.4	−0.9	−0.4
Cambodia	13,484	9,896	9,335	52.9	−2.4	−0.6
Philippines	11,194	6,676	5,789	19.4	−3.3	−1.4
Vietnam	10,663	9,303	9,819	30.2	−0.9	0.5
Nepal	5,580	4,683	3,900	27.3	−0.9	−1.8
Pakistan	2,749	2,755	2,361	3.2	−3.1	−1.5
Sri Lanka	2,094	2,288	1,940	30.0	−1.0	−1.6
Bangladesh	1,258	1,169	1,334	10.2	−1.8	1.3

a   Minor discrepancies in rates based on the 1980 and 1990 data are due to recent revisions by the Food and Agriculture Organization to 1990 forest area estimates.

Source: Food and Agriculture Organization, *Forest Resources Assessment 2000* and earlier issues.

although more difficult to quantify, has recently risen to the forefront of environmental concerns (Republic of the Philippines 1998; Myers 1988).[5]

Deforestation and the associated conversion of upland land to agriculture degrades the hydrological functions of watersheds. Annual fluctuations in stream flow are exaggerated in watersheds where water retention capacity has been lost along with forest cover and biomass, making such systems more prone to the effects of drought and flash flooding (Deutsch et al. 2001). Deforestation and the conversion of land to agriculture exacerbates soil erosion. Shifting cultivation (*kaingin*) systems traditionally practiced by indigenous upland communities were environmentally sustainable in the past, but increased population pressure in uplands has reduced fallow periods, and the more intensive farming practices of new immigrants to uplands are more land degrading (Table 12.3, and see David 1988; Cruz, Francisco, and Tapawan-Conway 1988). Soil run-off raises the total suspended sediment

Table 12.3 Philippine Erosion Rates by Land Use (tons/ha/year)

Land Use	Erosion Rate
Undisturbed forest	0.1– 0.4
Second-growth forests	1–7
Rice paddies	0.2–10
Plantations (depending on age and species)	2.4–75
Grasslands	1.5–3
Overgrazed lands	90–270
Kaingin areas (no conservation measures)	90–240
Annual cash crops (uplands)	30–180

Source: ENRAP (1994).

(TSS) loadings of rivers, and silt deposits in dams and canals diminish the capacity and efficiency of irrigation systems and hydroelectric power facilities. In areas where commercial agricultural production is pursued intensively, pesticide run-off is also a problem (Deutsch et al. 2001). Watershed degradation as a consequence of deforestation has emerged as perhaps the most important environmental problem in the Philippines, given that its impacts are felt not only in the uplands but also very widely in the lowlands.[6]

Agriculture and Croplands

Agriculture remains the single largest sector and employer in the Philippine economy (see Balisacan and Hill, Chapter 1, and David, Chapter 6). Well over half the population depends either directly or indirectly on income generated through agricultural production. Although investment in irrigation and episodes of technical progress have increased the productivity of some land and the yields of some crops, Philippine agriculture has experienced relatively low overall rates of productivity growth. Cereal and root crop yields and rates of fertilizer use are among the lowest in tropical Asia (Table 12.4).

Whereas expansion of agricultural land area was almost certainly an appropriate strategy in earlier decades when land was abundant, in the final quarter of the 20th century the conversion of forests and upper watershed areas to agriculture (and especially to production of annual crops) became a significant source of environmental problems. Recent evidence on long-term trends in the productivity of lowlands is equally disturbing. Staple grains (mainly rice and corn) account for most agricultural land use in developing countries. Intensive monoculture of any of these crops is known to be associated with a long-term decline in land productivity, a phenomenon sometimes disguised in recent years by technological progress (Cassman and Pingali 1995; Byerlee 1992). Moreover, the productivity of lowland cropland is

Table 12.4 Asian Fertilizer, Irrigation, and Crop Yields

Country	Crop Land, 1992–94 (ha)	Irrigated Land/Crop Land (%)		Fertilizer Use (kg/ha)		Average Crop Yield, 1994–96 (kg/ha)	
		1982–84	1992–94	1984	1994	Cereals	Roots & Tubers
Bangladesh	8,849	20	37	65	120	2,602	10,635
Cambodia	3,832	5	4	1	3	1,638	6,076
China	95,145	45	52	200	309	4,673	16,583
India	169,569	24	29	49	80	2,136	16,936
Indonesia	31,146	17	15	72	80	3,895	11,647
Lao PDR	900	16	16	0	2	2,561	9,005
Malaysia	7,536	6	5	105	159	3,052	9,701
Myanmar	10,067	10	11	19	12	3,015	8,995
Nepal	2,556	29	35	18	33	1,819	7,704
Pakistan	21,323	76	80	62	98	1,943	14,233
Philippines	9,320	16	17	29	64	2,283	6,880
Sri Lanka	1,889	29	29	102	113	2,568	8,903
Thailand	20,488	18	22	23	64	2,434	13,671
Vietnam	6,739	26	28	57	192	3,504	6,883

Source: WRI (2001).

directly dependent on the quality of irrigation services. Deforestation and the degradation of watersheds and hydrological systems have clearly diminished the quality of irrigation services in many parts of the country. Current estimates suggest that between 74 and 81 million tons of soil are lost annually, and that between 63% and 77% of the country's total land area is affected by erosion (FMB 1998). Recent studies show that sedimentation has reduced storage capacity at all of the Philippines' major reservoirs, and has measurably affected domestic water consumption, power generation, and irrigation. Furthermore, over the last 25 years, dry season irrigated area has fallen by 20–30% in several of the country's key irrigation systems (FMB 1998). With the upland frontier virtually closed and emerging signs of productivity growth slowdown—or even reversal—in the "best" lowland irrigated areas, the degradation of the agricultural land base is a source of serious concern. The decline of agricultural land productivity is of particular concern if the country is to continue to pursue a policy of self-sufficiency in cereals and/or if the dependence of the rural population on agricultural incomes remains high.

In cereal crops, production growth has been associated with increasingly intensive use of inorganic fertilizers and pesticides. Although "environment-friendly" techniques such as integrated pest management (IPM) are increasingly popular, chemical control of pests remains the norm. Rice cultivation accounts for a large proportion of total agricultural chemical demand in the Philippines: in 1987, 47% of all insecticides and 82% of all herbicides sold were for use in rice (Rola and Pingali 1993). Uncontrolled pesticide use and inappropriate application methods account for many deaths as well as eye, skin, respiratory, cardiovascular, and neurological illnesses among farmers and their families. Such health problems have been documented by Rola and Pingali (1993), who note that the mean pesticide-related health cost to Central Luzon rice farmers in their database far exceeded its net benefit in terms of improved crop yields. Offsite, inorganic fertilizers and agricultural chemicals further contribute to water pollution, loss of biological function in lakes, streams, and estuaries, and downstream health and abatement costs.

Coastal and Marine Ecosystems

The Philippines has 7,107 islands and a total coastline of 17,460 kilometers; its marine territorial waters cover nearly 2 million square kilometers of oceanic waters and 266,000 square kilometers of coastal waters. The coastal and marine ecosystems are clearly major components of the country's environmental resources, performing critical ecological functions (for example, breakwater and erosion control, nutrient recycling, beach sand deposition) and providing important resources such as mangroves, coral reefs, and seagrass beds that nurture a rich variety of fish and other aquatic life, while also providing facilities for recreation and tourism. These environmental resources are unique in many ways and, being major repositories of biodiversity, have international significance in terms of their importance in the global ecology. As with the Philippines' other environmental resources, these too have been significantly degraded. With more than half of the population residing in coastal areas, and most of the big cities located near the coast, these areas are subject to most of the environmental pressures emanating from population growth and the full range of human activities.[7]

The most tangible and direct economic impact of environmental degradation of marine ecosystems is reflected in the depletion of fish stocks (due primarily to overfishing, often using destructive methods such as bottom trawling, explosives, and harmful chemicals), the destruction of mangrove areas and corals, and the pollution of coastal waterways. But production levels have been maintained and even increased through greater fishing effort, further diminishing fish reproductive capacity.[8]

Mangrove swamps play a key role in the coastal ecosystems, forming the foundation of the coastal fisheries food chain and the breeding ground and nursery for many varieties of fish and crustaceans. They also provide timber, charcoal, and other types of wood for coastal households. Of approximately 450,000 hectares of mangroves that existed in 1918, more than two-thirds had been destroyed by 1987–88, so that only 149,000 hectares remained. With continuing conversion of mangrove land to fishponds and other forms of aquaculture, tourism development, and exploitation for wood and charcoal, mangrove area declined further to just 120,500 hectares by 1994, mostly located in isolated regions of Mindanao, Eastern Visayas, and Palawan. There is less quantitative information available on seagrass beds, whose importance in sustaining a viable marine ecosystem is considered to be underappreciated. However, they too are known to have experienced ongoing rapid degradation brought about by various forms of human activity such as coastal land development, mining, blast fishing, and run-off induced by deforestation and mining (Nickerson 1999).

The country's coral reefs not only provide a habitat for fish and other forms of marine life contributing some 10–15% of total fish production, but are also a major tourist attraction. Most (nearly 95%) of the reefs have suffered some degree of degradation, with nearly one-third being in poor condition. Human activities are not solely responsible for coral reef degradation, although they make a major contribution. Sediment deposit due to deforestation is considered a major source of coral damage, with other factors, such as direct extraction, mine tailings, pollution, destructive fishing methods, and coastal developments, also contributing to the problem.

Urban Systems

Rapid population growth and urbanization have contributed to urban population growth rates far in excess of the national average, and higher than in most major Asian economies, in recent decades (Table 12.5). Industrial growth has also been highly concentrated in and around urban areas (Pernia et al. 1983). Urban pollution thus consists of both industrial effluents (emissions into air and water, as well as solid waste) and post-consumer effluents (vehicle emissions, sewage, and solid waste). As a consequence, air and water pollution problems are most acute in urban regions, and especially in Metro Manila, which has the largest concentration of population and industry.

Air pollution in Metro Manila is quite serious.[9] In 1992, in locations in Metro Manila where 80% of the people live, annual average total suspended particulate (TSP) concentrations were found to be frequently more than five times higher than the World Health Organization Air Quality Guidelines (WHO AQG). Measures of PM_{10} (particulate matter of less than 10 microns) were also two to three times higher than WHO AQG, and long-term measured lead levels exceeded both national and WHO guidelines.[10] Although these emissions levels are not very high by the standards of Southeast Asian cities (for comparative TSP and sulfur dioxide (SO_2) levels, see Table 12.6), their impact on health is nevertheless large. Estimates for 1995 indicate that PM_{10} alone may have caused 1,300 deaths and respiratory diseases costing 4,594 million pesos (equivalent to 0.3% of 1995 GDP) per year. According to some official sources, TSP emissions are on an upward trend.[11] The primary source of air pollution has been increased fuel consumption, both by motor vehicles and for power generation. Bunker oil combustion in small to medium-sized industrial and commercial enterprises was the major contributor to high TSPs, followed by vehicle exhausts from diesel trucks, buses, and jeepneys; vehicle exhausts contributed a greater share to PM_{10}. Gasoline contributed most lead; the introduc-

Table 12.5 Population and Urbanization in Asian Developing Economies

Country	Total Population (million)		Urban Population (%)		Average Annual Growth Rate (%)	
	1970	2000	1970	2000	Total Population	Urban Population
Bangladesh	66.48	131.05	7.6	24.5	2.27	6.17
Cambodia	6.94	12.02	11.7	15.9	1.85	2.89
India	547.57	1015.92	19.8	28.4	2.07	3.26
Indonesia	117.54	210.42	17.1	40.9	1.96	4.82
Lao PDR	2.71	5.28	9.6	23.5	2.22	5.20
Malaysia	10.85	23.27	33.5	57.4	2.54	4.35
Myanmar	26.85	47.75	22.8	27.7	1.93	2.61
Nepal	11.88	23.04	3.9	11.9	2.20	5.87
Pakistan	60.61	138.08	24.9	37.0	2.75	4.07
Philippines	36.55	75.58	33.0	58.6	2.44	4.32
Sri Lanka	12.51	19.36	21.9	23.6	1.48	1.78
Thailand	35.75	60.73	13.3	21.6	1.81	3.39
Vietnam	42.73	78.52	18.3	24.0	2.04	2.98

Source: World Bank, *World Development Indicators 2001*, www.worldbank.org/WDI, accessed 19 June 2002.

tion of low lead gasoline in the early 1990s appears to have reduced ambient lead levels in air.

The development of the Philippine energy sector, the single largest source of industrial emissions, reveals an industry-level trend that merits discussion. Before 1977, hydropower constituted more than 80% of total national electricity-generating capacity. Major investments in oil-fired power generation during the late 1970s reduced this share to about one-third. In 1992–98, a period in which electricity-generating capacity increased by 76%, hydropower capacity increased by only 4%. The share of this source in total electricity generation diminished from one-third to less than one-fifth, with oil-fired plants contributing another two-fifths to one-half. The balance was made up primarily by increases in geothermal and coal-fired power generation; coal-fired generating capacity increased by a factor of five, and its share in total power generation rose from 6% to more than 17% (NSO 1988; NSCB, various years). Over three decades there has been a substantial swing in the composition of electricity generation, with fossil fuels now contributing nearly two-thirds of total supply. Urban populations are by far the worst-affected by air pollution from power-generating plants (Hordijk, Foell, and Shah 1995).

Table 12.6 Air Pollution in Selected Asian Cities, 1995[a]

	Total Suspended Particulates (micrograms/m^3)	Sulfur Dioxide (micrograms/m^3)
China		
Shanghai	246	53
Beijing	377	90
Tianjin	306	82
India		
Bombay	240	33
Calcutta	375	49
Delhi	415	24
Indonesia		
Jakarta	271	–
Malaysia		
Kuala Lumpur	85	24
Thailand		
Bangkok	223	11
Philippines		
Manila	200	33

a   WHO annual mean guidelines for air quality standards for total suspended particulates are 90 micrograms/m^3. For sulfur dioxide, the guideline is 50 micrograms/m^3.

Source: World Bank (1998), *World Development Indicators, 1998*.

Rapid growth of urban centers in the Philippines has not been matched by provision of infrastructure, including clean water, traffic control, and mass transit systems. Problems of urban decay are mounting. The country's large cities do not have adequate sewage and waste disposal facilities. Again, the problems are most acute in Metro Manila. Only 13% of households in Metro Manila are linked to a sewage system; 40% of solid household waste is dumped illegally, a part being burnt, adding to air pollution. Reporting these data, the 1998 Philippine National Development Plan summed up conditions in urban areas as follows:

The absence of far-reaching comprehensive land use and human settlement plans has resulted in the deterioration of the country's cities as human habitats beset with interrelated problems like inadequate mass transportation and road systems; pollution, and inadequate and inappropriate waste disposal systems; flooding; water shortage; deterioration and lack of basic social services; and proliferation of crime and other social evils (Republic of the Philippines 1998: 4–9).

Freshwater Systems

The freshwater ecosystem, comprising 384 major river systems and 54 lakes, and covering an area of about 569,600 hectares, faces severe problems through pollution and watershed degradation. Many of the major rivers and lakes, particularly those passing through or close to urban centers, are heavily polluted. The main river systems in Metro Manila are biologically dead,[12] and siltation and chemical residues are a serious problem for major lakes, including Laguna Lake, Lake Danao, Lake Lanao, and Lake Leonard.

Urban water pollution is caused primarily by the inappropriate disposal of household waste. Much is also contributed by industrial enterprises, the majority of which do not comply with existing water pollution standards. As mentioned earlier, inadequate sewage and other failings of waste disposal systems lead to much illegal dumping; a considerable proportion of daily household waste ends up in waterways. Elsewhere, with few river or lake system management systems in place and little effective control over effluent discharges or run-off, agricultural chemical residues and, in some locations, effluents from mining operations also contribute to the build-up of pollution.

The case of Laguna Lake illustrates many of these problems.[13] It is the second largest inland water body in southeast Asia, covering a surface area of 90,000 hectares. Its drainage region includes Metro Manila as well as many smaller cities, and 21 rivers and streams flow into it. In 1994, 1,481 factories were located in the catchment area, and the lake and its feeder rivers and streams were used as dumping grounds for industrial waste that contributed 30% of total lake pollution (agriculture and sewage respectively contributing 40% and 30%). Food processing, hog farms, slaughterhouses, beverage firms, and textile-makers were the largest sources of industrial pollutants. Although 60% of the local factories had nominally adopted pollution control measures, only 6% of these complied with legislated standards, demonstrating the utter inadequacy and ineffectiveness of traditional regulatory methods. Although new measures and new approaches adopted in the late 1990s have had some apparent success in abating effluent discharges (see section 5), the Laguna Lake ecosystem has already suffered long-term and possibly irreversible damage.

Costs of Environmental Degradation

The foregoing review, though brief and necessarily somewhat cursory, vividly illustrates the scope and severity of the challenges that human interventions now pose to the integrity of Philippine ecosystems. The postwar growth of the population and economy has been associated with decades of damage, both transitory and permanent, to these ecosystems and their component parts. In many cases the losses can-

not easily be aggregated or even calculated, let alone valued. Nonetheless it is undeniable that environmental degradation has imposed costs on the Philippine economy,
and it is conceivable that these have been quite large in relation to total income.

In the 1990s it became increasingly widespread practice for countries to augment
standard measures of national income from the system of national accounts with
"satellite accounts" that computed net additions to or reductions in estimated income
due to environmental damage and natural resource depletion. In developing countries, these exercises typically result in estimates of "adjusted" net domestic product
(ANDP) that are substantially below the measured net domestic product (WRI 1989;
TSC/WRI 1992). Our review of environmental developments in Philippine ecosystems suggests that past economic growth may have come at a significant cost in
terms of environmental resources lost and amenities foregone. However, in the
Philippines, a major natural resource accounting exercise completed in the early
1990s estimated that there was "no statistical difference" between ANDP and
unmodified GNP figures (ENRAP 1994).

This finding seems to us to reflect limitations inherent in the methodological
approach, rather than an accurate estimation of the real costs of long-term environmental degradation. First, the methodological procedure values waste disposal services as contributing positively to GDP. While common practice, this is the same kind
of procedure that gives rise to the statistical illusion that a plague among infants can
increase a country's GDP because it increases the value of health services.[14] Second,
it adds the value of unmarketed natural resource services (not hitherto counted in
GDP), which increases the value of adjusted GDP and thus largely offsets the negative effects of the depletion and degradation of the natural resource base. While this
procedure may produce a more statistically accurate one-off picture of national
income (which measures the flow of goods and services over the year), it also masks
the long-term costs of environmental depletion and degradation. After all, recognition of previously unrecorded benefits of environmental resources should not be
seen as somehow compensating for the long-term effects of the erosion of the very
resource base that provides those benefits. Third, and related to the first point, the
net costs detailed under specific items are rather small.[15] The authors attribute this
to the high costs of importing pollution abatement equipment and materials. This
assertion, if true, contradicts considerable evidence from other developing countries
indicating that control costs are often well below the cost of damages (see World
Bank 2000a).

Finally, a more fundamental point should be noted. Estimates of environmental
damage and abatement costs should recognize that the prevailing industry and price
structure and associated levels and intensities of environmental degradation reflect
the effects of distortionary policies. Ideally, environmental costs should be evaluated
at shadow prices rather than at distorted market prices. In principle, changes in policy may improve both efficiency and environmental outcomes. From this point of
view, it is useful to have direct estimates of the social cost of environmental damage, so that alternative policies for abatement can be assessed.

Although an adjusted measure of GDP of the kind now popular in satellite
accounts may be useful for some purposes, it disguises the full extent of environ-

mental degradation taking place in an economy and underestimates the environmental degradation costs that are being incurred. It follows that the goal of optimally utilizing natural resources for economic growth and poverty alleviation, while maintaining environmental quality, poses a formidable challenge for the future. The first task is to understand the causes and consequences of unsustainable rates of environmental degradation and natural resource depletion.

12.3 EXPLAINING THE CURRENT SITUATION AND PAST TRENDS

Economic Growth and the Environment

Nearly every form of economic activity is associated in some way with pollution or the depletion of natural resources. In production and trade, fossil fuels, timber, and minerals are consumed in the production and transport of goods and services, using processes that include waste emissions along with the desired output. Consumption by individuals and households also entails pollution in the form of solid waste, vehicle emissions, and sewage. While individuals or firms may correctly regard the environmental consequences of their actions as trivially small, in aggregate they contribute to a variety of social costs. These may include direct abatement or cleanup expenditures, loss of cultural and recreational amenities, and less direct and less easily quantified outcomes such as habitat and species extinction, biodiversity loss, and release of greenhouse gases. The fact that the full social cost of pollution and resource depletion is seldom internalized in private economic decisions lies at the core of virtually all economic analysis of environmental and resource problems.

In developing economies, the fundamental long-term source of economic change is growth. However, the pattern of economic growth is subject to many influences, among which a country's factor endowments, trade orientation, and economic policies and institutions (such as property rights regimes) figure very prominently. Moreover, it is inherent in growth that changes occur in the sectoral structure of production, the allocation of consumption expenditures, the emission–output ratio of industrial technologies, and the spatial distribution of population and economic activity in relation to the resource base. Poor countries that are growing relatively rapidly exhibit these changes in more pronounced fashion than do wealthier and more structurally stable industrialized economies.

A variety of factors broadly associated with economic growth influences interactions between the economy and the environment, and the long-run evolution of environmental quality. The effects of these factors can be grouped into three broad categories: scale, composition, and technique effects.[16]

The *scale effect* refers to the association between pollution or resource depletion and the size of an economy. More output, with no change in economic structure or in technology and consumption patterns, will lead to more pollution and more demands on the natural resource base. At first glance it may appear that the scale effect—arising as it does from economic growth and increasing per capita incomes—will be the dominant determinant of long-run environmental outcomes.

But such outcomes are also strongly influenced by initial conditions, and the aggregate rate of economic growth is not a complete predictor of trends in environmental quality or resource depletion.

The *composition effect* is the environmental impact of changes in the structure of production and consumption. Economies at early stages of economic development are endowed only with "raw" factors of production, such as labor and a variety of natural resources including land and soil, water, minerals, and animal and plant populations. Early economic growth entails the use of these resources to produce both final goods for direct consumption as well as investment goods: physical capital, knowledge, technology, and the legal and financial institutions that underpin exchange. Economic growth thus leads inevitably to changes in economic structure, both by altering the composition of national output, making possible the production of new goods, and—through growth in per capita incomes—by promoting changes in the composition of demand. An obvious example from developing economies is the decline of natural resource-intensive sectors such as mining, forestry, fishing, and agriculture as a percentage of GDP, and the corresponding rise of manufacturing and services. This structural shift has a scale effect (the decline of resource-based sectors is typically relative, not absolute, so there is more resource depletion overall), as well as a composition effect associated with the rise and decline of pollution-intensive industries.[17] Structural changes can also be triggered by exogenous changes in relative prices (such as those brought about by opening up to international trade), by changes in technology, endowments, or demand factors (tastes and preferences), and of course by policies.

In a typical example, a developing country in which the labor force is growing at 2% per year and net capital investment at 10% is one in which the most labor-intensive activities will decline over time, other things being equal, as capital growth raises labor productivity faster in sectors that are more capital-intensive (the "Rybczinski effect"). By extension, more capital-intensive industries that were initially below break-even point may come into existence as the capital–labor ratio increases; others may disappear and others still may both rise and fall (Leamer 1987; Deardoff 1999). It follows from these supply-side shifts that patterns of resource exploitation and pollution will also change with unequal factor growth rates, even if production technologies and relative output prices are fixed. Moreover, the changes may be non-monotonic, as the late 20th century decline of traditional manufacturing and rise of human capital-intensive industries in the United States and other wealthy nations made clear. A similar process can now be observed in the Philippines, where long-term investments in education, English-language training, and computer skills are beginning to pay off in the growth of human capital-intensive industries such as computer programming, software creation, and support systems for high-tech service-sector enterprises in the United States and elsewhere. Such processes are highly specific to the circumstances of an economy.

Changes in the composition of domestic consumer demand are captured in highly stylized form by Engel's law, which states that as per capita income expands, expenditure on food declines as a proportion of total consumer spending. This biased expansion of demand alters the relative weights of different goods in the consumption bundle over time as economic growth raises per capita income. In a closed economy, the Engel effect limits the growth rates of demand for food and other staples. Buoyant growth of spending out of new income on manufactures, personal services, education, and recreation are the primary sources of changes in relative commodity prices that in turn produce shifts in the structure of production. Engel effects and other endogenous relative price changes are also readily observed in an open economy, however, through changes in domestic demand for *non-tradables*—personal services, housing, education, health, recreational services, and goods that, by virtue of transport costs or other impediments, cannot be exchanged with other countries (Anderson and Warr 1987). Rising per capita incomes may alter emissions through changes in the composition of demand, as a result, for example, of preference for private automobiles over public transport.

Finally, emissions and resource depletion associated with any given output level depend also on techniques of production and consumption. Relative price changes may stimulate shifts in the input mix; new technologies developed domestically or acquired from abroad may alter the ratio of emissions or raw material demand to output. The *technique effect* reflects these supply-side changes and their underlying causes, including changes in consumer preferences for environmental quality, and in government policies limiting permissible emissions or intensities. The technique effect is normally expected to reduce environmental damage. There may be exceptions, however, such as "smokestack chasing" competition in which subnational or national governments relax environmental standards in order to attract investment.

In practice, the influence of composition and technique effects on changes in emissions over time, and their relationship to the scale effect, are likely to depend very much on country-specific circumstances. There is, however, some reason to believe that the three effects make different relative and even absolute contributions to total emissions over the range of development experience. This line of thinking has been formalized in a body of literature on the so-called "environmental Kuznets curve" (Grossman and Krueger 1993). It is conjectured that, for some types of pollutants at least, scale and composition effects tending to increase emissions intensities are the dominant environmental features of growth in poor countries. With sustained per capita income growth, the composition effect may eventually reverse itself as the relative importance of manufacturing diminishes and the structure of manufacturing output changes; technique effects driven by investments in new technologies and by changing preferences may then cause pollution production *at the margin* to decline. The net effect, it is hypothesized, is an inverse-U-shaped relationship between emissions and per capita income. As with the original Kuznets inverse-U hypothesis concerning the relationship between growth and income distribution, however, empirical tests of the environmental inverse-U hypothesis are largely inconclusive (Stern, Common, and Barbier 1996). Tests based on time-series data for single countries appear to provide some support for the hypothesis with respect to certain types of emissions (Grossman and Krueger 1995; Vincent, Rozali, and Associates 1997), but these are contradicted by numerous other studies, especially where the depletion of forests and other natural resources is concerned (Cropper and Griffiths 1994; Selden and Song 1994; Hettige, Mani, and Wheeler 1997;

World Bank 2000a). What most tests do reveal is that one of the most important factors governing the production, nature, and sectoral sources of pollution in developing economies is their exposure to international trade.

In open developing countries, trade policy (until very recently a major tool of industrialization policy) is unusual among microeconomic interventions in that its effects are both profound and pervasive in the economy, affecting both aggregate growth and the structure of production and demand. Thus it may be hypothesized that trade and trade policies (or their reform) have major effects on environmental quality and natural resource depletion. There are a number of normative analytical explorations of this question (Copeland 1994; Corden 1997; Ulph 1999), all of which focus on the general equilibrium welfare effects of trade policies in the presence of environmental externalities. By extrapolation, these results can also be used to identify differential effects on the welfare of groups within the economy, defined by their ownership of factors and/or their patterns of consumption. Obviously, it would be desirable to deploy an analytical model in which aggregate welfare, environmental outcomes, and the distributional effects of policy reforms are simultaneously determined. More generally still, which policy instruments are deployed and who bears the burden of pollution are determined in part by property rights (along with other political economy factors and the usual fiscal policy and efficiency considerations). Accordingly, in real world policy-making, an institutional failure such as open access to natural resources or free disposal of emissions into air and water could in principle acquire great economic significance.

But a general point does come through in these normative models: trade policy is not a substitute for environmental policy. Where environmental externalities exist, they should be addressed at the source by specific environmental policies. In particular, trade restrictions are not efficient instruments to address environmental problems. As Corden (1997) points out, in the presence of environmental externalities, the optimal policy for a "small country" is not laissez faire, but free trade *together with* targeted policies that address environmental externalities.

In the remainder of this section we explore the Philippine experience of development, trade policy reform, and environmental degradation, with emphasis on industrial emissions. In the subsequent section we make use of an applied general equilibrium model to provide some numerical results on the broader environmental implications of economic growth and policy reforms.

Industrialization and Industrial Emissions

At the aggregate level, industrial emissions growth in the Philippines displays a pattern shared with other developing countries. A first glance at data relating emissions to the size of economies (Brandon and Ramankutty 1992) or to increases in manufacturing output (Figure 12.1) suggests that the scale effect is the dominant manifestation of the environmental effects of economic growth. Toxic intensity (emissions per dollar of manufacturing output, discussed in more detail below) is positively related to growth in manufacturing output and GDP, and periods of rapid growth are associated with rapid increases in total emissions as well as in emissions

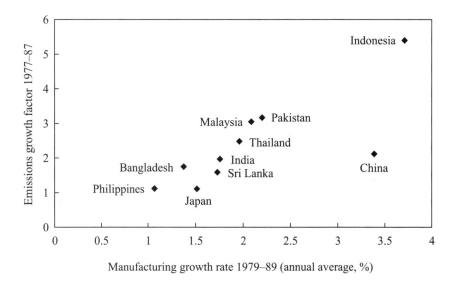

Manufacturing growth rate 1979–89 (annual average, %)

Figure 12.1 Growth of Manufacturing Output and Emissions in Asian Less Developed Countries

Source: Brandon and Ramankutty (1992); World Bank, *World Development Indicators 2001*, www.worldbank.org/WDI, accessed 19 June 2002.

per unit of income produced. Conversely, recessions or growth slowdowns, such as occurred in the 1980s in the Philippines as in most of Southeast Asia, are associated with slower increases, or even declines, in emissions output.

Figure 12.1, which plots industrial emissions growth against manufacturing sector growth in the Philippines and other developing Asian countries, provides a clear indication of the strength of the scale effect. In general, increases in manufacturing output are accompanied by increases in industrial emissions, and the figure suggests that the ratio of these two broad indicators is similar across economies.

Although these aggregate data are suggestive of a strong relationship between economic growth (or industrialization) and emissions growth, it should nevertheless be remembered that they reflect the joint impacts of scale, composition, and technique effects. Changes in the composition of output, between manufacturing and other sectors as well as within the manufacturing sector, may account for much of the apparently exponential growth of emissions in developing economies, as well as for much of the observed decline in emissions growth rates in wealthy countries (Lucas, Wheeler, and Hettige 1992). As seen in Figure 12.1, for example, the period from the late 1970s to the late 1980s saw a contraction of the Philippine manufacturing sector; nevertheless, aggregate industrial emissions still grew slightly. Variation in the relationship of emissions growth to manufacturing output growth thus has several sources, of which one is likely to be differences in the rate of change in the composition of industrial activity.

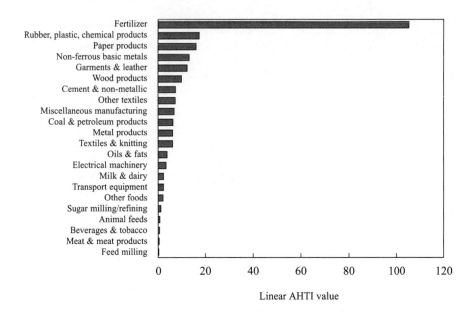

Figure 12.2 Acute Human Toxicity Indices for Manufacturing Industries
Source: Hettige et al. (1995).

In the Philippines, the composition of manufacturing sector activity has altered over time, though not monotonically (see Hill, Chapter 7). As in many newly industrializing countries, there has been a compositional shift over time from heavy industries and industries engaged in basic processing (basic metals, textiles, paper, cement, fertilizer), which are highly emissions-intensive, toward assembly and light manufacturing (vehicles, electronics, garments), which are substantially cleaner. An indication of this can be gleaned from Figure 12.2, which shows data on a widely used measure of industrial emissions, the acute human toxicity index (AHTI), for manufacturing industries.[18] What cannot be discovered from the data on the composition of production, however, is the extent to which changes in the composition of Philippine industrial production have occurred as the result of secular trends as opposed to policies—an analytical question to which we shall return shortly.

The Spatial Dimension

The breakdown of environmental changes by scale, composition, and technique effects can usefully be taken several steps further. One way to do so is to recognize geography. The Philippines, as noted above, is geographically and climatically diverse, and poverty, growth, and development are strongly spatially differentiated, perhaps to a greater degree than in countries with more uniform geographic conditions. As an example, the ratio of urban to rural populations, and especially the share of Metro Manila (the primate city) in total population, has increased greatly in the postwar era, as has the percentage of the population in the forest/upland ecosystem. The effects of various types of environmental degradation and resource degradation similarly have differential spatial impacts. In general, industrial emissions are concentrated in and around urban agglomerations, and problems of post-consumer waste such as sewage, solid waste, and vehicle emissions are more severe, even when adjusted for population, in urban ecosystems than elsewhere. Similarly, deforestation and the associated degradation of soils and watersheds in upland ecosystems affect rural (and within rural, upland) populations most directly. Assessing and aggregating such spatially distinct environmental problems is a major challenge for those who would evaluate the aggregate environmental benefits and costs of a given development strategy. We return to this point later, when we consider some possible trade-offs between environmental conservation, poverty alleviation, and the reduction of disparities in the real incomes of households.

Development Strategy and the Environment

Another useful way in which to extend the scale, composition, and technique effect analysis is to separate, where possible, the effects of economic policies from secular growth and economic change. This is especially important in a developing country like the Philippines, where (as is widely recognized) development strategies and the institutions that support them have had very significant impacts on the rate and nature of the growth and development of the economy. The country's long adherence to import-substituting industrialization (ISI) policies, its series of highly centralized and heavily corrupt administrations, and the boom–bust economic growth pattern that emerged partly as a result of both, have had both direct and indirect effects on resource use patterns and the growth of emissions. These effects are clearly seen in the pattern of industrial growth that took place behind protective trade barriers (Baldwin 1975; Bautista, Power, and Associates 1979). Moreover, periodic economic crises and related political upheavals that eroded investor confidence and blurred rate of return "signals" were partly responsible for the failure of the manufacturing sector to increase its share of GDP and total employment, and of the economy to diversify both sectorally and regionally until well into the 1990s.

Another indirect consequence of this pattern of growth is the spatial and sectoral distribution of increments to the Philippine population, as noted above. Philippine urbanization, and especially the growth of Manila relative to other urban centers, is partly a consequence of secular economic growth and partly a function of the ISI strategy, since the latter tended to diminish profitability and dampen employment growth in agriculture and traditional rural-based industries. With little substantive investment in urban infrastructure, rapid growth of urban populations both magnified and intensified the problems of water and air pollution and solid waste disposal. A low and uneven economic growth rate, as well as emphasis within ISI policies on capital-intensive industries, meanwhile, generated persistently high unemployment and underemployment rates. With few new opportunities in traditional, lowland-based agriculture and rural industry, internal migration and a high rate of natural increase created a boom in upland populations, a point given empirical support in Cruz and Francisco (1993). Land colonization, deforestation, and agricultural intensification on sloping and marginally arable lands ensued.[19] In this section we present a framework for considering such indirect effects of the ISI industrialization strategy and its attendant political economy features.

Inappropriate land use and associated migration patterns are not simply the inevitable consequences of rapid population growth and resulting pressure on the land frontier. They are to a considerable extent attributable to the effects of past policy decisions. Arguably some deforestation was inevitable, and even optimal from a national viewpoint, given that forests represented a valuable natural resource that could be exploited to generate much needed capital for growth and provide agricultural land for a rapidly growing and predominantly rural population. Past Philippine policies promoted deforestation both directly and indirectly. Current forestry policy promotes conservation, but many indirect pro-deforestation policy influences remain.

Policies that directly impacted on the forestry sector can be categorized into three groups. First, there were government programs that encouraged the conversion of forests to agricultural land uses, including state-sponsored settlement schemes (as was the case until relatively recently in parts of Palawan and Mindanao).[20] Second, the state did not always enforce regulations against conversion of forests to agricultural lands. This was the case not only with respect to the activities of large commercial interests, but also of small farmers, often new immigrants to uplands. Third, there was both legal and illegal logging, with logging concessions being disbursed as part of patronage politics to politically powerful groups, and a considerable proportion of "illegal" logging being carried out with the sanction and often the complicity of government officials at all levels (Cavanagh and Broad 1993). In practice legal and illegal logging facilitate land conversion to agriculture and hence play a critical role in this process, even though, in principle, selective logging need not cause deforestation.

Government programs that encouraged large-scale conversion of forests to agriculture were not unique to the Philippines; indeed they were ubiquitous throughout developing Asia and globally. With hindsight, the basic thrust of those programs can be criticized on both economic and environmental grounds, but it cannot be denied that they reflected mainstream development policy thinking of the time. Their environmental costs were in general poorly understood, and in any case were assumed to be much lower than the expected benefits. In both economic and political terms forest conversion was an attractive policy: it eased population pressure in the more densely populated regions, increased agricultural output and exports, and ameliorated the political pressures for land reform that fueled leftwing insurgencies. But when it came to logging—the activity central to the rapid deforestation process—government activities in the Philippines were driven much more directly by the priorities and interests of privileged elites who controlled the state rather than by any concerns about national development. Discussing the role of the state in the logging-induced deforestation process, Kummer (1992: 154–5) concludes that population growth was not the primary cause of deforestation in recent time; in reality, "the

Philippine government had a large control over this process and turned this control over to a small group of people. The process did not just happen; rather it served the financial interests of the wealthy and well connected." As in many other areas of Philippine economic life, national interests were made subservient to the narrow private interests of the politically powerful; political power and the control of the state became a tool for the rapacious exploitation of national resources by privileged groups. Not only did the country lose economic rents from timber extraction, logging also served as a conduit for capital outflows. With judicious undervaluation of export receipts, it served as a mechanism for circumventing prevailing exchange controls in the context of overvalued exchange rates, so that large funds could be repatriated overseas.

But these were not the only government policies and activities that impacted on deforestation and land degradation in the Philippines. Arguably at least as important were the indirect effects of macroeconomic and ISI-type trade policies, as well as sectoral policies targeting food crop agriculture such as the Green Revolution strategy in rice and, from the 1970s, high rates of protection for corn (Coxhead 2000). These impacts were transmitted through factor and product market linkages to the uplands, altering incentives for different forms of land use and interregional labor migration (Coxhead, Rola, and Kim 2001; Coxhead, Shively, and Shuai 2002). As their effects are not all immediately obvious, we identify them by considering a simple analytical model that captures some of the key stylized facts of the Philippine economy and the environmental issues of interest, the deforestation rate, and patterns of upland land use.[21] This model serves to elucidate some of the main economic forces that drive changes in production, consumption, and resource use in response to policy and other exogenous influences. In the next section we go on to demonstrate how these factors operate in a more richly specified applied general equilibrium model of the Philippine economy, and assess the quantitative importance of these forces in particular sets of circumstances.

Consider an economy that has two "regions," upland and lowland; these are distinguished by land endowments of different quality (productivity). This captures in stylized form the key distinction between irrigated (lowland) and rainfed (upland) agricultural systems. Two goods are produced in each region. The lowland produces "manufactures" and an agricultural crop, "food." The upland also produces "food," along with a non-food crop, "tree crops." Food is thus produced in two spatially separate sectors, with distinct technologies based on land quality differences. Manufactures and tree crops are traded with the rest of the world at given world prices, with tariffs added on imports. The use of quantitative restrictions to limit food imports means that domestic food prices are subject to fluctuations in domestic demand and supply. Philippine cereal imports have been subject to such restrictions, via a state trading monopoly, throughout the postwar era. Empirical studies confirm that domestic supply and demand influence cereal prices (Barker and Herdt 1985; David and Huang 1996). To reflect this, we assume that food, by contrast with the other goods, is non-traded.[22] Total food supply from lowlands and uplands is equal to total domestic demand, and its price adjusts relative to the prices of the traded goods to ensure that this market-clearing condition is satisfied.[23] The lowland sectors each use labor and "capital."[24] The two upland sectors both use labor and land. Labor is assumed to be freely mobile among sectors and regions; labor "migrates" across regions in response to changes in real wages. Labor supply grows at an exogenous rate, and wages adjust to clear the labor market. Land is region-specific; in uplands, land is mobile between the food and tree crops. Agricultural land in uplands can be created by clearing forest, an activity which requires labor inputs only; we assume open access to forest land, so there is no non-economic restraint on the amount of land that can be converted in this way.[25] The flow of services provided by standing forest is a public good; by assumption there is no market for these services, which are lost when forest is cleared to make land. In lowlands, the supply of land is fixed. Tree crops are normally much less soil-erosive (land degrading) than annual crops (Table 12.3), so a land use switch between the two has environmental implications. In addition, the negative off-site impacts of erosion are considered to cause a (factor-specific) technical *regress* in lowland sectors, by reducing the productivity of irrigated land and hydropower generating facilities through siltation, diminished overall flow and greater seasonal variation, and turbidity.

The model as specified immediately implies that there is more deforestation than is socially optimal. Upland producers devote labor to the clearing of forest to create upland agricultural land until the marginal value product of land is just equal to the marginal cost of labor used to clear it, but they do not take into account the social gain from the existence of a standing forest. Hence the extent of forest conversion to agriculture that is optimal for upland producers will be too high from the point of view of society. It also follows that, in general, labor force growth will increase deforestation by lowering the economy-wide wage rate, thereby reducing the cost of land conversion to both types of agriculture.

The impact of specific economic policies and exogenous factors ("shocks") on both environmental and other economic variables of interest depends on other structural features of the economy, including, for example, the relative factor intensities of the goods, whether manufacturing is an exportable or an importable, and the price and income elasticities of the non-traded food. Under ISI policy regimes, the manufacturing sector tends to be import competing and capital-intensive, while under export-oriented industrialization (EOI) policies, it tends to be exportable and labor-intensive. Upland food crops are assumed to be more labor-intensive than tree crops.

Let us consider three cases of interest that can shed light on Philippine developments. These are the effects of ISI and EOI policies on deforestation and soil erosion; the consequences of the Green Revolution in rice (primarily confined to lowlands); and the promotion of domestic self-sufficiency in corn through trade protection, subsidies on production, and the promotion of technological innovations.

ISI and EOI Policies

ISI policies protected import-competing, capital-intensive domestic industries, and also diverted investment funds through other means. Consider what happens if tariffs are increased in this model. The direct impact is to increase the relative price (and profitability) of the capital-intensive, import-competing manufacturing sector. This then leads to several product and factor market changes. Because manufacturing is capital-intensive, higher profitability in this sector tends to reduce the real wage (by the well-known Stolper–Samuelson effect), as it draws capital away from lowland food. Lower wages mean lower labor costs in food crop sectors, but this is not sufficient to offset the effect of higher capital costs in lowland food; hence it contracts at the prevailing price. However, if food demand remains more or less constant,[26] reduced lowland supply will put upward pressure on food prices, and the relative profitability of the more labor-intensive upland food will increase relative to tree crops. Further, lower wages will make land conversion to agriculture cheaper. Since the price of tree crops is exogenously determined in world markets, profitability in the tree crop sector will diminish because both the protection of manufactures and the consequent rise in food prices reduce its relative price in the domestic market. Hence it will tend to contract. The overall effect will be to promote movement of labor to uplands, to increase deforestation, and to increase soil erosion as more erosive food crops expand in upland areas at the expense of tree crops. Thus, in addition to having negative effects on efficiency and the real wage, ISI policies exacerbate both deforestation and soil erosion. These in turn reduce productivity in lowland ecosystems, through off-site effects. The exact opposite happens in the case of open, EOI policies, as can be illustrated by considering the case of import tariff reduction in a model variant with a labor-intensive, exported manufacturing good and a food crop sector that is a (protected) net importer.

Green Revolution (Productivity Improvement) in Lowland Food

The Green Revolution in rice, associated with modern technology and large irrigation and other supplementary investments, had a major impact on rice productivity in the Philippines, although this was primarily confined to lowland irrigated regions (David and Otsuka 1994). It was responsible for a significant decline in the real rice price during a period of rising demand (David and Huang 1996). Consider the impact of a Green Revolution-type productivity improvement in the context of our stylized model of an ISI economy.[27]

A productivity improvement in lowland rice pulls both capital and labor to that sector, increases lowland food supply and depresses food prices, and increases the economy-wide wage rate. Higher wages tend to cause the import-competing sector as well as both upland sectors to contract; the cost of land conversion rises and the rate of deforestation falls. The effect on upland food agriculture, such as corn, is more pronounced, as it is labor-intensive and suffers more than tree crops from an increase in wage costs.[28] Hence, there is a land use switch in uplands toward less erosive tree crops. Thus, even though the productivity impact of the Green Revolution is confined mainly to lowlands, it has an indirect environmentally beneficial effect on upland deforestation and soil erosion.[29] The combination of higher wages and lower food prices reduces incentives to open up forests and engage in low-productivity, erosive upland food crop agriculture.

Corn Policies

Corn has been increasingly protected in the Philippines, with effective protection rates rising from near zero in the late 1960s to as high as 70% in the early 1990s (Pagulayan 1998). Corn is grown very widely in uplands—with upland rice, it accounted for about 45% of cultivated land on slopes of above 18% in the late 1980s—and land area devoted to it has expanded significantly, often at the expense of forests, in the regions where deforestation continues. As mentioned earlier, Philippine agricultural policies have in essence converted corn into a non-traded good. Corn cultivation on sloping lands, particularly steeply sloping lands, is highly erosive (Table 12.3). We can evaluate the impact of protection for corn using a variant of the model outlined earlier, by considering corn and rice to be substitutes in consumption, with corn cultivated as the upland food crop.

Higher protection for corn raises its relative price and profitability, and switches land use in uplands away from tree crops. To the extent that expansion of corn cultivation lowers food prices, it also tends to cause the lowland food sector to contract. Moreover, higher profitability in corn increases pressure for the conversion of forests into land for corn cultivation.[30] Thus it tends to increase the labor pull toward uplands, increase deforestation, and aggravate soil erosion. The policy of high protection for corn has clear negative environmental outcomes.

After a long period of near-stagnation in productivity, corn has been experiencing significant yield increases in recent years, partly as a result of public sector investments in adaptive research and extension (Philippine Department of Agriculture 1990). What is the likely impact of such change? Productivity improvement generates two opposing forces impacting on corn profitability. First, at prevailing prices, it increases profitability. But, because trade restrictions weaken the link between domestic and world corn markets, the price of corn depends on domestic supply and demand. Productivity gains that increase supply have a depressing effect on price, and their effects are greater the lower is the demand elasticity for corn.[31] Policy experiments with an applied general equilibrium model of the Philippine economy have shown that, because corn demand is very inelastic, productivity improvements in corn can dampen prices to the point where land area under corn may actually go down, reducing land degradation (Coxhead and Shively 1998). But this result holds only when the trade regime completely insulates the sector from imports; under a more open policy regime, domestic prices will be more influenced by world prices, and domestic supply increases will not have such a large dampening effect. In such circumstances, productivity increases will increase land area under corn, and increase deforestation and erosion. In the Philippines, public sector interventions in defense of the producer prices of corn and rice had analogous, though much more limited, dampening effects during periods of rapid supply growth in relation to demand (Coxhead 2000).

Of course, in reality many of these effects are modified by market rigidities, a much more diversified economic structure, and other real-world complexities. Some of these are explicitly incorporated in the more detailed applied general equilibrium model discussed in the next section. Nevertheless, the overall picture and insights that emerge from this simple model are useful for understanding the effects of the broad policy regime and some of the important policies pursued in the food agriculture area. The ISI policy regime not only slowed aggregate economic growth but also had a harmful environmental impact—directly, by promoting the growth of generally emissions-intensive, capital-intensive industries, and indirectly, by promoting changes that accelerated resource depletion and environmental degradation in forest/upland ecosystems. The Green Revolution in rice (the negative effects of overuse of harmful pesticides and other chemicals notwithstanding) also reduced pressures for deforestation and upland land degradation. Protectionist policies in corn, on the other hand, had an offsetting negative effect to that of the Green Revolution in lowland rice.

What is the impact of trade liberalization on commercial logging activities? Because logs are exportables, trade liberalization will tend to increase their relative prices and the profitability of their production. Higher log prices imply higher stumpage values. In the absence of well-specified and enforced property rights (such as in an open access regime), the increase in stumpage values will accelerate deforestation. But with secure long-term property rights, more liberal trade policies will have the same impact on commercial forests as on other export sectors. Protectionist trade policies, the absence of appropriate environmental policies, and the direct complicity of government officials in deforestation for private gain have all combined to give the Philippines its present problems of deforestation and land degradation. They have also contributed to the emergence of Metro Manila as an overcrowded primate city. The pattern of migration to crowded cities and forested uplands that has characterized the Philippines in recent decades may not solely be due to the impact of policy regimes, but it has certainly played an important role.[32]

12.4 POLICY REFORMS, ENVIRONMENT, AND ECONOMIC WELFARE

In the 1990s, the Philippine government took some major legislative steps to address environmental problems. The Philippine Council for Sustainable Development, a multi-agency task force established in the wake of the 1992 Rio Conference, prepared *Philippine Agenda 21*, a document containing a comprehensive assessment of environmental problems and many proposals for regulatory and legislative reforms to address them.[33] Bills were passed to address property rights in forests and uplands, and others were formulated to protect forests, fisheries, and other natural resources. Conversion of mangrove lands was banned. Low-leaded and unleaded gasoline were introduced in 1993 and 1994 respectively, and it was planned that leaded gasoline would be completely phased out by 2001. The 1999 Clean Air Act laid out, for the first time in legislative form, guidelines for the control and reduction of emissions into air.

What are the likely environmental impacts of these policy and legislative initiatives? What economic trade-offs might be involved? The success or otherwise of explicitly environment-oriented measures in reducing deforestation and other forms of environmental degradation can be assessed only in the long run. In some cases, increased environmental protection may come at some cost in terms of foregone output; on the other hand, implementation may reduce abatement expenditures, thus delivering a benefit in the form of resources released for use in other activities.

At the same time, other legislative and policy changes are taking place which, although they do not specifically target environmental variables, can nevertheless be expected to have potentially large environmental effects. During the 1990s the Philippines took significant steps in the area of trade policy reform, the liberalization of foreign investment regulations, and the relaxation of some food and agricultural sector policies, including the longstanding quantitative restrictions on rice and corn importation. Significant reforms in each of these prominent areas of the economy can be expected to impact not only on the sectors or regions most directly affected, but also, through the kinds of general equilibrium linkages explored in section 3, on many other sectors and regions as well. Given the strength of factor and product market linkages, it may even be that the environmental implications of major economic reforms are more significant than those of any single environmental protection measure. There is, accordingly, a risk that the effects of environmental protection policy could be diminished or even negated by composition and technique effects induced by economic policy reforms.

These questions are exceptionally difficult to answer in a rigorous manner. Good-quality data are scarce; moreover, the answers in some cases must be traced through economic relationships that are quite indirect. Given these difficulties, one strategy is to simulate the effects of possible past or future changes on variables that are likely to provide indicators of environmental change, in a model that captures the main intersectoral and macroeconomic linkages through which the indirect effects of changes are transmitted.[34] In the remainder of this section we present the results of simulations using such a model, the APEX computable general equilibrium model of the Philippine economy (Clarete and Warr 1992). The APEX model, which originated in a joint Australian–Philippine research project, does not contain explicit environmental accounting; however, the results of policy simulations can readily be interpreted in terms of broad environmental outcomes by observing industry-level changes in output, input use, and prices, as explained below.[35] This enables intersectoral effects of the kind outlined in the previous discussion to be explicitly accounted for and their quantitative effects gauged—at least in terms of signs and orders of magnitude. Another advantage is that the model provides the means to calculate changes in important macroeconomic aggregates—such as trade and fiscal deficits, measures of economic welfare, and indicators of distributional change—simultaneously with information on production, input use, consumer demand, trade, and price formation. The general equilibrium structure thus permits evaluation of trade-offs, where they arise, between economic and environmental outcomes for a given set of policy changes.

As noted, APEX contains no explicit environmental information. However, for a given policy reform simulation, it does provide detailed predictions of input and output changes at the industry level. (The model contains 38 manufacturing and service sectors, and 12 agricultural sectors divided into three geographic regions.) These results can be used in conjunction with external information on the sectoral distribution of emissions, estimates of soil erosion rates under different crops, and so on, to calculate the likely effects of a given change on industrial pollution, deforestation, and agricultural expansion, as well as other outcomes of interest.[36]

To illustrate the possible environmental effects of a broad-based policy reform, we use the APEX model to examine the predicted outcomes of an across-the-board tariff reduction. As mentioned earlier, ISI has been a very prominent feature of Philippine development policy, and its effects have lingered in trade policy settings even until very recently. By asking what would happen if protection policies were relaxed, we obtain *ex post* insights into the effects of past protection policies on economic activity, and by extrapolation with additional information, on environmental phenomena such as industrial emissions.[37] Recognizing that trade policy reform is highly complex and that any such reform involves altering a range of different measures in different ways, we do not attempt to replicate any specific set of reforms. Rather, we simulate a uniform proportional tariff reduction of 25%. Tables 12.7a and 12.7b show, for the 50 APEX sectors, some basic information from the APEX database on sectoral size and labor intensity, as well as approximate protection levels. Table 12.7b also shows the AHTI emissions intensity data and rankings for manufacturing industries.

The trade reform simulation embodies numerous assumptions about the nature of the Philippine economy. External trade and the government budget are assumed to be in balance initially, and the economy must adjust following a "shock" (such as the exogenous revision of tariff rates) to restore these balances. Product differentiation means that the prices of imported tradables and similar products domestically produced do not necessarily move together. Supplies of some primary factors (land, skilled labor, and capital) are assumed to be fixed; the markets for these inputs clear through factor price adjustments. We assume, however, that there is initial slack in the market for unskilled labor, particularly in the lowest-income groups, so aggregate employment can rise or fall as a result of a shock, with no change in the nominal wage. The remaining details of the macroeconomic closure are chosen to ensure that the burden of adjustment to a shock falls entirely on households. The model thus yields a measure of welfare change based on increases or declines in real household consumption expenditure.

Sectoral results of the trade policy reform experiment are shown in Table 12.8. (More details of these simulations, including changes in macroeconomic variables and a complete description of APEX and solution procedures, are available from the authors upon request.) It can be seen from Table 12.8 that, broadly speaking, trade liberalization reduces activity in manufacturing sectors, which are mainly import competing and receive the highest initial protection, and increases it in food processing and primary industries, including forestry and mining. Aggregate agricultural output changes little, although output does exhibit considerable regional and sectoral variation, as discussed below. Within manufacturing, where there is a general correspondence between capital intensity, protection rates, and emissions intensity, some heavily emissions-intensive sectors contract. Declines in the prices of competing imports reduce domestic producer prices, although by less, since domestic and imported goods are imperfect substitutes. Conversely, many labor-intensive,

Table 12.7a Agricultural, Natural Resource and Service Sectors (%)[a]

Sector	GDP Share (%)	Labor Cost Share (%)	Implicit Tariff, 1994 (%)
Agriculture	0.14		
Irrigated rice	0.24	0.54	50.0
Rainfed rice	0.02	0.54	50.0
Corn	0.12	0.56	115.0
Coconut	0.08	0.37	0.0
Sugar	0.05	0.57	n.a.
Fruit	0.11	0.51	40.0
Vegetables	0.06	0.54	21.7
Rootcrops	0.02	0.55	n.a.
Other commercial crops	0.10	0.56	4.3
Hogs	0.16	0.38	n.a.
Chicken & poultry	0.03	0.49	n.a.
Other livestock	0.00	0.58	11.0
Natural resources	0.08		
Marine fisheries	0.47	0.47	19.1
Inland fisheries	0.15	0.38	–
Forestry	0.16	0.28	11.8
Crude oil & natural gas	0.03	0.22	29.2
Other mining	0.19	0.44	9.1
Services	0.57		
Agricultural services	0.07	0.46	–
Construction	0.08	0.59	–
Electricity, gas, & water	0.04	0.22	–
Transport & communications	0.08	0.48	–
Transport/storage/wholesale	0.37	0.36	–
Banks	0.02	0.65	–
Insurance	0.09	0.17	–
Government	0.14	0.98	–
Other	0.11	0.56	–

n.a. = not available; – = not applicable.
a   Value added shares shown for each sector are within-group shares. Value added and labor shares are calculated from 1989 data in the APEX database.

Table 12.7b Agricultural Processing and Manufacturing[a]

Sector	GDP Share (%)	Labor Cost Share (%)	Implicit Tariff, 1994 (%)	AHTI Score	AHTI Rank
Agricultural processing	0.07				
Rice & corn milling	0.35	0.47	51.58	n.a.	
Sugar milling/refining	0.07	0.31	59.21	1.121	18
Milk & dairy	0.06	0.28	29.23	2.251	15
Oils & fats	0.22	0.39	16.12	3.721	13
Meat & meat products	0.21	0.36	82.21	0.431	21
Feed milling	0.02	0.37	26.49	0.281	22
Animal feeds	0.05	0.44	72.69	0.701	19
Other foods	0.03	0.40	29.52	2.021	17
Manufacturing	0.15				
Beverages and tobacco	0.07	0.37	41.99	0.5921 0.272*	20
Textiles & knitting	0.08	0.49	14.50	6.071 1.312*	12
Other textiles	0.02	0.47	19.69	7.21 6.042*	8
Garments & leather	0.16	0.65	24.69	12.351 12.762*	5
Wood products	0.05	0.53	13.31	9.91 0.642*	6
Paper products	0.05	0.46	19.97	16.111 4.232*	3
Fertilizer	0.01	0.38	4.07	105.31	1
Rubber, plastic, chemical products	0.11	0.42	28.59	17.41 15.692*	2
Coal & petroleum products	0.04	0.12	28.88	6.231 1.442*	10
Non-ferrous basic metals	0.09	0.19	6.19	13.231	4
Cement & non-metallic	0.10	0.28	16.51	7.31 4.172*	7
Semiconductors	0.06	0.55	7.70	n.a.	
Metal products	0.07	0.49	17.24	6.081 3.382*	11
Electrical machinery	0.05	0.47	18.78	3.291 1.252*	14
Transport equipment	0.01	0.54	23.75	2.181 0.96*	16
Miscellaneous manufacturing	0.04	0.56	18.83	6.71 2.962*	9

a   Value added shares are within-group shares. Asterisks denote coefficient of variation of AHTI scores, when calculated as weighted average from several subsector values. Value added and labor shares are calculated from 1989 data in the APEX database.

Table 12.8 Result of a 25% Tariff Reduction (% change)[a]

Sector	Producer Price	Domestic Output	Sector	Producer Price	Domestic Output
Agriculture			**Manufacturing**		
Irrigated rice	−0.80	−0.56	Beverages & tobacco	−1.06	0.25
Rainfed rice	−0.80	−0.46	Textiles	−0.65	−0.84
Corn	−0.50	−0.26	Other textile	−0.11	0.24
Coconut	−0.02	0.29	Garments	0.09	−0.62
Sugar	−0.15	0.04	*Wood products*	*−0.35*	*2.16*
Fruit	−0.04	0.16	*Paper products*	*−0.46*	*−0.41*
Vegetables	0.12	0.25	*Fertilizer*	*−0.07*	*−0.09*
Rootcrops	0.11	0.24	*Other rubber products*	*−0.94*	*−0.05*
Other communal crops	0.11	0.12	Coal & petroleum products	−0.13	−0.11
Hogs	−0.05	0.05	*Basic/non-ferrous metals*	*0.08*	*−0.50*
Poultry	−0.28	0.02	Cement	−0.81	−0.44
Other livestock	−0.24	−0.02	Semiconductors	−0.29	1.83
			Metal products	*−2.68*	*−0.24*
Natural resources			Electrical machinery	−0.97	−0.40
Marine fisheries	0.20	−0.07	Transport equipment	−1.18	−0.48
Inland fisheries	0.35	0.08	Misc. manufacturing	−0.69	−0.80
Forestry	0.90	0.88			
Crude oil	−0.48	−0.04	**Services**		
Other mining	−0.19	0.63	Agricultural	0.13	−0.16
			Construction	−0.60	0.24
Agricultural processing			Electricity, gas, water	0.24	0.05
Rice & corn milling	−0.07	0.13	Telecommunications	0.50	0.08
Sugar milling	0.05	0.04	Transport/storage/wholesale	0.56	0.08
Dairy	−1.55	0.01	Bank	0.66	−0.03
Oils	−0.09	0.40	Insurance	0.70	0.05
Meat	0.14	0.07	Government	1.34	0.02
Feed milling	−1.81	0.32	Other services	0.01	−0.12
Animal feeds	−0.67	−1.52			
Other foods	−0.65	1.24			

a   Italics denotes manufacturing sectors with highest emissions intensity scores (see Table 12.7b).

export-oriented industries, which expand as a result of liberalization, are not especially emissions-intensive; the net result could be argued to be a composition effect that is positive for manufacturing.

In the forestry sector, the reforms bring about a rise in the producer price, and output expands. If property rights in forestry are well defined and enforced, as is assumed in the model, then an increase in the relative price of forestry should promote an expansion based on the planting of production forests, presumably at the expense of upland agriculture. On the other hand, if property rights are missing or not enforced, then the actual outcome will be quite different to that produced by the model; as discussed earlier, by raising the stumpage value of existing trees, trade liberalization enhances the incentive for logging of existing forests rather than for a longer-term increase in the forest sector. In this case trade liberalization is likely to promote accelerated deforestation.

Finally, the trade reforms raise the domestic prices of most exportable agricultural products, and reduce those of rice and corn, which are import-competing crops. Rice and corn prices fall modestly in nominal terms, but by greater amounts relative to the producer prices of other agricultural industries with which they compete for land. The structure of agricultural production thus shifts in the direction of exportables, especially tree crops such as coconut and fruit. Corn and upland rice, the two crops that account for virtually all agriculture-related soil erosion in uplands, both contract in area (Table 12.9). Overall, we may conclude that trade policy reform induces composition effects that are consistent with (or which at least do not run counter to) increased environmental protection in lowland and upland/forestry ecosystems, provided institutional failures (such as open access in forestry) are not severe.

That some agricultural sectors and some exportable manufacturing sectors should contract as a result of trade liberalization requires an explanation, given that these, along with traditional exportables such as forestry and mining, are normally assumed to be the industries most negatively affected by the ISI regime. In the simple model given in section 3, there was only one exportable and one importable, and the impact of liberalization was clear-cut. But when there are many goods in each category, using many inputs and with differing factor intensities, the net impact on a particular sector reflects not only the change in its output price but also the complex set of changes in input prices that affect the cost of production. Sometimes the change in output price may be more than offset by changes in input prices and overall costs of production, so that supply increases (decreases) may take place even when output prices fall (rise).

It should also be noted that rice and corn are both import-competing crops in APEX. The trade reform reduces the prices of imported grains substantially, and their domestic producer prices fall somewhat as a result. Moreover, the trade reforms promote activity in some highly labor-intensive sectors. Unskilled labor demand rises by 3.4% in semiconductors, 4.4% in wood products, 2.6% in "other foods" processing, 1.9% in mining, 2.5% in forestry, and 1.4% in construction. Although unskilled labor supply also increases (by 0.3%), agricultural profitability rises less than profitability in other exportable sectors, especially those that are relatively labor-intensive.

Table 12.9 Agricultural Land Use Changes due to a 25% Tariff Reduction (% change)

Agricultural Activity	Luzon	Visayas	Mindanao
Irrigated rice	−0.29	−0.49	−0.37
Rainfed rice	−0.21	−0.23	−0.31
Corn	−0.07	−0.06	−0.13
Coconut	0.51	0.20	0.54
Sugar	0.34	0.06	0.25
Fruits	0.42	0.11	0.34
Vegetables	0.53	0.31	0.48
Root crops	−1.62	1.03	−3.51
Other commercial crops	0.55	0.03	0.30
Hogs	0.37	0.00	0.23
Poultry	0.35	−0.03	0.17
Other livestock	0.36	−0.17	0.07

Source: APEX simulation results.

Macroeconomic and distributional results of the trade policy experiment (not shown, but available from the authors) show the reforms to have a very small positive effect on aggregate welfare, measured as the weighted sum of real household consumption expenditure. Because unskilled labor supply is elastic and because consumer prices fall in general, the reform has a slight positive effect on income distribution.

The trade policy reform simulation provides predictions about composition effects and, in comparative static sense, scale effects. Of course, longer-run growth outcomes are beyond the scope of the model; furthermore, it is known that this type of comparative static analysis tends to understate the growth stimulus of trade liberalization. In the longer run, if trade policy reform results in faster overall growth, then production of some kinds of environmental "bads" could increase in spite of the changes in industry structure toward less pollution-intensive industries. A mix of economic policy reforms and environmental protection measures is implied to ensure that the scale effect is not the dominant influence on the trajectory of environmental quality.

12.5 ISSUES AND PROSPECTS

It is clear that the Philippines faces several major environmental problems—deforestation, fisheries depletion, land and water system degradation, and urban pollution—that directly reduce the health and well-being of the population as well as the performance and growth potential of the economy. To some extent, these problems are almost inevitable outcomes of high population growth and changes in economic structure associated with early stages of economic growth. But they have been aggravated, quite severely in some cases, by the direct and indirect impact of government policies. Inward-looking protectionist policies, and the blatant use of state power to help favored elite groups exploit national resources, did more than simply constrain economic growth. By perpetuating poverty in rural areas, these policies and practices encouraged population movement to crowded cities and ecologically fragile uplands. By causing underinvestment in essential infrastructure for waste disposal, mass transport, and provision of clean water, they intensified urban environmental degradation. By undermining respect for property rights in nationally owned natural resources, they promoted deforestation. These legacies now weigh heavily on the Philippines.

Policy changes during the decade of the 1990s signaled a movement, broadly speaking, toward dismantling of protection and liberalization of other markets. This trend appears set to continue (although if history is any guide, the path may not be smooth). For the foreseeable future, environmental outcomes are likely to reflect the interaction of structural changes and patterns of growth in a more open policy context, along with such specific environmental policy and investment initiatives as might emerge in response to national and international environmental concerns. We have already outlined the structural impacts that seem likely in an open policy regime. They highlight that liberalization tends to improve overall export performance, while previously highly protected import-competing sectors contract. The environmental impact is not necessarily negative; indeed, there are some indications that land degradation and deforestation, and the intensity (if not the volume) of industrial emissions, may be lower under a more liberal trade regime. Such scale effects as are induced may thus be diminished by composition effects, shifting the country onto a "cleaner" growth path. Further, for a labor-rich country such as the Philippines, trade reforms have both distributional as well as growth benefits.

In a more open and liberal policy context, there appear to be several areas where government action seems essential, involving policies as well as resource expenditures. While policy liberalization may have a benign influence on the environment, specific environmental externalities need to be addressed through targeted environmental policies. Indeed, the cost of market failures may be higher under open trade and investment regimes. For example, where there is open access to natural resources, more liberal trade and investment policies can raise the incentives for ecologically sensitive natural resources to be even more intensively exploited, with no regard for sustainability concerns.[38] Finally, massive investment in essential infrastructure for waste disposal and clean water, particularly in crowded and fast-growing urban areas, is essential. These pose major challenges for Philippine administrations.

Considerable progress was made in the 1990s with the development of policies and programs specifically targeting the environment. But both international and Philippine experience demonstrates that enforcement of environmental legislation is not easy. It requires not only government will but also community support and action to overcome enforcement problems that are particularly serious in a low-income country. Such problems can be overcome to a considerable extent with institutional innovations that foster community mobilization and participation in environmental conservation. A number of recent developments are encouraging. The shift away from leaded gasoline has reduced atmospheric lead levels, and harmful effluents from industrial plants dropped significantly following a pilot scheme that implemented environmental user fees on plants operating near the Laguna Lake. EcoWatch, a program that combined standards-based ratings of the pollution performance of plants with public disclosure of non-compliant firms, has achieved remarkable success in reducing non-compliance in a group of selected factories in Manila. In upland ecosystems, several community-based programs have made progress with soil and forestry conservation through agroforestry, modified agricultural land management practices, and reforestation. These achievements all show that there is much untapped potential to utilize environment-friendly techniques without significant output reduction, and that considerable growth may be feasible with minimum damage to the environment.

These signs of progress will only signal a new chapter in the Philippine environmental story if economic growth is sufficiently rapid and equitable to generate both the resources and the political support for the preservation of environmental quality. Achieving growth at no environmental cost whatsoever seems unrealistic, and some difficult trade-offs will be unavoidable. As growth takes place, despite the demonstrated potential for technique changes to reduce or minimize environmental harm, the absolute levels of some environmental "bads"—such as certain types of industrial emissions—are likely to increase; in other words, the scale effect may overwhelm technique and composition effects. On the other hand, with proper policies to address externalities and market failures, growth can be compatible with maintenance of, or even improvement in, a range of other environmental variables. With the right combination of policies and community action, the country should be able to minimize environmental costs along the growth path, and ultimately deliver sustainable and equitable development. For the Philippines, in the environmental arena, as in many other aspects of economic development, the past century has been rich in experiences in what to avoid. It is to be hoped that the new millennium will be one that will be rich in positive lessons and satisfying achievements.

NOTES

With the usual caveats, we thank conference participants and Jerry Shively for helpful comments on an earlier draft. We also thank Tanya Silva and Toni Rose Domingo for research assistance. Financial support was provided by the Australian Centre for International Agricultural Research (ACIAR) and the United States Agency for International Development (USAID) through the Sustainable Agriculture and Natural Resources Management Collaborative Research Support Program (SANREM CRSP).

1. This classification of the Philippine ecosystems is based on Chapter 4 of *The Philippine National Development Plan: Directions for the 21st Century* (Republic of the Philippines 1998), *Philippine Agenda 21: A National Agenda for Sustainable Development for the 21st Century* (PCSD 1997), and *Philippines: Environment and Natural Resource Management Study* (World Bank 1989). The latter, though published in 1989, remains a very useful source of material on several aspects of the environmental issues facing the Philippines. See also the review of issues as of the late 1980s in de los Angeles and Lasmarias (1990).

2. About 45% of the "uplands" have 18–30% slopes, while more than half of the land area in the country is over 18% in slope (World Bank 1989)

3. The rate of 2.9% for the 1990–95 period is given in Republic of the Philippines (1998). As seen in Table 12.2, Food and Agriculture Organization (FAO) data indicate deforestation at rates of 3.3% per year in the 1980s, and 1.4% per year in the 1990s. Kummer (1992) presents a detailed discussion of data issues in the forestry sector. Fujisaka, Sajise, and del Castillo (1986) also provide a useful overview of the nature and evolution of the upland ecosystem.

4. Commercial logging facilitates subsequent conversion of logged forests to agriculture.

5. Of the endemic Philippine flora, 60% is considered already to be extinct, and a great many other species are endangered.

6. See, for example, World Bank (1989). By 1993, 17% of the total land area was estimated to be badly eroded, 28% moderately eroded, and a further 29% slightly eroded (Republic of the Philippines 1998). In this source the annual cost of on-site damage from erosion *only* was estimated to be about 0.25% of GDP.

7. For an excellent bibliographical survey of pre-1990 research on Philippine fisheries and aquatic resources, see de los Angeles et al. (1990).

8. "Philippine fishery resources ... are being depleted at an alarming rate due to overfishing" (Republic of the Philippines 1998: 4–8).

9. Data in this paragraph are from Shah and Nagpal (1997).

10. SO_2 levels appear not to be very serious in Metro Manila.

11. See Republic of the Philippines (1998). The figure given for 1995, however, is lower than the 1992 average.

12. The dissolved oxygen content is below the 5 mg/litre level needed to sustain aquatic life.

13. Data cited in this paragraph are from World Bank (2000a).

14. The authors note that while their figure is similar to those for other countries using this approach to the valuation of pollution abatement services, studies that use a different approach arrive at much higher differences between adjusted GDP and GDP.

15. For example, net environmental damage due to air pollution is estimated to be only 338 million pesos at 1988 prices, or 0.04% of GDP; a careful analysis of the health costs of air pollution in Metro Manila alone estimated these to be 0.03% of GDP (Shah and Nagpal 1997).

16. See Grossman and Krueger (1993). Although this taxonomy originated in the literature on trade and the environment, it is readily applicable to the broader setting of economic growth.

17. The pollution intensity of an industry can be defined in many ways. One is that an industry is pollution-intensive if the total level of pollution in the economy increases when it expands (drawing resources from other industries in an economy, thus making them contract) (Copeland 1994). We introduce a quantitative measure of pollution intensity in section 4.

18. The AHTI is an aggregate emissions score developed for developing countries by Hettige et al. (1995). The score is measured in risk-weighted pounds of toxic release inventory

(TRI) emissions per $1,000 of shipment value (the TRI aggregates 322 chemicals in an index developed by the U.S. Environmental Protection Authority). Higher AHTI scores indicate greater emissions intensity. These emissions measures are not based on Philippine data due to unavailability; however, "the present version [of the AHTI data] can be useful as a guide to probable pollution problems [in developing countries], even if exact estimates are not possible" (Hettige et al. 1995: 7).

19. Irrigation investments and the Green Revolution, by raising productivity in lowland agriculture, helped somewhat to offset these trends. However, the rapid rise in rice yields was not sustained for much more than a decade, and the derived labor demand effect was itself diminished by implicit and explicit subsidies on capital-intensive agricultural techniques (Jayasuriya and Shand 1986; Coxhead and Jayasuriya 1986).

20. See Paderanga (1986) for a historical review of land settlement policies in the Philippines.

21. A formal modeling exercise that describes the underlying assumptions and model limitations, together with analytical results for a range of different economic structures, and policy and exogenous changes, is in Coxhead and Jayasuriya (2002). The basic model, an extended version of the specific factors (Ricardo–Viner–Jones) model in its main features, builds on earlier work by the authors (Coxhead and Jayasuriya 1994, 1995; Coxhead 2000; Coxhead and Shively 1998; Jayasuriya 2001). (Where not specifically stated, the standard neoclassical assumptions are made.) This simple model is not, of course, meant to mimic the complexities of the Philippine economy, but rather to provide the flavor of the analytical insights that inform our basic arguments.

22. This is not an empirical assertion, nor is it maintained in our empirical work in the next section, but it enables us to capture the key fact that domestic prices are influenced by domestic markets.

23. From 1964 to 1988, rice imports constituted only 4.3% of total domestic supply (IRRI 1991).

24. Implicitly, we can think of lowland agriculture using a specific factor, "lowland," as well.

25. In other words, one factor of production is endogenously supplied. This same specification may equivalently be interpreted as a four-good economy with one intermediate good, land in the upland region, produced using only labor.

26. In principle, demand for food can go down because of the reduced national income that may result from the efficiency cost of the tariff, but usually this income effect is expected to be dominated by price effects.

27. This case is analyzed in Coxhead and Jayasuriya (1994), in a model without a forest sector. The inclusion of a forest sector does not change the basic thrust of the results.

28. Kikuchi and Hayami (1983) have documented the induced down-slope migration effect of the Green Revolution in Luzon. Shively (2001) quantifies the effects of irrigation development in a Palawan watershed on demand for labor in lowland agriculture, and through this on the diminution of upland activities that deplete forest resources.

29. Of course, the actual environmental impact of the Green Revolution has not been entirely positive; pesticide use that in reality had little productivity impact had costly health and environmental effects, as noted in section 2.

30. In principle, the higher wages that may accompany an expansion of corn production can dampen this effect. But, because the labor supply to uplands is probably quite elastic since it can draw on the larger population in the lowlands, this wage effect is unlikely to be strong.

31. We ignore income effects, which in principle could partially offset this result, on the grounds that they are likely to be very small in this case.

32. The urban bias in industrialization, particularly the Metro Manila bias, is often blamed on ISI policies, but it must be noted that there are powerful economic forces of agglomeration that would have operated even under a more open trade regime (see Fujita, Krugman, and Venables 1999).

33. See the list of legislative acts and policy initiatives in *Philippine Agenda 21* (PCSD 1997).

34. Ideally this approach should supplement detailed, data-driven analyses of individual environmental problems and sectoral economic experiences.

35. APEX is an applied general equilibrium model designed to address policy issues for the Philippines. It belongs to the class of models (sometimes known as Johansen models) that are linear in proportional changes of variables, and shares many features with the well-known ORANI model of the Australian economy (Dixon et al. 1982). Input–output data are drawn from the Philippine Social Accounting Matrix; all other parameters describing technology and preferences are constructed from original econometric estimates. The model contains 50 producer goods and services produced in 41 industries. There are five households, each representing a quintile of the income distribution. There are three distinct regional zones of agricultural production (Luzon, Visayas, and Mindanao), and agricultural sectors produce a vector of intermediate and final consumption goods using land, unskilled labor, and fertilizer. The model is solved using GEMPACK software (Harrison and Pearson 1996). Further description and some illustrative experiments may be found in Warr and Coxhead (1993). Coxhead (2000) uses APEX to examine the economic and environmental consequences of technical progress and food policy in Philippine agriculture.

36. There have been a number of earlier experiments along these lines, both using APEX for the Philippines (Coxhead and Shively 1998; Coxhead 2000) and using other applied general equilibrium models, for example for Indonesia (Anderson and Strutt 1996) and Sri Lanka (Bandara and Coxhead 1999).

37. Strictly speaking, changes in the prices of goods and services, and in the production and valuation of pollution, cause optimizing agents to respond by adjusting their abatement expenditures. These effects are not captured in the model.

38. Empirically, raising upland incomes through means that do not depend on resource exploitation has been demonstrated to diminish pressures on forest and wildlife stocks (Shively 1997).

Glossary

Unless otherwise indicated, "$" refers to U.S. dollars.

ACIAR	Australian Centre for International Agricultural Research
ADB	Asian Development Bank
AFTA	ASEAN Free Trade Area
AHTI	acute human toxicity index
ANDP	adjusted net domestic product
ANU	Australian National University
APEC	Asia Pacific Economic Cooperation
APT	Asset Privatization Trust
AQG	Air Quality Guidelines
ARMM	Autonomous Region of Muslim Mindanao
ASEAN	Association of Southeast Asian Nations
AusAID	Australian Agency for International Development
barangay	barrio (the smallest political unit in the country)
BLES–DOLE	Bureau of Labor and Employment Statistics, Department of Labor and Employment
BM	base money
BOI	Board of Investment
BOT	build–operate–transfer
BSP	Bangko Sentral ng Pilipinas
CAR	Cordillera Administrative Region
CARP	Comprehensive Agrarian Reform Program
CD	cumulative distribution
CGE	computable general equilibrium
CPI	consumer price index
DBP	Development Bank of the Philippines

419

DRC	domestic resource cost
E.U.	European Union
EDSA	Epifanio De Los Santos Avenue
ENRAP	Environmental and Natural Resources Accounting Project
EO	Executive Order
EOI	export-oriented industrialization
EPR	effective protection rate
ESCAP	Economic and Social Commission for Asia and the Pacific
FAO	Food and Agriculture Organization
FDI	foreign direct investment
FIES	Family Income and Expenditure Survey
FMB	Forest Management Bureau
FNRI	Food and Nutrition Research Institute
FRA	foreign reserve assets
GATS	General Agreement on Trade in Services
GATT	General Agreement on Tariffs and Trade
GATT-UR	General Agreement on Tariffs and Trade, Uruguay Round
GDP	gross domestic product
GNP	gross national product
GRDP	gross regional domestic product
GVA	gross value added
HDN	Human Development Network
IGF	international gateway facility
ILO	International Labour Office
IMF	International Monetary Fund
IP	internet protocol
IPM	integrated pest management
IRA	internal revenue allotment
IRRI	International Rice Research Institute
ISI	import-substituting industrialization
ISIC	International Standard Industrial Classification
IT	information technology
ITU	International Telecommunications Union
LGU	local government unit
M1	narrow money
M2	broad money
M3	total liquidity
MAV	minimum access volume
MDF	Municipal Development Fund
Mercosur	Free Trade Agreement between Argentina, Brazil, Paraguay, and Uruguay
MI	Macro International, Inc.
MNC	multinational corporation
MVA	manufacturing value added
MWSC	Manila Waterworks and Sewerage Corporation
NAFTA	North American Free Trade Area
NCR	National Capital Region
NDA	net domestic assets
NDP	net domestic product

NDS	net differential shift
NEAT	National Elementary Assessment Test
NEDA	National Economic and Development Authority
NFA	National Food Authority
NFA	net foreign assets
NGO	non-government organization
NIA	National Irrigation Administration
NIE	newly industrializing economy
NIR	net international reserves
NPC	National Power Corporation
NPR	nominal protection rate
NPS	net proportional shift
NSAT	National Secondary Assessment Test
NSCB	National Statistical Coordination Board
NSO	National Statistics Office
NTC	National Telecommunications Commission
OECD	Organization for Economic Cooperation and Development
OFW	overseas Filipino worker
ORRP	overnight reverse repurchase rates
PCSD	Philippine Council for Sustainable Development
PEZA	Philippine Economic Zone Authority
PHILEXPORT	Philippine Exporters' Confederation
PIDS	Philippine Institute for Development Studies
PLDT	Philippine Long Distance Telephone Company
PM	particulate matter
PNB	Philippine National Bank
PNOC	Philippine National Oil Company
POPCOM	Commission on Population
PPP	purchasing power parity
PSIC	Philippine Standard Industrial Classification
QR	quantitative restriction
QTM	quantity theory of money
R&D	research and development
RA	Republic Act
RAIC	regional agro-industrial center
RCA	revealed comparative advantage
REER	real effective exchange rate
RER	real exchange rate
RM	reserve money
RRP	reverse repurchase rate
SAM	social accounting matrix
SAS	Service Area Scheme
SER	shadow exchange rate
SITC	Standard Industrial Trade Classification
SME	small and medium-sized enterprises
SO_2	sulfur dioxide
SOE	state-owned enterprise
SRA	Social Reform Agenda
TFP	total factor productivity

TFR	total fertility rate
TNS	total net shift
TRP	trade reform policy
TRRP	term reverse repurchase rate
TSP	total suspended particulate
TSS	total suspended sediment
U.S.	United States
UNCTAD	United Nations Conference on Trade and Development
UNDP	United Nations Development Program
USAID	United States Agency for International Development
VAT	value added tax
WHO	World Health Organization
WPI	wholesale price index
WRI	World Resources Institute
WTO	World Trade Organization

References

Abrenica, J. (1998), "The Asian Automotive Industry: Assessing the Roles of State and Market in the Age of Global Competition," *Asian-Pacific Economic Literature*, 12(1): 12–26.

Abrenica M.J.V. (1999a), *Reforming the Telecommunications Industry: Prospects and Challenges*, Quezon City: Foundation for Economic Freedom.

Abrenica, M.J.V. (1999b), "Technological Convergence and Competition: The Telecommunications Industry," in D.B. Canlas and S. Fujisaki (eds), *Studies in Governance and Regulation: The Philippines*, Tokyo: Institute of Developing Economies and Japan External Trade Organization, pp. 166–85.

Abrenica, M.J.V. (2000), Competition Policy in the Telecommunications Industry: A Survey of Interconnection Issues, Paper submitted to the Center for Integrative Studies, University of the Philippines, Manila.

Abrenica, M.J.V., and E.S. de Dios (2000), Information Asymmetry and the Design of the Regulatory Regime: Interconnection Issues, Paper presented at the workshop, "Regulation and Governance," School of Economics, University of the Philippines, and School of Economic Studies, University of Manchester, Manila, 29–30 March.

Abueva, Jose V. (1970), "The Philippines: Tradition and Change," *Asian Survey*, 10(1): 56–64.

ADB (Asian Development Bank) (1997), *Emerging Asia: Changes and Challenges*, Manila: ADB.

ADB (Asian Development Bank) (2000), *Development Outlook 2000*, Manila: Oxford University Press.

ADB/WB (Asian Development Bank and World Bank) (1999), *Philippine Education for the 21st Century: The 1998 Philippines Education Sector Study*, Manila: ADB and World Bank.

Adlung, R. (2000), "Services Trade Liberalization from Developed and Developing Country Perspectives," in P. Sauve and R.M. Stern. (eds), *GATS 2000: New Directions in Services*

Trade Liberalization, Washington, D.C.: Centre for Business and Government, Harvard University, and Brookings Institution Press, pp. 112–31.

Aganon, M. (2000), "National Report—Philippines," in Asian Productivity Organization (ed.), *Changing Labor Market and Women Employment*, Tokyo: Asian Productivity Organization, pp. 291–356.

Alba, Michael M. (2001), "Household Vulnerability to Employment Shocks, 1997–1998," *Philippine Review of Economics*, 38: 53–91.

Alburo, F.A. (1993), "Political Economy of Liberalizing Foreign Trade: Philippine Experiences," *Philippine Review of Economics and Business*, 30(1): 122–40.

Alesina, Alberto (1997), "The Political Economy of High and Low Growth," in B. Pleskovic and J. Stiglitz (eds), *Annual World Bank Conference on Development Economics*, Washington, D.C.: World Bank, pp. 217–37.

Almonte, Jose (1996), "Building State Capacity for Reform," Speech to the Philippine Economic Society, Metro Manila, 9 February.

Alonzo, R.P., E.S. de Dios, and G.R. Tecson (1992), "Role of Small and Medium-scale Enterprises in Industrial Restructuring in the Philippines," *Small Industry Bulletin for Asia and the Pacific*, 26/27: 46–54.

Alston, Julian M., C. Chan-Kong, M.C. Marra, P.G. Pardey, and T.G. Wyatt (2000), "A Meta-analysis of Rates of Return to Agricultural R&D," *Research Report*, Washington, D.C.: International Food Policy Research Institute.

Amel, D.F., and J.N. Liang (1997), "Determinants of Entry and Profits in Local Banking Markets," *Review of Industrial Organization*, 12: 59–78.

Anderson, Benedict (1988), "Cacique Democracy and the Philippines: Origins and Dreams," *New Left Review*, 169(May–June): 3–33.

Anderson, K. (1994), "Food Price Policy in East Asia," *Asian-Pacific Economic Literature*, 8(2): 15–30.

Anderson, K. (1998), "Environmental and Labor Standards: What Role for the WTO?," in A.O. Krueger (ed.), *The WTO as an International Organization*, Chicago: University of Chicago Press, pp. 231–55.

Anderson, K., and A. Strutt (1996), "On Measuring the Environmental Impact of Agricultural Trade Liberalization," in M.E. Bredahl et al. (eds), *Agriculture, Trade, and the Environment: Discovering and Measuring the Critical Linkages*, Boulder and London: HarperCollins and Westview Press, pp. 151–72.

Anderson, K., and P.G. Warr (1987), "General Equilibrium Effects of Agricultural Price Distortions: A Simple Model for Korea," *Food Research Institute Studies*, 20(3): 245–63.

Anderson, K., Y. Hayami, et al. (1986), *The Political Economy of Agricultural Protection: East Asia in International Perspective*, Sydney: Allan & Unwin.

Aristotle (1985), *The Politics*, Translated by T.A. Sinclair, Edited by Trevor J. Saunders, Harmondsworth: Penguin Books.

Asian Policy Forum (2000), Policy Recommendations for Preventing another Capital Account Crisis, Asian Development Bank Institute, Tokyo, mimeo.

Aswicahyono, H.H., and H. Hill (1993), "Explaining Foreign Investment Shares in LDC Industry: Incorporating the Policy Factor," *Economics Letters*, 41: 167–70.

Athukorala, P., and C. Manning (1999), *Structural Change and International Migration in East Asia: Adjusting to Labour Scarcity*, Melbourne: Oxford University Press.

Atkinson, A.B. (1983), *The Economics of Inequality*, 2nd edition, Oxford: Clarendon Press.

Austria, M. (1996), "Textiles and Garments Industries: Impact of Trade Policy Reforms on Performance, Competitiveness and Structure," in E.M. Medalla, G.R. Tecson, R.M. Bautista, J.H. Power, and Associates (eds), *Philippine Trade and Industrial Policies:*

Catching Up with Asia's Tigers, Vol. 2, Makati: Philippine Institute for Development Studies, pp. 67–138.

Austria, M. (1998), "Productivity Growth in the Philippines after the Industrial Reforms," *Discussion Paper Series No. 98-26*, Makati: Philippine Institute for Development Studies.

Austria, M. (2000), "Assessing the Competitiveness of the Philippine IT Industry," *Discussion Paper Series No. 2000-03*, Makati: Philippine Institute for Development Studies.

Balassa, B. (1965), "Trade Liberalisation and 'Revealed' Comparative Advantage," *Manchester School of Economic and Social Studies*, 33(1): 99–123.

Balassa, B. (1978), "Exports and Economic Growth: Further Evidence," *Journal of Development Economics*, 5: 181–9.

Baldwin, Robert E. (1975), *Foreign Trade Regimes and Economic Development: The Philippines*, New York: National Bureau for Economic Research.

Bale, Malcolm, and E. Lutz (1981), "Distortions in Agriculture and Their Effects: An International Comparison," *American Journal of Agricultural Economies*, 63(1): 8–22.

Balisacan, A.M. (1992), "Rural Poverty in the Philippines: Incidence, Determinants and Policies," *Asian Development Review*, 10: 125–63.

Balisacan, A.M. (1993), "Agricultural Growth, Landlessness, Off-farm Employment, and Rural Poverty in the Philippines," *Economic Development and Cultural Change*, 41(April): 533–62.

Balisacan, A.M. (1994), *Poverty, Urbanization and Development Policy: A Philippine Perspective*, Quezon City: University of the Philippines Press.

Balisacan, A.M. (1995), "Anatomy of Poverty during Adjustment: The Case of the Philippines," *Economic Development and Cultural Change*, 44: 33–62.

Balisacan, A.M. (1996), "Philippines," in M.G. Quibria (ed.), *Rural Poverty in Developing Asia*, Vol. 2, Manila: Asian Development Bank, pp. 407–585.

Balisacan, A.M. (1997), "Getting the Story Right: Growth, Redistribution and Poverty Alleviation in the Philippines," *Philippine Review of Economics and Business*, 34(June): 1–37.

Balisacan, A.M. (1998), "What Do We Really Know—or Don't Know—About Economic Inequality and Poverty in the Philippines," in A.M. Balisacan and S. Fujisaki (eds), *Growth, Poverty and Income Inequality in the Philippines*, ASEAN Economic Development Program 46, Tokyo: Institute of Developing Economies, pp. 1–42.

Balisacan, A.M. (2001a), "Poverty in the Philippines: An Update and Reexamination," *Philippine Review of Economics*, 38: 16–51.

Balisacan, A.M. (2001b), "Rural Development in the 21st Century: Monitoring and Assessing Performance in Rural Poverty Reduction," in D.B. Canlas and S. Fujisaki (eds), *The Philippine Economy: Alternatives for the 21st Century*, Quezon City: University of the Philippines Press, pp. 162–201.

Balisacan, A.M., and E.M. Pernia (2001), Probing beneath Cross-national Averages: Poverty, Inequality, and Growth in the Philippines, Economics and Research Department, Asian Development Bank, mimeo.

Balisacan, A.M., M.H. Debuque, and N. Fuwa (2001), The Political Economy of Philippine Rural Development since the 1960s, World Bank: Washington, D.C., mimeo.

Balisacan, A.M., R.G. Edillon, A.B. Brillantes, and D.B. Canlas (2000), *Approaches to Targeting the Poor.* Manila: United Nations Development Program and National Economic and Development Authority.

Bandara, J.S., and Ian Coxhead (1999), "Can Trade Liberalization Have Environmental Benefits in Developing Countries? A Sri Lankan Case Study," *Journal of Policy Modeling*, 21(3): 349–74.

Bardhan, Pranab (1996), "Efficiency, Equity and Poverty Alleviation: Policy Issues in Less Developed Countries," *Economic Journal*, 106(September): 1,344–56.

Barker, R., and R.W. Herdt, with Beth Rose (1985), *The Rice Economy of Asia*, Washington, D.C.: Resources for the Future.

Barro, Robert J., and Xavier Sala-i-Martin (1993), "Regional Growth and Migration: A Japan–United States Comparison," *Journal of Japanese and International Economies*, 6(December): 312–46.

Barro, Robert J., and Xavier Sala-i-Martin (1995), *Economic Growth*, New York: McGraw-Hill.

Basilio, Leilanie Q., and Debbie M. Gundaya (1997), The Impact of Collective Public Infrastructure on Regional Income Disparities, Unpublished undergraduate thesis, School of Economics, University of the Philippines, Manila, April.

Battad, J. (1978), "Determinants of Nutritional Status of Preschoolers," *Philippine Economic Journal*, 17(1–2): 154–67.

Bautista, Maria Cynthia (2002) "People Power 2: The Revenge of the Elite on the Masses?" in Amando Doronila (ed.), *Between Fires: Fifteen Perspectives on the Estrada Crisis*, Pasig: Anvil Publishing and Philippine Daily Inquirer, pp. 1–42.

Bautista, R.M. (1975), "Employment Effects of Export Expansion in the Philippines," *Malayan Economic Review*, 20: 49–69.

Bautista, R.M. (1986a), "Domestic Price Distortions and Agricultural Income in Developing Countries," *Journal of Development Economics*, 23: 19–39.

Bautista, R.M. (1986b), "Multisectoral Analysis of Trade Liberalization: The Philippines," *Philippine Economic Journal*, 25: 135–71.

Bautista, R.M. (1987), "Production Incentives in Philippine Agriculture: Effects of Trade and Exchange Rate Policies," *Research Report No. 59*, Washington, D.C.: International Food Policy Research Institute.

Bautista, R.M. (1988), "Foreign Borrowing as Dutch Disease," *International Economic Journal*, II(Autumn): 35–49.

Bautista, R.M. (1990), "Development Strategies, Foreign Trade Regimes, and Agricultural Incentives in Asia," *Journal of Asian Economics*, 1: 115–34.

Bautista, R.M. (1992), *Development Policy in East Asia: Economic Growth and Poverty Alleviation*, Singapore: Institute of Southeast Asian Studies.

Bautista, R.M. (1993), "Trade and Agricultural Development in the 1980s and the Challenges for the 1990s: Asia," *Agricultural Economics*, 8: 345–75.

Bautista, R.M. (1995), "Rapid Agricultural Growth is Not Enough: The Philippines, 1965–80," in J.W. Mellor (ed.), *Agriculture on the Road to Industrialization*, Baltimore: Johns Hopkins University Press, pp. 113–49.

Bautista, R.M. (1997), "Income and Equity Effects of the Green Revolution in the Philippines: A Macroeconomic Perspective," *Journal of International Development*, 9: 151–68.

Bautista, R.M., and M.B. Lamberte (1996), "The Philippines: Economic Developments and Prospects," *Asian-Pacific Economic Literature*, 10: 16–31.

Bautista, R.M., and S. Robinson (1997), "Income and Equity Effects of Crop Productivity Growth under Alternative Foreign Trade Regimes: A CGE Analysis for the Philippines," *Asian Journal of Agricultural Economics*, 2: 177–94.

Bautista, R.M., and A. Valdes (eds) (1993), *The Bias against Agriculture: Trade and Macroeconomic Policies in Developing Countries*, San Francisco: Institute for Contemporary Studies Press.

Bautista, R.M., J.H. Power, and Associates (1979), *Industrial Promotion Policies in the Philippines*, Manila: Philippine Institute for Development Studies.

Bee, O.J. (1987), "Depletion of Forest Reserves in the Philippines," *Field Report Series No. 18*, Singapore: Institute of Southeast Asian Studies.

Behrman, J.R., A.B. Deolalikar, and B.L. Wolfe (1988), "Nutrients: Impacts and Determinants," *World Bank Economic Review*, 2: 299–320.

Berry, A., E. Rodriguez, and H. Sandee (1999), "Firm and Group Dynamics in the Role of the SME Sector in Indonesia and the Philippines," Paper presented to a World Bank conference on "The Role of Small and Medium Enterprises in Development," Chiang Mai.

Berthelemy, J.C., and A. Varoudakis (1996), *Financial Development Policy and Growth*, Paris: OECD Development Centre.

Bevis, Gwendolyn G. (2001), Party Time? The Formation of Programmatic Parties in the Philippines, Unpublished manuscript, University of Wisconsin-Madison, Madison.

Bhagwati, J.N., and T.N. Srinivasan (1978), "Trade Policy and Development," in R. Dornbush and J. Frenkel (eds), *International Economic Policy: Theory and Evidence*, Baltimore: Johns Hopkins University Press, pp. 1–35.

Binswanger, Hans P., and Mark R. Rosenzweig (1986), "Behavioral and Material Determinants of Production Relations in Agriculture," *Journal of Development Studies*, 22: 503–39.

Bird, K. (1999), "Concentration in Indonesian Manufacturing, 1975–93," *Bulletin of Indonesian Economic Studies*, 35(1): 43–73.

Blaxall, Martha, and T. Lenagham (1994), Prospects for Filipino Banana Exports: Market Trends and Policy, Final Report, Agribusiness System Assistance Program Policy Studies No. 93-07, Quezon City: Department of Agriculture.]

BLES–DOLE (Bureau of Labor and Employment Statistics, Department of Labor and Employment) (1998), *Trends and Patterns of Non-regular Employment in the Philippines: 1992–1996*, Manila: BLES–DOLE.

BLES–DOLE (Bureau of Labor and Employment Statistics, Department of Labor and Employment) (2000), "The 1999 Employment Situation," *Labstat Update*, 4(2): 1–4.

Bonner, Raymond (1987), *Waltzing with a Dictator: The Marcoses and the Making of American Policy*, New York: Times Books.

Borras, Saturnino M., Jr. (2000), "CARP in Its 12th Year: A Closer Look at the Agrarian Reform Performance," *Political Brief* (http://www.ipd.ph/pub/polbrief/2000/june/carp12.shtml).

Bouis, H.E. (1982), Rice Policy in the Philippines, PhD dissertation, Stanford University, Stanford.

Bouis, H.E. (1989), *The Relationship between Nutrition and Income Sources for the Rural Poor in a Southern Philippine Province*, Washington, D.C.: International Food Policy Research Institute.

Bouis, H.E., and L.J. Haddad (1990), "Effects of Agricultural Commercialization on Land Tenure, Household Resource Allocation, and Nutrition in the Philippines," *Research Report 79*, Washington, D.C.: International Food Policy Research Institute.

Boulier, B.L., and N.G. Mankiw (1986), "An Econometric Investigation of Easterlin's 'Synthesis Framework': The Philippines and the United States," *Population Studies*, 40: 473–86.

Brandon, C., and R. Ramankutty (1992), "Toward an Environmental Strategy for Asia," *World Bank Discussion Papers No. 224*, Washington, D.C: World Bank.

Brash, Donald T. (1999), Inflation Targeting: An Alternative Way of Achieving Price Stability, Paper presented to a symposium on the 50th anniversary of central banking in the Philippines, Manila, 5 January.

BSP (Bangko Sentral ng Pilipinas) (various years), *Selected Philippine Economic Indicators*, Manila: BSP.

Byerlee, D. (1992), "Technical Change, Productivity and Sustainability in Irrigated Cropping Systems of South Asia: Emerging Issues in the Post Green-revolution Era," *Journal of International Development*, 4(5): 477–96.

Cabanilla, L. (1995), Devolution of Agricultural Extension to LGU: A Socioeconomic Analysis, Paper written under a research grant from the Local Government Academy, University of the Philippines, Los Baños.

Cabigon, J.V., and W. Flieger (1999), *1995 Gender-specific Life Tables for the Philippines, Its Regions and Provinces*, Manila: National Statistics Office.

Caprio, G., and D. Klingebiel (1996), "Bank Insolvencies: Bad Luck, Bad Policy or Bad Banking?" in M. Bruno and B. Pleskovic (eds), *Annual World Bank Conference on Development Economics 1996*, Washington, D.C.: World Bank, pp. 79–104.

Cashin, Paul, and Ratna Sahay (1996), "International Migration, Center–State Grants and Economic Growth in the States of India," *IMF Staff Papers*, 43(March): 123–71.

Cassman, K.G., and P.L. Pingali (1995), "Intensification of Irrigated Rice Systems: Learning from the Past to Meet Future Challenges," *Geo-Journal*, 35(3): 299–305.

Cavanagh, John, and Robin Broad (1993), *Plundering Paradise: The Struggle for the Environment in the Philippines*, Berkeley, CA: University of California Press.

Chenery, H., S. Robinson, and M. Syrquin (1986), *Industrialization and Growth: A Comparative Study*, New York: Oxford University Press.

Claessens, S., A. Demirguc-Kunt, and H. Huizinga (1998), "How Does Foreign Entry Affect the Domestic Banking Market?" *Working Paper Series No. 50*, Washington, D.C.: World Bank.

Claessens, S., S. Djankov, and H. Lang (2000), "The Separation of Ownership and Control for East Asian Firms," *Journal of Financial Economics*, 58: 81–112.

Clarete, R.L., and J.A. Roumasset (1983), "An Analysis of the Economic Policies Affecting the Philippine Coconut Industry," *Working Paper No. 83-08*, Makati: Philippine Institute for Development Studies.

Clarete, R.L., and J. Roumasset (1987), "A Shoven–Whalley Model of a Small Open Economy: An Illustration with Philippine Tariffs," *Journal of Public Economics*, 32: 247–61.

Clarete, R.L., and P.G. Warr (1992), The Theoretical Structure of the APEX Model of the Philippine Economy, Workshop on the APEX CGE Model of the Philippine Economy, Philippine Department of Agriculture and Philippine Economic Society, Makati, July 1992.

Collas-Monsod, Solita (1998), "The War against Poverty: A Status Report," in David G. Timberman (ed.), *The Philippines: New Directions in Domestic Policy and Foreign Relations*, New York: Asia Society, pp. 85–110.

Collas-Monsod, Solita, and Toby C. Monsod (1999), "International and Intranational Comparisons of Philippine Poverty," in A.M. Balisacan and S. Fujisaki (eds), *Causes of Poverty: Myths, Facts, and Policies*, Quezon City: University of the Philippine Press, pp. 51–95.

Copeland, B. (1994), "International Trade and the Environment: Policy Reform in a Polluted Small Open Economy," *Journal of Environmental Economics and Management*, 26(1): 44–65.

Corden, W.M. (1965), "Recent Developments in the Theory of International Trade," *Special*

Papers in International Economics No. 7, Princeton University: International Finance Section, Department of Economics.

Corden, W.M. (1997), *Trade Policy and Economic Welfare*, 2nd edition, Oxford: Clarendon Press; New York: Oxford University Press.

Coronel, Sheila (ed.) (2000), *Investigating Estrada: Millions, Mansions, and Mistresses*, Quezon City: Philippine Center for Investigative Journalism.

Cororaton, C.B., et al. (1995), "Total Factor Productivity of Philippine Manufacturing Industries," *Journal of Philippine Development*, 22(2): 303–90.

Corpuz, Onofre D. (1965), *The Philippines*, Englewood, NJ: Prentice-Hall.

Coxhead, I. (2000), "The Consequences of Philippine Food Self-sufficiency Policies for Economic Welfare and Agricultural Land Degradation," *World Development*, 28(1): 111–28.

Coxhead, I., and S. Jayasuriya (1986), "Labour-shedding with Falling Real Wages in the Philippines," *Asian Survey*, 26(10): 1,056–66.

Coxhead, I., and S. Jayasuriya (1994), "Technical Change in Agriculture and the Rate of Land Degradation in Developing Countries: A General Equilibrium Analysis," *Land Economics*, 70(3): 20–37.

Coxhead, I., and S. Jayasuriya (1995), "Trade and Tax Reforms and the Environment: The Economics of Soil Erosion in Developing Countries," *American Journal of Agricultural Economics*, 77: 631–44.

Coxhead, I., and S. Jayasuriya (2002), *The Open Economy and the Environment: Development, Trade and Resources in Asia*, Cheltenham, UK and Northampton, MA., USA: Edward Elgar (in press).

Coxhead, I., and G.E. Shively (1998), "Some Economic and Environmental Implications of Technical Progress in Philippine Corn Agriculture: An Economy-wide Perspective," *Journal of Agricultural Economics and Development*, 26(1/2): 60–90.

Coxhead, I., A.C. Rola, and K. Kim (2001), "How Do National Markets and Price Policies Affect Land Use at the Forest Margin? Evidence from the Philippines," *Land Economics*, 77(2): 250–67.

Coxhead, I., G.E. Shively, and X. Shuai (2002), "Development Policies, Resource Constraints, and Agricultural Expansion on the Philippine Land Frontier," *Environment and Development Economics*, 7: 341–63.

Cropper, I., and C. Griffiths (1994), "The Interaction of Population Growth and Environmental Quality," *American Economic Review*, 84(2): 250–54.

Crouch, Harold (1985), *Economic Change, Social Structure and the Political System in Southeast Asia: Philippine Development Compared with the other ASEAN Countries*, Singapore: Institute of Southeast Asian Studies.

Cruz, M.C., C.A. Meyer, R. Repetto, and R. Woodward (1992), *Population Growth, Poverty, and Environmental Stress: Frontier Migration in the Philippines and Costa Rica*, Washington, D.C.: World Resources Institute.

Cruz, W., and H. Francisco (1993), Poverty, Population Pressure and Deforestation in the Philippines, Paper presented at the workshop, "Economy-wide Policies and the Environment," World Bank, Washington, D.C., 14–15 December.

Cruz, W., H. Francisco, and Z. Tapawan-Conway (1988), "The On-site and Downstream Costs of Soil Erosion," *PIDS Working Paper No. 88–11*, Manila: Philippine Institute for Development Studies.

Cuaderno, Miguel, Sr. (1964), *Problems of Economic Development*, no publishing information given.

Dakila, Francisco, G. Jr. (2001), Alternative Monetary Policy Rules for the Philippines, Draft PhD dissertation, School of Economics, University of the Philippines, Manila.

Datt, Gaurav, and Hans Hoogeveen (2000), El Niño or El Peso? Crisis, Poverty, and Income Distribution in the Philippines, World Bank, Washington, D.C., mimeo.

Datt, Gaurav, and Martin Ravallion (1992), "Growth and Redistribution Components of Changes in Poverty Measures: A Decomposition with Applications to Brazil and India in the 1980s," *Journal of Development Economics*, 38: 275–95.

David, C.C. (1983), "Economic Policies and Agricultural Incentives," *Philippine Economic Journal*, 11: 154–82.

David, C.C. (1994), "GATT-UR and Philippine Agriculture: Facts and Fallacies," *Journal of Philippine Development*, 21(38): 141–70.

David, C.C. (1996), Agricultural Policy and the WTO Agreement: The Philippine Case, Paper presented at a conference on "Food and Agricultural Policy Challenges for the Asia-Pacific," Manila, October.

David, C.C. (1997) "Agricultural Policy and the WTO Agreement: The Philippine Case," *Discussion Paper Series No. 97-13*, Makati: Philippine Institute for Development Studies.

David, C.C. (1999), *Constraints to Food Security: The Philippine Case*, Makati: Philippine Institute for Development Studies, June.

David, C.C., and J. Huang (1996), "Political Economy of Rice Price Protection in Asia," *Economic Development and Cultural Change*, 44(3): 463–83.

David, C.C., and K. Otsuka (eds) (1994), *Modern Rice Technology and Income Distribution in Asia*, Boulder and London: Lynne Reinner Publishers; Los Baños, Philippines: International Rice Research Institute.

David, C.C., et al. (1998), "Philippine Agricultural and Natural Resource Allocation: Issues and Directions for Reform," *Discussion Paper No. 99-33*, Makati: Philippine Institute for Development Studies.

David, W.P. (1988), "Soil and Water Conservation Planning: Policy Issues and Recommendations," *Journal of Philippine Development*, 15(1): 47–84.

de Dios, Emmanuel (ed.) (1984), *An Analysis of the Philippine Economic Crisis: A Workshop Report*, Quezon City: University of the Philippines Press.

de Dios, Emmanuel (1988), "The Erosion of the Dictatorship," in Aurora Javate-de Dios, Petronilo Bn. Daroy, and Lorna Kalaw-Tirol (eds), *Dictatorship and Revolution: Roots of People's Power*, Metro Manila: Conspectus, pp. 70–131.

de Dios, Emmanuel (1990), "A Political Economy of Philippine Policy-making," in John W. Langford and K. Lorne Brownsey (eds), *Economic Policy-making in the Asia-Pacific Region*, Halifax, Nova Scotia: Institute for Research on Public Policy, pp. 109–147.

de Dios, Emmanuel (1993), *Poverty, Growth, and the Fiscal Crisis*, Makati: Philippine Institute for Development Studies and International Development Research Centre.

de Dios, Emmanuel S., and Associates (1993), "Poverty, Growth and the Fiscal Crisis," Makati: Philippine Institute for Development Studies and International Development Research Center.

de Dios, Emmanuel, Benjamin Diokno, Raul Fabella, Felipe Medalla, and Solita Collas Monsod (1997), "Exchange Rate Policy: Past Mistakes and Future Tasks," *Public Policy*, 1(1): 15–41.

de los Angeles, M.S., and N.C. Lasmarias (1990), "A Review of Philippine Natural Resource and Environmental Management," *Working Paper Series No. 90-08*, Manila: Philippine Institute for Development Studies.

de los Angeles, M.S., E.P. Gonzales, R. Pelayo, and L.A. Ygrubay (1990), "Economics of Philippine Fisheries and Aquatic Resources," *Working Paper Series No. 90-17*, Manila: Philippine Institute for Development Studies.

de los Reyes, R.P., and S.G. Jopillo (1986), *An Evaluation of the Philippine Participatory*

Communal Irrigation Program, Quezon City: Institute of Philippine Culture, Ateneo de Manila University.

Dean, J.M. (1999), "Testing the Impact of Trade Liberalization on the Environment: Theory and Evidence," in P.G. Fredriksson (ed.), *Trade, Global Policy, and the Environment*, Washington, D.C.: World Bank, pp. 55–63.

Deardoff, A. (1999), "Patterns of Trade and Growth across Cones," *Discussion Paper No. 443*, Ann Arbor, MI: Research Seminar in International Economics, University of Michigan School of Public Policy.

Deaton, Angus (1997), *The Analysis of Household Surveys: A Microeconometric Approach to Development Policy*, Baltimore: Johns Hopkins University Press for the World Bank.

Deaton, Angus (2001), "Counting the World's Poor: Problems and Possible Solutions," *World Bank Research Observer*, 16(2): 125–47.

DeGraff, D.S, R.E. Bilsborrow, and A.N. Herrin (1996), "Children's Education in the Philippines: Does High Fertility Matter?" *Population Research and Policy Review*, 15(June): 219–47.

Deininger, Klaus, and Lyn Squire (1998), "New Ways of Looking at Old Issues: Inequality and Growth," *Journal of Development Economics*, 57: 259–87.

Deininger, Klaus, Francisco Lara Jr., Pedro Olinto, and Miet Maertens (2000), Redistribution, Investment and Human Capital Accumulation: The Case of Agrarian Reform in the Philippines, Unpublished paper, World Bank, Manila.

Deolalikar, Anil B. (1988), "Nutrition and Labor Productivity in Agriculture: Estimates for Rural South India," *Review of Economics and Statistics*, 70(3): 406–13.

Deutsch, W.G, J.L. Orprecio, A.L. Busby, J.P. Bago-Labis, and E.Y. Cequiña (2001), "Community-based Water Quality Monitoring: From Data Collection to Sustainable Management of Water Resources," in I. Coxhead and G. Buenavista (eds), *Challenges of Natural Resource Management in a Rapidly Developing Economy: A Case Study from a Philippine Watershed*, Los Baños: Philippine Council on Agricultural Research, Natural Resources and Development, pp. 138–60.

Deutsche Morgan Grenfell (1998), *Philippine Banks*, Manila: Deutsche Morgan Grenfell, March.

Dixon, P., B.R. Parmenter, J, Sutton, and D.P. Vincent (1982), *ORANI: A Multisectoral Model of the Australian Economy*, Amsterdam: North-Holland.

Dobson, W., and Chia S.Y. (eds) (1997), *Multinationals and East Asian Integration*, Singapore: Institute of Southeast Asian Studies.

Dohner, R.S., and P. Intal Jr. (1989), "The Marcos Legacy: Economic Policy and Foreign Debt in the Philippines," in J.D. Sachs and S.M. Collins (eds), *Developing Country Debt and Economic Performance*, Vol. 3, Chicago: University of Chicago Press for the National Bureau of Economic Research, pp. 371–614.

Dollar, D. (1992), "Outward-oriented Developing Economies Do Grow More Rapidly: Evidence from 95 LDCs, 1976–1985," *Economic Development and Cultural Change*, 40: 523–44.

Dollar, David, and Aart Kraay (2001), "Growth Is Good for the Poor," *World Bank Policy Research Paper No. 2587*, Washington, D.C.: World Bank.

DOTC (Philippine Department of Transportation and Communications) (1993), *National Telecommunications Development Plan, 1991-2020, July 1993 update*, Manila: DOTC.

Dy, Rolando (1990), *Economic Evaluation of Communal Irrigation Systems*, Report prepared for the World Bank, Pasig City: University of Asia and thePacific.

Engracia, L.T., and A.N. Herrin. (1984), "Employment Structure of Female Migrants to the Cities in the Philippines," in G.W. Jones (ed.), *Women in the Urban and Industrial Work-*

force: Southeast and East Asia, Canberra: Development Studies Centre, Australian National University, pp. 293–303.

ENRAP (Philippine Environmental and Natural Resources Accounting Project) (1994), *ENRAP-Phase II: Main Report*, Manila: ENRAP.

ESCAP (Economic and Social Commission for Asia and the Pacific) (1998), *Population Data Sheet*, Bangkok: ESCAP, United Nations.

ESCAP (Economic and Social Commission for Asia and the Pacific) (2000), *Population Data Sheet*, Bangkok: ESCAP, United Nations.

Esguerra, E. (1995), "Employment, Competitiveness and Growth," in R. Fabella and H. Sakai (eds), *Toward Sustained Growth*, Tokyo: Institute of Developing Economics, pp. 193–221.

Fabella, R.V. (1989), "Trade and Industry Reforms in the Philippines: Process and Performance," in Manuel F. Montes and Hideyoshi Sakai (eds), *Philippine Macroeconomic Perspective: Developments and Policies*, Tokyo: Institute of Developing Economies, pp. 183–214.

Fabella, R.V. (1991), "Trade and Industry Reforms in the Philippines," in S. Ostry (ed.), *Authority and Academic Scribblers*, San Francisco: ICS Press, pp. 73–91.

Feder, G., et al. (1988), *Land Policies and Farm Productivity in Thailand*, Baltimore: Johns Hopkins University Press for the World Bank.

Feketekuty, G. (2000), "Regulatory Reform and Trade Liberalization in Services," in P. Sauve and R.M. Stern (eds), *GATS 2000: New Directions in Services Trade Liberalization*, Washington, D.C.: Centre for Business and Government, Harvard University, and Brookings Institution Press, pp. 85–111.

Ferguson, C. (1987), *Returns to Irrigation Intensification in Philippine Gravity Systems*, Unpublished PhD dissertation, Cornell University, Ithaca, New York.

Fields, Gary S. (2002), *Accounting for Income Inequality and Its Change: A New Method, with Application to the Distribution of Earnings in the United States*, Unpublished paper, Cornell University, Ithaca, N.Y.

Findlay, C. (2001), "Services Sector Reform and Development Strategies: Issues and Research Priorities," *Policy Issues in International Trade and Commodities Study Series No. 8*, Geneva: UNCTAD.

Flieger, W., and J. Cabigon (1994), *Life Table Estimates: For the Philippines, Its Regions and Provinces, by Sex: 1970, 1980 and 1990*, Health Finance Development Project Monograph No. 5, Manila: Department of Health, Republic of the Philippines; United States Agency for International Development; and UPecon Foundation.

Florentino, R.F, M.R.A. Pedro, L.V. Candelaria, B.D. Ungson, R.U. Zarate, Jr., M.A.R.M. Ramirez, and E.M. Lanot (1993), "An Evaluation of the Impact of Home Gardening on the Consumption of Vitamin A and Iron among Preschool Children," Manila: Food and Nutrition Research Institute, Department of Science and Technology.

FMB (Forest Management Bureau) (1998), *The Philippines' Strategy for Improved Watershed Resources Management*, Manila: Department of Environment and Natural Resources.

FNRI (Food and Nutrition Research Institute) (1988), *Third National Nutrition Survey, Philippines 1987*, Manila: FNRI, Department of Science and Technology.

FNRI (Food and Nutrition Research Institute) (1994), *Fourth National Nutrition Survey, Philippines 1993*, Manila: FNRI, Department of Science and Technology.

FNRI (Food and Nutrition Research Institute) (1997), "1996 Updating of Nutritional Status of Filipino Children at the Provincial Level," *FNRI Special Bulletin*, Manila: FNRI, Department of Science and Technology, July.

FNRI (Food and Nutrition Research Institute) (1999*), Initial Results of the Fifth National*

Nutrition Survey, Philippines 1998, Manila: FNRI, Department of Science and Technology.

Forbes, Kristin J. (2000), "A Reassessment of the Relationship between Inequality and Growth," *American Economic Review*, 90: 869–87.

Foster, James E., and A.F. Shorrocks (1988), "Poverty Orderings," *Econometrica*, 56: 173–7.

Foster, James E., Joel Greer, and Erik Thorbecke (1984), "A Class of Decomposable Poverty Measures," *Econometrica*, 52: 761–6.

Frankel, Jeffrey A. (1993), " Monetary Regime Choices for a Semi-open Country," *Working Paper No. 93-02*, Federal Reserve Bank of San Francisco Center for Pacific Basin Monetary and Economic Studies, San Francisco, February.

Frankel, Jeffrey A. (1997), *Regional Trading Blocs in the World Economic System*, Washington D.C.: Institute for International Economics.

Fujisaka, S., P. Sajise, and R. del Castillo (eds) (1986), *Man, Agriculture and the Tropical Forest: Change and Development in the Philippine Uplands*, Bangkok: Winrock International.

Fujita, M., P. Krugman, and A.J. Venables (1999), *The Spatial Economy: Cities, Regions and International Trade*, Cambridge, MA: MIT Press.

Gallup, John Luke, and Jeffrey D. Sachs, with Andrew D. Mellinger (1998), "Geography and Economic Development," in Boris Pleskovic and Joseph E. Stiglitz (eds), *Annual World Bank Conference on Development Economics*, Washington, D.C.: World Bank, pp. 127–70.

Garbaccio, R.F., and S.J. La Croix (1998), Regional Convergence in Output and Consumption in China: Evidence from the Maoist and Reform Periods, Unpublished paper, Department of Economics, University of Hawaii, Honolulu.

Garcia, M., and P. Pinstrup-Andersen (1987), "The Pilot Food Price Subsidy Scheme in the Philippines: Its Impact on Income, Food Consumption, and Nutritional Status," *Research Report 61*, Washington, D.C.: International Food Policy Research Institute.

Go, G.L., D.R. Kamerschen, and C.D. Delorne (1999), "Market Structure and Price–Cost Margins in Philippine Manufacturing Industries," *Applied Economics*, 31(7): 857–64.

Gochoco, Maria Socorro (1991a), "Financial Liberalization and Interest Rate Determination: The Case of the Philippines, 1981–1985," *Journal of Macroeconomics*, 13(2): 335–50.

Gochoco, Maria Socorro (1991b), "Targets, Instruments, and Monetary Policy in an Open Economy: A GARCH Application," *Working Paper No. 91-05*, Federal Reserve Bank of San Francisco Center for Pacific Basin Monetary and Economic Studies, San Francisco, October.

Gochoco, Maria Socorro (1993), "Are Money, Interest Rates, Output and the Exchange Rate Cointegrated? Implications for Monetary Targeting," *Philippine Review of Business and Economics*, 30(1): 91–101.

Gochoco-Bautista, Maria Socorro (1997/2000), "Capital Flows and the Integration of International Financial Markets," Draft paper. Published in 2000 in Cayetano Paderanga Jr. (ed.), *Coming to Grips with Globalization*, Manila: University of the Philippines Center for Integrative and Development Studies, pp. 63–88.

Gochoco-Bautista, Maria Socorro (1999a), "The Past Performance of the Philippine Banking System and Challenges in the Postcrisis Period," in Asian Development Bank (ed.), *Rising to the Challenge in Asia: A Study of Financial Markets, Volume 10: Philippines*, Manila: Asian Development Bank, pp. 29–77.

Gochoco-Bautista, Maria Socorro (1999b), The Security Implications of the Liberalization and Globalization of Financial Markets, Paper written for a project on development and security in Southeast Asia, sponsored by the Canadian International Development Agency, Manila, March.

Gochoco-Bautista, Maria Socorro (2001), "What Drives Monetary Policy?" *University of the Philippines School of Economics Discussion Paper No. 0015*, Quezon City: University of the Philippines, March.

Gochoco-Bautista, Maria Socorro (2002), "Financial Liberalization and Economic Reform: The Philippine Experience," in Chung Lee (ed.), *Financial Liberalization and the Economic Crisis in Asia*, London: Routledge, forthcoming.

Golay, Frank H. (1961), *The Philippines: Public Policy and National Economic Development*, Ithaca: Cornell University Press.

Goldman Sachs (1999), "Asia Banks: Prudential Norms and CAMELOT II," Goldman Sachs, 1 March.

Gonzales, Leonardo, and N.D. Perez (1991), The Economics of Hog and Poultry Production, Unpublished paper in M.W. Rosegrant and L.A. Gonzales (eds), The Corn–Livestock Sector: Performance and Policy Implications, International Food Policy Research Institute, Washington, D.C.

Gonzalez, A. (2000), "Philippine Basic Education 1999–2004: Analysis, Recommendations, and Plans," in Human Development Network and United Nations Development Program (eds), *Philippine Human Development Report 2000*, Manila: Human Development Network and United Nations Development Program.

Gonzalez, Eduardo (1996), "Intergovernmental Fiscal Relations: An Institutional Analysis," in Alonzo, Ruperto P. et al. (eds), *Developing an Action Plan for the Financing of Local Government Projects with Social and Environmental Objectives*, Vol. 2, Institutional and Sectoral Studies, Quezon City: University of the Philippines School of Economics Foundation, October, pp. 234–79.

GOP/UNICEF (Government of the Republic of the Philippines and United Nations International Children's Emergency Fund) (1997), *Situation of Children and Women in the Philippines, 1997*, Manila: GOP and UNICEF.

Grossman, G., and A.B. Krueger (1993), "The Environmental Impacts of a North American Free Trade Agreement," in P. Garber (ed.), *The U.S–Mexico Free Trade Agreement*, Cambridge, MA: MIT Press: 13–56.

Grossman, G., and A.B. Krueger (1995), "International Trade and the Environment," *Quarterly Journal of Economics*, May: 353–77.

Guinigundo, Diwa C. (1999), Current State of the Philippine Banking System, Paper presented to the Annual Meeting of the Philippine Economic Society, Makati, 12 March.

Guinigundo, Diwa C. (2000), Problems and Issues on Inflation Targeting: The Case of the Philippines, Unpublished paper presented to the Bangko Sentral ng Pilipinas public hearings on inflation targeting, Manila, March.

Habito, C.F. (1987), Intersectoral Linkages and Agricultural Policies: A General Equilibrium Analysis, Philippine Institute for Development Studies, Makati, mimeo.

Haddad, L., and H. Bouis (1991), "The Impact of Nutritional Status on Agricultural Productivity: Wage Evidence from the Philippines," *Oxford Bulletin of Economics and Statistics*, 53(1): 45–69.

Halcrow Fox (1999), "Transport Infrastructure and Capacity Development Project," Vols 1–3, Technical Assistance No. 2968, Asian Development Bank, Manila.

Harrigan, F. (1998), "Asian Saving: Theory, Evidence, and Policy," in F.G. Adams and S. Ichimura (eds), *East Asian Development: Will the East Asian Growth Miracle Survive?* Westport: Praeger, pp. 127–57.

Harrison, W. Jill, and K.R. Pearson (1996), "Computing Solutions for Large General Equilibrium Models Using GEMPACK," *Computational Economics*, 9(2): 83–127.

Hathaway, Dale, and M. Ingco (1995), "Agricultural Liberalization and the Uruguay Round," in W. Martin and L. Alan Winters (eds), *The Uruguay Round and the Developing Economies*, World Bank Discussion Paper No. 307, Washington, D.C.: World Bank.

Haustmann, R., and M. Gavin (1996), "Securing Stability and Growth in a Shock-prone Region: The Policy Challenge for Latin America," *IDB Working Paper Series 315*, Washington, D.C.: Office of the Chief Economist, Inter-American Development Bank.

Hawes, Gary (1987), *The Philippine State and the Marcos Regime: The Politics of Export*, Ithaca: Cornell University Press.

Hayami, Yujiro (2000), An Ecological and Historical Perspective on Agricultural Development in Southeast Asia, Paper prepared for the World Bank, Washington, D.C.

Hayami, Yujiro, and M. Kikuchi (1978), "Investment Inducement to Public Infrastructure: Irrigation in the Philippines," *Review of Economics and Statistics*, 60(1): 70–77.

Hayami, Yujiro, and M. Kikuchi (2000), *A Rice Village Saga: Three Decades of Green Revolution in the Philippines*, Maryland: Barnes and Noble.

Hayami, Y., M. Kikuchi, and E.B. Marciano (1998), "Structure of Rural-based Industrialization: Metal Craft Manufacturing on the Outskirts of Greater Manila, Philippines," *Developing Economies*, 36(2): 132–54.

HDN/UNDP (Human Development Network and United Nations Development Program) (2000), *Philippine Human Development Report 2000*, Makati: HDN and UNDP.

Heaver, R.A. and J.M. Hunt (1995), *Improving Early Childhood Development: An Integrated Program for the Philippines*, Washington, D.C.: World Bank.

Heller, Peter, Richard Haas, and Ahsan Mansur (1986), "A Review of Fiscal Impulse Measures," *IMF Occasional Paper*, Washington, D.C.: IMF, May.

Herrin, A.N. (1990a), Nutrition: Consequences, Determinants and Policy Interventions, Report prepared for National Nutrition Council, Philippines, December.

Herrin, A.N. (1990b), "Philippines," in Asian Development Bank (ed.), *Human Resource Policy and Economic Development: Selected Country Studies,* Manila: Asian Development Bank.

Herrin, A.N. (1993), "Studies on Consequences of Population Change in Asia: Philippines," *Asian Population Studies Series No. 121*, New York: Economic and Social Commission for Asia and the Pacific, United Nations.

Herrin, A.N., and M.P. Costello (1998), "Policy Responses to Future Population Growth in the Philippines," *Journal of Philippine Development*, Number Forty-Five, First Semester, 25(1): 127–46.

Hettige, H.P., M. Mani, and D. Wheeler (1997), Industrial Pollution in Economic Development: Kuznets Revisited, Development Research Group, World Bank, mimeo.

Hettige, H., P. Martin, M. Singh, and D. Wheeler (1995), "IPPS: The Industrial Pollution Projection System," *Policy Research Department Working Paper*, Washington, D.C.: World Bank.

Hill, H. (1985), "Subcontracting, Technological Diffusion and the Development of Small Enterprise in Philippine Manufacturing," *Journal of Developing Areas*, 19(2), 245–61.

Hill, H. (1995), "Small–Medium Enterprise and Rapid Industrialization: The ASEAN Experience," *Journal of Asian Business*, 11(1): 1–31.

Hobday, M. (2001), "The Electronics Industries of Pacific Asia," *Asia-Pacific Economic Literature*, 15(1): 13–29.

Hoekman, B. (1995), "Tentative First Steps: An Assessment of the Uruguay Round Agreement on Services," *World Bank Policy Research Working Paper 1455*, Washington, D.C.: World Bank, May.

Hooley, R. (1985), *Productivity Growth in Philippine Manufacturing: Retrospect and Future Prospects*, PIDS Monograph Series No. 9, Makati: Philippine Institute for Development Studies.

Hordijk, L., W. Foell, and J. Shah (1995), RAINS-ASIA: An Assessment Model for Air Pollution in Asia, Report prepared for a World Bank project, "Acid Rain and Emission Reductions in Asia," http://www.iiasa.ac.at/~heyes/docs/rains.asia.html, accessed 13 September 2000.

Horton, S. (1988), "Birth Order and Child Nutritional Status: Evidence from the Philippines," *Economic Development and Cultural Change*, 36(2): 341–54.

Hutchcroft, Paul D. (1998), *Booty Capitalism: The Politics of Banking in the Philippines*, Ithaca: Cornell University Press, and Quezon City: Ateneo de Manila University Press.

Hutchcroft, Paul D. (1999a), "After the Fall: Prospects for Political and Institutional Reform in Post-crisis Thailand and the Philippines," *Government and Opposition*, 34(4): 473–98.

Hutchcroft, Paul D. (1999b), "Neither Dynamo nor Domino: Reforms and Crises in the Philippine Political Economy," in T.J. Pempel (ed.), *The Politics of the Asian Economic Crisis*, Ithaca: Cornell University Press, pp. 163–83.

Hutchcroft, Paul D. (2000), "Colonial Masters, National Politicos, and Provincial Lords: Central Authority and Local Autonomy in the American Philippines, 1900–1913," *Journal of Asian Studies*, 59(2): 277–306.

ILO (International Labour Office) (1974), *Sharing in Development: A Program of Employment, Equity and Growth for the Philippines*, Geneva: ILO.

Imbat, M.M.C., and E.M.F. Tanlapco (1993), "Influence of Import Competition and Seller Concentration on the Profitability of the Philippine Manufacturing Sector," *Philippine Review of Economics and Business*, 30(2): 234–55.

IMF (International Monetary Fund) (1999), *Yearbook of International Financial Statistics 1999*, Washington, D.C.

IMF (International Monetary Fund) (2000), *Yearbook of International Financial Statistics 2000*, Washington, D.C.: IMF.

IMF (International Monetary Fund) (2001), *Yearbook of International Financial Statistics 2001*, Washington, D.C.

Ingco, Merlinda, and F. Ng (1998), Distortionary Effects of State Trading for Agriculture: Issues for the Next Round of Multilateral Trade Negotiations, Unpublished paper, World Bank, Washington, D.C.

Intal, P.S. (1996), "Beyond WTO: Meeting the Challenges of the New Trade and Environment Regime: Perspectives from the Philippines and the ASEAN," *Discussion Paper Series No. 96-08*, Makati: Philippine Institute for Development Studies.

Intal, P.S., and G.M. Llanto (1998a), "Financial Reform and Development in the Philippines, 1980–1997: Imperatives, Performance, and Challenges," *PIDS Discussion Paper Series No. 98-02*, Makati: Philippine Institute for Development Studies, January.

Intal, P.S., and G.M. Llanto (1998b), "Financial Reform and Development in the Philippines, 1980–1997: Imperatives, Performance and Challenges," *Journal of Philippine Development*, 25: 1–77.

Intal, P.S., and J.H. Power (1990), *Trade, Exchange Rate and Agricultural Pricing Policies in the Philippines*, Comparative Studies on the Political Economy of Agricultural Pricing Policy, Washington D.C.: World Bank.

Intal, P.S., and J.H. Power (1991), "The Philippines," in A.O. Krueger et al. (eds.), *The Polit-*

ical Economy of Agricultural Pricing Policy, Vol. 2: Asia, Baltimore and London: Johns Hopkins University Press, pp. 149–94.

IRRI (International Rice Research Institute) (1991), *World Rice Statistics 1990*, Los Baños: IRRI.

ITU (International Telecommunications Union) (1998), *World Telecommunications Development Report 1998: Universal Service*, Geneva: ITU.

ITU (International Telecommunications Union) (1999a), *Trends in Telecommunication Reform: Convergence and Regulation*, Geneva: ITU.

ITU (International Telecommunications Union) (1999b), *World Telecommunication Development Report 1999: Mobile Cellular*, Geneva: ITU.

Jamison, Dean T. (1986), "Child Malnutrition and School Performance in China," *Journal of Development Economics*, 20: 299–309.

Jayasuriya, S. (2001), "Agriculture and Deforestation in Tropical Asia: An Analytical Framework," in A. Angelsen and D. Kaimowitz (eds), *Agricultural Technologies and Tropical Deforestation*, Oxon, U.K. and New York, U.S.: CAB International, pp. 317–34.

Jayasuriya, S., and R.T. Shand (1986), "Technical Change and Labour Absorption in Asian Agriculture: Some Emerging Trends," *World Development*, 14(3): 415–28.

Jha, S., A. Deolalikar, and E.M. Pernia (1993), "Population Growth and Economic Development Revisited with Reference to Asia," *Asian Development Review*, 11(2): 1–46.

Johnson, D. Gale (1991), *World Agriculture in Disarray*, 2nd edition, New York: St. Martins Press.

Jurado, Gonzalo M. (1976), "Foreign Trade and External Debt," in José Encarnación, Jr. (ed.), *Philippine Economic Problems in Perspective*, Quezon City: School of Economics, University of the Philippines, pp. 262–326.

Kamin, Steven B., and Paul R. Wood (1996), Capital Flows, Financial Intermediation, and Aggregate Demand: Empirical Evidence from Mexico and Other Pacific Basin Countries, Paper presented at a conference on "Managing Capital Flows and Exchange Rates in the Pacific Basin," sponsored by the Federal Reserve Bank of San Francisco, San Francisco, September.

Kikuchi, M., and Y. Hayami (1983), "New Rice Technology, Intrarural Migration, and Institutional Innovation in the Philippines," *Population and Development Review*, 9(2): 247–57.

Kikuchi, M., A. Maruyama, H. Fujie, and Y. Hayami (2000), Investment Inducements to Public Infrastructure: Irrigation in the Philippines and Sri Lanka since Independence, Unpublished paper, International Food Policy Research Institute.

Krugman, P. (ed.) (1987), *Strategic Trade Policy and the New International Economics*, Cambridge, MA: MIT Press.

Kummer, D.M (1992), *Deforestation in the Postwar Philippines*, Manila: Ateneo de Manila Press.

La Croix, S.J. (1998), Convergence in Malaysia, Unpublished paper, University of Hawaii, Honolulu.

La Croix, S.J., R. Garbaccio, and M. Southichak (1998), "Regional Economic Development in Asia: Progress, Pitfalls and Policy," in United Nations Development Program (ed.), *Sustainable and Balanced Development in the Asia Pacific*, EDAP Joint Policy Studies No. 4, Seoul: Korea Development Institute.

Lall, S. (2000), "The Technological Structure and Performance of Developing Country Manufactured Exports," *Oxford Development Studies*, 28(3): 337–69.

Lamberte, M. (1985), "Financial Liberalization: What Have We Learnt?" *Journal of Philippine Development*, 12: 274–89.

Lamberte, M. (1993), "Assessment of Financial Market Reforms in the Philippines: 1980–1992," *Journal of Philippine Development*, 20: 231–59.

Lamberte, M. (1995), "Managing Surges in Capital Inflows: The Philippine Case," *Journal of Philippine Development*, 22(1): 43–88.

Lamberte, M. (1999), Some Issues on the Liberalization of the Entry and Scope of Operations of Foreign Banks, Unpublished notes, Philippine Institute for Development Studies, Makati.

Lamberte, M., and G.M. Llanto (1995), "A Study of Financial Sector Policies: The Philippine Case," in S.N. Zahid (ed.), *Financial Sector Development in Asia: Country Study*, Manila: Asian Development Bank, pp. 235–301.

Lamberte, M.B., M.S. Casuga, and D.C.E. Erge (1997), Assessment of the Role and Performance of Government Nonfinancial Agencies in Implementing Directed Credit Programs, Unpublished paper, Credit Policy Improvement Program, Makati.

Lamberte, M.B., R.G. Manasan, G.M. Llanto, W.M. Villamil, E.S. Tan, F.C. Fajardo, and M. Kramer (1993), *Decentralization and Prospects for Regional Growth*, Manila: Philippine Institute for Development Studies.

Lamberte, M., et al. (1999), "Impacts of the Southeast Asian Financial Crisis on the Philippine Manufacturing Sector," *Discussion Paper Series No. 99-09*, Makati: Philippine Institute for Development Studies.

Landé, Carl H. (2001), "The Return of 'People Power' in the Philippines," *Journal of Democracy*, 12(2): 88–102.

Lary, H.B. (1968), *Imports of Manufactures from Less Developed Countries*, New York: Columbia University Press.

Lawas, Jose M. (1990), Evolution of Regional Planning in the Philippines: A Process Documentation, Unpublished material, Philippine Institute for Development Studies, Manila.

Leamer, E. (1987), "Paths of Development in the Three-factor, n-good General Equilibrium Model," *Journal of Political Economy*, 95(5): 961–99.

Legarda, Benito (1999), *After the Galleons: Foreign Trade, Economic Change and Entrepreneurship in the Nineteenth-century Philippines*, Monograph No. 18, Madison: Center for Southeast Asian Studies, University of Wisconsin-Madison.

Levine, R. (1994), Does the Financial System Matter? World Bank, Washington, D.C., mimeo.

Li, Hongyi, and Heng-fu Zou (1998), "Income Inequality Is Not Harmful for Growth: Theory and Evidence," *Review of Development Economics*, 2(3): 318–34.

Lim Chong Yah (2001), *Southeast Asia: The Long Road Ahead*, Singapore: World Scientific Publishing.

Lim, J. (2000), *The East Asian Crisis and Employment: The Gender Dimension*, Quezon City: Philippine Center for Policy Studies.

Lim, Joseph Y. (1999), The Social Impact and Responses to the Current East Asian Economic and Financial Crisis: The Philippine Case, Country paper prepared for the United Nations Development Program/Regional Bureau for Asia and the Pacific, Bangkok.

Lindert, Peter H. (1991), "Historical Patterns of Agricultural Policy," in C.P. Timmer (ed.), *Agriculture and the State: Growth, Employment, and Poverty in Developing Countries*, Ithaca and London: Cornell University Press, pp. 29–83.

Lindsey, C.W. (1977), "Market Concentration in Philippine Manufacturing, 1970," *Philippine Economic Journal*, 16(3): 289–312.

Lindsey, C.W., and E.M. Valencia (1981), "Foreign Direct Investment in the Philippines: A Review of the Literature," *Discussion Paper Series*, Makati: Philippine Institute for Development Studies.

Lipton, Michael (1995), "Market, Redistributive and Proto-reform: Can Liberalization Help the Poor?" *Asian Development Review*, 13(1): 1–35.

Liviatan, Oded (1994), "Impact of Public Financial Institutions in Fiscal Stance," in Mario Blejer and A. Cheasty (eds), *How to Measure the Fiscal Deficit*, Washington, D.C.: IMF, pp. 259–76.

Llanto, G.M., and M.B. Lamberte (1998), "The Philippines: Recent Financial Reforms, Surges in Foreign Capital and the Government's Response," in *Financial Deregulation, Capital Flows and Macroeconomic Management in the Asia Pacific*, EDAP Joint Policy Studies 5, Seoul: Korea Development Institute, pp. 157–84.

Llanto, Gilbert M., Ma. Piedad S. Geron, and Marie-Christine G. Tang (2000), "Directed Credit Programs: Issues and Framework for Reform," Credit Policy Improvement Program, National Credit Council, Department of Finance, Manila.

Loehr, William, and Rosario G. Manasan (1999), Fiscal Decentralization and Economic Efficiency: Measurement and Evaluation, Draft, January, Submitted to United States Agency for International Development, Manila.

Lucas, R.E., D. Wheeler, and H. Hettige (1992), "Economic Development, Environmental Regulation and the International Migration of Toxic Industrial Pollution: 1960–88," in P. Low (ed.), *International Trade and the Environment*, World Bank Discussion Papers No. 159, Washington, D.C.: World Bank, pp. 67–86.

Macapagal-Arroyo, Gloria (1987), "An Investigation of the Real Effects of Government Expenditure," *Philippine Review of Economics and Business*, 24: 55–78.

Madriaga, J.R., et al. (1999a), "Prevalence of Anemia among Filipinos," in Food and Nutrition Research Institute (ed.), *Initial Results of the Fifth National Nutrition Survey, Philippines 1998*, Manila: Food and Nutrition Research Institute, Department of Science and Technology.

Madriaga, J.R., et al. (1999b), "Prevalence of Iodine Deficiency in the Philippines," in Food and Nutrition Research Institute (ed.), *Initial Results of the Fifth National Nutrition Survey, Philippines 1998*, Manila: Food and Nutrition Research Institute, Department of Science and Technology.

Maglen, L., and R. Manasan (1999), "Education Costs and Financing in the Philippines," *Technical Background Paper No. 2*, Philippine Education for the 21st Century, The 1998 Philippines Education Sector Study, Manila: Asian Development Bank.

Magno, Alexander R. (1995), "The Market Consensus," *Far Eastern Economic Review*, 10 August: 31.

Magno, Alexander R. (1996), "The Philippines in 1995: Completing the Market Transition," in *Southeast Asian Affairs 1996*, Singapore: Institute of Southeast Asian Studies.

Manasan, R.G. (1991), "Employment Effects of Selected Structural Adjustment Policies in the Philippines," *Philippine Economic Journal*, 30: 143–77.

Manasan, R.G. (1995), "Fiscal Decentralization: The Early Years of Code Implementation," *Development Research News*, 13(4), Makati: Philippine Institute for Development Studies.

Manasan, R.G. (1997), *Fiscal Adjustment in the Context of Growth and Equity, 1986–1996*, Makati: Philippine Institute for Development Studies.

Manasan, R.G. (1999), *Impact of Local Government Code and Proposed Amendments on Ability to Finance Infrastructure: Towards a Framework for LGU Finance*, Manila: United States Agency for International Development.

Manasan, R.G. (2001), *Budget Allocation for Human Development Expenditures: Measuring Progress on the 20:20 Initiative of Provinces and Cities 1995–1998*, Manila: United Nations International Children's Emergency Fund.

Manasan, R.G., and R.G. Mercado (1999), "Regional Economic Growth and Convergence in the Philippines: 1975–1997," in Eduardo T. Gonzales (ed.), *Reconsidering the East Asian Economic Model: What's Ahead for the Philippines*, Pasig City: Development Academy of the Philippines.

Manasan, R.R. and V. Pineda (1999), *Assessment of Philippine Tariff Reform: 1998 Update*, Makati: Philippine Institute of Development Studies.

Manasan, R.G., and R.G. Querubin (1997), "Assessment of Tariff Reform in the 1990s," *Discussion Paper Series No. 97-10*, Makati: Philippine Institute for Development Studies.

Mangahas, Mahar (1995), "Self-rated Poverty in the Philippines, 1981–1992," *International Journal of Public Opinion Research*, 7(1): 39–55.

Manning, C. (2000), Labour Markets and the Financial Crisis in East Asia: Context, Outcomes and Strategies for the Future, Paper presented to a policy seminar on "Coping with the Social Impact of the Crisis," Asia Development Forum 2000, Singapore 6–8 June.

Marcos, Ferdinand E. (1979), *The Democratic Revolution in the Philippines*, Englewood Cliffs, NJ: Prentice-Hall International.

Martinez, Edmund (1996), "Fidel Ramos's Unfinished Business," *Politik*, 2(February): 37–41.

Maxfield, Sylvia, and James H. Nolt (1990), "Protectionism and the Internationalization of Capital: U.S. Sponsorship of Import Substitution Industrialization in the Philippines, Turkey, and Argentina," *International Studies Quarterly*, 34: 49–81.

McCoy, Alfred W. (1983), "'In Extreme Unction': Philippine Sugar Industry," in Third World Studies Program (ed.), *Political Economy of Philippine Commodities*, Quezon City: Third World Studies Center, University of the Philippines, pp. 135–79.

McCoy, Alfred W. (1999), *Closer than Brothers: Manhood at the Philippine Military Academy*, New Haven: Yale University Press.

McCoy, Alfred W., and Eduardo C. de Jesus (eds) (1982), *Philippine Social History: Global Trade and Local Transformations*, Quezon City: Ateneo de Manila University Press.

McHale, Thomas R. (1959), An Econecological Approach to Economic Development, PhD thesis, Harvard University, Cambridge MA.

McKendrick, D.G., R.E. Doner, and S. Haggard (2000), *From Silicon Valley to Singapore: Location and Competitive Advantage in the Hard Disk Drive Industry*, Stanford: Stanford University Press.

McKinnon, R.I. (1973), *Money and Capital in Economic Development*, Washington, D.C.: Brookings Institution.

Medalla, E.M. (1986), "Assessment of the Tariff Reform Program and Trade Liberalization," *Tariff Commission-PIDS Staff Paper Series No. 86-03*, Makati: Philippine Institute for Development Studies.

Medalla, E.M. (1998), "Trade and Industrial Policy beyond 2000: An Assessment of the Philippine Economy," *Discussion Paper Series No. 98-05*, Makati: Philippine Institute for Development Studies.

Medalla, E.M., G.R. Tecson, R.M. Bautista, J.H. Power, and Associates (1995/96), *Philippine Trade and Industrial Policies: Catching Up with Asia's Tigers*, 2 volumes, Makati: Philippine Institute for Development Studies.

Mercado-Aldaba, R.A. (1995), "Foreign Direct Iinvestment in the Philippines: A Reassessment," Special Paper No. 2 in E.M. Medalla, G.R. Tecson, R.M. Bautista, and J.H. Power (eds), *Catching Up with Asia's Tigers: Philippine Trade and Investment Policies*, Makati: Philippine Institute for Development Studies: 239–309.

Michaely, M.D. (1977), "Exports and Growth: An Empirical Investigation," *Journal of Development Economics*, 4: 49–53.

Michaely, M.D., D. Papengiorgiou, and A.M. Choksi (eds) (1991), *Liberalizing Foreign Trade: Lessons of Experience in the Developing World*, Vol. 7, Cambridge: Basil Blackwell.

Mincer, Jacob (1974), *Schooling, Experience and Earnings*, New York: National Bureau of Economic Research.

Montes, Manuel F. (1987), *The Philippines: Stabilization and Adjustment Policies and Programmes*, Helsinki: World Institute for Development Economics Research.

Montes, Manuel F. (1989a), "Financing Development: The 'Democratic' versus the 'Corporatist' Approach in the Philippines," in Miguel Urrutia, Shinicihi Ichimura, and Setsuko Yukawa (eds), *The Political Economy of Fiscal Policy*, Tokyo: United Nations University, pp. 84–148.

Montes, Manuel F. (1989b), "Philippine Structural Adjustments, 1970–1987," in Manuel F. Montes and Hideyoshi Sakai (eds), *Philippine Macroeconomic Perspective: Developments and Policies*, Tokyo: Institute of Developing Economies, pp. 45–90.

Montinola, Gabriella R. (1999), "Parties and Accountability in the Philippines," *Journal of Democracy*, 10(1): 126–40.

Myers, Norman (1988), "Environmental Degradation and Some Economic Consequences in the Philippines," *Environmental Conservation*, 15: 205–14.

NEDA (National Economic and Development Authority) (1993), National Framework for Regional Development, Unpublished material, NEDA, Manila, December.

Nickerson, D.J. (1999), "Trade-offs of Mangrove Area Development in the Philippines," *Ecological Economics*, 28(2): 279–98.

Noland, M. (2000), "The Philippines in the Asian Financial Crisis: How the Sick Man Avoided Pneumonia," *Asian Survey*, 40(3): 401–12.

NSCB (National Statistical Coordination Board) (1990), *1988 Economic and Social Indicators*, NSCB: Manila.

NSCB (National Statistical Coordination Board) (1995), *Philippine Statistical Yearbook*, Manila: NSCB.

NSCB (National Statistical Coordination Board) (2001), *Philippine Statistical Yearbook*, NSCB: Manila

NSCB (National Statistical Coordination Board) (2002), *1991–2000 Philippine National Health Accounts*, NSCB: Manila.

NSCB (National Statistical Coordination Board) (various years), *Philippine Statistical Yearbook*, Manila: NSCB.

NSO (National Statistics Office) (1988), *Philippine Energy Statistics 1988*, Manila: NSO.

NSO (National Statistics Office) (1989), *Functional Literacy, Education and Mass Media Survey*, NSO: Manila.

NSO (National Statistics Office) (1994), *Functional Literacy, Education and Mass Media Survey*, NSO: Manila.

NSO (National Statistics Office) (1997), *1995 Census-based National and Regional Population Projections*, NSO: Manila.

NSO, DOH, and MI (National Statistics Office, Department of Health, and Macro International, Inc.) (1999), *National Demographic and Health Survey 1998*, Manila: NSO, DOH, and MI.

NTC (National Telecommunications Commission) (2001), Annual Report 2000, Manila, mimeo.

Ogawa, N., G.W. Jones, and J.G. Williamson (eds) (1993), *Human Resources in Development along the Asia-Pacific Rim*, Singapore: Oxford University Press.

Orbeta, A. (2000), E-commerce in Southeast Asia: A Review of Developments, Challenges and Issues, Paper prepared for the ASEAN Roundtable 2000, "New Development Paradigms in Southeast Asia: The Challenge of Information Technology," Institute for Southeast Asian Studies, Singapore, 11–12 October.

Orbeta, A., and E.M. Pernia (1999), "Population Growth and Economic Development in the Philippines: What Has Been the Experience and What Must Be Done?," *Discussion Paper Series*, Makati: Philippine Institute for Development Studies.

Otsuka, Keijiro (1991), "Determinants and Consequences of Land Reform Implementation in the Philippines," *Developing Economies*, 35(2): 339–55.

Otsuka, K., H. Chuma, and Y. Hayami (1992), "Land and Labor Contracts in Agrarian Economies: Theories and Facts," *Journal of Economic Literature*, 30: 1,965–2,018.

Paderanga, C. (1986), A Review of Land Settlement Policies in the Philippines, 1900–1975, *School of Economics Discussion Paper No. 8613*, Manila: University of the Philippines.

Paderanga, Cayetano Jr. (1996), "Philippine Financial Developments: 1980–1995," in Raul V. Fabella and Kazuhisa Ito (eds), *Financial Sector Issues in the Philippines*, Tokyo: Institute of Developing Economies, pp. 1–26.

Pagulayan, A.C. Jr. (1998), "Philippines," in Asian Productivity Organization (ed.), *Agricultural Price Policy in Asia and the Pacific*, Tokyo: Asian Productivity Organization, pp. 265–78.

Paqueo, V.B. (1985), "An Econometric Analysis of Educational Attainment among Elementary School Age Children: Preliminary Analysis," in *Transactions of the National Academy of Science and Technology, Republic of the Philippines,* Vol. 2, Metro Manila: The Academy, pp. 359–82.

Pardey, P.G., J. Roseboom, and J.R. Anderson (eds) (1991), *Agricultural Research Policy: International Quantitative Perspective*, Cambridge, UK: Cambridge University Press.

Paredes, Ruby R. (ed.) (1989), *Philippine Colonial Democracy*, Monograph Series No. 32, New Haven: Yale University Southeast Asia Studies.

Payer, Cheryl (1974), *The Debt Trap: The International Monetary Fund and the Third World*, New York: Monthly Review Press.

PCSD (Philippine Council for Sustainable Development) (1997), *The Philippine Agenda 21: A National Plan for Sustainable Development for the 21st Century,* Manila: PCSD.

Pernia, E.M., and R. Israel (1994), "Spatial Development, Urbanization and Migration Patterns in the Philippines," in A.M. Balisacan, F.M. Medalla, and E.M. Pernia (eds), *Spatial Development, Land Use, and Rural–Urban Linkages in the Philippines*, Manila: National Economic and Development Authority, pp. 13–46.

Pernia, E.M., C.W. Paderanga Jr., V.P. Hermoso, and Associates (1983), *The Spatial and Urban Dimensions of Development in the Philippines*, Manila: Philippine Institute for Development Studies.

Philippine Department of Agriculture (1990), *Philippine Agricultural Development Plan 1991–1995*, Manila: Philippine Department of Agriculture.

Philippine Tariff Commission (1979), *Tariff Profiles in ASEAN*, Manila: Philippine Tariff Commission.

PIDS/TC (Philippine Institute for Development Studies and Tariff Commission) (1986), *Tariff Profiles in ASEAN*, Manila: National Economic and Development Authority.

Pineda, Virginia S. (1997), "Effects of the Uniform Five Percent Tariff on Manufacturing," *Discussion Paper Series No. 97-16*, Makati: Philippine Institute for Development Studies, September.

POPCOM (Commission on Population) (2000), *The Directional Plan of the Philippine Population Management Program 2001–2004*, Mandaluyong City: POPCOM.

Population Council (1994), "Reconsidering the Rationale, Scope, and Quality of Family Planning Programs," *Population Council Issue Papers*, Manila: Population Council.

Power, J.H. (1983), "Response to Balance of Payments Crises: Korea and the Philippines," *Staff Paper Series No. 83-05*, Makati: Philippine Institute for Development Studies.

Power, J.H., and G.P. Sicat (1971), *The Philippines: Industrialization and Trade Policies*, London: Oxford University Press.

Putzel, James (1992), *A Captive Land: The Politics of Agrarian Reform in the Philippines*, Quezon City: Ateneo de Manila University Press.

Quizon, M.D., et al. (1994), "Part D: Biomedical Nutrition Survey," in Food and Nutrition Research Institute (ed.), *Fourth National Nutrition Survey, Philippines 1993*, Manila: Food and Nutrition Research Institute, Department of Science and Technology.

Radelet, S., and J.D. Sachs (1998), "The East Asian Financial Crisis: Diagnosis, Remedies, Prospects," *Brookings Papers in Economic Activity*, 1: 1–90.

Ram, R. (1985), "Exports and Economic Growth: Some Additional Evidence," *Economic Development and Cultural Change*, 33: 415–25.

Ranis, G., and F. Stewart (1993), "Rural Nonagricultural Activities in Development: Theory and Experience," *Journal of Development Economics*, 40: 75–101.

Ranis, G., and F. Stewart (1999), "V-Goods and the Role of the Urban Informal Sector in Development," *Economic Development and Cultural Change*, 47(2): 259–88.

Ravallion, Martin (1994), *Poverty Comparisons*, Chur, Switzerland: Harwood Academic Publishers.

Ravallion, Martin, and Jyotsna Jalan (1996), "Growth Divergence due to Spatial Externalities," *Economics Letters*, 53: 227–32.

Ravallion, Martin, and Shaohua Chen (1997), "What Can New Survey Data Tell Us about Recent Changes in Distribution and Poverty?" *World Bank Economic Review*, 11(May): 357–382.

Remolona, E.M., M. Mangahas, and F. Pante, Jr. (1986), "Foreign Debt, Balance of Payments, and the Economic Crisis of the Philippines in 1983–84," *World Development*, 14(8): 993–1,018.

Republic of the Philippines (1998), *The Philippine National Development Plan: Directions for the 21st Century*, Manila: Republic of the Philippines.

Reyes, E., E. Milan, and T. Sanchez (1989), "Employment, Productivity and Wages in the Philippine Labor Market: An Analysis of Trends and Policies," *Working Paper Series No. 89-03*, Makati: Philippine Institute for Development Studies.

Reyes, Celia M., Generoso G. de Duzman, Rosario G. Manasan, and Aniceto C. Orbeta (1999), Social Impact of the Regional Financial Crisis in the Philippines, Philippine Institute for Development Studies, Makati, mimeo.

Riedinger, Jeffrey M. (1995), *Agrarian Reform in the Philippines: Democratic Transitions and Redistributive Reform*, Stanford: Stanford University Press.

Rivera, Temario C. (1994), *Landlords and Capitalists: Class, Family, and State in Philippine Manufacturing*, Quezon City: University of the Philippines Press.

Rocamora, Joel (1994), *Breaking Through*, Metro Manila: Anvil Publishing, Inc.

Rocamora, Joel (1995), "The Political Requirements of Economic Reform," *Issues & Letters*, 4(October): 1–4.

Rodlauer, M., et al. (2000), "Philippines: Toward Sustainable and Rapid Growth. Recent Developments and the Agenda Ahead," *Occasional Paper 187*, Washington D.C.: International Monetary Fund.

Rodriguez, E. (1998), "International Migration and Income Distribution in the Philippines," *Economic Development and Cultural Change*, 46(2): 329–50.

Rodrik, D. (1992), "The Limits of Trade Policy Reform in Developing Countries," *Journal of Policy Perspectives*, 6: 87–105.

Rola, A.C., and P.L. Pingali (1993), *Pesticides, Rice Productivity and Farmers' Health: An Economic Assessment*, Los Baños and Washington, D.C.: International Rice Research Institute and World Resources Institute.

Roumasset, James (1995), "The Nature of the Agricultural Firm," *Journal of Economic Behavior and Organization*, 26: 171–7.

Roumasset, James (2000), Market Friendly Food Security: Alternatives for Restructuring NFA, Unpublished paper, Department of Economics, University of Hawaii, Honolulu.

RP/UNFPA (Republic of the Philippines and United Nations Population Fund) (1999), *Country Population Assessment: Philippines*, Manila: RP/UNFPA.

Sachs, J.D. et al. (1998), *Promotion of Broad-based Economic Growth in the Philippines*, Pasig City: National Economic and Development Authority.

Sakai, H. (1989), "Postwar Economic Development in the Philippines: Thrust, Zeal and Achievement," in M.F. Montes and H. Sakai (eds), *Philippine Macroeconomic Perspective: Developments and Policies*, Tokyo: Institute of Developing Economies, pp. 1–43.

Sala-i-Martin, Xavier X. (1996), "The Classical Approach to Convergence Analysis," *Economic Journal*, 106(July): 1,019–36.

Saldana, Cesar G. (1999), Philippine Corporate Governance Environment and Policy and Their Impact on Corporate Performance and Finance, Paper submitted to the Asian Development Bank under RETA 5802: "A Study of Corporate Governance and Financing in Selected Developing Member Countries," Pasig, 19 October.

Selden, T., and D. Song (1994), "Neoclassical Growth, the J-curve for Abatement, and the Inverted U curve for Pollution," *Journal of Environmental Management and Control*, 29: 162–8.

Shah, J., and T. Nagpal (eds) (1997), "Urban Air Quality Management in Asia: Metro Manila Report," *World Bank Technical Paper No. 380*, Washington, D.C.: World Bank.

Shalom, Stephen Rosskamm (1981), *The United States and the Philippines: A Study of Neocolonialism*, Philadelphia: Institute for the Study of Human Issues.

Shaw, E. (1973), *Financial Deepening and Economic Growth*, New York: Oxford University Press.

Shively, G.E. (1997), "Poverty, Technology, and Wildlife Hunting in Palawan," *Environmental Conservation*, 24(1): 57–63.

Shively, G.E. (2001), "Agricultural Change, Rural Labor Markets, and Forest Clearing: An Illustrative Case from the Philippines," *Land Economics* 77(2): 268–84.

Siamwalla, A., A. Brillantes, S. Chunharas, C. McAndrews, A. Mcintyre, and F. Roche (2000), *The Evolving Roles of the State, Private, and Local Actors in Rural Asia*, Manila: Asian Development Bank.

Sicat, G. (1994), "Tax Reform in the Philippines," in Richard A. Musgrave, C.H. Chang, and J. Riew (eds), *Taxation and Economic Development among Pacific Asian Countries*, Boulder: Westview Press: pp. 64–82.

Sicat, G. (1999), "The Philippines," in H.W. Arndt and H. Hill (eds), *Southeast Asia in Crisis*, Singapore: Institute of Southeast Asian Studies, pp. 41–50.

Sicat, G. (2000), "Estrada's Ruinous Economic Leadership," *BusinessWorld*, 4 December: 4.

Sicat, G. (2002), "The Next President Could Be an Economist, or Gloria Macapagal as an Economist," *Development Research News*, 29(1): 8–19.]

Sidel, John T. (1999), *Capital, Coercion, and Crime: Bossism in the Philippines*, Stanford: Stanford University Press.

Solon, O., A.N. Herrin, R.H. Racelis, M.G. Manalo, V. Ganac, and G. Amoranto (1999),

"Health Care Expenditure Patterns in the Philippines: Analysis of National Health Accounts, 1991–1997," *Philippine Review of Economics and Business*, 36(2): 335–64.

Southichak, M., and S.J. La Croix (1998), Output Convergence in Thailand, Unpublished paper, University of Hawaii, Honolulu.

Stanley, Peter W. (1974), *A Nation in the Making: The Philippines and the United States, 1899–1921*, Cambridge, MA: Harvard University Press.

Stern, D.I., M.S. Common, and E.B. Barbier (1996), "Economic Growth and Environmental Degradation: The Environmental Kuznets Curve and Sustainable Development," *World Development*, 24(7): 1,151–60.

Takacs, W.E. (1994), "Domestic Content and Compensatory Export Requirements: Protection of the Motor Vehicle Industry in the Philippines," *World Bank Economic Review*, 8(1): 127–49.

Tan, E. (1993), "Interlocking Directorates, Commercial Banks, Other Financial Institutions and Non-financial Corporations," *Philippine Review of Economics and Business*, 30(1): 1–50.

Tan, E. (1995), "Trade Reform in the 1990s: Effects of E.O. 470 and the Import Liberalization Program," in E.M. Medalla, G.R. Tecson, R.M. Bautista, and J.H. Power (eds), *Catching Up with Asia's Tigers: Philippine Trade and Investment Policies*, Makati: Philippine Institute for Development Studies.

Tan, E. (2000), "Filipino Overseas Employment—An Update," *Discussion Paper 0003*, Manila: School of Economics, University of the Philippines.

Tan, Lina (2000), Postwar Philippine–Japan Trade Relations, Unpublished manuscript, Quezon City.

Tan, N. (1979), "The Structure of Protection and Resource Flows in the Philippines," in R.M. Bautista, J.H. Power, and Associates (eds), *Industrial Promotion Policies in the Philippines*, Makati: Philippine Institute for Development Studies, pp. 126–71.

Tan, N. (1986), "The Philippines: The Structure and Causes of Manufacturing Sector Protection," in C. Findlay and R. Garnaut (eds), *The Political Economy of Manufacturing Protection: Experiences of ASEAN and Australia*, Sydney: Allen & Unwin, pp. 48–76.

Tanggol, Sukarno D. (1990), "Regional Autonomy and Social Development: Some Notes on the Case of Muslim Mindanao," *Philippine Journal of Public Administration*, 34(1): 1–26.

Tecson, G.R. (1996), "Philippine Manufacturing Industries and the Effects of Trade Policy Reforms on Structure and Efficiency," in E.M. Medalla, G.R. Tecson, R.M. Bautista, J.H. Power, and Associates (eds), *Philippine Trade and Industrial Policies: Catching Up with Asia's Tigers*, Vol. 2, Makati: Philippine Institute for Development Studies, pp. 1–66.

Tecson, G.R. (1999), "The Hard Disk Drive Industry in the Philippines," *Report 99-01*, San Diego: Graduate School of International Relations and Pacific Studies, University of California.

Tecson, G.R. (2000), "Industrial Development in the Philippines : Issues and Prospects for the 21st Century," in S. Fujisaki and D.B. Canlas (eds), *The Philippine Economy: Alternatives for the 21st Century*, Tokyo: Institute of Developing Economies and Japan External Trade Organization.

Thompson, Mark R. (1996), "Off the Endangered List: Philippine Democratization in Comparative Perspective," *Comparative Politics*, 28(2): 179–205.

Tidalgo, R., and E. Esguerra (1984), *Philippine Employment in the Seventies*, Makati: Philippine Institute for Development Studies.

Timmer, C.P. (1988), "The Agricultural Transformation," in H. Chenery and T.N. Srinivasan (eds), *Handbook of Economics*, Vol. 1, Amsterdam: North Holland.

Tolentino, Bruce (2000), "Monitoring the Implementation of the 1999-2004 MTPDP with Regard to the Provision of Rural Roads," in Government of the Philippines and World Bank, *Rural Development and Natural Resources Management: Trends, Strategy Implementation, and Framework Performance Indicator System*, Manila, Government of the Philippines and World Bank, pp. 1–17, Annex 10.

Tordesillas, Ellen (2000), "The Nocturnal President," in Sheila Coronel (ed.), *Investigating Estrada: Millions, Mansions, and Mistresses*, Quezon City: Philippine Center for Investigative Journalism, pp. 15–25.

TSC/WRI (Tropical Science Center and World Resources Institute) (1991), *Accounts Overdue: Natural Resource Deprecation in Costa Rica*, Washington, D.C.: World Resources Institute.

Tyers, Rodney, and K. Anderson (1992), *Disarray in World Food Markets: A Quantitative Assessment*, New York: Cambridge University Press.

Ulph, A. (1999), *Trade and the Environment,* Cheltenham: Edward Elgar.

Umali, Dina L. (1990), The Structure and Price Performance of the Philippine Rice Marketing System, PhD dissertation, Stanford University, Stanford.

UNCTAD (United Nations Conference on Trade and Development) (2000), *World Investment Report 2000*, Geneva: World Bank.

UNDP (United Nations Development Program) (1996, 2000), *Philippine Human Development Report*, Manila: UNDP.

Ungarte, E., and M.J. Sullivan (2000), "Reform and the Corporate Environment in the Philippines," in P. Drysdale (ed.), *Reform and Recovery in East Asia: The Role of the State and Economic Enterprise*, London: Routledge, pp. 191–213.

Velandria, F.V., et al. (1994), "Part C: Clinical Nutrition Survey," in Food and Nutrition Research Institute (ed.), *Fourth National Nutrition Survey, Philippines 1993*, Manila: Food and Nutrition Research Institute, Department of Science and Technology.

Vincent, J.R., Md A. Rozali, and Associates (1997), *Environment and Development in a Resource-rich Economy: Malaysia under the New Economic Policy*, Cambridge, MA: Harvard Institute for International Development; and Kuala Lumpur: Institute of Strategic and International Studies.

Warr, P. (1989), "Export Processing Zones: The Economics of Enclave Manufacturing," *World Bank Research Observer*, 4: 65–88.

Warr, P.G., and I. Coxhead (1993), "The Distributional Impact of Technical Change in Philippine Agriculture: A General Equilibrium Analysis," *Food Research Institute Studies*, 22(3): 253–74.

Warren, T. (2000), "The Identification of Impediments to Trade and Investment in Telecommunication Services," in C. Findlay and T. Warren (eds), *Impediments to Trade in Services: Measurement and Policy Implications*, London: Routledge, pp. 71–84.

Wells, L.T. (1994), "Mobile Exporters: New Foreign Investors in East Asia," in K.A. Froot (ed.), *Foreign Direct Investment*, Chicago: University of Chicago Press, pp. 173–91.

Winters, L. Alan (1995), "Implications of the Uruguay Round Agreements: Critical Issues and Adjustment Requirements," in *Implications of the Uruguay Round Agreements for the Asian and Pacific Region*, New York: United Nations.

World Bank (1981), "Philippines Staff Appraisal Report on the Industrial Finance Project," *Report No. 3331-PH*, Washington, D.C.: World Bank.

World Bank (1988), "Philippines: Financial Sector Study," *Report No. 7177-PH*, Washington, D.C.: World Bank.

World Bank (1989), *Philippines: Environment and Natural Resource Management Study*, Washington, D.C.: World Bank.

World Bank (1991), Philippine Irrigated Agriculture Sector Review, Unpublished paper, World Bank, Washington, D.C.

World Bank (1992), "The Philippines: Country Economic Report: Public Sector Resource Mobilization and Expenditure Management," *Report No. 100056-PH*, Washington, D.C.: World Bank.

World Bank (1993), *The East Asian Miracle*, New York: Oxford University Press.

World Bank (1995), "Philippines Public Expenditure Management for Sustained and Equitable Growth," *Report No. 14680-Ph*, Vol. 2, East Asia and Pacific Region, World Bank, Washington, D.C.

World Bank (1997a), "Philippines: Managing Global Integration," *Background Papers*, 2, Washington D.C.: World Bank, 17 November.

World Bank (1997b), *Private Capital Flows to Developing Countries: The Road to Financial Integration*, New York: Oxford University Press.

World Bank (1998a), *East Asia: The Road to Recovery*, Washington D.C.: World Bank.

World Bank (1998b), *World Bank Support for Small and Medium Industries in the Philippines: An Impact Evaluation*, Washington, D.C.: World Bank.

World Bank (2000a), *Greening Industry: New Roles for Communities, Markets and Governments*, Washington, D.C.: Oxford University Press for the World Bank.

World Bank (2000b), *Philippines—Growth with Equity: The Remaining Agenda*, Washington, D.C.: East Asia and Pacific Regional Office, World Bank.

WRI (World Resources Institute) (1989), *Wasting Assets: Natural Resources in the National Income Accounts*, Washington, D.C.: WRI.

WRI (World Resources Institute) (1999), *World Resources 1998–99*, Washington, D.C.: WRI.

WRI (World Resources Institute) (2001), *World Resources 2000–2001*, Washington, D.C.: WRI.

Ybanez, R. (1983), "Ancillary Firm Development in the Philippine Automobile Industry," in K. Odaka (ed.), *The Motor Vehicle Industry in Asia*, Singapore: Singapore University Press, pp. 228–85.

Yoshihara, Kunio (1994), *The Nation and Economic Growth: The Philippines and Thailand*, Kuala Lumpur: Oxford University Press.

Author Index

Subject Index